FARMAX essentially means compressing a population vertically and horizontally so as to give that population more space.

0.01

0.10

0.25

0.30

0.45

0.45

0.17 0.22

0.30 0.40

0.45 0.50

0.70

0.86

1.52

1.60

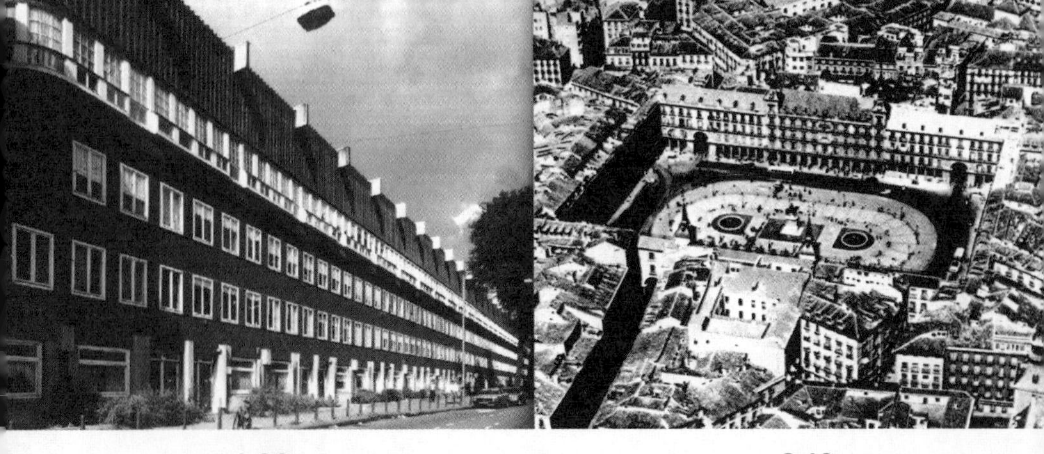

1.88

2.10

1.10

1.30

1.64

1.65

2.10

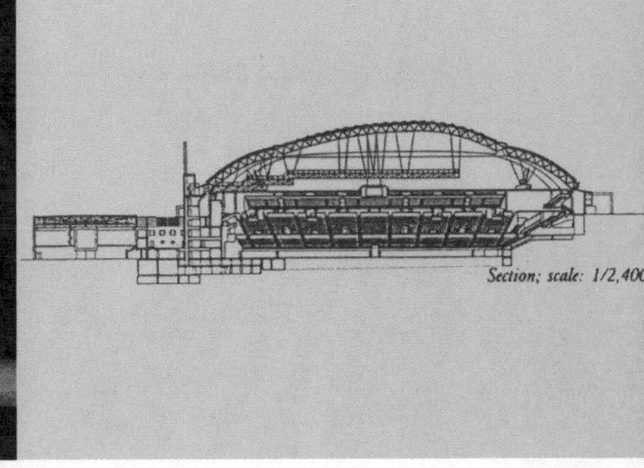

2.30

2.78 2.80

3.00 3.00

3.25 3.25

2.88 2.96

3.00 3.20

3.25 3.60

4.00

5.67

10.0

10.0

13.6

13.6

6.50

6.80

10.0

12.0

16.9

22.8

MVRDV

FARMAX

Excursions on density

Edited by Winy Maas and Jacob van Rijs with Richard Koek

010 publishers, Rotterdam

Acknowledgements

FARMAX is conceived and edited by
Winy Maas and Jacob van Rijs with Richard Koek.

It is construed as an architectural narrative composed of studies and designs done by MVRDV in Rotterdam and by students of Delft University of Technology, the Berlage Institute in Amsterdam and the Academy of Architecture and Urban Planning in Rotterdam, between 1994 and 1998, plus various contributions by other authors.

The research and the production for the book have been carried out by MVRDV: Winy Maas, Jacob van Rijs and Nathalie de Vries with Tom Mossel, Joost Grootens, Eline Strijkers, Nicole Meijer, Bas van Neijenhof, Bart Reuser and Frank van Maanen.

The book has been designed by Roelof Mulder (Arnhem/Amsterdam) in association with Annemarie van Pruyssen.

Translations from Dutch into English were made by John Kirkpatrick.

First published in the Netherlands in 1998 by 010 Publishers, Watertorenweg 180, 3063 HA Rotterdam, The Netherlands.
www.archined.nl/010

CIP/ISBN 90-6450-266-8

We gratefully acknowledge the generous support of the Netherlands Architecture Fund in Rotterdam.

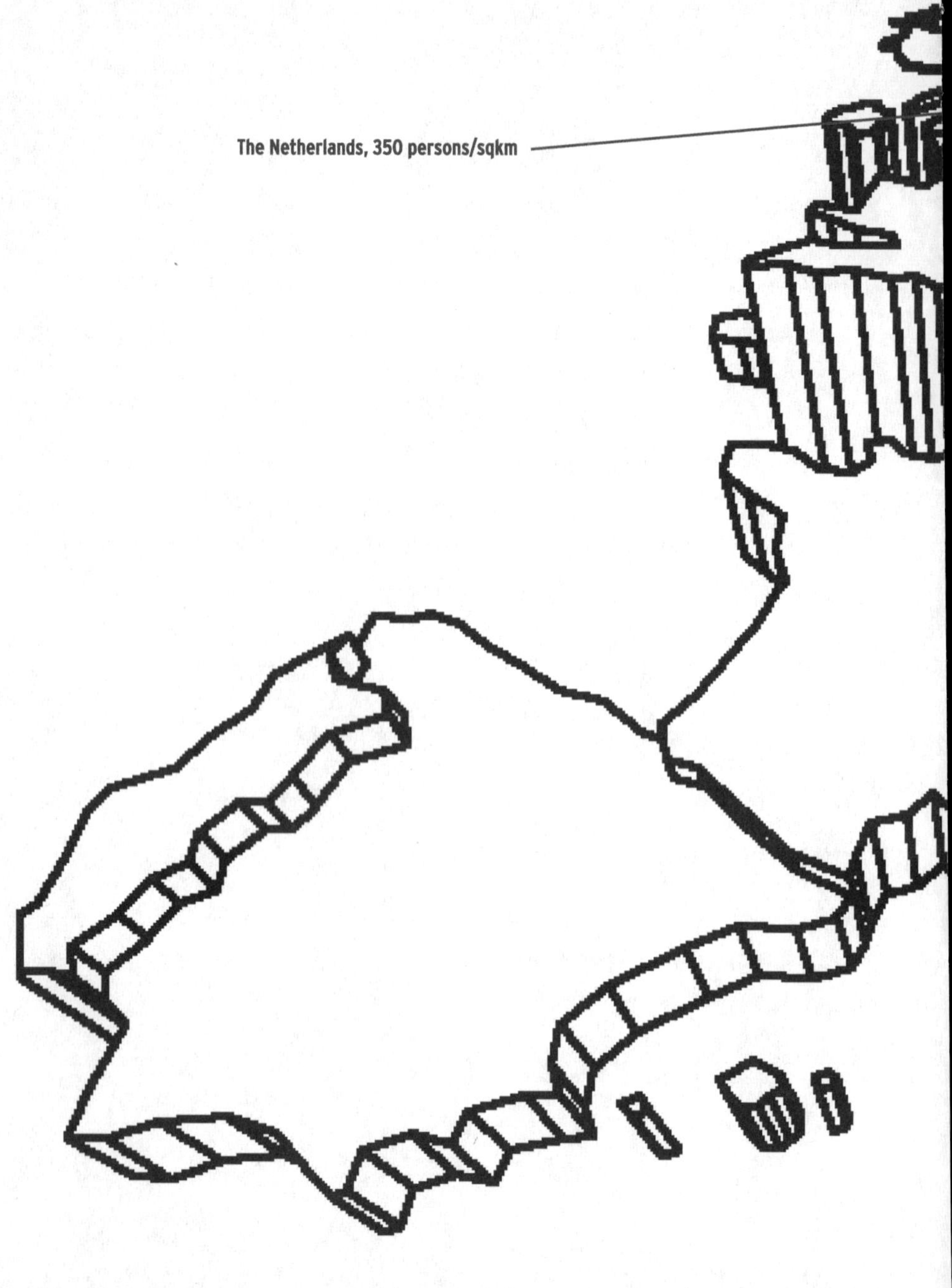
The Netherlands, 350 persons/sqkm

Greyness on the Dutch Mesa

Text

1994

Richard Koek, Winy Maas and Jacob van Rijs

is reputed to have the highest average density in the world.

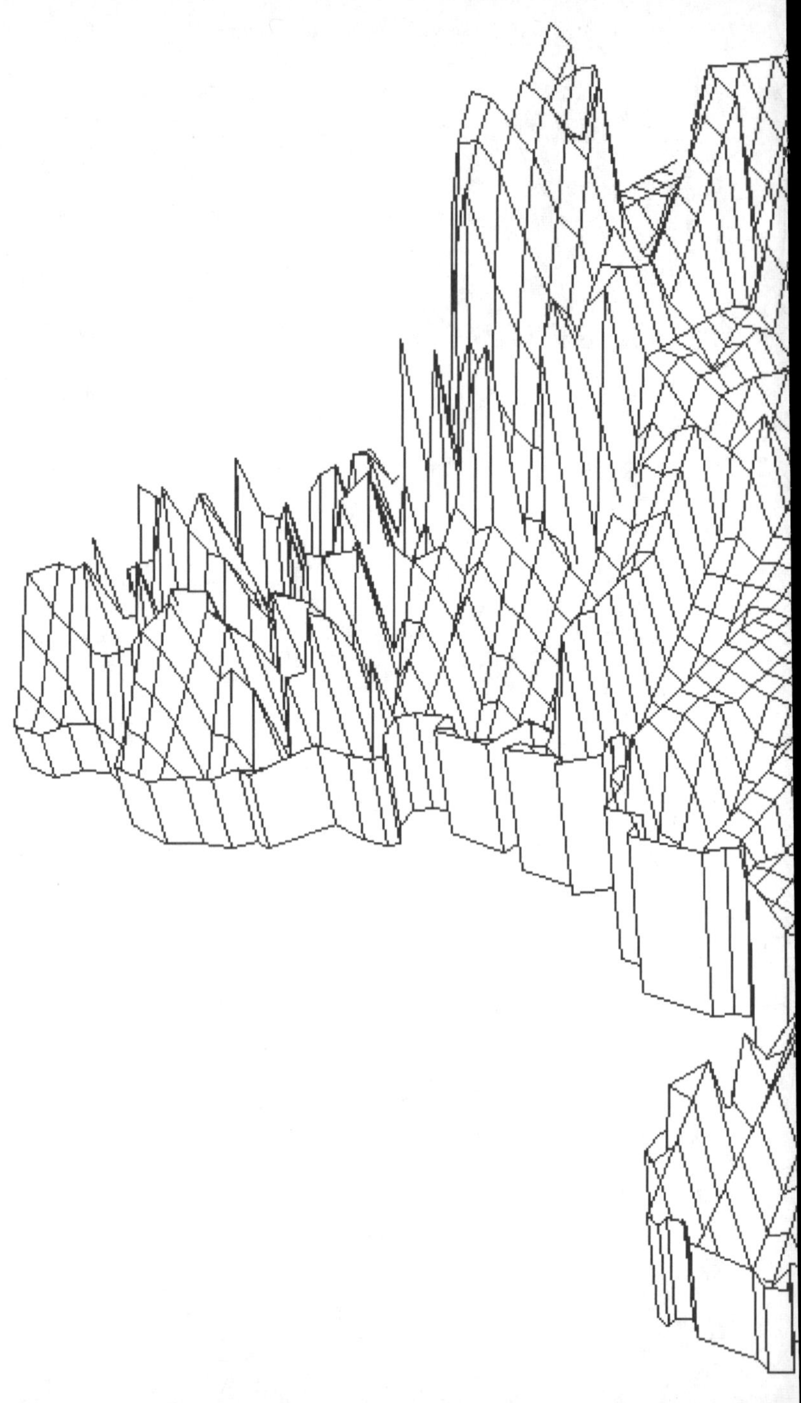

Yet nowhere in the country itself is there the impression

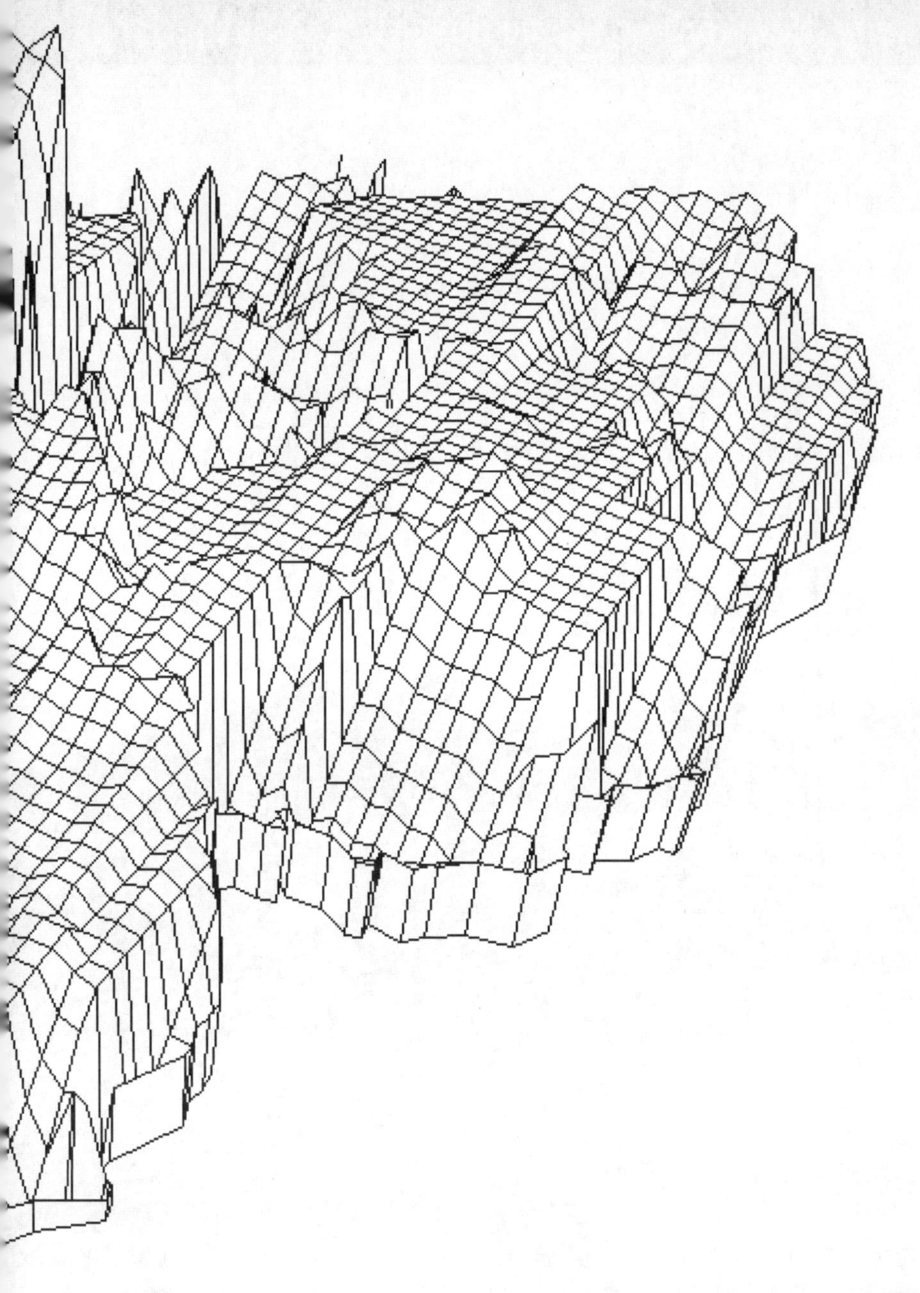

that this really is the case. Certainly not when compared to

Hong Kong, New York or Rio de Janeiro. The Netherlands may

it seem to be filling up with a suburban 'matter' of low cost

be well populated generally but not unduly so. Vast areas of

housing-with-gardens, low rent offices, warehouses, factory-style farms, motorcycle scrambling areas and other elements

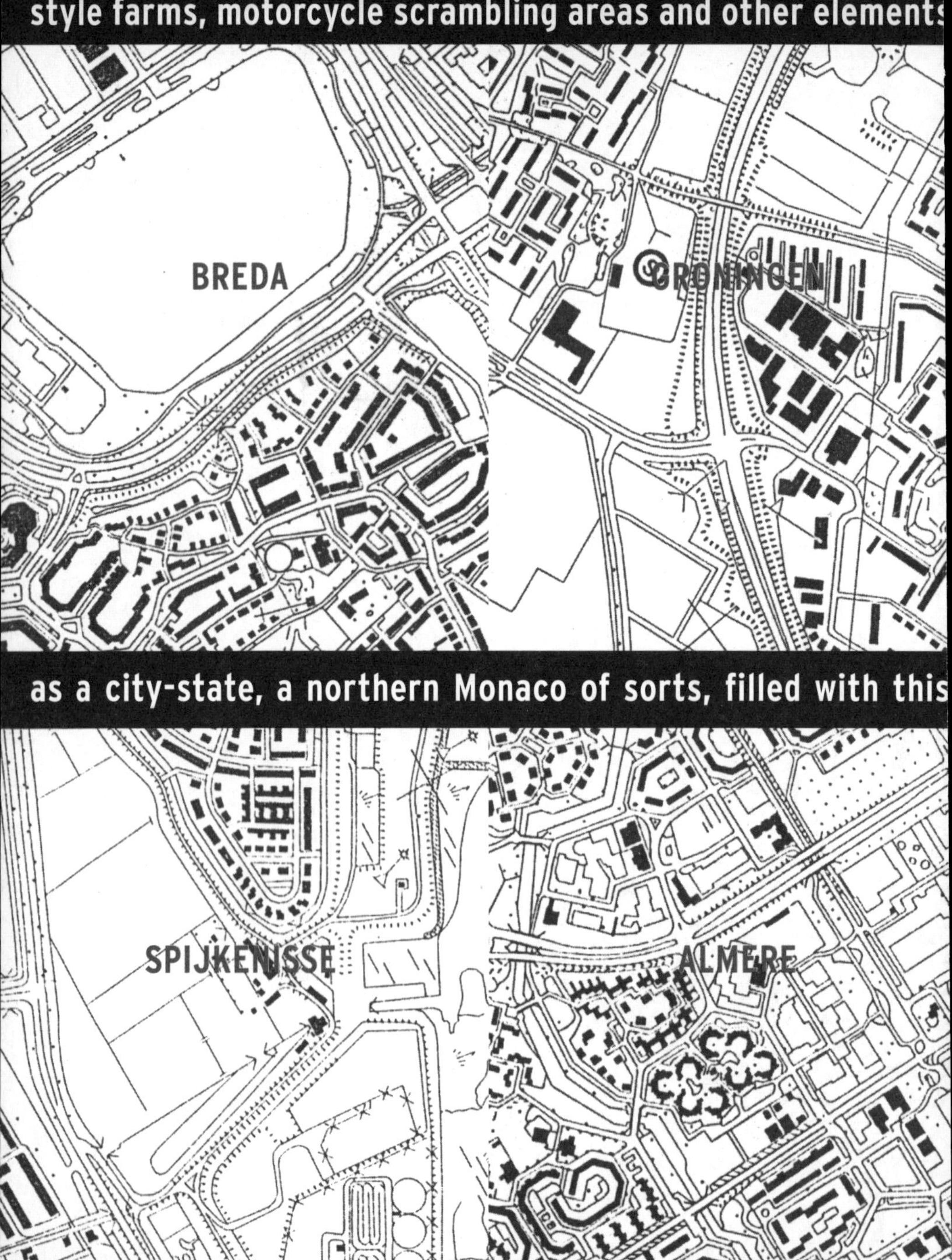

as a city-state, a northern Monaco of sorts, filled with this

organization, consisting as it does of development that has

with a lowish density. The country can steadily be regarded

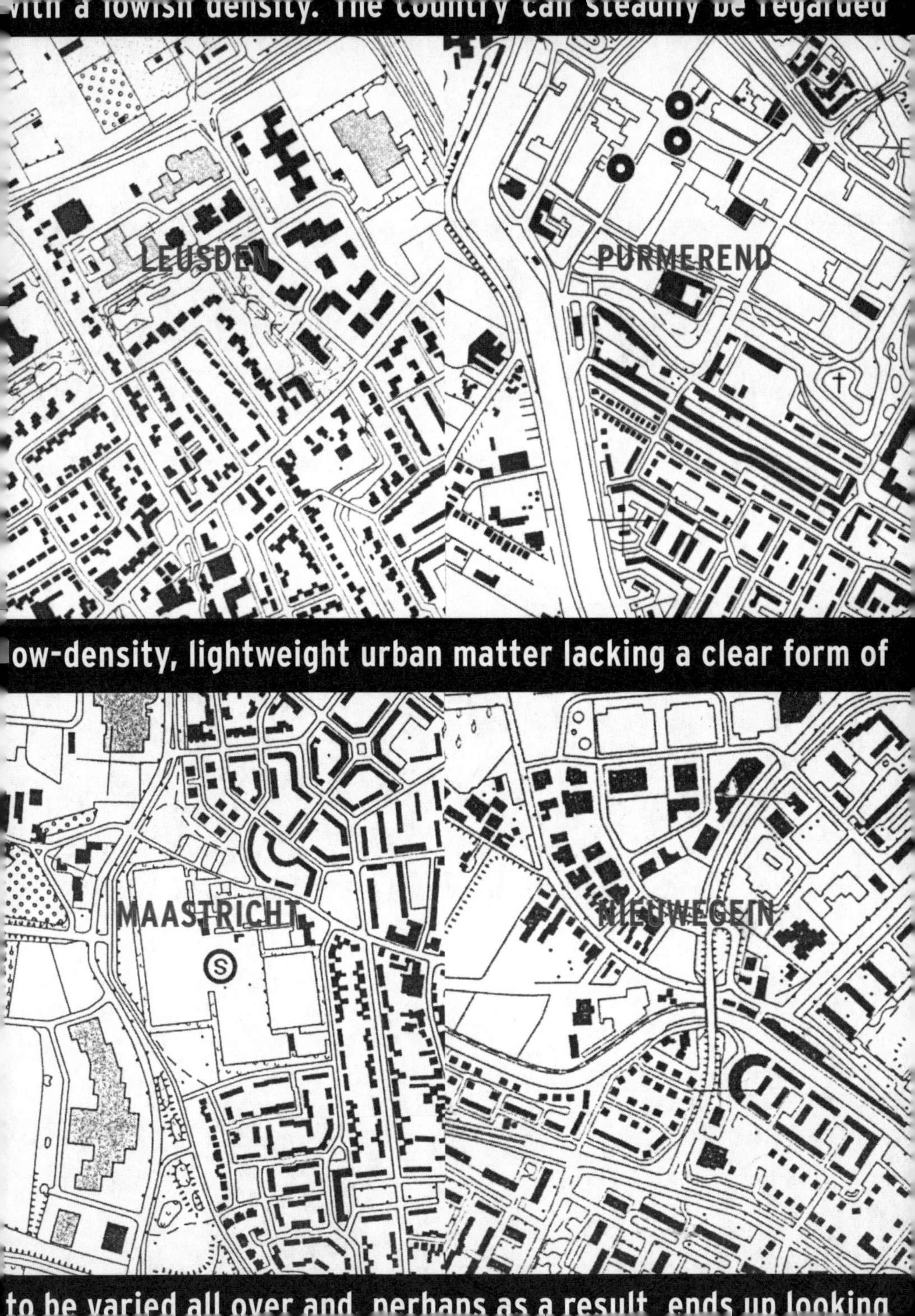

ow-density, lightweight urban matter lacking a clear form of

to be varied all over and, perhaps as a result, ends up looking the same. This urbanity is more concerned with quantity than

that cannot be considered entirely valuable? Accepting this

will cover most of the areas still open and envelop our entire

situation by carrying densities to an extreme and ruffling the

with quality. How then are we to cope with an urban matter

condition as fixed and simply continuing the present trend

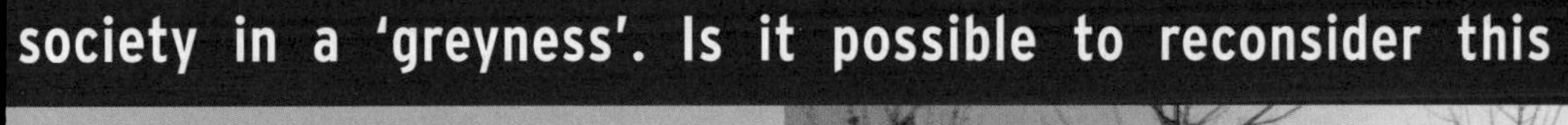

society in a 'greyness'. Is it possible to reconsider this

texture with inserts or polarities? Is it possible to imagine ultra-dense areas that can soak up programme like a sponge

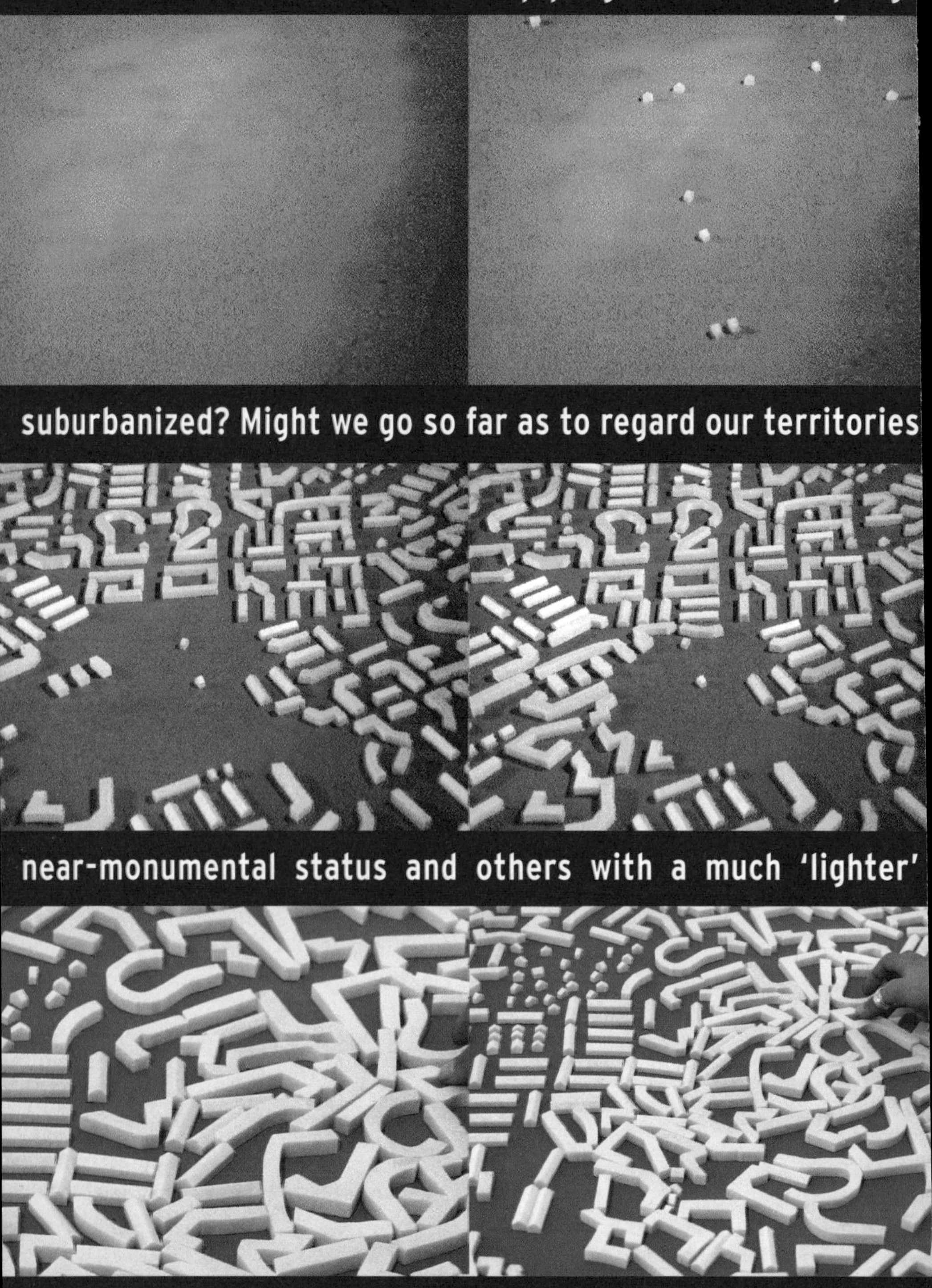

suburbanized? Might we go so far as to regard our territories

near-monumental status and others with a much 'lighter'

impossibilities of these extremes and discover their

and save our pastoral landscapes from being totally

as a confluence of areas with a dense and more permanent,

mode of urbanism? Can we examine the possibilities and

prospects and limitations?

The world of the extreme Floor Area Ratio,

CONTENTS

LITENESS

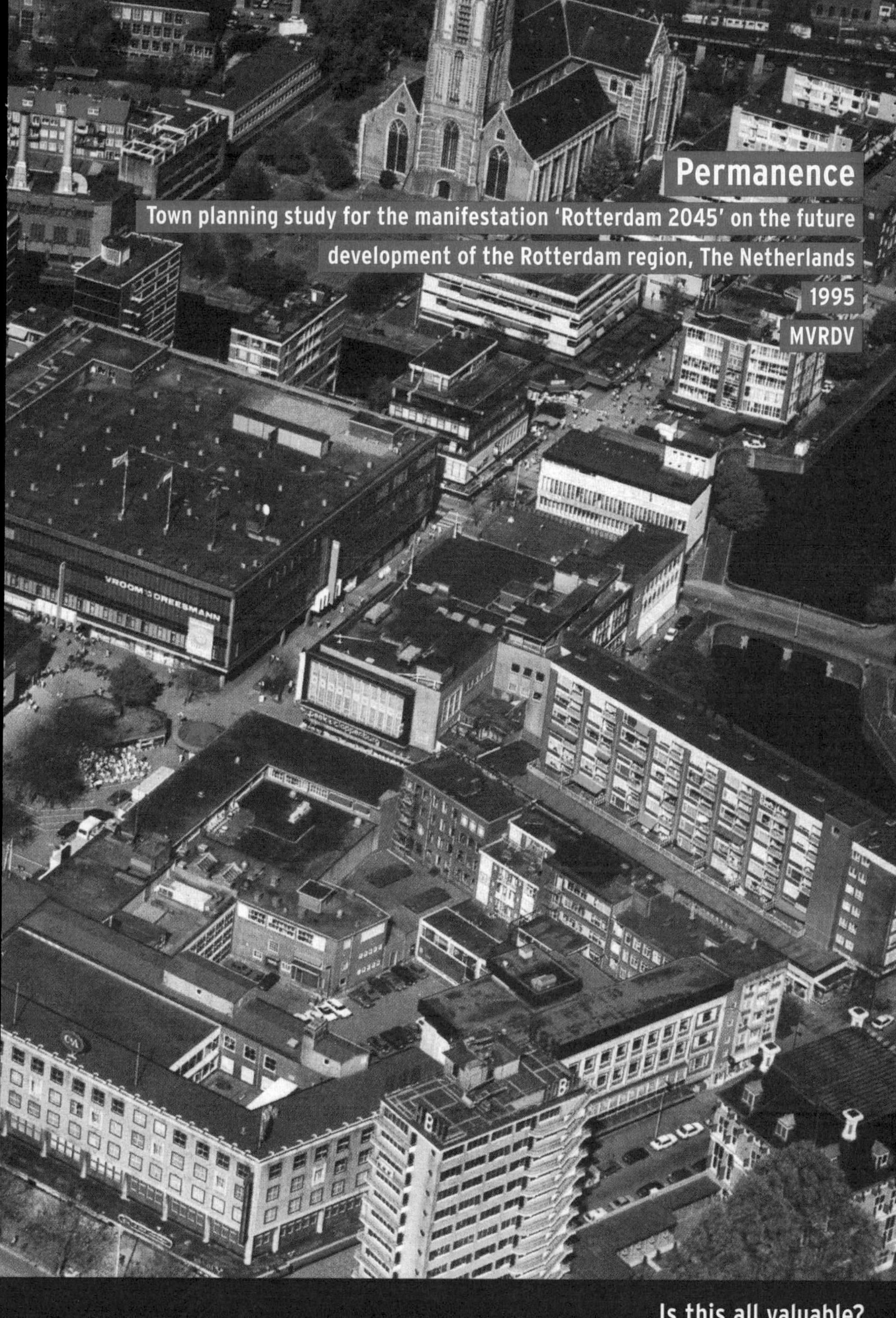

Permanence

Town planning study for the manifestation 'Rotterdam 2045' on the future development of the Rotterdam region, The Netherlands

1995

MVRDV

Is this all valuable?

Can we define an environment that can be broken down or cleared more easily

we imagine a 'lighter' mode of urbanism, one that can be considered as non-

manifests itself more with temporary and short-term behaviour than with a

can be more connected with the word landscape than with the word city. This

so that we can change our urbanistic goals within a relatively short time? Can

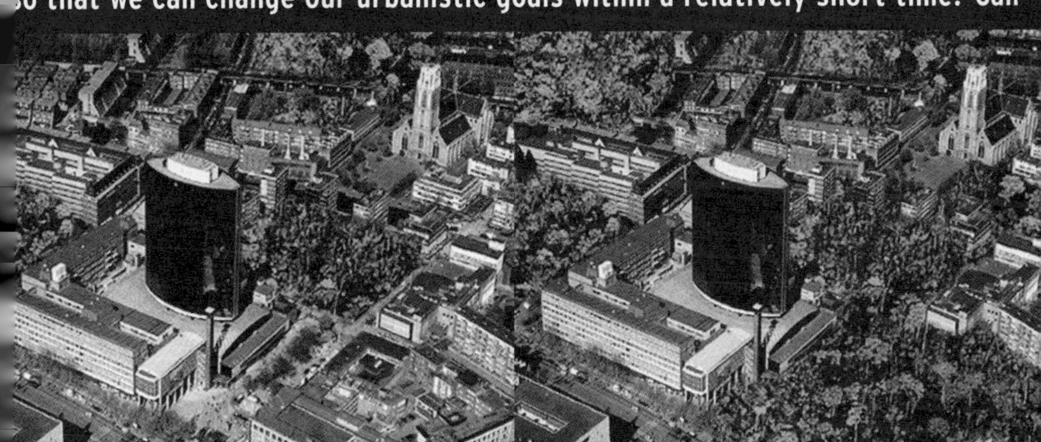

designed, non-designated, less regulated and more free? An urbanism that

'frozen' eternal condition. An urbanism that cultivates the unexpected and that

'lite' urbanism questions the permanence of the city; should we regard all of

the existing urban fabric as permanent? Are all our buildings that beautiful o-
heavy and fixed mode of urbanistic behaviour be replaced by a lighter form
the economical value of the built environment, we can estimate its necessity
cars (six years), many houses have an economical value of thirty to forty years

valuable that we have to work with them as if they were monuments? Can this

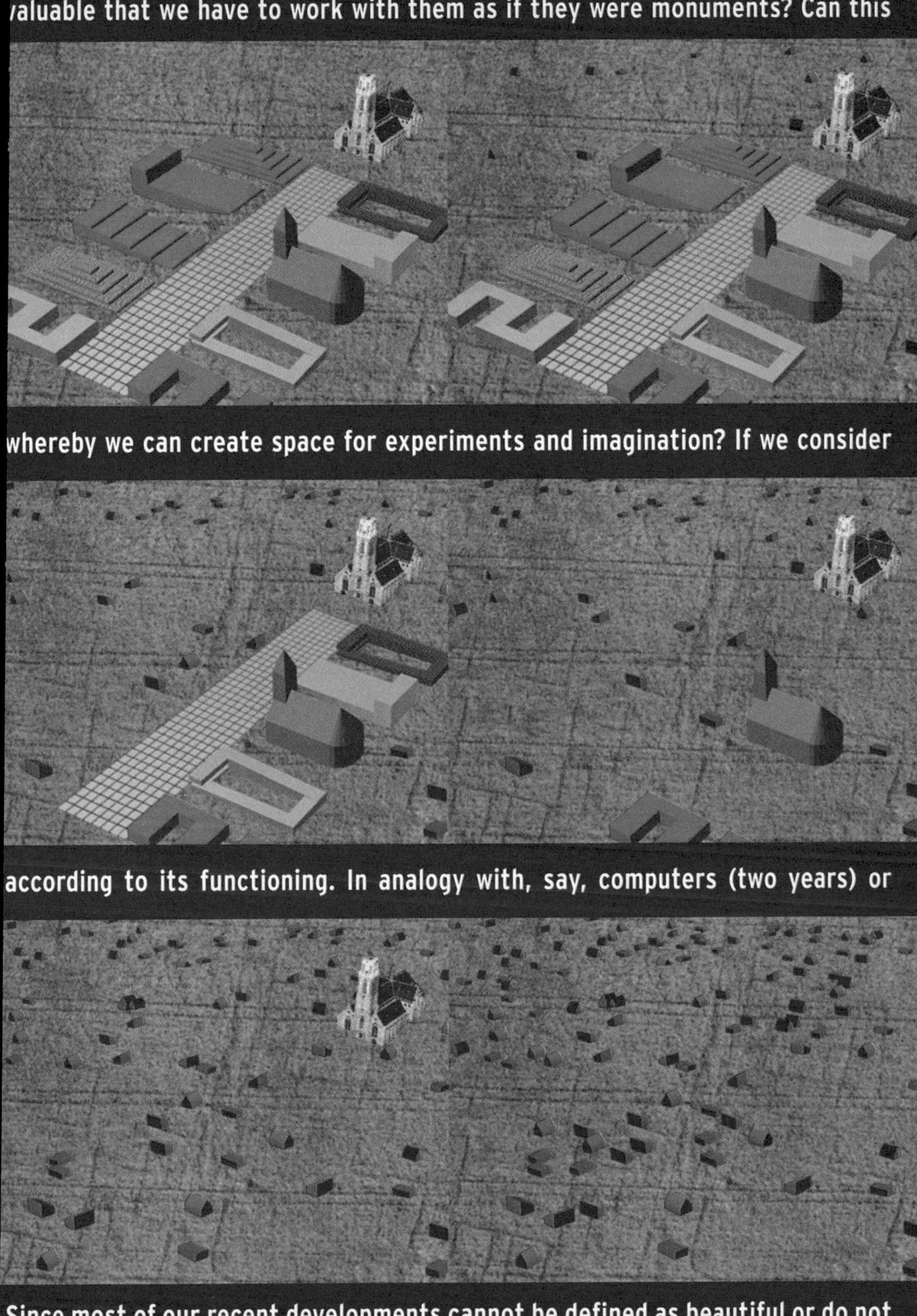

whereby we can create space for experiments and imagination? If we consider

according to its functioning. In analogy with, say, computers (two years) or

Since most of our recent developments cannot be defined as beautiful or do not possess eternal value, gigantic 'voids' and multiple fantasies can be foresee

so that islands of monuments appear as Mont St. Michels in an expanse of

within thirty years. Vast areas of our towns can be broken down and redesigned

emptiness. Existing towns have the opportunity to dissolve in 'landscape'

Extreme mixes of programmes become imaginable: from living at a farm to

Broadacre City, in which an agro-urban society can be developed through a

arming within the town. This Lite City registers as an 'echo' of Wright's

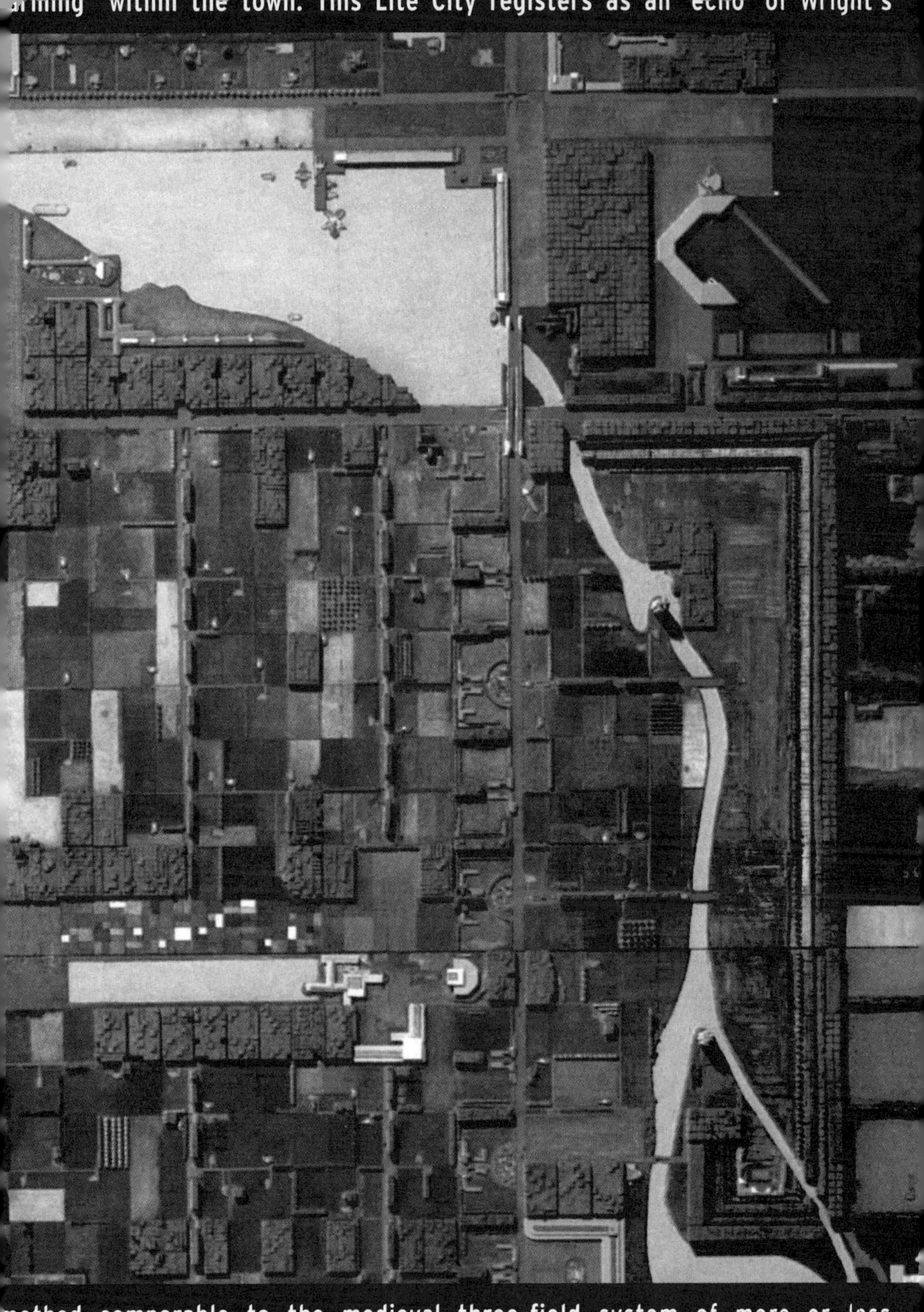

method comparable to the medieval three-field system of more or less temporary occupation. A town with its own logic and logistics, in which 'change

urbanism can be enforced by reducing the economical value of extensive part

instead of sewage pipes, electricity cables for heating instead of gas pipes

as a place. One that defines space for the unpredictable. This lighter form of

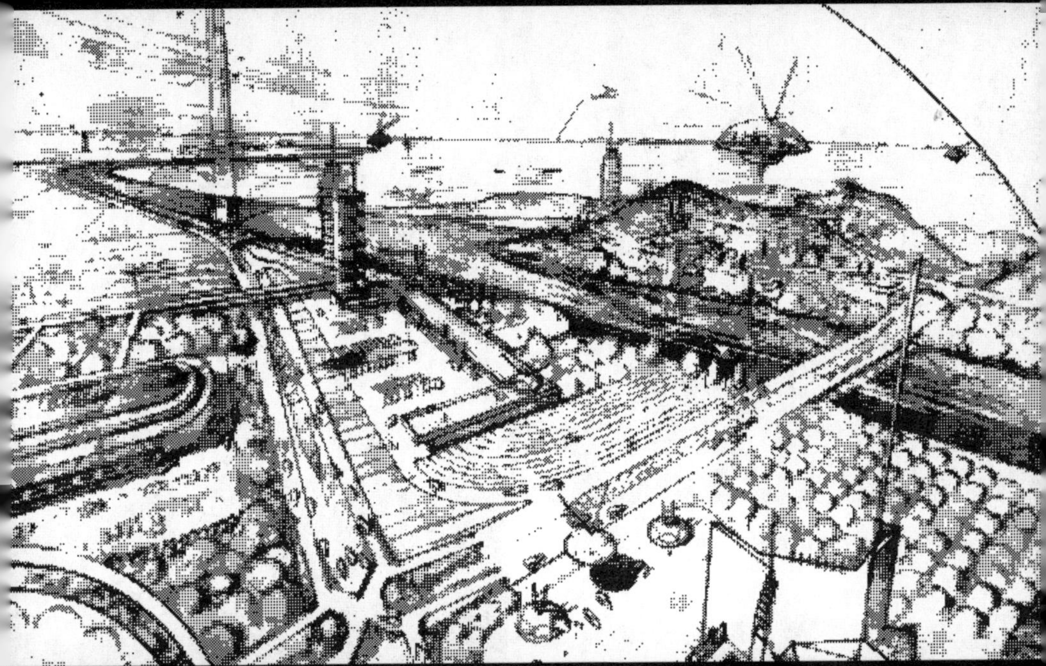

of our building production: grass roads instead of asphalt, ecological pools

mobile phones instead of telecom lines, timber piles instead of sand foundations, minibuses or buses-on-demand instead of expensive metro lines

COSTS COSTS

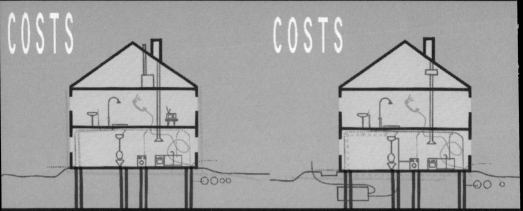

affordable within the existing budget, so that we can develop big gardens

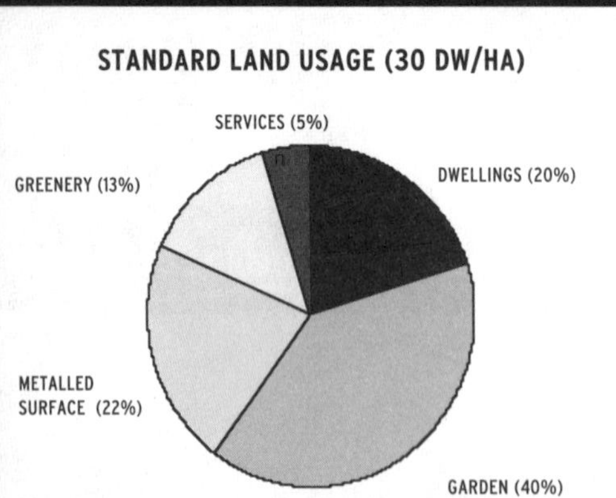

view. So that the claustrophobia of the suburb can be put into perspective by

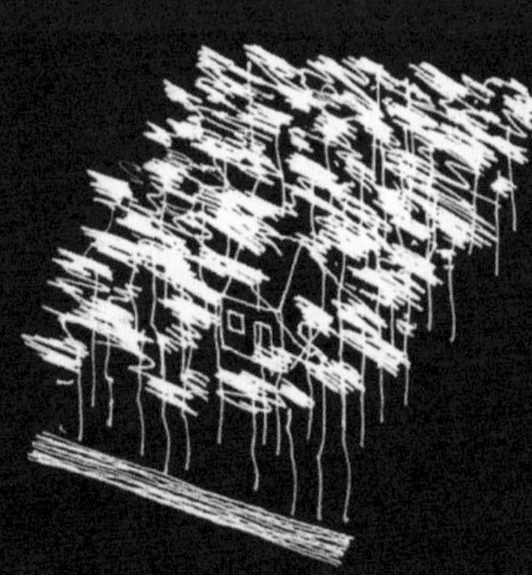

ecology. It gives rise to the paradoxical feeling that ecological sustainability

his economy can create exciting possibilities. Very low densities are

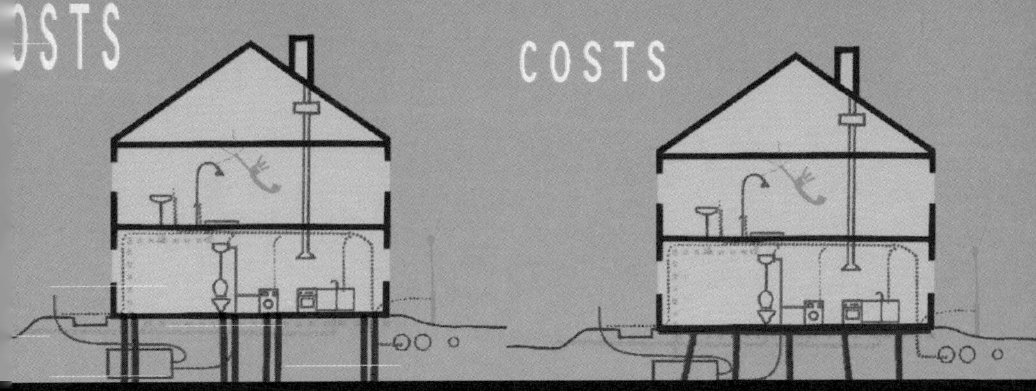

around the houses. Or a communal forest in which the houses disappear from

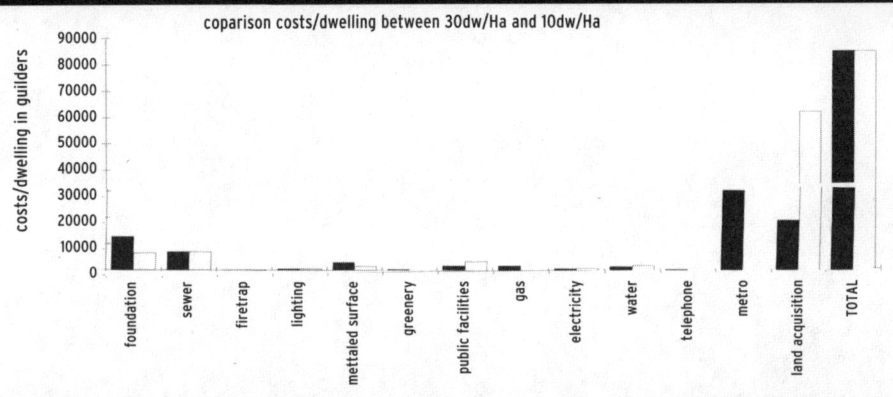

one's own private idyll or by a communal gesture. Economy thus links arms with

LAND USAGE WITH LESS DWELLINGS (10 DW/HA)

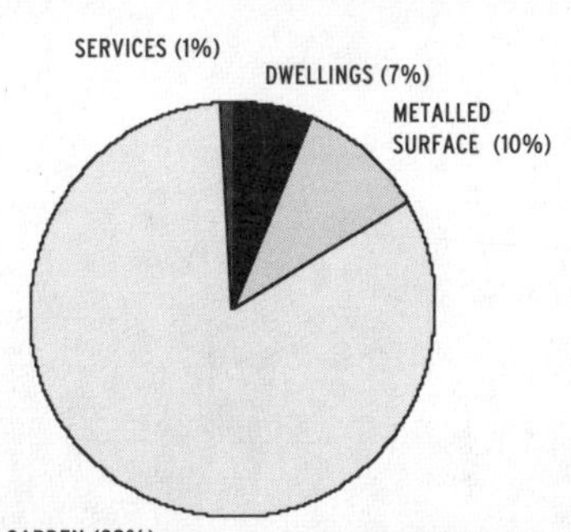

ECOLOGY = ECONOMY

has been translated into liteness and temporariness. This liteness can impact

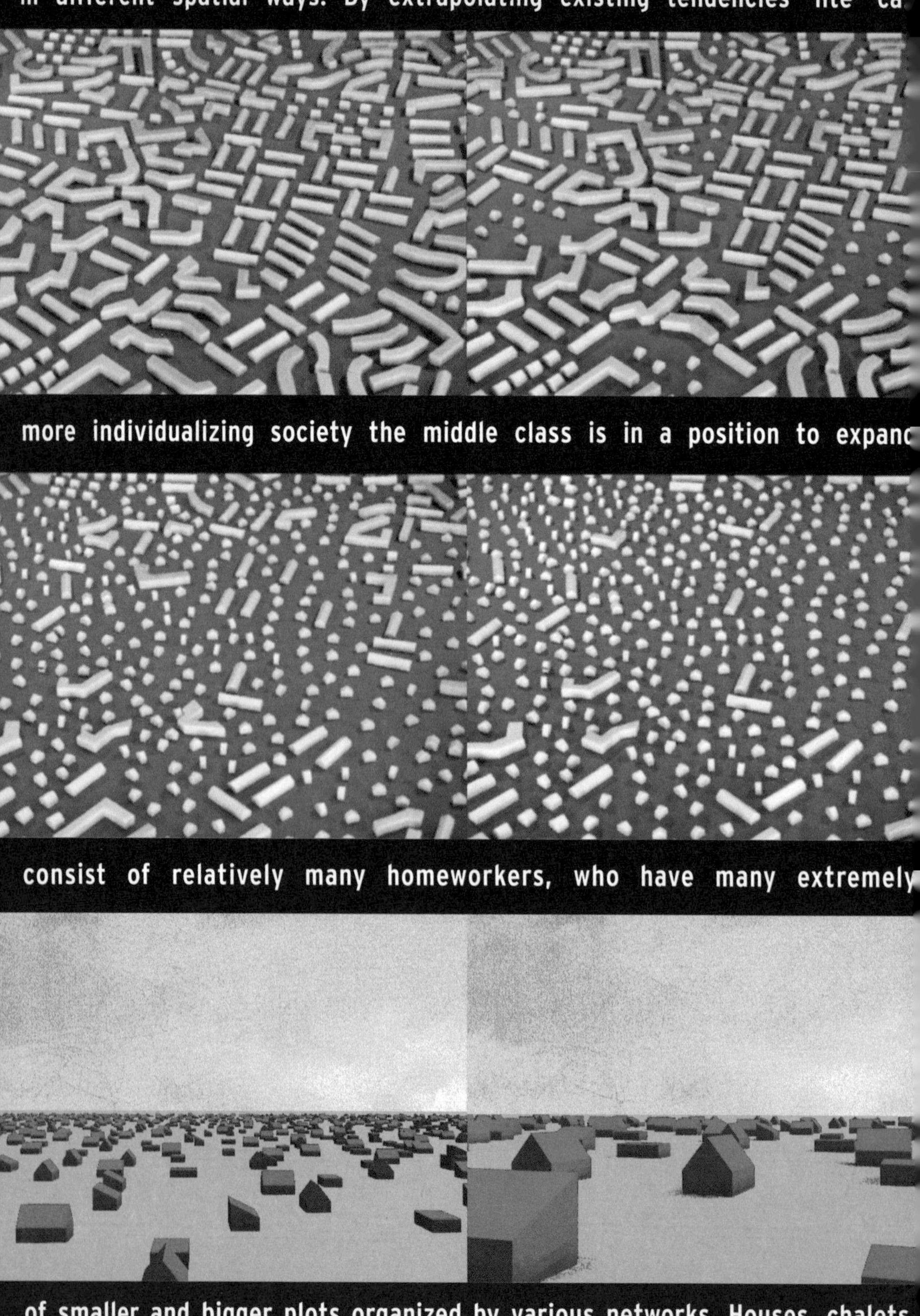

in different spatial ways. By extrapolating existing tendencies lite ca

more individualizing society the middle class is in a position to expand

consist of relatively many homeworkers, who have many extremely

of smaller and bigger plots organized by various networks. Houses, chalets

naterialize in a 'campingland' or a 'villageland'. **Campingland** In a more and

enormously, with more people working fewer hours. This middle class will then

differentiated working and living relationships. The city dissolves into a 'land'

ZUIDBUURT 57
Landhuis "Paddenburg" met rondom fraai uitzicht over de weilanden. Entree via eigen brug. Terras met natuurstenen vloer en glazen afscheiding. Entree: ruime hal met gard., meterkast, toilet met afzuiger, fontein en vloerverw. Inpandige berging met aansl. wasmach. en droger, c.v.-combiketel (1992). Ruime, mod. eetkeuken met plavuizen en vloerverw., alle moderne app., kookeiland met ker. kookplaat en

fermettes, homes, farms, condominiums and colonies are gathered together in

one big supercamp, where the holiday feeling is part of day-to-day life

fittest', those who have and those who have not will rally to protect or fight fo

colonies. The bigger the differences among the groups, the greater the

these villages with 'fields of fire' their relative autonomy can be assured. This

Villageland In a society that can be characterized by the 'survival of the

their property. This leads to towns composed of communities, villages or

complexity and the intenser the potential need for cohesion. By surrounding

Mölnlycke en Hay Management Consultants
kozen voor de inspirerende
omgeving van landgoed "De Breul"...
HayGroup
Mölnlycke

gives space for the necessary ecological fields.

KM PER CAR FOR HOLIDAY TRAVEL
(IN %)

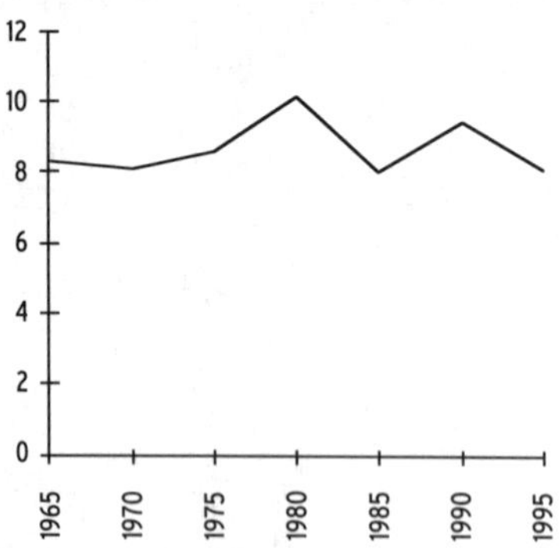

KM PER CAR FOR TRAVEL TO AND FROM WORK (IN %)

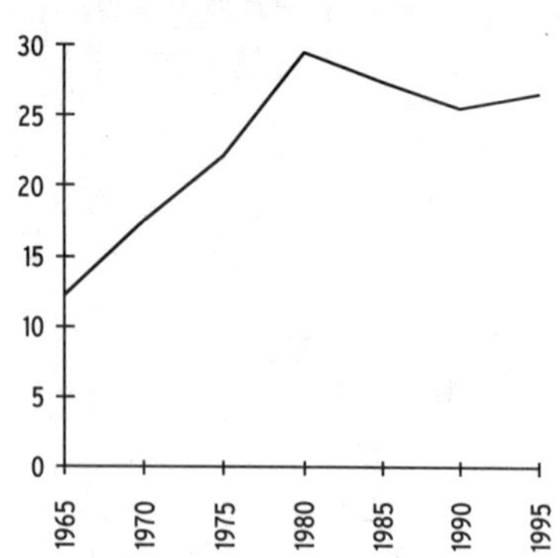

PERSONS GOING ON HOLIDAY
(IN % OF POPULATION)

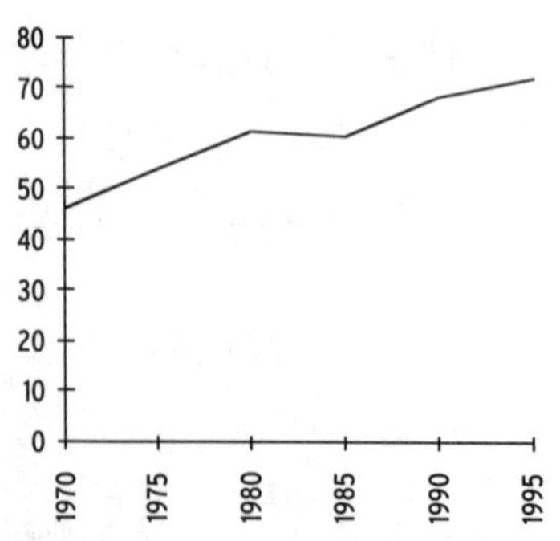

HOLIDAY OUTLAYS IN THE NETHERLANDS (IN MILLIONS)

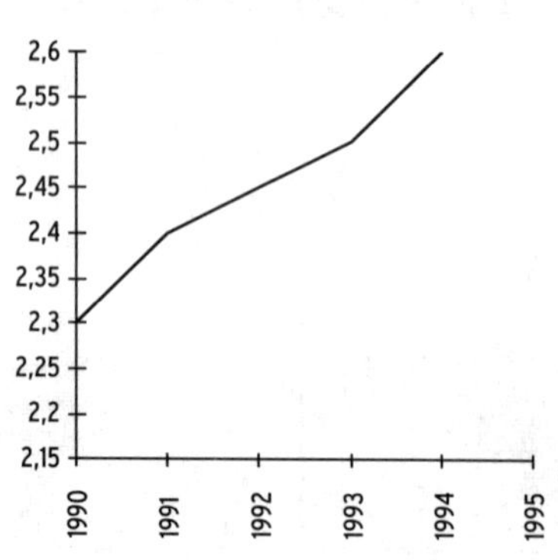

Dutch tendencies

Statistics

1996

Arnold Reijndorp and Vincent Kompier

Re-editing: MVRDV

KM PER CAR, TOTAL
(X 1000)

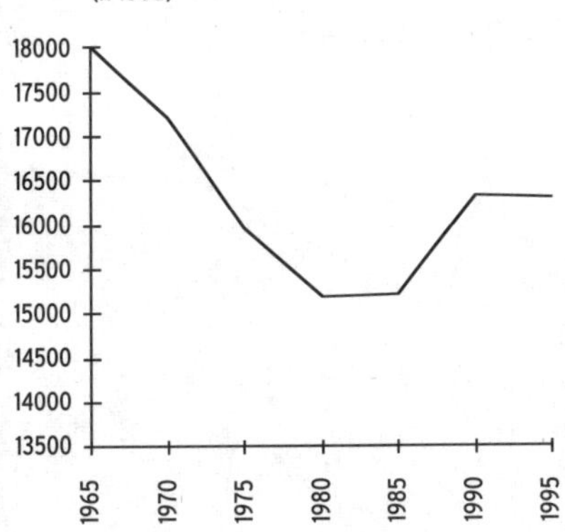

KM PER CAR, OTHER
(IN %)

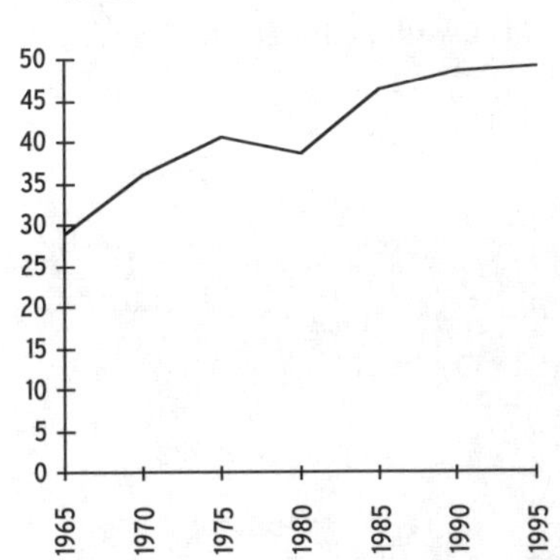

RETAIL SALES OF DIY ARTICLES
(INDEX 1985 = 100)

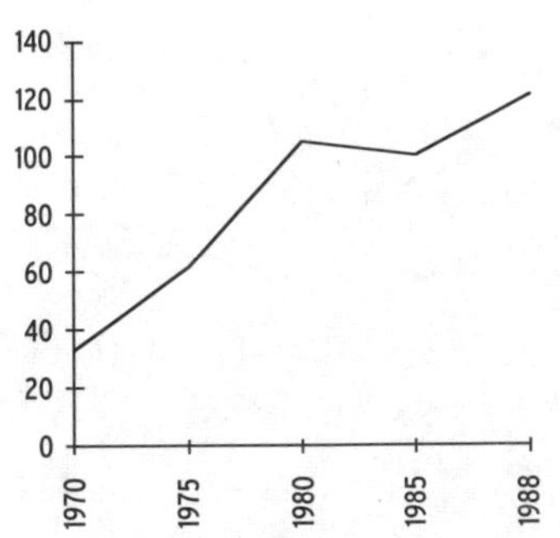

WORK RELATING TO PERSONAL OBLIGATIONS
(IN %)

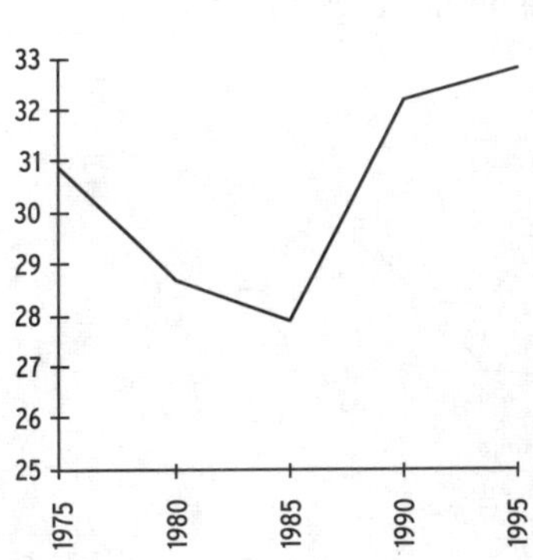

HOLIDAY OUTLAYS ABROAD
(IN MILLIONS)

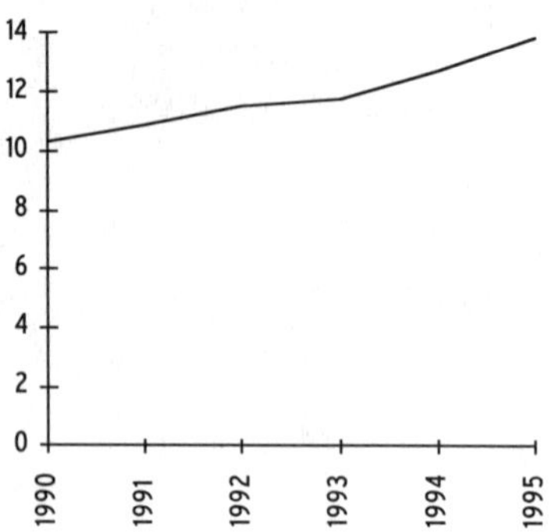

HOLIDAY OUTLAYS IN OTHER COUNTRIES
(IN MILLIONS)

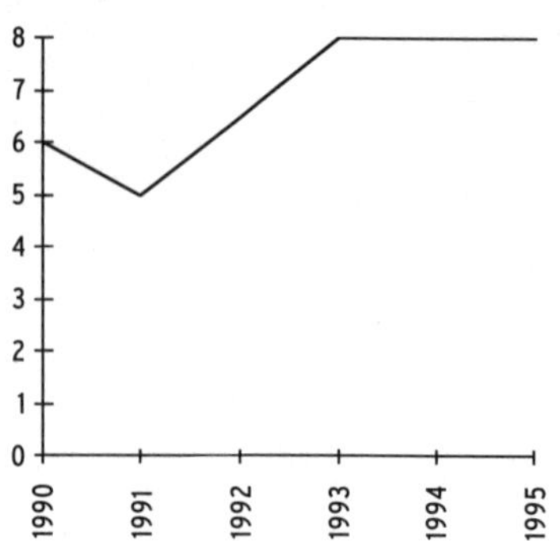

TELEPHONE CONNECTIONS
(X 1000)

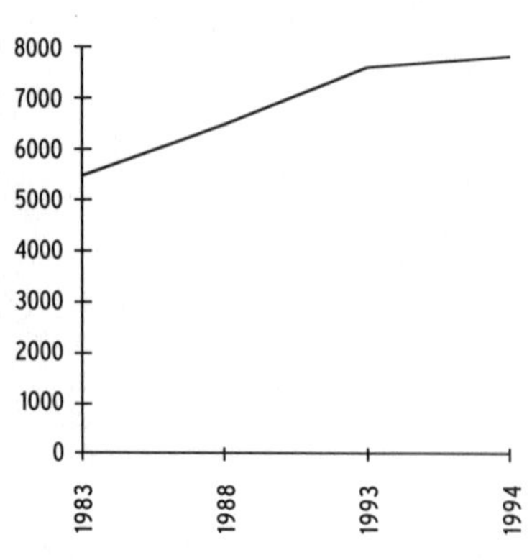

TELEPHONE USE IN NL
(X MLD)

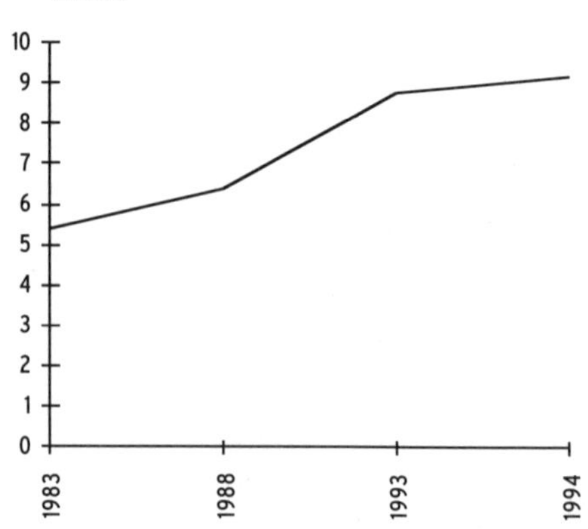

HOUSEHOLDS WITH A CAR
(IN %)

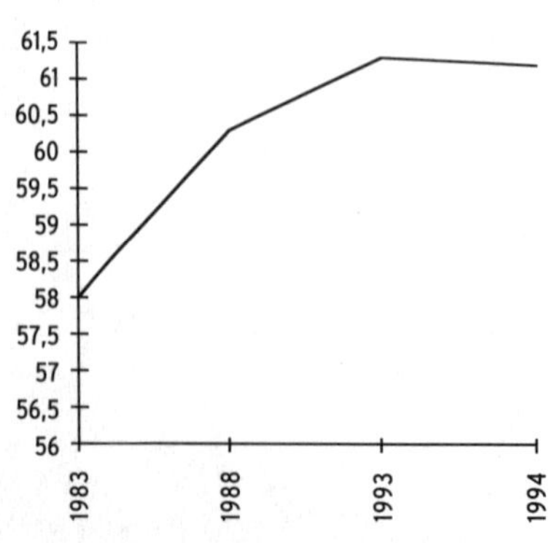

HOUSEHOLDS WITH MORE THAN TWO CARS
(IN %)

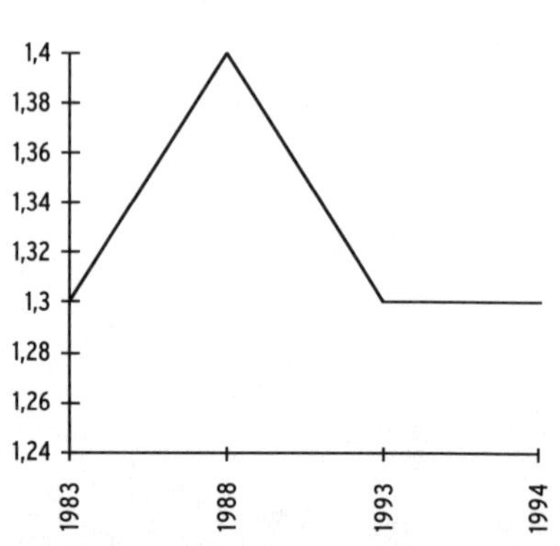

PERSONAL OBLIGATIONS
(HOUR/WEEK)

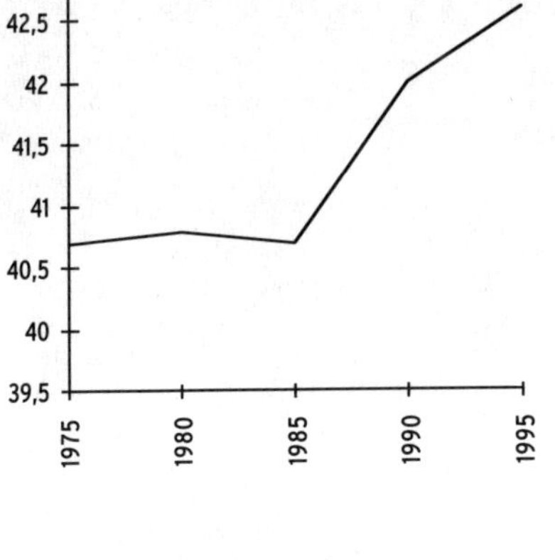

TOTAL NUMBER OF CRIMES
(IN THOUSANDS)

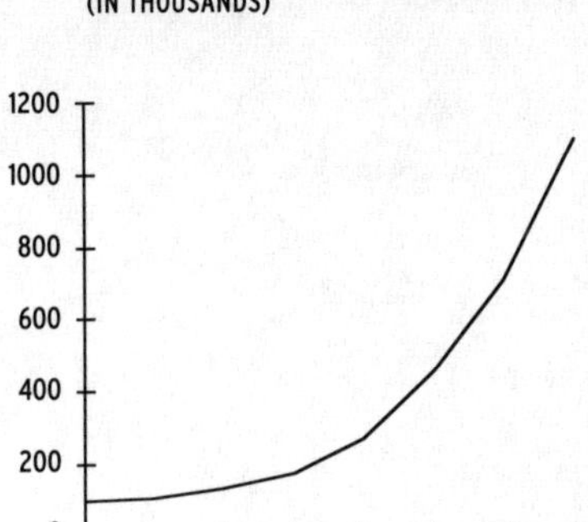
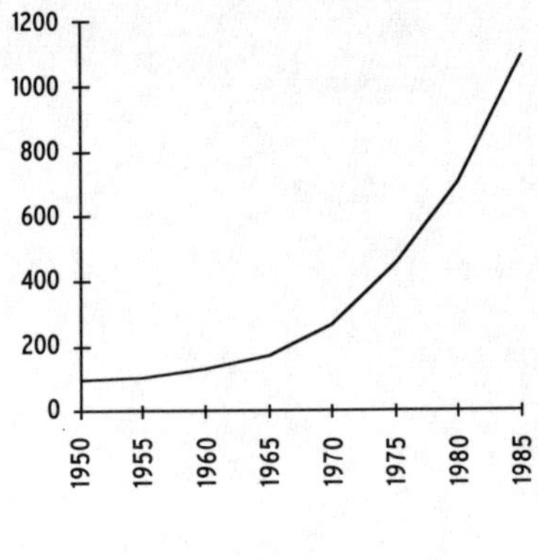

TELEPHONE USE ABROAD
(IN BILLIONS)

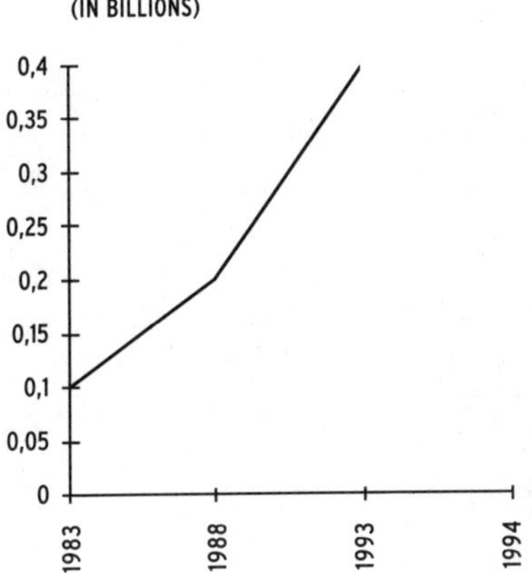

HOUSEHOLDS WITHOUT A CAR
(IN %)

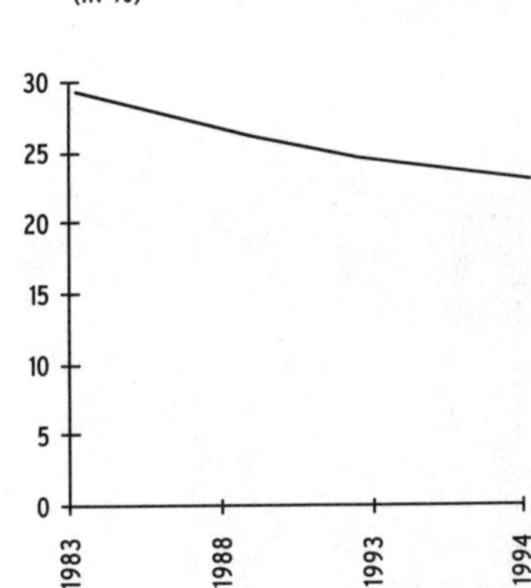

AVERAGE NUMBER OF WORKING HOURS
(PER WEEK)

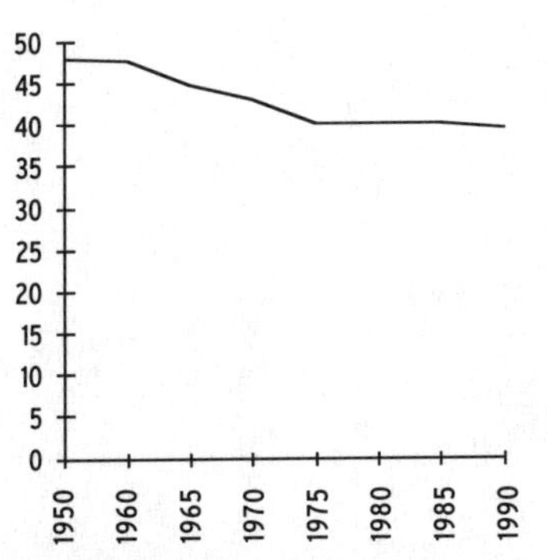

HOUSEHOLDS WITH TWO CARS
(IN %)

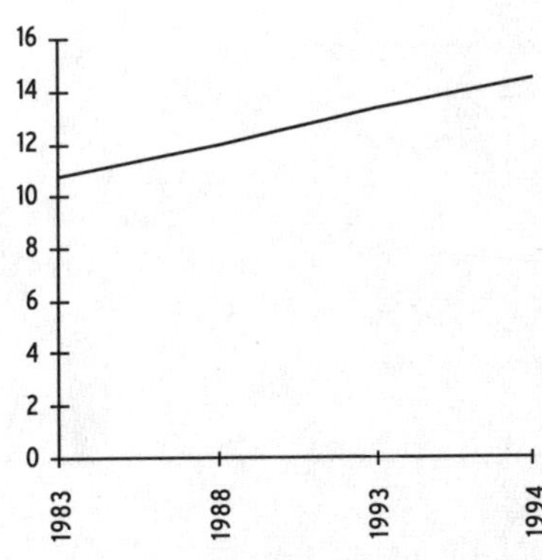

NUMBER OF INHABITANTS
(PER DWELLING)

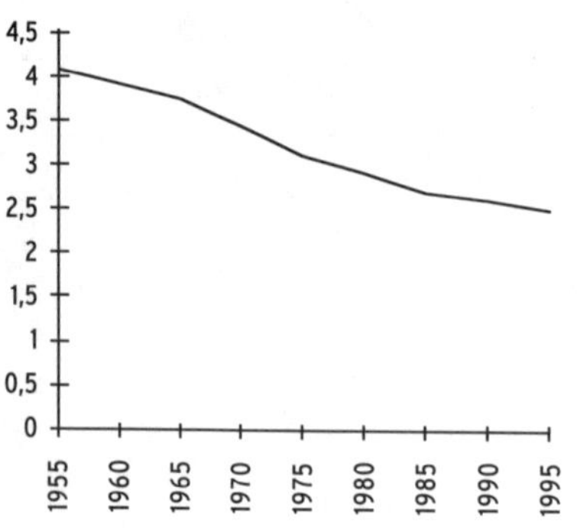

CARS
(X 1000)

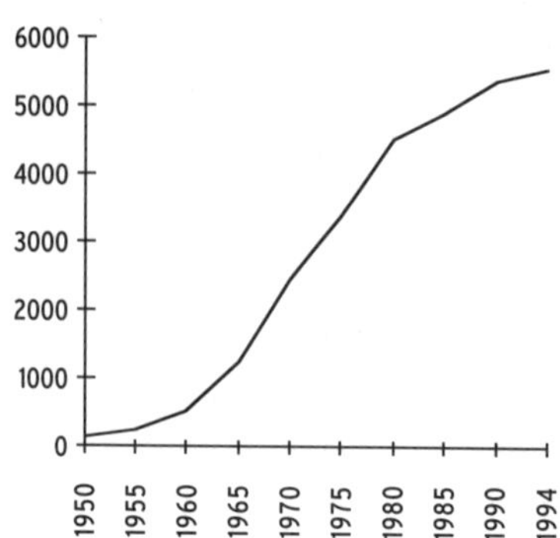

DIVORCED
(IN %)

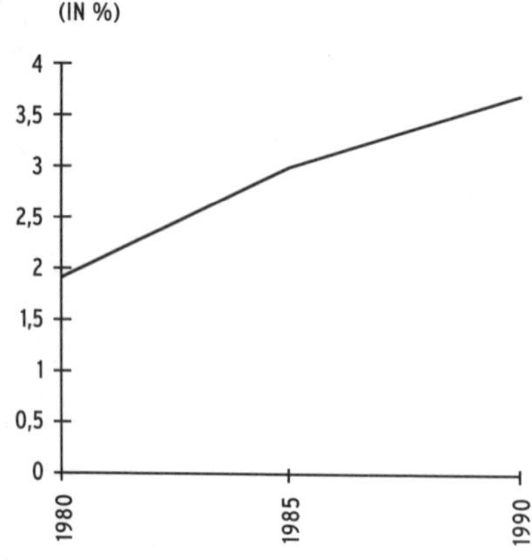

UNMARRIED
(IN %)

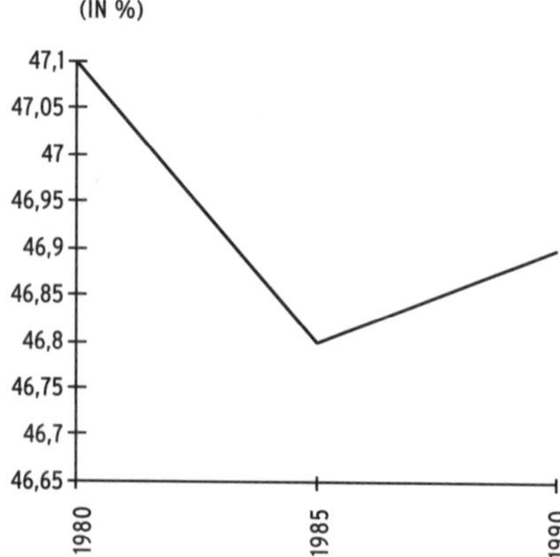

MARRIED
(IN %)

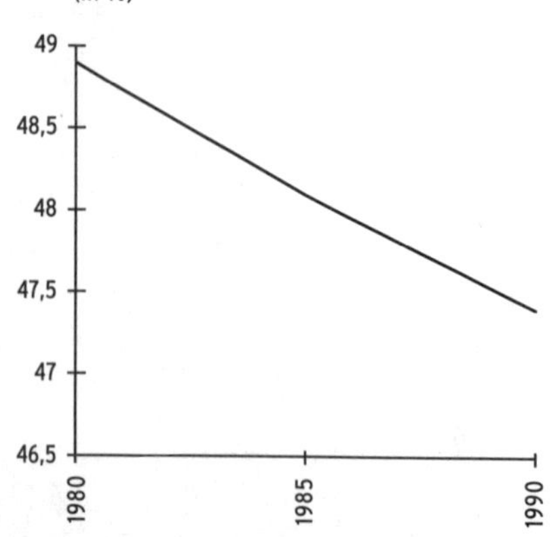

ACTIVE ENGAGEMENT IN SPORT
(IN %)

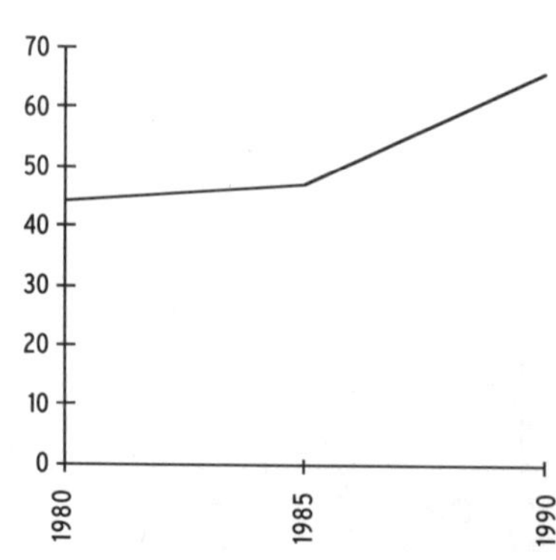

MEMBERSHIPS, ENTRANCE FEES SPORTS OUTINGS, HOLIDAYS
(INDEX 1990 = 100)

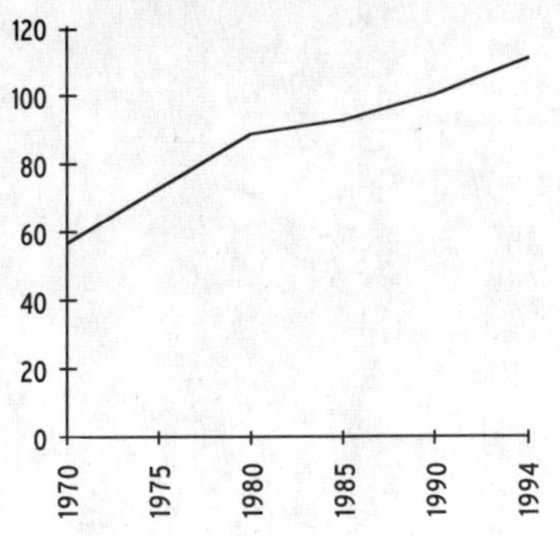

BOOKS, NEWSPAPERS AND MAGAZINES
(INDEX 1990 = 100)

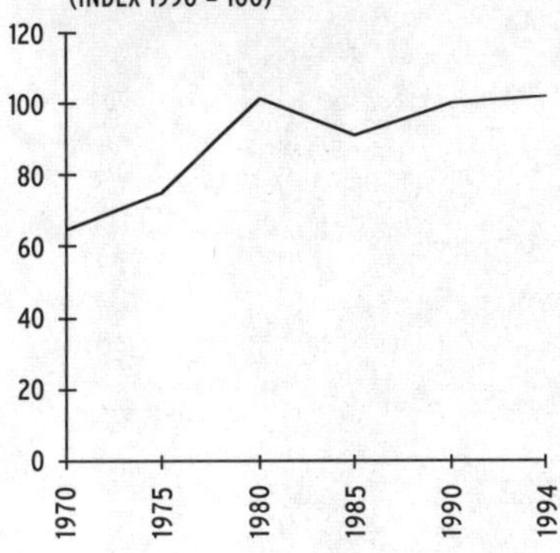

KM PER CAR FOR BUSINESS TRAVEL
(IN %)

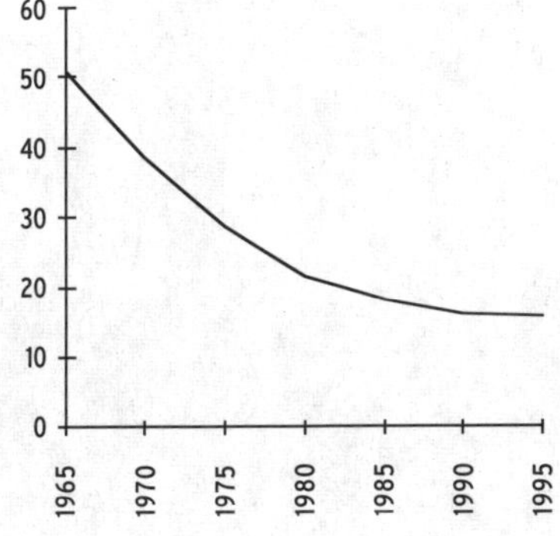

APPLIANCES AND ACCESSORIES FOR ADVANCEMENT AND RECREATION
(INDEX 1990 = 100)

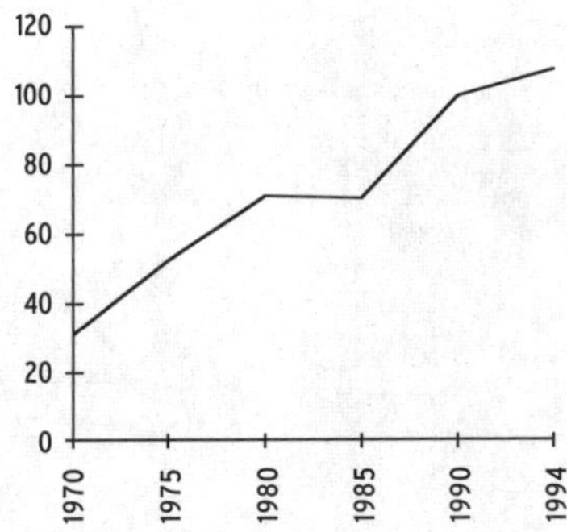

Campingland

Text

1997

Arnold Reijndorp and Vincent Kompier

Individualization Individualizing is on the increase. Having said that, its manifestation as loneliness, insecurity and unease is being fought with all possible means. Anything able to soften this negative development has priority. 'Organized' forms of confluence are impossible these days. Spontaneous organically evolved confluences, on the other hand, are certainly possible but need time. The question for the individualist is still: 'What do I gain from this, what does it give me?' The individualizing of leisure time means a decreasing interest in group sports, with the occasional exception of small groups. Community only counts here when it's convenient; freedom from obligations is more important. Often this sense of community is just an impulse - to go with a group to the laser games, or for a walk in the country.

The collective ordering of time is ceding to individual ordering of time. One product of this process of individualization is that everyone divides up their time according to their needs as individuals. This relates as much to families with children as to those without. Taking meals together has been replaced by an agenda of encounters. Yet the temporal division between work and family has remained pretty well the same over the years. Almost half of the women with children refuse to work, the other half will only work part-time. The shifting division of roles within households signifies a greater transport mobility. If car use is to be further restrained in future this will put the already overburdened timetable of symmetrical households under even greater pressure.
For a certain group, leisure time activity is occupying a more and more central place in life. Not work but free time gives life meaning for this group. The diversity of leisure time activity is increasing, there is the desire to maximize the number of free-time activities. It is no longer so that one hobby is indulged to the hilt; many hobbies practiced in tandem mean more status. Even in one's leisure time a full diary means prestige. A major aspect is part-time work or work done on an irregular basis. This situation has mades it almost impossible to synchronize activities with others.

In identifying leisure activity we can make a differentiation by age: a generation or more of older people entering the 'leisure time market' now and in the future grew up in post-war prosperity and are better educated. Because of this they exhibit a far more modern free-time behaviour than their predecessors. Advertisements and media capitalize on this: take the Dutch TV ad showing a 55-plusser extemporising on a drumkit, or the Golden Girls comedy series in which four ladies of riper years share a house in the Sun Belt. This trend is going to continue. With the decrease in the number of young people a more dominant 'oldies culture' will emerge.

Life style At present lifestyle is strongly focused on the image presented to the outside world. The media are particularly responsible in defining what today's home should look like; the number of TV programmes that feature home furnishing and garden design is still on the increase. Kiosks also have special shelves set aside for home and garden magazines.

The importance of material property is waning as a hallmark of status. Social status can no longer be read from one's car alone. The burgeoning prosperity has brought consumer goods within easier reach of most people, thus lessening their exclusiveness and status value. Taste counts more than cash these days. The design lookalike lamp selling like hot cakes for fifty guilders looks the spitting image of the original on sale at Cappelini's for nine times that much (though an expert eye can immediately spot the 'negligible' difference).

This has led in the last few years to a drop in retail profits. Particularly because the number of young people is on the decrease, and the fashion sensitivity of the young no longer manifests itself in pricey consumer articles, the retail trade has had to rethink its strategy to turn the drop in profits back into a rise.

Individualism in social behaviour is not easing off, however, and so new means of distinguishing are required. You are no longer what you have (house, job, car, microwave) but what you do (bungee-jumping, parachute jumping, own business, following a course, going to lectures, visiting museums). This has its impact in practice: outlays in the retail trade have dropped in recent years. Retail trade specialists are busy considering new formulas. It could well be that the traditional shopping chains are on the way out with a subsequent greater interest in small-scale shopping facilities in tandem with large-scale department store cum leisure developments combining recreation, entertainment and retail.

Culture is another means of making an individual of yourself, of which the clearest expression is lifestyle. The rise in the average level of education

means that people are thinking more about these aspects.
'They don't want to end up in the umpteenth row house in Hoofddorp West,' according to a real estate agent in an interview. Research has proved that the scale of identification with dwelling is restricted to one's house and the most immediate vicinity. The exterior and interior of the house are used as a means to stress one's own style and uniqueness/identity. The identity of the neighbourhood and the district is of lesser value, save for the presence of facilities.
A further means of personal expression besides the look of the house and the garden is the degree and type of recreation indulged in.

Organizing daily life The collective ordering of time is ceding to an individual ordering of time. One product of this process of individualization is that everyone divides up their time according to their needs as individuals. This relates as much to families with children as to those without. Taking meals together has been replaced by an agenda of encounters. Yet the temporal division between work and family has remained pretty well the same over the years. Almost half of the women with children refuse to work, the other half will only work part-time.

Man (52) works as a housing official at Amersfoort Municipality, and lives with a schoolmistress teaching at a primary school in Nieuwland, the latest residential district in Amersfoort. They have four children. He and his girlfriend each work 32 hours a week, variously divided over five days: 'The children arrive home from school in varying order. In principle we have a childminder from three o'clock on. I myself don't work on Wednesday and Friday afternoons, so we don't need one then. The childminder makes the evening meal and leaves at half-past five. By this time everyone should be home. The boys have piano lessons, they've usually been there. One goes to basketball, another to football, a third to volleyball, and I go to volleyball as well. My partner is presently on a course, which means she is studying evenings. Sometimes I have to spend an evening at a board meeting of the foundation dealing with reception centres. My partner used to work before and had a son at that time, so she was used to childminders. I myself had home help for a long time as my wife had died. Our attitude was to the effect that we would
both carry on working, even though it was only four days in the week, and we wanted a childminder. The other children are older so you don't have to do everything for them. Many things they do for themselves. And our motto is 'do the things you want to do'. We

do take them once every so often to their sports clubs, but in principle they should be able to manage it themselves.'

Timing problems A woman from Overkroeten-Noord (42) sells cosmetics and uses her home as a base. She has trouble getting the agendas of the members of her family to coincide at those special times: 'Actually we don't eat together any more in the evening. Well, I often have supper with the children, the three of us. Or we have to wait until eight or half-past for my husband, but that doesn't work either because then the children have other things to do.'

The daily life in Diemen-Noord of a husband (44) and wife (42), who both work in Amsterdam and have a son, as told by the woman: 'I get up at half-past six, feed the boy and then we all leave the house at a quarter to eight. First Richard drops me at my work. Then he brings Jan to the crèche and carries on to his work. I work until four or thereabouts, Richard until half five. We usually give each other a ring in the afternoon. Often it happens that I'm in the town and so we arrange to meet at the crèche and then all drive home together. On the way back we buy some meat and vegetables, as the shops here are open until half six. Sometimes Richard picks up Jan, in which case I come home by train. On average we have two evenings a week for ourselves. So every two weeks we spend an evening out together. Otherwise, we're at home; if one goes out the other babysits.'

Use of the car The shifting division of roles within households signifies a greater car mobility. If car use is to be further restrained in future this will put the already overburdened timetable of symmetrical households under even greater pressure.

A family in Prinsenland with two children got rid of their car, with the result that they almost never get out of Rotterdam, as: 'This requires a certain amount of planning. What time does the train leave, what time does it go back. It's just too complicated. With a car you just jump in and drive off.' If you have a car you're going to make use of it: 'The thing is, if it's just you in the car it can be expensive, if there are two of you it's cheaper. You're going to use it anyway.'

A woman of 36 works forty hours a week as a receptionist in Leiden. Her husband works as a chauffeur in Amsterdam, and has set up his own travel agency. She now travels to work by train: 'I'd buy a second car if I had the money. It takes from half an hour to an hour to travel to or from work by public transport. I often miss the bus on the way back and have to wait half an hour. That's not much fun particularly in the evenings.'

Leisure time For a particular group, leisure time activity is occupying a more and more central place in life. The diversity of leisure time activity is increasing, there is the desire to maximize the number of free-time activities. It is no longer so that one hobby is indulged to the hilt; many hobbies practiced in tandem mean more status. A full diary means prestige. A major factor is part-time work or work done on an irregular basis. This situation has made it difficult to synchronize activities with others. Activities indulged in in leisure time are often contingent on a whim, your mood or the weather. Your time is only really your own when you can fill it in as you please: 'The only thing you're tied to is work times, what you do with the rest is up to you.' Variation and improvisation seem to be the key factors in leisure time. In a household in Hoofddorp, the husband (39) works 40 hours a week as a fire safety consultant, his wife (38) works 38 hours a week as a product manager; they have two children: 'If it's nice weather we go to the beach and if it isn't so nice we head into the town. There are times when we go to the woods and then carry on to the town, or the other way around.'

Privacy Individualizing is on the increase. However, its manifestation as loneliness, insecurity and unease is being fought with all possible means. Anything able to soften this negative developed has priority. 'Organized' forms of confluence are impossible these days. Spontaneous organically evolved confluences, on the other hand, are certainly possible but these need time. The question for the individualist is still: 'What do I gain from this, what does it give me?' The individualizing of leisure time means a decreasing interest in group sports, with the occasional exception of small groups. Community only counts here when it's convenient; freedom from obligations is more important. Often this sense of community is an impulse - to go with a group to the laser games, or for a walk in the country. This trend holds just as true for the setting up of residents' associations.

An older couple in Amersfoort - he (62) given an early retirement after years of working in the Amsterdam docks, she (58) a retired schoolteacher now active as the secretary of the residents' association in the apartment complex where the couple lives - have discovered the value of privacy after moving to an apartment. Privacy was something they had missed in the daily living environment of the single-family house they had moved from. 'Making friends is more difficult here than in a family house. There you see everyone sitting in the garden. But that has its disadvantages, for we really do like our privacy. You didn't have that at all where we used to live. You weren't even eating your meals in private.'

A forty-year-old woman, with academic training as a psychotherapist but not working any more, lives with her husband (40, organization consultant for approx. 40 hours a week) and is the mother of an eighteen -month- old boy: 'We set up a residents' association. It's been discontinued since then, the problems we wanted to solve have now been dealt with. A spin-off of that venture is that there is still a barbecue once a year, but we don't go to it. I do notice that others enjoy more intensive contact, to the extent of going away together at weekends. I keep thinking; in a year such friendships will have blown over, and then they are left living in such close proximity. Try and do without the other for a change.'

Garden centres At present lifestyle is strongly focused on the image presented to the outside world. The media are particularly responsible in defining what today's home should look like; the number of TV programmes that feature home furnishing and garden design is still increasing. Kiosks also have special shelves set aside for home and garden magazines.
The exterior and interior of the house is used as a means to stress one's own style and uniqueness/identity. The identity of the neighbourhood and the district is of lesser value, save for the presence of facilities.

A housewife (53) living in Kattenbroek was asked what she spent most of her time doing: 'In the summer it's the garden. This always amuses the children who think: oh they've always got an excuse to go to the garden centre. An awful lot of capital must have gone into laying them out. People who may be rather slapdash about the home still let themselves be pulled up by others. If you've got a tidy garden, your neighbour is bound to make sure his is tidy too.'

Villageland

Text

1997

Arnold Reijndorp and Vincent Kompier

Clanning Despite the apparent trend towards an ever greater individualization there is also evidence of a counter-trend. When it comes to organizing our daily lives two polarized movements are of significance. On the one hand the radius of action has increased, both for work and recreation. Globalization and internationalization are indulged in by just about everyone, even if this goes no further than vacations. Going out/night life in Groningen, working in Rotterdam, conventions in Rome, holidays in Florida, friends in Brabant - the 'universe' as daily living environment. The multiplicity of lifestyles combined with the increase of individualism and self-realization is forcing the community aspect into the background. On the other hand, just this enlargement of the living environment has brought increased interest in 'community' at the small scale, the need for something of your own, something for yourself. Advertisements are a good indication of this trend: 'we've got Dommelsch beer'.

Increase in residents' associations The following remarks were made by a resident (38) living with her husband (46) and child (3) in a single-family house in Prinsenland. The woman, who set up the association, works as a consultant for a non-profit organization; her husband's work as project leader has made him familiar with the municipal services: 'Of course we have quite a network of expertise in the neighbourhood. The people here know how you can get things set up. They don't how to make things, though. One of them calculated those little pillars at the entrance to our local park but we got bricklayers in to actually build them. On the other hand, the people here are willing enough to roll their sleeves up and get on with it. The willows along the ring canal we pollarded ourselves. When you're mentally active all day it's great to get stuck into lopping branches off trees. We make a nice day of it, with soup and bread rolls.'

The success of residents' associations is largely due to the expertise and professional input of locals who are academically trained or occupying important posts. Lawyers draw up the association statutes, a photographer takes pictures for the neighbourhood paper, a designer at an advertising agency designs the logo and a magistrate living locally is asked for advice in the event of a legal action.

A woman in her mid forties living in Hoofddorp - a training coordinator for 20 hours a week, with a husband (47, an automation manager) and two children of 10 and 8 - put it this way: 'At one point we had a buyers' association, so you got to know one another right at the start. Because you all have to put up your fence, lay out your garden, you make contact more easily, all being in the same boat. The kitchen needs fitting and the bathroom needs whatever. And then it gets to the point that if something goes wrong with your house or its completion, you're soon round at the neighbours' to see if they're having this trouble as well. Is this the normal thing or should we do something about it? Things like that. And I think if that's the case, if you all move in at the same time, you usually get to know your neighbours much earlier on. We Dutch are not that open and full of hospitality along the lines of hi, I've just moved into the area. When you're a stranger and have to integrate in an existing community, it's quite a different start from the one we had.'

A 33-year-old man working in Hilversum for a telecommunications company, lives in a freestanding house in Kattenbroek with his girlfriend, 32, an accountant at the University Hospital in Utrecht. They moved to this detached house from a subsidized owner-occupied house elsewhere in the district, where they had set up a residents' association: 'We drew up a joint contract for boiler maintenance and had some agreement with a shop about paint. We did make use of that paint; we also had discounts on cheese, but that didn't work too well.'

Fear This urge to individualize proceeds in part from a fear of insecurity. This fear, which actually is a lot less acute than the media would have us believe, is a major stimulus towards clarity of purpose and organization. Clarity in respect of the daily living environment and how this is designed, but also as regards the type of people there. A revived desire for the neighbourhood then.

A couple at early retiring age living in Amersfoort (he was a company consultant, she a director's secretary) deliberately chose a house in an apartment complex, on one of the upper floors: 'Safety. That's the main thing. I wanted to live in a freestanding bungalow, but if one of us dies the other is left alone there with all that space. Safety in the sense of little chance of break-ins. That's why we are up here on the second floor. Where we lived first, in our own house, there were five locks on the door including four of those standard spring-action affairs. But anyone can make short work of those with a screwdriver. And we had a break-in as well.'

We require 'trustworthy' people with whom to share a neighbourhood, who need not necessarily be friends or acquaintances. The neighbourhood as framework of integration in which to arrive, despite differences in lifestyle, standards and values, at a sense of community. In spite of the far-reaching individualization we see this urge for community expressed in architecture, social control and so on. This longing for community is serious, though one that has no truck with the cosy rusticity of seventies housing ideology.

Contact with the neighbours This involves a form of social control but not the faultfinding variety that there used to be. We require 'trustworthy' people with whom to share a neighbourhood, who need not necessarily be friends or acquaintances. The neighbourhood as framework of integration in which to arrive, despite differences in lifestyle, standards and values, at a sense of community. In spite of the far-reaching individualization we see this urge for community in architecture, social control and so on. This longing for community is serious, though one that has no truck with the cosy rusticity of seventies housing ideology. Mutual contact is rooted in helping each other.

A 36-year-old woman in Haagse Beemden: 'The man next door helped my husband to put the pond in place. If the neighbour has a problem, then my husband helps him. The neighbour's wife has just begun a computer course. So my husband is often next door helping her if she needs it.'

A 57-year-old woman was another to point to this mutual help: 'The neighbours needed to sell their car. So I said type it in the computer, I'll put it on the board next time I go to the supermarket. That's how you help each other.'

This sense of a dwelling arena is a major development that should not be underestimated. A key element here is the immediately adjoining private domain, a guarantee if you like of personal property and status. The call for clarity, also in the spatial sense, proceeds from the feelings of insecurity and the wish for a home that truly is one's own. In this respect a sense of involvement, activated by the inhabitants themselves, in the residential setting can be important. A renewed feeling of 'civic pride' or 'decency' is then back with us, also as regards the legal aspect. This can proceed in tandem with an aversion to rules; the idea lives that occupants should draw up the rules themselves, simply because the authorities are too tied up with red tape to stimulate such individual ventures. On the other hand, the government is singularly inactive when it comes to regulating traffic safety, neighbourhood watches and the like. This is another aspect often taken care of by the residents. Back as well is the need to help one another, whether in immaterial things (babysitting, advice) or more material matters (borrowing a drill, sharing a car). This collective use of such resources or services is prompted less by financial considerations as by such diverse issues as the Chinese puzzle of dividing up one's time, the less central place of work, the network society that is making inroads into our daily life, and an increasing awareness of environmental issues. For many it is a way of keeping the worries of daily life under control (e.g. a double-income household with children looking for a babysitter and a housekeeper/cleaner).

A socially active household, a young pair of double-incomers (he a director of an insurance office, she a personnel and organization manager) used to live in a drive-in house in Bleiswijk. There they had little contact with the other people in the street, nor could they identify with them. Now they are living among people who know more about enjoying life, and feel more at home: 'People here are always paying each other visits. Going cycling together. We have laid a drainage channel together with the neighbours. We help each other in the garden. We see each other at parties, for drinks and birthdays. Quite a lot actually. More than one person takes the initiative. Some are members of a tennis club and then we all go to the club do. It all just happens naturally.'

Sometimes a beautiful garden is cause for a chat.

A 47-year-old woman in Haagse Beemden tells how she met a couple further up the street this way. 'They were walking past the house and said how nice the front garden looked and asked who'd designed it. That's how it started. Then we met again at the supermarket and once at the Chinese here in the square.'

A single woman, a school teacher, living in an apartment in Prinsenland put it this way: 'Once when I went away for a weekend I dropped the key in the neighbours' letterbox with a note: you weren't home but could you please empty my letterbox. That for me is neighbourly contact, when you can do things like that for each other. And to be able to ask such favours, it's easier when you're on more familiar terms. Not that I feel the need to be always in each other's homes.'

A forty-year-old woman had this to say: 'We were living in Asterd as one of twelve families in a dead-end street. Then there's incentive enough to do something like organize a party or go to dancing lessons together. One thing leads to another.

Perhaps the age-group had something to do with it. The average age there in Asterd was around forty. There were a whole bunch of men with a mid-life crisis who decided to get off with the woman next door. There were plenty of divorces. Sometimes as many as two or three in each street. Perhaps the fact that everyone was earning a packet had something to do with it. A lot of money went into the social life there and there were enough parties. That could be a disadvantage of being prosperous like that.'

Sport A member of the board of Haagse Beemden tennis club described it as follows: 'Most of the members here are not your average earners. There's a lot of money pumped into the club. Plenty of businessmen, many self-employed, executives and stuff. We attract sponsors like flies. So we never have much difficulty getting funds. We don't go to them, they come to us. Oranjeboom the beer people have just given us a small fortune to do up the clubhouse and the other accommodations as we see fit.'

Another tennis-playing inhabitant of Haagse Beemden, a 29-year-old driving instructress from Rotterdam, is also a member of a small hockey club in Prinsenbeek. Her 34-year-old husband (director of a logistics company) prefers to stick to his old football team in Rotterdam: 'The only people who play football here went to university or have a certain type of profession.'
This man, who studied law in Leiden, has yet to find a suitable club in Haagse Beemden.

Next, a pair of double-earners in Kattenbroek, she (33) in public relations for a pharmaceutical company in Naarden, he (30) a freelance journalist: '500 metres from here is a huge sports complex where you can do everything, from tennis to fitness and badminton to aerobics, you name it. And we're members. We go there more than one evening a week after work. We usually take the car.'

Many respondents aspired to combining being on their own at home with a degree of familiarity with the surroundings. A couple (the husband aged 33 and a coordinator at a flower auction market, his wife aged 31 and manager of a customers' service) had moved from Veghel to Hoofddorp: 'You feel like you're at home. I mean, if you take a walk up the street you make conversation or you might have a beer together at the tennis club. These things are all part of life, aren't they, I feel they add the personal touch.'

A further means of expression besides the look of the house and the garden is the degree and type of recreation indulged in.

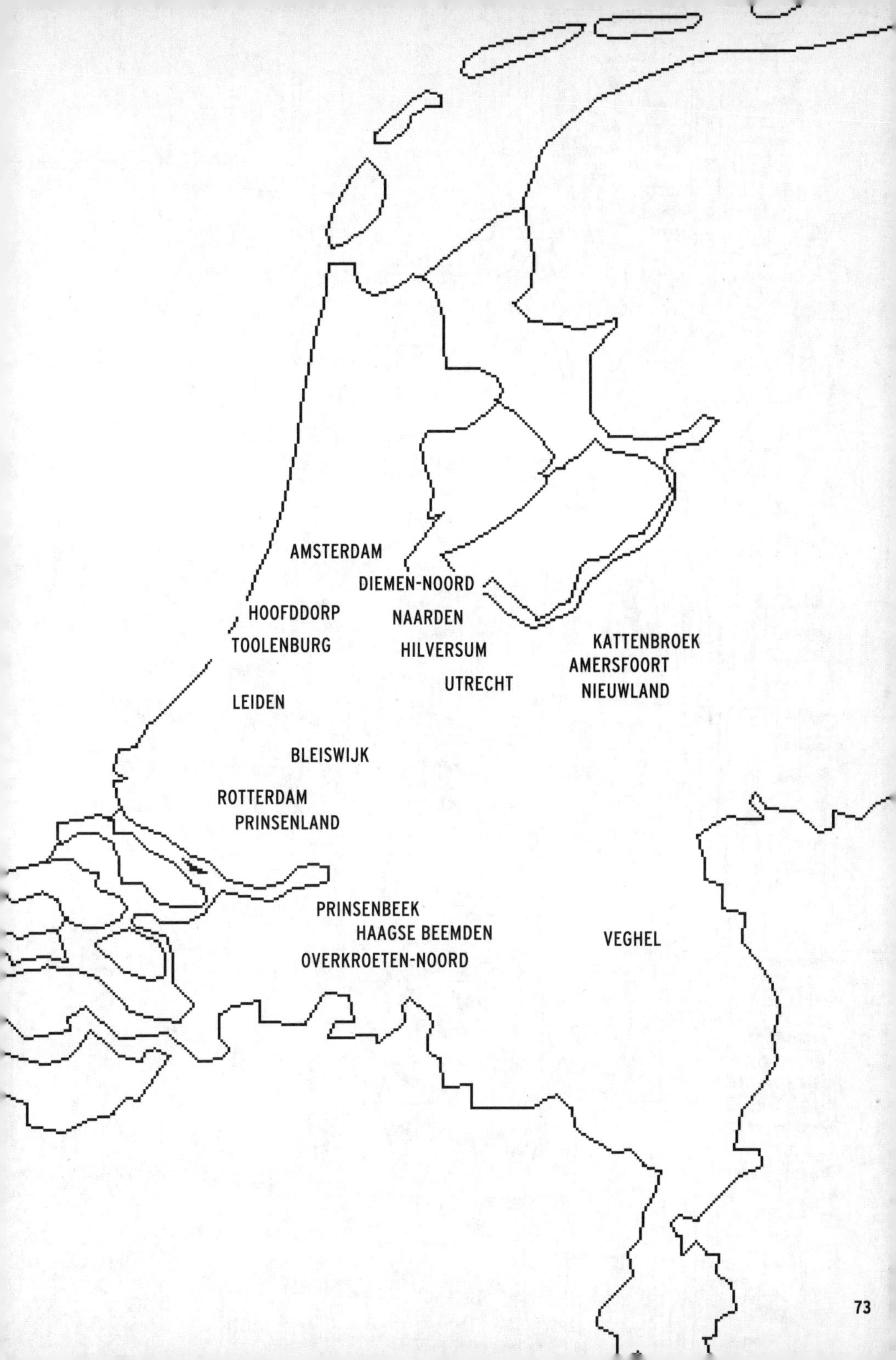
AMSTERDAM
DIEMEN-NOORD
HOOFDDORP
NAARDEN
TOOLENBURG
HILVERSUM
KATTENBROEK
AMERSFOORT
UTRECHT
NIEUWLAND
LEIDEN
BLEISWIJK
ROTTERDAM
PRINSENLAND
PRINSENBEEK
HAAGSE BEEMDEN
VEGHEL
OVERKROETEN-NOORD

C
C
C
C
C
C

Lelyland

Study for the development of Lelystad, The Netherlands

1994

Tom Mossel

Re-editing: MVRDV, 1996

Slack water in overpriced Lelystad Number 23 is still showing signs of life, the rest of the street is utterly silent. Since Ria next door moved out, that's a month ago, the Boonstra family in Lelystad has no neighbours any more. 'The ones opposite left for Drenthe a year ago,' Mrs. Boonstra explained, 'and the house next to them was already empty when we moved here. That was two years back.'

Four of the six houses in this row of Lelystad's Wold district are empty. As are five of the nine across the road. The remaining occupants have stuck posters on their windows: 'This is a no-can-pay zone'.

Large chunks of Kamp, the abutting system of streets, are just as dead. You can see right through the houses here. The only signs that they were ever occupied are the crumbling kitchen units. And the gardens, where the plumes of fancy grass are slowly being strangled by rampant gypsophila. The shrubs have been pruned right back. Sand is blowing everywhere.

Lelystad is caving in. Begun almost thirty years ago as a boomtown, with until 1980 a doubling of population every two to three years, the polder town has seen more people leave than arrive this past year and a half.

The exodus is proceeding apace. In 1995, an average of 307 inhabitants left each month to be replaced by a smaller number of arrivals. Even the natural increase in population fails to compensate. For four years now the town has had no more than 60,000 inhabitants on average.

These days, the slack water in the demographic trend here is less the aftermath of difficult conditions in Lelystad than the prime cause of those conditions. The town had been built for growth and was a long way from being full-blown. Its planners based its construction on a population of 100,000 inhabitants by the year 2000.

Over the years, such expectations have of course been continually adjusted downwards. Yet the housing stock, bureaucratic machinery and public services are still geared to many more than the 60,000 inhabitants of today.

The results? Empty property, sky-high expenses and cutbacks on services. Since 1986 the council is under the control of the Minister of Finance. Of the more than 700 officials 170 have been siphoned off elsewhere. There were three libraries to begin with, now there is only one.

And yet Lelystad in 1995, with an unemployment rate of over 17 percent, was the most expensive municipality in the Netherlands. In that year the Lelystad-dweller paid an average of 1,262.27 guilders per property in living expenses - over 6 percent more than in 1994.

'We simply don't know how much longer we can hold out', says Mrs. Boonstra. Her rent is almost 850 guilders a month. When she and her family moved to the Wold two years ago it was 750. And that was already too much in her opinion. She had in fact asked for a smaller house. 'We were given a bigger one.' Then there was the annual rise in rent of up to 6.5 percent. 'And the housing corporation does nothing in the way of repairs. Six months ago somebody came to take an order for a new front door. Three months later the order went through, and I'm still waiting.' This year she has refused to pay the rise in rent. Together with all the remaining neighbours.
B. Doorten of the Lelystad Housing Foundation admits that the high rents, if not actually driving people out, are not exactly enticing them in either. The rents in Lelystad according to Doorten are 100 guilders higher on average than in the rest of the country. 'The thing is, there are no old, cheap houses here. Lelystad is too new for that.'
R. van Otterloo, acting manager of De Opdracht, a housing corporation feeling the pinch, defends the rent increase. The ratio between price and quality is right, he feels. The houses (two storeys, garden front and back) are in good condition and therefore 'eminently rentable'. There's little amiss with the houses, Van Otterloo insists. 'It's just that there are too few occupants for the number available.'
The council is trying to do something about it. This year it is to present a 'master plan for accelerated growth'. A solid chunk of good intentions - including a 'cultural about-face' and a 'qualitative leap forwards' - with which the town hopes to achieve greater things. In ten years Lelystad needs to have reached 80,000 residents. And preferably more wealthy ones than at present. This is a hard enough task in itself, considering that there are no universities or colleges in the Flevopolders, so the town's young contingent heads off elsewhere to study and generally doesn't come back.
Yet in the face of all this, more new houses are programmed to be built during the coming years. In case this seems illogical, these are to be houses for private ownership. Council spokesman K. Cloo refers to the eagerness to acquire the beautiful, expensive houses in the former sports grounds of Beukenhof. There 550 prospective buyers vied for 54 lots. 'Living' and 'space' as positive points for the polder are as strong as ever. 'Move from here? Not on your life!' was how one resident put it.
But outside the polder Lelystad has 'no image', Cloo sighs.
The Amsterdammer who decides to leave the capital looks for a house in

Almere, not in Lelystad. In Almere they put you on a waiting list of approximately three years. If fifty applicants were to turn up in Lelystad tomorrow, the De Opdracht corporation can help all fifty, Van Otterloo claims. Trouble is, they're not coming. To the outside world Lelystad represents a decided lack of excitement ('Chair thief arrested promptly' is headline news in the local rag) and seems like the original back of beyond. When the parents of jeweller R. Jansen tell their neighbour in Hilversum that they are off to visit their son in Lelystad, he asks whether they will be coming back that same evening. 'As if they were off to the bush. Hilversum's a mere fifty kilometres away!'

Jansen, a board member of the shopkeepers' association of Lelycenter, the oldest shopping centre, knows how hard it is to fill empty spaces in the centre of town. If anything, it is even more important to draw industry and commerce to Lelystad than new inhabitants. And more difficult. The master plan hopes to 'up considerably' the number of jobs there. But, Jansen adds: 'Just try convincing the headquarters of a lamp shop in Badhoevendorp that it is worth setting up a branch in Lelystad. A high crime rate, an impoverished clientele, that's what they think there.'

Jansen earns a 'comfortable' living in Lelystad: 'My average outlay per client is higher than in the rest of the Netherlands.' He puts this into perspective with 'I cater to the top layer of the market'.The shopkeepers catering to the bottom layer have a much harder time of it. Their customers have to think twice before they shop.

The less well-off Mr. and Mrs. Weber are sitting on a bench in front of their house on the Kamp. He has his puzzle-book open, she is busy embroidering. Now that they live from Mr. Weber's pension the expenses - their rent has risen in four years from 700 to 900 guilders - are all the more harsh.

'We have a new hobby,' says Mrs. Weber as she pours out the fermented elderberry juice, 'home winemaking.'

The housing corporation is turning rented property into owner-occupied houses. The propitious interest rate makes that ultimately more advantagious for the occupant. De Opdracht, says acting manager Van Otterloo, has made a deal with the local bank. Whoever buys a house instead of renting one can pay 200 to 300 guilders a month less on mortgage than they would on rent.

The Webers would love to buy the house but wonder if they could. Mr. Weber points to his car parked across the road. 'It's ten, twelve years old. But I can't buy a new one. That's all in the past.'

Bas Blokker, 'Lelystad', NRC Handelsblad 24 July 1996, pp. 1,3

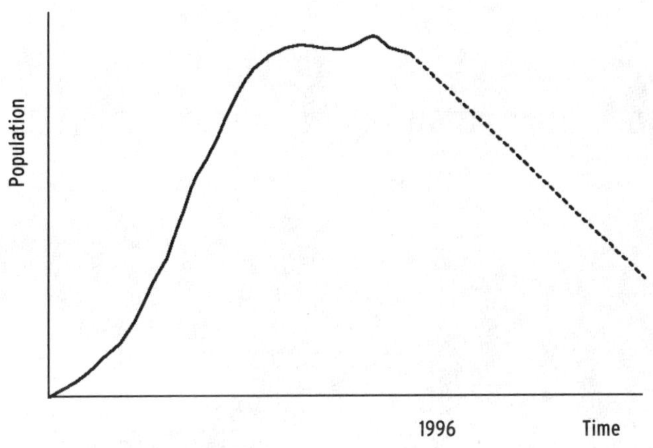

Lelystad is the capital of the Flevopolders, areas of land recently reclaimed from the IJsselmeer which was once part of the North Sea. It was planned in the 1950s to attrack people from the densifying urban areas nearby such as Amsterdam and Utrecht. According to the planners it would grow into a town of 100,000 inhabitants by the year 2000, a full-blown centre for the Polders.

But not all of the polders have been realized. And Almere, the proposed second town, which was situated closer to the donor cities and being designed later was more aware of the demands of potential occupants, turned out to be more successful in

attracting a population.
The repercussions for Lelystad were no growth, no centre and masses of empty property. Lelystad became a town too many.
For all that, this failure can be seen as an advantage, for nowhere in Holland is the density so low.
By redistributing the land and the built areas, it should be possible to house those who want to escape from the densities of Almere or Amsterdam and find empty, colonizable spaces in this town.
Wherever inhabitants leave, an enormous potential becomes available for those who stay: bigger houses, bigger gardens, more nature, more agriculture.

LELYLAND,

a sun city

for the elderly,

an oasis for

second homers,

a quiet retreat

for the urbanite,

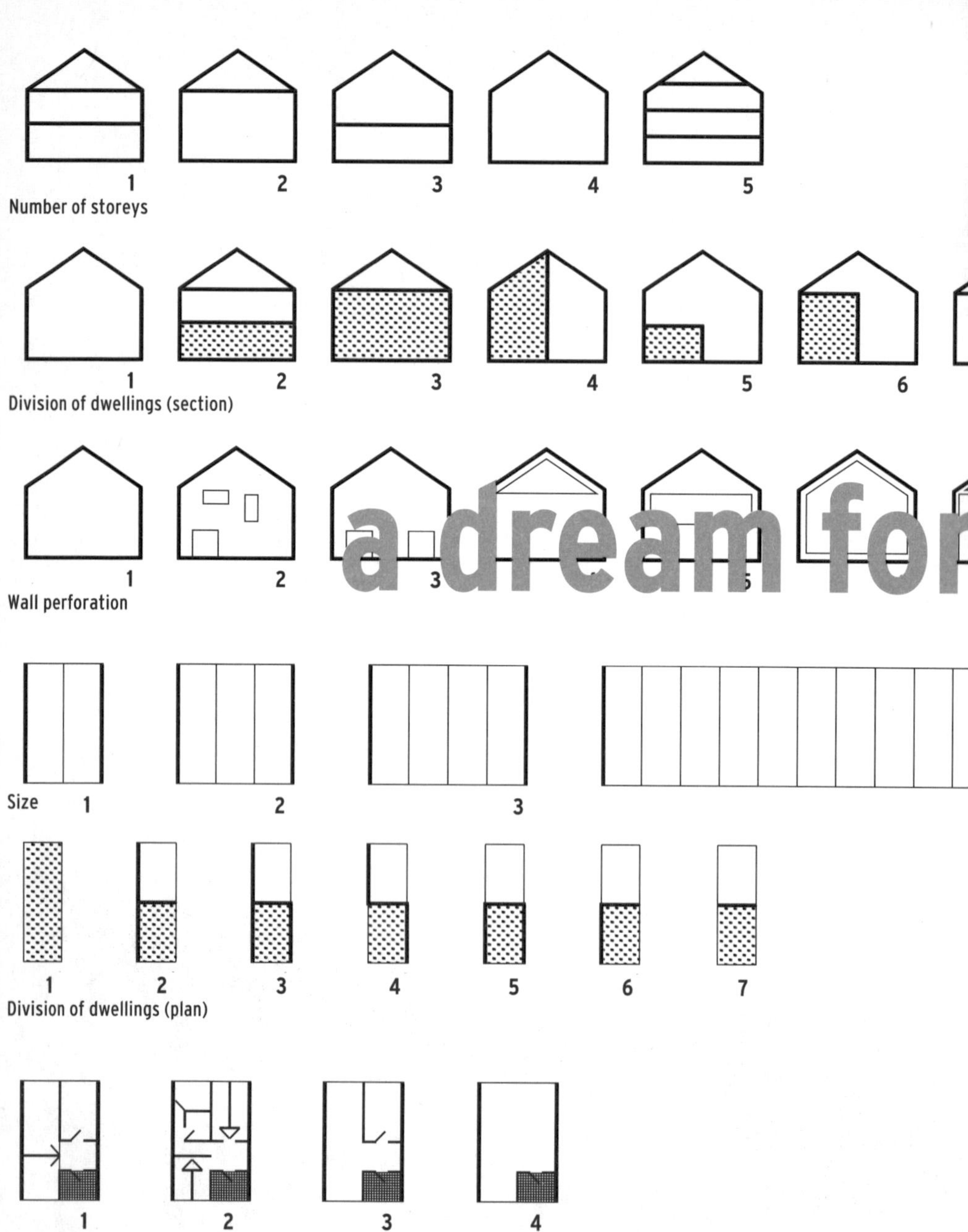
1
2
3
4
5
Number of storeys
1
2
3
4
5
6
Division of dwellings (section)
a dream for
1
2
3
Wall perforation
Size
1
2
3
1
2
3
4
5
6
7
Division of dwellings (plan)
1
2
3
4
Walls

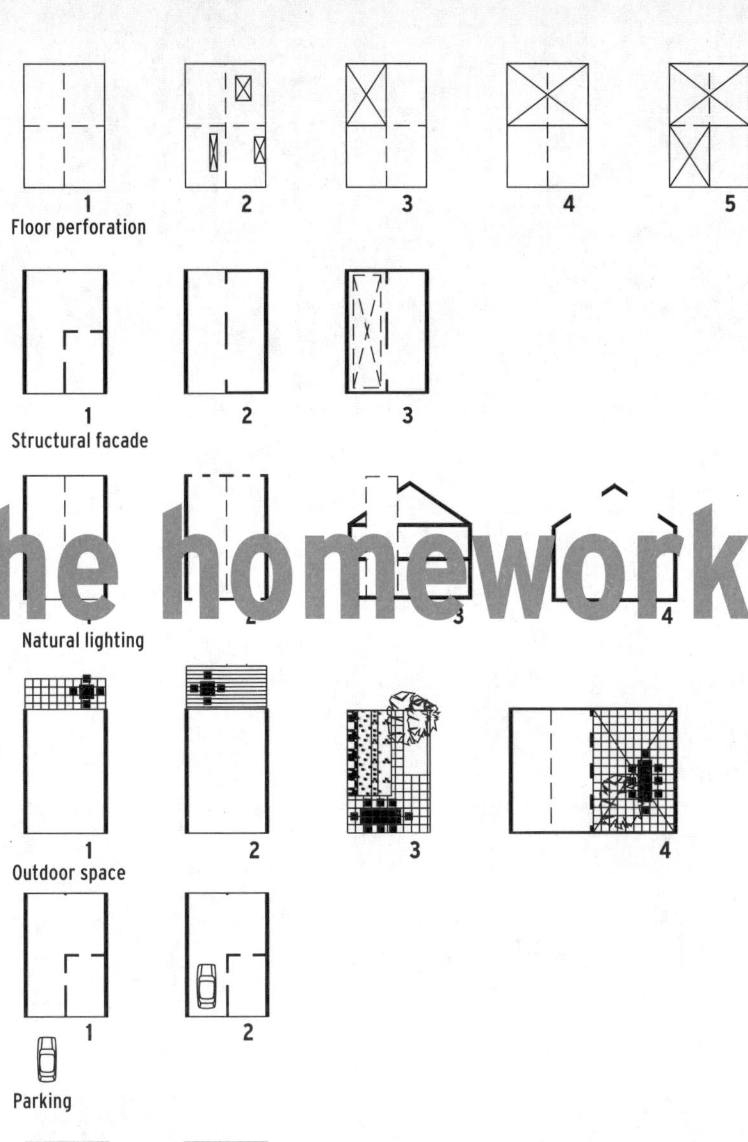

the homeworker,

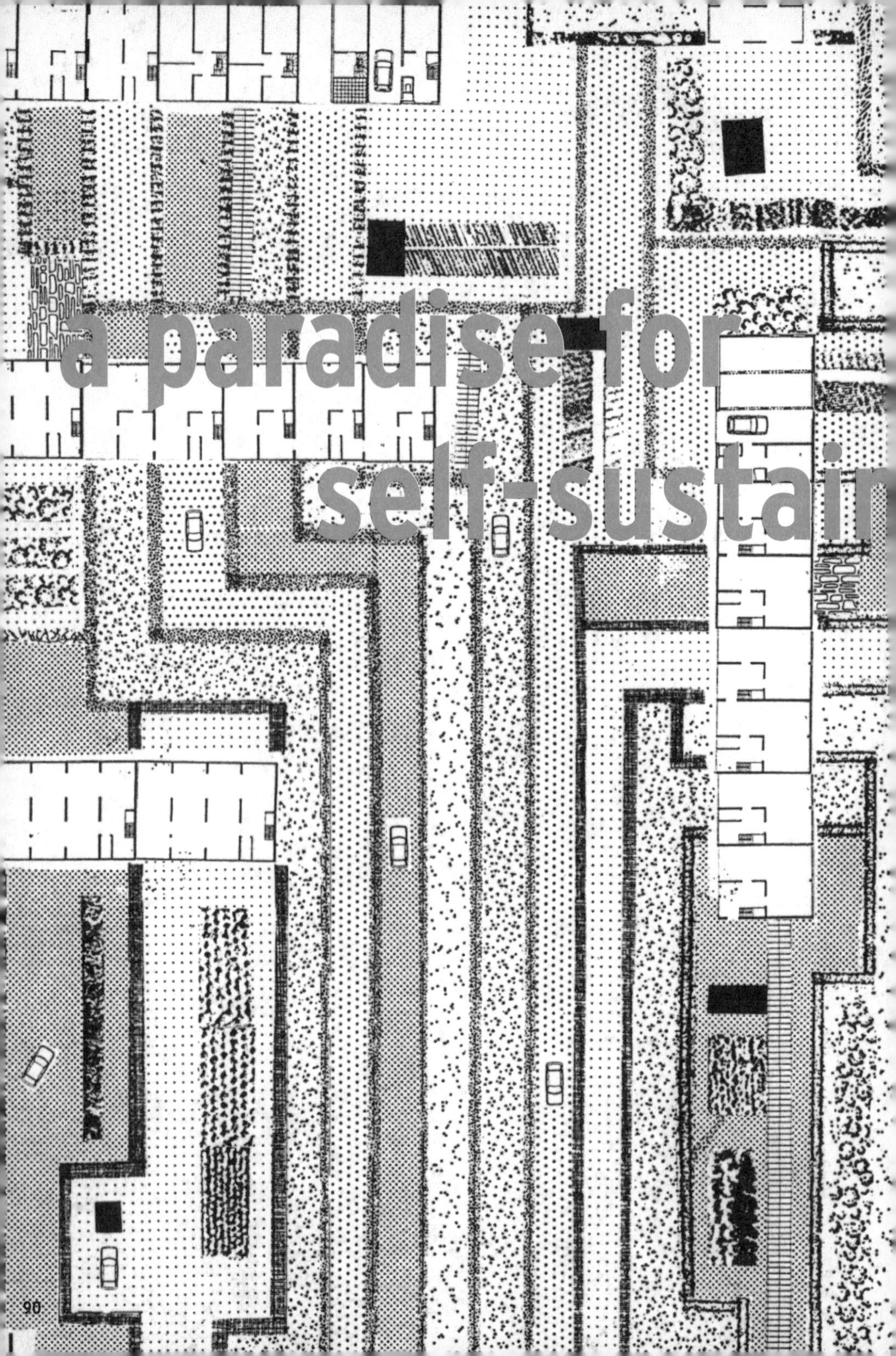

a paradise for self-sustain

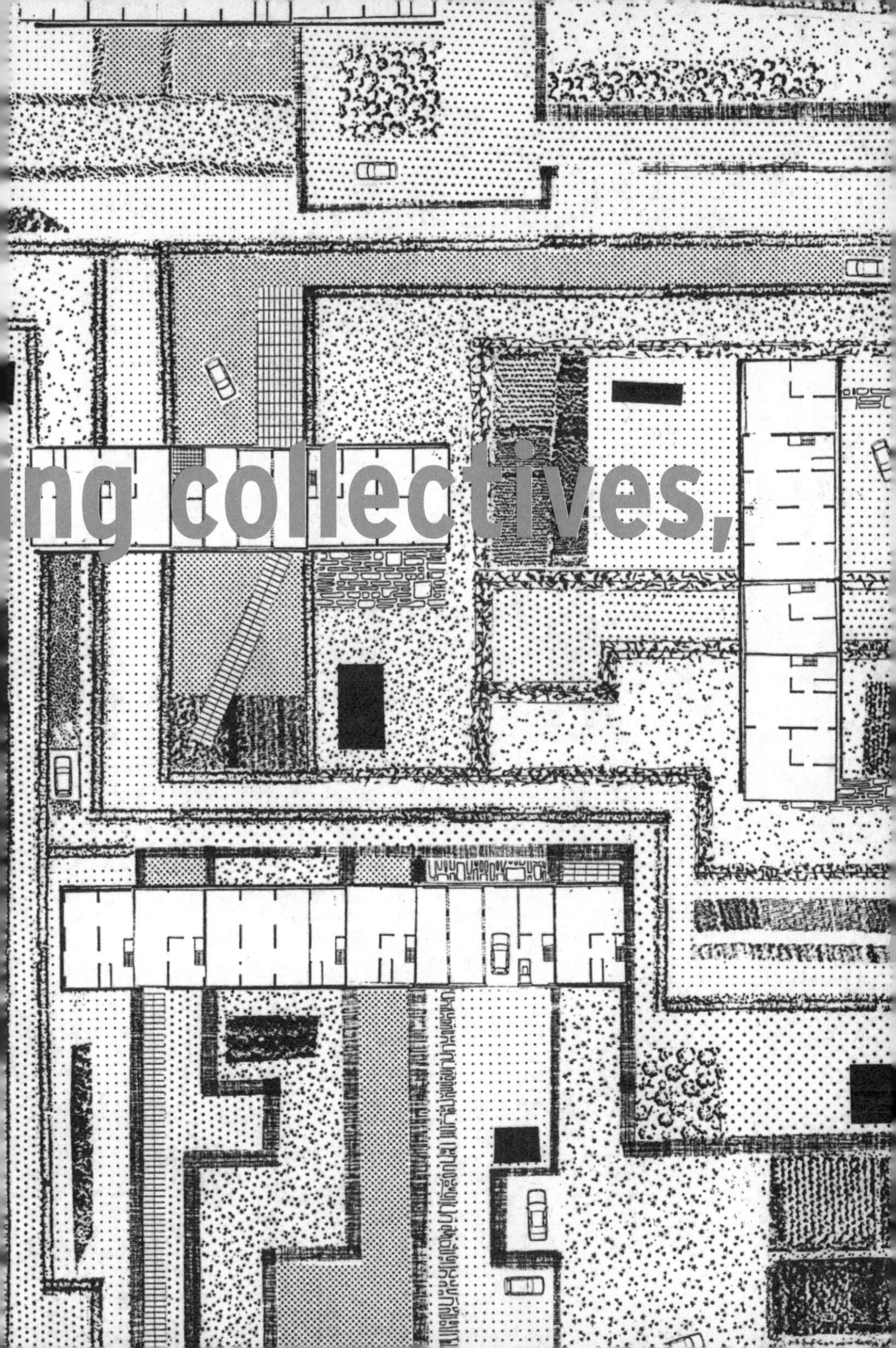
ng collectives,

land for the

ecofarmer

Landscape

Text

1995

Winy Maas

Landscape is in the air! Landscape is everywhere! The word 'landscape' has so much zipped into the recent architectural discourse, that it is even more often used than Americans use the word 'fuck'. Landscape emerges as the solution in times when architecture and urbanism are losing out on significance. This process coincides with the diagnosis that the discipline of Landscape Architecture is entering an era of doubt. After conquering the doom and pessimism of the seventies with an ecological answer and meeting the economic hype of the eighties and nineties with 'design', the profession is now confronted with the question of how to address the overwhelming number of paradoxical demands surrounding it. How to embody the multi-cultural and multiform in a profession that is historically swallowed up by the paradigms of 'purity', 'harmony' and 'nobility'. The landscape architect is seen as the personification of the pastoral, the harmonious, the environmentally friendly: truly 'good' and noble aims. And in that respect one could argue that he is often misused for political objectives. Yet that very innocence is false and saturated with a oversimplified moralism. For if landscape calls upon 'endlessness', 'awe' and 'gigantism' and expresses itself in panoramas and distant prospects, then it is indeed the synonym for 'overview', encompassing good and bad, is about multiplicity and pluralism. It has the potential to manipulate this field of ideas, opinions and expressions. Instead of a mere argument for goodness, this domain has the capacity of putting into perspective. This position obliges it to study the substance of the 'moral'.

Datascape

Text

1996

Winy Maas

Beyond chaos How to deal with the moral in an era where architecture has been overoccupied by chaos theories, that function as rhetorical hide-aways and mythical retreats? Should architecture still aspire to expressing 'chaos' even when it is already surounded by it?

Massive uniqueness: the final extravaganza Everything can be made, every object is imaginable, nothing seems strange or extravagant anymore.

What should we make under these circumstances? Do we still aspire to the ultimate extravaganza? Are we suffering from 'object fatigue', a consequence of the multitude of objects competing for our attention, all these buildings clamouring to tell us something?

In our search for the 'one-off' in a veritable slew of the 'unique', the expression of the individual object has become ridiculous: in a massive 'sea of uniqueness' the individual object simply ceases to exist. In this massiveness, architecture bifurcates: on one side it introverts, which leads to a stronger emphasis on the role of the interior. On the other side architecture becomes synonymous with urbanism.

Majorities The lion's share of the building production is concerned with the banal and the normal. In our desire to be avant-garde, this signifies an all-absorbing massiveness, a prescribed experience, a pasteurized reality. Why are we still not interested in it? Are we afraid of the banal in ourselves?

It has become the emblem of something that is past its peak, a vivid illustration of the twentieth century dilemma: in our search for the unique we all make or find the same things; desiring en masse the authentic and exceptional, it all turns out banal.
If we regard this phenomenon ironically, we are denying all its humanity. The way we look down on it, must be the same as the way the Victorian bourgeoisie looked down on the working classes, with contempt, mixed with shame. Now as then, a Dickensian type is needed to give back to banality that human face.

Urbanism When architecture becomes urbanism, it enters the realms of quantities and infrastructure, of time and relativism.
Things come, things go. Events take place in apparently unorganized patterns, the very chaos of which possesses hidden logics, allowing 'gravities' to emerge from within this endless tapestry of objects.
These gravities reveal themselves when sublimated beneath certain assumed maximized circumstances or within certain maximized constraints.
Because of tax differences the borders between Belgium and the Netherlands are occupied with vast numbers of villas generating a linear town along the frontier. Market demands have precipitated a 'slick' of houses-with-a-small-garden in Holland. Political constraints in Hong Kong generate 'piles' of dwellings around its

boundaries. The popularity of white brick in Friesland causes a 'white cancer' of housing estates alongside all the villages. In its desire for a cosmetic nineteenth-century identity, Berlin forces its new buildings into tight envelopes. This pushes larger programmes underground, turning the streets into mere components in the midst of vast programmes.

Monumental regulations in Amsterdam limit the demand for modern programmes, generating 'mountains of programme' invisible from the street behind the medieval facades. Throughout the Ruhr, accessibility demands create virtually enclosed types of infrastructure precipitating a string of linear towns. In La Defense in Paris, to avoid the high-rise rules massive programmes manifest themselves as ziggurats with 18 metre high accessible 'steps' so that all offices can be entered by the maximum length of the fire ladders. Psychological issues, anti-disaster patterns, lighting regulations, acoustic treatments.

All these manifestations can be seen as 'scapes' of the data behind it.

Extremities If 'progress' remains the main reason for 'research', the hypothesis remains the most effective way to deal with it. In order to understand the behaviour of massiveness, we have to push it to the limits and adopt this 'extremizing' as a technique of architectural research. Assuming a possible maximization (the word 'maximum'

already implies rules), society will be confronted with the laws and by-laws that it has set up and that are extrapolated with an iron logic. It will begin questioning these regulations.
The protection of certain areas push programmes to the left-over corners of our countries. Do we want that? More comfort raises the issue that we are becoming dependent on it. Do we want that?
More massiveness and higher densities leads to the question of whether we still should use our light and air regulations. Or if we should cope with noise in another way. And so on.

Datascapes: sublimized pragmatism? Under maximized circumstances, every demand, rule or logic is manifested in pure and unexpected forms that go beyond artistic intuition or known geometry and replace it with 'research'. Form becomes the result of such an extrapolation or assumption as a 'datascape' of the demands behind it. It shows the demands and norms, balancing between ridicule and critique, sublimizing pragmatics.
It connects the moral with the normal. Having found the opportunity to criticize the norm and the moral behind it, it constructs a possible 'argument'. Artistic intuition is replaced by 'research': hypotheses that observe, extrapolate, analyse and criticize our behaviour.

Emptyscape

Locus seminar

1992

Patricia Bijvoet, Winy Maas and Christian Zalm

Re-editing: MVRDV, 1997

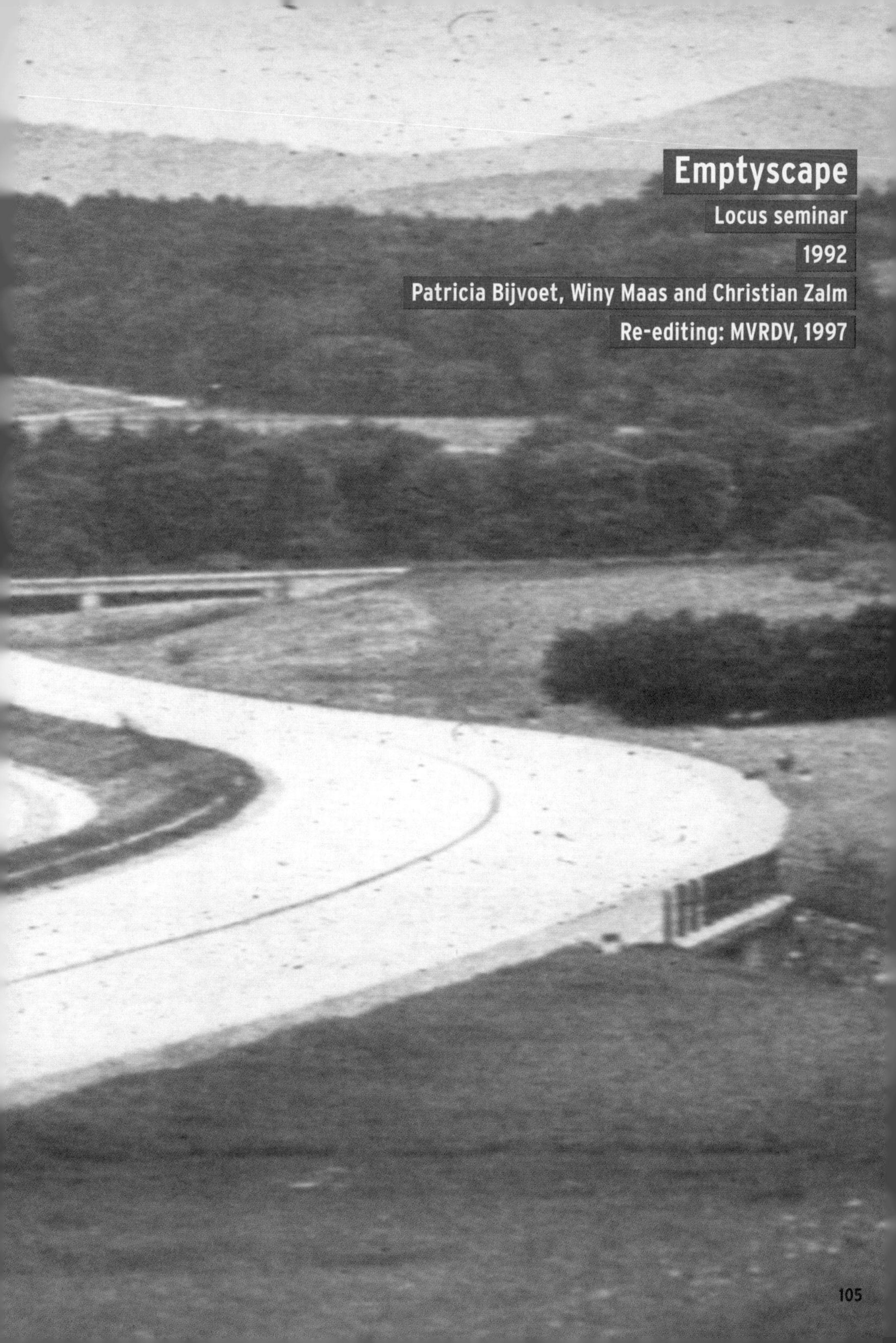

The wish for 'empty land' seems so resolutely present in Dutch art and culture as to suggest a tradition going back to the skies of the painter Jacob van Ruijsdael. But the emptiness in the landscape is fast diminishing. How are we to define 'emptiness' in these times of want? Can 'classic' empty spaces (nature reserves, ecological zones, sustainable agriculture production zones) be combined with contemporary ones?
Can The Emptiness be read as a cumulation of sectors and zones of differently defined emptinesses?
For instance, to prevent the traveller being totally cut off from the environment by acoustic baffles,

plantations and office buildings, areas around highways and railway lines could be opened up. These could become scenic parkways with unforeseeable possibilities for programmes that beg accessibility and visibility. So-called 'fields of fire' could be set up to bring out the grandeur of protected historical towns and objects listed under the Monument Acts. And so on. By mapping these specific requirements and limitations, an offbeat though contextual figure emerges as a series of 'generous voids' in self-filling surroundings - a minimal counterbalance in a densifying society.

Parkways

Possible building zones

Parks

Possible building zones

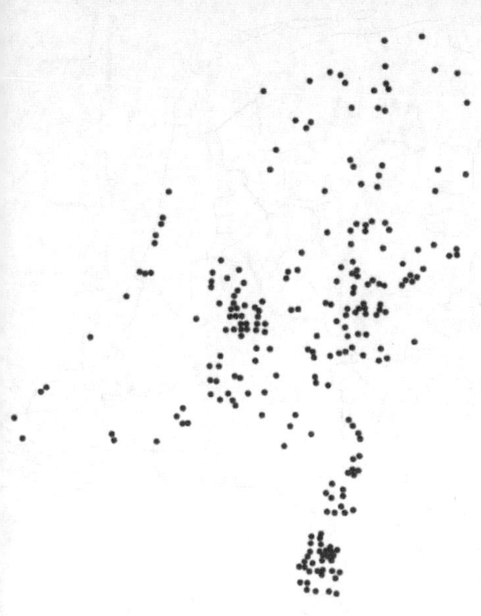

Fields of fire

Possible building zones

Parkscape Holland

Holland town

Detail

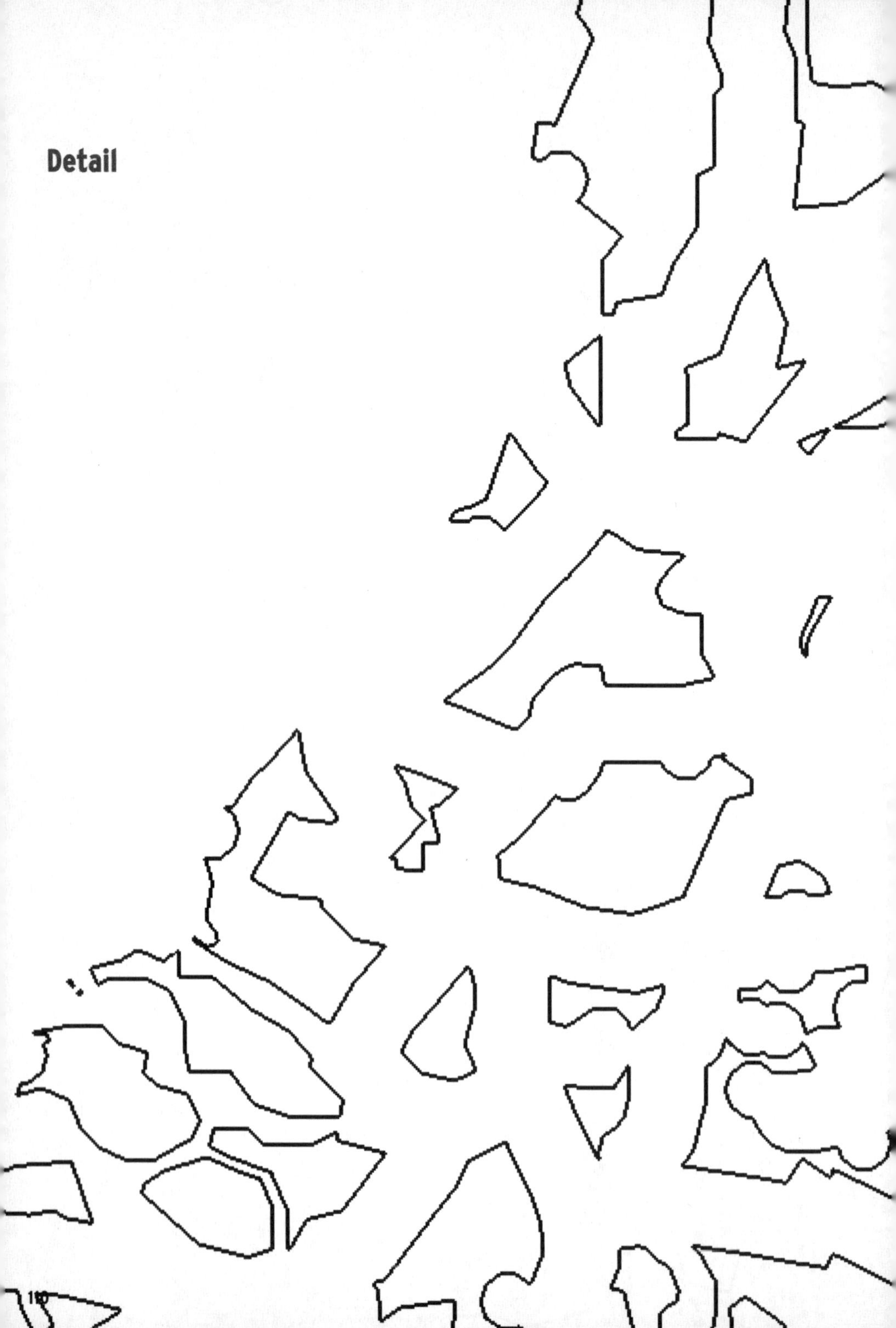

classified monument
1500 metres: field of fire

M
highway
1500 metres: parkway
M

THAT'LL BE THE

DUTCH SETTLERS

Windscape

Case study on the location of windmill parks in The Netherlands

1997

MVRDV

It would take 54 billion guilders (the equivalent of 600 km of High-Speed Trainline) to finance enough windmills to supply all the energy this country requires. 54,000 windmills for the Netherlands - it then occurs that fears for a terminating energy source one dispelled: instead of all that effort trying to conserve energy you would then have energy literally to waste. After all, it would be freely available in inexhaustible quantities. So open your windows, turn up the heating, throw away the facades, let the birds in! The ultimate transparency!
Should the total open space of the Netherlands be filled with windmills this energy supply would be so gigantic that in the post-gas era the Netherlands could begin exporting this type of energy.

'The building industry has long had to make do with constructions and materials that are primitive for our day, compared with the technological means and scientific collaboration in, say, space travel.
'The more architecture (which continues to use thousands of tonnes of material) is availed of scientific information, the more economically it could function.
I can even imagine that it will eventually prove possible to insulate an empty space thermically, acoustically and hydraulically, merely with physical forces.
This would change the very nature of architecture.'

(From a short speech by Gerrit Rietveld on being granted an honorary doctorate in the technical sciences by the senate of the TU Delft on 11 January, 1964 (Bless, 1982)

45,000 MW =
54,000 windmills =
54,000,000,000,000 guilders =
600 KM highspeed trainline =
6 government periods =
4500 KM^2

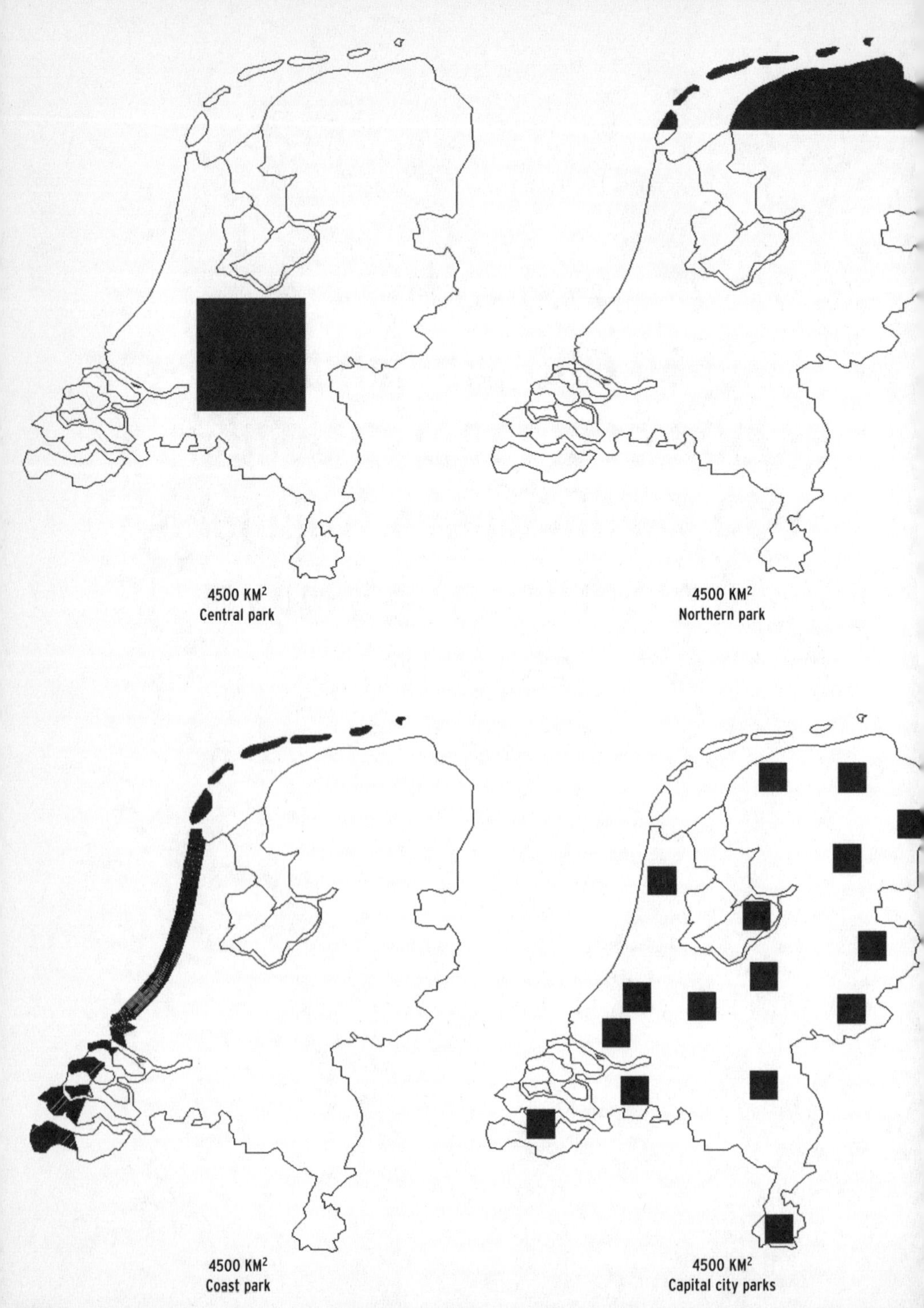
4500 KM²
Central park
4500 KM²
Northern park
4500 KM²
Coast park
4500 KM²
Capital city parks

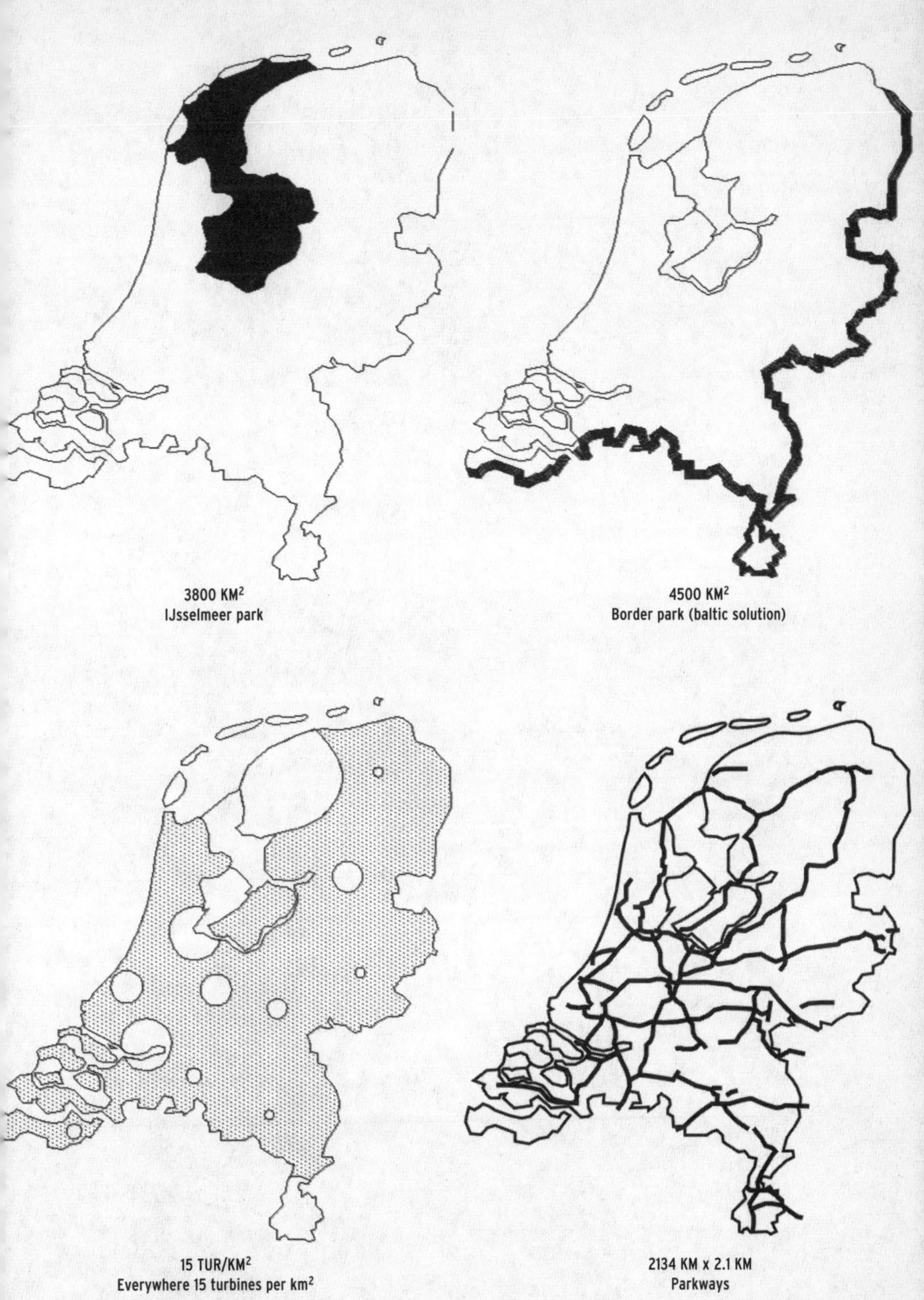

3800 KM^2
IJsselmeer park

4500 KM^2
Border park (baltic solution)

15 TUR/KM^2
Everywhere 15 turbines per km^2

2134 KM x 2.1 KM
Parkways

When dense, when lite?

Text

1997

Harm Tilman

The expectations these days are that our cities will continue to grow. According to an urban survey published in the English paper The Economist, this is because they are forever reinventing themselves.[1]
This new urban growth is spreading the cities further outwards, generating new urban centres or edge cities.
By this means polynuclear regions emerge, where the centres might once again play a binding role.
In the coming years, urban policy will need to encourage further growth in the existing central city areas especially. This means among other things that our cities will have to become modernized, organized, transformed. As a result, we will have to operate in the centre in a much more active manner that of late. And this is where urban density comes in.

Farewell contained cities The issue of concentration and deconcentration has long been central to urban design. The siting and dimensions of urban functions were at the core of research begun in the nineteenth century into functional specialization and urban hierarchy and into the role played by land ownership in urban development. In 1826 Johannes von Thünen was the first to succeed in establishing a link between ground rent and siting. His book Der isolierte Staat in Beziehung auf Landwirtschaft und Nationalökonomie opened the way for further research into links between the value of the location and the siting of urban activities. Links, however, that cannot be forged today, as the authoritative planner Peter Hall has pointed out. An explosion of density can now occur at any random point in the city. This phenomenon is quite detached from the traditional interpretation of the city as an unbroken field, or an area whose parts add up to more than the whole. Built containers are springing up at random points in the city[2], containers that accommodate a great variety of activities with a bewildering flexibility. According to Rem Koolhaas any such parts of the world might be 'turned with savage competence into idyllic tapestries that connect these points of density'.[3]

City of general relativity Massimo Cacciari probes deeper into this problematic in a marvellous essay.[4] Sociology, philosophy and urbanism, he suggests, have trained us to see the metropolis as a functional system of relations and links. Premised on this whole, the various 'sciences' seek to programme the metropolitan dimension (that is, the dimension in which the

individual as abstract intellect is placed). His is a convincing argument, that the urban sciences derive from spatially defining the metropolis as a Whole of the parts, as a Relation of the relations. The spatializing of the urban dynamic is the upshot of this move.
This problem can be overcome by reopening the discourse on the metropolis. Cacciari uses Einstein's comparison of the American grid with the European city to generate the image of a city shaped by social subjects of obscure identity, by indeterminate soft bodies whose form changes depending on the gravitational field they occupy and the information they receive; bodies that lead a nomadic existence in the urban space. The spatial configuration of this city is no longer given but deconstructed in the purest of processes. Rather than the place where certain movements make their home, the city now is the totality of these events. Deprived of qualities of its own, the urban space can only be described in terms of the 'adventure' of named bodies.
In the city of total relativity the issue according to Deleuze is not making a point, but drawing lines. The lines we draw, he continues, have no source and are designed in a preexisting environment; it is impossible to create a tabula rasa. The more we take the world as it is, the greater our chance of changing it.[5] Virtual urbanism is an urbanism whose plan, space, process and intelligence generate the most up-to-date relations and links, as well as the greatest potential for unpredicted events. Such events are never actualized in the image of the virtual force generating them. Virtual reality is something we can see only by experimenting with it.

The scheme as event The urban issue this raises is that of which principles to deploy in order to organize or reorganize the composition of wide-ranging programmes. A Krier-style model of a continuous and contained city is of little help to us here. One thing is certain - the design for the urban landscape in the transformation areas cannot be dictated by urbanists. The rules the latter prescribe, if they are to be efficient, will have to allow a maximum of freedom to urban operations, particularly those of private enterprise.
The most pressing problem, then, is not one of 'image quality', but relates to programmatic givens of an economic and social nature. Two aspects play a part here. First, there is the uncertainty surrounding the allocation of such areas, the method of approach and the planning limits. This uncertainty pertains to the financial/operational programme, where it encourages

large-scale mixed-use developments with monitored internal courts. But the influence of and dependence on the market remain great.
At the same time other relations spring up between the social issue and the spatial design. A design that fixes beforehand all functions and the structure to house them, is absurd. It would fail to plug into the new life-rhythm of the metropolis. This calls for other designs and new ways of making them, but also for new relations between design and scheme. There are at present attempts to link space design with the human sense of time, where it can express the shaky equilibrium of individual and collective life and exploit the restlessness of the urban landscape.
Such designs embrace the time factor as the constituent element in urban analysis and urban planning. In view of the countless uncertainties surrounding the urban task, as well as its complexity, these designs will require a high-powered conceptual framework as well as the space created for countless combinations and substitutions.[6]

Differences The urbanization of today may be the premise for a new geography and typology of 'luoghi notevoli', of urban spaces marked by functional complexity, spatial articulation and symbolic values. At the same time it should not be forgotten - and this is in itself an argument for a design embracing the entire urban space - that this development may ultimately mean an urban landscape of homogeneous configuration, an endless proliferation of non-places.[7]
Take the increased distinction between dwelling and the collective space; add to that the new office districts and shopping malls in the periphery; the suburban strip, an urban space wholly geared to the car; the distribution of specialized citadels (theme parks, university campuses, etc) and ultra-commercialized pedestrian precincts; and finally the rise of residential areas heavily segregated on the social and typological front. These phenomena show just how far processes of functional specialization and dissolution of public space can reach.
They express the steadily advancing process of homogenization of the whole urban space (the urban landscape). Against that process, one unmistakably operative in the Netherlands - 'Californication' hits the Randstad - we can pit an alternative best described as the exploiting of local differences and specific qualities.

High and low density That utterly dissimilar models and lines of approach obtain for different areas is made clear if we compare the American cities of Atlanta and Portland. Each evolved during the eighties in very much its own direction.[8] Atlanta is the paradigmatic sprawled American city. Its suburbs have exploded and generated suburbs of their own.
The three largest Edge Cities each contain more office and retail surface area than the entire Downtown Atlanta. These days the city centre's share in the total employment figures is no more than ten percent. Portland by contrast has burgeoned into a prototypical, compact metropolitan region. Although this city is not bounded by mountains or water like other compact cities (Tokyo for example or San Francisco), its urban form is being shaped for it. The area where development is permitted, is cordoned off using Urban Growth Boundaries. The idea here is less to limit urban growth than to accommodate it. This means that urban redevelopment get the emphasis, that links are sought between land use and public transport. In Portland the key aims are to achieve higher densities and a more lucid decision-making and regional planning, as well as develop a regional rail infrastructure.
One can scarcely imagine a greater difference than that contained in these two approaches to regional development policy. Each has its own impact on the respective city centre. According to the American planner, Arthur C. Nelson, an uncontrolled regional development makes for a less than efficient distribution of urban development, the city centres aside. Distribution, after all, means higher costs. But, continues Nelson, 'the bottom line is that more compact patterns of urban development, anchored by relatively high-density central cities, result in greater economic development. The emerging literature is beginning to show that gross domestic product is improved by both larger city size and higher densities.'

Density as formula Until recently, functional and economic considerations were such that a higher density in the central city was deemed desirable if not inevitable. It obviously made sense to draw together a galaxy of urban organizations enabling visitors and users to access them with a minimum of effort. Similarly, the high density was justified by high land values in the inner urban areas. The proportionately high development density expressed the concentration of urban life, satisfying the legitimate claim to urbanity, experiential value, intimacy and attractiveness.
Density is a variable whereby in principle the built surface area, floor surface

area or built mass is related to the surface area of the plot or the entire urban area. In city planning a FAR of 1.5 to 1.8 was long considered the optimum. In an impeccable East German study made in 1967 it was argued that 'a value of 1.5 for a development ratio of 30% permits a development in five storeys and for 15% a development in ten storeys.'[9] This line of reasoning does lead to a certain homogenization taking the compact city as ideal. In a virtual urbanism, however, the concepts of density are directed related to the material problems of transforming the city.

Accordingly, countless experiments are done on density in all its aspects. Density is the city's third dimension and a vehicle for provocative statements. Stronger means than just housing are required to produce a truly compact city with a density comparable to that of New York or Hong Kong. Dutch legislation restricts housing to comparatively low densities. To build more densely requires implementing more light-insensitive functions.[10] Hence the concept of mix is essential alongside those of densification and modernization to make an attractive compact city. Urban density, then, is more than simply upping the Floor Area Ratio. It also entails densifying and stacking functional, social and economic systems and levels in the city.

In the Floor Area Ratio is expressed the degree of economic exploitation of a given piece of land or city. Density is a critical tool, linked as much to the dimensions and disposition of the urban plan as to the traffic flows evoked by the untold relations between parts of the city. By processing density, the city is shaped in plan and section and its areas and individual buildings fixed. A proposal attendant on research done on densities is that of the monolithic city: this is the outcome of the numerous possibilities of combining this variable.

Virtual urbanism 'The ideal of the city has been dismantled; the city is now a constellation of densities forever avoiding a condition of critical mass. Density can now only exist on condition that it is surrounded by nothingness.'[11] In urban design there exists the need for a programme of a non-standard mode of production. Urban objects are utterly reproducible, yet at the same time utterly deformable by modifying the density variables. This latter move encourages new forms; an urbanism that draws lines and is premised on the developing of mathematical formulas. Density increase/density decrease thus considered is a mathematical function that can be used to design a virtual urbanism one step ahead of the new urban

reality. Density increase and decrease occur in concert, particularly when a great need for transformation obtains. The discussion about whether it should be one or the other is a simplistic and misleading line of argument. It is not a matter of low density versus city, or of high- versus low-density dwelling, but rather of the modelling of functional regions from all of its wide range of components. Nor is it a conflict between car and public transport, but a question of providing more options in our daily life. Not the open market versus social control, but simply recognition of the new demographic and economic reality of the city.

Notes: [1] The Economist, 29 July 1995 [2] See Harm Tilman, 'Metapool uitdagend werkveld voor architecten. UIA-congres in Barcelona', de Architect, 27 (1996) 9, pp. 46-53; 'De Haagse Hogeschool als stedelijke infrastructuur', in De Haagse Hogeschool en de stedelijke vernieuwing van het Laakhavengebied, NAi Publishers, Rotterdam 1997, pp. 27-39 [3] Rem Koolhaas, 'Atlanta', in Robin Middleton (ed.), The Idea of the City, p. 89 [4] Massimo Cacciari, 'Metropoli della mente', Casabella no. 523, 1986, pp. 14-15 [5] Gilles Deleuze and Claire Parnet, Dialogues, Flammarion, Paris 1977 [6] Bernard Tschumi, Architecture and Disjunction, The MIT Press, Cambridge 1996 [7] Arturo Lanzani, Il territorio al plurale, Franco Angeli, Milan 1991, p. 256
[8] Arthur C. Nelson with Jeffrey H. Milgroom, 'Regional Growth Management and Central-City Vitality', in Fritz W. Wagner, Timothy E. Joder and Anthony J. Mumphrey Jr (eds.), Urban Revitalization. Policies and Programs, Sage, 1995 [9] Hans Schmidt et al., Funktion und Komposition der Stadtzentren. Untersuchungen am Beispiel der Stadtzentren Berlin, Leipzig, Dresden und Karl-Marx-Stadt, Deutsche Bauinformation, Berlin 1967, p. 75 [10] Mutaties, p. 44 [11] Rem Koolhaas, 'Atlanta', in the Idea of the City, p. 90

MASSIVENESS

Rat tests

Opinions

1997

MVRDV

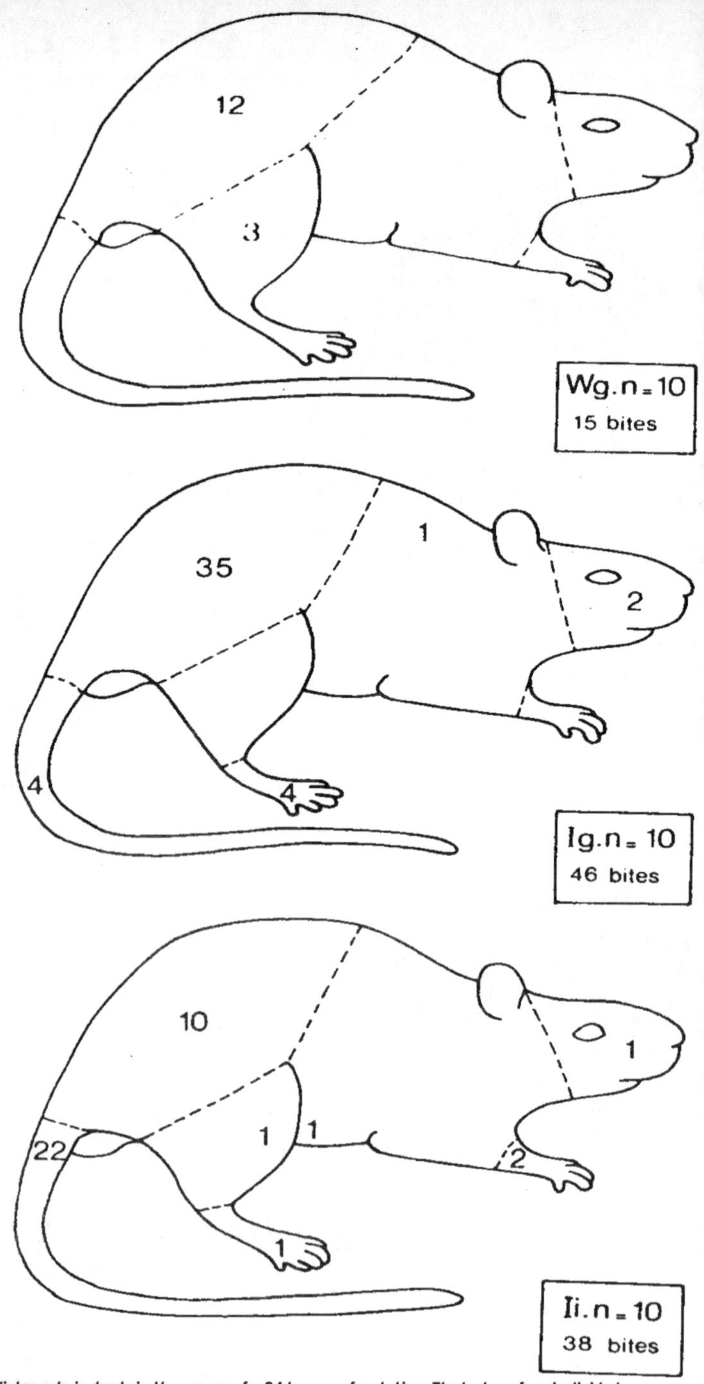

Bites inflicted to 160 days old male Wistar rats in dyads in the course of a 24 hour confrontation. The bodysurface is divided into parts to show the approximate localization of the wounds. Wg, within group-dyads or familiar rats. Bg, between group-dyads or unfamiliar rats. Ig, isolation-reared rats in dyads with groupreared rats. Gi, group-reared rats in dyads with isolation-reared rats. Tot., the distribution of all bites on the bodysurface.

rat test source: P.J.A. Timmermans, Social Behavior in the Rat, J.L. van Kaauwen, and Th. J. Fuchten, 1978

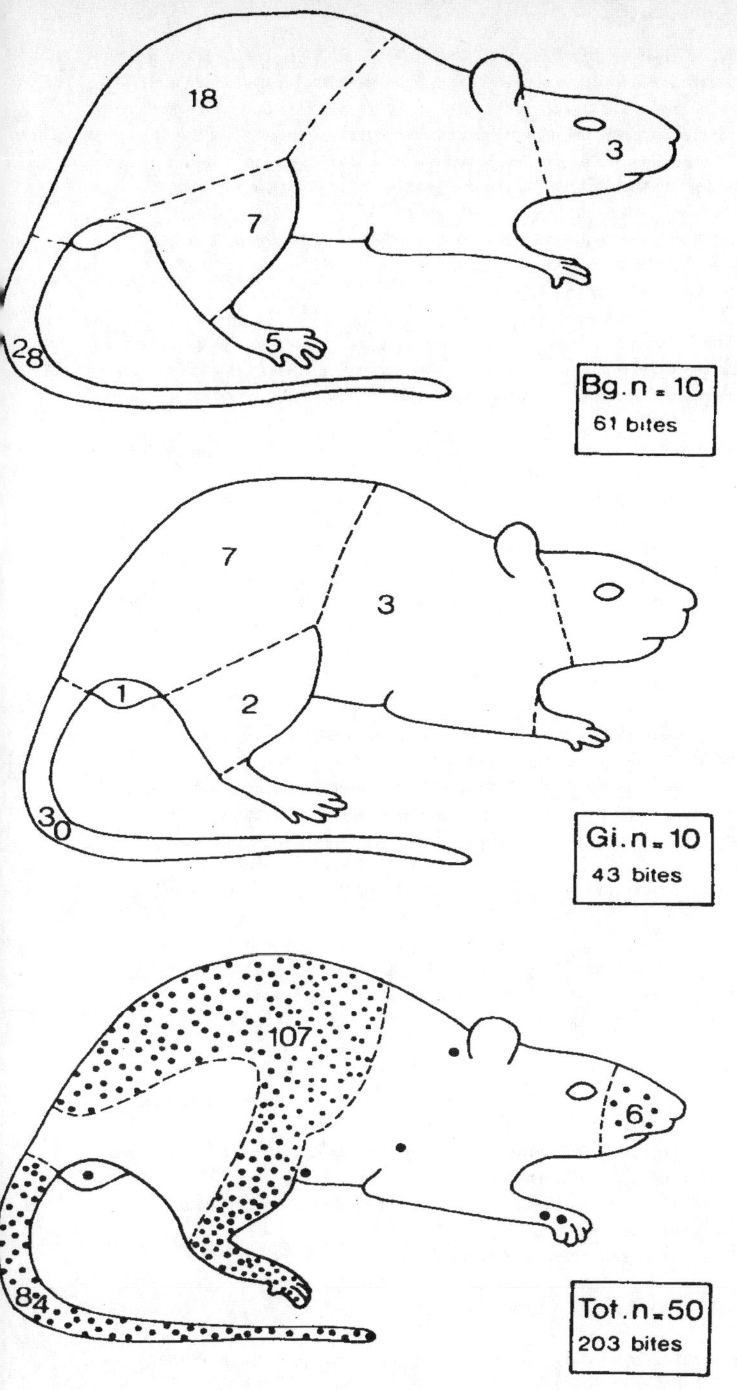
18
3
7
5
28
Bg.n = 10
61 bites
7
3
1
2
30
Gi.n = 10
43 bites
107
6
84
Tot.n = 50
203 bites

• The word 'sink' is used figuratively to mean a receptacle of foul or waste things. Calhoun invented the term 'behavioral sink' to designate the gross distortions of behavior which appeared among the majority of the rats in the Rockville barn. Such a phenomenon, he believes, is 'the outcome of any behavioral process that collects animals together in unusually great numbers. The unhealthy connotations of the term are not accidental: a behavioral sink does act to aggravate all forms of pathology that can be found within a group.'
The behavioral sink included disruptions of nest building, courting, sex behavior, reproduction, and social organization. Autopsied rats showed serious physiological effects as well.
The sink was reached when the population density was approximately double that which had been observed to produce a maximum of stress in the wild rat colony.
(Edward T. Hall, The Hidden Dimension, Double & Company, inc. 1966 p. 24)

• Two groups with which I have had some experience - the Japanese and the Arabs - have much higher tolerance for crowding in public spaces and in conveyances than do Americans and northern Europeans. However, Arabs and Japanese are apparently more concerned about their own requirements for the spaces they live in than are Americans.
(Edward T. Hall, The Hidden Dimension, Double & Company, inc. 1966, p. 58)

• This index revealed very little and Chombart de Lauwes then decided to use a new index to establish crowding - the number of square meters per person per unit.
The results of this index were startling; when the space available was below eight to ten square meters per person social and physical pathologies doubled! Illness, crime, and crowding were definitely linked. When the space available rose above fourteen square meters per person, the incidence of pathology of both types also increased, but not so sharply... A note of caution must be introduced here. There is nothing magic about ten to thirteen square meters of space.
(Edward T. Hall, The Hidden Dimension, Double & Company, inc. 1966 p. 161)

• Hall's 'Aha Erlebnis' emerged from research done by the ethnologist John Calhoun into the consequences of overcrowding among Norway rats. The rats Calhoun studied had everything they required except space. The repercussions of this one deprivation were spectacular: cannibalism, homosexuality, disruption of pregnancies, miscarriages, rejection and destruction of young, serious physiological effects and general aggression.
It appeared as though all the social aspects of behaviour were thrown overboard leaving only a gross distortion, what Calhoun calls a 'behavioural sink'.
(Lodewijk Brunt, Samenleven onder druk; Openbaar gedrag in Hong Kong. See also Edward T. Hall, The Hidden Dimension, Double & Company, Inc., 1966)

• C. and W. Russell cite this experiment of Calhoun's and add that from these and similar observations it emerges that violence erupts in an animal community when the population is too great, and that this violence serves to limit the population and disperse the survivors as before. It begins to look as though we have discovered the function of violence among animals.
This seems plausible enough. But what are we to make of the following facts?
A] In the wild, more than a hundred and fifty rats are able to coexist in perfect peace in a territory a great deal less that 1000 m^2.
B] In three of the six experiments Calhoun carried out there was nothing of what he has termed a behavioural sink, though there were difficulties in these experiments in bearing and raising the young rats.
C] If you take ten rats that have coexisted peacefully in a cage of 60 by 40 cm and place them in a space of 2 by 50 cm they will become aggressive and remain so...
It is still extremely premature to conclude from experiments like these that aggression is caused by overpopulation.
(Maarten 't Hart, Ratten, Amsterdam wetenschappelijke uitgeverij 1977)

• A list compiled by the United Nations of societies in order of violent crime ratings, places Hong Kong in the lowest regions.
(Adapted from Michael Harris Bond, Beyond the Chinese Face. Insights from Psychology, Oxford University Press, 1991, Hong Kong/Oxford/New York. Quoted in Lodewijk Brunt, Samenleven onder druk; Openbaar gedrag in Hong Kong)

• **Taken as a whole, the research and theories indicate that high density, by itself, is not always unhealthy or even unpleasant. However, when high density is associated with such factors as overstimulation, loss of personal control, and violation of personal space, the experience of crowding is likely to result.**
(Stephen Worchel, Joel Cooper and George R. Goethals, Understanding Social Psychology, Brooks/Cole Publishing Company, Pacific Grove, California 1991)

• **Crowding: A motivational state aroused through the interaction of spatial, social and personal factors.**
Density: The amount of space available for each individual in a defined area.
(Stephen Worchel, Joel Cooper and George R. Goethals, Understanding Social Psychology, Brooks/Cole Publishing Company, Pacific Grove, California 1991)

• **Hong Kong is a paradigm for this increase in density, a paradigm that certainly cannot and should not be adopted in every detail, but one that must be studied carefully so that we may learn from the example of its shadows and its splendour.**
(Lampugnani, Victorio Magnano 1993, The Aesthetics of Density, Prestel Verlag, New York/Munich. Quoted in Samenleven onder druk; Openbaar gedrag in Hong Kong, Lodewijk Brunt 1994)

• **Despite the fact that Hong Kong possesses an extreme population density, this does not necessarily lead to the type of pathological phenomenon often associated with it, particularly influenced by the ethnological range of ideas. On the contrary, despite all manner of serious problems that accompany such a heavy population concentration, public life in the city in general seems to proceed in orderly fashion.**
(Lodewijk Brunt, Samenleven onder druk; Openbaar gedrag in Hong Kong 1994)

• **It stands to reason that such an extreme population density is far more difficult to assimilate in large cities with a lower level of prosperity than Hong Kong.**
(Lodewijk Brunt, Samenleven onder druk; Openbaar gedrag in Hong Kong 1994)

• **Despite the extreme population density in Hong Kong, there seems nothing at all in public life there resembling a 'behavioral sink'.**
(Lodewijk Brunt, Samenleven onder druk; Openbaar gedrag in Hong Kong 1994)

• **Overcrowding gets the adrenalin going, and the adrenalin gets them hyped up. And here they are, hyped up, turning bilious, nephritic, queer, autistic, sadistic, barren, batty, sloppy, hot-in-the-pants, chancred-on-the-flankers, leering, puling, numb...**
(Tom Wolfe, 1968. Quoted in Lodewijk Brunt, Samenleven onder druk; Openbaar gedrag in Hong Kong 1994)

• **The implosion of the world population into cities everywhere is creating a series of destructive behavioral sinks more lethal than the hydrogen bomb. Man is faced with a chain reaction and practically no knowledge of the structure of the cultural atoms producing it. If what is known about animals when they are crowded or moved to an unfamiliar biotope is at all relevant to mankind, we are now facing some terrible consequences in our urban sinks.**
(Edward T. Hall, The Hidden Dimension, Double & Company, inc. 1966. Quoted in Lodewijk Brunt, Samenleven onder druk; Openbaar gedrag in Hong Kong 1994)

• **The basic design parameters for the HDB housing estates has been based on the assumption that high-rise equals high-density. High-density in the Singapore context means floor space ratio of the current maximum of 2.8. The error in HDB studies on alternative heights was in assuming an unchanged block depth/unit type design. The relationship between layout planning and unit type design can be seen to be closely connected. This relationship is precise and exacting. For example, for block depths to be increased in the interest of variety and block lengths, the internal planning of unit types has to change. Airwells, courtyards and the internalising of kitchens and bathrooms have to be considered. Site coverage is a critical factor. The increase beyond the current 12 to 15% site coverage liberates building from options.**
(Robert Powell and Akitek Tenggara, Line, edge and shade, The search For a Design Language in Tropical Asia, (Tien Wah Press), Singapore, 1997)

More square metre
No context? More
More autonomy? Le
Less sense of time
Less soil? Less sex
More murders?
Less children? Less
Less crime? Less s
Higher temperatur
Higher energy effic

?

ntasy?

s light?

Less sky?

al offences?

traffic victims?

cides?

s?

ency? Less wind?

Who is afraid of massiveness?

Global statistics

1996

MVRDV

POPULATION

COUNTRY	DENSITY PEOPLE PER SQ. KM	POPULATION × MILLION
AFRICA		
MAURATANIA	1.90	1.92
NAMIBIA	2.10	1.76
BOTSWANA	2.20	1.21
LIBYA	2.40	4.23
CHAD	4.20	5.40
GABON	4.50	1.20
CAR	4.50	2.77
NIGER	5.30	6.69
CONGO	5.50	1.89
MALI	7.20	8.92
ANGOLA	7.50	9.40
SUDAN	9.50	23.80
ALGERIA	10.00	23.84
ZAMBIA	10.00	7.53
SOMALIA	11.20	7.11
ZAIRE	14.30	33.46
MOZAMBIQUE	18.70	14.93
MADAGASCAR	19.00	11.24
GUINEA	20.60	5.07
LIBERIA	22.50	2.51
ZIMBABWE	22.70	8.88
CAMEROON	23.40	11.10
SOUTH AFRICA	24.20	29.60
TANZANIA	24.60	23.20
BURKINA FASO	31.00	8.50
MOROCCO	33.60	23.91
COTE D IVOIRE	36.00	11.61
SENEGAL	36.10	7.11
ETHIOPIA	39.10	47.88
BENIN	39.50	4.45
KENYA	41.00	23.88
TUNESIA	47.70	7.81
EGYPT	52.00	51.90
SIERRA LEONE	55.10	3.95
LESOTHO	55.40	1.68
TOGO	57.20	3.25
GHANA	59.20	14.13
MALAWI	65.4	7.75
UGANDA	87.3	17.19
NIGERIA	113.6	104.96
BURUNDI	185.0	5.15
RWANDA	256.3	6.75
MAURITIUS	591.4	1.10
BAHRAIN	694.6	0.48
ASIA		
MONGOLIA	1.3	2.09
OMAN	4.6	1.38
SAUDI ARABIA	6.5	14.02
SOUTH YEMEN	7.0	2.35
PAPUA NG	7.7	3.56
LAOS	16.3	3.87
UAE	17.9	1.50
AFGHANISTAN	23.9	15.51
QATAR	28.9	0.33
BHUTAN	30.9	1.45
IRAN	31.9	52.52
INDONESIA	34.4	174.95
IRAQ	39.0	17.25
FIJI	39.4	0.72
BRUNEI	41.6	0.24
JORDAN	42.9	3.94
CAMBODIA	43.5	7.87
NORTH YEMEN	49.1	9.83
MALAYSIA	51.3	16.92
BURMA	59.1	39.97
SYRIA	61.2	11.34
THAILAND	106.1	54.54
KUWAIT	110.0	1.96
CHINA	115.5	1104
NEPAL	129.5	18.23
PAKISTAN	132.4	105.41
N. KOREA	178.4	21.9
VIETNAM	194.9	64.23
PHILIPPINES	195.7	58.72
ISRAEL	218.9	4.43
INDIA	242.3	796.6
SRI LANKA	252.9	16.59
LEBANON	272.1	2.83
JAPAN	324.5	122.61
S. KOREA	423.3	41.97
TAIWAN	552.8	19.9
BANGLADESH	725.9	104.53
SINGAPORE	4288.0	2.65
HONG KONG	5308.4	5.68
MACAO	25882.3	0.44
EUROPE + U.S.		
AUSTRALIA	2.1	16.53
ICELAND	2.4	0.25
CANADA	2.8	25.95
NORWAY	10.8	4.2
NEW ZEALAND	12.3	3.29
USSR	12.7	283.68
FINLAND	14.6	4.95
SWEDEN	18.8	8.44
US	26.3	246.33
IRELAND	51.4	3.54
CYPRUS	59.5	0.55
TURKEY	68.0	52.42
GREECE	77.0	10.01
SPAIN	77.4	39.05
BULGARIA	81.1	8.99
AUSTRIA	90.6	7.6
ROMANIA	97.0	23.05
FRANCE	102.1	55.87
YUGOSLAVIA	104.3	23.56
ALBANIA	109.2	3.14
PORTUGAL	113.0	10.41
HUNGARY	113.9	10.6
DENMARK	119.0	5.13
POLAND	121.1	37.86
CZECHOSLOVAKIA	122.2	15.62
LUXEMBOURG	143.1	0.37
E. GERMANY	153.9	16.67
SWITZERLAND	160.3	6.62
ITALY	195.4	57.44
UK	233.8	57.08
W. GERMANY	246.1	61.2
BELGIUM	299.7	9.92
NETHERLANDS	395.8	14.76
LATIN AMERICA		
GUYANA	4.7	1.01
BOLIVIA	6.4	6.99
PARAQUAY	9.9	4.04
ARGENTINIA	11.5	31.96
PERU	16.5	21.26
CHILE	16.8	12.75
BRAZIL	17.0	144.4
BAHAMAS	17.2	0.24
URUQUAY	17.6	3.06
VENEZUELA	20.6	18.75
COLOMBIA	26.5	30.24
NICARAGUA	30.4	3.62
PANAMA	30.5	2.32
ECUADOR	37.7	10.20
MEXICO	41.9	82.73
HONDURAS	42.8	4.80
COSTA RICA	56.0	2.85
GUATAMALA	79.7	8.68
CUBA	93.8	10.40
DOMINICAN REP.	141.0	6.87
NETH. ANTILLES	191.3	0.19
HAITI	198.9	5.52
JAMAICA	222.9	2.45
TRINIDAD	241.8	1.24
EL SALVADOR	242.9	5.11
PUERTO RICO	369.8	3.29
BARBADOS	580.0	0.25
BERMUDA	1132.1	0.06

PHONE

COUNTRY	DENSITY	PEOPLE PER TELEPHONE
AFRICA		
MAURATANIA	1.90	358
BOTSWANA	2.20	8
LIBYA	2.40	4.6
CHAD	4.20	4
CAR	4.50	376
NIGER	5.30	561
CONGO	5.50	97
ANGOLA	7.50	211
SUDAN	9.50	280
ALGERIA	10.00	27
ZAMBIA	10.00	81
SOMALIA	11.20	26
ZAIRE	14.3	766
MOZAMBIQUE	18.70	233
MADAGASCAR	19.00	263
GUINEA	20.60	31.5
ZIMBABWE	22.70	33
BURKINA FASO	31.00	482
COTE D IVOIRE	36.00	712
SENEGAL	36.10	9
ETHIOPIA	39.10	340
BENIN	39.50	270
KENYA	41.00	73
EGYPT	52.00	35.6
SIERRA LEONE	55.10	298
GHANA	59.20	178
MALAWI	65.40	4
UGANDA	87.30	276
NIGERIA	113.60	367
BURUNDI	185.00	615
MAURITIUS	591.40	19
BAHRAIN	694.60	3.4
ASIA		
OMAN	4.60	1.5
SAUDI ARABIA	6.50	8
PAPUA NG	7.7	53.8
LAOS	16.3	8
UAE	17.90	4.7
AFGHANISTAN	23.9	543
QATAR	28.90	3.2
BHUTAN	30.9	66
IRAN	31.90	26.5
IRAQ	39.00	18.6
FIJI	39.4	1.7
BRUNEI	41.6	6.5
JORDAN	42.90	20.5
CAMBODIA	43.5	9
MALAYSIA	51.3	11.7
BURMA	59.1	743
SYRIA	61.20	16.8
THAILAND	106.1	52.6
KUWAIT	110.00	5.8
CHINA	115.5	150
PAKISTAN	132.4	164
N. KOREA	178.4	9
VIETNAM	194.9	10
ISRAEL	218.90	2.6
INDIA	242.3	191
SRI LANKA	252.90	128
JAPAN	324.5	1.8
S. KOREA	423.3	5.4
BANGLADESH	725.9	730
SINGAPORE	4288	2.3
HONG KONG	5308.4	2.2
MACAO	25882.3	4.2
EUROPE + U.S.		
AUSTRALIA	2.1	1.8
CANADA	2.8	1.3
NORWAY	10.8	1.3
NEW ZEALAND	12.3	1.5
USSR	12.7	10.3
FINLAND	14.6	1.4
SWEDEN	18.8	1
US	26.3	1.3
IRELAND	51.4	3.7
TURKEY	68	7.9
GREECE	77	2.5
SPAIN	77.4	4.1
BULGARIA	81.1	4.5
AUSTRIA	90.6	1.9
FRANCE	102.1	1.6
YUGOSLAVIA	104.3	7.6
PORTUGAL	113	4.8
HUNGARY	113.9	16.2
DENMARK	119	1.2
POLAND	121.1	8.5
CZECHOSLOVAKIA	122.2	2.6
LUXEMBOURG	143.1	1.4
E. GERMANY	153.9	4.3
SWITZERLAND	160.3	1.2
ITALY	195.4	1.5
UK	233.8	1.9
W. GERMANY	246.1	1.6
BELGIUM	299.7	2.2
NETHERLANDS	395.8	1.6
LATIN AMERICA		
BOLIVIA	6.40	41.4
ARGENTINIA	11.50	9.7
PERU	16.50	32.8
CHILE	16.80	15.5
BRAZIL	17.00	11.3
BAHAMAS	17.20	2.2
URUQUAY	17.60	7.6
VENEZUELA	20.60	11.3
COLOMBIA	26.50	13
NICARAGUA	30.40	63.4
PANAMA	30.50	9.4
ECUADOR	37.70	27.4
MEXICO	41.90	10.4
HONDURAS	42.80	86.6
GUATAMALA	79.70	62
CUBA	93.80	18.9
NETH. ANTILLES	191.30	4
TRINIDAD	241.80	11
EL SALVADOR	242.90	38.1
BARBADOS	580.00	3.3

T.V.

COUNTRY	DENSITY PEOPLE PER SQ KM	PEOPLE PER TELEVISION
AFRICA		
MAURATANIA	1.90	1810
BOTSWANA	2.20	53
CHAD	4.20	1085
GABON	4.50	82
CAR	4.50	548
NIGER	5.30	455
CONGO	5.50	298
MALI	7.20	8400
ANGOLA	7.50	225
SUDAN	9.50	20
ALGERIA	10.00	14
ZAMBIA	10.00	69
ZAIRE	14.3	2100
MOZAMBIQUE	18.70	144
MADAGASCAR	19.00	187
LIBERIA	22.50	55
ZIMBABWE	22.70	64
CAMEROON	23.40	210
SOUTH AFRICA	24.20	9
TANZANIA	24.60	1684
BURKINA FASO	31.00	213
MOROCCO	33.60	20
COTE D IVOIRE	36.00	19
SENEGAL	36.10	449
ETHIOPIA	39.10	607
BENIN	39.50	260
KENYA	41.00	184
TUNESIA	47.70	15
EGYPT	52.00	12
SIERRA LEONE	55.10	121
LESOTHO	55.40	112
TOGO	57.20	190
GHANA	59.20	89
MALAWI	65.40	162
UGANDA	87.30	160
NIGERIA	113.60	179
BURUNDI	185.00	4860
RWANDA	256.30	1843
MAURITIUS	591.40	9
BAHRAIN	694.60	2.4
ASIA		
MONGOLIA	1.3	46
OMAN	4.60	17
SAUDI ARABIA	6.50	3.5
SOUTH YEMEN	7.00	44
PAPUA NG	7.7	82.9
LAOS	16.3	435
UAE	17.90	12
AFGHANISTAN	23.9	170
QATAR	28.90	3
IRAN	31.90	19
INDONESIA	34.4	25.3
IRAQ	39.00	17
FIJI	39.4	16.9
BRUNEI	41.6	6.1
JORDAN	42.90	15
NORTH YEMEN	49.10	211
MALAYSIA	51.3	9
BURMA	59.1	1313
SYRIA	61.20	17
THAILAND	106.1	10
KUWAIT	110.00	4
CHINA	115.5	101
NEPAL	129.5	884
PAKISTAN	132.4	68
VIETNAM	194.9	531
PHILIPPINES	195.70	28
ISRAEL	218.90	4
INDIA	242.3	155
SRI LANKA	252.90	35
LEBANON	272.10	3
JAPAN	324.5	1.7
S. KOREA	423.3	5.2
TAIWAN	552.8	3
BANGLADESH	725.9	325
SINGAPORE	4288	5
HONG KONG	5308.4	4.2
MACAO	25882.3	8.8
EUROPE + U.S.		
AUSTRALIA	2.1	2
ICELAND	2.4	1.7
CANADA	2.8	2
NORWAY	10.8	2.6
NEW ZEALAND	12.3	2.7
USSR	12.7	9.4
FINLAND	14.6	3.3
SWEDEN	18.8	3.5
US	26.3	1.2
IRELAND	51.4	4.3
TURKEY	68	12.2
GREECE	77	3
SPAIN	77.4	2.8
BULGARIA	81.1	3.3
AUSTRIA	90.6	3
ROMANIA	97	4
FRANCE	102.1	2.7
YUGOSLAVIA	104.3	2.2
PORTUGAL	113	3.7
HUNGARY	113.9	13
DENMARK	119	2.5
POLAND	121.1	4.4
CZECHOSLOVAKIA	122.2	3
LUXEMBOURG	143.1	1.4
E. GERMANY	153.9	5.8
SWITZERLAND	160.3	2.8
ITALY	195.4	3.4
UK	233.8	2.8
W. GERMANY	246.1	2.4
BELGIUM	299.7	3
NETHERLANDS	395.8	2.7
LATIN AMERICA		
GUYANA	4.70	23
BOLIVIA	6.40	13
PARAQUAY	9.90	43
ARGENTINIA	11.50	5
PERU	16.50	12
CHILE	16.80	6
BRAZIL	17.00	5
BAHAMAS	17.20	5
URUQUAY	17.60	6
VENEZUELA	20.60	7
COLOMBIA	26.50	10
NICARAGUA	30.40	17
PANAMA	30.50	6
ECUADOR	37.70	214
MEXICO	41.90	8
HONDURAS	42.80	15
COSTA RICA	56.00	8
GUATAMALA	79.70	27
CUBA	93.80	5
DOMINICAN REP.	141.00	12
NETH. ANTILLES	191.30	5
HAITI	198.90	214
JAMAICA	222.90	9
TRINIDAD	241.80	4
EL SALVADOR	242.90	14
PUERTO RICO	369.80	4
BARBADOS	580.00	4
BERMUDA	1132.10	1

CAR

COUNTRY	DENSITY PEOPLE PER SQ KM	PEOPLE PER CAR
AFRICA		
MAURATANIA	1.90	239.9
BOTSWANA	2.20	84.9
LIBYA	2.40	9.8
GABON	4.50	50.8
CAR	4.50	195.4
NIGER	5.30	450.8
CONGO	5.50	82.8
MALI	7.20	412.6
ANGOLA	7.50	67.5
SUDAN	9.50	706.3
ALGERIA	10.00	33.4
ZAMBIA	10.00	78.6
SOMALIA	11.20	3300
ZAIRE	14.3	354.2
MOZAMBIQUE	18.70	177.9
MADAGASCAR	19.00	230.7
GUINEA	20.60	630
LIBERIA	22.50	307.9
ZIMBABWE	22.70	56.2
CAMEROON	23.40	117
SOUTH AFRICA	24.20	11.4
TANZANIA	24.60	565
BURKINA FASO	31.00	771.4
MOROCCO	33.60	44.2
COTE D IVOIRE	36.00	66.6
SENEGAL	36.10	30.9
ETHIOPIA	39.10	1122.4
BENIN	39.50	204.4
KENYA	41.00	182.4
TUNESIA	47.70	45.3
EGYPT	52.00	125.5
SIERRA LEONE	55.10	172.8
LESOTHO	55.40	1580
TOGO	57.20	133.4
GHANA	59.20	247.6
MALAWI	65.40	511.9
UGANDA	87.30	530.5
NIGERIA	113.60	144.8
BURUNDI	185.00	644.4
MAURITIUS	591.40	33.3
BAHRAIN	694.60	4.4
ASIA		
MONGOLIA	1.3	31.9
OMAN	4.60	10.9
SOUTH YEMEN	7.00	220.5
PAPUA NG	7.7	121.6
UAE	17.90	7.5
AFGHANISTAN	23.9	467.1
QATAR	28.90	3.8
INDONESIA	34.4	190.6
FIJI	39.4	24.7
BRUNEI	41.6	4.8
CAMBODIA	43.5	130.9
NORTH YEMEN	49.10	336.6
MALAYSIA	51.3	14.1
BURMA	59.1	1467.9
THAILAND	106.1	107.7
CHINA	115.5	1093.3
NEPAL	129.5	777.3
PAKISTAN	132.4	247.6
N. KOREA	178.4	80
VIETNAM	194.9	29.8
PHILIPPINES	195.70	179
INDIA	242.3	542.4
SRI LANKA	252.90	112.5
JAPAN	324.5	4.2
S. KOREA	423.3	50.7
TAIWAN	552.8	15.9
BANGLADESH	725.9	3441.9
SINGAPORE	4288	10.7
HONG KONG	5308.4	29.8
SAUDI ARABIA	6.50	11.6
SYRIA	61.20	124.4
IRAN	31.90	33.3
IRAQ	39.00	70.1
ISRAEL	218.90	6.2
JORDAN	42.90	21
KUWAIT	110.00	3.4
LEBANON	272.10	5.9
EUROPE + U.S.		
AUSTRALIA	2.1	2.3
ICELAND	2.4	2
CANADA	2.8	2.2
NORWAY	10.8	2.6
NEW ZEALAND	12.3	2.2
USSR	12.7	22.8
FINLAND	14.6	2.9
SWEDEN	18.8	2.5
US	26.3	1.8
IRELAND	51.4	4.8
CYPRUS	59.50	5
TURKEY	68	45.4
GREECE	77	7
SPAIN	77.4	3.8
BULGARIA	81.1	7.9
AUSTRIA	90.6	2.8
ROMANIA	97	81.1
FRANCE	102.1	2.5
YUGOSLAVIA	104.3	7.8
PORTUGAL	113	8.1
HUNGARY	113.9	6.4
DENMARK	119	3.2
POLAND	121.1	9
CZECHOSLOVAKIA	122.2	5.7
E. GERMANY	153.9	4.8
SWITZERLAND	160.3	2.4
ITALY	195.4	2.5
UK	233.8	2.8
W. GERMANY	246.1	2.2
BELGIUM	299.7	2.8
NETHERLANDS	395.8	2.9
LATIN AMERICA		
GUYANA	4.70	37.8
BOLIVIA	6.40	86
PARAQUAY	9.90	73.1
ARGENTINIA	11.50	7.8
PERU	16.50	54.5
CHILE	16.80	21.4
BRAZIL	17.00	15.8
BAHAMAS	17.20	3.5
URUQUAY	17.60	18.3
VENEZUELA	20.60	11.7
COLOMBIA	26.50	49.5
NICARAGUA	30.40	109.9
PANAMA	30.50	15.7
ECUADOR	37.70	163.2
MEXICO	41.90	15.5
HONDURAS	42.80	184.1
COSTA RICA	56.00	12.9
GUATAMALA	79.70	93
CUBA	93.80	533.5
DOMINICAN REP.	141.00	62.6
NETH. ANTILLES	191.30	2.7
HAITI	198.90	196
JAMAICA	222.90	26.4
TRINIDAD	241.80	5.2
EL SALVADOR	242.90	103.6
PUERTO RICO	369.80	2.6
BARBADOS	580.00	7.5
BERMUDA	1132.10	2.4

ROAD

COUNTRY	DENSITY OF PEOPLE PEOPLE/SQ.KM	ROAD DENSITY KM/SQ. KM
AFRICA		
BOTSWANA	2.20	0.02
GABON	4.50	0.03
CAR	4.50	0.03
NIGER	5.30	0.01
ANGOLA	7.50	0.06
ALGERIA	10.00	0.03
ZAMBIA	10.00	0.05
SOMALIA	11.20	0.03
ZAIRE	14.3	0.06
MADAGASCAR	19.00	0.09
LIBERIA	22.50	0.08
ZIMBABWE	22.70	0.2
SOUTH AFRICA	24.20	0.15
TANZANIA	24.60	0.09
BURKINA FASO	31.00	0.04
MOROCCO	33.60	0.13
COTE D IVOIRE	36.00	0.17
SENEGAL	36.10	0.08
ETHIOPIA	39.10	0.04
BENIN	39.50	0.07
KENYA	41.00	0.1
TUNESIA	47.70	0.18
EGYPT	52.00	0.03
LESOTHO	55.40	0.14
TOGO	57.20	0.14
GHANA	59.20	0.09
MALAWI	65.40	0.13
UGANDA	87.30	0.14
NIGERIA	113.60	0.12
BURUNDI	185.00	0.2
RWANDA	256.30	0.48
MAURITIUS	591.40	0.98
ASIA		
SAUDI ARABIA	6.50	0.04
AFGHANISTAN	23.9	0.03
IRAN	31.90	0.08
IRAQ	39.00	0.1
JORDAN	42.90	0.06
NORTH YEMEN	49.10	0.19
MALAYSIA	51.3	0.12
BURMA	59.1	0.03
SYRIA	61.20	0.16
THAILAND	106.1	0.15
KUWAIT	110.00	0.23
PAKISTAN	132.4	0.14
VIETNAM	194.9	0.2
PHILIPPINES	195.70	0.53
ISRAEL	218.90	0.23
INDIA	242.3	0.52
SRI LANKA	252.90	0.32
LEBANON	272.10	0.68
JAPAN	324.5	2.93
S. KOREA	423.3	0.56
SINGAPORE	4288	4.33
EUROPE + U.S.		
AUSTRALIA	2.1	0.11
ICELAND	2.4	0.11
CANADA	2.8	0.09
NORWAY	10.8	0.29
NEW ZEALAND	12.3	0.35
USSR	12.7	0.07
FINLAND	14.6	0.25
SWEDEN	18.8	0.32
US	26.3	0.68
IRELAND	51.4	1.34
CYPRUS	59.50	1.32
TURKEY	68	0.42
GREECE	77	0.26
SPAIN	77.4	0.64
BULGARIA	81.1	0.33
AUSTRIA	90.6	1.29
ROMANIA	97	0.32
FRANCE	102.1	1.46
PORTUGAL	113	0.56
HUNGARY	113.9	1.03
DENMARK	119	1.67
LUXEMBOURG	143.1	2
W. GERMANY	246.1	2.02
BELGIUM	299.7	3.91
NETHERLANDS	395.8	2.14
LATIN AMERICA		
BOLIVIA	6.40	0.04
PARAQUAY	9.90	0.03
ARGENTINIA	11.50	0.08
CHILE	16.80	0.11
BRAZIL	17.00	0.2
URUQUAY	17.60	0.28
VENEZUELA	20.60	0.11
COLOMBIA	26.50	0.1
NICARAGUA	30.40	0.13
PANAMA	30.50	0.11
ECUADOR	37.70	0.14
MEXICO	41.90	0.12
HONDURAS	42.80	0.13
COSTA RICA	56.00	0.57
DOMINICAN REP.	141.00	0.37
JAMAICA	222.90	1.53
TRINIDAD	241.80	1.01
EL SALVADOR	242.90	0.59
PUERTO RICO	369.80	1.06

ROAD ACCIDENT

COUNTRY	DENSITY	ROAD ACCIDENTS INVOLVING INJURY TO PERSONS PER 100000 PEOPLE
AFRICA		
BOTSWANA	2,20	286,28
CAR	4,50	17,36
NIGER	5,30	5,41
CAMEROON	23,40	51,68
BURKINA FASO	31,00	10,87
MOROCCO	33,60	104,71
COTE D IVOIRE	36,00	36,93
SENEGAL	36,10	85,11
ETHIOPIA	39,10	8,56
BENIN	39,50	9,60
TUNESIA	47,70	104,26
TOGO	57,20	50,12
UGANDA	87,30	28,37
RWANDA	256,30	49,32
MAURITIUS	591,40	518,82
ASIA		
IRAN	31,90	29,90
JORDAN	42,90	144,92
NORTH YEMEN	49,10	38,50
MALAYSIA	51,30	470,92
SYRIA	61,20	36,09
THAILAND	106,10	18,70
KUWAIT	110,00	1004,49
PAKISTAN	132,40	15,16
PHILIPPINES	195,70	17,45
JAPAN	324,50	472,38
S. KOREA	423,30	366,40
HONG KONG	5308,40	259,42
EUROPE + U.S.		
AUSTRALIA	2,10	159,64
ICELAND	2,40	212,80
CANADA	2,80	646,31
NORWAY	10,80	217,71
NEW ZEALAND	12,30	428,57
FINLAND	14,60	156,75
SWEDEN	18,80	197,48
US	26,30	916,52
IRELAND	51,40	163,16
CYPRUS	59,50	573,82
TURKEY	68,00	47,12
GREECE	77,00	224,51
SPAIN	77,40	128,34
BULGARIA	81,10	53,53
AUSTRIA	90,60	592,30
FRANCE	102,10	330,46
PORTUGAL	113,00	621,31
HUNGARY	113,90	184,56
DENMARK	119,00	224,21
CZECHOSLOVAKIA	122,20	154,19
LUXEMBOURG	143,10	360,00
SWITZERLAND	160,30	367,10
ITALY	195,40	276,90
UK	233,80	432,73
W. GERMANY	246,10	558,59
BELGIUM	299,70	552,68
NETHERLANDS	395,80	295,26
LATIN AMERICA		
CHILE	16,80	12,89
VENEZUELA	20,60	114,34

CRIME

COUNTRY	DENSITY	TOTAL CRIME RATE PER PEOPLE PER SQ KM 100000 POPULATION
AFRICA		
BOTSWANA	2.2	5046.33
LIBYA	2.4	1022.27
GABON	4.5	134.48
NIGER	5.3	32.51
CONGO	5.5	10.28
ANGOLA	7.5	240.05
SUDAN	9.5	1770.94
ZAMBIA	10.0	2569.33
ZIMBABWE	22.7	1425.16
TANZANIA	24.6	63.90
MOROCCO	33.6	718.73
COTE D IVOIRE	36.0	294.80
SENEGAL	36.1	235.30
KENYA	41.0	479.77
LESOTHO	55.4	1643.00
TOGO	57.2	10.75
MALAWI	65.4	1055.18
NIGERIA	113.6	311.96
BURUNDI	185.0	82.11
MAURITIUS	591.4	2365.84
ASIA		
PAPUA NG	7.7	833.72
QATAR	28.9	212.57
INDONESIA	34.4	44.4
BRUNEI	41.6	479.77
JORDAN	42.9	629.92
MALAYSIA	51.3	607.41
SYRIA	61.2	54.40
THAILAND	106.1	348.57
KUWAIT	110.0	575.65
PHILIPPINES	195.7	33.87
LEBANON	272.1	489.23
JAPAN	324.5	1453.33
SINGAPORE	4288.0	1412.68
HONG KONG	5308.4	1759.07
EUROPE + U.S.		
AUSTRALIA	2.1	6897.37
CANADA	2.8	10802.36
NORWAY	10.8	3871.38
NEW ZEALAND	12.3	12509.08
FINLAND	14.6	13380.94
SWEDEN	18.8	11785.22
US	26.3	5031.29
IRELAND	51.4	2898.68
CYPRUS	59.5	643.98
TURKEY	68.0	178.6
GREECE	77.0	3564.08
SPAIN	77.4	2573.27
AUSTRIA	90.6	5185.55
FRANCE	102.1	6714.06
PORTUGAL	113.0	774.45
HUNGARY	113.9	1470.54
DENMARK	119.0	8823.5
LUXEMBOURG	143.1	3946.75
SWITZERLAND	160.3	5134.02
ITALY	195.4	2124.47
UK	233.8	6545.53
W. GERMANY	246.1	6755
BELGIUM	299.7	2349.74
NETHERLANDS	395.8	7424.95
LATIN AMERICA		
CHILE	16.8	1372.73
VENEZUELA	20.6	837.27
COLOMBIA	26.5	687.24
ECUADOR	37.7	292.01
DOMINICAN REP.	141.0	294.68
TRINIDAD	241.8	3016.21
BERMUDA	1132.1	7.41

MURDER

COUNTRY	DENSITY PEOPLE PER SQ. KM	MURDER RATE PER 100000 PEOPLE
AFRICA		
BOTSWANA	2.2	7.49
LIBYA	2.4	1.60
GABON	4.5	1.12
NIGER	5.3	0.21
CONGO	5.5	1.06
ANGOLA	7.5	10.30
SUDAN	9.5	4.46
ZAMBIA	10.0	9.73
ZIMBABWE	22.7	21.11
TANZANIA	24.6	8.67
MOROCCO	33.6	0.78
COTE D IVOIRE	36.0	1.78
SENEGAL	36.1	1.67
KENYA	41.0	4.53
EGYPT	52.0	1.53
LESOTHO	55.4	53.19
TOGO	57.2	0.16
MALAWI	65.4	2.93
NIGERIA	113.6	1.69
BURUNDI	185.0	3.67
RWANDA	256.3	6.71
MAURITIUS	591.4	2.33
ASIA		
SAUDI ARABIA	6.5	1.15
PAPUA NG	7.7	9.23
QATAR	28.9	1.71
INDONESIA	34.4	0.9
FIJI	39.4	2.89
JORDAN	42.9	2.72
MALAYSIA	51.3	1.97
SYRIA	61.2	2.25
THAILAND	106.1	16.56
KUWAIT	110.0	1.06
PHILIPPINES	195.7	42.51
ISRAEL	218.9	1.83
LEBANON	272.1	19.20
JAPAN	324.5	1.47
S. KOREA	423.3	1.36
SINGAPORE	4288.0	2.73
HONG KONG	5308.4	1.64
EUROPE + U.S.		
AUSTRALIA	2.1	3.42
CANADA	2.8	6.33
NORWAY	10.8	0.92
NEW ZEALAND	12.3	2.54
FINLAND	14.6	5.62
SWEDEN	18.8	5.74
US	26.3	7.91
IRELAND	51.4	1.08
CYPRUS	59.5	2.06
TURKEY	68.0	1.41
GREECE	77.0	1.83
SPAIN	77.4	2.16
AUSTRIA	90.6	2.44
FRANCE	102.1	4.63
PORTUGAL	113.0	4.6
HUNGARY	113.9	3.72
DENMARK	119.0	5.77
LUXEMBOURG	143.1	5.25
SWITZERLAND	160.3	2.24
ITALY	195.4	5.25
UK	233.8	1.37
W. GERMANY	246.1	4.51
BELGIUM	299.7	3.27
NETHERLANDS	395.8	12.26
LATIN AMERICA		
CHILE	16.8	6.26
VENEZUELA	20.6	9.93
COLOMBIA	26.5	2.54
ECUADOR	37.7	4.53
DOMINICAN REP.	141.0	9.93
TRINIDAD	241.8	6.76
BARBADOS	580.0	6.14
BERMUDA	1132.1	10.79

SEX OFFENCE

COUNTRY	DENSITY PEOPLE SQ KM	SEX OFFENCES (INCLUDING RAPE) PER 100000 POPULATION
AFRICA		
KENYA	41.0	7.70
EGYPT	52.0	0.41
BOTSWANA	2.2	55.81
LIBYA	2.4	19.70
GABON	4.5	0.48
NIGER	5.3	1.44
ANGOLA	7.5	18.31
SUDAN	9.5	11.62
ZAMBIA	10.0	7.79
ZIMBABWE	22.7	33.35
TANZANIA	24.6	0.46
MOROCCO	33.6	26.07
COTE D IVOIRE	36.0	8.03
SENEGAL	36.1	4.88
MALAWI	65.4	7.07
NIGERIA	113.6	1.79
BURUNDI	185.0	1.26
RWANDA	256.3	10.81
MAURITIUS	591.4	6.88
ASIA		
SAUDI ARABIA	6.5	19.28
PAPUA NG	7.7	31.36
QATAR	28.9	30.00
INDONESIA	34.4	3.22
FIJI	39.4	32.56
JORDAN	42.9	19.31
MALAYSIA	51.3	5.02
SYRIA	61.2	6.18
THAILAND	106.1	11.31
ISRAEL	218.9	48.86
LEBANON	272.1	3.17
JAPAN	324.5	3.57
S. KOREA	423.3	37.6
SINGAPORE	4288.0	23.01
EUROPE + U.S.		
AUSTRALIA	2.1	7723
CANADA	2.8	58.88
NORWAY	10.8	21.73
NEW ZEALAND	12.3	110.35
FINLAND	14.6	21.74
SWEDEN	18.8	46.1
US	26.3	35.67
IRELAND	51.4	7.7
CYPRUS	59.5	5.61
TURKEY	68.0	6.57
GREECE	77.0	5.1
SPAIN	77.4	12.52
AUSTRIA	90.6	43.91
FRANCE	102.1	32.14
PORTUGAL	113.0	2.98
HUNGARY	113.9	19.14
DENMARK	119.0	42.86
LUXEMBOURG	143.1	26.5
SWITZERLAND	160.3	57.65
UK	233.8	41.14
W. GERMANY	246.1	6.25
BELGIUM	299.7	35.28
NETHERLANDS	395.8	62.18
LATIN AMERICA		
CHILE	16.8	36.04
VENEZUELA	20.6	45.89
DOMINICAN REP.	141.0	4.36
TRINIDAD	241.8	10.21
BARBADOS	580.0	51.59

THEFT

COUNTRY	DENSITY PEOPLE SQ. KM	THEFTS PER 100000 POPULATION
AFRICA		
BOTSWANA	2.2	1650.55
LIBYA	2.4	270.07
GABON	4.5	48.24
NIGER	5.3	10.20
ANGOLA	7.5	76.16
SUDAN	9.5	249.82
ZAMBIA	10.0	1006.19
MOROCCO	33.6	216.69
COTE D IVOIRE	36.0	150.76
SENEGAL	36.1	92.05
KENYA	41.0	85.61
EGYPT	52.0	36.15
LESOTHO	55.4	631.87
TOGO	57.2	3.69
MALAWI	65.4	684.50
NIGERIA	113.6	63.16
BURUNDI	185.0	25.26
RWANDA	256.3	100.62
MAURITIUS	591.4	1003.46
ASIA		
SAUDI ARABIA	6.5	54.90
PAPUA NG	7.7	324.03
QATAR	28.9	131.71
INDONESIA	34.4	56.97
FIJI	39.4	1642.26
BRUNEI	41.6	280.95
JORDAN	42.9	149.91
SYRIA	61.2	37.63
THAILAND	106.1	78.61
KUWAIT	110.0	129.76
PHILIPPINES	195.7	55.54
ISRAEL	218.9	4113.64
JAPAN	324.5	1137.68
S. KOREA	423.3	274.99
SINGAPORE	4288.0	897.63
HONG KONG	5308.4	1012.86
EUROPE + U.S.		
AUSTRALIA	2.1	4610.47
CANADA	2.8	5114.14
NORWAY	10.8	2862.84
NEW ZEALAND	12.3	7245.08
FINLAND	14.6	1914.42
SWEDEN	18.8	6930.99
US	26.3	4697.49
IRELAND	51.4	2591.39
CYPRUS	59.5	437.17
TURKEY	68.0	77.11
GREECE	77.0	227.78
SPAIN	77.4	1624.34
AUSTRIA	90.6	2388.66
FRANCE	102.1	4111.64
PORTUGAL	113.0	351.93
HUNGARY	113.9	720
DENMARK	119.0	7110.28
LUXEMBOURG	143.1	2065.75
SWITZERLAND	160.3	4585.66
ITALY	195.4	1548.39
W. GERMANY	246.1	4268.72
BELGIUM	299.7	1864.29
NETHERLANDS	395.8	5588.54
LATIN AMERICA		
CHILE	16.8	738.39
BAHAMAS	17.2	1815.04
VENEZUELA	20.6	560.77
COLOMBIA	26.5	213.21
DOMINICAN REP.	141.0	72.79
TRINIDAD	241.8	1346.34
BARBADOS	580.0	1841.31

PHONE

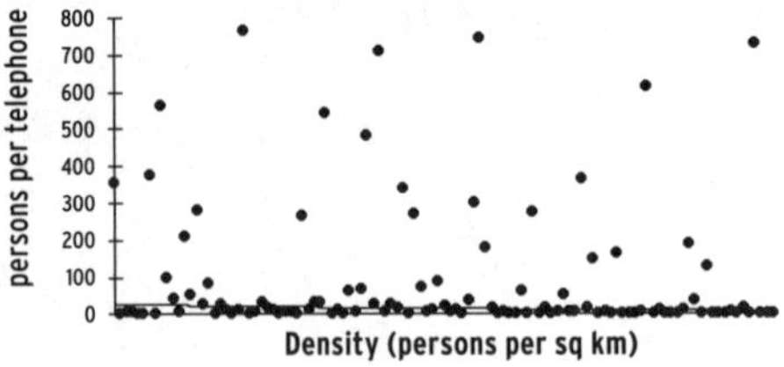
persons per telephone
Density (persons per sq km)

TV

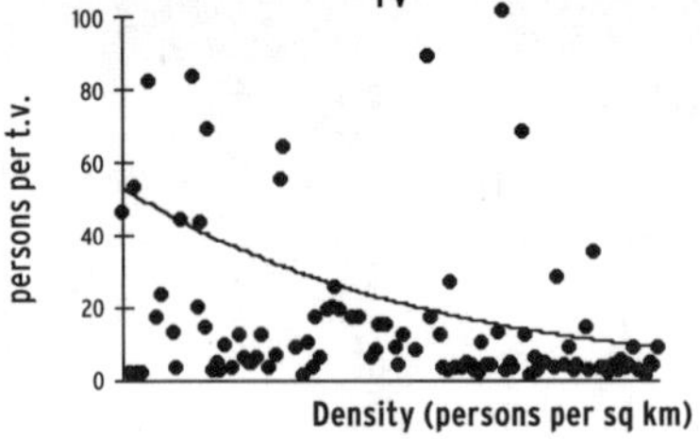
persons per t.v.
Density (persons per sq km)

AFRICA

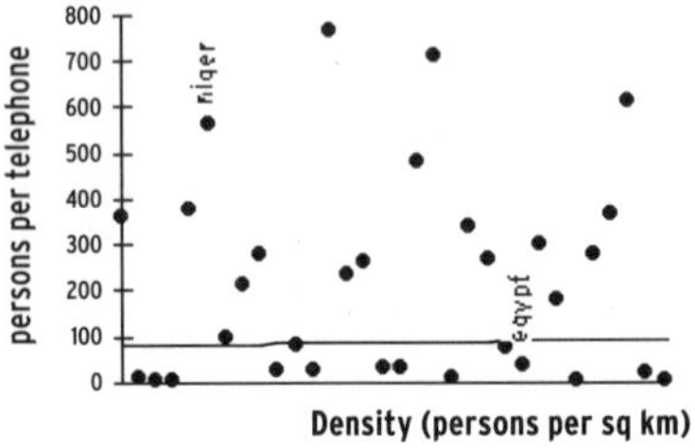
persons per telephone
niger
egypt
Density (persons per sq km)

AFRICA

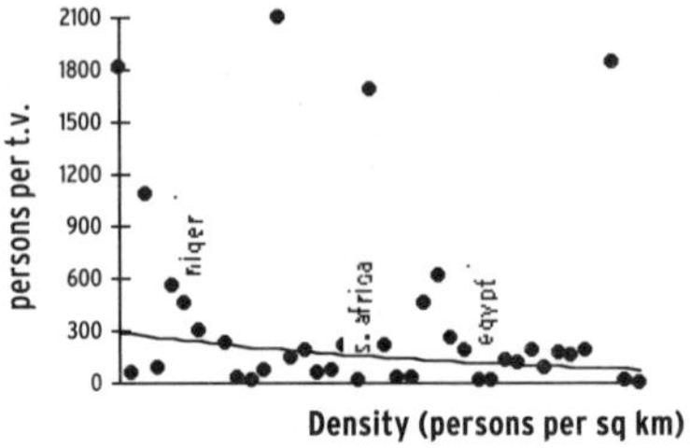
persons per t.v.
niger
s. africa
egypt
Density (persons per sq km)

ASIA

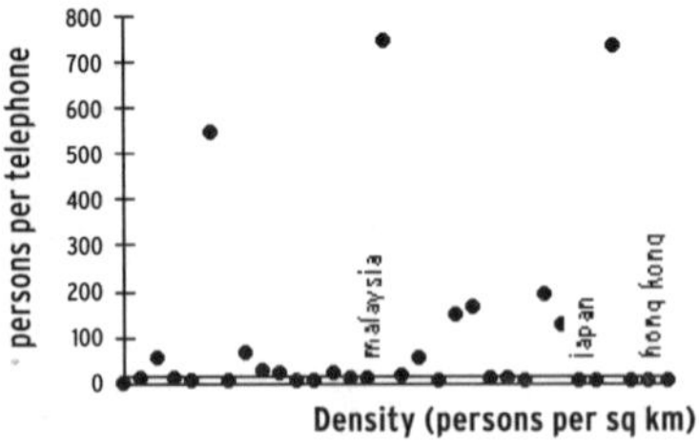
persons per telephone
malaysia
japan
hong kong
Density (persons per sq km)

ASIA

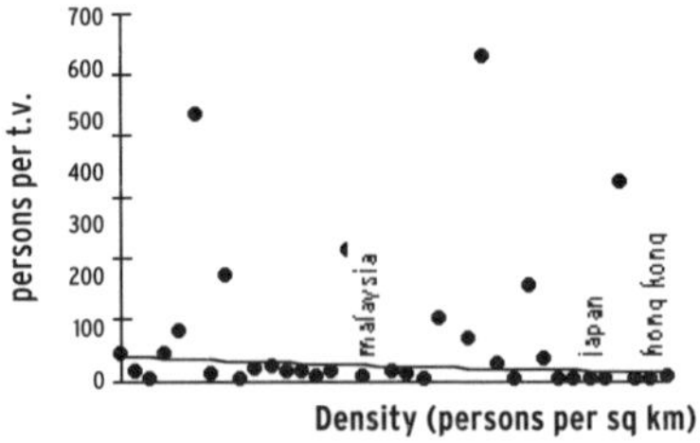
persons per t.v.
malaysia
japan
hong kong
Density (persons per sq km)

EUROPE & U.S.

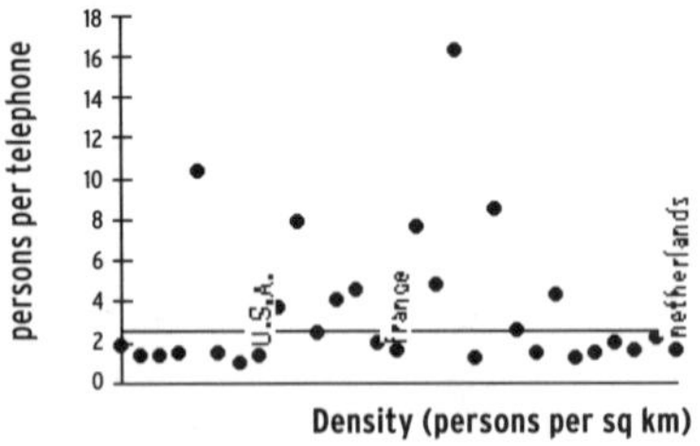
persons per telephone
U.S.A.
france
netherlands
Density (persons per sq km)

EUROPE & U.S.

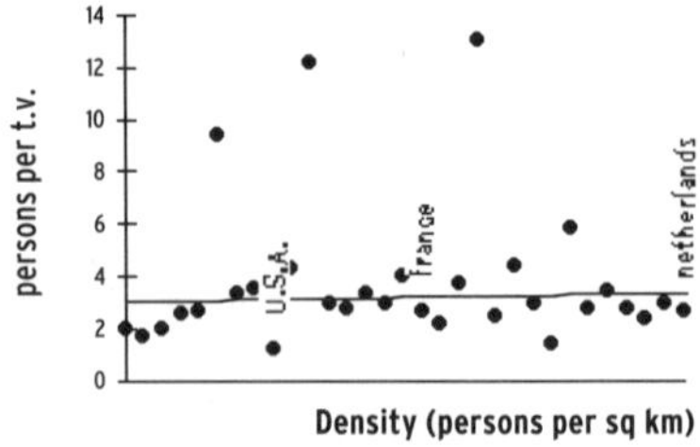
persons per t.v.
U.S.A.
france
netherlands
Density (persons per sq km)

LATIN AMERICA

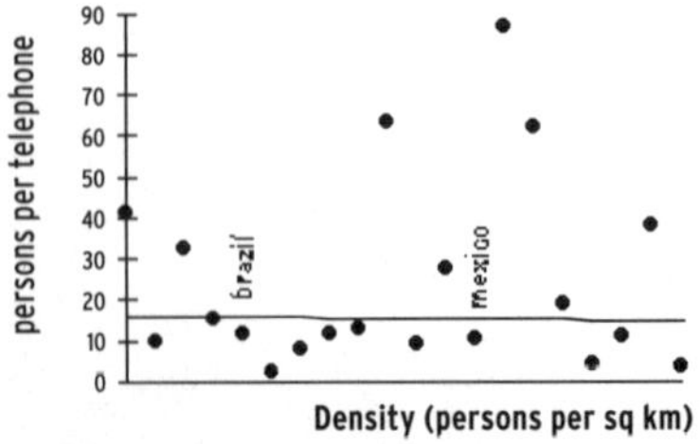
persons per telephone
brazil
mexico
Density (persons per sq km)

LATIN AMERICA

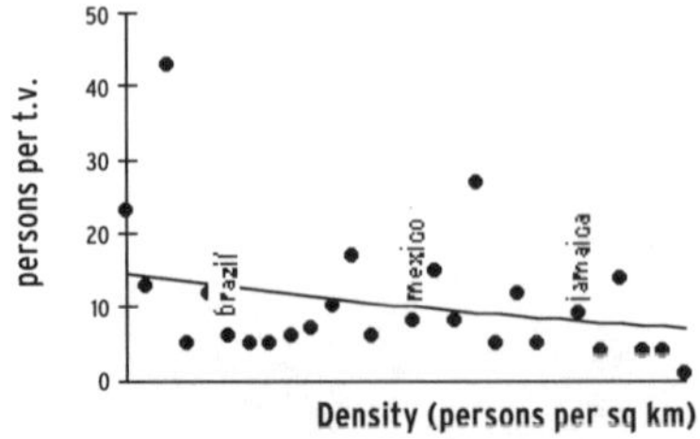
persons per t.v.
brazil
mexico
jamaica
Density (persons per sq km)

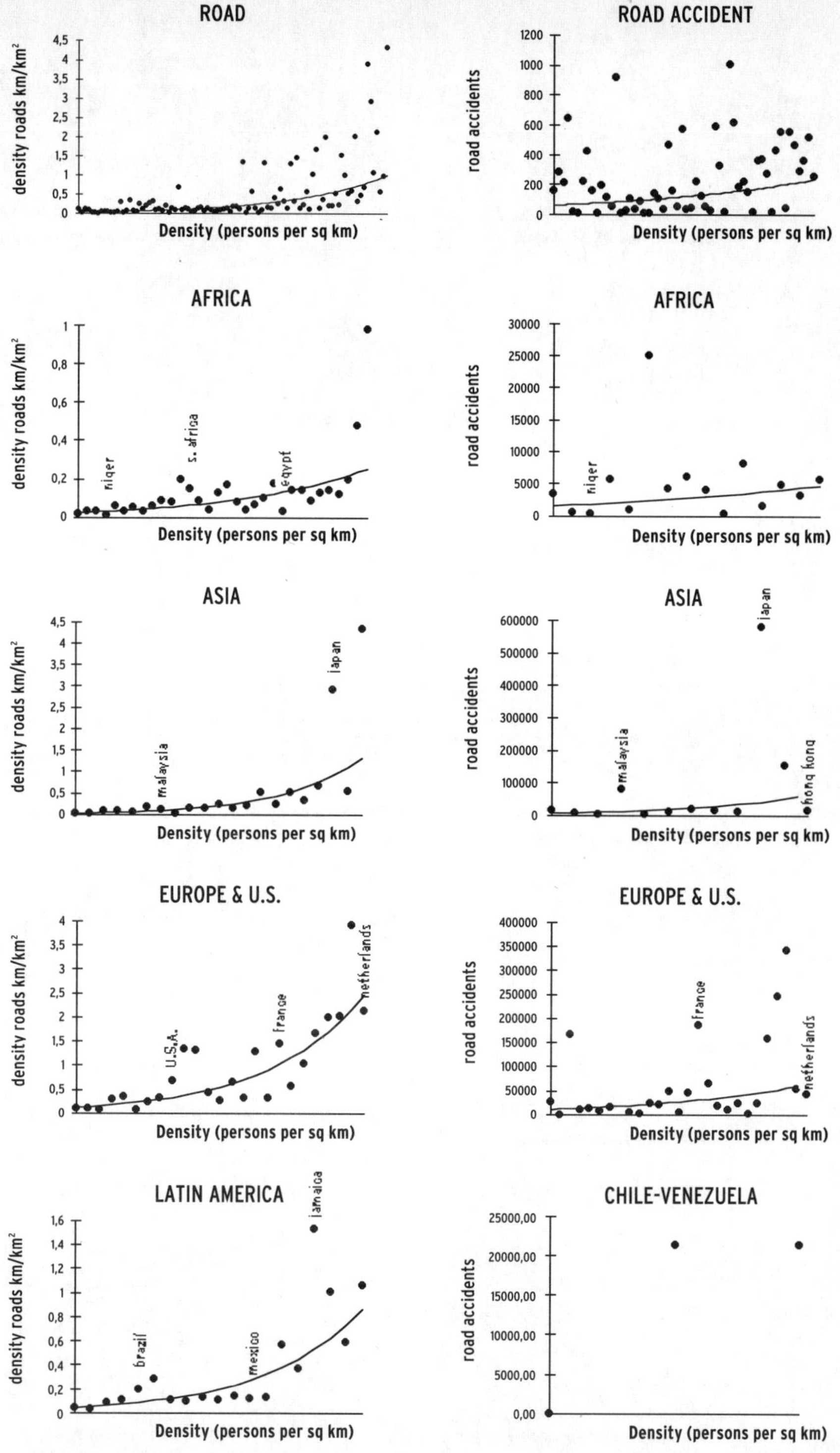
ROAD
density roads km/km²
4,5
4
3,5
3
2,5
2
1,5
1
0,5
0
Density (persons per sq km)
ROAD ACCIDENT
road accidents
1200
1000
800
600
400
200
0
Density (persons per sq km)
AFRICA
density roads km/km²
1
0,8
0,6
0,4
0,2
0
niger
s. africa
egypt
Density (persons per sq km)
AFRICA
road accidents
30000
25000
20000
15000
10000
5000
0
niger
Density (persons per sq km)
ASIA
density roads km/km²
4,5
4
3,5
3
2,5
2
1,5
1
0,5
0
malaysia
japan
Density (persons per sq km)
ASIA
road accidents
600000
500000
400000
300000
200000
100000
0
japan
malaysia
hong kong
Density (persons per sq km)
EUROPE & U.S.
density roads km/km²
4
3,5
3
2,5
2
1,5
1
0,5
0
U.S.A.
france
netherlands
Density (persons per sq km)
EUROPE & U.S.
road accidents
400000
350000
300000
250000
200000
150000
100000
50000
0
france
netherlands
Density (persons per sq km)
LATIN AMERICA
density roads km/km²
1,6
1,4
1,2
1
0,8
0,6
0,4
0,2
0
brazil
mexico
jamaica
Density (persons per sq km)
CHILE-VENEZUELA
road accidents
25000,00
20000,00
15000,00
10000,00
5000,00
0,00
Density (persons per sq km)

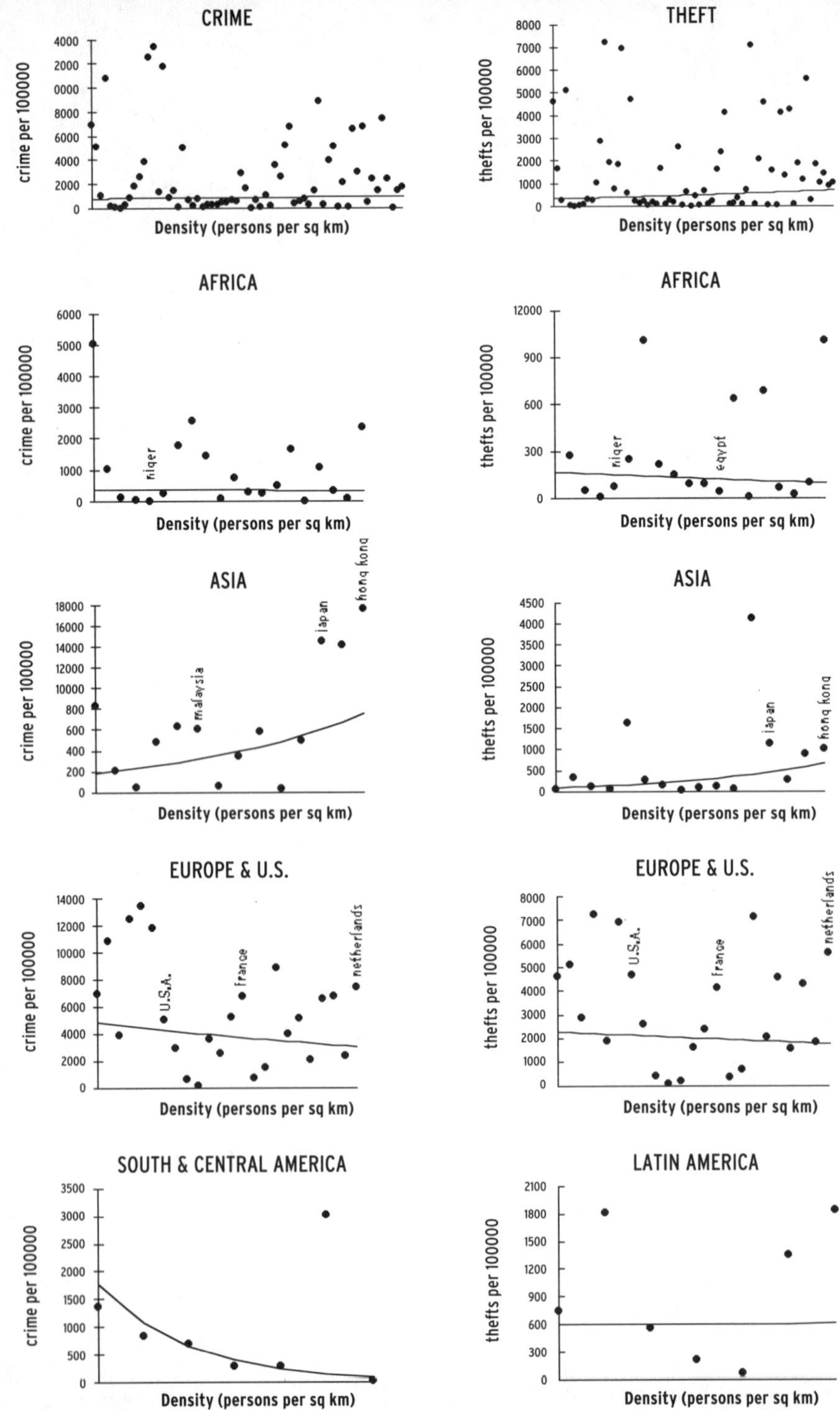
CRIME
crime per 100000
Density (persons per sq km)
THEFT
thefts per 100000
Density (persons per sq km)
AFRICA
crime per 100000
niger
Density (persons per sq km)
AFRICA
thefts per 100000
niger
egypt
Density (persons per sq km)
ASIA
crime per 100000
malaysia
japan
hong kong
Density (persons per sq km)
ASIA
thefts per 100000
japan
hong kong
Density (persons per sq km)
EUROPE & U.S.
crime per 100000
U.S.A.
france
netherlands
Density (persons per sq km)
EUROPE & U.S.
thefts per 100000
U.S.A.
france
netherlands
Density (persons per sq km)
SOUTH & CENTRAL AMERICA
crime per 100000
Density (persons per sq km)
LATIN AMERICA
thefts per 100000
Density (persons per sq km)

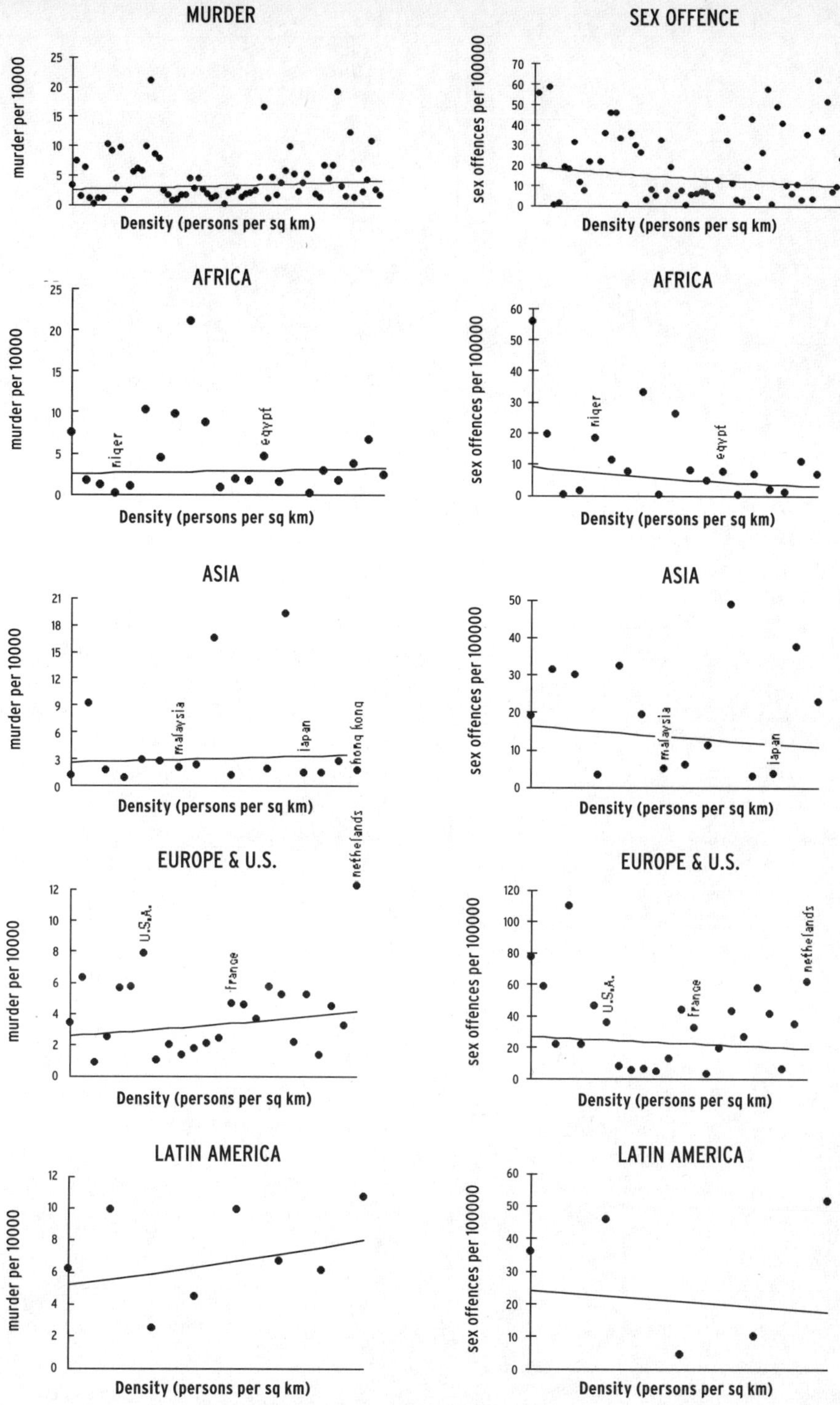
MURDER
murder per 10000
Density (persons per sq km)
SEX OFFENCE
sex offences per 100000
Density (persons per sq km)
AFRICA
murder per 10000
niger
egypt
Density (persons per sq km)
AFRICA
sex offences per 100000
niger
egypt
Density (persons per sq km)
ASIA
murder per 10000
malaysia
japan
hong kong
Density (persons per sq km)
ASIA
sex offences per 100000
malaysia
japan
Density (persons per sq km)
EUROPE & U.S.
murder per 10000
U.S.A.
france
nethelands
Density (persons per sq km)
EUROPE & U.S.
sex offences per 100000
U.S.A.
france
nethelands
Density (persons per sq km)
LATIN AMERICA
murder per 10000
Density (persons per sq km)
LATIN AMERICA
sex offences per 100000
Density (persons per sq km)

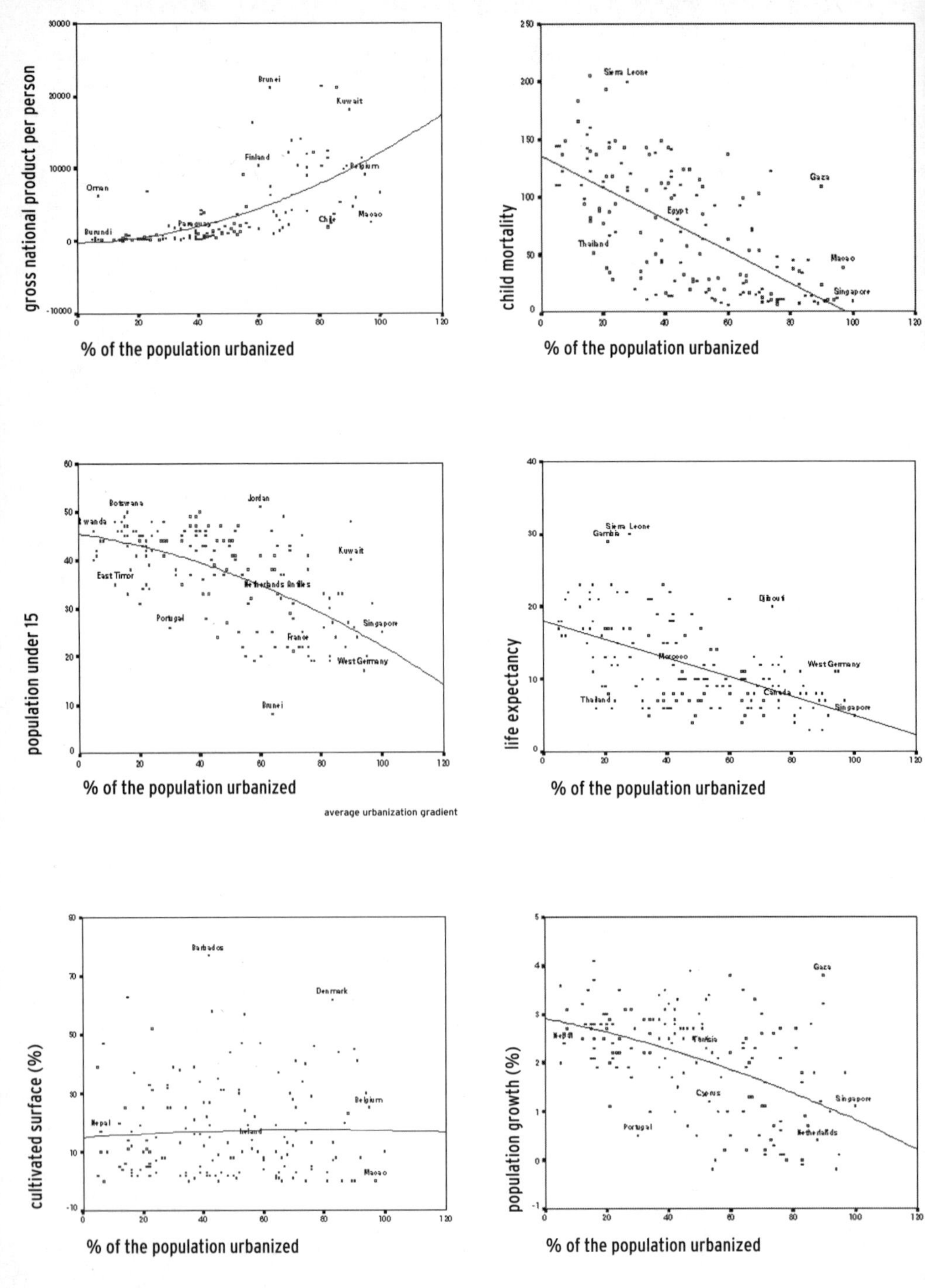

average urbanization gradient

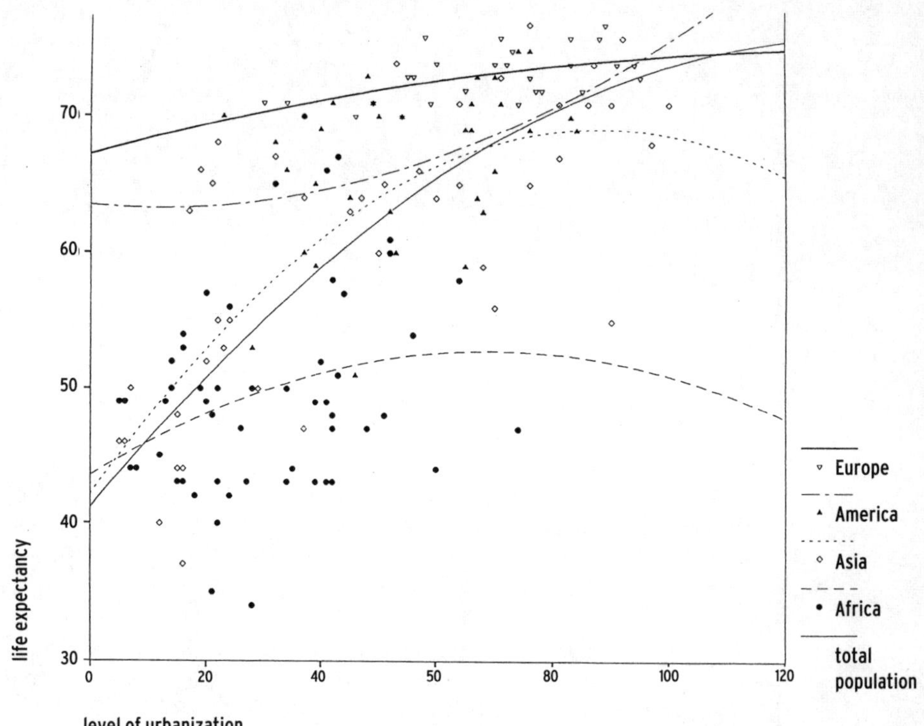
life expectancy
70
60
50
40
30
0
20
40
50
80
100
120
level of urbanization
Europe
America
Asia
Africa
total population

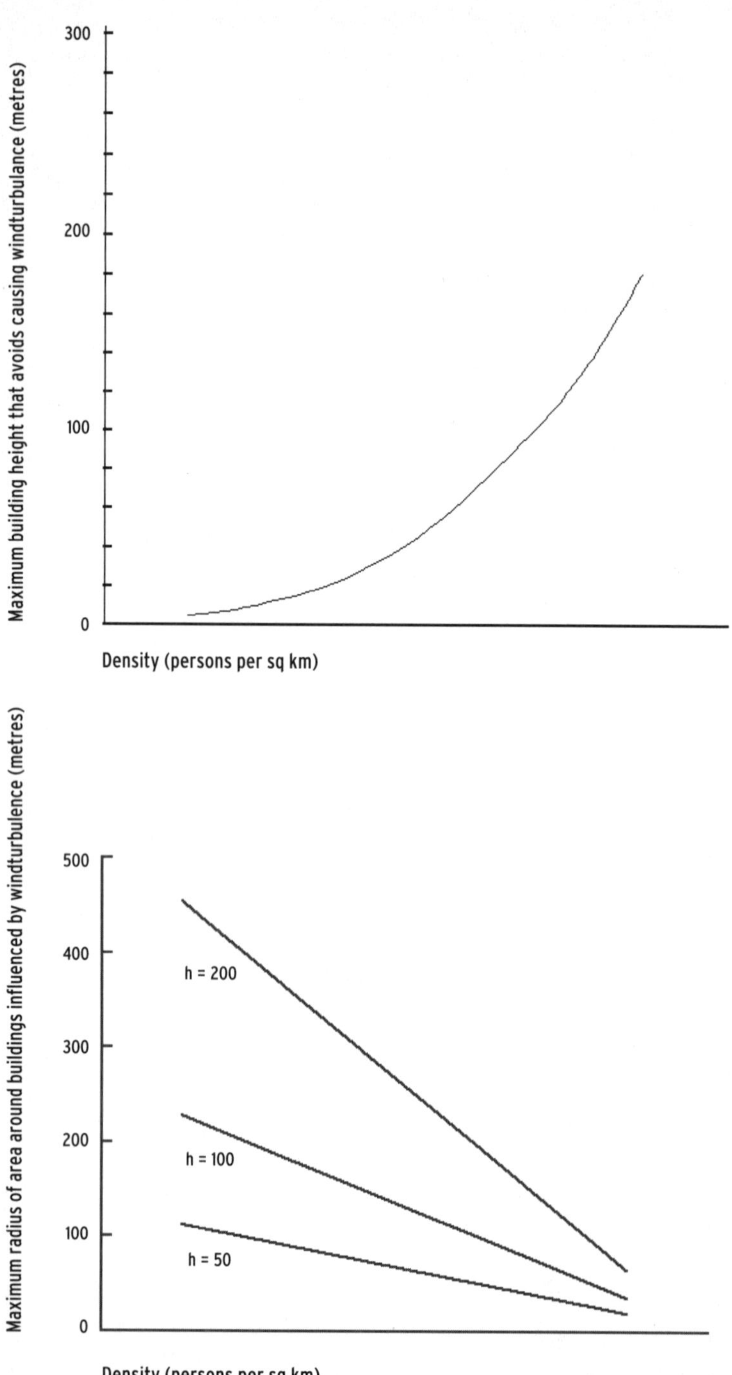
Maximum building height that avoids causing windturbulance (metres)
300
200
100
0
Density (persons per sq km)
Maximum radius of area around buildings influenced by windturbulence (metres)
500
400
300
200
100
0
h = 200
h = 100
h = 50
Density (persons per sq km)

Climate
Statistics
1996
MVRDV

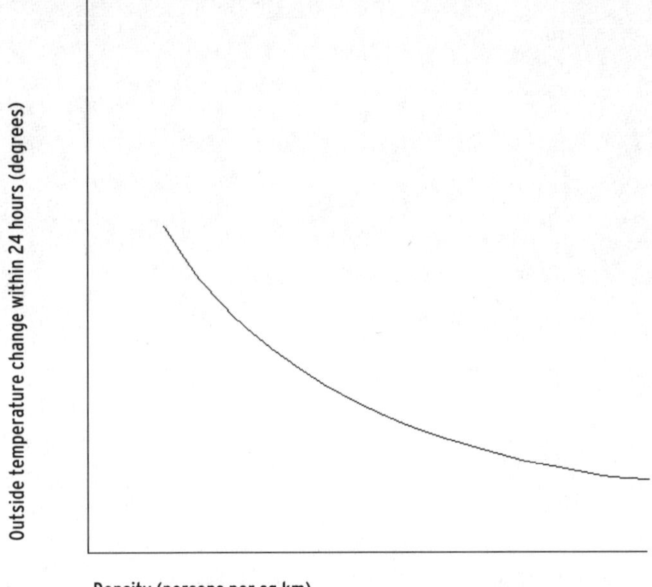
Outside temperature change within 24 hours (degrees)
Density (persons per sq km)

Temperature difference between town and hinterland (degrees)

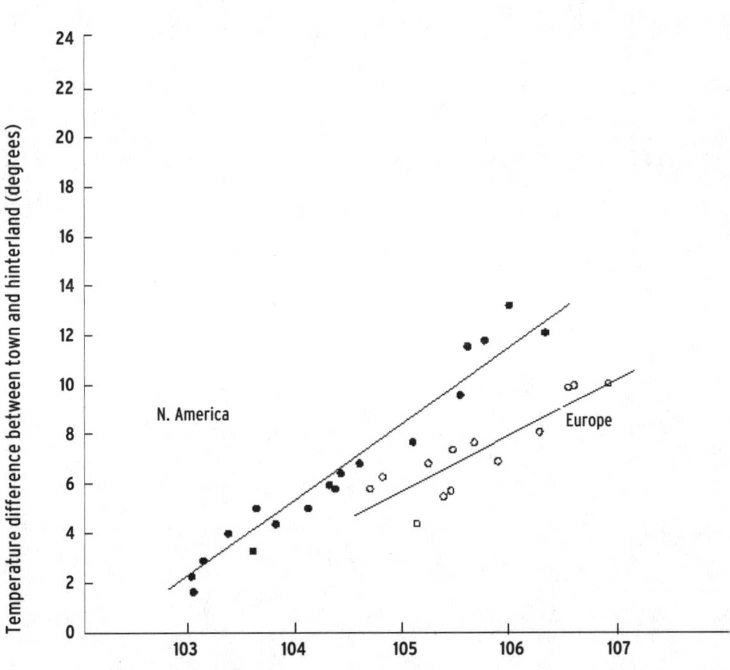
24
22
20
18
16
14
12
10
8
6
4
2
0
N. America
Europe
10^3
10^4
10^5
10^6
10^7
Size of town (amount of people)

Traffic

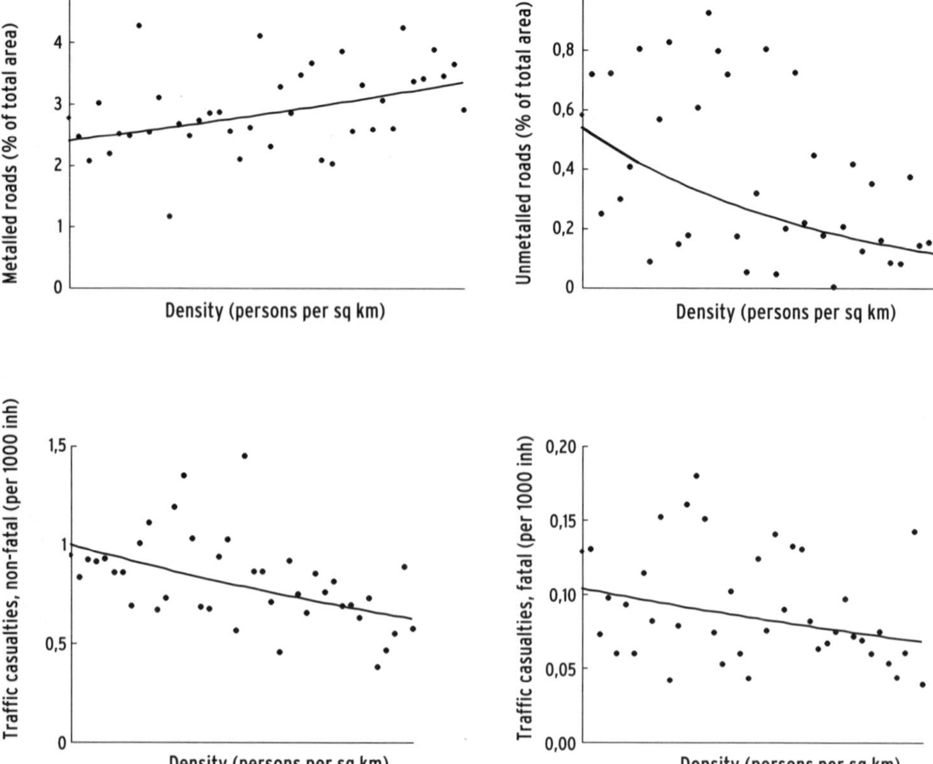

Metalled roads (% of total area)
5
4
3
2
1
0
Density (persons per sq km)
Unmetalled roads (% of total area)
1
0,8
0,6
0,4
0,2
0
Density (persons per sq km)
Traffic casualties, non-fatal (per 1000 inh)
1,5
1
0,5
0
Density (persons per sq km)
Traffic casualties, fatal (per 1000 inh)
0,20
0,15
0,10
0,05
0,00
Density (persons per sq km)

And Holland?

Statistics

1996

MVRDV

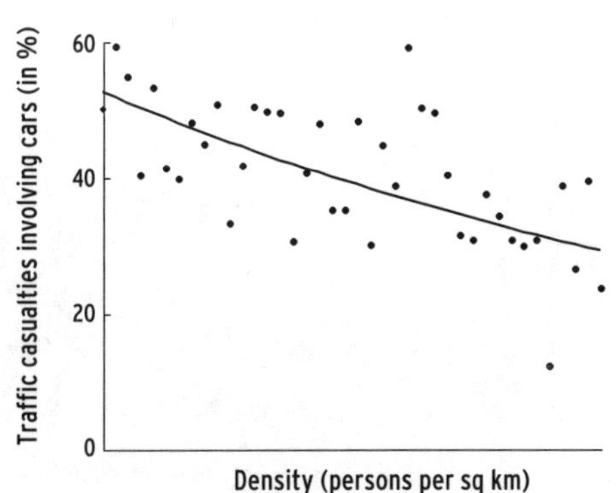

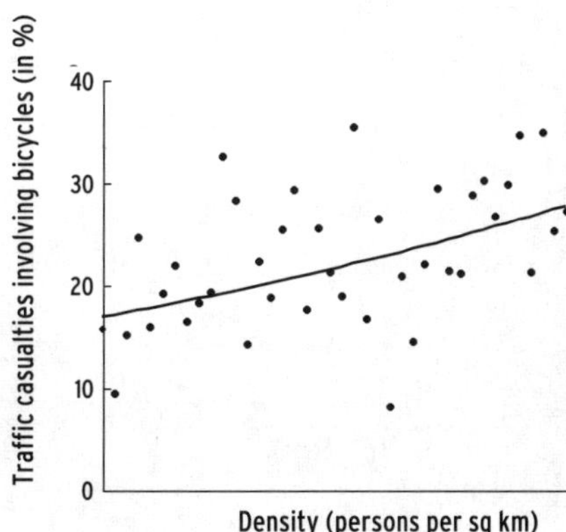

Ecology

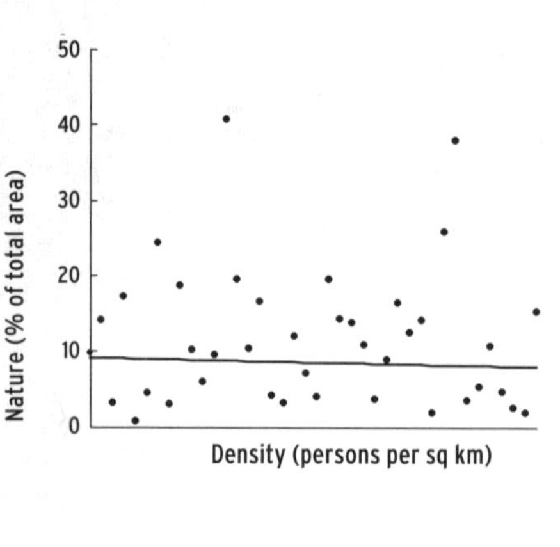

Nature (% of total area)
50
40
30
20
10
0
Density (persons per sq km)

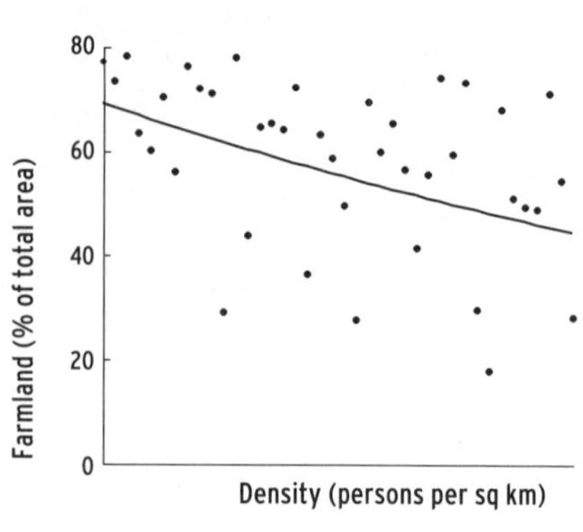

Farmland (% of total area)
80
60
40
20
0
Density (persons per sq km)

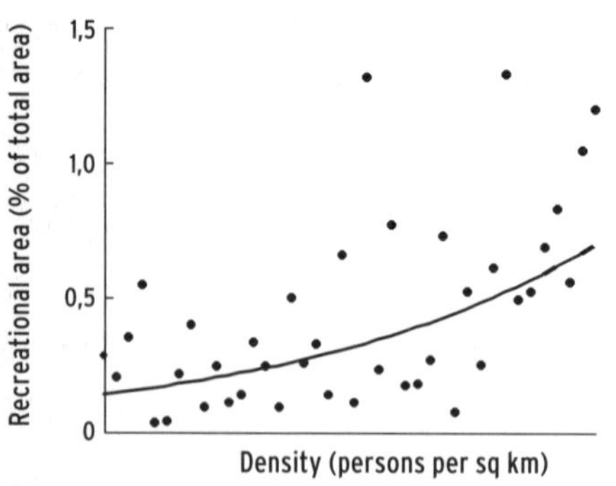

Recreational area (% of total area)
1,5
1,0
0,5
0
Density (persons per sq km)

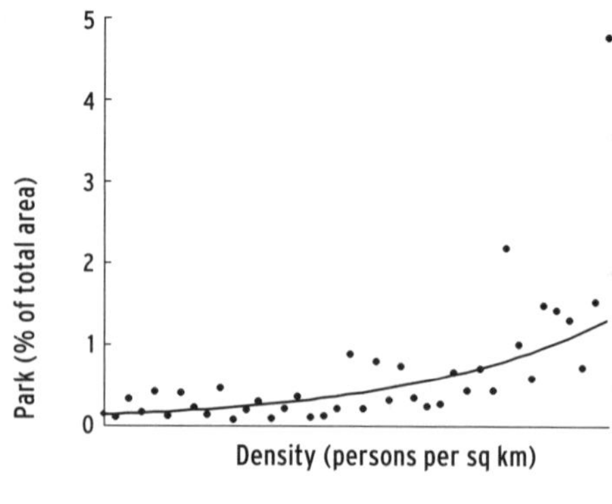

Park (% of total area)
5
4
3
2
1
0
Density (persons per sq km)

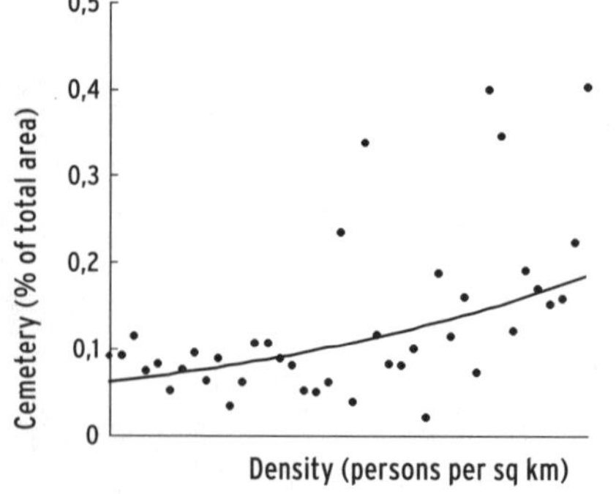

Cemetery (% of total area)
0,5
0,4
0,3
0,2
0,1
0
Density (persons per sq km)

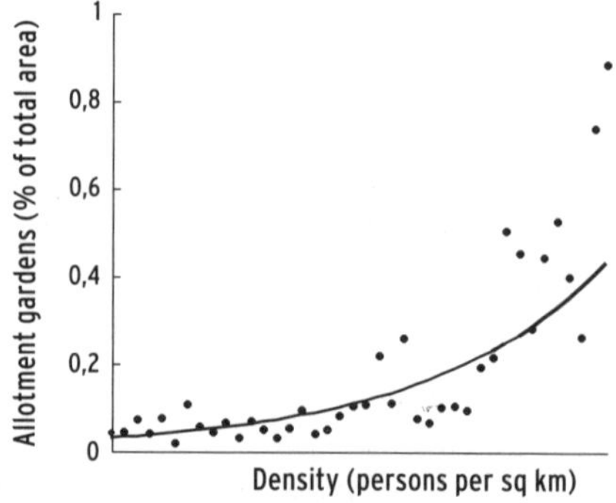

Allotment gardens (% of total area)
1
0,8
0,6
0,4
0,2
0
Density (persons per sq km)

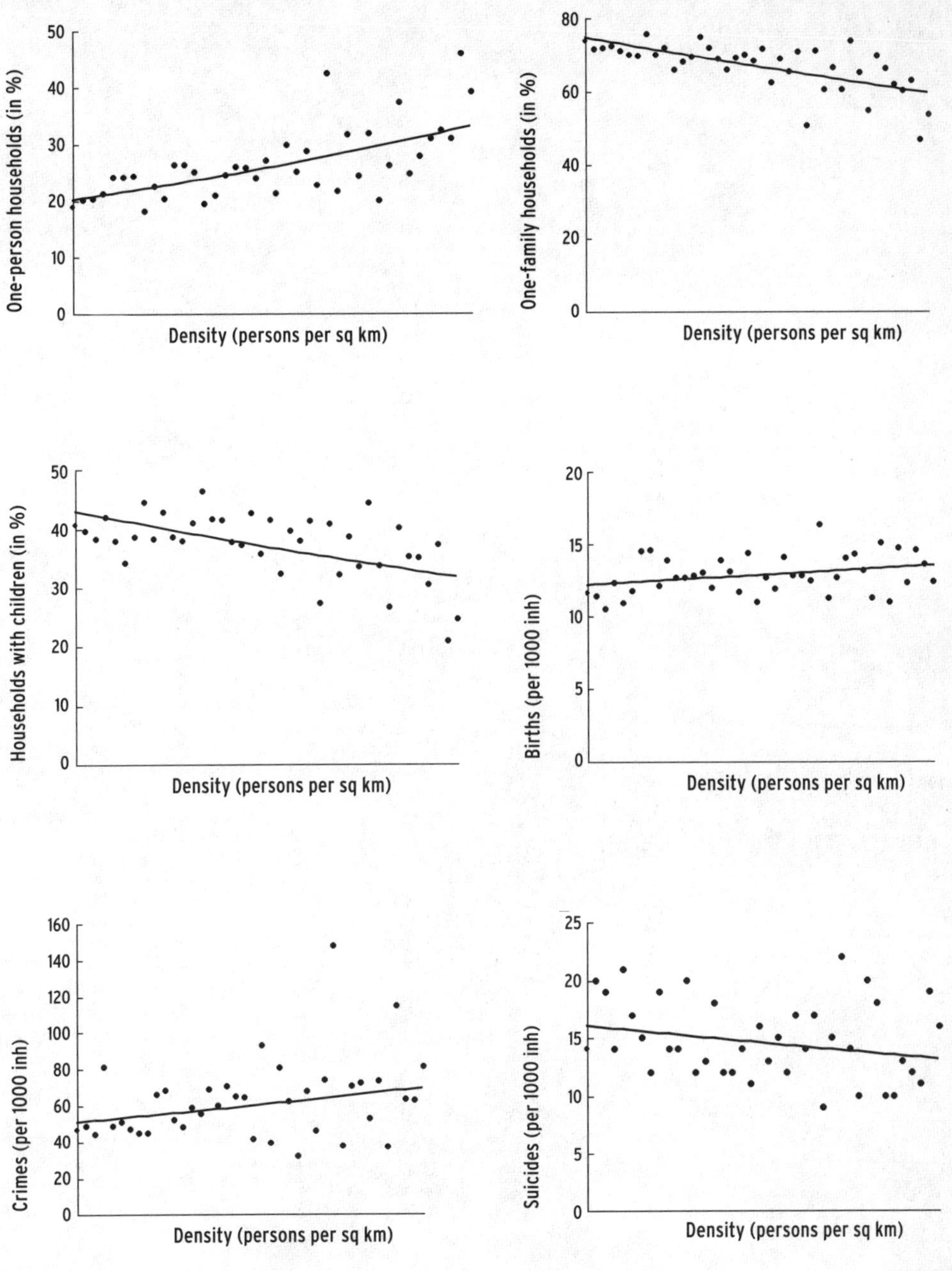
One-person households (in %)
50
40
30
20
10
0
Density (persons per sq km)
One-family households (in %)
80
60
40
20
0
Density (persons per sq km)
Households with children (in %)
50
40
30
20
10
0
Density (persons per sq km)
Births (per 1000 inh)
20
15
10
5
0
Density (persons per sq km)
Crimes (per 1000 inh)
160
140
120
100
80
60
40
20
0
Density (persons per sq km)
Suicides (per 1000 inh)
25
20
15
10
5
0
Density (persons per sq km)

KWC FAR 12

Kowloon Walled City density study

1995

Laurence Liauw

An aberration At ten to fourteen storeys high, its 2.5 hectares of urban fabric held a capacity of 35,000 inhabitants, making it the world's densest settlement. For many years Kowloon Walled City was synonymous with all the darkest aspects of China - opium dens, gambling, Triad gangs, cramped living conditions.

Dating back to 1843, KWC is the mutation of a historical slippage: two powers struggling not to lose face and economic and symbolic control, resulting in a diplomatic black hole. It was a massive attractor for illicit activities to run rampant.

The superblock became an unplanned artificial city, offering itself as a synthetic reality. It contained in a single block virtually all the components that make up a city-state, a 'war machine'. Out-of-control self-organization meant not only no government, but an urban form generated from a multiplicity of errors.

KWC was eight times as densely populated as the Unite D'habitation and ten times the most congested European district. There were no laws, no taxes, no foundations, no light. All classical and modern planning models had been ignored. However, it managed to contain a thriving community of residents, businesses and institutions. It was an Edge City within a city, acting as an in-between space between two conflicting ideologies.

Where there is nothing, anything is possible.

Hyperdensity:

KWC average	13,000 persons per hectare
New York City	91 persons per hectare
KWC average	3.75 m^2 per person
Corbusier's biological unit	14 m^2 per person

In KWC, normal scales - of the block, street, room, courtyard, open spaces, light incidence, staircase - collapsed. There, scale radically distorted the space-time continuum.

A super-deep plan caused one to be engulfed by darkness. Daylight cycles had been eliminated, allowing KWC's 24 hour programme to be free of the constraints of natural biorhythms. Some activities were even averse to light.

KWC was a 'domino' structure of interlocking self-supporting blocks. Tenants literally built over, through and around each other. Nearly all elevations were blocked, causing severe interiorization and placelessness

within the monolith. Freedom from context. Boundary facades were illegally extended as a pleated quilt of cages. The only break in density was the roofscape, a 'continuous' surface 45m above ground level.
Mass in KWC behaved in a fluid manner, flowing into cracks between buildings. As new structures were erected, remaining space was displaced running into the nearest empty spot. As density increased, spatial blobs and strands got compressed and subdivided into a trickle. Form and matter crystallized from drifting particles searching for clusters with which to coagulate. Spatial greed has no predictable form.

Fluid organizations Fluid organizations in KWC fall into three categories - circulation, population and services.
A network of branching 'streets' were interconnected for multiple access. Often less than 1 m wide, they slowed movement down within KWC and encouraged maximum mixing. Along alleys, activities spilled out - boundaries between inside and outside were blurred by flexible barriers. Staircases suddenly forked and entered other buildings. Narrow streets were complemented at higher levels by a secondary circulation system allowing smooth movement across KWC. The roofscape was a vast topography that encouraged continuous movement across, into and out of circulation gaps.
End-users of KWC came and went as waves of immigrants and 'tourists' cruised its depths. Some settled, others got swept out again. Thus a transient 'community' was formed where populations and programmes flowed through its mass, changing character over time.
Services infrastructure existed in chaotic yet continuous organizations. Hyperdensity forced these regimes to be used on a time-share basis, some residents stealing water, gas, electricity and space from each other by illegally redirecting routes.

Blurred typologies Conventional boundaries defining typologies were blurred as unstable programmes changed both their spatial and functional characteristics. A cafeteria would transform into a mah-jong parlour at certain hours, while a plastic toy factory doubled as an illegal drugs den. Most stores and manufacturing units were at street level but also on upper floors, where a sweatshop and social club would occupy the same space. These non-domestic units (NDU) were often incorporated into residential quarters, with even distribution at all levels. This implies a typological

blurring of KWC in section (as well as plan) where levels no longer typify the programme. Form and surface iconography had likewise been erased by hyperdensity.
Ultimately, the power of KWC lay in its ability to subvert reality over time to its advantage: from customs house to spy centre, from garrison to tourist destination, from administration centre to gambling house, from rebel base to educational establishment, from refugee camp to vice den, from residential units to industrial complex, from gangland to community centre.

Combat zone On the 14th of January 1987, the Hong Kong government announced that Kowloon Walled City was to be demolished.
KWC had previously survived due to the differences between the British and China. It had become an embarrassment, symbolizing 'undesirable' images. Demolition was seen as a way to wipe the slate clean: tabula rasa. It marked the lobotomy of a threatening ideology. Health and safety was the surrogate excuse invented by the authorities.
'Metropolitan shock value' was what made KWC monumental and defamiliarized. Ascribing to the discursive space of the sublime, beauty was eliminated, making it uncanny. It was the 'other', the monstrous, the magnificent, the ugly, the dense and varied, the shocking, the political, the revolutionary. Pushing at moral and spatial boundaries: a latterday Babel.

KWC was an ideological combat zone that became political even though it was itself a non-political domain. It formed an aggressive alternative reality intent on discrediting all 'natural reality' and becoming an imperfect conjecture of an ideal state, the manifestation of a city in perpetual crisis.

An aberration of history

1668	Signal station with fortifications. Salt mines.
1841	British occupation of HK island.
1843	Chinese magistrate transfers soldiers to KWC, to defend Kowloon from British. KWC as 'war machine' begins.
1847	Wall built entirely around fort by Viceroy of Canton. Symbol of Imperial control to show the British 'barbarians'.
1854	Chinese anti-Manchu rebels attack KWC. Emergence of Triads (secret societies). External events continue to influence KWC beyond its control.
1859	Civic functions are installed (religion, customs, health, education, law, markets). Chinese moral defence against 'barbarians' outside.
1890	Gambling dens and other vices frequented by locals colonials. British infuriated. Irresistible attraction of illegal practices emerges.
1898	Peking Convention for lease of HK until 1997, KWC excluded. China plants spy and secret deterrent within enemy grounds.
1899	200 British troops attack KWC only to find an abandoned fort. Fata morgana: invasion of a phantom entity.
1904	KWC left alone by both governments, and becomes a tourist destination. Diplomatic black hole as a spectacle of ruin.
1905	Schools, churches and almshouses established from converted offices. Seeds of programmatic confusion sown.
1934	British government clears squatters to transform KWC into resort. Anticipation of future 'tourists' flooding KWC.
1940	Japanese occupation. KWC walls to be used to lay airport runway. KWC stripped bare by her bachelors, even.
1947	Refugee and squatter population swells to 2000. Evacuation announced. Riots. Maximum freedom and depravity flourish in the absence of control.
1950	Organized vice and crime flourish with refugee influx. KWC as massive vice attractor perpetuated by 'tourists'.
1962	High-rise boom begins within KWC. Beginning of spatial compression leading to implosion.
1971	Census records a population of 10,000. HK government starts providing basic services. Ratio of 5 persons per household already exceeds HK average.
1974	Police campaign against crime leads to 2580 arrests. Crime still flourishes. Authorities bid to control illegal entertainment.
1983	Crime more or less squeezed out. Population already exceeds 350,000. Self-organization reaches its peak.
1984	Sino-British Joint Declaration on the handover of HK in 1997. Global issues determine local outcomes.
1987	Plans to demolish KWC revealed suddenly by both governments.
1992	Demolition, eviction and compensation carried out at cost of $3.2 billion. Tabula rasa. Lobotomy of a dangerous ideology.

Playground
ROAD
MEI TUNG ESTATE
TUNG TAU TSUEN RO
ALMS HOUSE BACK STREET
TAI CHANG ST
WEST CITY RD
TAI CHANG STREET
SZ KUNG ST

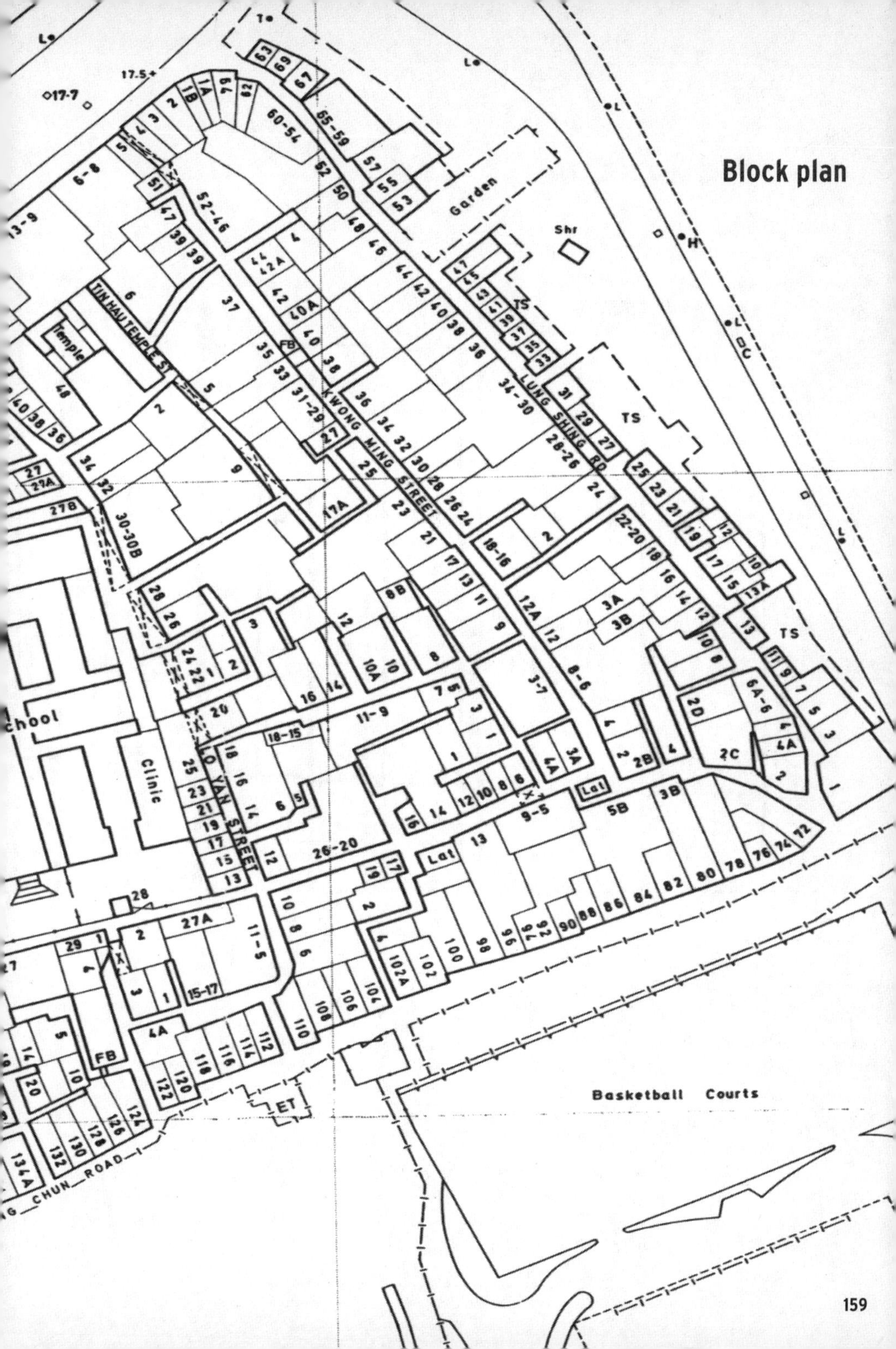

Garden
Shr
TS
LUNG SHING RD
KWONG MING STREET
TIN HAU TEMPLE ST
Temple
LO YAN STREET
School
Clinic
Lat
ET
FB
CHUN ROAD
Basketball Courts

Block plan

Longitudinal section

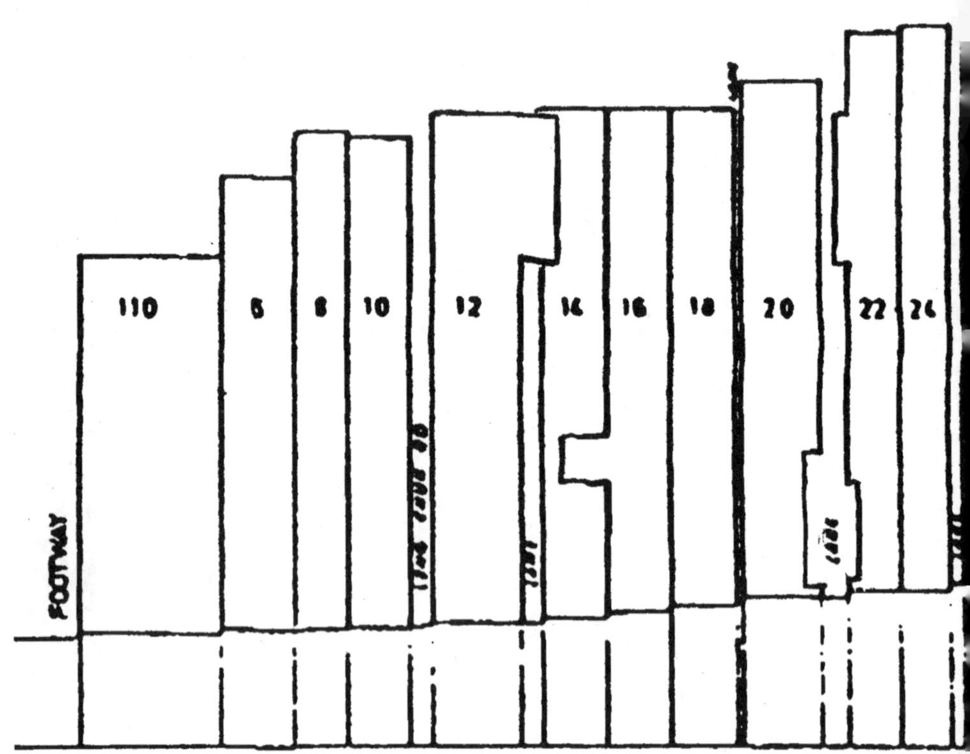

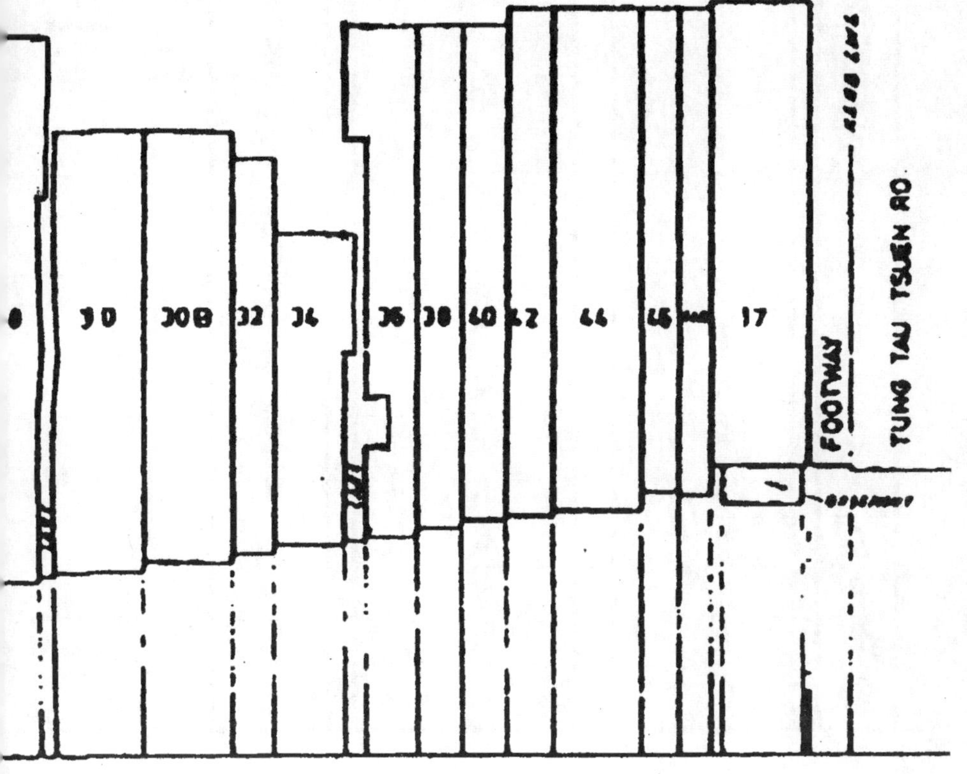

30
30B
32
34
36
38
40
42
44
46
17
FOOTWAY
TUNG TAU TSUEN RD

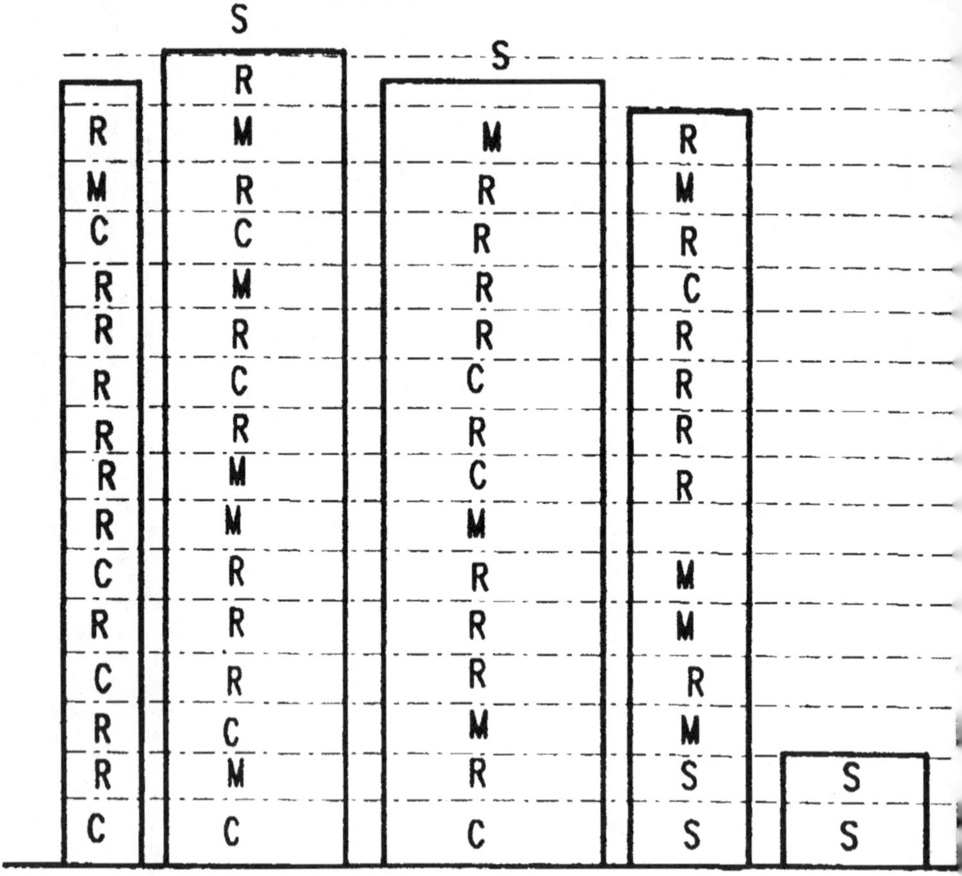

Vertical discontinuity of programs produce both horizontal and vertical social intercourse

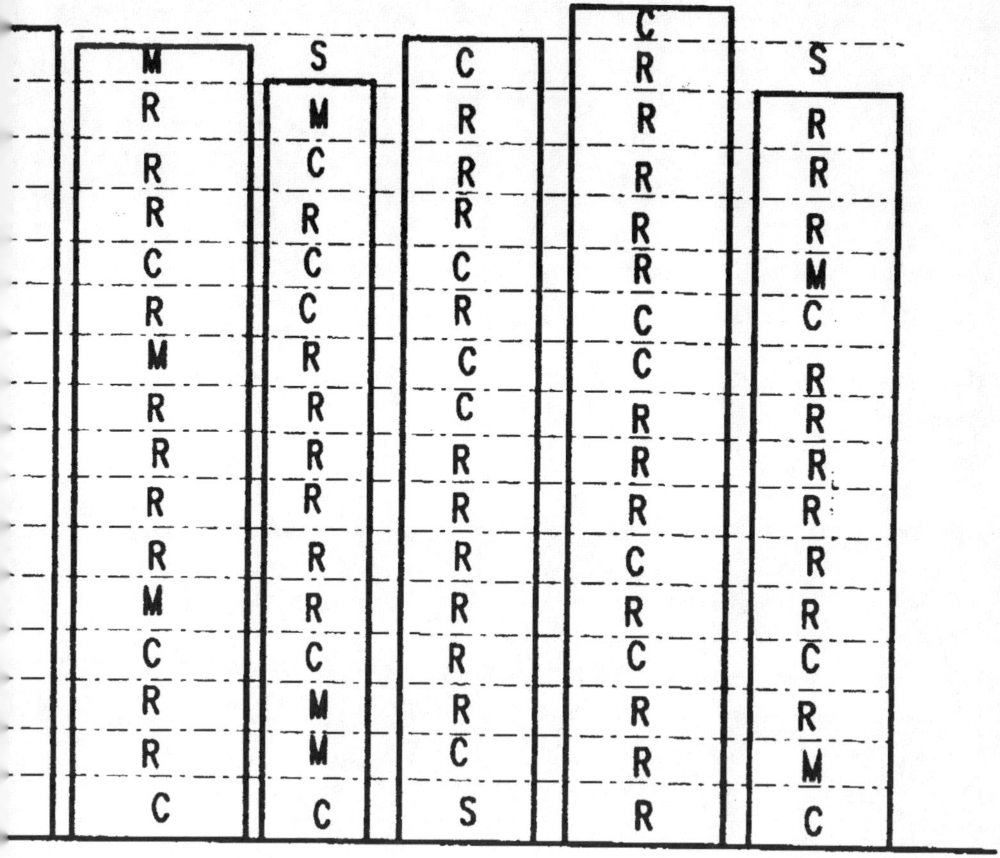

M R R R C R M R R R R M C R R C

S M C R C C R R R R R R C M M C

C R R R C R C C R R R R R R C S

C R R R R R C C R R R C R C R R R

S R R R M C R R R R R R C R M C

R - Residental

M - Mixed

C - Commercial

S - Social

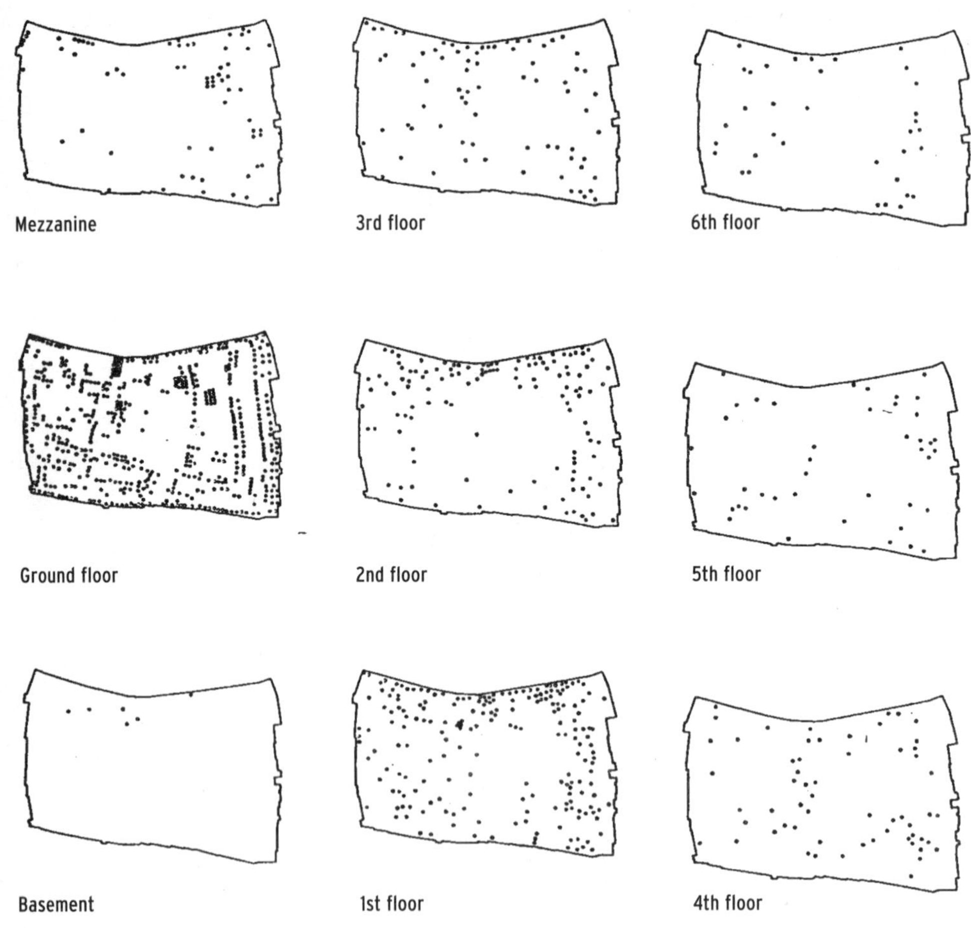

Distribution of non-domestic units

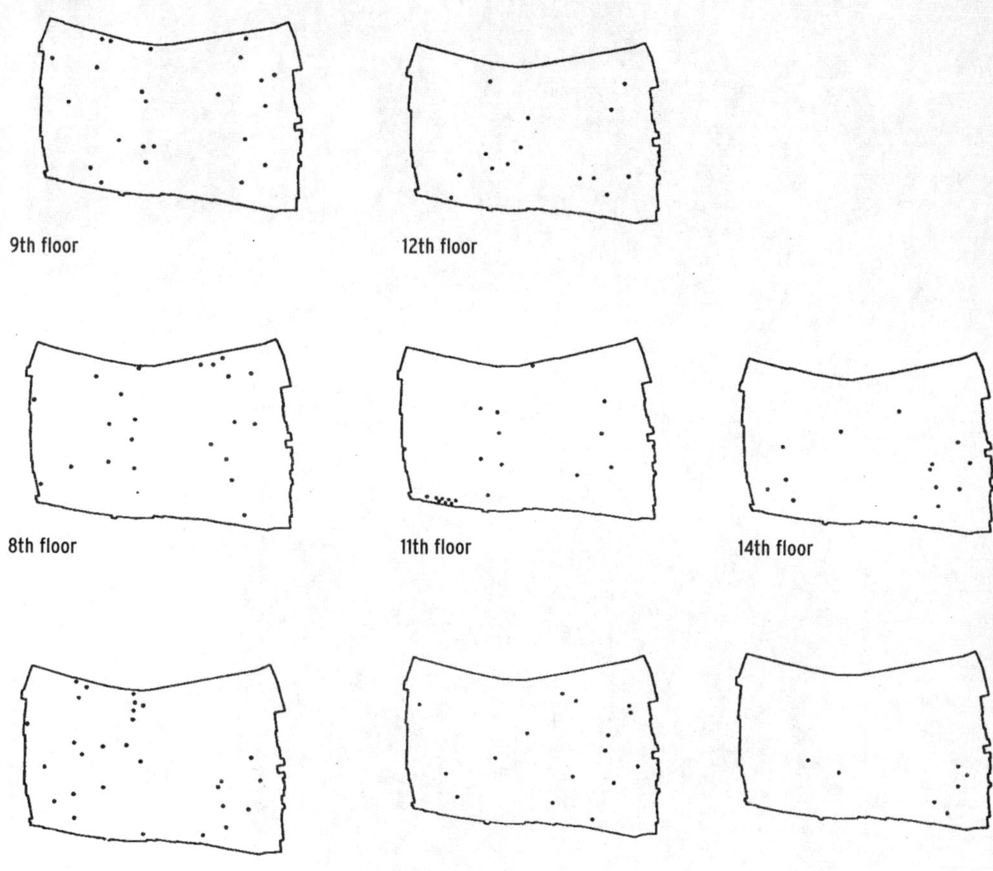
9th floor
12th floor
8th floor
11th floor
14th floor
7th floor
10th floor
13th floor

Streets

Compression of programmes

Roofscape: a continuous topography

Demolition

獅子山

Far East

Hong Kong Tower typology

1998

Jacob van Rijs

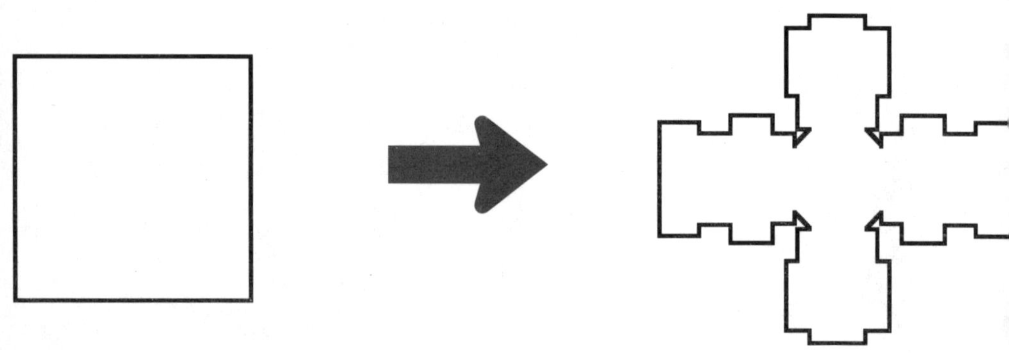

There is something otherworldly about residential tower blocks in Hong Kong. It is as though they have been pulled straight up out of the earth through a hole decided on beforehand. Their verticality is further enhanced by the articulated, almost flower-like floor plans. Instead of a contour that is filled in, individual houses are tacked onto a central core. Each apartment, each room even, thereby contributes to distorting the tower's circumference, giving it a facade surface area double that of a rectangular tower.
The volatile real estate market, the tremendous demand for housing and restricted availability of building sites seem to be at the bottom of this phenomenon, though these aspects in themselves fail to explain the specific form. One would expect the limited influence of construction costs on the total sum - land costs are many times greater - to yield a greater diversity. But the minor differences that there are between towers are veiled by the ubiquitous uptakes, air-conditioning units (one for each room) and cage-like built-on appurtenances.
The buildings' eventual form would appear to be a direct consequence of pumping up the legislation to a maximum and the fact that every room in a flat has to have at least one outside wall.
The building regulations of the Town Planning Department are of an uncomplicated nature and are premised on three aspects: plot ratio, site coverage and building height. Plot ratio is a measure of the admissible density on site, the maximum number of built-up square metres. Site coverage indicates the maximum percentage of land to be developed. These combine with the maximum building height to define the contours of the built development. A maximum number of houses per hectare (a normal unit of measurement in the Netherlands) is not given, resulting in very many small dwellings and efficient circulation spaces, one every square metre.
The greatest permissible plot ratio for housing development in Hong Kong is 10, added to which is a maximum site coverage of 40% and a minimum building height of 61 metres. Given these figures, towers are the unavoidable outcome. The higher the density, the more slender the built development, the slogan would seem to be. For Hong Kong, almost inevitably, this leads to the extruded floor plans one invariably finds there.

Plans

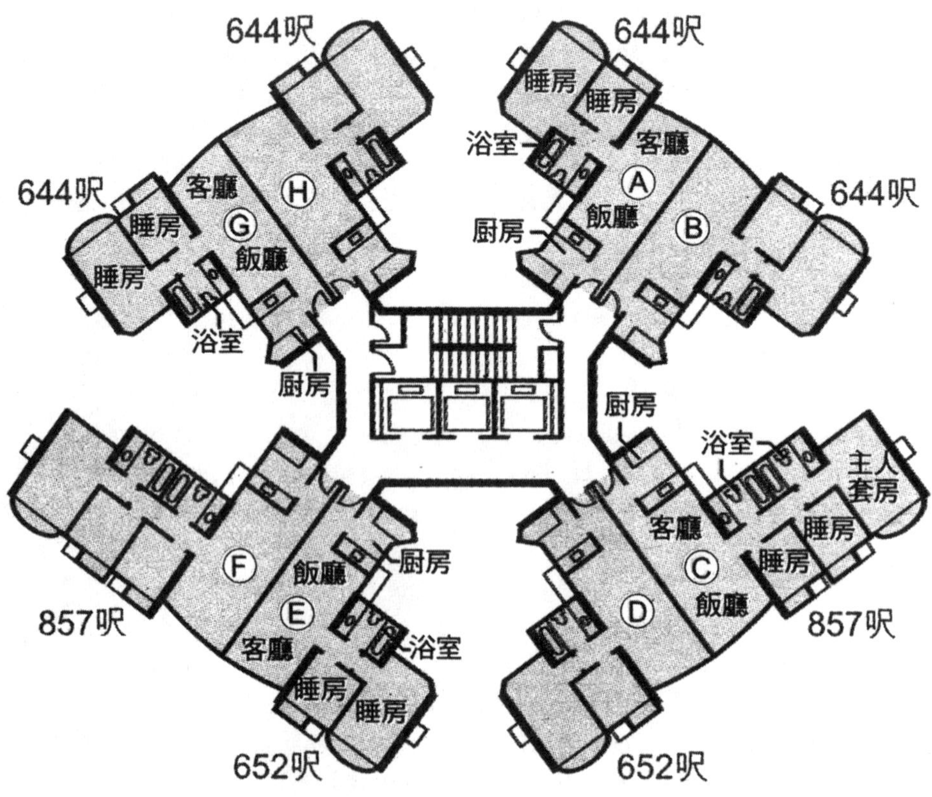
644呎
644呎
644呎
644呎
睡房
睡房
浴室
客廳
Ⓐ
飯廳
廚房
Ⓑ
客廳
Ⓗ
Ⓖ
睡房
睡房
飯廳
浴室
廚房
廚房
浴室
主人
套房
睡房
客廳
睡房
Ⓒ
飯廳
Ⓓ
857呎
Ⓕ
飯廳
廚房
Ⓔ
浴室
客廳
睡房
睡房
857呎
652呎
652呎

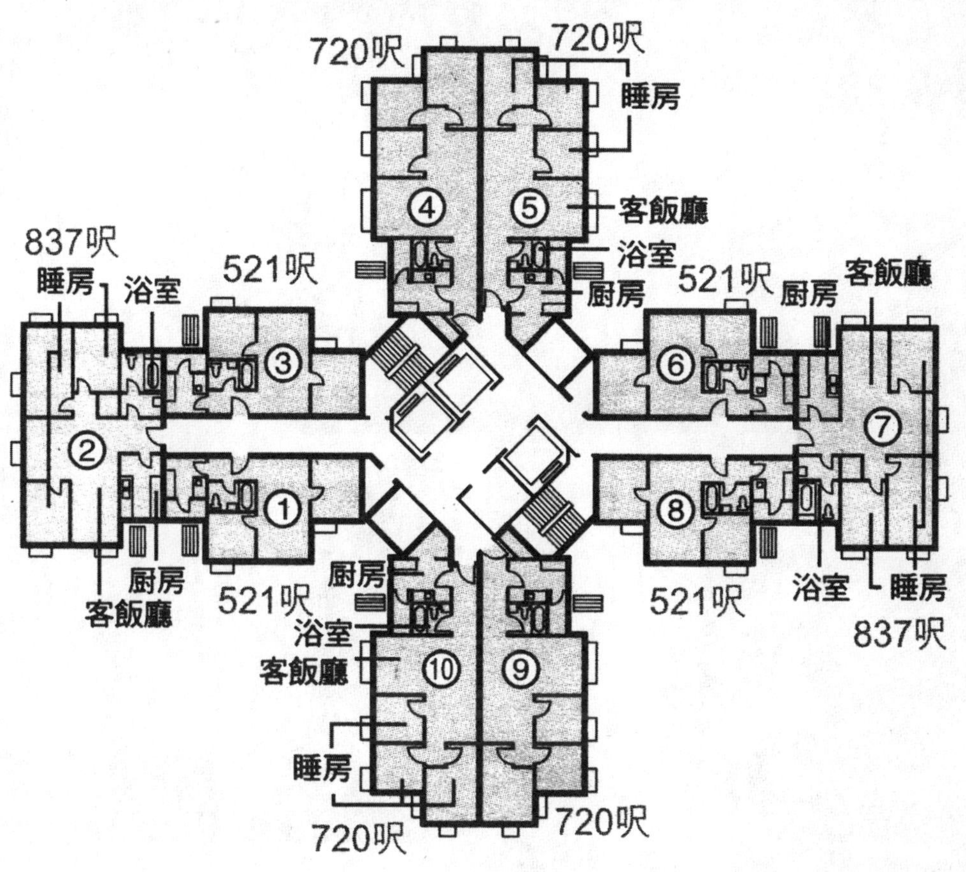
720呎
720呎
睡房
客飯廳
837呎
睡房
浴室
521呎
浴室
521呎
廚房
客飯廳
廚房
3
4
5
6
7
2
1
8
10
9
廚房
客飯廳
521呎
廚房
浴室
客飯廳
521呎
浴室
睡房
837呎
睡房
720呎
720呎

Showhouse

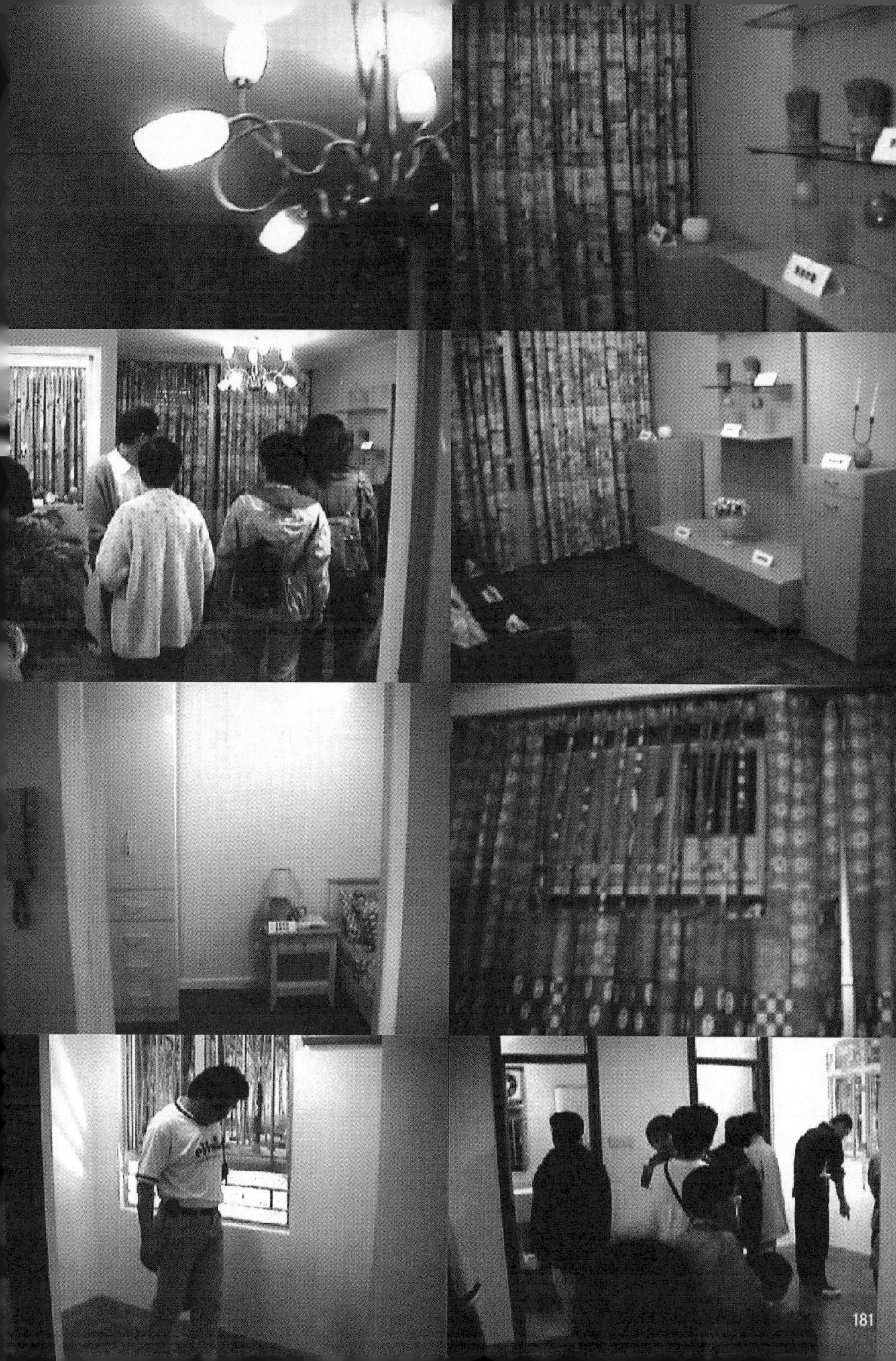

Extruded optimisation

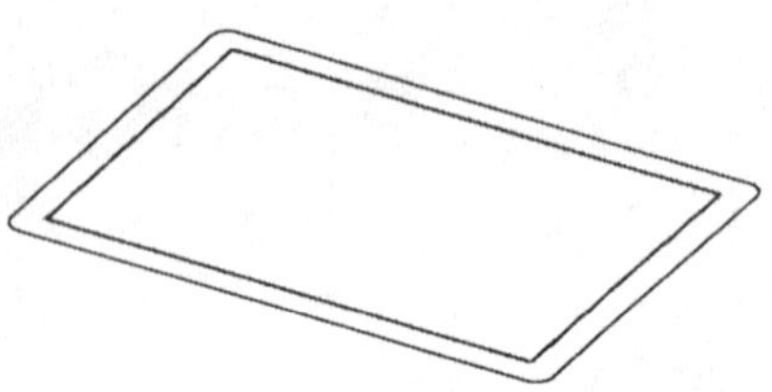

1. Take a plot somewhere in Hong Kong

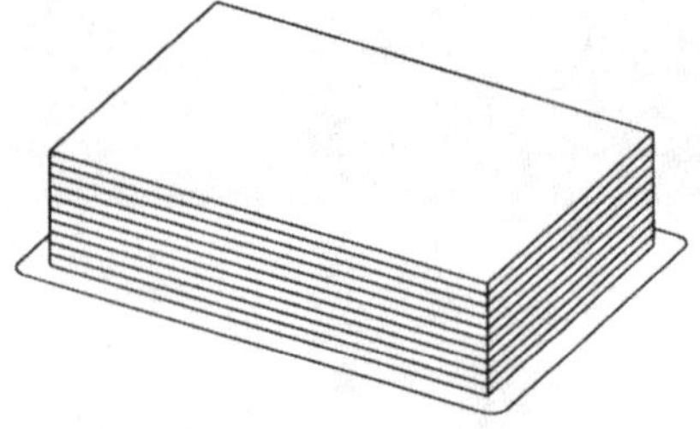

2. The plot ratio is 10. This means that the maximum gross floor area of a building on this site is 10 times the surface of the site.

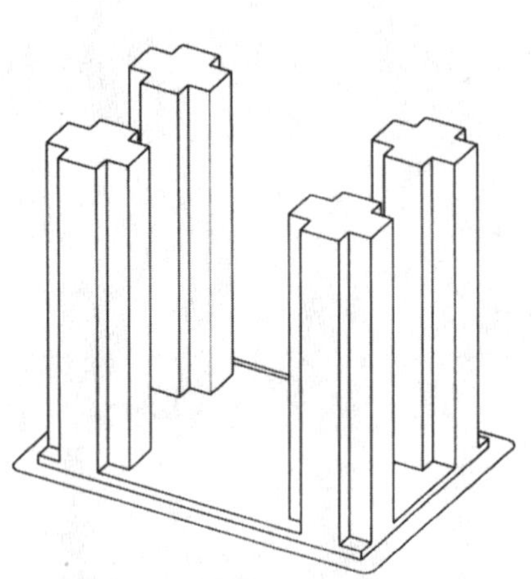

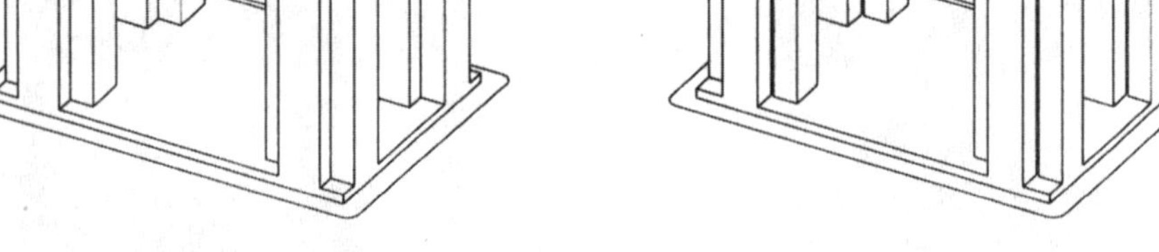

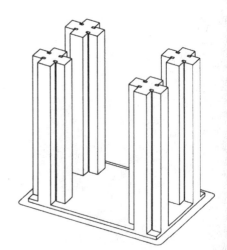

5,6. Optimasation of the plan: more smaller apartments with more frontage.

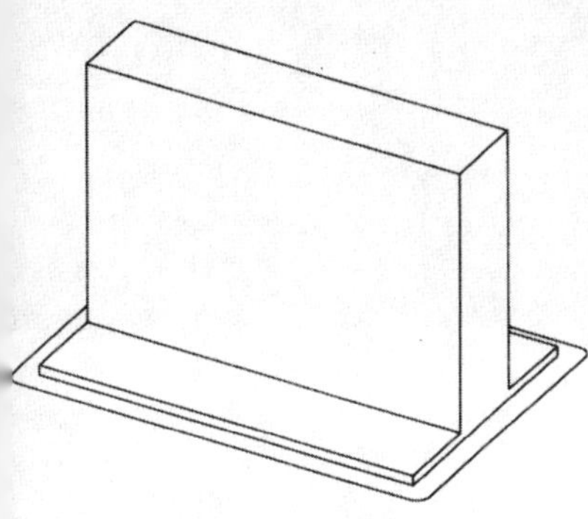

3. For domestic buildings and a plot ratio of 10, the building should be higher than 61 metres and the site coverage should be no more than 40%.

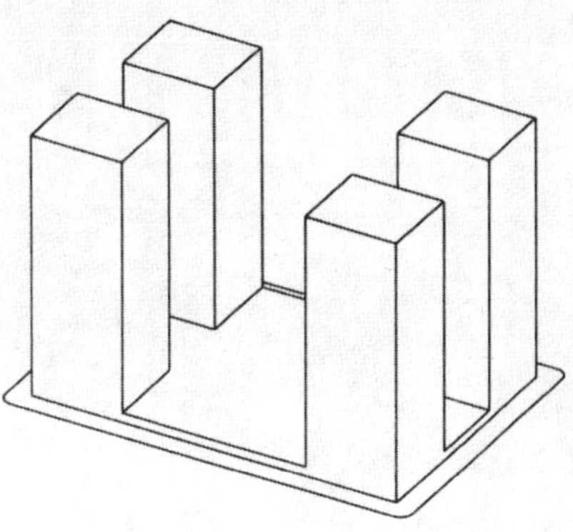

4. There is less circulation in 4 towers than in 1 slab.

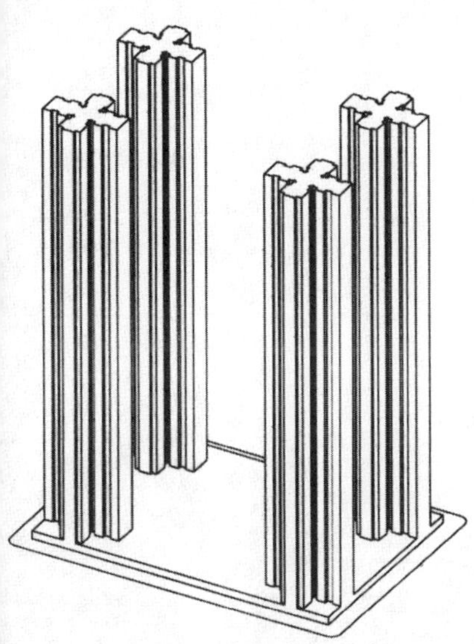

7. The optimum plan is there, but the towers are now too slender.

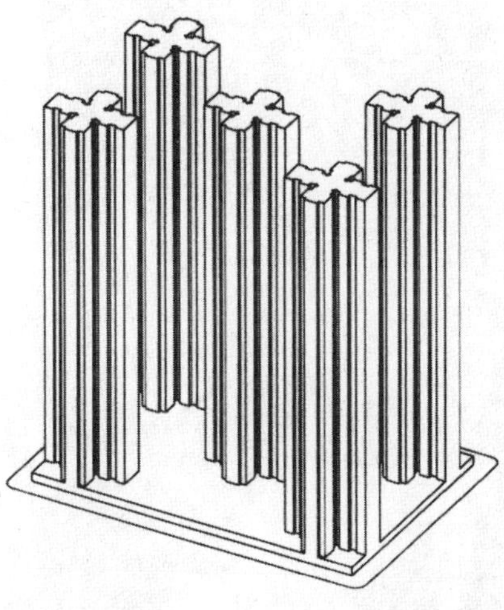

8. The towers are lowered and another one is added in such a way that the plot ratio remains the same.

Plot ratio and site coverage in Hong Kong (Selected parts from an article by Kenneth J.K. Chan, FHKIS, FRICS, ACIArb, RPS(BSD)

The determination of plot ratio and site coverage of a building project is amongst the most important factors in contemplating developments in Hong Kong.

1. Plot Ratio

1. The plot ratio of a building is obtained by dividing the gross floor area of the building by the area of the site on which the building is erected. For the purposes of determining the permitted plot ratio, sites are classified into 3 classes, They are:

(a) Class A site means a site that abuts on one street not less than 4.5m wide.

(b) Class B site means a corner site that abuts on 2 streets with at least 40 per cent of the boundary of the site abuting on the streets neither of which is less than 4.5m wide.

(c) Class C site means a corner site that abuts on 3 streets with at least 60 per cent of the boundary of the site abuting on the streets none of which is less than 4.5m wide.

2. The permitted plot ratio is the maximum plot ratio permitted under paragraph (1) & (2) of Building (Planning) Regulation 21.

3. Plot ratio calculation applicable to composite buildings are as follows:

Domestic Plot Ratio = (Permitted Non-Domestic Plot Ratio - Actual Non-Domestic Plot Ratio) x Permitted Domestic Plot Ratio / Permitted Non-Domestic Plot Ratio

e.g. PRpnd = 15, PRand = 10, PRpd = 10, Domestic Plot Ratio = (15-10) x 10 /15 = 3.33

(Table 1) plot ratio

Height of Buildings(m)	Domestic Building			Non-domestic Building		
	A Site	B Site	C Site	A Site	B Site	C Site
not exceeding 15m	3.3	3.8	4.0	5.0	5.0	5.0
over 15m but not exceeding 18 m	3.6	4.0	4.3	5.8	5.8	5.8
over 18m but not exceeding 21m	3.9	4.3	4.7	6.7	6.7	6.7
over 21m but not exceeding 24m	4.2	4.6	5.0	7.4	7.4	7.4
over 24m but not exceeding 27m	4.4	4.9	5.3	8.0	8.1	8.1
over 27m but not exceeding 30m	4.6	5.2	5.5	8.5	8.7	8.8
over 30m but not exceeding 36m	5.0	5.7	6.0	9.5	9.9	10.2
over 36m but not exceeding 43m	5.4	6.1	6.5	10.5	10.8	11.2
over 43m but not exceeding 49m	5.9	6.5	7.0	11.0	11.6	12.0
over 49m but not exceeding 55m	6.3	7.0	7.5	11.5	12.1	12.6
over 55m but not exceeding 61m	6.8	7.6	8.0	12.2	12.5	13.0
exceeding 61m	8.0	9.0	10.0	15.0	15.0	15.0

2. Site coverage

1 The site coverage of a site is the area of the site that is covered by the building that is erected thereon. For the purposes of determining the permitted site coverage, sites are classified into 3 classes, They are:

(a) Class A site means a site that abuts on one street not less than 4.5m wide.

(b) Class B site means a corner site that abuts on 2 streets with at least 40 per cent of the boundary of the site abuting on the streets neither of which is less than 4.5m wide.

(c) Class C site means a corner site that abuts on 3 streets with at least 60 per cent of the boundary of the site abuting on the streets none of which is less than 4.5m wide.

2 The permitted site coverage is the maximum site coverage permitted under paragraph (1) & (2) of Building (Planning) Regulation 21. (see table 2)

3 The permitted site coverage may be exceeded in some cases where:

(a) building is set back from boundary at ground with no vertical obstruction of 5.5m/3.3m; and

(b) part of lot abutting street is acquired by the Crown for the purposes of street widening. The excess site coverage shall not exceed the figure obtained by dividing the product of 1500 and the dedicated area by the product of the area of the site and the height of the building.

(Table 2) site coverage in %

Height of Buildings(m)	Domestic Building			Non-domestic Building		
	A Site	B Site	C Site	A Site	B Site	C Site
not exceeding 15m	66.6	75.0	80 .0	100	100	100
over 15m but not exceeding 18m	60.0	67.0	72.0	97.5	97.5	97.5
over 18m but not exceeding 21m	56.0	62.0	67.0	95.0	95.0	95.0
over 21m but not exceeding 24m	52.0	58.0	63.0	92.0	92.0	92.0
over 24m but not exceeding 27m	49.0	55.0	59.0	89.0	90.0	90.0
over 27m but not exceeding 30m	46.0	52.0	55.0	85.0	87.0	88.0
over 30m but not exceeding 36m	42.0	47.5	50.0	80.0	82.5	85.0
over 36m but not exceeding 43m	39.0	44.0	47.0	75.0	77.5	80.0
over 43m but not exceeding 49m	37.0	41.0	44.0	69.0	72.5	75.0
over 49m but not exceeding 55m	35.0	39.0	42.0	64.0	67.5	70.0
over 55m but not exceeding 61m	34.0	38.0	41.0	60.0	62.5	65.0
exceeding 61m	33.3	37.5	40.0	60.0	62.5	65.0

Taikoo Shing, Hong Kong

LIGHT

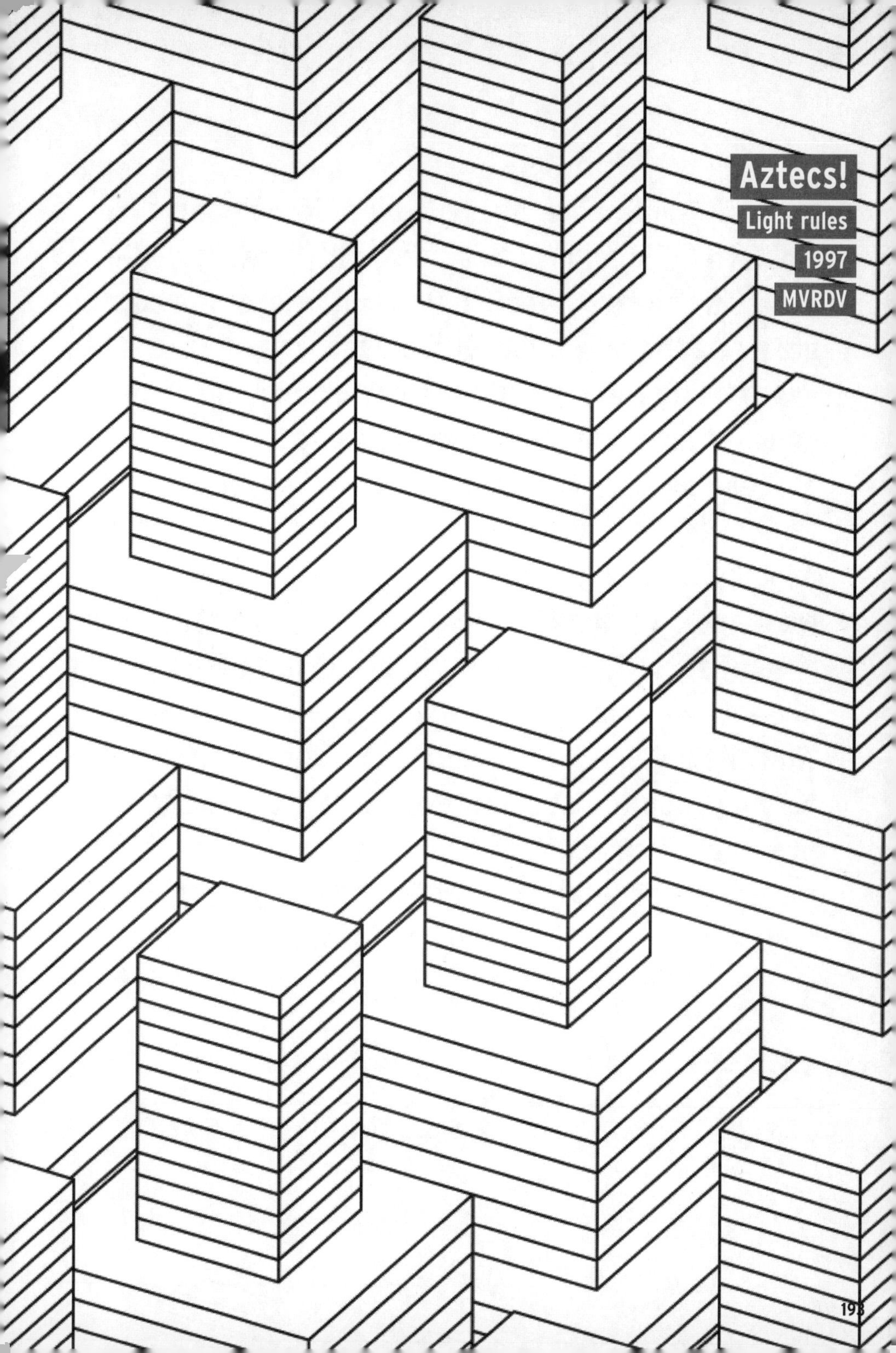
Aztecs!
Light rules
1997
MVRDV

With the emergence of the Modern Movement, Western building practice began introducing codes for achieving more hygienic living conditions. In order to provide adequate light, Dutch byelaws required that every living room should receive a minimum of three hours of direct sunlight on its facade every day, proceeding from the values of 21 March and 21 September. This means that such rooms require an unbuilt zone of 32 degrees when facing east or west and 38 when facing south. For an average floor area of some $75m^2$, the depth of these houses should not exceed 10 metres. The same byelaws stipulated that the level of light within an office necessitates leaving unbuilt a sun angle of 52 degrees for an average office depth of 7 metres. These regulations were to be of seminal influence on the potential density; increasing the number of floors doesn't

automatically mean that the total Floor Area Ratio is enlarged. This is effected by the need for bigger interjacent spaces so as to fully occupy the lower floors. Given these constraints, we might envisage a maximum density when we use housing only.
This maximum, with a FAR of 3 to 4, might be three to four times denser than the current average Western European densities: even the most profitable ones (i.e. the 'modernistic' linear building blocks in a northeast-southwest direction) have a density lower than that of La Défense and only a third of that of Hong Kong.
If we want to reach more competitive densities and maintain the byelaws, we will HAVE TO MIX housing with other programmes: offices, storage space, retail, parking, services. The almost historical plea for 'mixed use' has been translated into an obligation!

Light laboratory test VPRO building 1994

Light formulas

Dwellings

h	= building height
V	= number of floors (dwellings)
Vhw	= floor height (dwellings)
α	= shading angle E-W orientation (dwellings)
β	= shading angle E-W orientation (dwellings)
x	= shadow, E-W direction
y	= shadow, N-S direction
Cx	= number of buildings, E-W direction
Cy	= number of buildings, N-S direction
Ctot	= total number of dwellings
Ow	= floor area (dwellings)
b	= dimensions of residential building in E-W direction
l	= dimensions of residential building in N-S direction
Opw	= floor area used for parking
dw	= total number of parking lots (dwellings)
w	= parking norm (dwellings)

Situation

Osit	= total area size
Bg	= dimensions of area in E-W direction
Lg	= dimensions of area in N-S direction
m	= depth of dwellings with block types in E-W direction
n	= depth of dwellings with block types in N-S direction

Offices

htot	= building height
Vk	= number of floors (offices)
Vhk	= floor height (offices)
λ	= shading angle of offices in E-W direction
δ	= shading angle of offices in N-S direction
xk	= shadow, E-W direction
yk	= shadow, N-S direction
Ok	= floor area (offices)
bk	= dimensions of office building in E-W direction
lk	= dimensions of office building in N-S direction
Opk	= floor area used for parking
dk	= number of parking lots (offices)
k	= parking norm (offices)
mk	= depth of offices with block types in E-W direction
nk	= depth of offices with block types in N-S direction

General formulas for dwelling types

h = Vh*V
x = h/tanα
x = (Vh*V)/tanα
y = h/tanβ
y = (Vh*V)/tanβ
Cx = Bg/(b+x)
Cy = Lg/(l+y)
Ctot = Cx*Cy

Ow = b*l*V*Ctot
Osit = Bg*Lg
FAR dwellings, parking excluded = Ow/Osit
d = Ow/w
Opw = d*30
Ototw = Ow+Opw
FAR dwellings, parking included = Ototw/Osit

Row e-w orientation

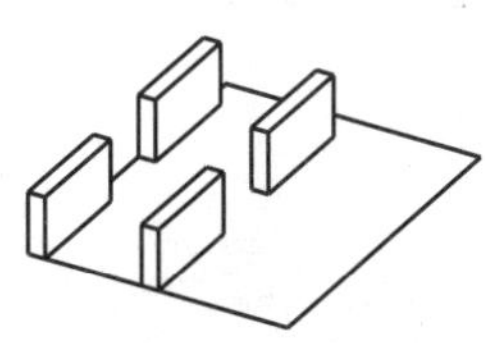

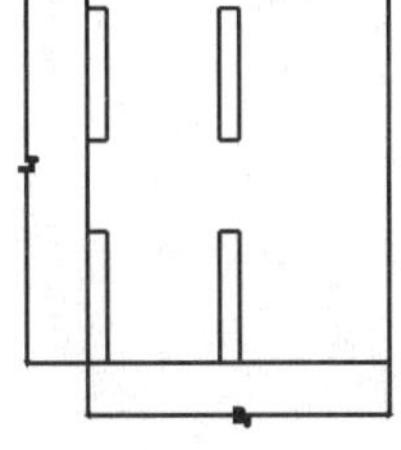

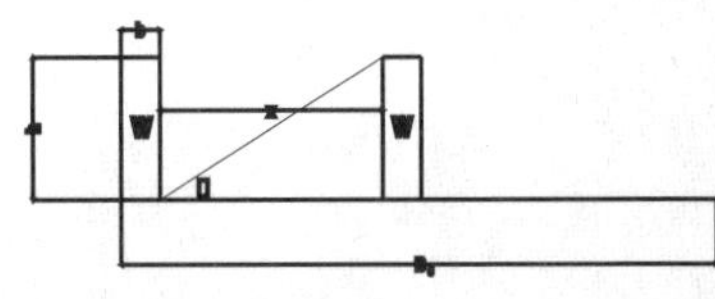

Ctot = Cx

FAR dwellings, parking included = (30+w)/w*(b*l*V)/(Lg*(b+Vh*V/tanα))
FAR dwellings, parking excluded = (b*l*V)/(Lg*(b+Vh*V/tanα))

Row ne-sw orientation

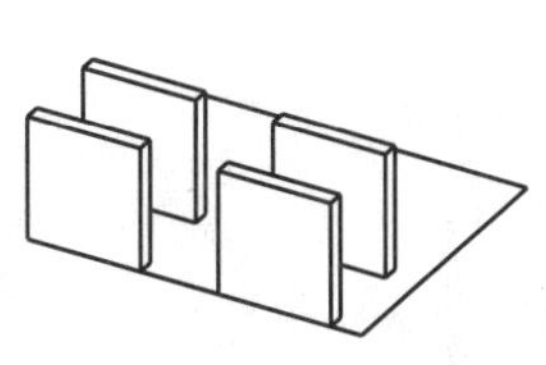

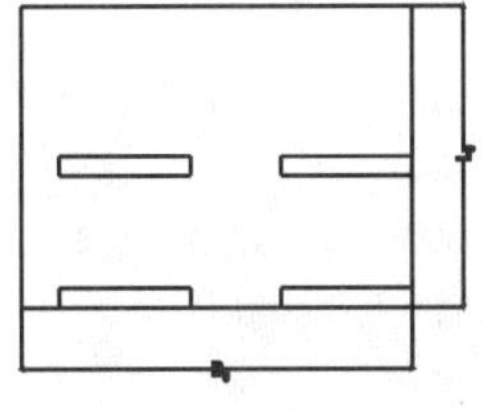

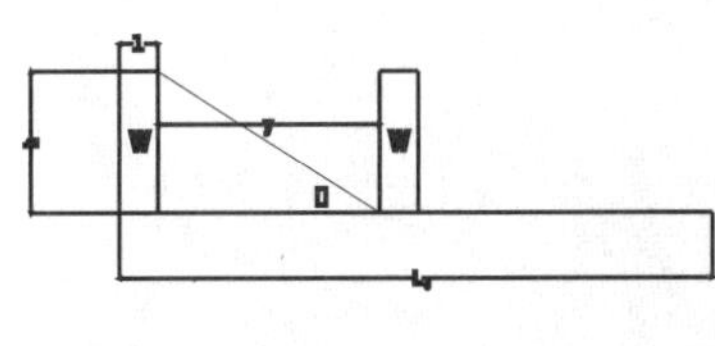

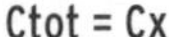

Ctot = Cx

FAR dwellings, parking included = (30+w)/w*(b*l*V)/(Lg*(b+Vh*V/tanα))
FAR dwellings, parking excluded = (b*l*V)/(Lg*(b+Vh*V/tanα))

Block

$b = 2m+x$

$b = 2m+Vh*V/\tan\alpha$

$l = 2n+y$

$l = 2n+Vh*V/\tan\beta$

$Ow = (b*l-x*y)*V*Ctot$

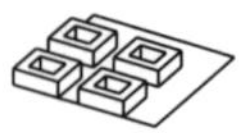

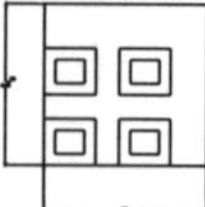

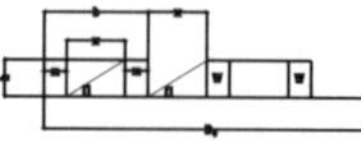

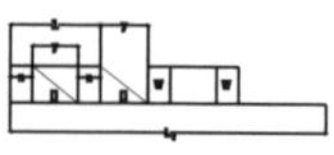

FAR dwellings, parking included =

$(30+w)/w*((4m*n+Vh*V(2m/\tan\beta+2n/\tan\alpha))*V)/(2\ (Vh*V)/\tan\alpha+2m)*(2\ (Vh*V)/\tan\beta+2n)$

FAR dwellings, parking excluded =

$((4m*n+Vh*V(2m/\tan\beta+2n/\tan\alpha))*V)/(2\ (Vh*V)/\tan\alpha+2m)*(2\ (Vh*V)/\tan\beta+2n)$

Tower

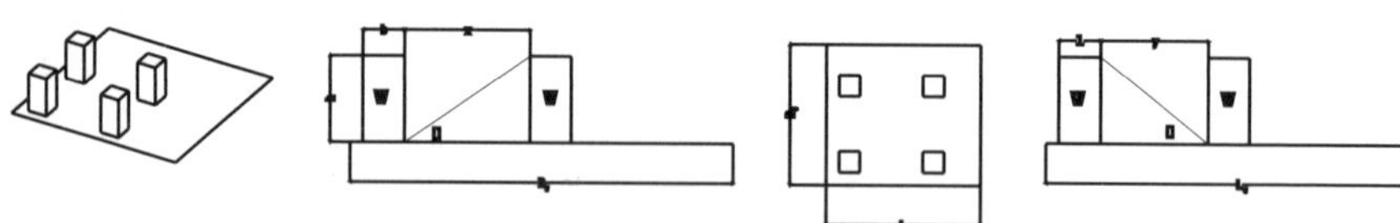

FAR dwellings, parking included = $(30+w)/w*(b*l*V)/(b+Vh*V/tana)(l+Vh*V/\tan\beta)$

FAR dwellings, parking excluded = $b*l*V/(b+Vh*V/\tan\alpha)(l+Vh*V/\tan\beta)$

General formulas for office types

$hk = Vhk*V$

$xk = hk/\tan\lambda$

$xk = (Vhk*V)/\tan\alpha$

$yk = hk/\tan\delta$

$yk = (Vhk*V)/\tan\delta$

$Cx = Bg/(bk+xk)$

$Cy = Lg/(lk+yk)$

$Ctot = Cx*Cy$

$Ok = bk*lk*V*Ctot$

$Osit = Bg*Lg$

FAR offices, parking excluded = $Ok/Osit$

$d = Ok/w$

$Opw = d*30$

$Ototk = Ok+Opw$

FAR offices, parking included = $Ototk/Osit$

Row e-w orientation

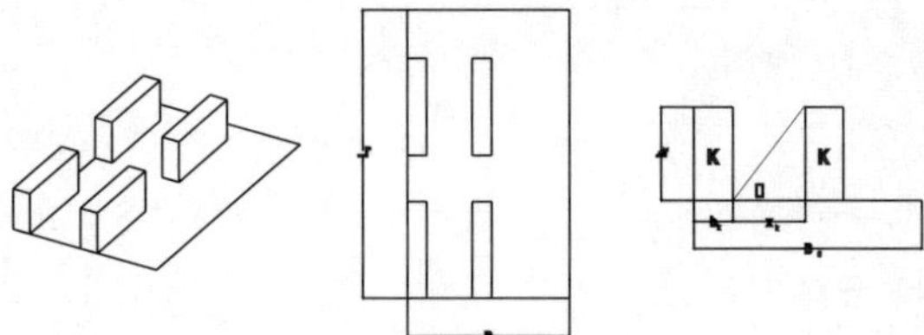

$Ctot = Cx$

FAR offices, parking included = $(30+k)/k*(bk*lk*V)/(Lg*(bk+Vhk*V/\tan\lambda))$
FAR offices, parking excluded = $(bk*lk*V)/(Lg*(b+Vhk*V/\tan\lambda))$

Block

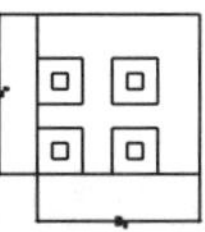

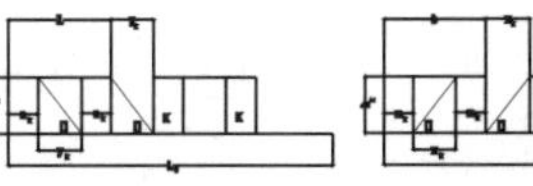

$bk = 2mk+xk$
$bk = 2mk+Vhk*V/\tan\lambda$
$lk = 2nk+yk$
$lk = 2nk+Vhk*V/\tan\delta$
$Ok = (bk*lk-xk*yk)*V*Ctot$

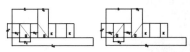

FAR offices, parking included =
$(30+k)/k*((4mk*nk+Vhk*V(2mk/tand+2nv/\tan\alpha))*V)/(2\ (Vhk*V)/\tan\lambda+2mk)*(2\ (Vhk*V)/\tan\delta+2nk)$
FAR offices, parking excluded =
$((4mk*nk+Vhk*V(2mk/\tan\delta+2nk/\tan\alpha))*V)/(2\ (Vhk*V)/\tan\lambda+2mk)*(2\ (Vhk*V)/\tan\delta+2nk)$

Tower

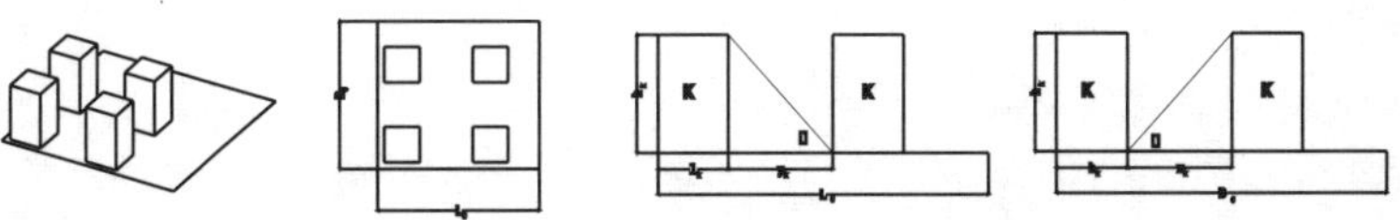

FAR offices, parking included = $(30+k)/k*(bk*lk*V)/(bk+Vhk*V/\tan\lambda)(lk+Vhk*V/\tan\delta)$
FAR offices, parking excluded = $bk*lk*V/(bk+Vhk*V/\tan\lambda)(lk+Vhk*V/\tan\delta)$

Mix

xk = x-(bk-b)

htot = xk*tanλ

Vk = (htot-h)/Vhk

Ok = bk*lk*Vk*Ctot Ok≥0

dk = Ok/k

Opk = dk*30

Osit = Bg*Lg

FAR offices, parking excluded = Ok/Osit

FAR dwellings, parking included = (Ok+Opk)/Osit

FAR dwellings+offices, parking excluded = (Ow+Ok)/Osit

FAR dwellings+offices, parking included = (Ow+Opw+Ok+Opk)/Osit

L shape orientation

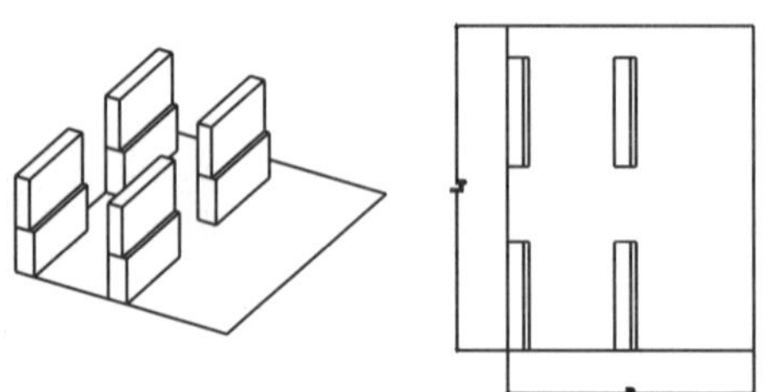

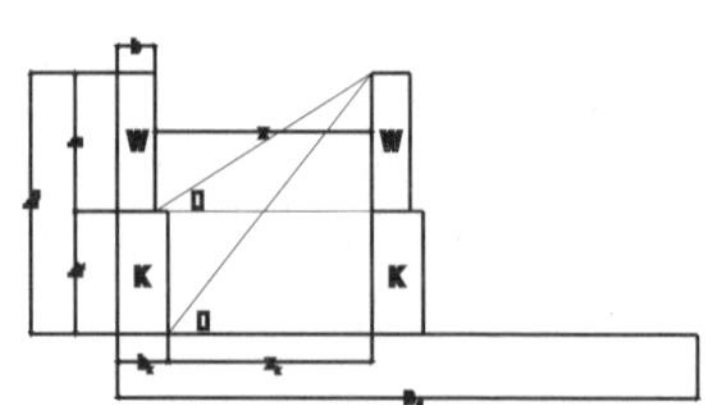

FAR dwellings+offices, parking excluded = (Ow+Ok)/Osit

FAR dwellings+offices, parking included = (Ow+Opw+Ok+Opk)/Osit

Ctot = Cx

Ok≥0

FAR dwellings+offices, parking included =
(30+w)/w*(b*l*V)/(Lg*(b+Vh*V/tanα))+(30+k)/k*(bk*lk*((Vh*V/tanα-(bk-b))
tanλ-h))/Lg(b+Vh*V/tanα)*Vhk

FAR offices, parking excluded =
(b*l*V)/(Lg*(b+Vh*V/tanα))+(bk*lk*((Vh*V/tanα-(bk-b))*tanλ-h))/Lg*(b+Vh*V/tanα)*Vhk

L pyramid shape e-w orientation

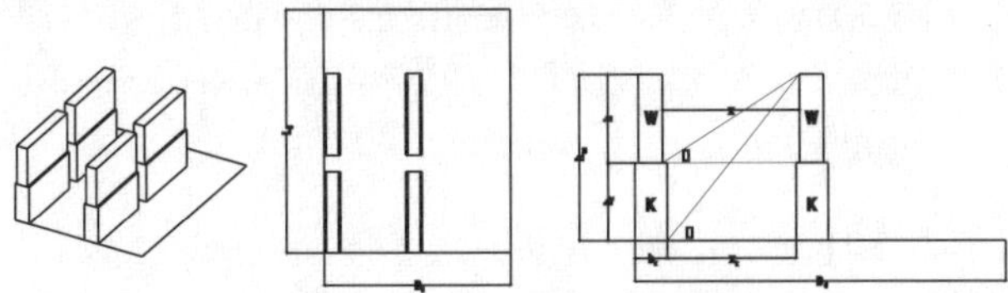

FAR dwellings+offices, parking excluded = (Ow+Ok)/Osit

FAR dwellings+offices, parking included = (Ow+Opw+Ok+Opk)/Osit

Ctot = Cx

xk = x-(bk-b)/2

$Ok \geq 0$

FAR dwellings+offices, parking included =

$$(30+w)/w*(b*l*V)/(Lg*(b+Vh*V/\tan\alpha))+(30+k)/k*(bk*lk*((Vh*V/\tan\alpha-(bk-b)/2)*\tan\lambda-h))/Lg*(b+Vh*V/\tan\alpha)*Vhk$$

FAR dwellings+offices, parking excluded =

$$(b*l*V)/(Lg*(b+Vh*V/\tan\alpha))+(bk*lk*((Vh*V/\tan\alpha-(bk-b)/2)*\tan\lambda-h))/Lg*(b+Vh*V/\tan\alpha)*Vhk$$

Block

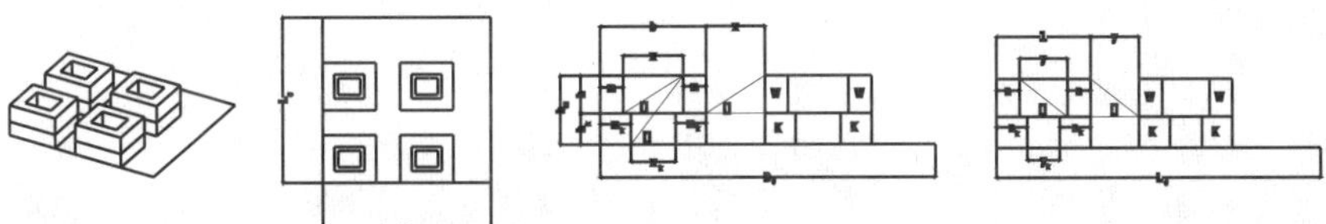

FAR dwellings+offices, parking excluded = (Ow+Ok)/Osit

FAR dwellings+offices, parking included = (Ow+Opw+Ok+Opk)/Osit

xk = x-2(mk-m)

yk = y-2(nk-n)

bk = $2\ mk+(Vh*V/\tan\alpha-2(mk-m))$

lk = $2\ nk+(Vh*V/\tan\beta-2(nk-n))$

Ok = (bk*lk-xk*yk)*Vk*Ctot

$Ok \geq 0$

FAR dwellings+offices, parking included =
(30+w)/w*((4m*n+Vh*V(2m/tanβ+2n/tanα))*V)/(2(Vh*V)/tanα+2m)*(2(Vh*V)/tanβ+2n)+
(30+k)/k*((2 mk+(Vh*V/tanα-2(mk-m))*(2nk+(Vh*V/tanβ-2(nk-n))-(Vh*V/tanα-2(mk-m))
*(Vh*V/tanβ-2(nk-n)))*((Vh*V/tanα-2(mk-m))*tanλVh*V))/((2m+2Vh*V/tanα)*(2n+2Vh*V/tanβ)*Vhk)

FAR offices, parking excluded =
((4m*n+Vh*V(2m/tanβ+2n/tanα))*V)/(2 (Vh*V)/tanα+2m)*(2 (Vh*V)/tanβ+2n)+
((2 mk+ (Vh*V/tanα-2(mk-m))* (2nk+(Vh*V/tanβ-2(nk-n))-(Vh*V/tanα-2(mk-m))*
(Vh*V/tanβ-2(nk-n)))*((Vh*V/tanα-2(mk-m))*tanλ-Vh*V))/((2m+2Vh*V/tanα)*
(2n+2Vh*V/tanβ)*Vhk)

Block pyramid

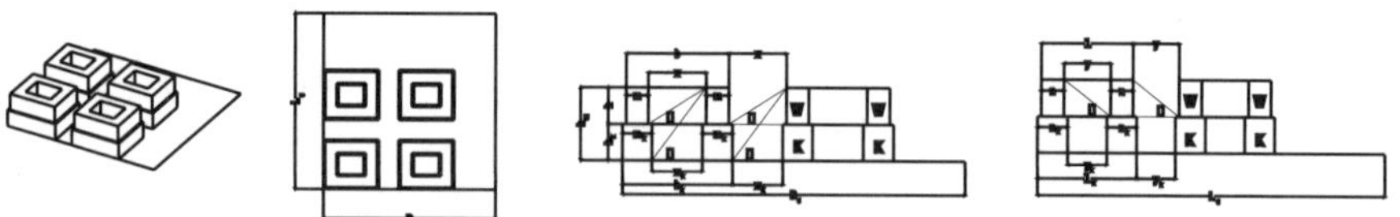

FAR dwellings + offices, parking excluded = (Ow+Ok)/Osit
FAR dwellings + offices, parking included = (Ow+Opw+Ok+Opk)/Osit
xk = x-(mk-m)
yk = y-(nk-n)
Ok = (bk*lk-xk*yk)*Vk*Ctot
Ok≥0

FAR dwellings + offices, parking included =
(30+w)/w*((4m*n+Vh*V(2m/tanβ+2n/tanα))*V)/(2 (Vh*V)/tanα+2m)*
(2 (Vh*V)/tanβ+2n)+(30+k)/k* ((2 mk+(Vh*V/tanα-(mk-m))*(2nk+(Vh*V/tanβ-(nk-n))-
(Vh*V/tanα-(mk-m))*(Vh*V/tanβ-(nk-n)))*((Vh*V/tanα-(mk-m))*tanλ-Vh*V))/((2m+2Vh*V/tanα)
*(2n+2Vh*V/tanβ)*Vhk)

FAR offices, parking excluded =
((4m*n+Vh*V(2m/tanβ+2n/tanα))*V)/(2 (Vh*V)/tanα+2m)*(2 (Vh*V)/tanβ+2n)+
((2 mk+(Vh*V/tanα-(mk-m))*(2nk+(Vh*V/tanβ-(nk-n))-(Vh*V/tanα-(mk-m))*
(Vh*V/tanβ-(nk-n)))*((Vh*V/tanα-(mk-m))*tanλ-Vh*V))/((2m+2Vh*V/tanα) *(2n+2Vh*V/tanβ)*Vhk)

Pyramid

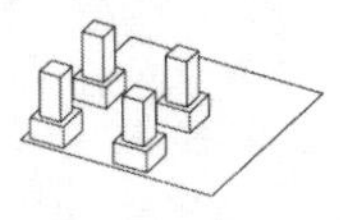

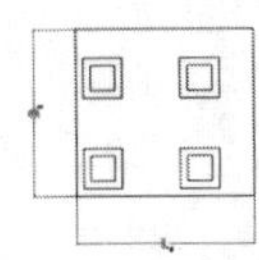

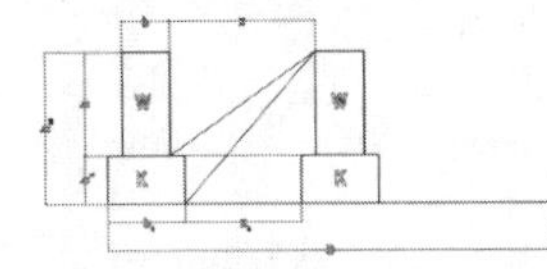

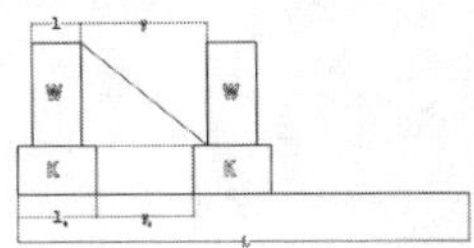

FAR dwellings + offices, parking excluded = $(Ow+Ok)/Osit$

FAR dwellings + offices, parking included = $(Ow+Opw+Ok+Opk)/Osit$

$xk = x-(bk-b)/2$

$Ok \geq 0$

FAR dwellings+offices, parking included =

$$(30+w)/w*(b*l*V)/(b+Vh*V/\tan\alpha)(l+Vh*V/\tan\beta)+(30+k)/k *(bk*lk*((Vh*V/\tan\alpha-(bk-b)/2)*\tan\lambda-h))/(b+Vh*V/\tan\alpha)(l+Vh*V/\tan\beta)*Vhk$$

FAR dwellings+offices, parking excluded =

$$(b*l*V)/(b+Vh*V/\tan\alpha)(l+Vh*V/\tan\beta)+(bk*lk*((Vh*V/\tan\alpha-(bk-b)/2)* \tan\lambda-h))/(b+Vh*V/\tan\alpha)(l+Vh*V/\tan\beta)*Vhk$$

Dutch parameters

Housing parameters

1. total gross upper storey height: Vhw = 2,70m

2. House depth including access: (l or b) = 15m

3. 1.2 parking places for each house; this corresponds to 1 parking place per 70m² living surface area (w = 70). 30m² floor (Opw =30) surface area is reserved for each parking place; this includes the necessary access.

4. 3 hours direct sunlight on the facades fronting the principal rooms, proceeding from the values of 21 March and 21 September: α = 32° in an east-west orientation, β = 38° in an north-south orientation.

Office parameters

1. total gross upper storey height: Vhk = 4m

2. Office depth when lit from two sides: (l or b) = 20m

3. 1 parking place for each 80m² floor surface area. (k = 90); 30m² floor surface area is reserved for each parking place (Opk = 30); this includes the necessary access.

4. λ = 52° sun angle offices in east-west orientation
   δ = 52° sun angle offices in north-south orientation

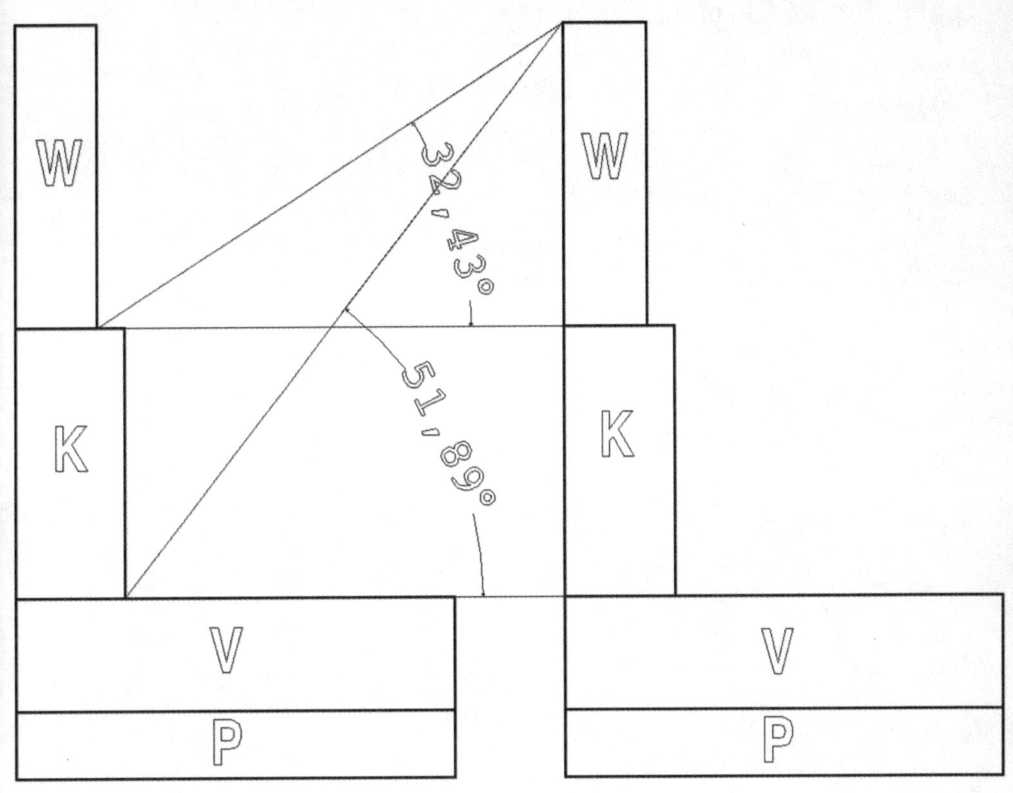
W
W
32,43°
51,89°
K
K
V
V
P
P

Application of Dutch parameters

NO. OF LEVELS HOUSES	NO. OF LEVELS OFFICES L.SCAPE	TOTAL NUMBER OF LEVELS	FAR L. SHAPE L. SHAPE	NO. OFFI
0	0,00	0,00	0,00	0,00
1	0,00	1,00	1,11	0,00
2	0,00	2,00	1,81	0,62
3	0,52	3,52	2,80	1,32
4	1,23	5,23	3,67	2,03
5	1,94	6,94	4,34	2,74
6	2,65	8,65	4,87	3,45
7	3,35	10,35	5,29	4,15
8	4,06	12,06	5,64	4,86
9	4,77	13,77	5,94	5,57
10	5,48	15,48	6,19	6,28
11	6,19	17,19	6,41	6,99
12	6,89	18,89	6,60	7,69
13	7,60	20,60	6,76	8,40
14	8,31	22,31	6,91	9,11
15	9,02	24,02	7,04	9,82
16	9,72	25,72	7,16	10,52
17	10,43	27,43	7,26	11,23
18	11,14	29,14	7,36	11,94
19	11,85	30,85	7,45	12,65
20	12,56	32,56	7,53	13,36
21	13,26	34,26	7,60	14,06
22	13,97	35,97	7,67	14,77
23	14,68	37,68	7,73	15,48
24	15,39	39,39	7,79	16,19
25	16,09	41,09	7,84	16,89
26	16,80	42,80	7,89	17,60
27	17,51	44,51	7,94	18,31
28	18,22	46,22	7,98	19,02
29	18,93	47,93	8,03	19,73
30	19,63	49,63	8,06	20,4
31	20,34	51,34	8,10	21,14
32	21,05	53,05	8,14	21,85
33	21,76	54,76	8,17	22,56
34	22,46	56,46	8,20	23,26
35	23,17	58,17	8,23	23,97
36	23,88	59,88	8,26	24,68
37	24,59	61,59	8,28	25,39
38	25,30	63,30	8,31	26,10
39	26,00	65,00	8,33	26,8
40	26,71	66,71	8,35	27,51
41	27,42	68,42	8,38	28,22
42	28,13	70,13	8,40	28,93
43	28,83	71,83	8,42	29,63
44	29,54	73,54	8,44	30,34
45	30,25	75,25	8,45	31,05
46	30,96	76,96	8,47	31,76
47	31,67	78,67	8,49	32,47
48	32,37	80,37	8,51	33,17
49	33,08	82,08	8,52	33,88
50	33,79	83,79	8,54	34,59
51	34,50	85,50	8,55	35,30
52	35,20	87,20	8,56	36,00
53	35,91	88,91	8,58	36,71
54	36,62	90,62	8,59	37,42
55	37,33	92,33	8,60	38,13
56	38,04	94,04	8,62	38,84
57	38,74	95,74	8,63	39,54
58	39,45	97,45	8,64	40,25
59	40,16	99,16	8,65	40,96
60	40,87	100,87	8,66	41,67
61	41,57	102,57	8,67	42,37
62	42,28	104,28	8,68	43,08
63	42,99	105,99	8,69	43,79
64	43,70	107,70	8,70	44,50
65	44,41	109,41	8,71	45,21
66	45,11	111,11	8,72	45,91
67	45,82	112,82	8,73	46,62
68	46,53	114,53	8,74	47,33
69	47,24	116,24	8,74	48,04
70	47,94	117,94	8,75	48,74
71	48,65	119,65	8,76	49,45
72	49,36	121,36	8,77	50,16
73	50,07	123,07	8,77	50,87
74	50,78	124,78	8,78	51,58
75	51,48	126,48	8,79	52,28
76	52,19	128,19	8,79	52,99
77	52,90	129,90	8,80	53,70
78	53,61	131,61	8,81	54,41
79	54,31	133,31	8,81	55,11
80	55,02	135,02	8,82	55,82
81	55,73	136,73	8,83	56,53
82	56,44	138,44	8,83	57,24
83	57,15	140,15	8,84	57,95
84	57,85	141,85	8,84	58,65
85	58,56	143,56	8,85	59,36
86	59,27	145,27	8,85	60,07
87	59,98	146,98	8,86	60,78
88	60,68	148,68	8,86	61,48
89	61,39	150,39	8,87	62,19
90	62,10	152,10	8,87	62,90
91	62,81	153,81	8,88	63,61
92	63,52	155,52	8,88	64,32
93	64,22	157,22	8,89	65,02
94	64,93	158,93	8,89	65,73
95	65,64	160,64	8,90	66,44
96	66,35	162,35	8,90	67,15
97	67,05	164,05	8,91	67,85
98	67,76	165,76	8,91	68,56
99	68,47	167,47	8,91	69,27
100	69,18	169,18	8,92	69,98

NUMBER ·AMID SHAPE	FAR L. PYRAMID LEVELS	NO. OF LEVELS L. PYRAMID SHAPE	TOTAL NUMBER OFFICE BLOCK	FAR BLOCK LEVELS BLOCK	NO. OF LEVELS OFFICES	NUMBER OF LEVELS BLOCK PYRAMID	FAR BLOCK PYRAMID LEVELS	NO. OF LEVELS BLOCK PYRAMID	TOTAL NUMBER OFFICES PYRAMID	FAR PYRAMID LEVELS PYRAMID
	0,00	0,00	0,00	0,00	0,00	0,00	0,00	0,00	0,00	0,00
	1,11	0,00	1,00	1,14	0,00	1,00	1,14	0,00	1,00	1,07
	2,51	0,00	2,00	1,88	0,00	2,00	1,88	0,00	2,00	1,66
	3,56	0,00	3,00	2,42	0,00	3,00	2,42	0,00	3,00	1,99
	4,33	0,00	4,00	2,81	0,00	4,00	2,81	0,43	4,43	2,74
	4,92	0,34	5,34	3,35	1,94	6,94	4,63	1,14	6,14	3,50
	5,39	1,05	7,05	4,01	2,65	8,65	5,22	1,85	7,85	3,99
	5,76	1,75	8,75	4,55	3,35	10,35	5,70	2,55	9,55	4,30
	6,07	2,46	10,46	5,02	4,06	12,06	6,10	3,26	11,26	4,50
	6,33	3,17	12,17	5,41	4,77	13,77	6,44	3,97	12,97	4,60
	6,56	3,88	13,88	5,75	5,48	15,48	6,73	4,68	14,68	4,65
	6,75	4,59	15,59	6,05	6,19	17,19	6,98	5,39	16,39	4,66
	6,91	5,29	17,29	6,32	6,89	18,89	7,20	6,09	18,09	4,64
	7,06	6,00	19,00	6,55	7,60	20,60	7,40	6,80	19,80	4,60
	7,19	6,71	20,71	6,76	8,31	22,31	7,57	7,51	21,51	4,55
2	7,31	7,42	22,42	6,95	9,02	24,02	7,72	8,22	23,22	4,48
2	7,41	8,12	24,12	7,12	9,72	25,72	7,86	8,92	24,92	4,41
3	7,50	8,83	25,83	7,28	10,43	27,43	7,99	9,63	26,63	4,33
4	7,59	9,54	27,54	7,42	11,14	29,14	8,10	10,34	28,34	4,25
	7,67	10,25	29,25	7,55	11,85	30,85	8,21	11,05	30,05	4,17
	7,74	10,95	30,95	7,67	12,55	32,55	8,30	11,76	31,76	4,09
5	7,80	11,66	32,66	7,78	13,26	34,26	8,39	12,46	33,46	4,01
	7,86	12,37	34,37	7,88	13,97	35,97	8,47	13,17	35,17	3,94
3	7,92	13,08	36,08	7,97	14,68	37,68	8,54	13,88	36,88	3,86
	7,97	13,79	37,79	8,06	15,39	39,39	8,61	14,59	38,59	3,78
	8,02	14,49	39,49	8,14	16,09	41,09	8,68	15,29	40,29	3,71
)	8,06	15,20	41,20	8,22	16,80	42,80	8,74	16,00	42,00	3,64
	8,10	15,91	42,91	8,29	17,51	44,51	8,80	16,71	43,71	3,57
2	8,14	16,62	44,62	8,36	18,22	46,22	8,85	17,42	45,42	3,50
3	8,18	17,32	46,32	8,42	18,92	47,92	8,90	18,13	47,13	3,43
3	8,21	18,03	48,03	8,48	19,63	49,63	8,95	18,83	48,83	3,37
4	8,24	18,74	49,74	8,54	20,34	51,34	8,99	19,54	50,54	3,30
5	8,27	19,45	51,45	8,59	21,05	53,05	9,03	20,25	52,25	3,24
6	8,30	20,16	53,16	8,64	21,76	54,76	9,07	20,96	53,96	3,18
5	8,33	20,86	54,86	8,69	22,46	56,46	9,11	21,66	55,66	3,13
7	8,36	21,57	56,57	8,73	23,17	58,17	9,14	22,37	57,37	3,07
3	8,38	22,28	58,28	8,78	23,88	59,88	9,18	23,08	59,08	3,02
9	8,40	22,99	59,99	8,82	24,59	61,59	9,21	23,79	60,79	2,96
)	8,43	23,69	61,69	8,86	25,29	63,29	9,24	24,50	62,50	2,91
0	8,45	24,40	63,40	8,89	26,00	65,00	9,27	25,20	64,20	2,86
	8,47	25,11	65,11	8,93	26,71	66,71	9,30	25,91	65,91	2,82
2	8,49	25,82	66,82	8,96	27,42	68,42	9,32	26,62	67,62	2,77
3	8,51	26,53	68,53	9,00	28,12	70,12	9,35	27,33	69,33	2,73
3	8,52	27,23	70,23	9,03	28,83	71,83	9,37	28,03	71,03	2,68
4	8,54	27,94	71,94	9,06	29,54	73,54	9,40	28,74	72,74	2,64
5	8,56	28,65	73,65	9,09	30,25	75,25	9,42	29,45	74,45	2,60
5	8,57	29,36	75,36	9,11	30,96	76,96	9,44	30,16	76,16	2,56
7	8,59	30,06	77,06	9,14	31,66	78,66	9,46	30,87	77,87	2,52
	8,60	30,77	78,77	9,17	32,37	80,37	9,48	31,57	79,57	2,48
8	8,62	31,48	80,48	9,19	33,08	82,08	9,50	32,28	81,28	2,45
9	8,63	32,19	82,19	9,21	33,79	83,79	9,52	32,99	82,99	2,41
0	8,64	32,89	83,89	9,24	34,49	85,49	9,54	33,70	84,70	2,38
0	8,65	33,60	85,60	9,26	35,20	87,20	9,55	34,40	86,40	2,34
	8,67	34,31	87,31	9,28	35,91	88,91	9,57	35,11	88,11	2,31
2	8,68	35,02	89,02	9,30	36,62	90,62	9,59	35,82	89,82	2,28
3	8,69	35,73	90,73	9,32	37,33	92,33	9,60	36,53	91,53	2,25
4	8,70	36,43	92,43	9,34	38,03	94,03	9,62	37,24	93,24	2,22
4	8,71	37,14	94,14	9,36	38,74	95,74	9,63	37,94	94,94	2,19
5	8,72	37,85	95,85	9,38	39,45	97,45	9,65	38,65	96,65	2,16
6	8,73	38,56	97,56	9,40	40,16	99,16	9,66	39,36	98,36	2,13
7	8,74	39,26	99,26	9,41	40,86	100,86	9,67	40,07	100,07	2,11
37	8,75	39,97	100,97	9,43	41,57	102,57	9,68	40,77	101,77	2,08
08	8,76	40,68	102,68	9,44	42,28	104,28	9,70	41,48	103,48	2,05
79	8,77	41,39	104,39	9,46	42,99	105,99	9,71	42,19	105,19	2,03
50	8,77	42,10	106,10	9,48	43,70	107,70	9,72	42,90	106,90	2,00
21	8,78	42,80	107,80	9,49	44,40	109,40	9,73	43,61	108,61	1,98
1	8,79	43,51	109,51	9,50	45,11	111,11	9,74	44,31	110,31	1,95
62	8,80	44,22	111,22	9,52	45,82	112,82	9,75	45,02	112,02	1,93
33	8,80	44,93	112,93	9,53	46,53	114,53	9,76	45,73	113,73	1,91
04	8,81	45,63	114,63	9,54	47,23	116,23	9,77	46,44	115,44	1,89
74	8,82	46,34	116,34	9,56	47,94	117,94	9,78	47,14	117,14	1,87
45	8,83	47,05	118,05	9,57	48,65	119,65	9,79	47,85	118,85	1,84
16	8,83	47,76	119,76	9,58	49,36	121,36	9,80	48,56	120,56	1,82
87	8,84	48,46	121,46	9,59	50,06	123,06	9,81	49,27	122,27	1,80
58	8,84	49,17	123,17	9,60	50,77	124,77	9,82	49,98	123,98	1,78
28	8,85	49,88	124,88	9,62	51,48	126,48	9,83	50,68	125,68	1,76
99	8,86	50,59	126,59	9,63	52,19	128,19	9,84	51,39	127,39	1,75
70	8,86	51,30	128,30	9,64	52,90	129,90	9,84	52,10	129,10	1,73
41	8,87	52,00	130,00	9,65	53,60	131,60	9,85	52,81	130,81	1,71
11	8,87	52,71	131,71	9,66	54,31	133,31	9,86	53,51	132,51	1,69
82	8,88	53,42	133,42	9,67	55,02	135,02	9,87	54,22	134,22	1,67
53	8,88	54,13	135,13	9,68	55,73	136,73	9,88	54,93	135,93	1,66
24	8,89	54,83	136,83	9,69	56,43	138,43	9,88	55,64	137,64	1,64
95	8,89	55,54	138,54	9,70	57,14	140,14	9,89	56,35	139,35	1,62
65	8,90	56,25	140,25	9,70	57,85	141,85	9,90	57,05	141,05	1,61
36	8,90	56,96	141,96	9,71	58,56	143,56	9,90	57,76	142,76	1,59
07	8,91	57,67	143,67	9,72	59,27	145,27	9,91	58,47	144,47	1,58
78	8,91	58,37	145,37	9,73	59,97	146,97	9,92	59,18	146,18	1,56
48	8,92	59,08	147,08	9,74	60,68	148,68	9,92	59,88	147,88	1,55
9	8,92	59,79	148,79	9,75	61,39	150,39	9,93	60,59	149,59	1,53
90	8,93	60,50	150,50	9,75	62,10	152,10	9,93	61,30	151,30	1,52
61	8,93	61,20	152,20	9,76	62,80	153,80	9,94	62,01	153,01	1,50
32	8,94	61,91	153,91	9,77	63,51	155,51	9,95	62,72	154,72	1,49
02	8,94	62,62	155,62	9,78	64,22	157,22	9,95	63,42	156,42	1,48
73	8,94	63,33	157,33	9,78	64,93	158,93	9,96	64,13	158,13	1,46
44	8,95	64,04	159,04	9,79	65,63	160,63	9,96	64,84	159,84	1,45
15	8,95	64,74	160,74	9,80	66,34	162,34	9,97	65,55	161,55	1,44
85	8,95	65,45	162,45	9,81	67,05	164,05	9,97	66,25	163,25	1,42
56	8,96	66,16	164,16	9,81	67,76	165,76	9,98	66,96	164,96	1,41
27	8,96	66,87	165,87	9,82	68,47	167,47	9,98	67,67	166,67	1,40
98	8,97	67,57	167,57	9,83	69,17	169,17	9,99	68,38	168,38	1,39

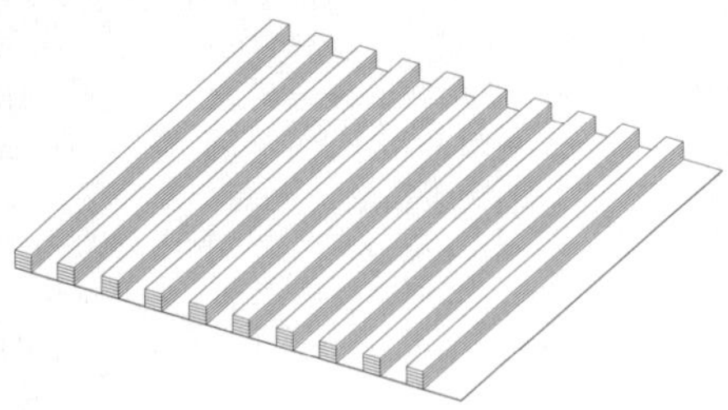

Row houses
5 floors
24m in between distance

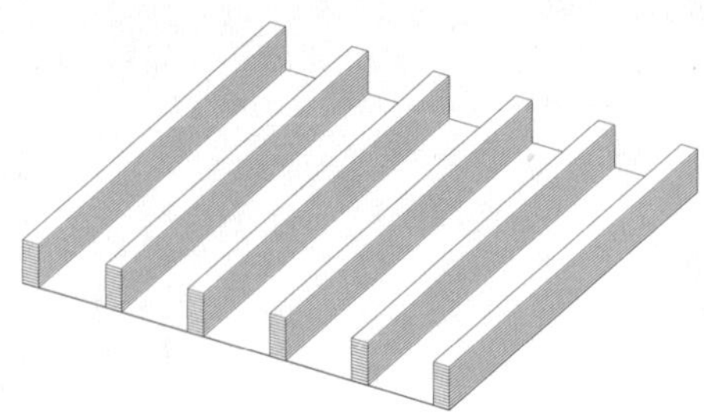

13 floors
62m in between distance

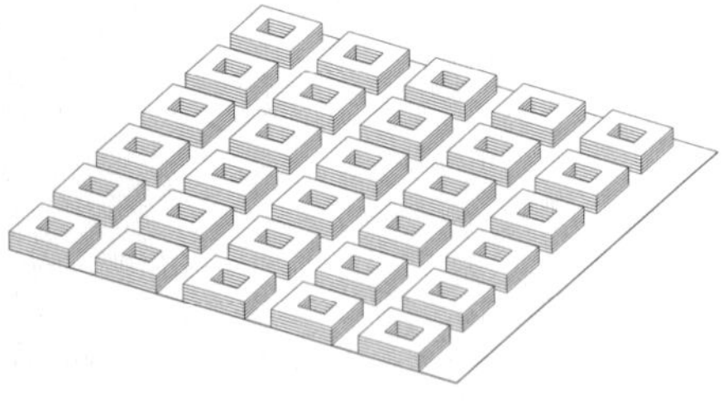

Blocks
5 floors
24m in between distance (x-dir)
19m in between distance (y-dir)

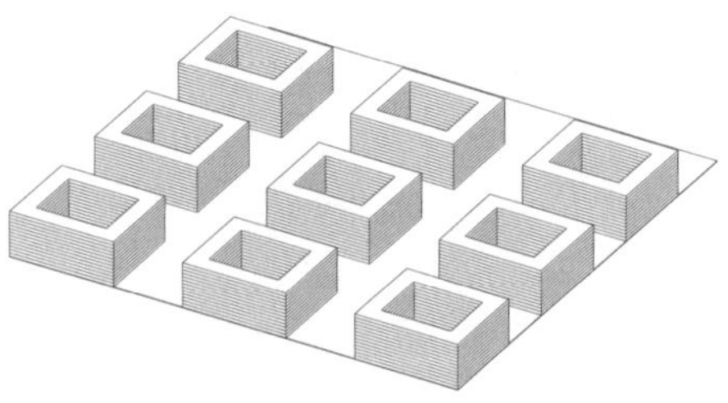

13 floors
62m in between distance (x-dir)
50m in between distance (y-dir)

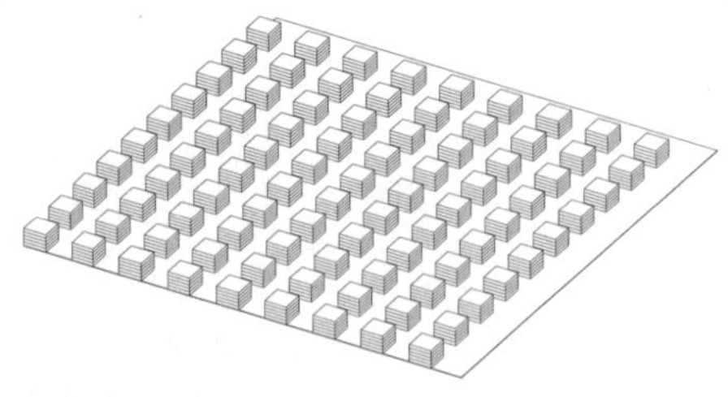

Towers
5 floors
24m in between distance (x-dir)
19m in between distance (y-dir)

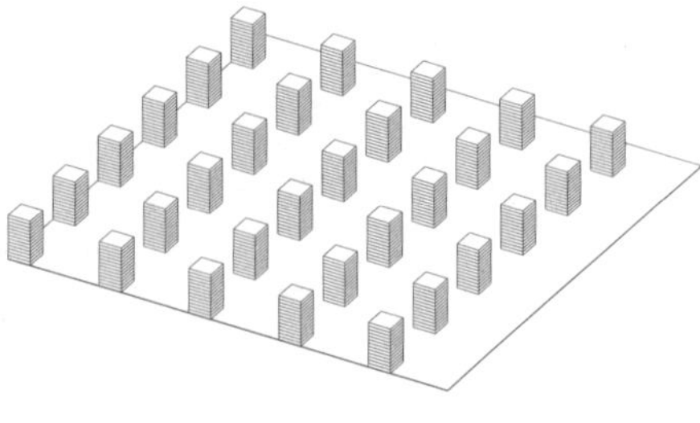

13 floors
62m in between distance (x-dir)
50m in between distance (y-dir)

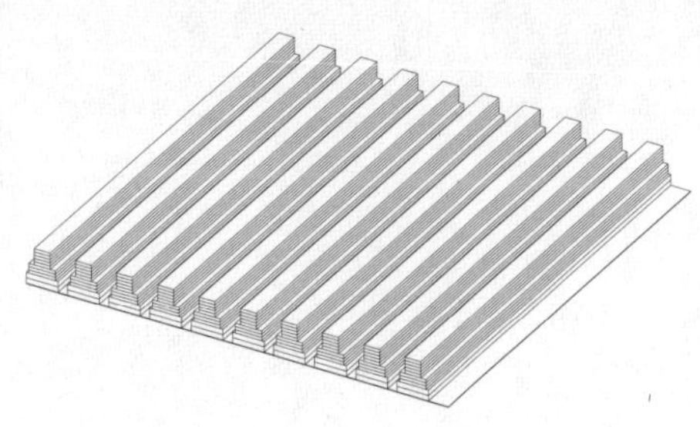

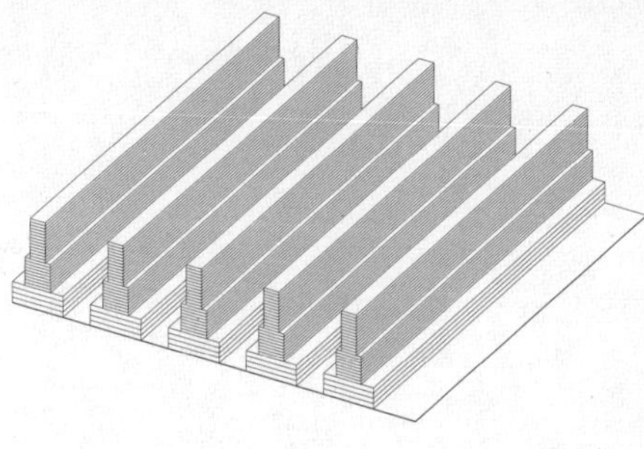

L-shape pyramid

10 floors

9m in between distance

26 floors

27m in between distance

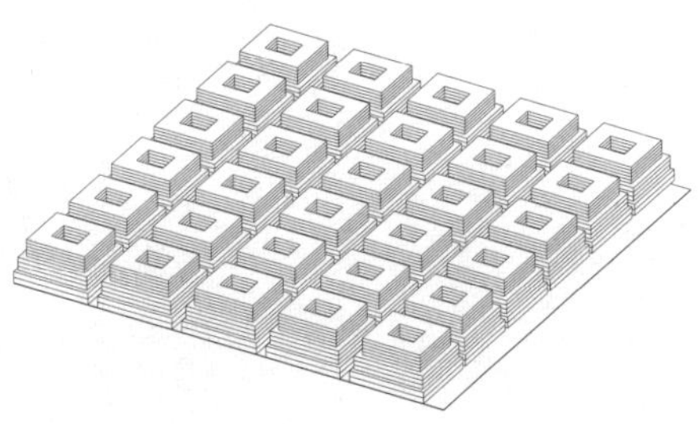

Block pyramid

10 floors

9m in between distance (x-dir)

4,2m in between distance (y-dir)

26 floors

32m in between distance (x-dir)

20m in between distance (y-dir)

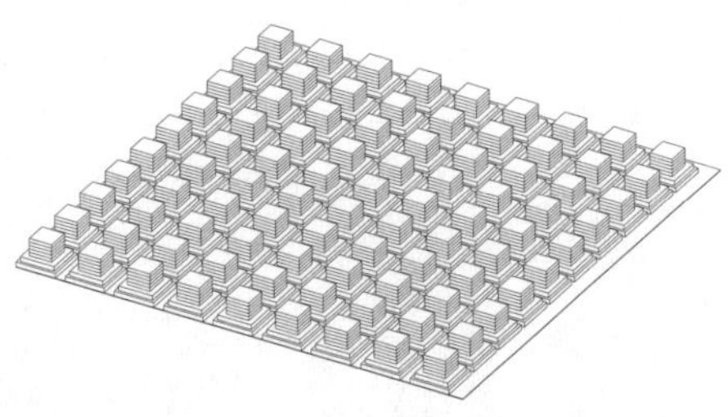

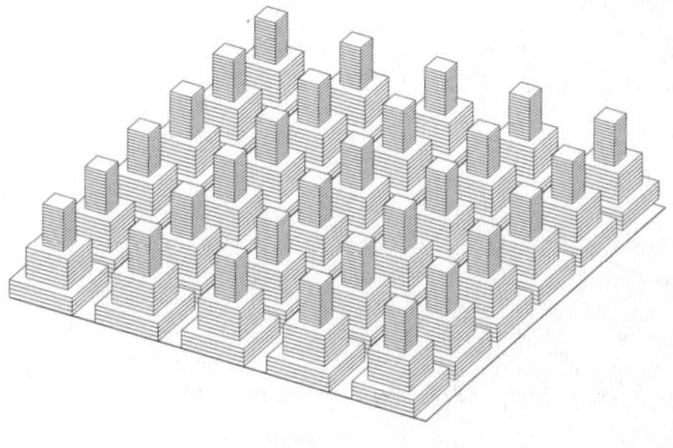

Pyramid

7 floors

9m in between distance (x-dir)

4,2m in between distance (y-dir)

24 floors

22m in between distance (x-dir)

10m in between distance (y-dir)

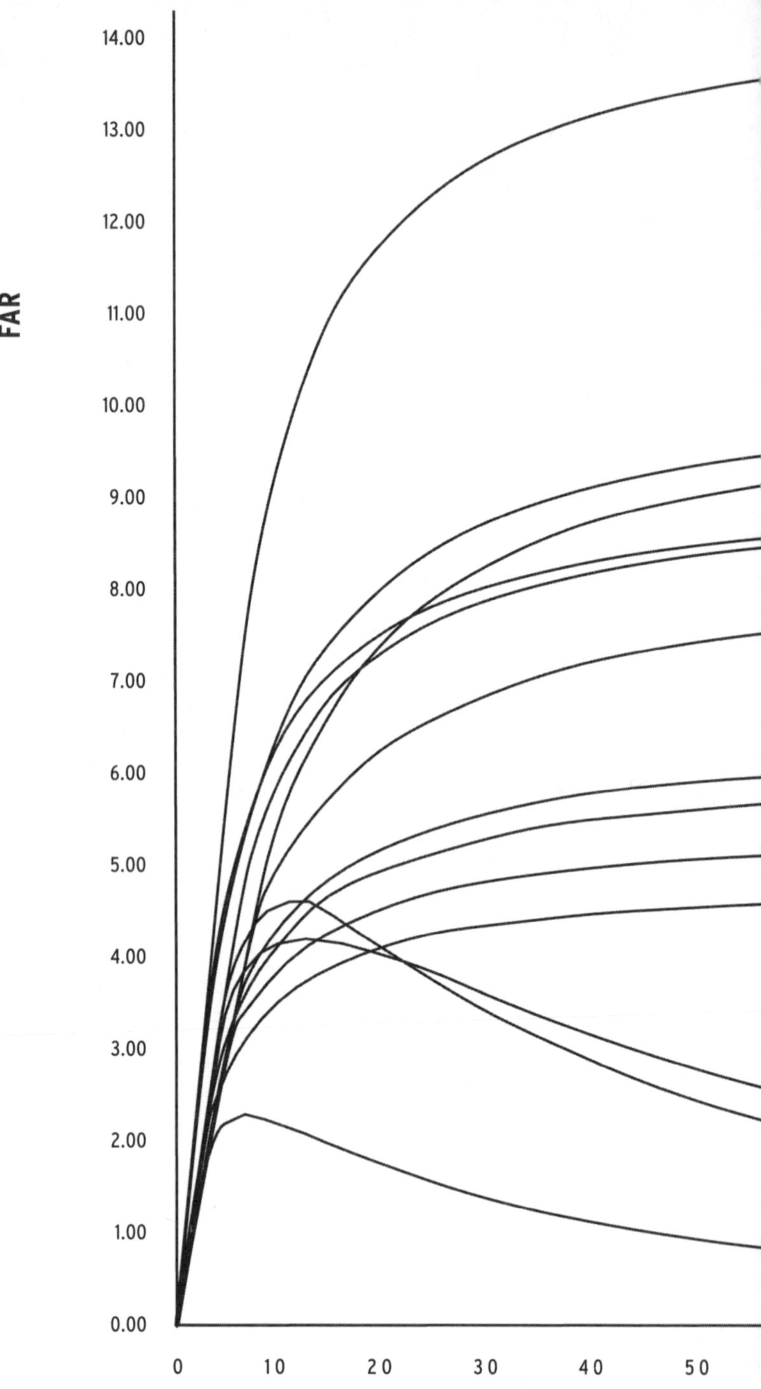
FAR
14.00
13.00
12.00
11.00
10.00
9.00
8.00
7.00
6.00
5.00
4.00
3.00
2.00
1.00
0.00
0
10
20
30
40
50

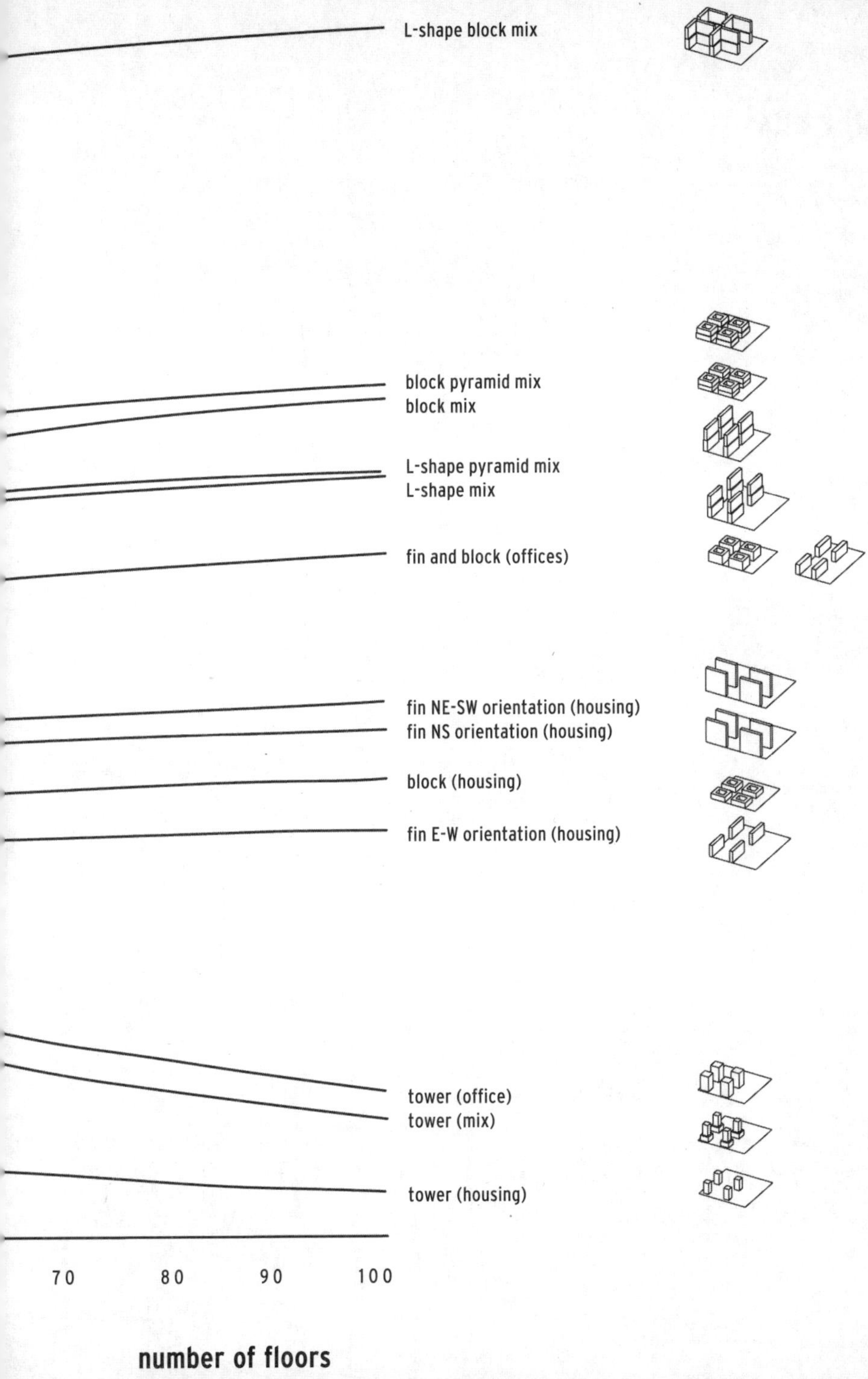

L-shape block mix

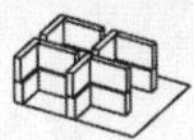

block pyramid mix
block mix

L-shape pyramid mix
L-shape mix

fin and block (offices)

fin NE-SW orientation (housing)
fin NS orientation (housing)

block (housing)

fin E-W orientation (housing)

tower (office)
tower (mix)

tower (housing)

70 80 90 100

number of floors

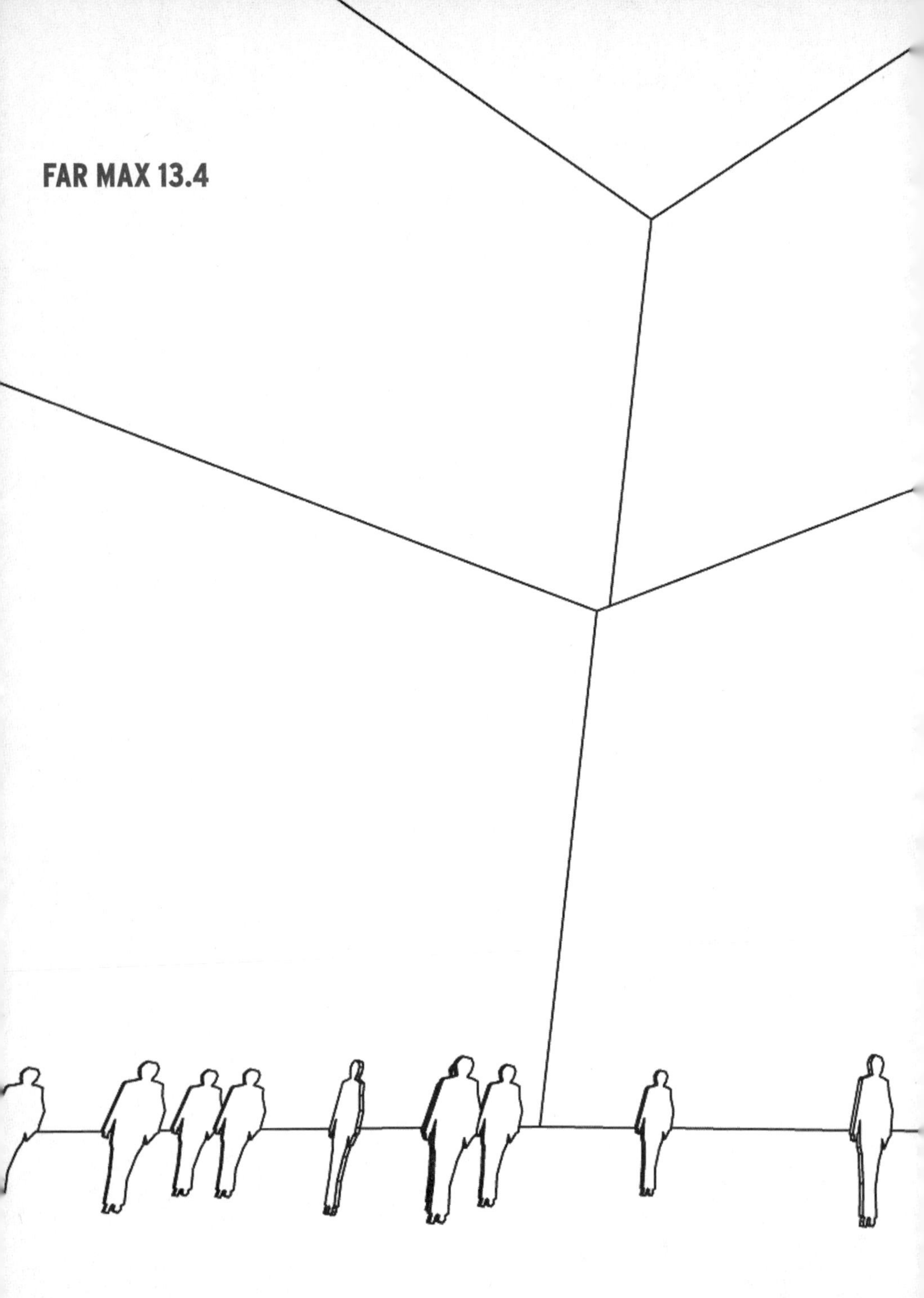
FAR MAX 13.4

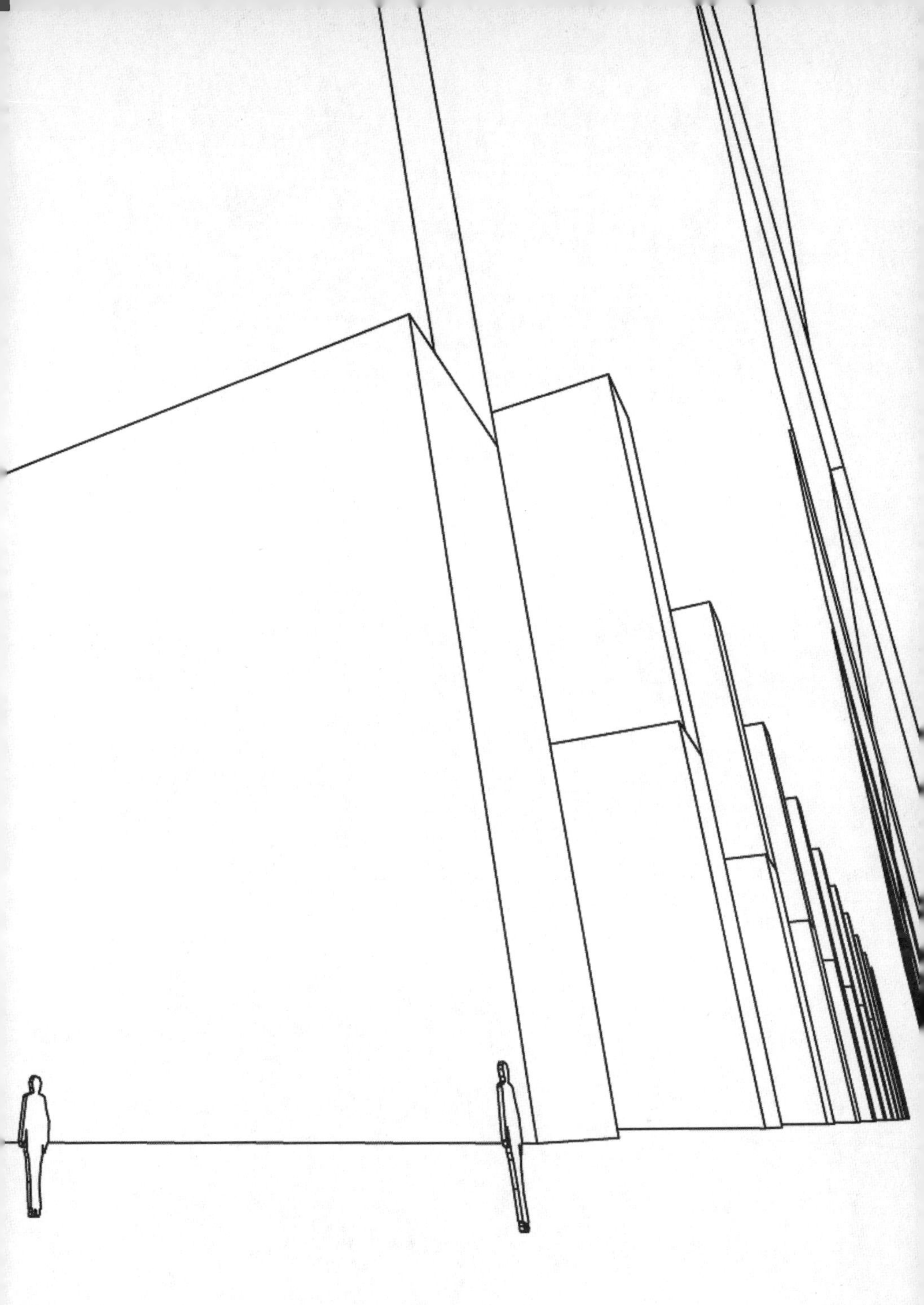

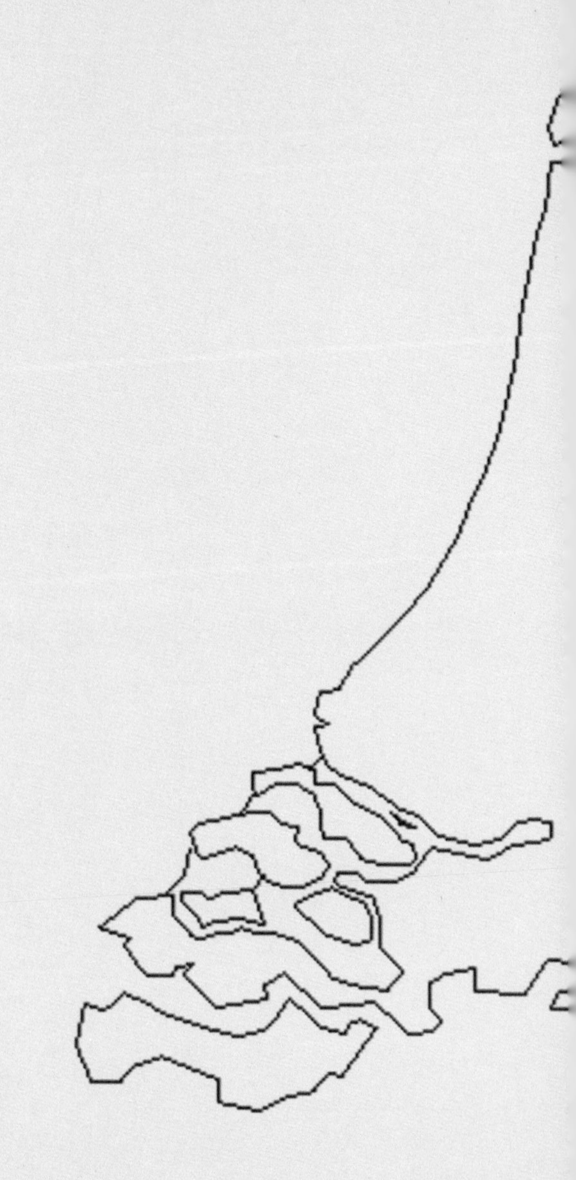

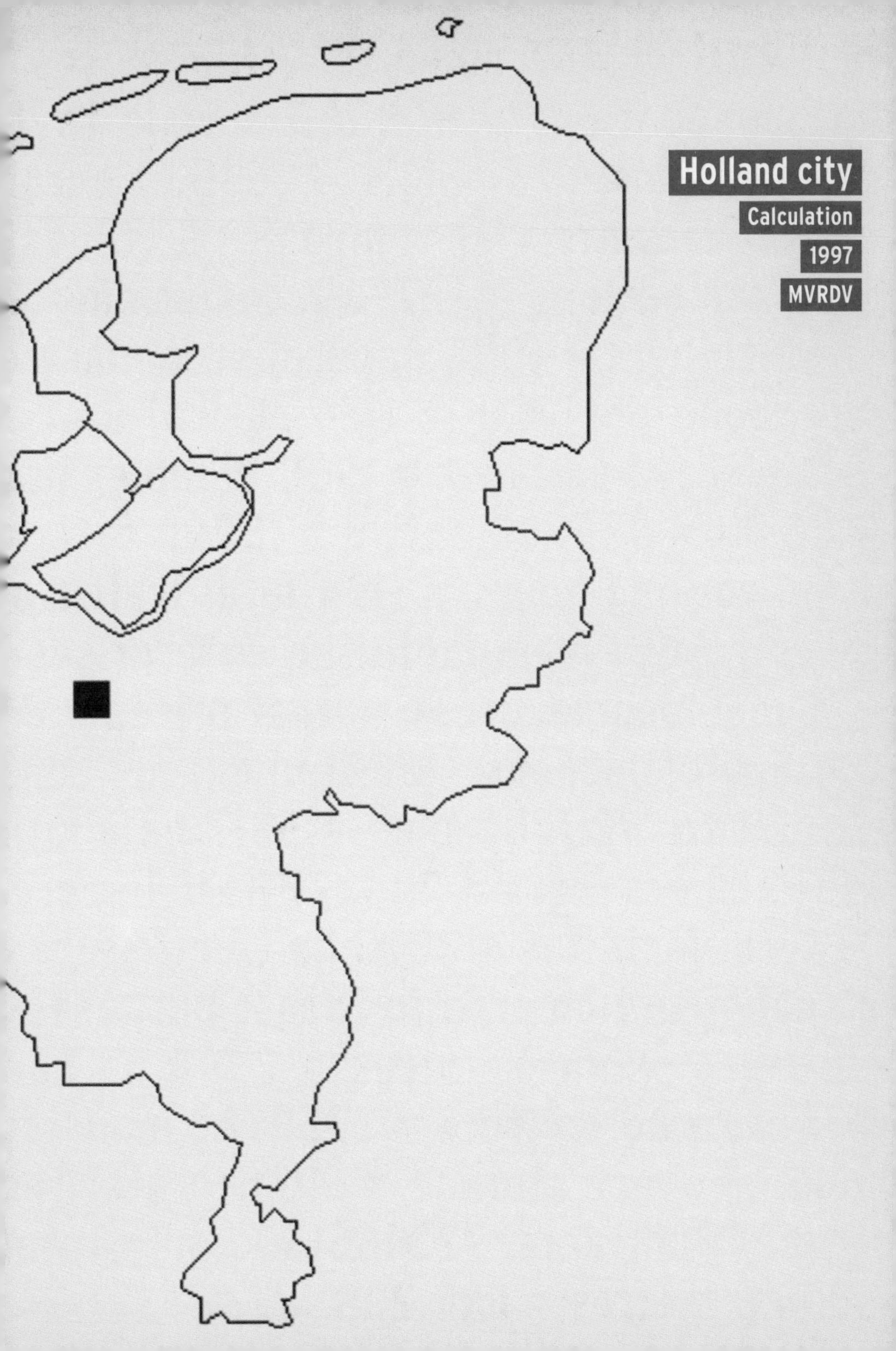

Holland city

Calculation

1997

MVRDV

Holland = 467 cinemas & filmhouses
accommodations = 868000 bicycle thef
museums open to public = 263500 burgl
mln inhabitants = 97 companies & orchest
accommodations = 22760 performing a
practitioners = 1008 general secondary e
telephone per year = 1178 agricultural a
constructed per year = 196819 babies bor
tourists = 235000 cattle = 18000 taxis =
time working hours = 1194 fatal traffic a
firms = 6681 manufacturing enterprises
national income, gross market prices = 24
= 4.5 mln chickens = 2851 pj energy cons
received = 720000 pigs = 5317 ha allotm
15310 ha greenery = 284227 ha living are
cultural facilities = 3070 ha tram/metro &
ha construction area for other purposes =
ha other public services = 2894 ha hor
117774 ha agriculture = 79581 ha industry
= 46 ha wreck storage = 610 ha water res
= total floor area 7224661500 m^2 = total
5884.6 metres = FAR 208

26 art galleries = 4120 outdoor sports
er Year = 85 vocational colleges = 632
s per year = 705 swimming pools = 15.5
= 6.2 mln dwellings = 1770 indoor sports
performances per year = 7013 general
cational colleges = 1 mln harassments via
horticultural holdings = 16377 dwellings
er year = 8.6 mln overnight stays foreign
6 mln cars = 5.7 mln jobs = 26.9 bln full-
lents per year = 1942 private architect's
8150 sports schools = 610.7 mln guilders
mln kg potatoes for consumption per year
ption per year = 164.3 bln guilders taxes
t gardens = 5393 ha unmetalled roads =
31146 ha sports area = 244435 ha social-
ail = 6600 ha daytime recreation = 16463
7074 ha gouvernment & services = 10508
ulture = 9513 ha nocturnal recreation =
business = 186621 ha industrial purposes
voir = 1993 ha cementery = 1408 ha dump
lume 25408123800 m^3 = 800 x 5884.6 x

Dutch Volume

function		floor height
housing	light	3 m
greenery	light	15 m
allotment gardens	light	10 m
gouvernment & services	mix	3 m
nocturnal recreation	mix	3 m
daytime recreation	mix	5 m
agriculture	dark	2 m
industry & business	dark	4 m
metalled roads	dark	5 m
sports	dark	7 m
sociol-cultural facilities	dark	4 m
planned area for industrial purposes	dark	4 m
planned area for other purposes	dark	3 m
other public services	dark	3 m
unmetalled roads	dark	5 m
tram-metro & rail	dark	5 m
horticulture	dark	2 m
cemetery	dark	4 m
dump	dark	5 m
water reservoir	dark	5 m
wreck storage	dark	5 m
total		

floor area Lightcondition	volume Lightcondition	
2842268000 m^2	7389896800 m^3	
153100000 m^2	2296500000 m^3	
53172000 m^2	531720000 m^3	
105210000 m^2	273546000 m^3	
95125000 m^2	247325000 m^3	
65995000 m^2	329975000 m^3	
1177739000 m^2	2355478000 m^3	
795810000 m^2	3183240000 m^3	
770742000 m^2	3468339000 m^3	
311461500 m^2	2180230500 m^3	
244350000 m^2	977400000 m^3	
186210000 m^2	744840000 m^3	
164265000 m^2	492795000 m^3	
105080000 m^2	315240000 m^3	
53930000 m^2	242685000 m^3	
30699000 m^2	138145500 m^3	
28944000 m^2	57888000 m^3	
19925000 m^2	79700000 m^3	
14075000 m^2	70375000 m^3	
6100000 m^2	30500000 m^3	
461000 m^2	2305000 m^3	
7224661500 m^2	25408123800 m^3	= 800 x 5885 x 5885 m

Meteorite city

Light rules

1997

Eric Drieënhuizen

Re-editing: MVRDV

Dutch law proclaims that the elevation of houses should obtain minimally three hours of direct sunlight per day.

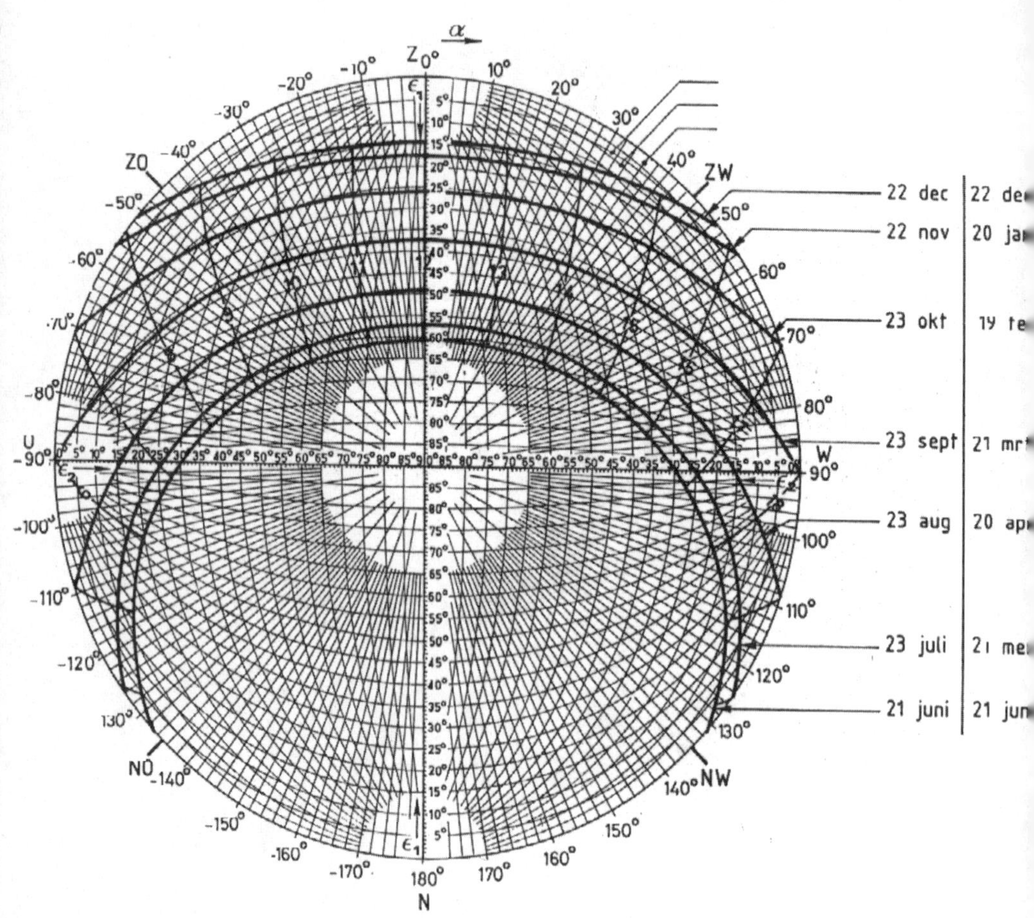

Sun diagram

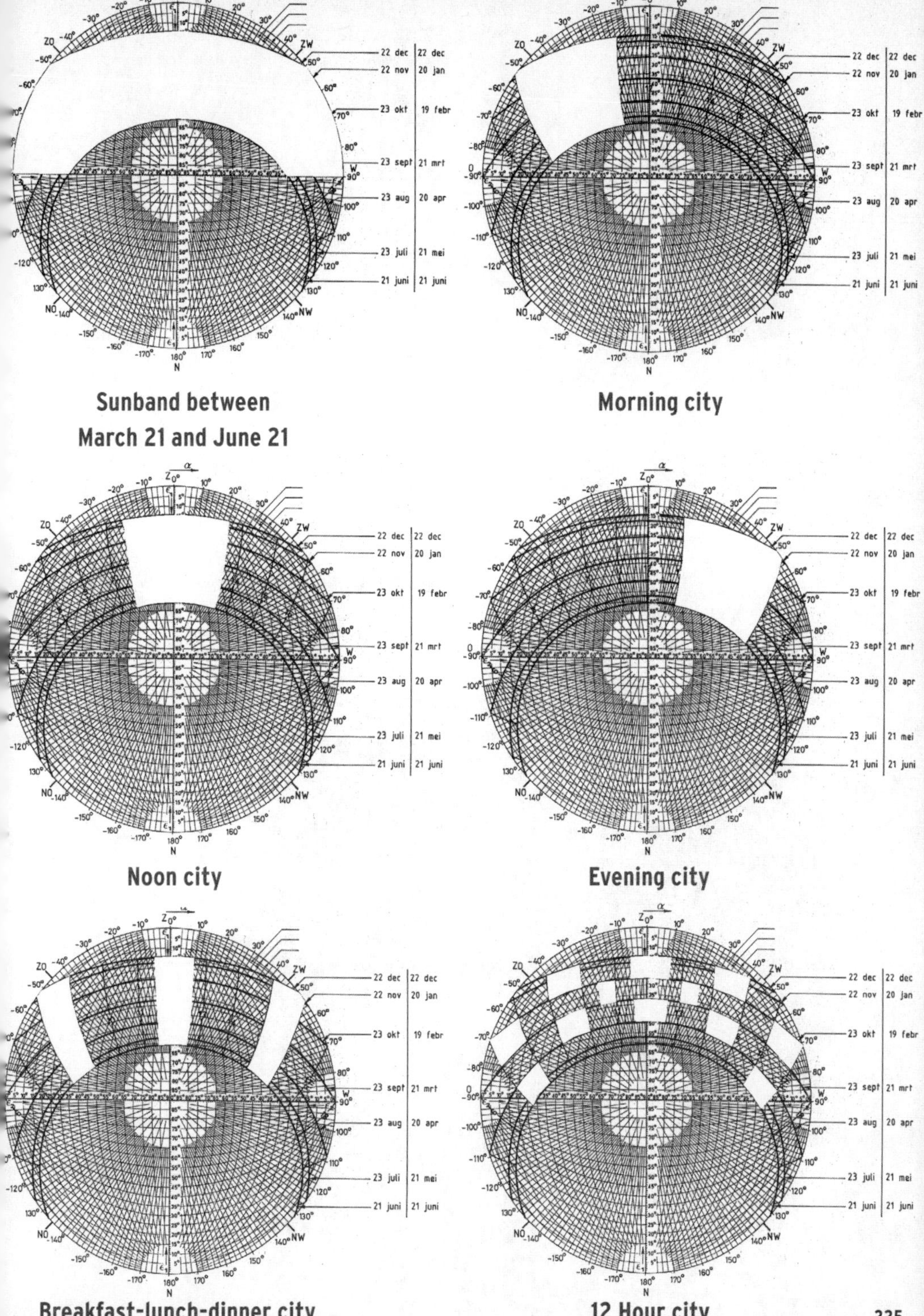

Sunband between March 21 and June 21

Morning city

Noon city

Evening city

Breakfast-lunch-dinner city

12 Hour city

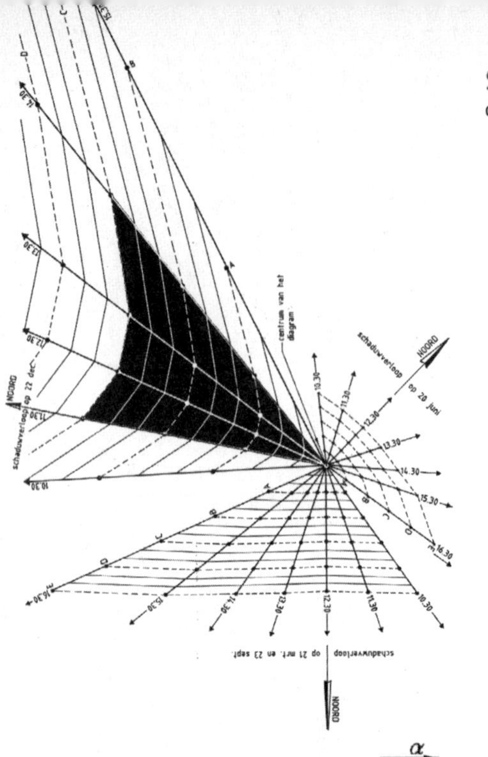

Shadow diagram Length of the shadow during one hour of a vertical rod during several days throughout the year.

NOORD
centrum van het diagram
schaduwverloop op 20 juni
schaduwverloop op 22 dec
schaduwverloop op 21 mrt. en 23 sept.
10.30
11.30
12.30
13.30
14.30
15.30
16.30

Sun diagram Unbuilt zone inorder to allow for three hours sunlight at one position at ground floor

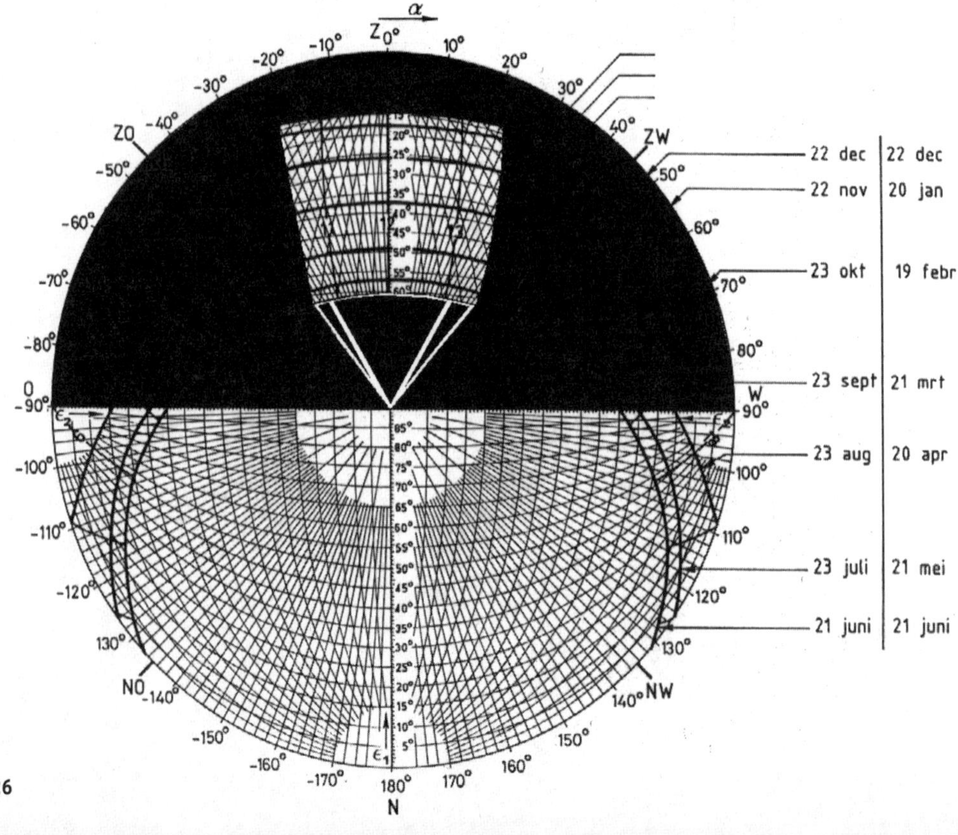

α
Z
ZO
ZW
O
W
NO
NW
N
22 dec | 22 dec
22 nov | 20 jan
23 okt | 19 febr
23 sept | 21 mrt
23 aug | 20 apr
23 juli | 21 mei
21 juni | 21 juni

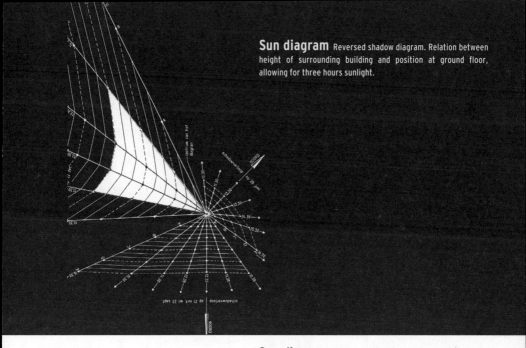

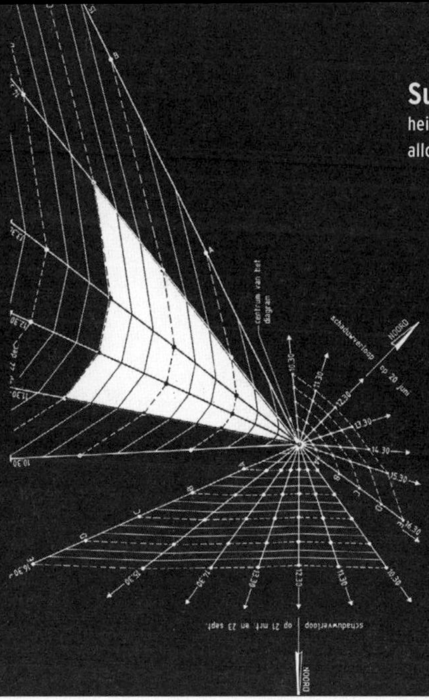

Sun diagram Reversed shadow diagram. Relation between height of surrounding building and position at ground floor, allowing for three hours sunlight.

Sun diagram Unbuilt zone inorder to allow for three hours sunlight at one point on the ground floor corresponds with 95% of the available sky.

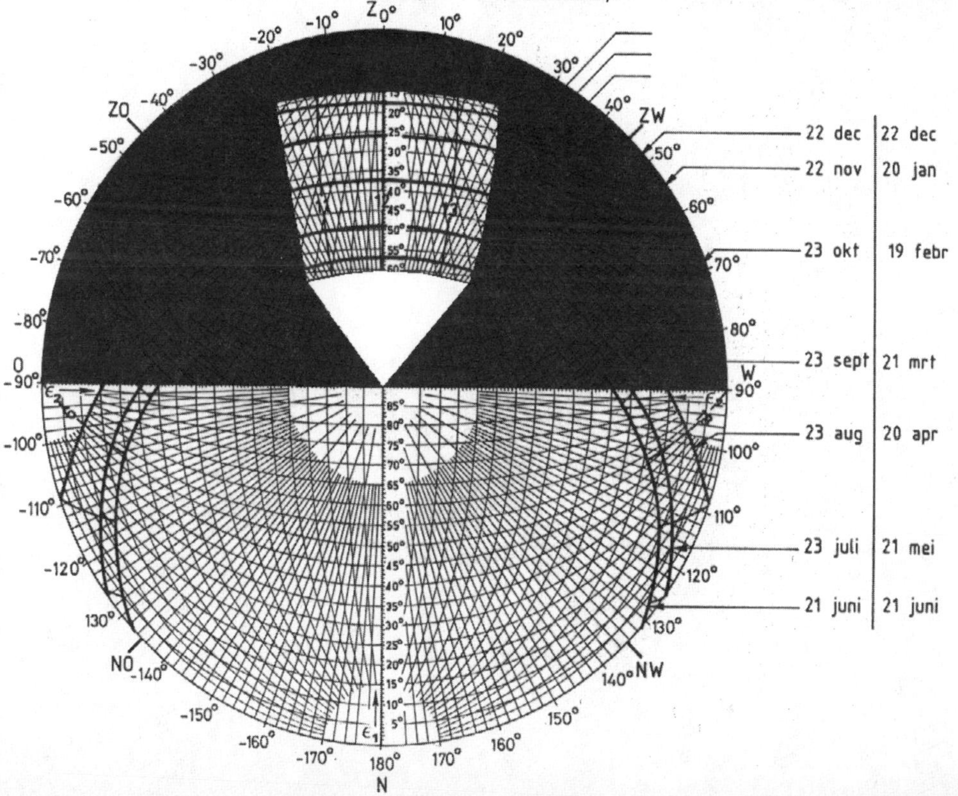

Meteorite

Using sun diagrams, we can calculate light cones that penetrate the imagined building mass so that even the lowest floors acquire sufficient sunlight for housing.

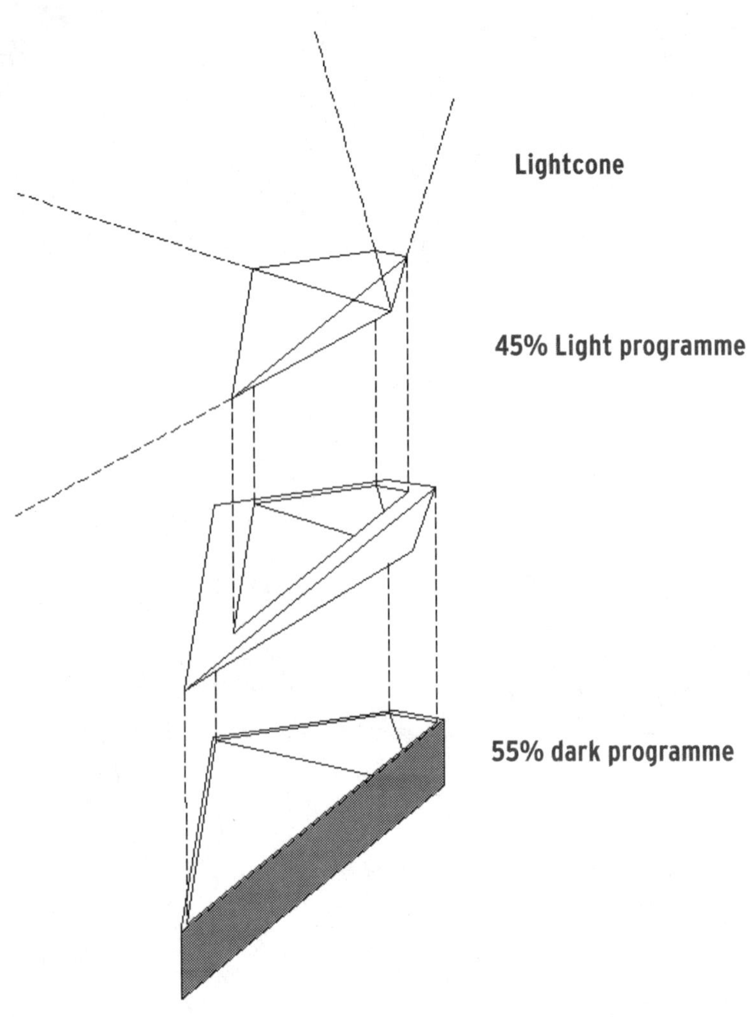

Meteorite city

If we conceive of a Holland City that honours the prescribed three hours a day of direct sunlight by means of a shower of light-meteorites, this city will measure 40 x 40 x 0.025 km with a FAR of 4.5.

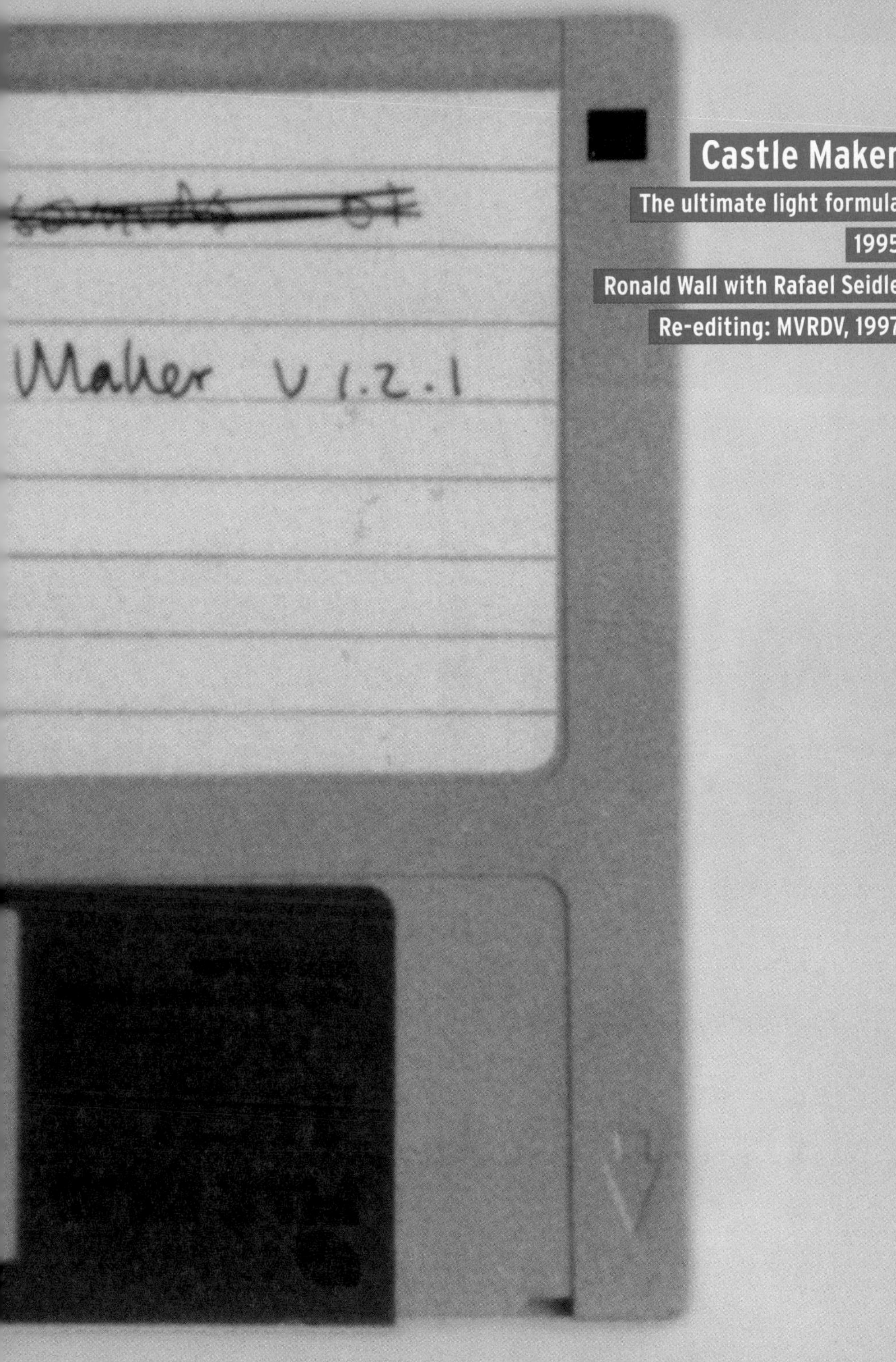

Castle Maker

The ultimate light formula

1995

Ronald Wall with Rafael Seidle

Re-editing: MVRDV, 1997

Castle maker gives a method to generate optimized buildings within the constraints of light and

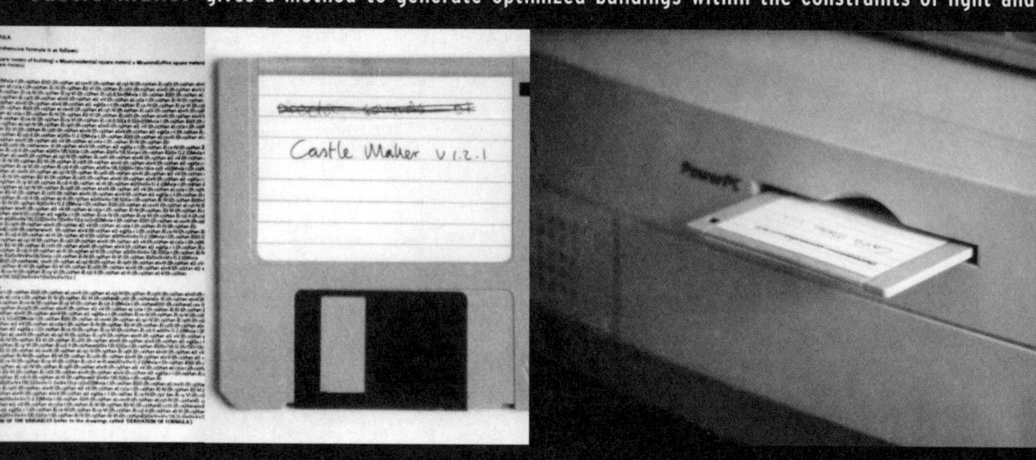

or anywhere where a planet depends on one sun. On earth an identical assignment in Helsinki,

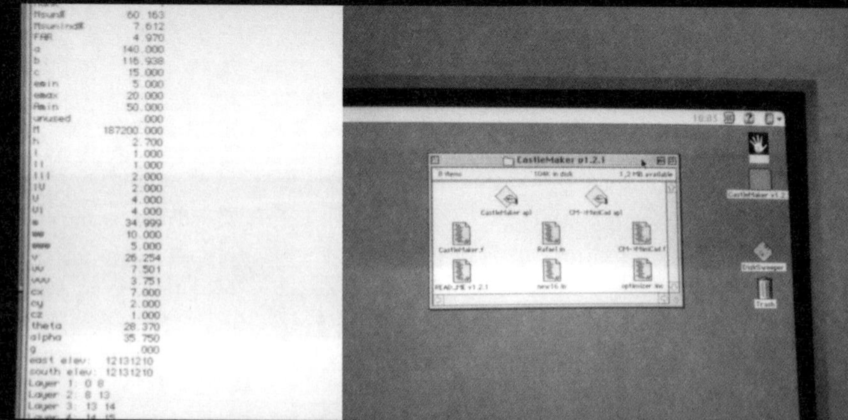

and sun angles. The location determines the form. Castle Maker uses a handful of parameters but can be

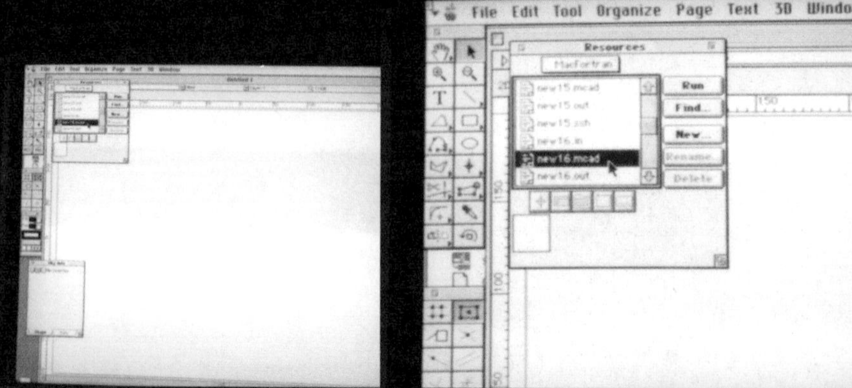

given Floor Area Ratio, building height, length and depth, sun angles, height and depth of apartments and programme. Castle Maker is flexible (all parameters are variable) and can be used anywhere in the world,

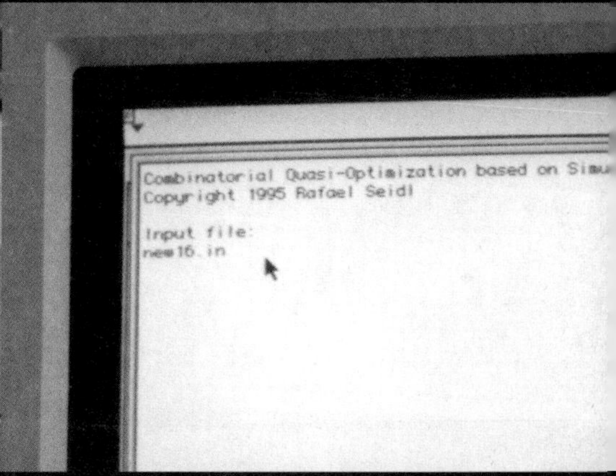

Johannesburg or Rotterdam will generate different optimal buildings, due to the difference in programme

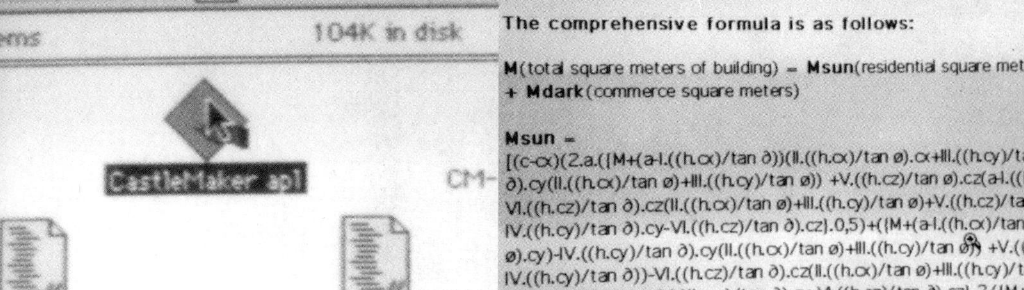

extended if necessary. For this book the program consists of parameters on building site, desired or

them open. The coherence of the parameters has been expressed by the formula. This formula can

office (Msunind) and commercial programs (Mdark). The slightest change in any given parameter will

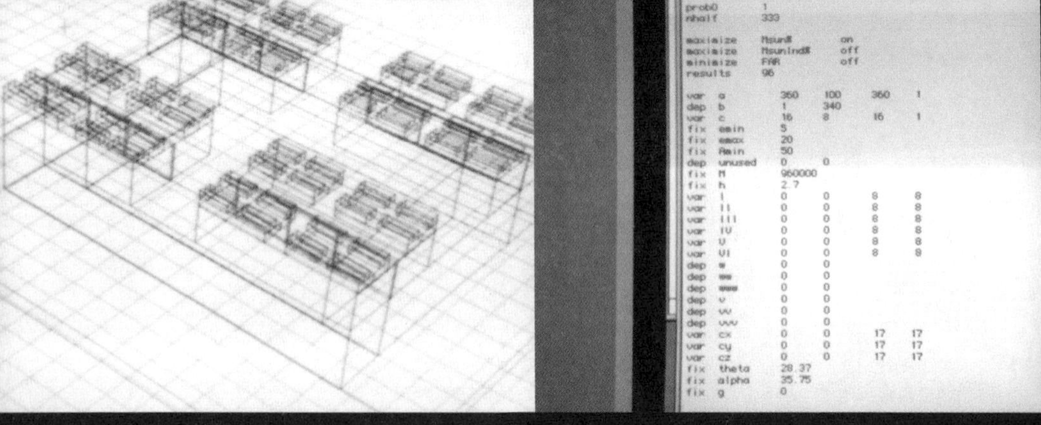

easily reach into the millions. The formula calculates an optimal result using the 'Simulated Annealing'

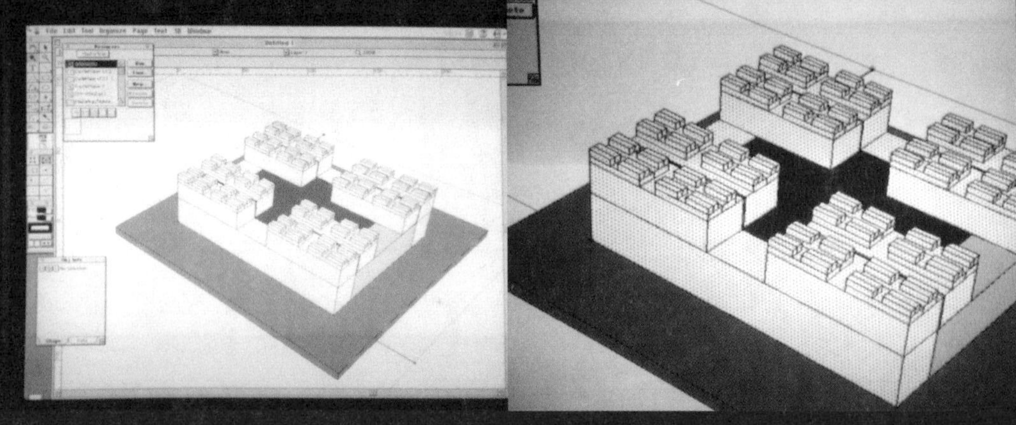

the best buildings in order of rank. Linking the outcome of this investigation with a CAD program, Castle

escribe any given manipulation resulting in the percentage of building suitable for residential (Msun),

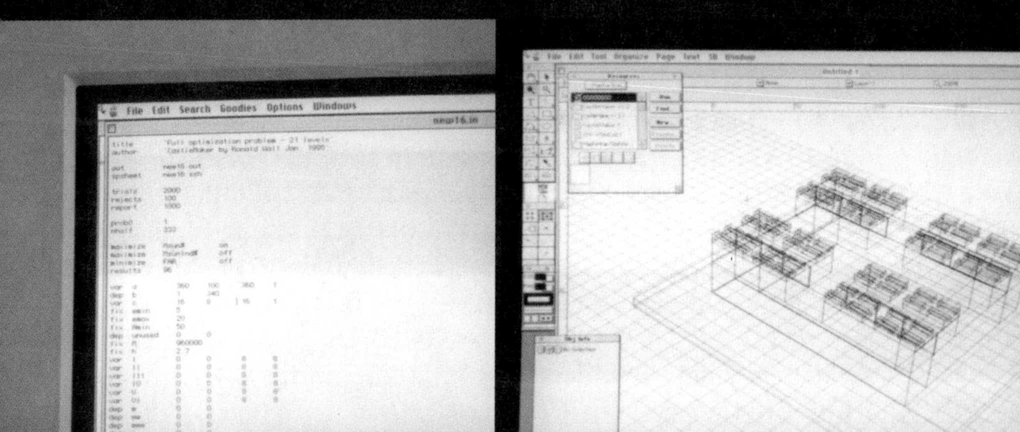

deliver a totally new result (building). The number of results (buildings) within a given assignment can

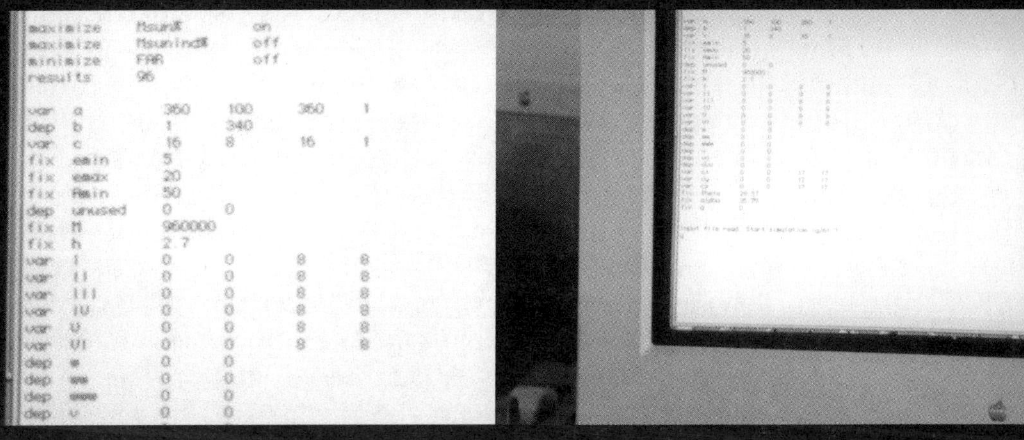

method through which it can quickly calculate millions of possible solutions, searching for and recording

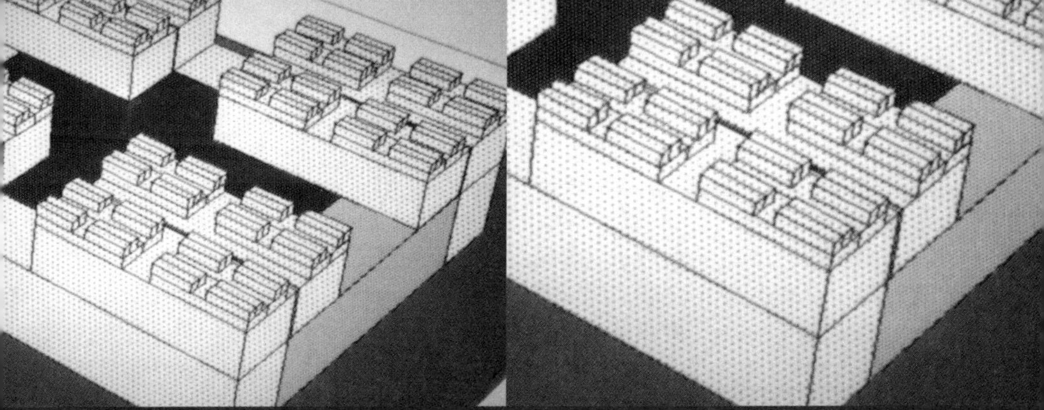

Maker automatically draws the optimized building for you.

The ultimate light formula is as follows: M(total square metres of building) = Msun(resident
cx)(2.a.({M+(a-I.((h.cx)/tan ‡))(II.((h.cx)/tan ø).cx+III.((h.cy)/tan ø).cy)-IV.((h.cy)/tan ‡
VI.((h.cz)/tan ‡).cz(II.((h.cx)/tan ø)+III.((h.cy)/tan ø)+V.((h.cz)/tan ø)) +g}/{a.c-I.((h.c
ø).cx+III.((h.cy)/tan ø).cy)-IV.((h.cy)/tan ‡).cy(II.((h.cx)/tan ø)+III.((h.cy)/tan ø)) +V.((h.c
ø)+V.((h.cz)/tan ø)) +g}/{a.c-I.((h.cx)/tan ‡).cx-IV.((h.cy)/tan ‡).cy-VI.((h.cz)/tan ‡).cz}-2.
ø)+III.((h.cy)/tan ø)) +V.((h.cz)/tan ø).cz(a-I.((h.cx)/tan ‡)-IV.((h.cy)/tan ‡))-VI.((h.cz)/tan
‡).cy-VI.((h.cz)/tan ‡).cz}.0,5))(a.0,5))]+[(({M+(a-I.((h.cx)/tan ‡))(II.((h.cx)/tan ø).cx+III.
I.((h.cx)/tan ‡)-IV.((h.cy)/tan ‡))-VI.((h.cz)/tan ‡).cz(II.((h.cx)/tan ø)+III.((h.cy)/tan ø)+V
ø))/(II+1)-2.(({M+(a-I.((h.cx)/tan ‡))(II.((h.cx)/tan ø).cx+III.((h.cy)/tan ø).cy)-IV.((h.cy)/ta
VI.((h.cz)/tan‡).cz(II.((h.cx)/tanø)+ III.((h.cy)/tan ø)+V.((h.cz)/tan ø)) +g}/{a.c-I.((h.cx)
‡))/(I+1)0,5)+(a-I.((h.cx)/tan ‡))/(I+1).2.(({M+(a-I.((h.cx)/tan ‡))(II.((h.cx)/tan ø).cx+III.(
I.((h.cx)/tan ‡)-IV.((h.cy)/tan ‡))-VI.((h.cz)/tan ‡).cz(II.((h.cx)/tan ø)+III.((h.cy)/tan ø)+V
ø))/(II+1)0,5))][(II+1)(I+1)(cx-cy)] +[(({M+(a-I.((h.cx)/tan ‡))(II.((h.cx)/tan ø).cx+III.((h
I.((h.cx)/tan ‡)-IV.((h.cy)/tan ‡))-VI.((h.cz)/tan ‡).cz(II.((h.cx)/tan ø)+III.((h.cy)/tan ø)+V.((
III.((h.cy)/tan ø))/(II+III+1)-2.(({M+(a-I.((h.cx)/tan ‡))(II.((h.cx)/tan ø).cx+III.((h.cy)/tan ø
IV.((h.cy)/tan ‡))-VI.((h.cz)/tan ‡).cz(II.((h.cx)/tan ø)+III.((h.cy)/tan ø)+V.((h.cz)/tan ø)) +
ø))/(II+III+1)0,5))((a-I.((h.cx)/tan ‡)-IV.((h.cy)/tan ‡))/(I+IV+1)0,5)+(a-I.((h.cx)/tan ‡)-
IV.((h.cy)/tan ‡).cy(II.((h.cx)/tan ø)+III.((h.cy)/tan ø)) +V.((h.cz)/tan ø).cz(a-I.((h.cx)/tan ‡)
I.((h.cx)/tan ‡).cx-IV.((h.cy)/tan ‡).cy-VI.((h.cz)/tan ‡).cz}-II.((h.cx)/tan ø)-III.((h.c
ø).cx+III.((h.cy)/tan ø).cy)-IV.((h.cy)/tan ‡).cy(II.((h.cx)/tan ø)+III.((h.cy)/tan ø)) +V.((h.c
ø)+V.((h.cz)/tan ø)) +g}/{a.c-I.((h.cx)/tan ‡).cx-IV.((h.cy)/tan ‡).cy-VI.((h.cz)/tan ‡).cz}-II.((
ø).cx+III.((h.cy)/tan ø).cy)-IV.((h.cy)/tan ‡).cy(II.((h.cx)/tan ø)+III.((h.cy)/tan ø)) +V.((h.cz
ø)+V.((h.cz)/tan ø)) +g}/{a.c-I.((h.cx)/tan ‡).cx-IV.((h.cy)/tan ‡).cy-VI.((h.cz)/tan ‡).cz}-II.
‡)-VI.((h.cz)/tan ‡))/(I+IV+VI+1)0,5)+(a-I.((h.cx)/tan ‡)-IV.((h.cy)/tan ‡)-VI.((h.cz)/tan
‡).cy(II.((h.cx)/tan ø)+III.((h.cy)/tan ø)) +V.((h.cz)/tan ø).cz(a-I.((h.cx)/tan ‡)-IV.((h.cy)/ta
‡).cx-IV.((h.cy)/tan ‡).cy-VI.((h.cz)/tan ‡).cz}-II.((h.cx)/tan ø)-III.((h.cy)/tan ø)-V.((h.
‡))(II.((h.cx)/tan ø).cx+III.((h.cy)/tan ø).cy)-IV.((h.cy)/tan ‡).cy(II.((h.cx)/tan ø)+III.((h.cy)/
III.((h.cy)/tan ø)+V.((h.cz)/tan ø)) +g}/{a.c-I.((h.cx)/tan ‡).cx-IV.((h.cy)/tan ‡).cy-VI.((
‡).cy(II.((h.cx)/tan ø)+III.((h.cy)/tan ø)) +V.((h.cz)/tan ø).cz(a-I.((h.cx)/tan ‡)-IV.((h.cy)/ta
‡).cx-IV.((h.cy)/tan ‡).cy-VI.((h.cz)/tan ‡).cz}.0,5))(a.0,5)]+[(({M+(a-I.((h.cx)/tan ‡))(II.
+V.((h.cz)/tan ø).cz(a-I.((h.cx)/tan ‡)-IV.((h.cy)/tan ‡))-VI.((h.cz)/tan ‡).cz(II.((h.cx)/tan ø
‡).cz}-II.w)/(II+1)-2.(({M+(a-I.((h.cx)/tan ‡))(II.((h.cx)/tan ø).cx+III.((h.cy)/tan ø).cy)-I
IV.((h.cy)/tan ‡))-VI.((h.cz)/tan ‡).cz(II.((h.cx)/tan ø)+III.((h.cy)/tan ø)+V.((h.cz)/tan ø)) +
I.((h.cx)/tan ‡))/(I+1)0,5).(II+1)(I+1)(cx-cy)]+[(({M+(a-I.((h.cx)/tan‡)) (II.((h.cx)/tan ø).cx+
I.((h.cx)/tan ‡)-IV.((h.cy)/tan ‡))-VI.((h.cz)/tan ‡).cz(II.((h.cx)/tan ø)+III.((h.cy)/tan ø
III.ww)/(II+III+1)-2.(({M+(a-I.((h.cx)/tan ‡))(II.((h.cx)/tan ø).cx+III.((h.cy)/tan ø).cy)-IV.((h.c
‡))-VI.((h.cz)/tan ‡).cz(II.((h.cx)/tan ø)+III.((h.cy)/tan ø)+V.((h.cz)/tan ø)) +g}/{a.c-I.
(II+III+1)0,5))((a-I.((h.cx)/tan ‡)-IV.((h.cy)/tan‡))/(I+IV+1)0,5)(II+III+1) (I+IV+1)(cy-cz)]+[((
ø)+III.((h.cy)/tan ø)) +V.((h.cz)/tan ø).cz(a-I.((h.cx)/tan ‡)-IV.((h.cy)/tan ‡))-VI.((h.cz)/tan
‡).cy-VI.((h.cz)/tan ‡).cz}-II.w-III.ww-V.www)/(II+II+V+1)-2.(({M+(a-I.((h.cx)/tan ‡))(II.((
+V.((h.cz)/tan ø).cz(a-I.((h.cx)/tan ‡)-IV.((h.cy)/tan ‡))-VI.((h.cz)/tan‡).cz(II.((h.cx)/tanø)+
‡).cz}-II.((h.cx)/tan ø)-III.((h.cy)/tan ø)-V.((h.cz)/tanø))/(II+III+V+1)0,5))((a-I.((h.cx)/tan ‡)-

re metres) + Msunind(office square metres) + Mdark(commerce square metres) Msun = [(c-h.cx)/tan ø)+III.((h.cy)/tan ø)) +V.((h.cz)/tan ø).cz(a-I.((h.cx)/tan ‡)-IV.((h.cy)/tan ‡))-‡).cx-IV.((h.cy)/tan ‡).cy-VI.((h.cz)/tan ‡).cz}.0,5)+({M+(a-I.((h.cx)/tan ‡))(II.((h.cx)/tan).cz(a-I.((h.cx)/tan ‡)-IV.((h.cy)/tan ‡))-VI.((h.cz)/tan ‡).cz(II.((h.cx)/tan ø)+III.((h.cy)/tan I.((h.cx)/tan ‡))(II.((h.cx)/tan ø).cx+III.((h.cy)/tan ø).cy)-IV.((h.cy)/tan ‡).cy(II.((h.cx)/tan ((h.cx)/tan ø)+III.((h.cy)/tan ø)+V.((h.cz)/tan ø)) +g}/{a.c-I.((h.cx)/tan ‡).cx-IV.((h.cy)/tan tan ø).cy)-IV.((h.cy)/tan ‡).cy(II.((h.cx)/tan ø)+III.((h.cy)/tan ø)) +V.((h.cz)/tan ø).cz(a-'tan ø)) +g}/{a.c-I.((h.cx)/tan ‡).cx-IV.((h.cy)/tan ‡).cy-VI.((h.cz)/tan ‡).cz}-II.((h.cx)/tan I.((h.cx)/tan ø)+III.((h.cy)/tan ø)) +V.((h.cz)/tan ø).cz(a-I.((h.cx)/tan ‡)-IV.((h.cy)/tan ‡))-).cx-IV.((h.cy)/tan ‡).cy-VI.((h.cz)/tan ‡).cz}-II.((h.cx)/tan ø))/(II+1)0,5))((a-I.((h.cx)/tan an ø).cy)-IV.((h.cy)/tan ‡).cy(II.((h.cx)/tan ø)+III.((h.cy)/tan ø)) +V.((h.cz)/tan ø).cz(a-'tan ø)) +g}/{a.c-I.((h.cx)/tan ‡).cx-IV.((h.cy)/tan ‡).cy-VI.((h.cz)/tan ‡).cz}-II.((h.cx)/tan ø).cy)-IV.((h.cy)/tan ‡).cy(II.((h.cx)/tan ø)+III.((h.cy)/tan ø)) +V.((h.cz)/tan ø).cz(a-an ø)) +g}/{a.c-I.((h.cx)/tan ‡).cx-IV.((h.cy)/tan ‡).cy-VI.((h.cz)/tan ‡).cz}-II.((h.cx)/tan ø)-((h.cy)/tan ‡).cy(II.((h.cx)/tan ø)+III.((h.cy)/tan ø)) +V.((h.cz)/tan ø).cz(a-I.((h.cx)/tan ‡)--I.((h.cx)/tan ‡).cx-IV.((h.cy)/tan ‡).cy-VI.((h.cz)/tan ‡).cz}-II.((h.cx)/tan ø)-III.((h.cy)/tan)/tan ‡))/(I+IV+1).2.(({M+(a-I.((h.cx)/tan ‡))(II.((h.cx)/tan ø).cx+III.((h.cy)/tan ø).cy)-y)/tan ‡))-VI.((h.cz)/tan ‡).cz(II.((h.cx)/tan ø)+III.((h.cy)/tan ø)+V.((h.cz)/tan ø)) +g}/{a.c- ø))/(II+III+1)0,5))][(II+III+1)(I+IV+1)(cy-cz)]+[(({M+(a-I.((h.cx)/tan ‡))(II.((h.cx)/tan ø).cz(a-I.((h.cx)/tan ‡)-IV.((h.cy)/tan ‡))-VI.((h.cz)/tan‡).cz(II.((h.cx)/tanø)+III. ((h.cy)/tan an ø)-III.((h.cy)/tan ø)-V.((h.cz)/tan ø))/(II+III+V+1)-2.(({M+(a-I.((h.cx)/tan ‡))(II.((h.cx)/tan).cz(a-I.((h.cx)/tan ‡)-IV.((h.cy)/tan ‡))-VI.((h.cz)/tan ‡).cz(II.((h.cx)/tan ø)+III.((h.cy)/tan 'tan ø)-III.((h.cy)/tan ø)-V.((h.cz)/tan ø))/(II+III+V+1)0,5))((a-I.((h.cx)/tan ‡)-IV.((h.cy)/tan V+VI+1).2.(({M+(a-I.((h.cx)/tan‡))(II.((h.cx)/tanø). cx+III.((h.cy)/tan ø).cy)-IV.((h.cy)/tan .((h.cz)/tan ‡).cz(II.((h.cx)/tan ø)+III.((h.cy)/tan ø)+V.((h.cz)/tan ø)) +g}/{a.c-I.((h.cx)/tan ø))/(II+III+V+1)0,5))][(II+III+V+1)(I+IV+VI+1)cz] Msunind=[(c-cx)({M+(a-I.((h.cx)/tan +V.((h.cz)/tan ø).cz(a-I.((h.cx)/tan ‡)-IV.((h.cy)/tan ‡))-VI.((h.cz)/tan‡).cz(II.((h.cx)/tanø)+n ‡).cz}-2.({M+(a-I.((h.cx)/tan‡))(II.((h.cx)/tanø).cx+ III.((h.cy)/tan ø).cy)-IV.((h.cy)/tan .((h.cz)/tan ‡).cz(II.((h.cx)/tan ø)+III.((h.cy)/tan ø)+V.((h.cz)/tan ø)) +g}/{a.c-I.((h.cx)/tan /tan ø).cx+III.((h.cy)/tan ø).cy)-IV.((h.cy)/tan ‡).cy(II.((h.cx)/tan ø)+III.((h.cy)/tan ø)) n.cy)/tan ø)+V.((h.cz)/tan ø)) +g}/{a.c-I.((h.cx)/tan ‡).cx-IV.((h.cy)/tan ‡).cy-VI.((h.cz)/tan)/tan ‡).cy(II.((h.cx)/tan ø)+III.((h.cy)/tan ø)) +V.((h.cz)/tan ø).cz(a-I.((h.cx)/tan ‡)--I.((h.cx)/tan ‡).cx-IV.((h.cy)/tan ‡).cy-VI.((h.cz)/tan ‡).cz}-II.((h.cx)/tanø))/(II+1)0,5))((a-y)/tan ø).cy)-IV.((h.cy)/tan ‡).cy(II.((h.cx)/tan ø)+III.((h.cy)/tan ø)) +V.((h.cz)/tan ø).cz(a-n.cz)/tan ø)) +g}/{a.c-I.((h.cx)/tan ‡).cx-IV.((h.cy)/tan ‡).cy-VI.((h.cz)/tan ‡).cz}-II.w-‡).cy(II.((h.cx)/tan ø)+III.((h.cy)/tan ø)) +V.((h.cz)/tan ø).cz(a-I.((h.cx)/tan ‡)-IV.((h.cy)/tan /tan ‡).cx-IV.((h.cy)/ tan ‡).cy-VI.((h.cz)/tan ‡).cz}-II.((h.cx)/tan ø)-III.((h.cy)/tanø))/-I.((h.cx)/tan ‡))(II.((h.cx)/tan ø).cx+III.((h.cy)/tan ø).cy)-IV.((h.cy)/tan ‡).cy(II.((h.cx)/tan .((h.cx)/tan ø)+III.((h.cy)/tan ø)+V.((h.cz)/tan ø)) +g}/{a.c-I.((h.cx)/tan ‡).cx-IV.((h.cy)/ tan tan ø).cx+III.((h.cy)/tan ø).cy)-IV.((h.cy)/tan‡). cy(II.((h.cx)/tan ø)+III.((h.cy)/tan ø)) .cy)/tanø)+ V.((h.cz)/tan ø)) +g}/{a.c-I.((h.cx)/tan ‡).cx-IV.((h.cy)/tan ‡).cy-VI.((h.cz)/tan .cy)/tan ‡)-VI.((h.cz)/tan‡))/(I+IV+VI+1)0,5) (II+III+V+1)(I+IV+VI+1)cz]

Derivation of the Formula

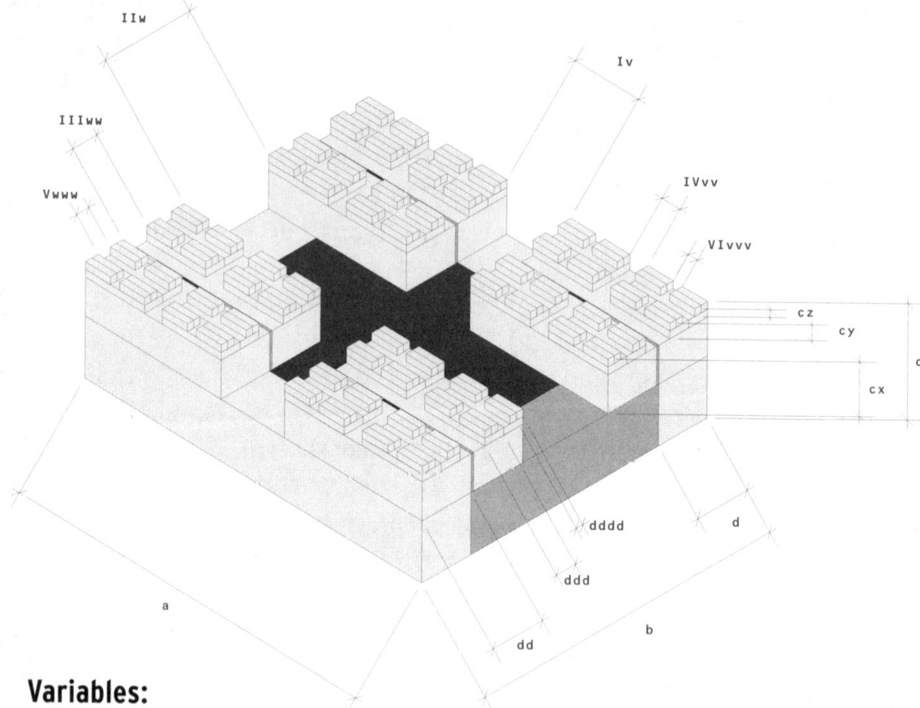

Variables:

a	= block length North to South
b	= block length East to West
c	= total no. of layers
d	= apartment depth of c-cx East to West
dd	= apartment depth of cx-cy
ddd	= apartment depth of cy-cz
dddd	= apartment depth of cz
e	= apartment depth of c-cx North to South
ee	= apartment depth of cx-cy
eee	= apartment depth of cy-cz
eeee	= apartment depth of cz
h	= apartment height
M	= Total square metres
I	= no. of v holes
II	= no. of w holes
III	= no. of ww holes
IV	= no. of vv holes
V	= no. of www holes
VI	= no. of vvv holes
w	= largest hole width E/W
ww	= medium hole width E/W
www	= small hole width E/W
v	= largest hole width N/S
vv	= medium hole width N/S
vvv	= small hole width N/S
cx	= depth of v and w
cy	= depth of vv and ww
cz	= depth of vvv and www
Ø	= angle of sun E/W
↕	= angle of sun N/S
g	= sun independent perforation

Derivation of the Formula

M = The total number of square metres of the building

Msun = The percentage of square metres (of the whole building) which has the required direct sunlight and which is suitable for residential spaces

Msunind = The percentage of square metres (of the whole building) which has indirect sunlight and which is suitable for office spaces

Mdark = The percentage of square metres (of the whole building) which has no natural sun light, but which is suitable for commercial spaces

M = Msun + Msunind + Mdark

Msun = [(c-cx)(2.a.d+(b-2.d)e)] + [((b-II.w)/(II+1)-2.dd)ee + (a-I.v)/(I+1).2.dd)] [(II+1)(I+1)(cx-cy)] + [((b-II.w-III.ww)/(II+III+1) - 2.ddd)eee+(a-1.v-IV.vv)/(I+IV+1).2.ddd)][(II+III+1)(I+IV+1)(cy-cz)] + [((b-II.w-III.ww V.www)/(II+III+V+1)-2.dddd)eeee + (a-I.v-IV.vv-VI.vvv)/(I+IV+VI+1).2.dddd)][(II+III+V+1)(1+IV+VI+1)cz]

Msunind = [(c-cx)(b-2.d)e)] + [((b-II.w)/(II+1)-2.dd)ee.(II+1)(I+1)(cx-cy)] + [((b-II.w-III.ww)/(II+III+1)-2.ddd)eee(II+III+1)(I+IV+1)(cy-cz)] + [((b-II.w-III.ww-V.www)/(II+III+V+1)-2.dddd)eeee.(II+III+V+1) (1+IV+VI+1)cz]

Width Formulas

w = ((h.cx)/tan Ø)
v = ((h.cx)/tan ‡)
ww = ((h.cy)/tan Ø)
vv = ((h.cy)/tan ‡)
www = ((h.cz)/tan Ø)
vvv = ((h.cz)/tan ‡)

Depth Formulas

Rule: If d's or e's > 20m, make 20,
If d's or e's < 2,5m cancel operation,

If d.2 = breadth of block, then the respective e = 0m
d = b.0,5
dd = (b-II.w)/(II+1)o,5
ddd = (b-II.w-III.ww)/(II+III+1)o,5
dddd = (b-II.w-III.ww-V.www)/(II+III+V+1)o,5
e = b.0,5
ee = (a-I.v)/(I+1)o,5
eee = (a-I.v-IV.vv)/(I+IV+1)o,5
eeee = (a-I.v-IV.vv-V.vvv)/(I+IV+VI+1)o,5

B Formula

b =[M+(a-I.v)(II.w.cx+III.ww.cy)-IV.vv.Cy(II.w+III.ww) + V.www.cz (a-1.v-IV.vv)-VI.vvv.cz(II.w+III.ww+V.www)+g)/(a.c-I.v.cx-IV.vv.cy-VI.vvv.cz]

Example, stage 1

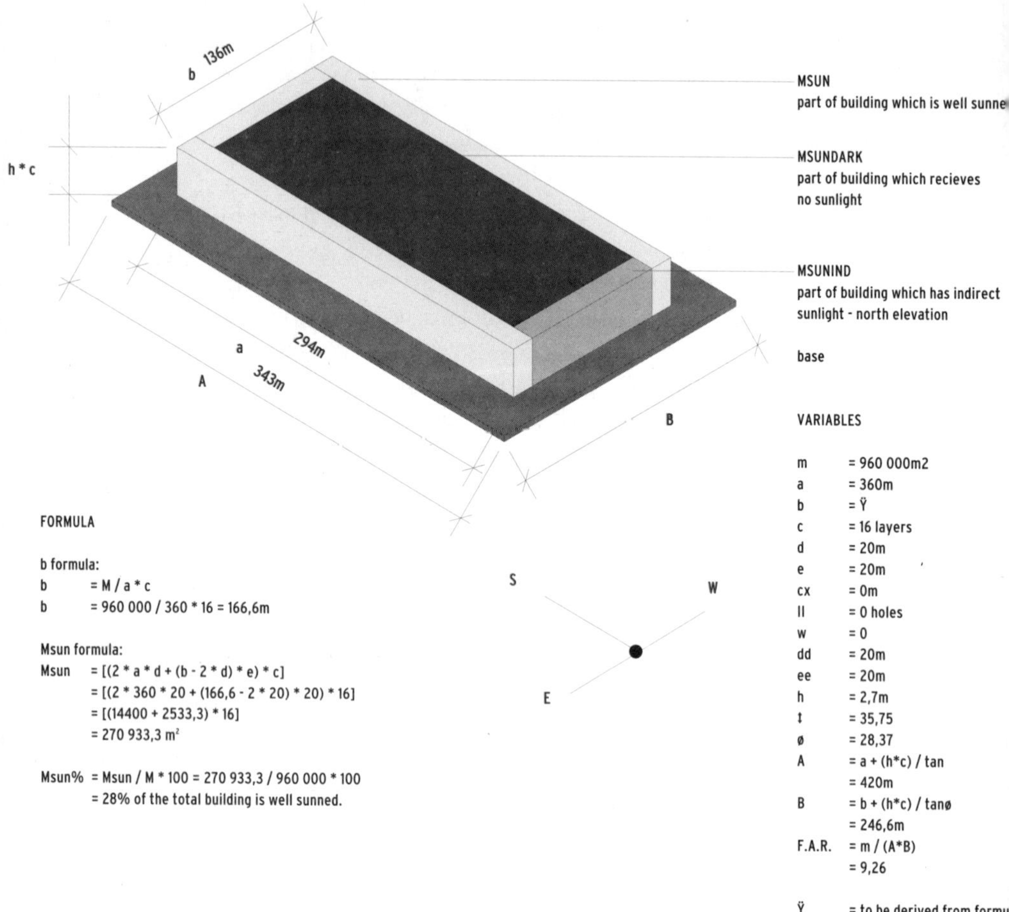

FORMULA

b formula:

b = M / a * c
b = 960 000 / 360 * 16 = 166,6m

Msun formula:

Msun = [(2 * a * d + (b - 2 * d) * e) * c]
= [(2 * 360 * 20 + (166,6 - 2 * 20) * 20) * 16]
= [(14400 + 2533,3) * 16]
= 270 933,3 m²

Msun% = Msun / M * 100 = 270 933,3 / 960 000 * 100
= 28% of the total building is well sunned.

VARIABLES

m	= 960 000m2
a	= 360m
b	= Ÿ
c	= 16 layers
d	= 20m
e	= 20m
cx	= 0m
ll	= 0 holes
w	= 0
dd	= 20m
ee	= 20m
h	= 2,7m
↕	= 35,75
ø	= 28,37
A	= a + (h*c) / tan
	= 420m
B	= b + (h*c) / tanø
	= 246,6m
F.A.R.	= m / (A*B)
	= 9,26
Ÿ	= to be derived from formu

The example consists of two stages. In stage one, there are no holes made in the building. That results in a low percentage of well sunned built area: 25%. In stage two, one hole is made in the building. The building enlarges from 166.6m to 186.6m. More sunlight is found because of the hole. The sunned percentage equals 39.16%. Obviously the more holes and the deeper the hole, the greater the sunned area. The computer does thousands of trials where it cuts out holes in both directions and in many variations. It stores the best sunned percentages found.

Example, stage 2

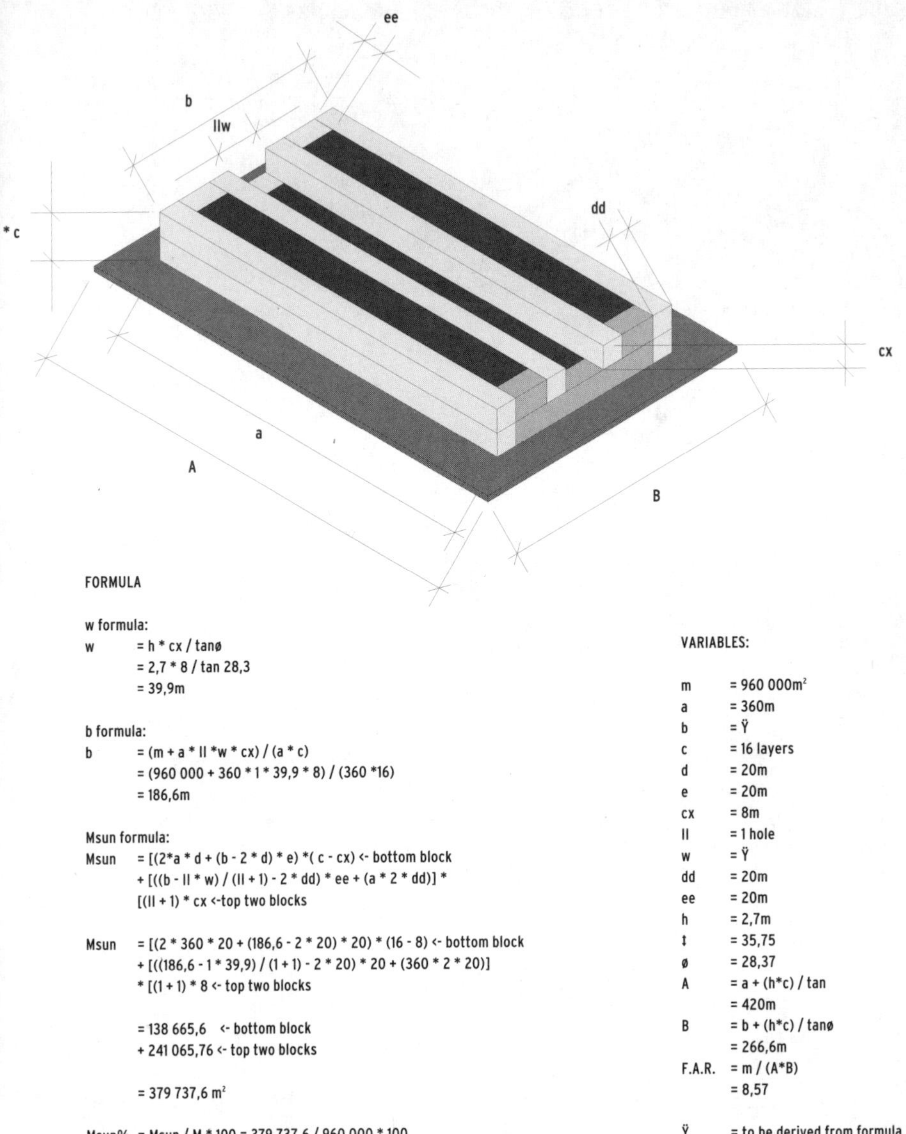

FORMULA

w formula:

w = h * cx / tanø
= 2,7 * 8 / tan 28,3
= 39,9m

b formula:

b = (m + a * ll *w * cx) / (a * c)
= (960 000 + 360 * 1 * 39,9 * 8) / (360 *16)
= 186,6m

Msun formula:

Msun = [(2*a * d + (b - 2 * d) * e) *(c - cx) <- bottom block
+ [((b - ll * w) / (ll + 1) - 2 * dd) * ee + (a * 2 * dd)] *
[(ll + 1) * cx <-top two blocks

Msun = [(2 * 360 * 20 + (186,6 - 2 * 20) * 20) * (16 - 8) <- bottom block
+ [((186,6 - 1 * 39,9) / (1 + 1) - 2 * 20) * 20 + (360 * 2 * 20)]
* [(1 + 1) * 8 <- top two blocks

= 138 665,6 <- bottom block
+ 241 065,76 <- top two blocks

= 379 737,6 m²

Msun% = Msun / M * 100 = 379 737,6 / 960 000 * 100
= 39,16 % of the total building is well sunned.

VARIABLES:

m	= 960 000m²
a	= 360m
b	= Ÿ
c	= 16 layers
d	= 20m
e	= 20m
cx	= 8m
ll	= 1 hole
w	= Ÿ
dd	= 20m
ee	= 20m
h	= 2,7m
↕	= 35,75
ø	= 28,37
A	= a + (h*c) / tan
	= 420m
B	= b + (h*c) / tanø
	= 266,6m
F.A.R.	= m / (A*B)
	= 8,57

Ÿ = to be derived from formula

Samples

Equal square metres but different cities, different sun angles

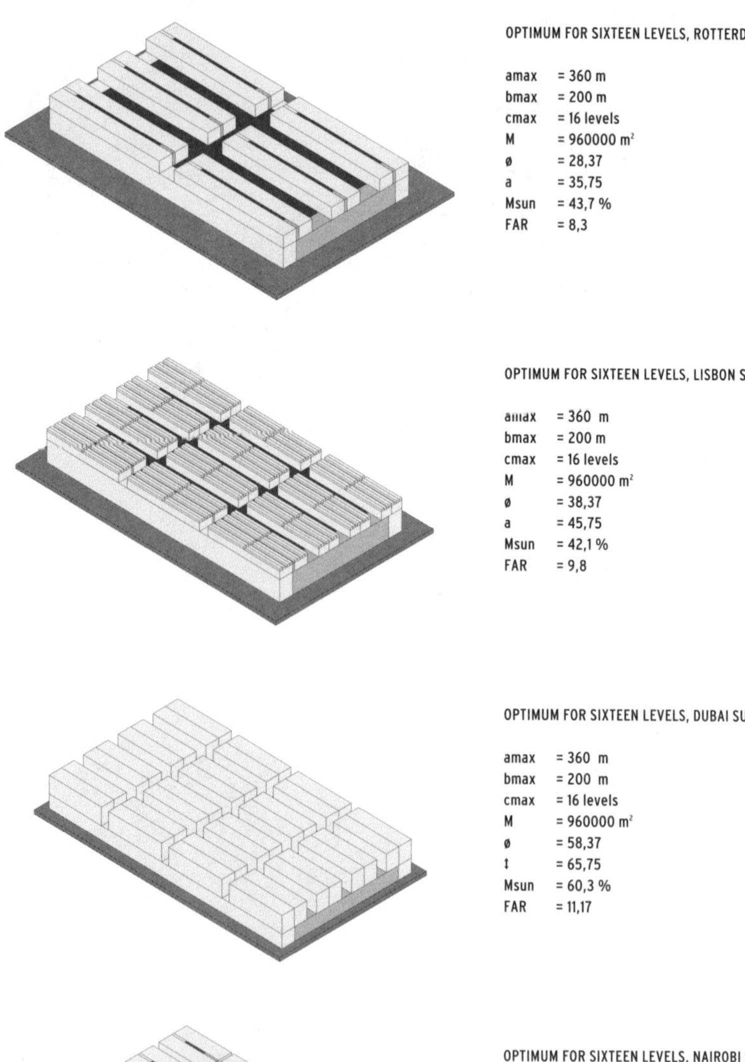

OPTIMUM FOR SIXTEEN LEVELS, ROTTERDAM SUN

amax = 360 m
bmax = 200 m
cmax = 16 levels
M = 960000 m^2
ø = 28,37
a = 35,75
Msun = 43,7 %
FAR = 8,3

OPTIMUM FOR SIXTEEN LEVELS, LISBON SUN

amax = 360 m
bmax = 200 m
cmax = 16 levels
M = 960000 m^2
ø = 38,37
a = 45,75
Msun = 42,1 %
FAR = 9,8

OPTIMUM FOR SIXTEEN LEVELS, DUBAI SUN

amax = 360 m
bmax = 200 m
cmax = 16 levels
M = 960000 m^2
ø = 58,37
t = 65,75
Msun = 60,3 %
FAR = 11,17

OPTIMUM FOR SIXTEEN LEVELS, NAIROBI SUN

amax = 360 m
bmax = 200 m
cmax = 16 levels
M = 960000 m^2
ø = 78,37
a = 85,75
Msun = 94 %
FAR = 12,6

Samples

Equal square metres but with different height restrictions

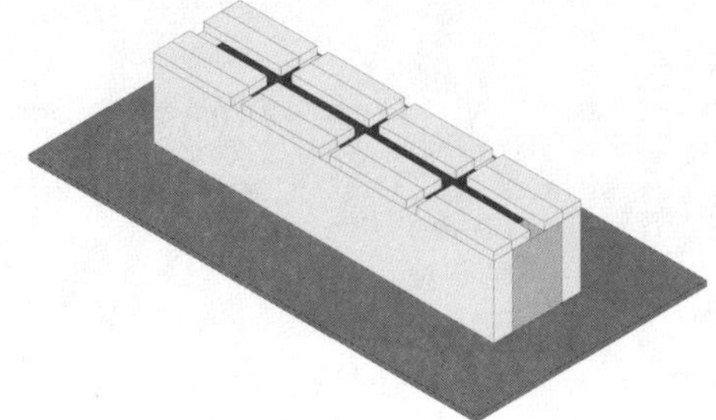

OPTIMUM FOR THIRTY LEVELS,

amax = 360 m
bmax = 200 m
cmax = 30 levels
M = 960 000 m²
ø = 28,37°
↕ = 35,75°
Msun = 51,1 %
FAR = 8,4

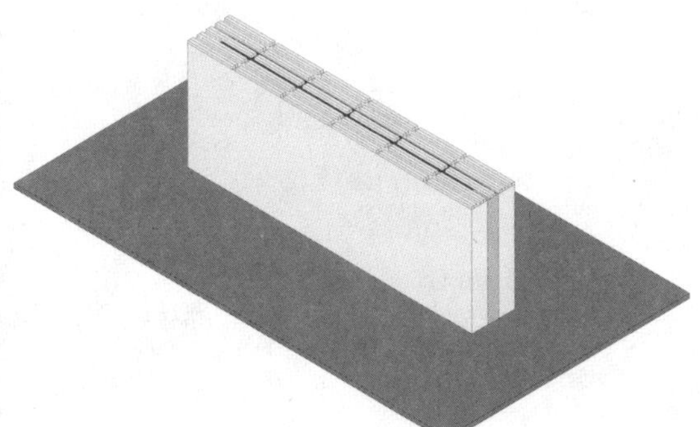

OPTIMUM FOR FIFTY LEVELS

amax = 360 m
bmax = 200 m
cmax = 50 levels
M = 960000 m²
ø = 28,37
↕ = 35,75
Msun = 76 %
FAR = 5,7

OPTIMUM FOR ONE HUNDRED LEVELS

amax = 360 m
bmax = 200 m
cmax = 100 levels
M = 960000 m²
ø = 28,37
↕ = 35,75
Msun = 100 %
FAR = 2,48

optimizer.README

Combinatorial Quasi-Optimization based on Simulated Annealing

Introduction

Simulated Annealing is a well-known method in Combinatorial Programming. It may be used to find clusters of near-optimal solutions to a combinatorial problem in a finite variable space. In that these clusters are sought by trial and error, the method represents a refinement on the better-known Monte Carlo method. One difference lies in the way a new set of trial variables is determined.

In the Monte Carlo method, the two sets are completely unrelated, each set being determined at random from scratch. In Simulated Annealing, the each new set is determined by randomly perturbing the current set. The maximum amounts by which the variable may be perturbed decline exponentially with a suitable time-like parameter (see below).

Certain trial sets of variables may be inadmissible and must be discarded. However, the equations determining the bounds on the permissible space may be highly non-linear. It is possible, for example to compute dependent parameters as functions of the trial set, and use them to determine the admissability of the set.
This contrasts starkly with the limitations of traditional direct optimization by Linear Programming (Simplex method).

If a trial set is admissable, it is ranked with respect to the current set of retained parameters using one or more suitable optimization functions. Optimalization with regard to multiple functions is complex in that it represents an attempt to determine near-optimal compromises between usually contrary demands.

If the current trial set represents an improvement on the worst of the the currently retained sets, or if that set is not yet complete, the trial set is always insert-sorted into the list of retained solutions. Otherwise, it is not retained but it is used as the basis for the next trial with a probability that declines exponentially with a suitable time-like parameter, usually related to the number of admissable trials performed. In this way, disjunct clusters of near-optimal solutions are readily found.
It is important to bear in mind that the optimization functions may be far from smooth, and that there is no guarantee that a particular cluster will be found at all. If a large number of small optimum clusters is suspected, it is recommended that the problem space be split to produce reliable results in a number of seperate optimization runs. These may later be combined to produce the full solution.

If the probability is not met then the next trial set is determined on the basis of one of the currently retained solutions, chosen at random. Combined with the exponentially declining parameters, this automatically leads to further optimization within the clusters found.

The process may be terminated when the total number of trial sets, whether admissable or not, exceeds a threshold specified by the user. Another useful criterion for termination is the number of admissable trial sets since the last improvement.

Combinatorial Quasi-Optimization based on Simulated Annealing
Copyright 1995 Rafael Seidl

Title: Full optimization problem - 30 levels
Author: CastleMaker by Ronald Wall Jan. 1995

Parameter definitions:

Parameter	Type	Value	Minimum	Maximum	Divisions
a	variable	360.000	100.000	360.000	1
b	dependent		1.000	200.000	
c	variable	30.000	2.000	30.000	1
emin	fixed	5.000			
emax	fixed	20.000			
Amin	fixed	50.000			
unused	dependent		.000	.000	
M	fixed	960000.000			
h	fixed	2.700			
I	variable	.000	.000	9.000	9
II	variable	.000	.000	9.000	9
III	variable	.000	.000	9.000	9
IV	variable	.000	.000	9.000	9
V	variable	.000	.000	9.000	9
VI	variable	.000	.000	9.000	9
w	dependent		.000	.000	
ww	dependent		.000	.000	
www	dependent		.000	.000	
v	dependent		.000	.000	
vv	dependent		.000	.000	
vvv	dependent		.000	.000	
cx	variable	.000	.000	30.000	30
cy	variable	.000	.000	30.000	30
cz	variable	.000	.000	30.000	30
theta	fixed	28.370			
alpha	fixed	35.750			
g	fixed	.000			

Simulated Annealing parameters:

Initial probability: 1.000
Half life in valid trials: 333
Maximum number of trials: 1000
Maximum number of inferior trials between improvements: 100

Output parameters:

Number of optima to be produced: 96
Number of quality functions to be considered: 3

Completed 1000 trials in all.
Completed 18 valid trials.
No improvement in last 1 valid trials.

Optimization results:

Parameter	Rank 1	Rank 2	Rank 3	Rank 4	Rank 5	Rank 6
a	360.000	360.000	360.000	360.000	360.000	360.000
b	91.102	94.023	90.563	91.111	90.723	91.315
c	30.000	30.000	30.000	30.000	30.000	30.000
emin	5.000	5.000	5.000	5.000	5.000	5.000
emax	20.000	20.000	20.000	20.000	20.000	20.000
Amin	50.000	50.000	50.000	50.000	50.000	50.000
unused	.000	.000	.000	.000	.000	.000
M	960000.000	960000.000	960000.000	960000.000	960000.000	960000.000
h	2.700	2.700	2.700	2.700	2.700	2.700
I	3.000	6.000	9.000	9.000	9.000	5.000
II	1.000	1.000	1.000	2.000	.000	3.000
III	.000	.000	.000	.000	5.000	.000
IV	.000	.000	.000	.000	1.000	.000
V	.000	.000	.000	.000	.000	.000
VI	.000	.000	.000	.000	.000	.000
w	14.999	19.999	10.000	10.000	10.000	10.000
ww	.000	.000	.000	.000	5.000	.000
www	.000	.000	.000	.000	.000	.000
v	11.252	15.002	7.501	7.501	7.501	7.501
vv	.000	.000	.000	.000	3.751	.000
vvv	.000	.000	.000	.000	.000	.000
cx	3.000	4.000	2.000	2.000	2.000	2.000
cy	.000	.000	.000	.000	1.000	.000
cz	.000	.000	.000	.000	.000	.000
theta	28.370	28.370	28.370	28.370	28.370	28.370
alpha	35.750	35.750	35.750	35.750	35.750	35.750
g	.000	.000	.000	.000	.000	.000
Msun%	51.133	50.254	49.848	49.315	49.211	49.113
MsunInd%	2.875	2.926	2.960	2.981	5.541	2.993
FAR	8.427	8.326	8.446	8.427	8.440	8.419

Parameter	Rank 7	Rank 8	Rank 9	Rank 10	Rank 11	Rank 12
a	360.000	360.000	360.000	360.000	360.000	360.000
b	89.622	89.774	100.158	91.699	89.925	93.680
c	30.000	30.000	30.000	30.000	30.000	30.000
emin	5.000	5.000	5.000	5.000	5.000	5.000
emax	20.000	20.000	20.000	20.000	20.000	20.000
Amin	50.000	50.000	50.000	50.000	50.000	50.000
unused	.000	.000	.000	.000	.000	.000
M	960000.000	960000.000	960000.000	960000.000	960000.000	960000.000
h	2.700	2.700	2.700	2.700	2.700	2.700
I	9.000	9.000	9.000	2.000	9.000	9.000
II	3.000	4.000	.000	4.000	5.000	2.000
III	.000	.000	.000	.000	.000	.000
IV	.000	.000	.000	.000	.000	.000
V	.000	.000	.000	.000	.000	.000
VI	.000	.000	.000	.000	.000	.000
w	5.000	5.000	29.999	10.000	5.000	14.999
ww	.000	.000	.000	.000	.000	.000
www	.000	.000	.000	.000	.000	.000
v	3.751	3.751	22.503	7.501	3.751	11.252
vv	.000	.000	.000	.000	.000	.000
vvv	.000	.000	.000	.000	.000	.000
cx	1.000	1.000	6.000	2.000	1.000	3.000
cy	.000	.000	.000	.000	.000	.000
cz	.000	.000	.000	.000	.000	.000
theta	28.370	28.370	28.370	28.370	28.370	28.370
alpha	35.750	35.750	35.750	35.750	35.750	35.750
g	.000	.000	.000	.000	.000	.000
Msun%	49.034	48.878	48.865	48.732	48.723	48.668
MsunInd%	2.998	3.007	3.008	3.016	3.016	3.020
FAR	8.479	8.474	8.122	8.406	8.468	8.338

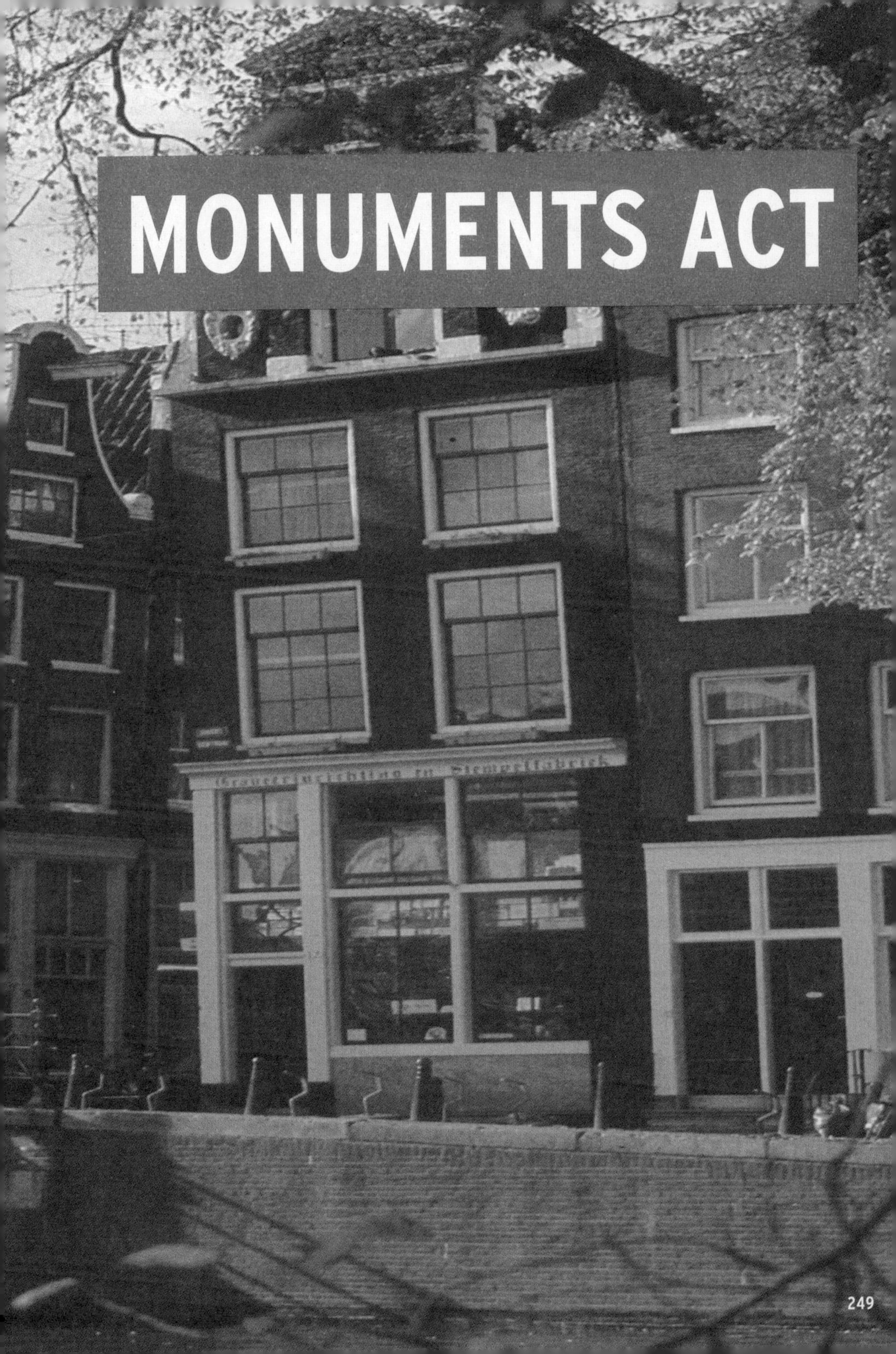

MONUMENTS ACT

Shadowtown

Competition design for the Railway station area in Bergen op Zoom, The Netherlands

1993

MVRDV

Bergen op Zoom is a beautiful medieval town in the southern part of the Netherlands that is surrounded by forests, rural hills and the Oosterschelde Bay. An untypically dutch parlour.

foto: gemeentearchief Bergen op Zoom

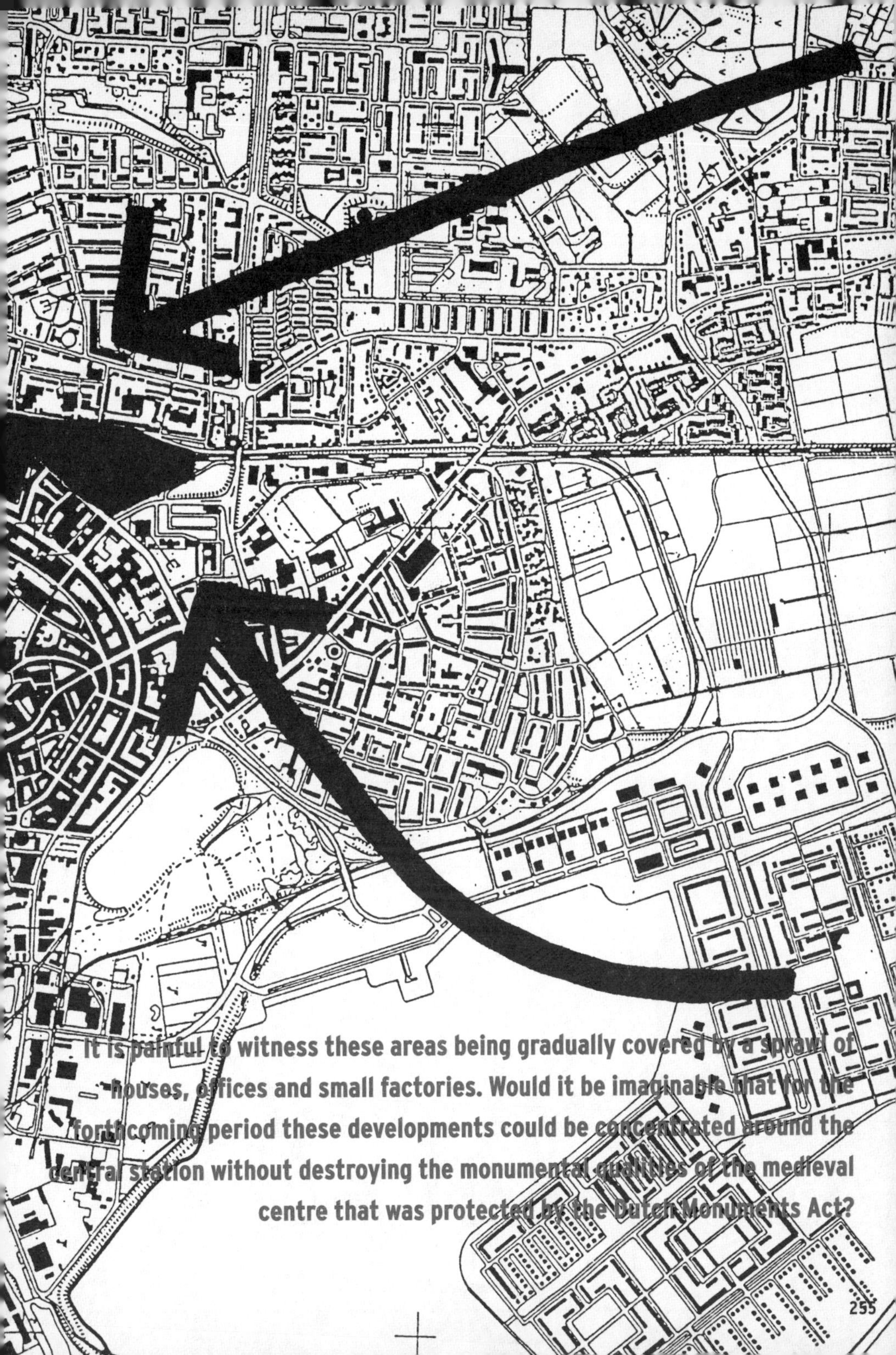

It is painful to witness these areas being gradually covered by a sprawl of houses, offices and small factories. Would it be imaginable that for the forthcoming period these developments could be concentrated around the central station without destroying the monumental qualities of the medieval centre that was protected by the Dutch Monuments Act?

This act states that new buildings in and around the centre should be so erected as to be 'invisible' from within the Protected Zone in order to preserve the character of the old town. By projecting all possible viewing lines from the old town over the planning zone, the potential envelope reaches up to eighteen storeys.

Envelope

Planning zone

1. Grote markt
2. Kerkstraat
3. Zuivelstraat
4. Passage
5. Stationsstraat
6. Meeussenstraat
7. Rijksweg A58
8. Iepstraat
9. Randweg oost

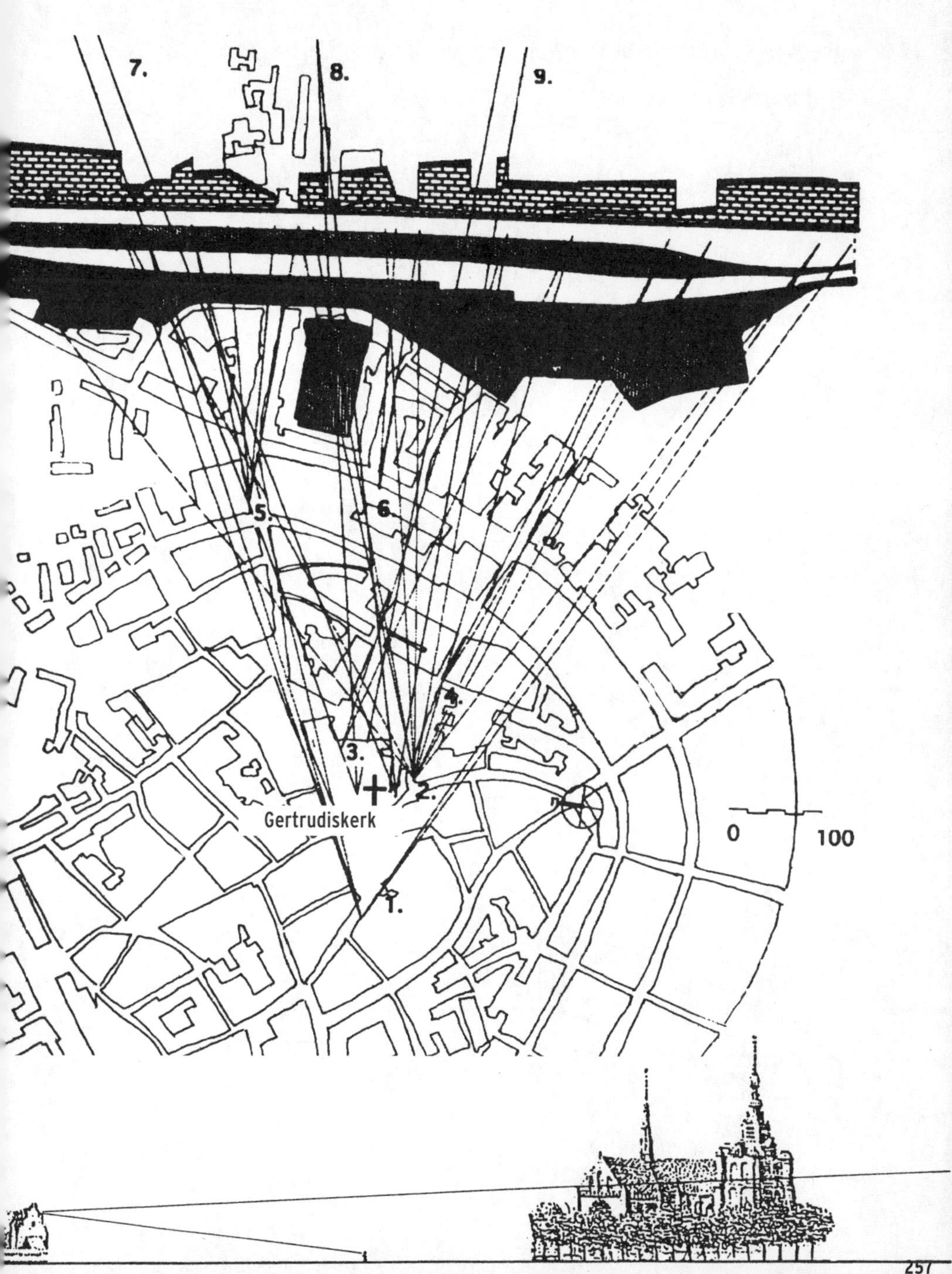
7.
8.
9.
5.
6.
4.
3.
2.
Gertrudiskerk
1.
0
100

This envelope is to contain the building production in the Bergen op Zoom region for decades to come!

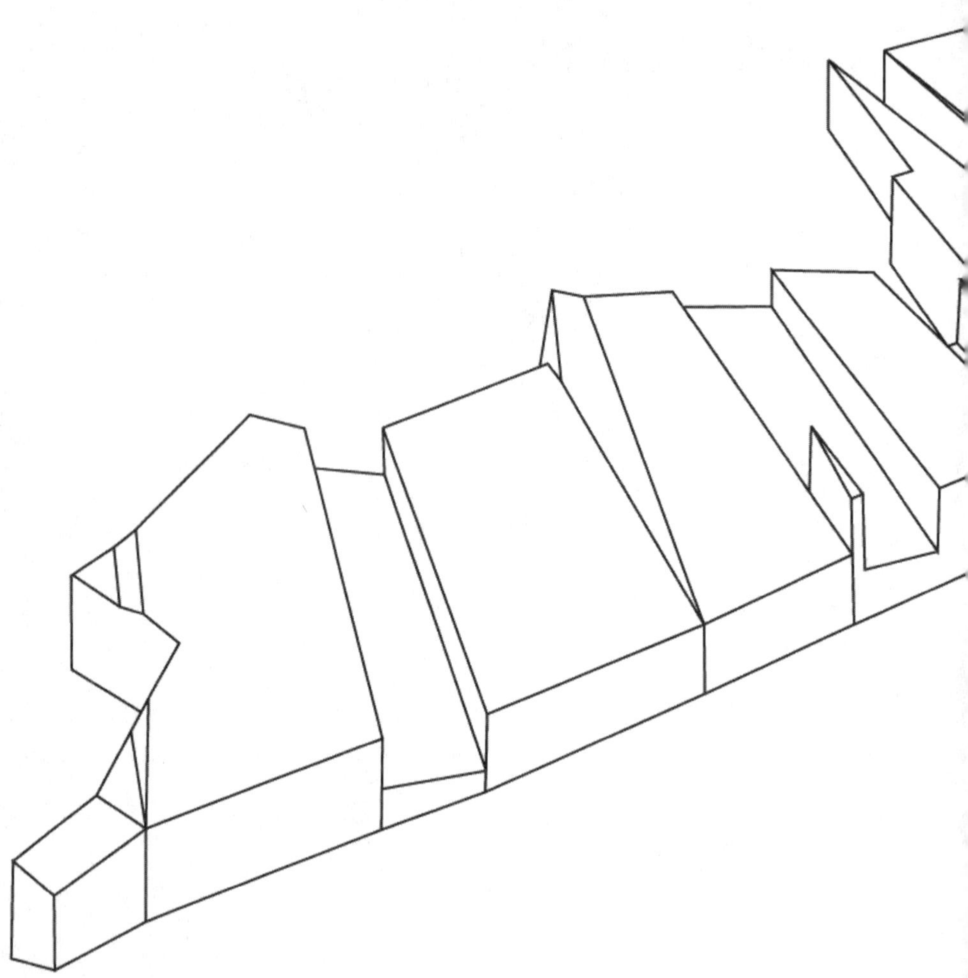

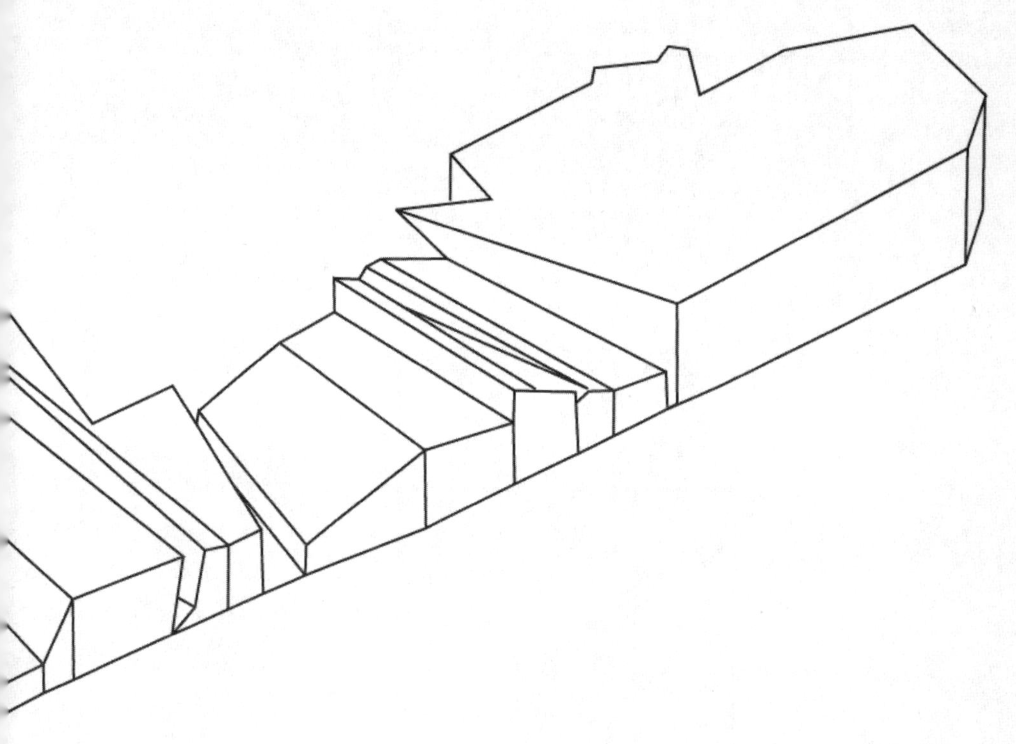

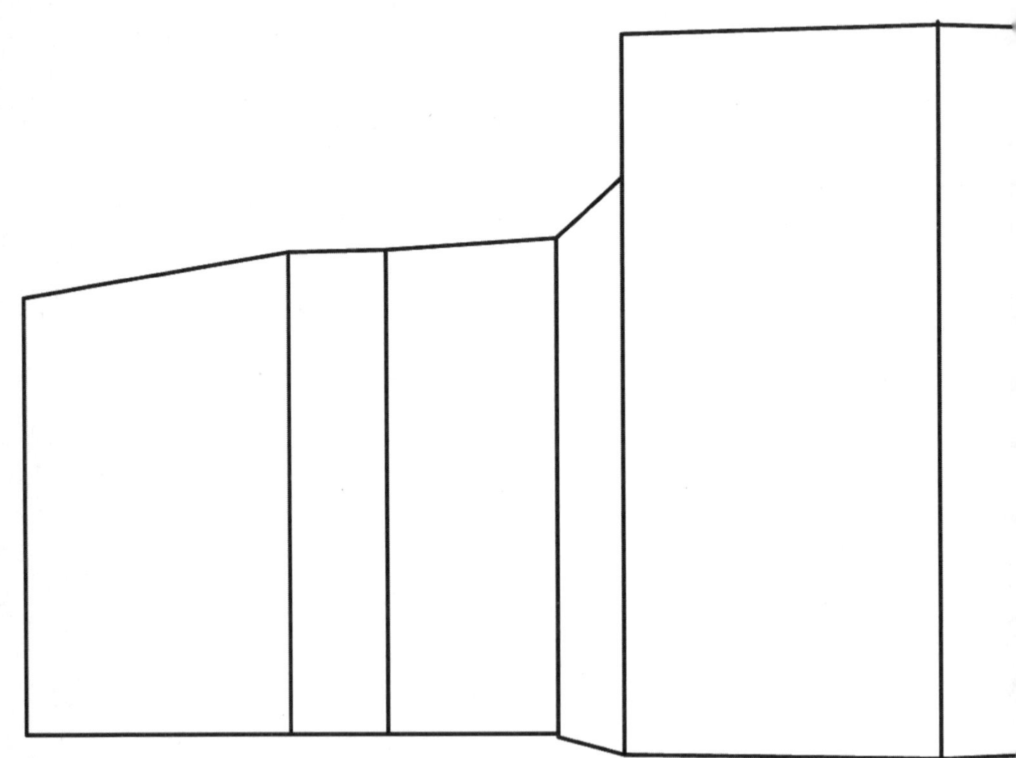

The envelope creates streets that defy all imagining.

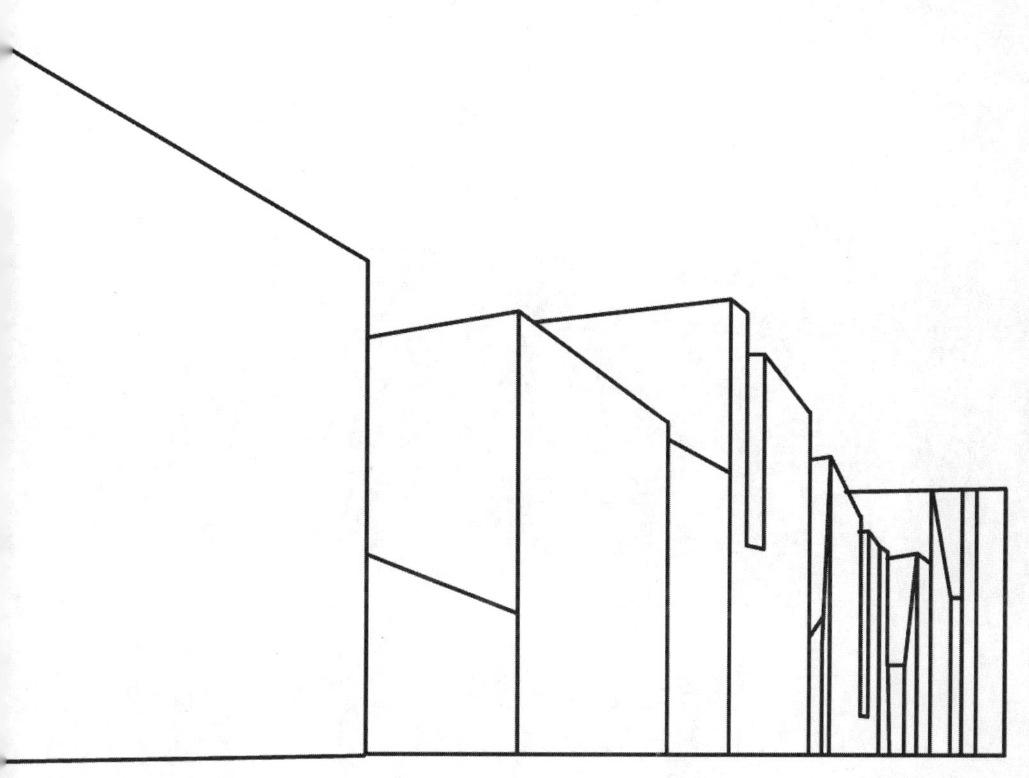

The potential mass manifests itself as a mountain of hidden modernity, the shadow of the 'eternal idyll' of Bergen op Zoom.

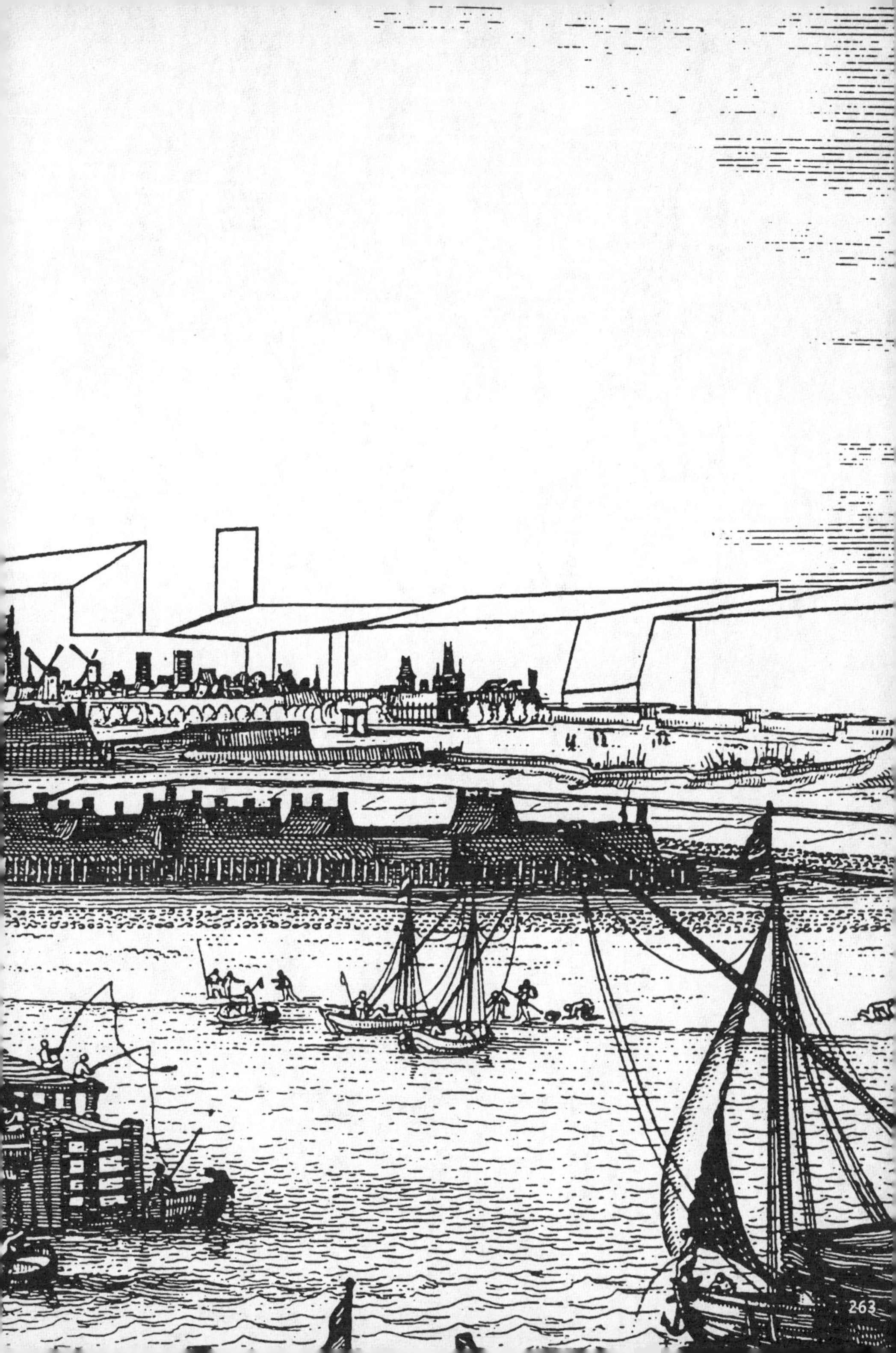

Gothics

Design study for densification of the centre of Amsterdam, The Netherlands

1996

MVRDV

The inner courts of the old European towns have up till now been exempted from giant programmes. But the success formula of shopping in authenticity is gradually turning these centres into European variants on malls. Supermarkets, Chinese restaurants, megastores, department stores and parking garages are encroaching upon and violating the interiors of the blocks, keeping the ancient facades upright as precious elements of a successful marketing strategy, as masks for modernity. But how far can we densify these areas without destroying their illusion?

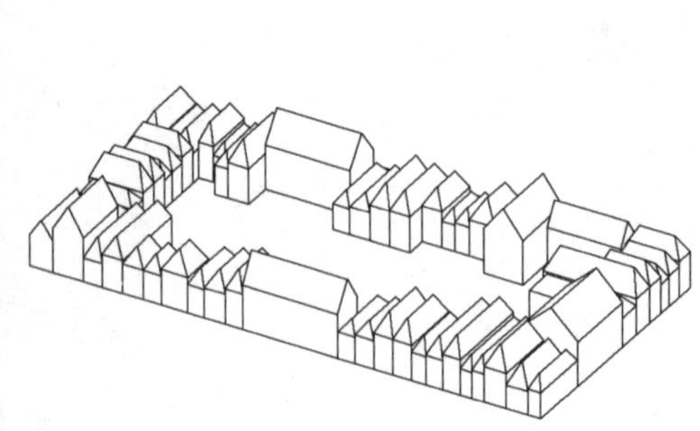

1. 18th century block
FAR = 0,8

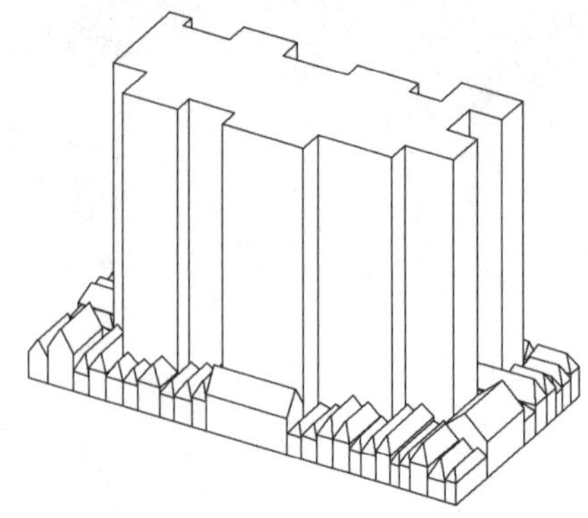

2. extrusion of the inner court

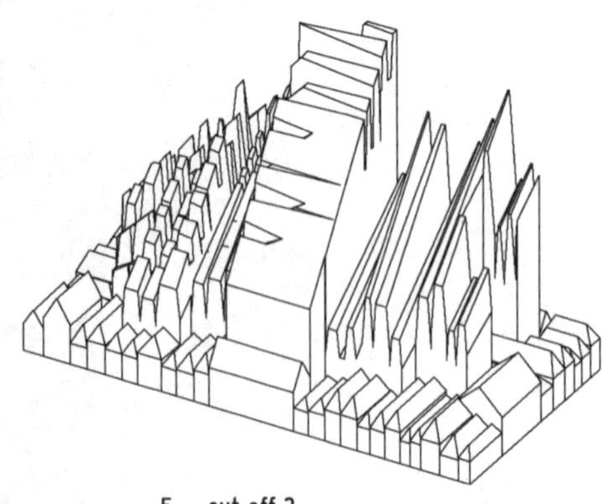

5. cut off 2

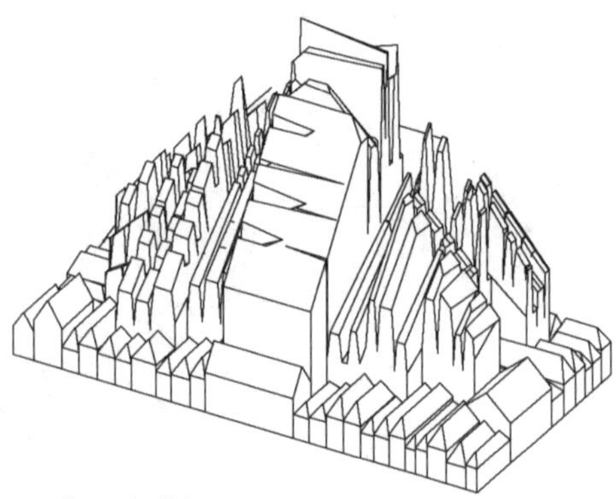

6. cut off 3

By projecting all possible viewing lines from the medieval streets over these blocks, a potential maximum envelope can be considered, that multiplies the existing density.

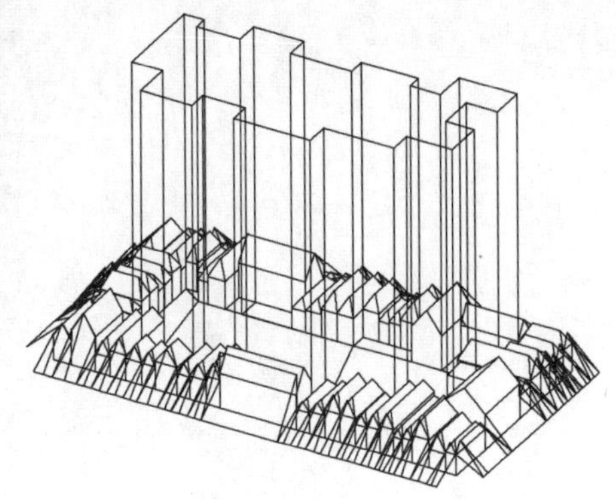

3. viewlines from the street

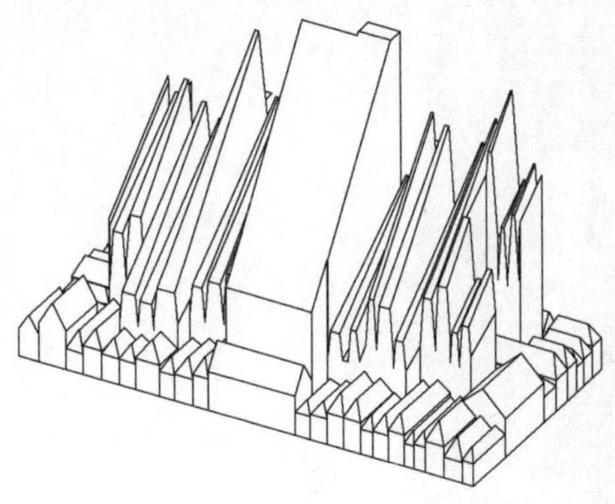

4. cut off 1

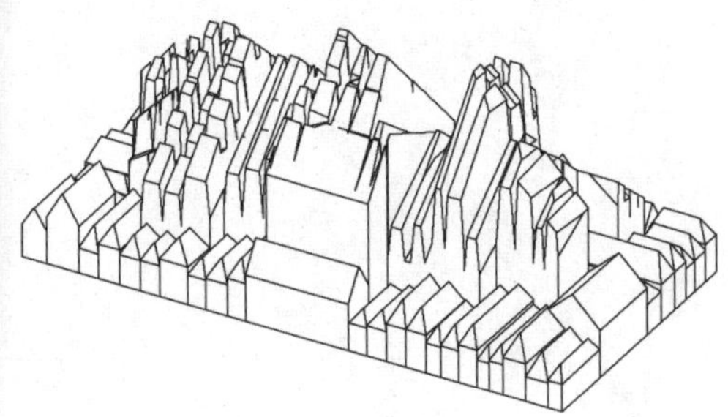

7. cut off 4

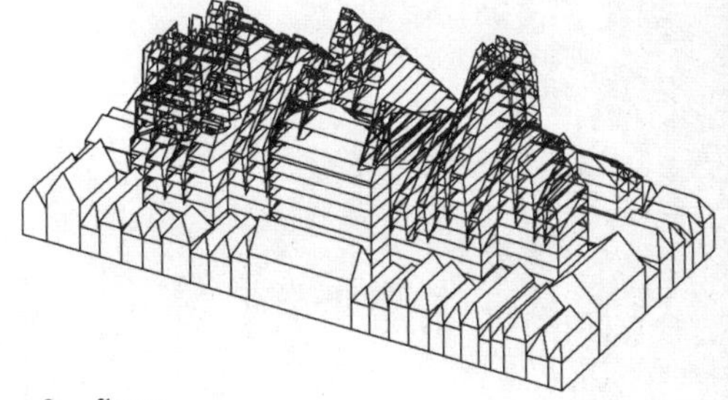

8. floors
FAR = 7.8

This envelope echoes the configuration of the classical buildings with invisible'Mont Saint Michels'

that have an even more Gothic air than the originals.

Pompeiian Carpet

Urban study for Molensloot, The Hague, The Netherlands

1994

MVRDV

How are we to densify the monumental urban compositions of the 1930s by Van Eesteren and others without destroying their delicate qualities?

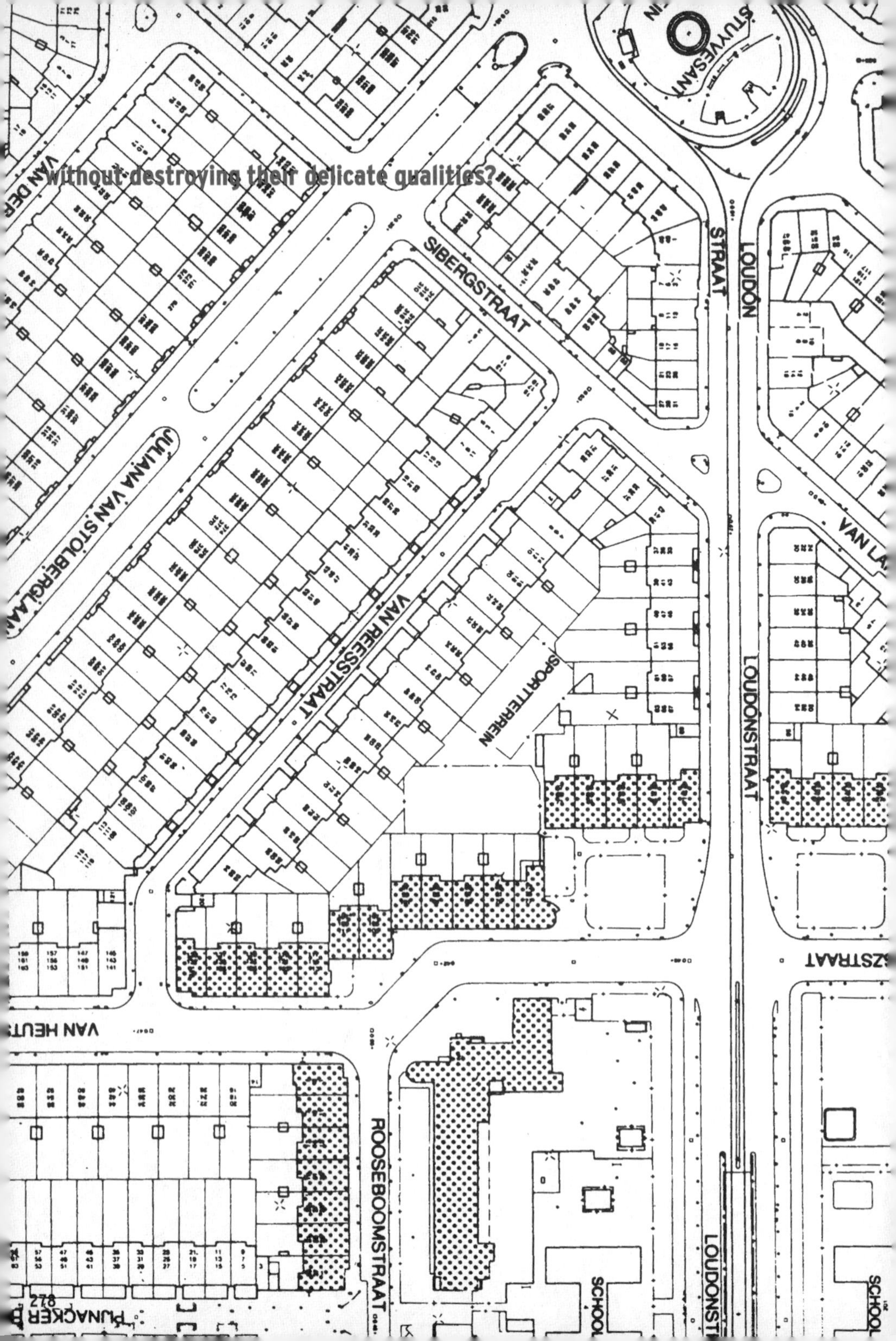

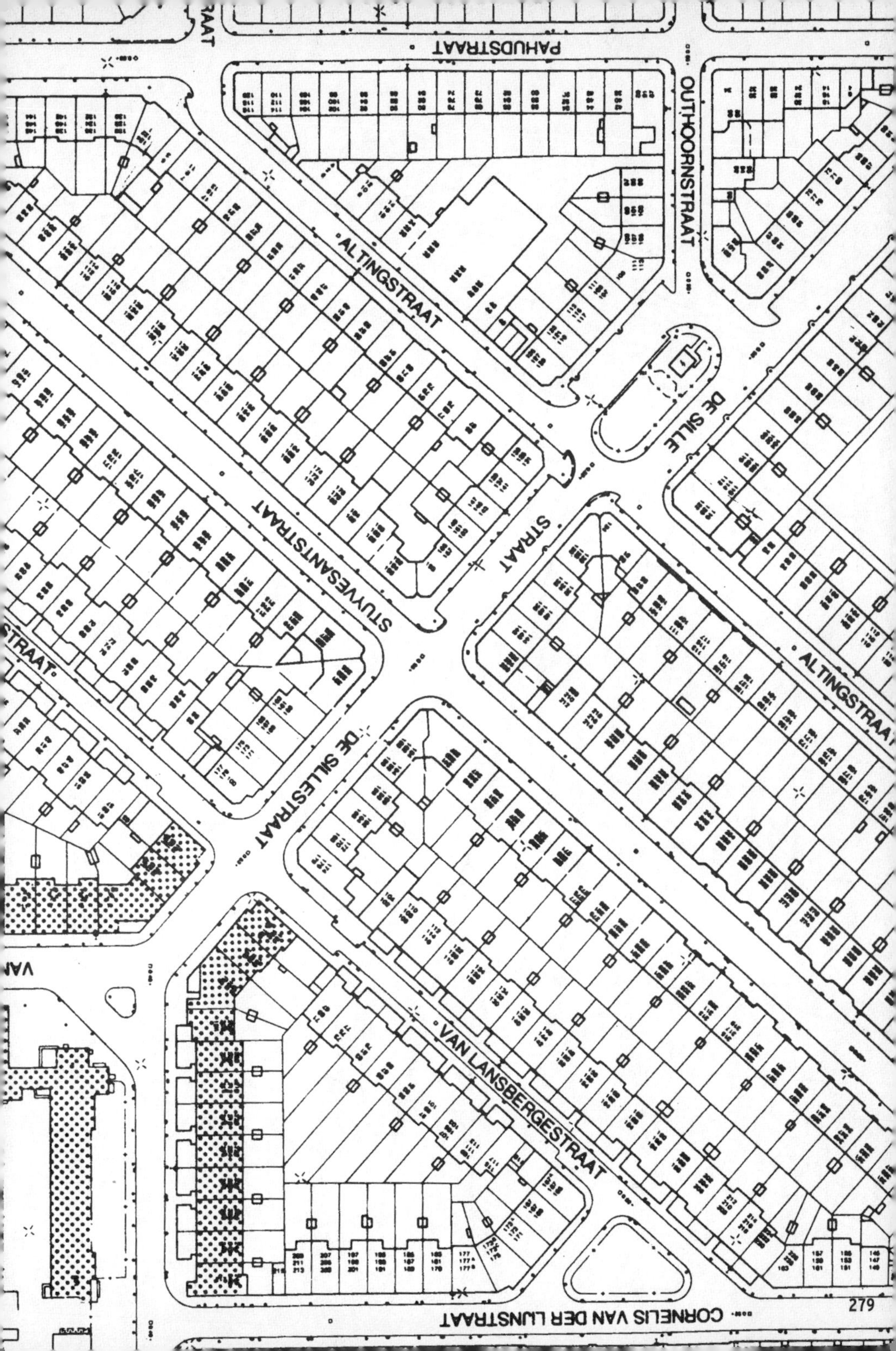
PAHUDSTRAAT
OUTHOORNSTRAAT
ALTINGSTRAAT
STUYVESANTSTRAAT
STRAAT
DE SILLE
ALTINGSTRAAT
DE SILLESTRAAT
STRAAT
VAN
VAN LANSBERGESTRAAT
CORNELIS VAN DER LIJNSTRAAT

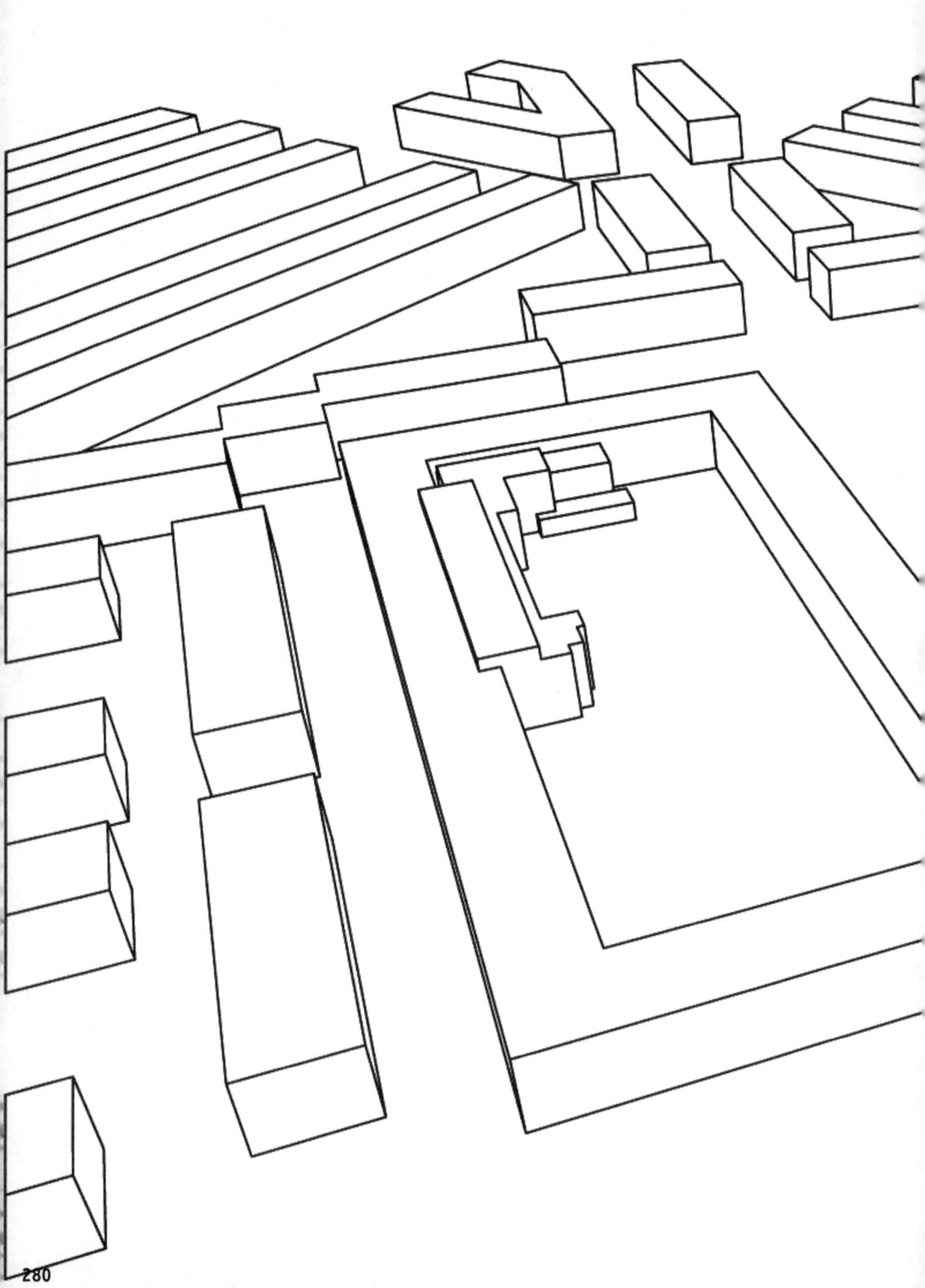

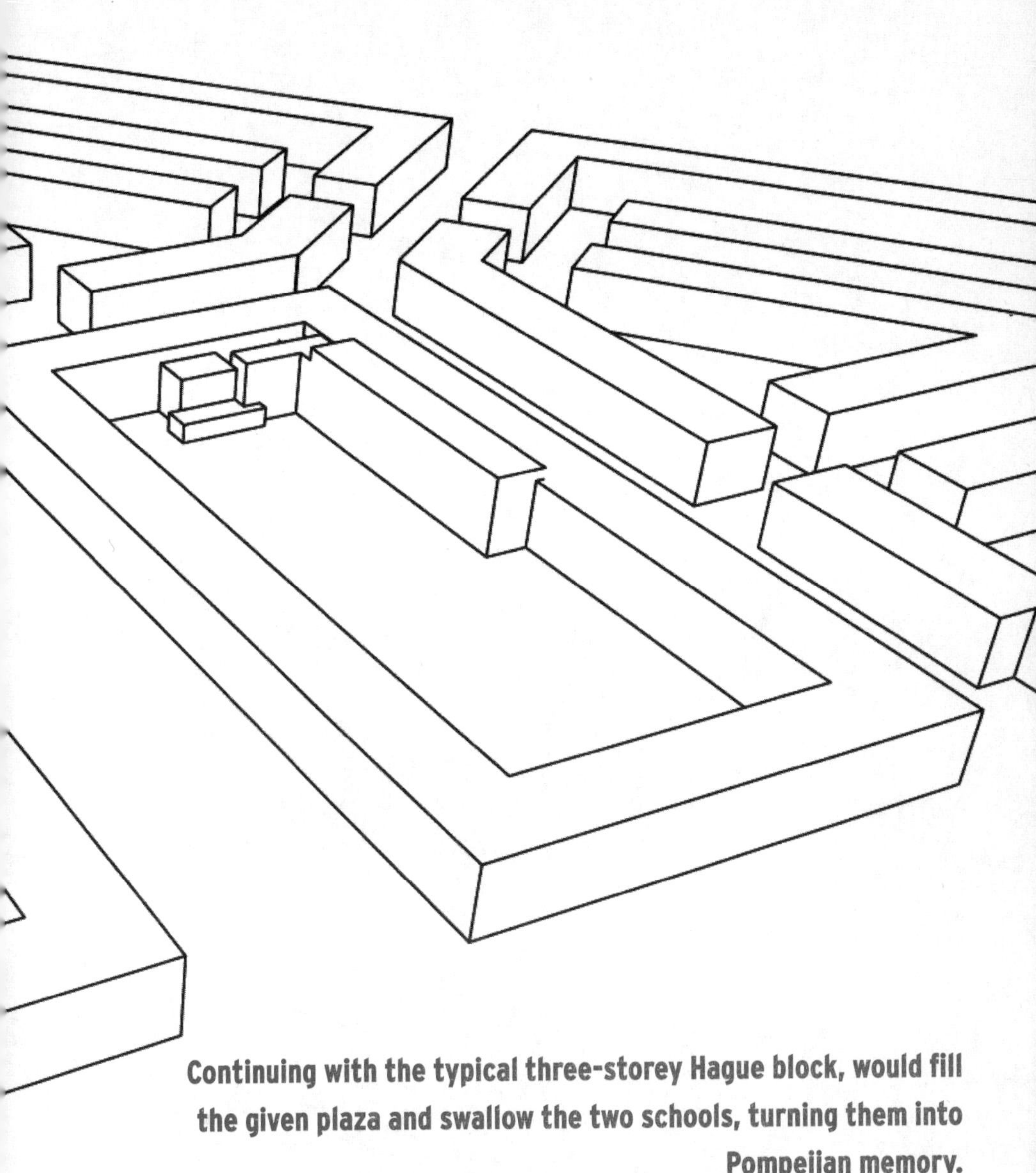

Continuing with the typical three-storey Hague block, would fill the given plaza and swallow the two schools, turning them into Pompeiian memory.

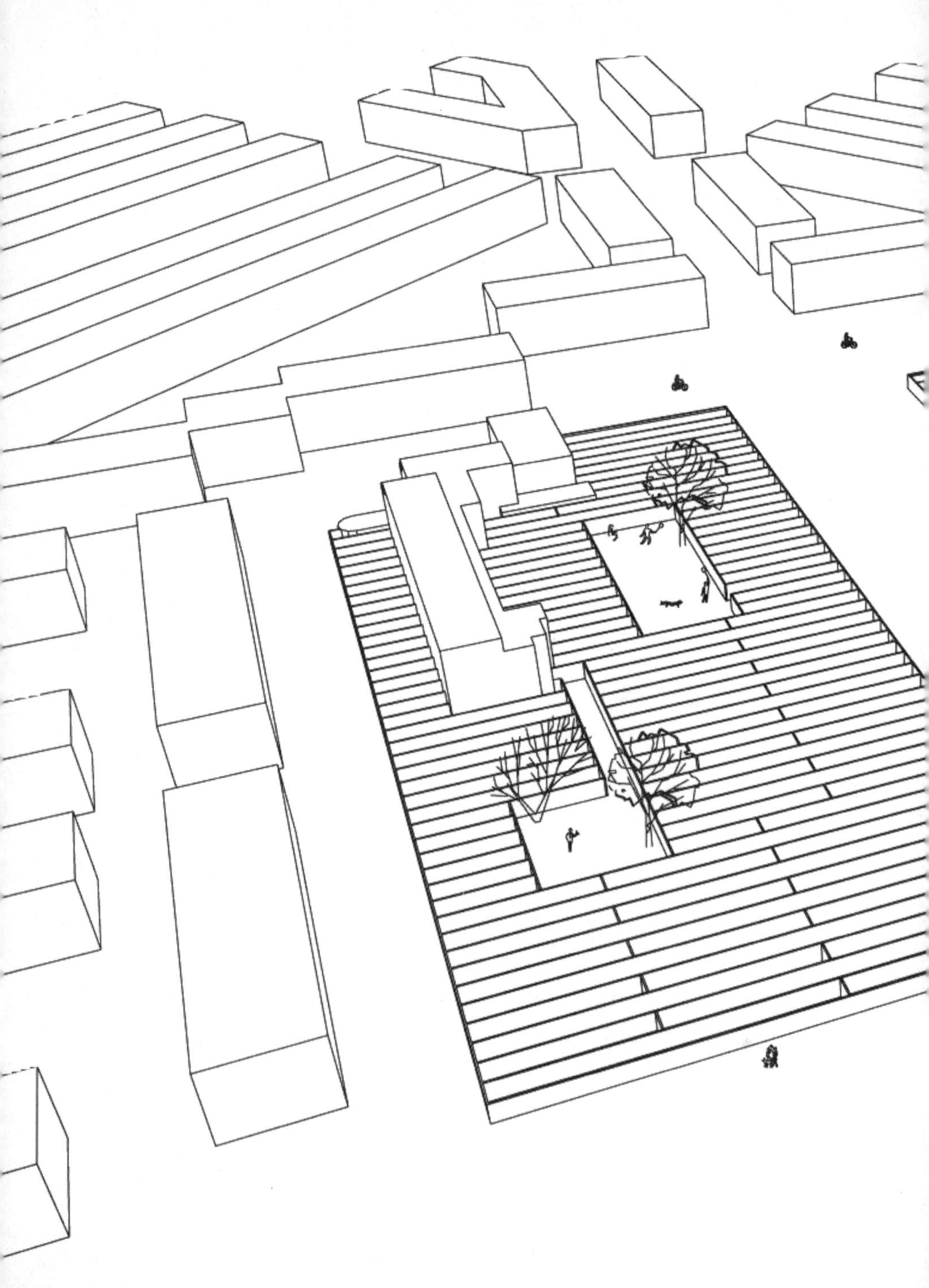

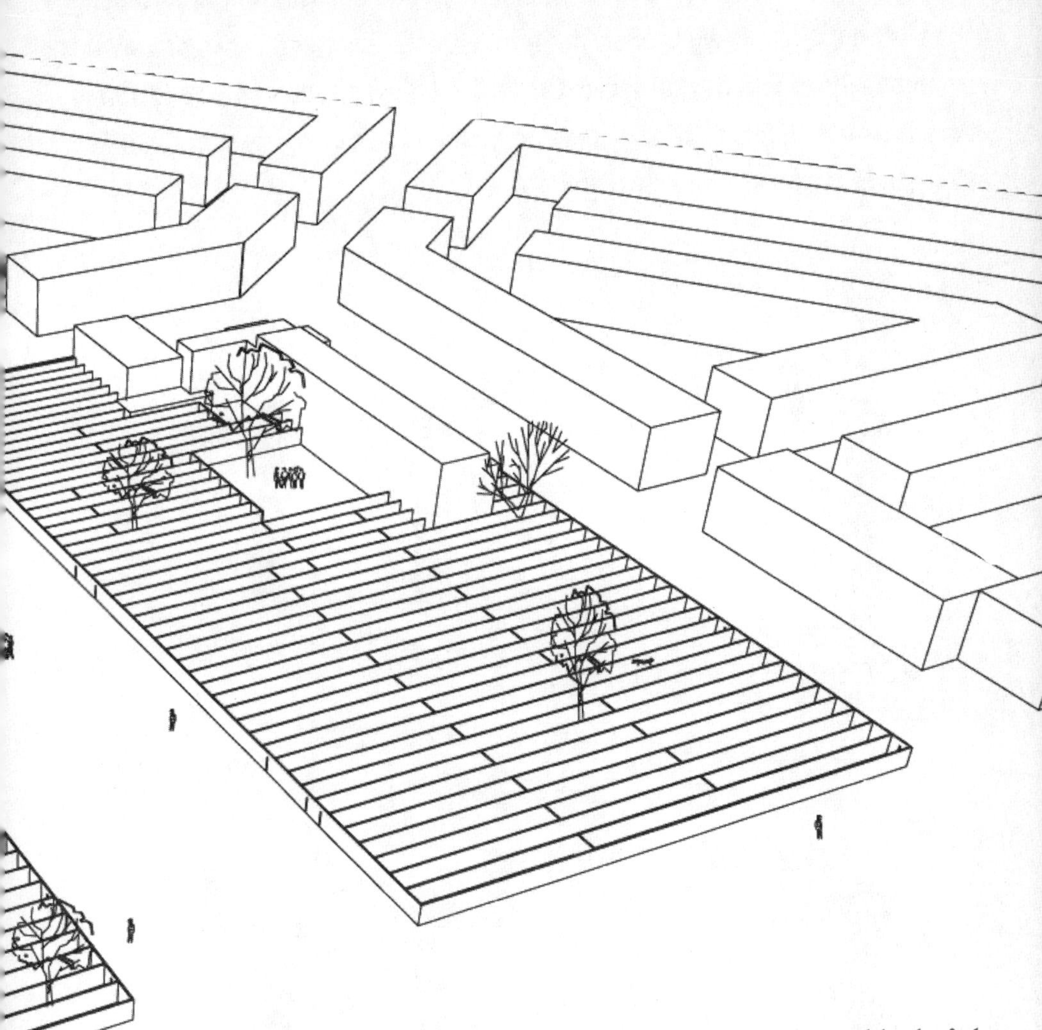

In turning the existing Hague envelope of three-storey blocks into an allotment garden-like 'carpet' of dwellings, the existing monumental school buildings, also designed by Van Eesteren, end up surrounded by a three metre high 'plinth'. These monuments rise phoenix-like from this new volume. The monumental composition of the urban space has been preserved.

Since the roof can be regarded as the main facade and window, architecture will manifest itself only through its interior. This 'chopped urbanism' avoids any competitive architectural representation. Every type of parcellation, every type of 'idealism' can be imagined, since the cut-off connects all differences : it turns them into one object.

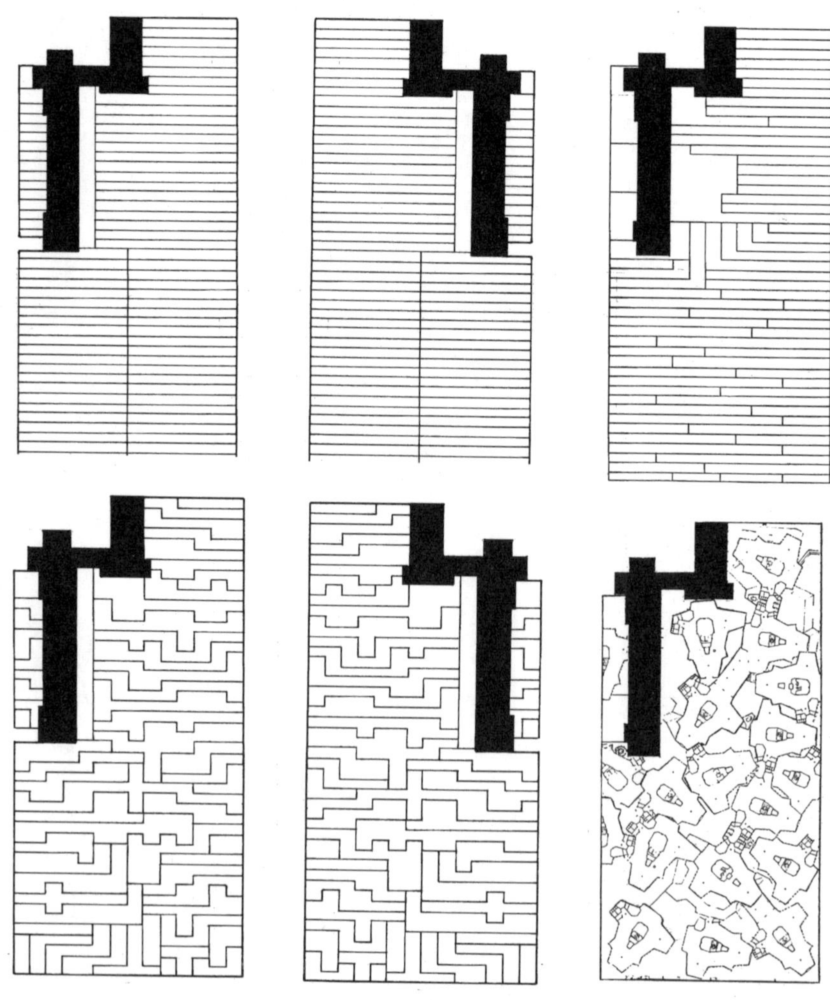

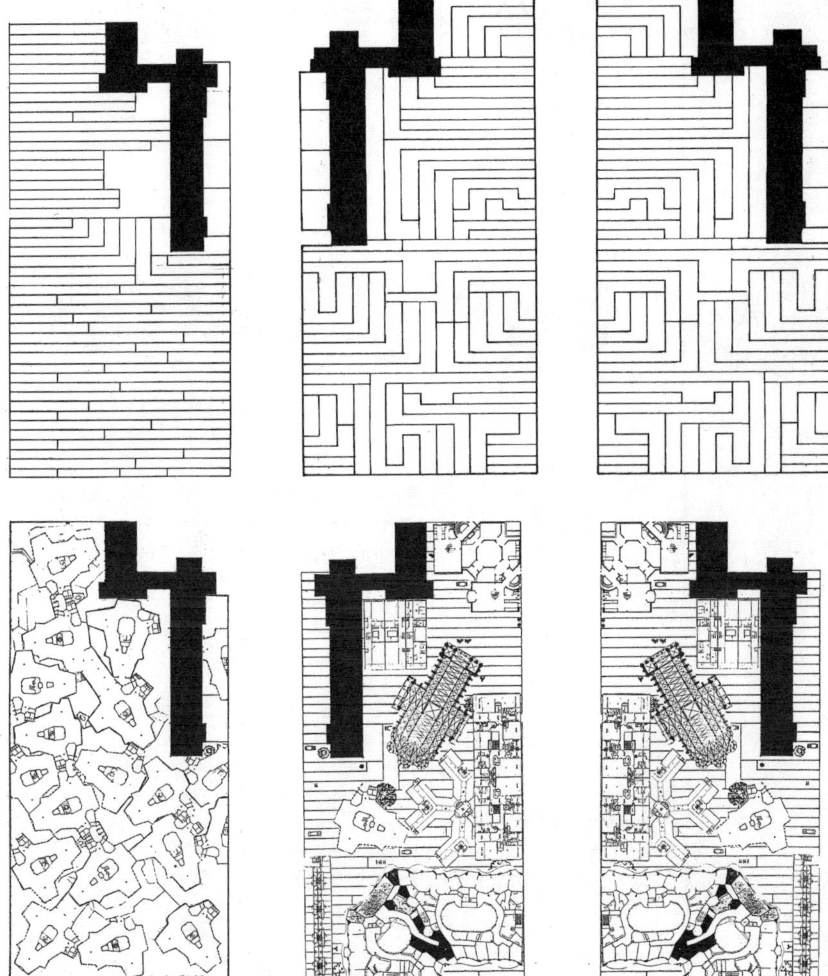

In the proposed plan, long narrow houses with glass roofs connect the streets with the public gardens.

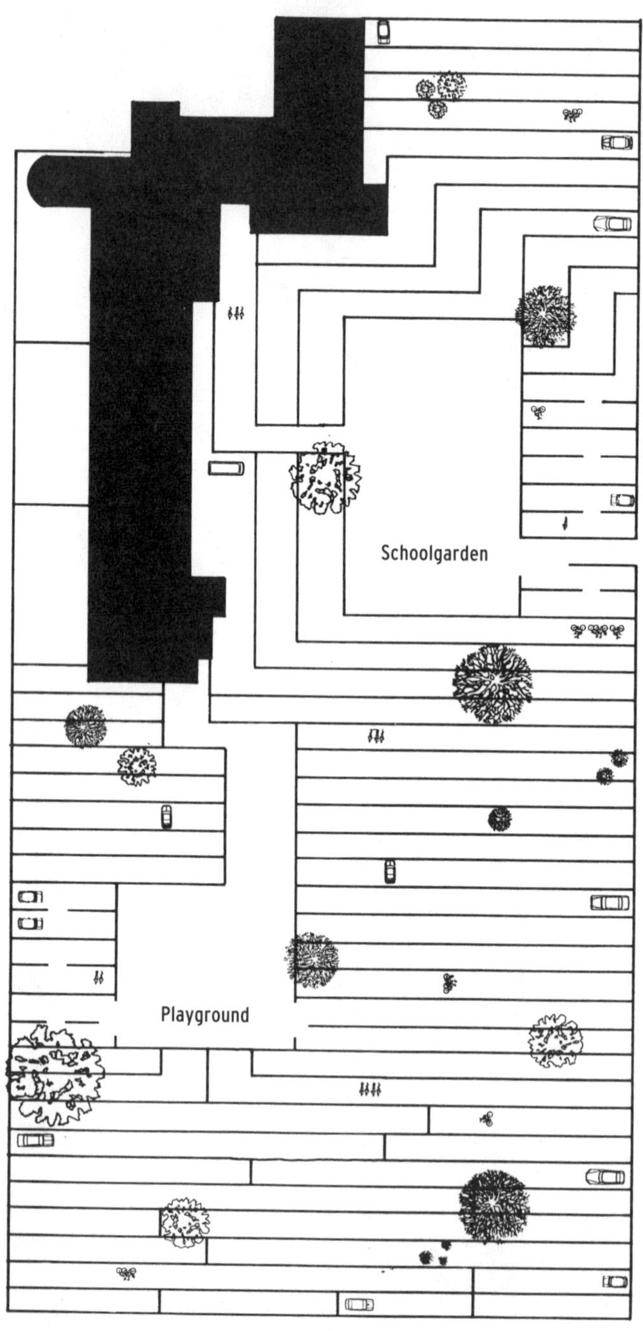

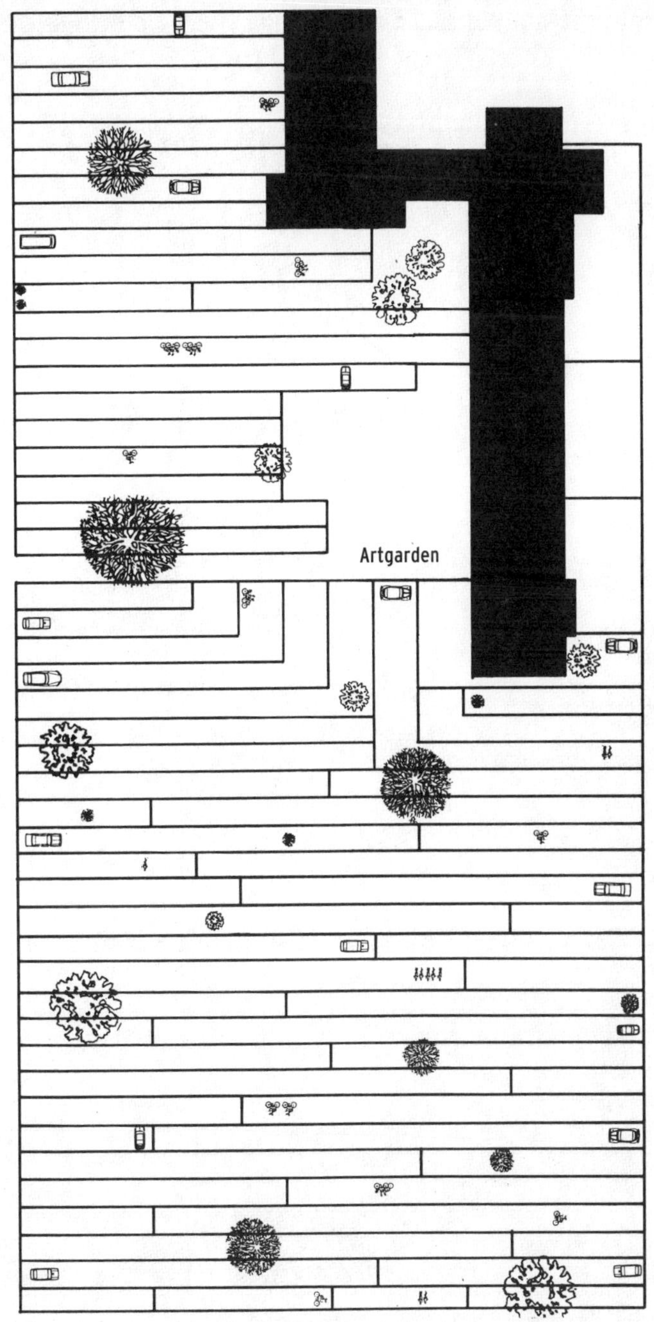
Artgarden

Existing trees and shrubs can be easily maintained in this lowness, leading to unexpected charactarizations of the houses. They can be used as special elements within the houses and that will give them a distinguishing character:

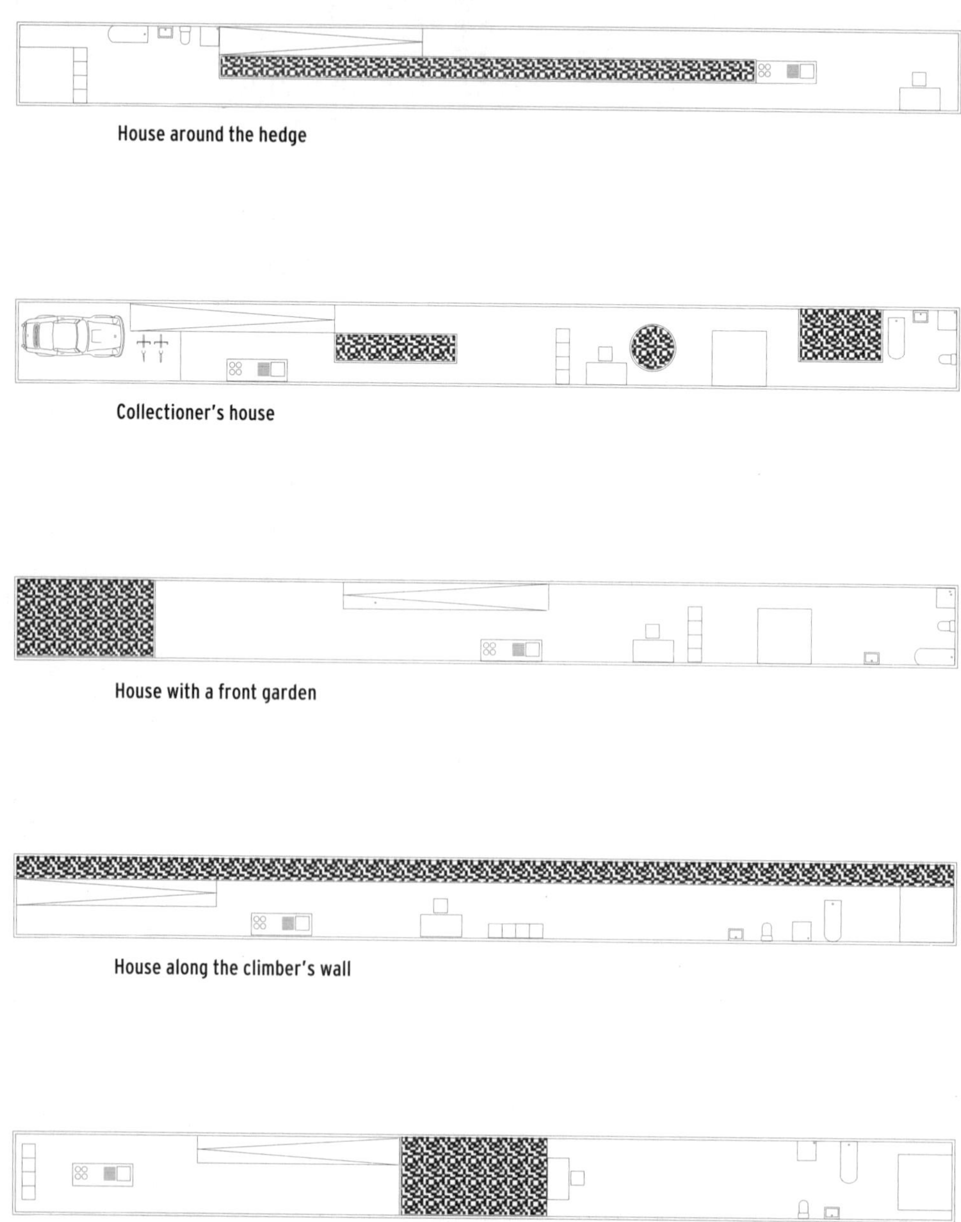

House around the hedge

Collectioner's house

House with a front garden

House along the climber's wall

House with a garden-house

Patio house

House with a back garden

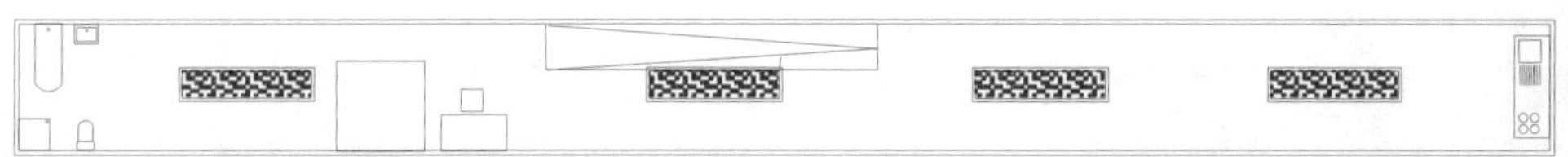

House under the plane trees

House within the forest

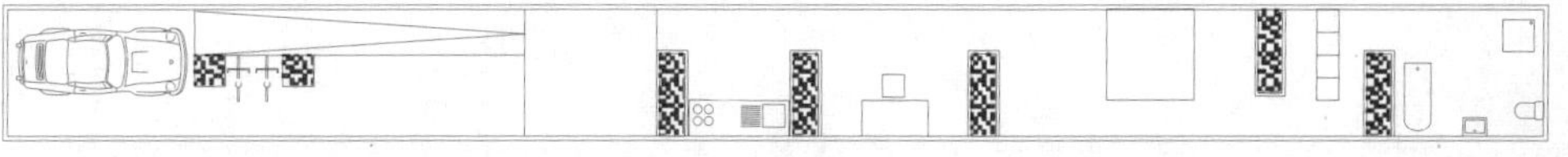

Hedge house

Within this potential claustrophobia,

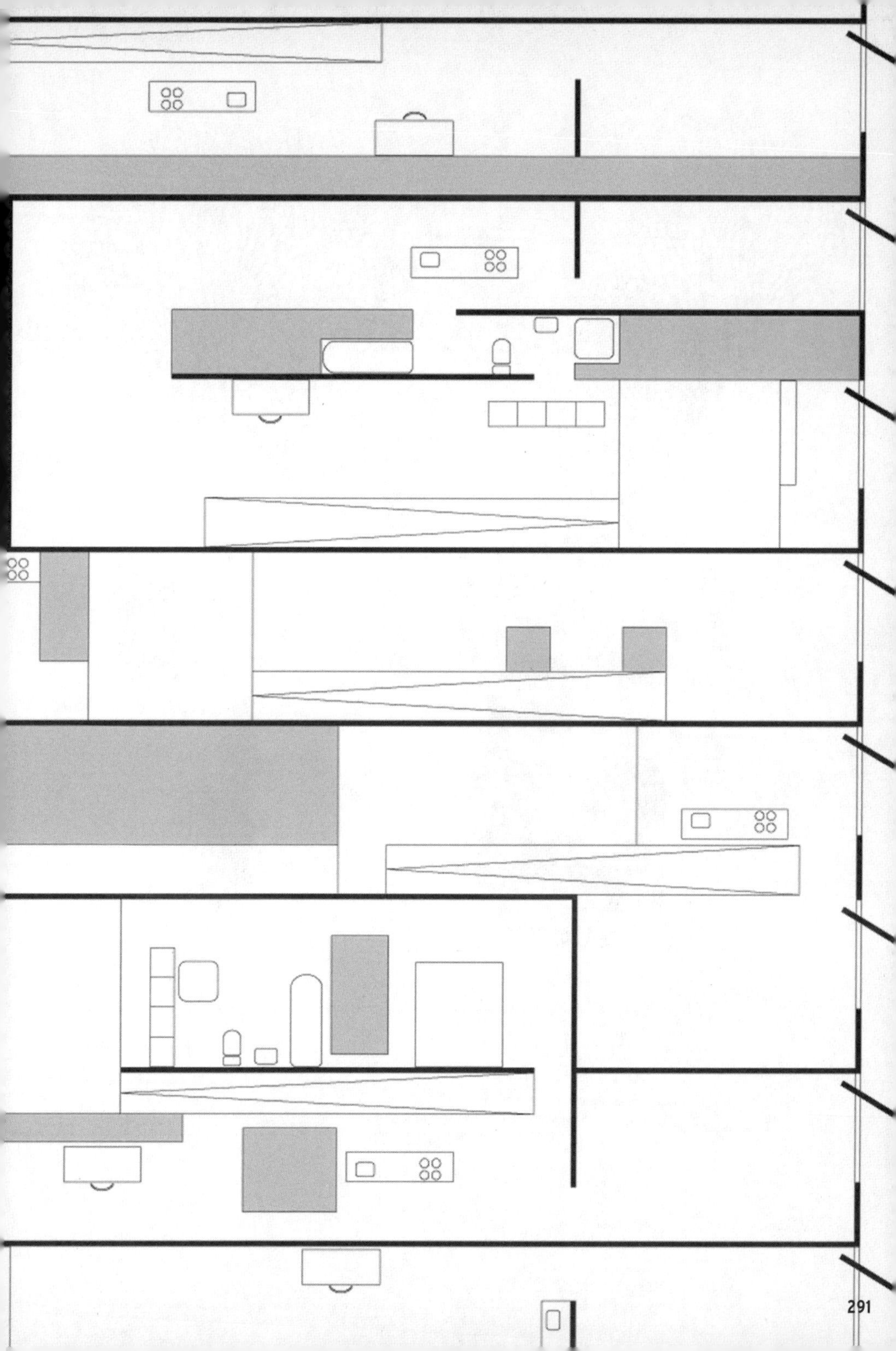

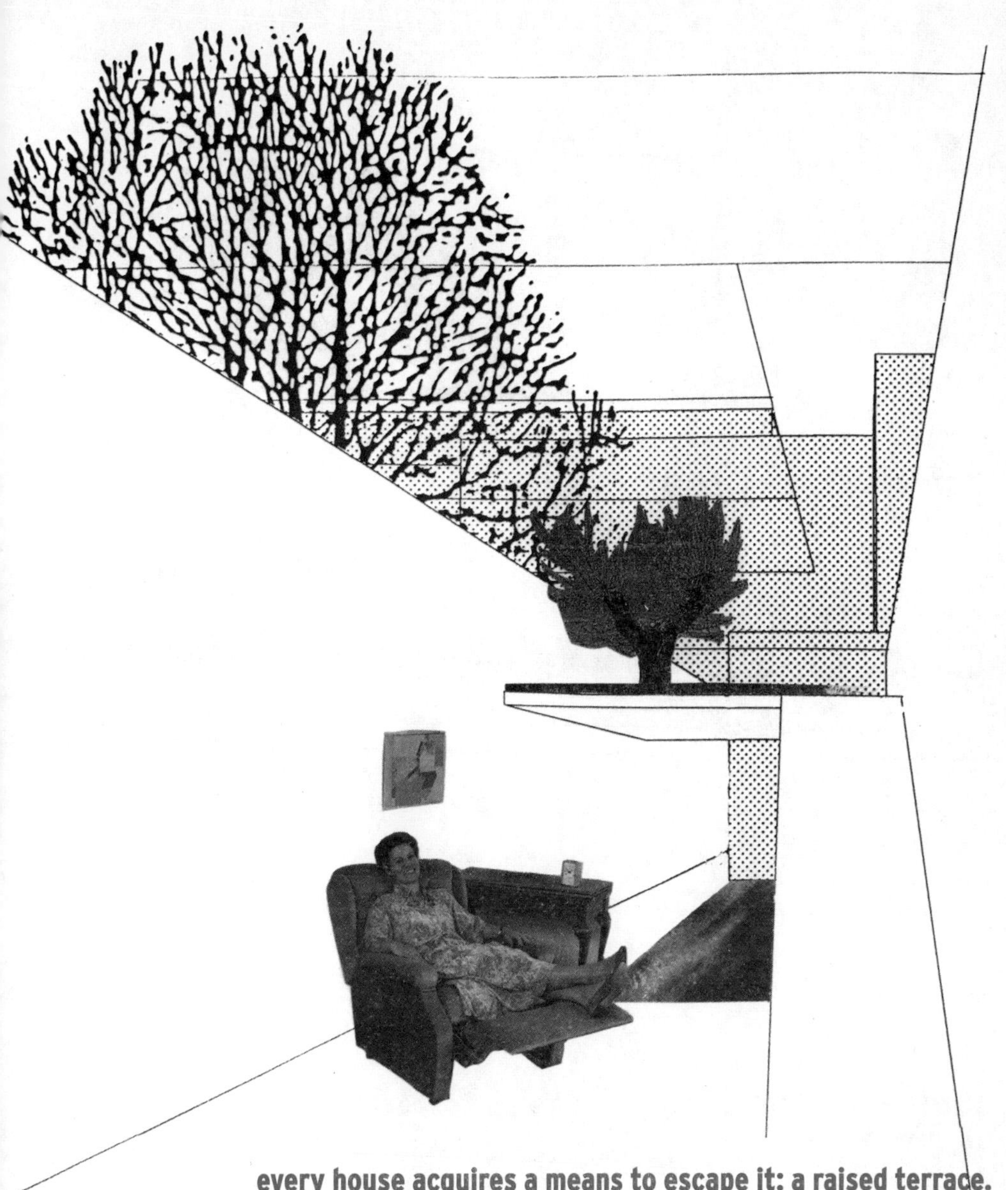

every house acquires a means to escape it: a raised terrace.

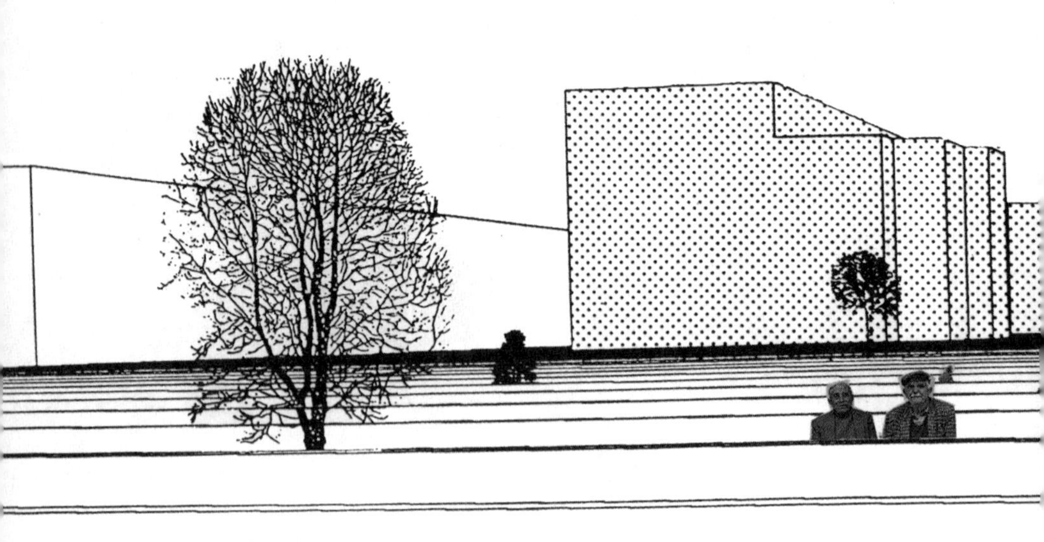

It gives a panoramic view over this 'carpet' of houses, which registers as a 'barbecue field' crowded with neighbours.

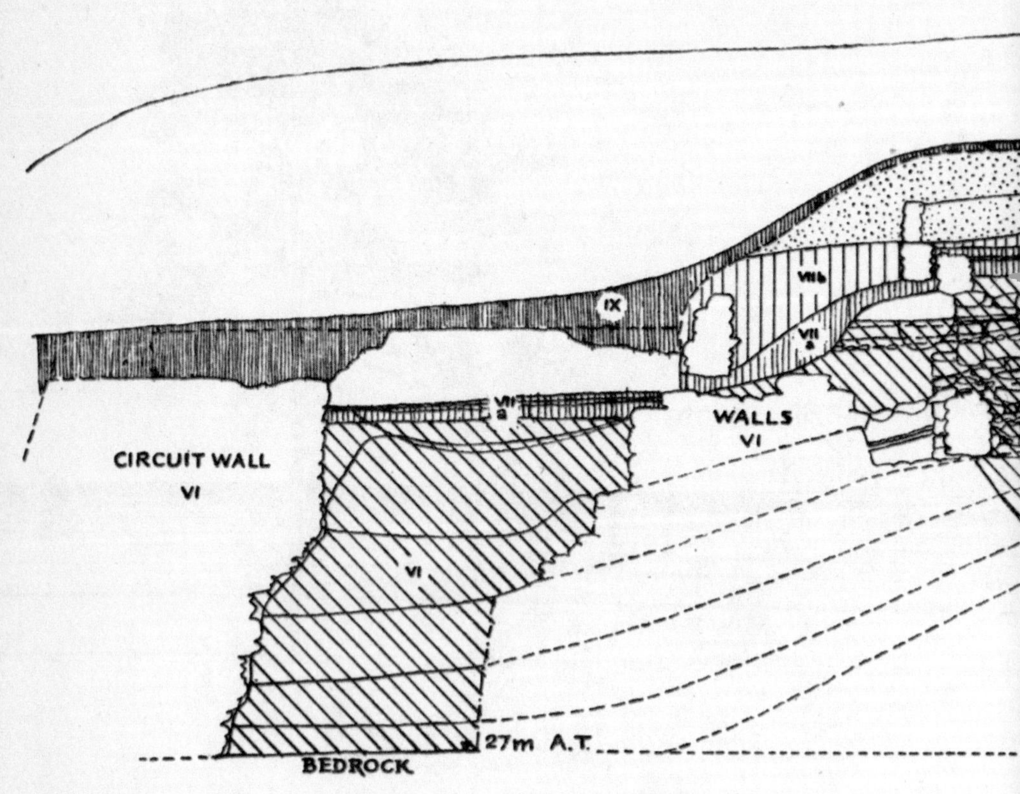

Fig. 3 Diagrammatic section of deposit in south part of mound

Trojan Extrusion

Densification study for Rotterdam centre, The Netherlands

1995

Mark Verheijen

Re-editing: MVRDV, 1997

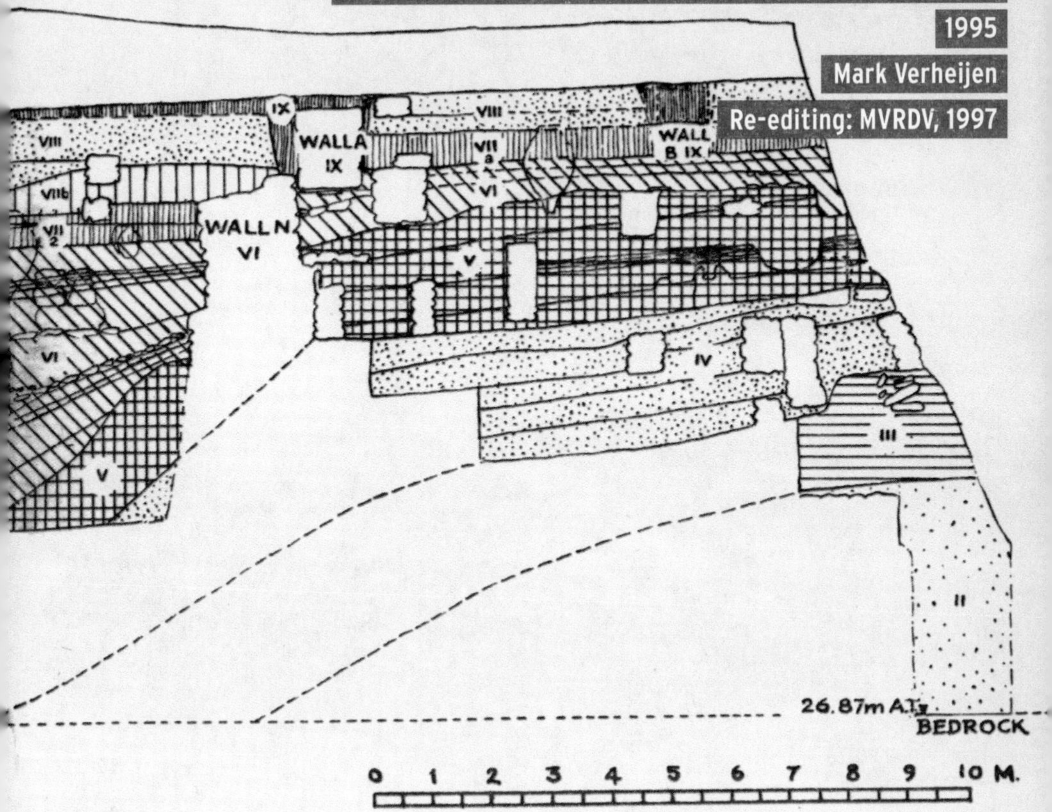

Existing building lines often seem sacrosanct.

1945

This gives them a monumental status with far-reaching consequences

1995

In a radical densification of Rotterdam, raising the existing development by consistent and concerted action to a single new height would generate the perspective of an infinite open roofscape; a potential new ground level where the church and office towers 'float' in a sea of programme.

Section through existing situation

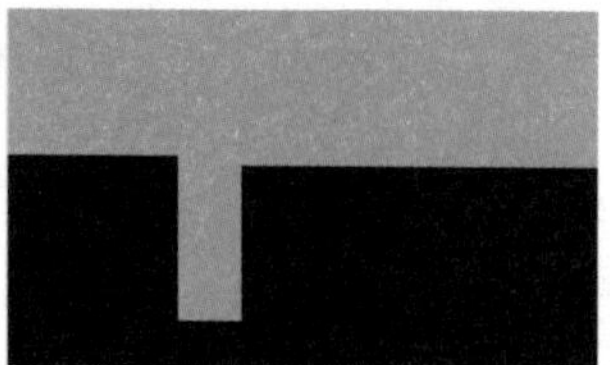

Section through concept

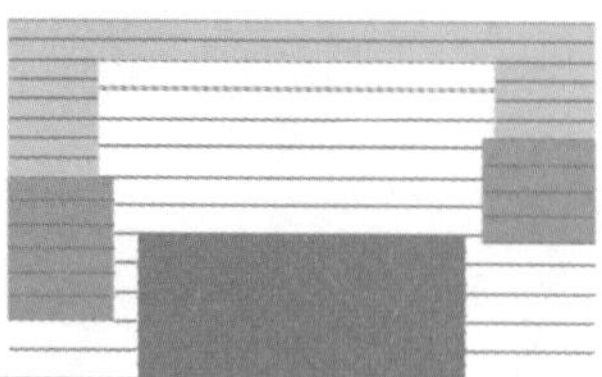

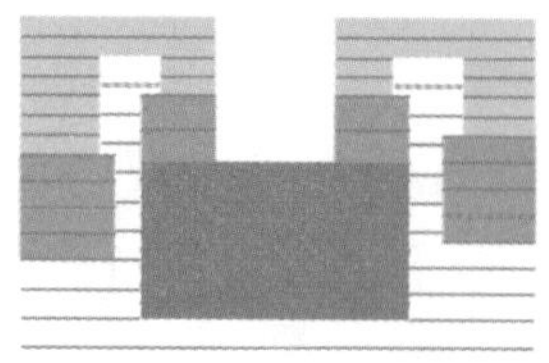

Section through new programme

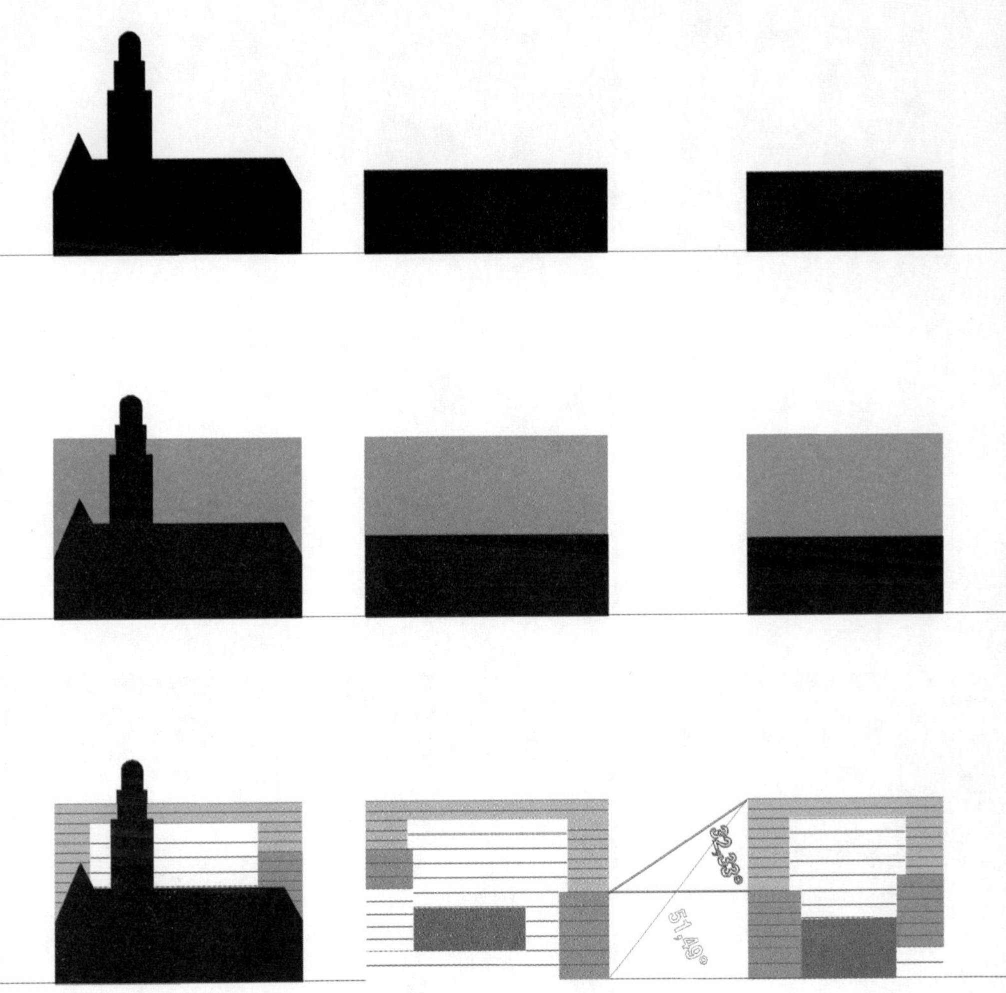

In this 'plateau' the existing streets resonate as gullies. Their configuration, in view of the light incidence, generates a strict programmatic division among the building blocks.

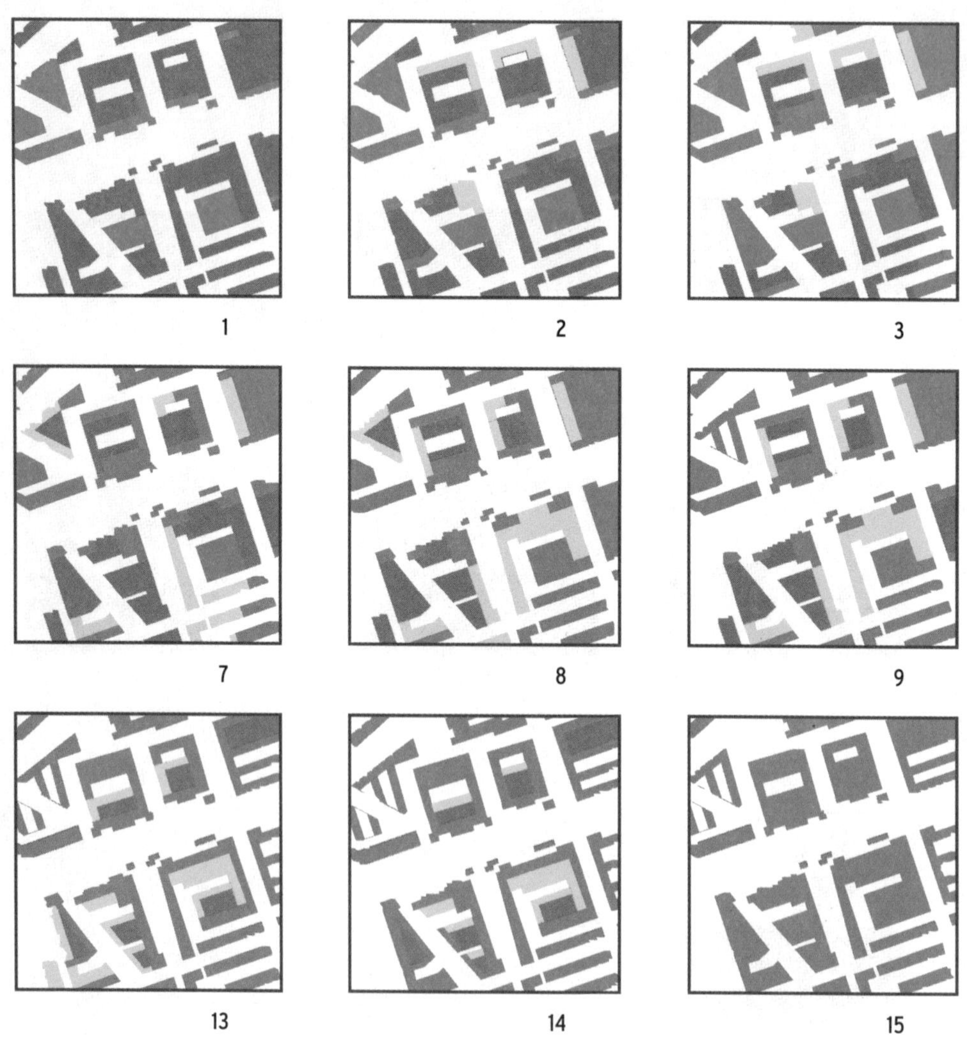
1
2
3
7
8
9
13
14
15

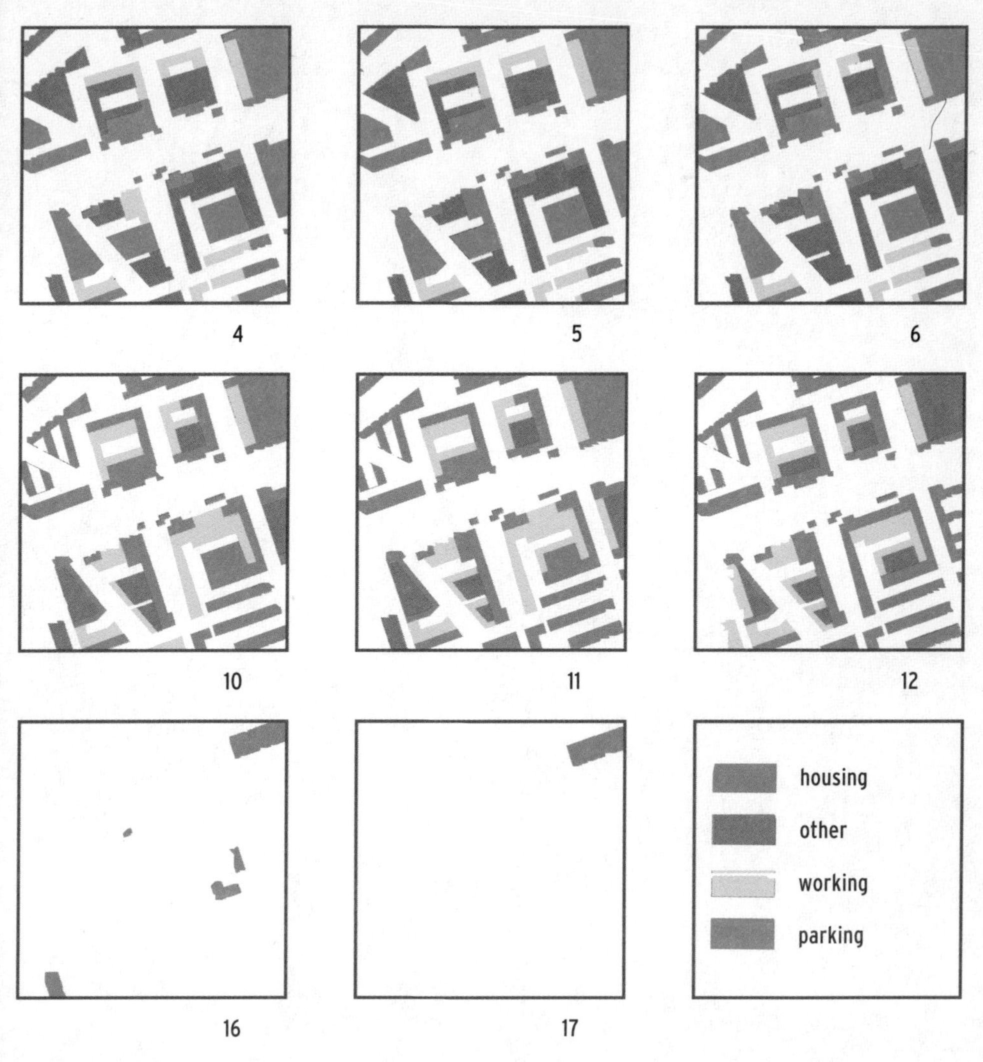

The wider the street the more habitation,

as a stratified petrification of the current streetscape.

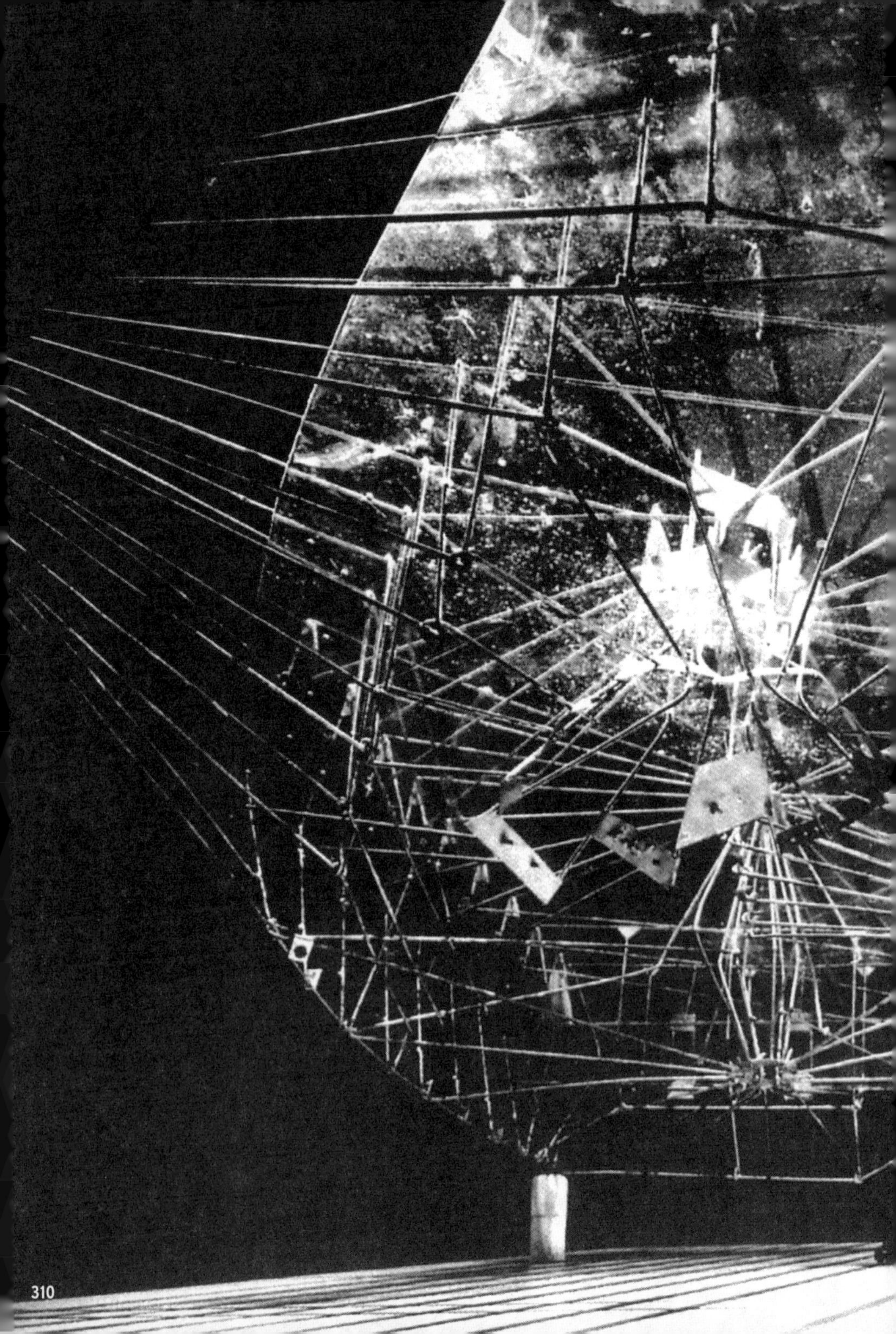

New! New Babylon

Densification study for Rotterdam centre, The Netherlands

1995

Ronald Wall

Re-editing: MVRDV, 1997

Large-scale densification makes it feasible (at last) to develop a vertical zoning of the city following the horizontal one: shopping on the third floor, keep-fit on the eighth, public transport on the tenth, jogging on the fifteenth, parking on the eighteenth, and so on. The city can then be read literally as a stack of networks. The question then arises as to which parts are to be kept open and which filled in.

If the existing public space including trees were to be declared a protected area, building development could then only begin some twenty-five metres up.

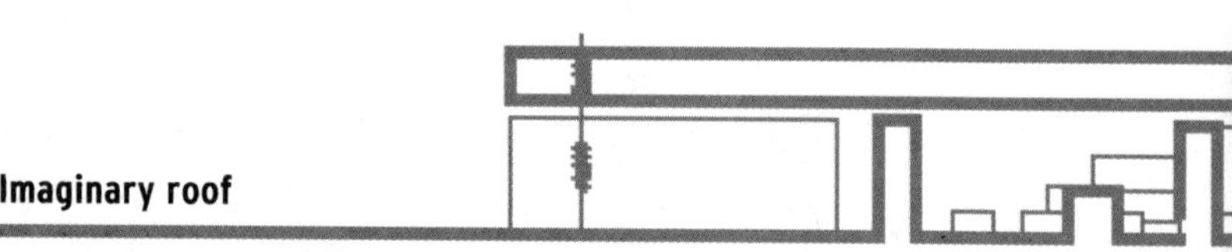

This would create an urban 'attic-level', a New Babylon; a network above the existing city with its own laws and logic, one free of the burden and impracticalities of the existing ground level.

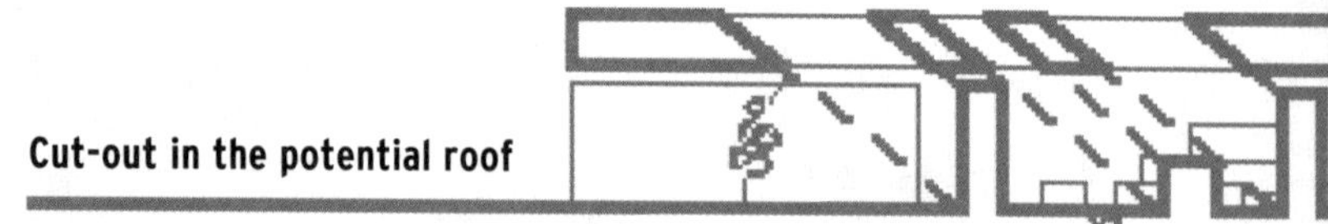

By punching holes in this 'attic-level', the existing development would be provided with light and dwelling would not be relegated to the roofscape of the city.

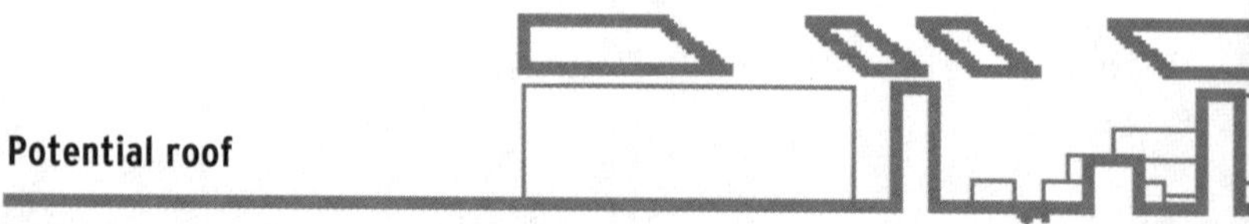

The existing city would then be blessed with a permanent 'Paulus Potter': a landscape of sunbeams.

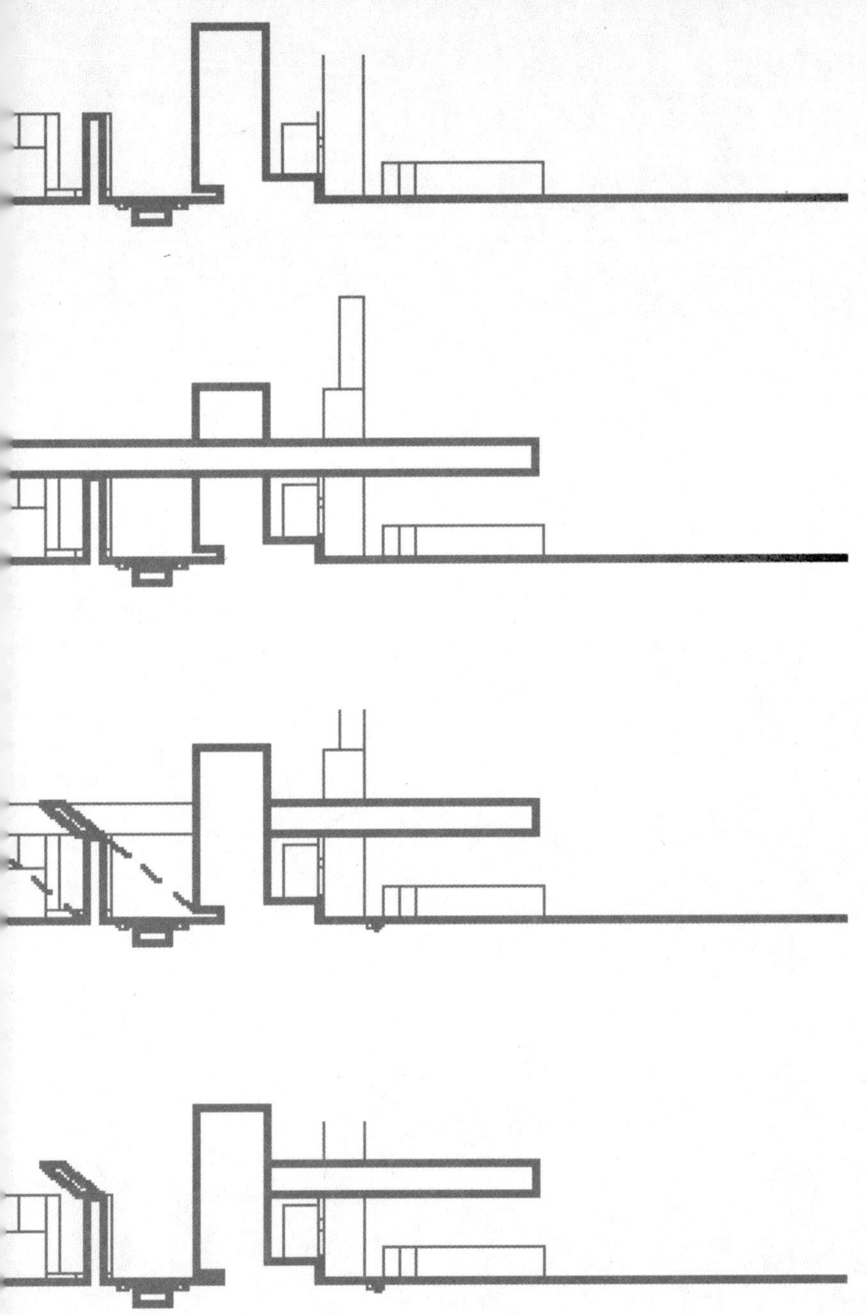

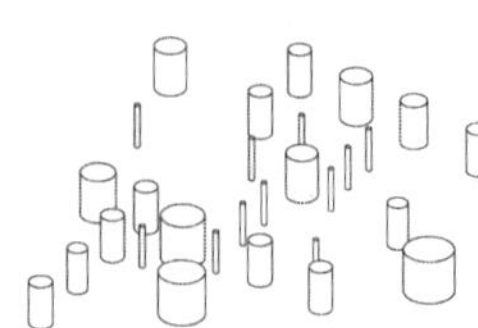

parking towers

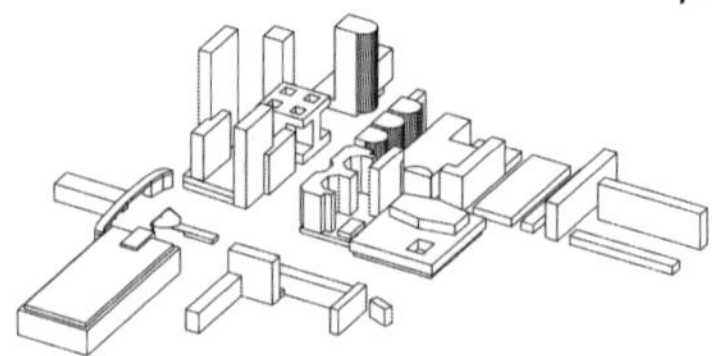

exisiting situation

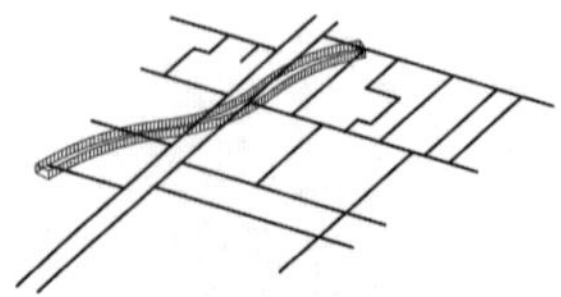

underground network

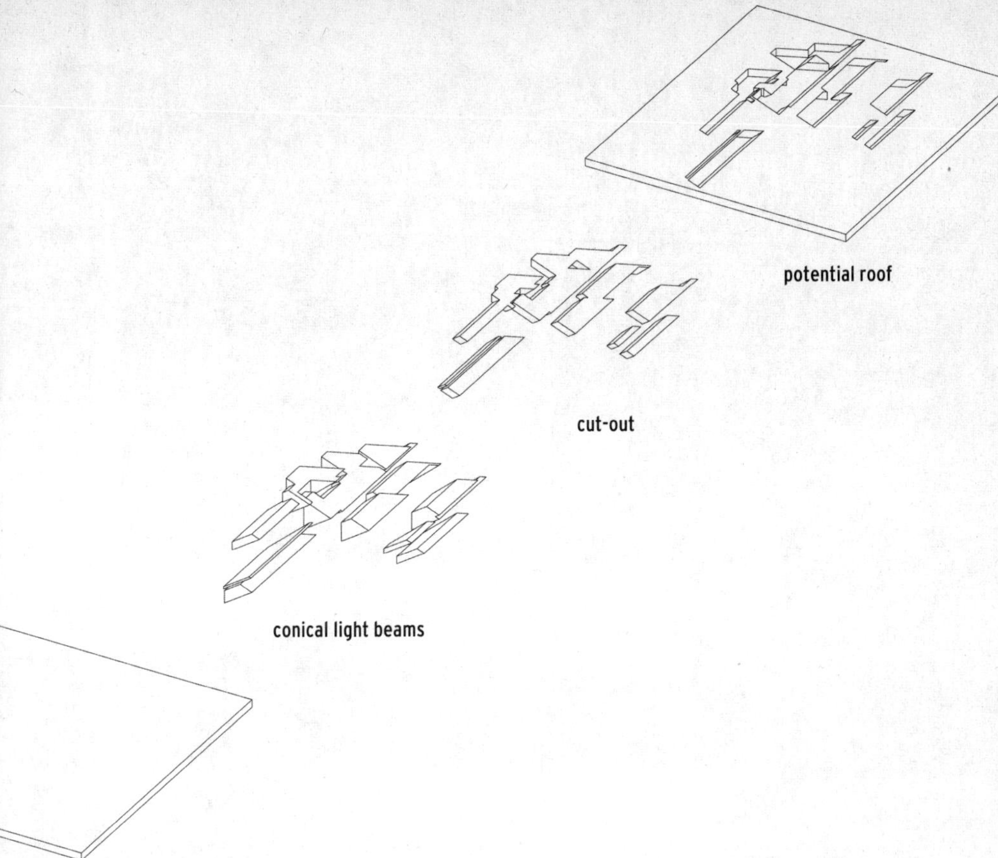
potential roof
cut-out
conical light beams
imaginary roof

It allows for a 'cloud of potential' above the current public space of the city.

The Cantilever

100 apartments for elderly people in Amsterdam-Osdorp, The Netherlands

1997

MVRDV

In the garden city developments in the west of Amsterdam, we are confronted with comprehensive densification operations that threaten to disrupt the continuous open and green space, the key quality of this portion of the city.
As part of an operation of this type we proposed a slab of 100 apartments for 55-plussers marking the end of an old-age services belt. This slab would add to the existing arsenal of old-age housing types. Following up the warden-assisted flat and sheltered housing models, we proposed building apartments close by central services with a greater degree of independence. In this light, it became conceivable that once the ageing population tendency had subsided, the housing could just as easily be occupied by younger people.

To keep allowing sufficient sunlight to the surrounding development in respect to Van Eesteren's tenets, it was only possible to place 87 of the 100 apartments in the slab.
The remaining 13 were left in limbo; where on earth were they to be accommodated?
Place them elsewhere on the site and the existing open space would shrink even more.
A deeper slab with narrower bay measures proved equally impracticable. The north-south orientation of the apartments elicited a bay of 7.20m as basic premise. By hanging the 13 apartments on the north side of the slab and leaving them literally 'in the air', the elevation along Ookmeerweg, with its shades of Eastern Europe, gets the articulation it badly needs. The north-south units in the slab are now supplemented with types oriented to east and/or west that look out over the polder.
By restricting the number of partitions in the basic (internal) units it was possible to save 7 or 8 per cent of space there, enough to finance the suspended dwellings which cost one and a half times as much.
The spartan gallery-access flats are immediately enlivened by this move, each gallery gaining a perspective of its own.

The otherwise utterly regular units have their own distinct if self-effacing air thanks to the variety of window positions and balcony dimensions and the welter of balustrading materials. This spatial variety likewise generates a potential chatterzone among the balconies of the various apartments.
Capitalizing on the fact that for soundproofing purposes party walls have to be 8 cm thicker than is structurally necessary, this extra zone is able to receive rods from which to hang the cantilevering frameworks of the suspended units without needing to strengthen the loadbearing walls.
These frameworks might have elicited an uncomfortable sense of the skeletal were it not that in most units sound-reduction and fire regulations necessitated covering them up.
Here, then, sheltered housing has been reconfigured as 'outboard units'. This way, the ground level is kept as open and green as possible. The outboard unit signifies a potential prototype for densifying post-war residential areas.

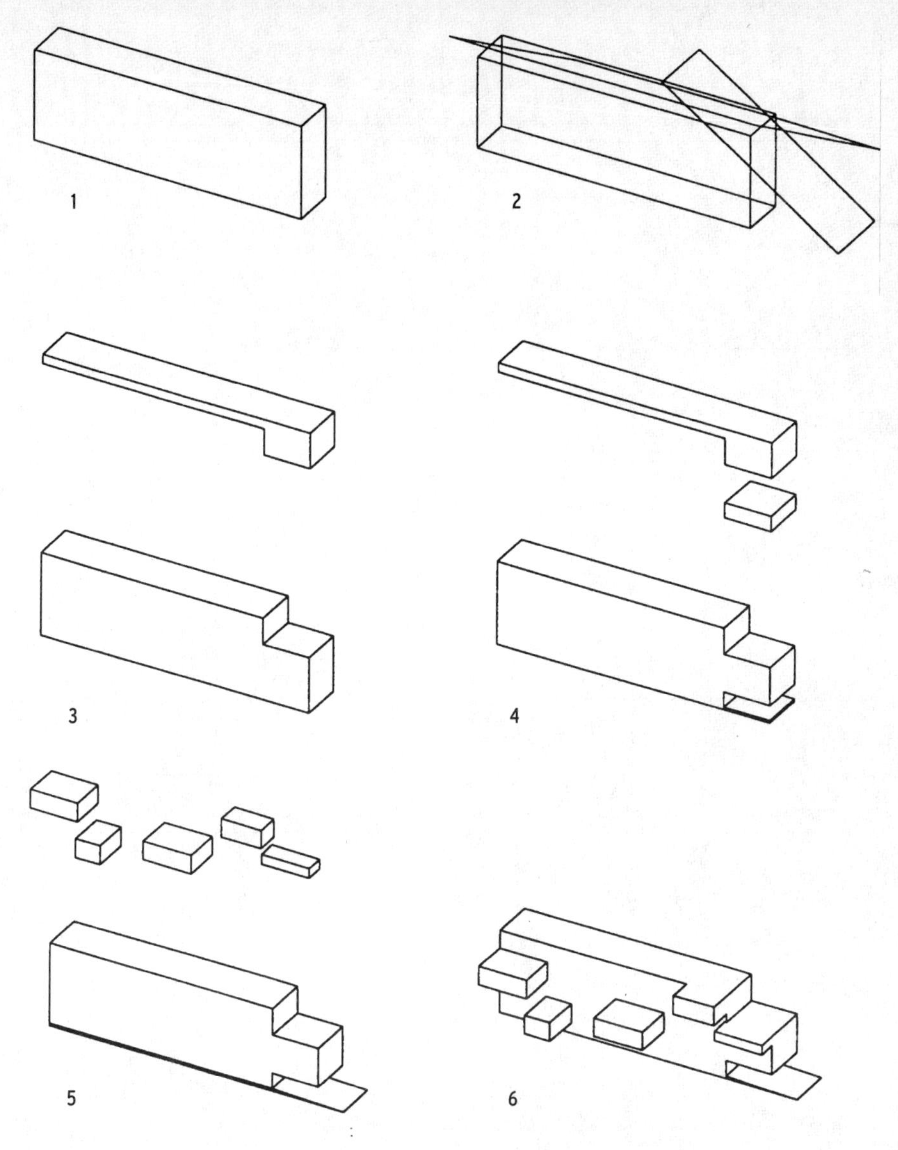

Effect of the shading angle:
from sheltered housing units to suspended outboard units

Plans

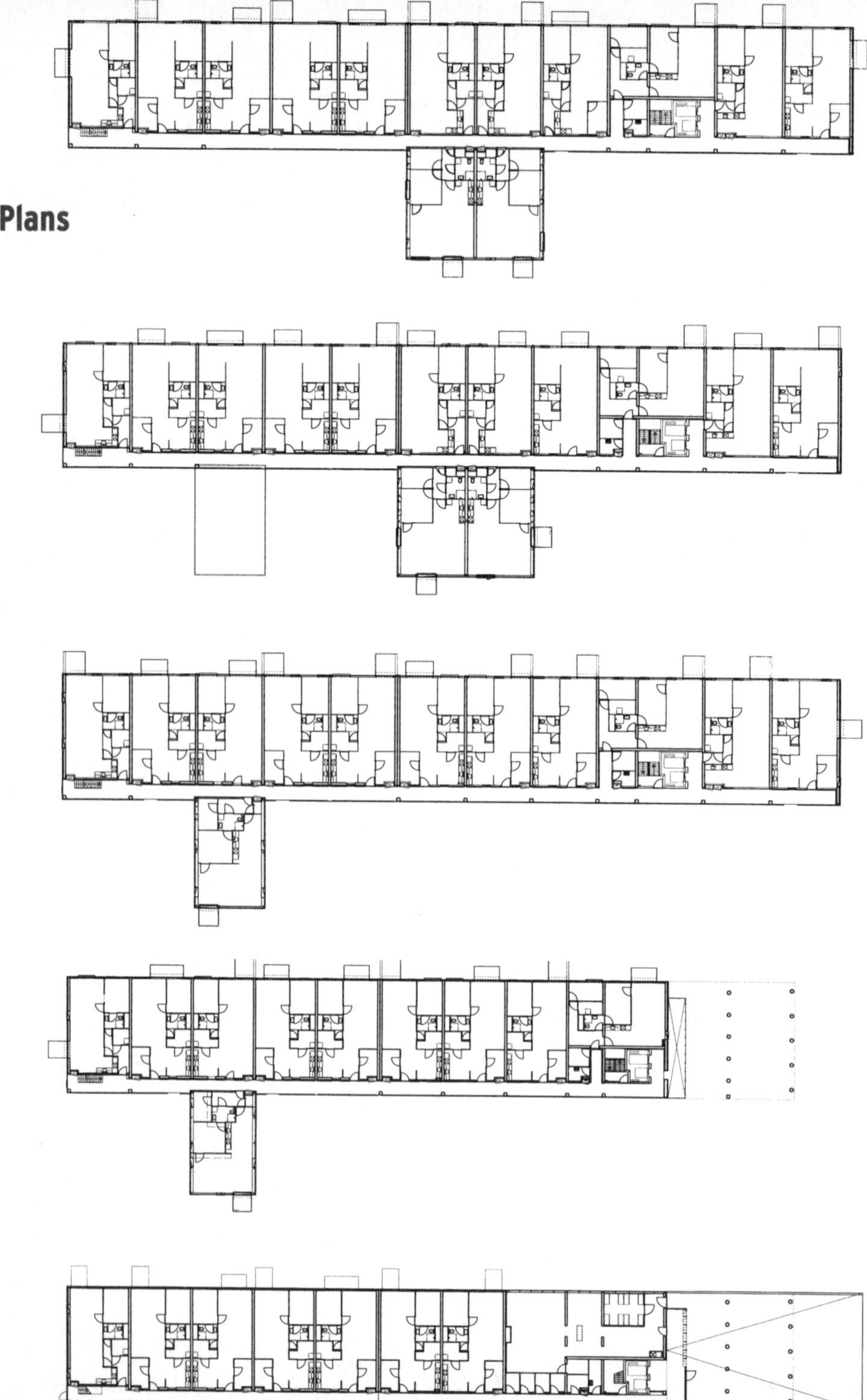

Floors

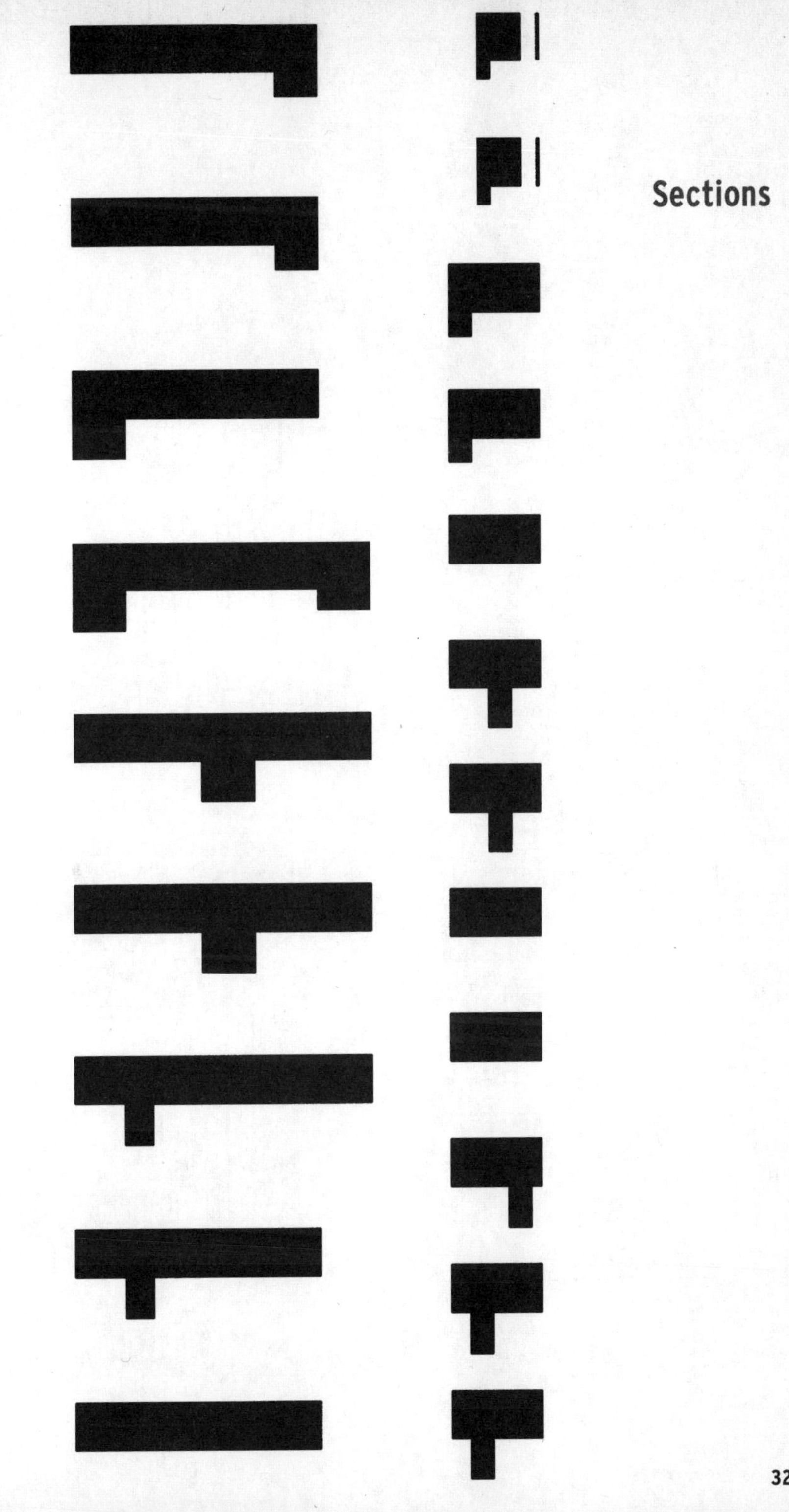

Sections

View

X-ray: structure

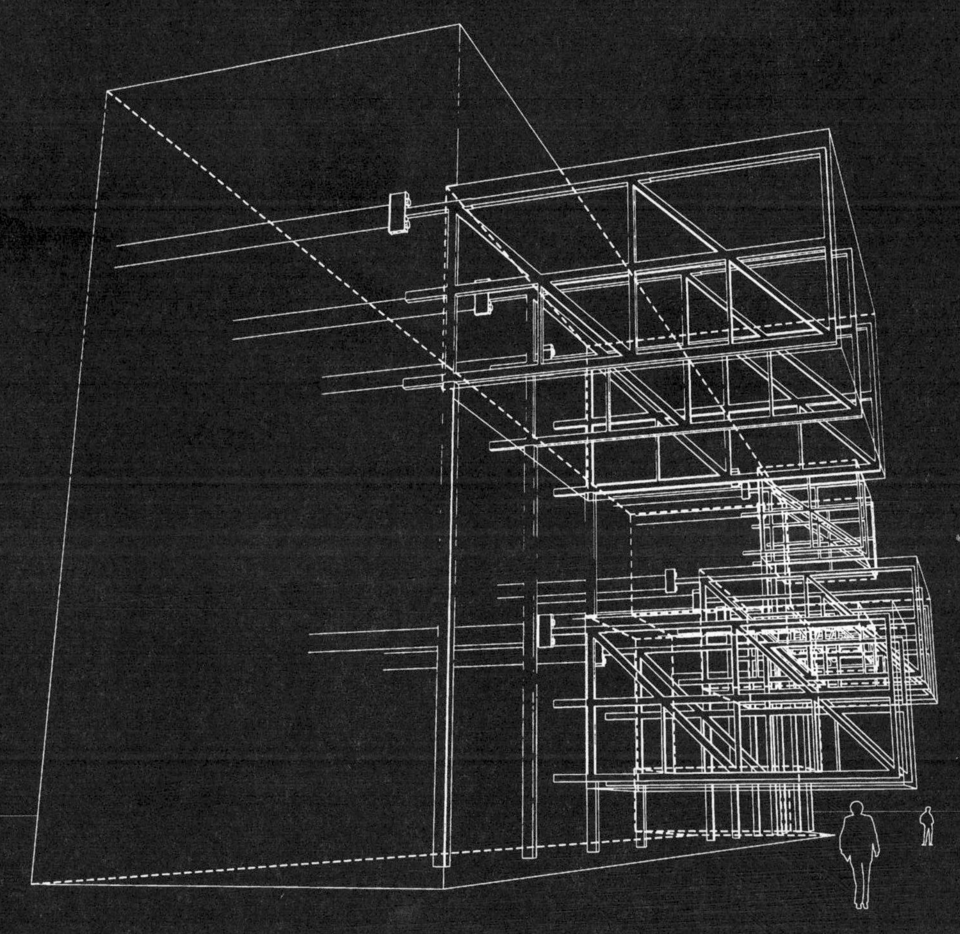

3d urban space

Interiors

Occupied interiors

Interiors of suspended houses

Occupied interiors of suspended houses

Galleries

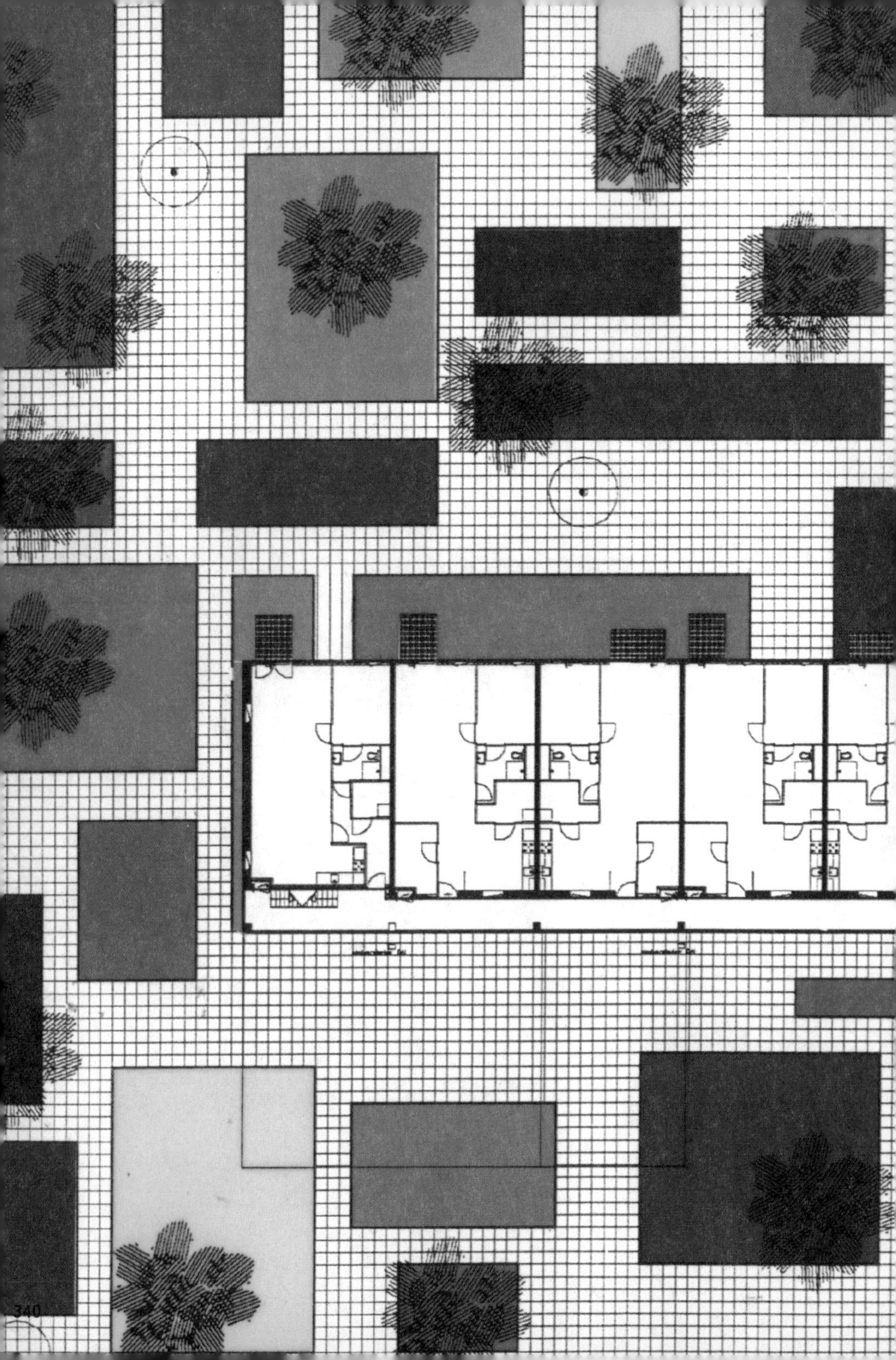

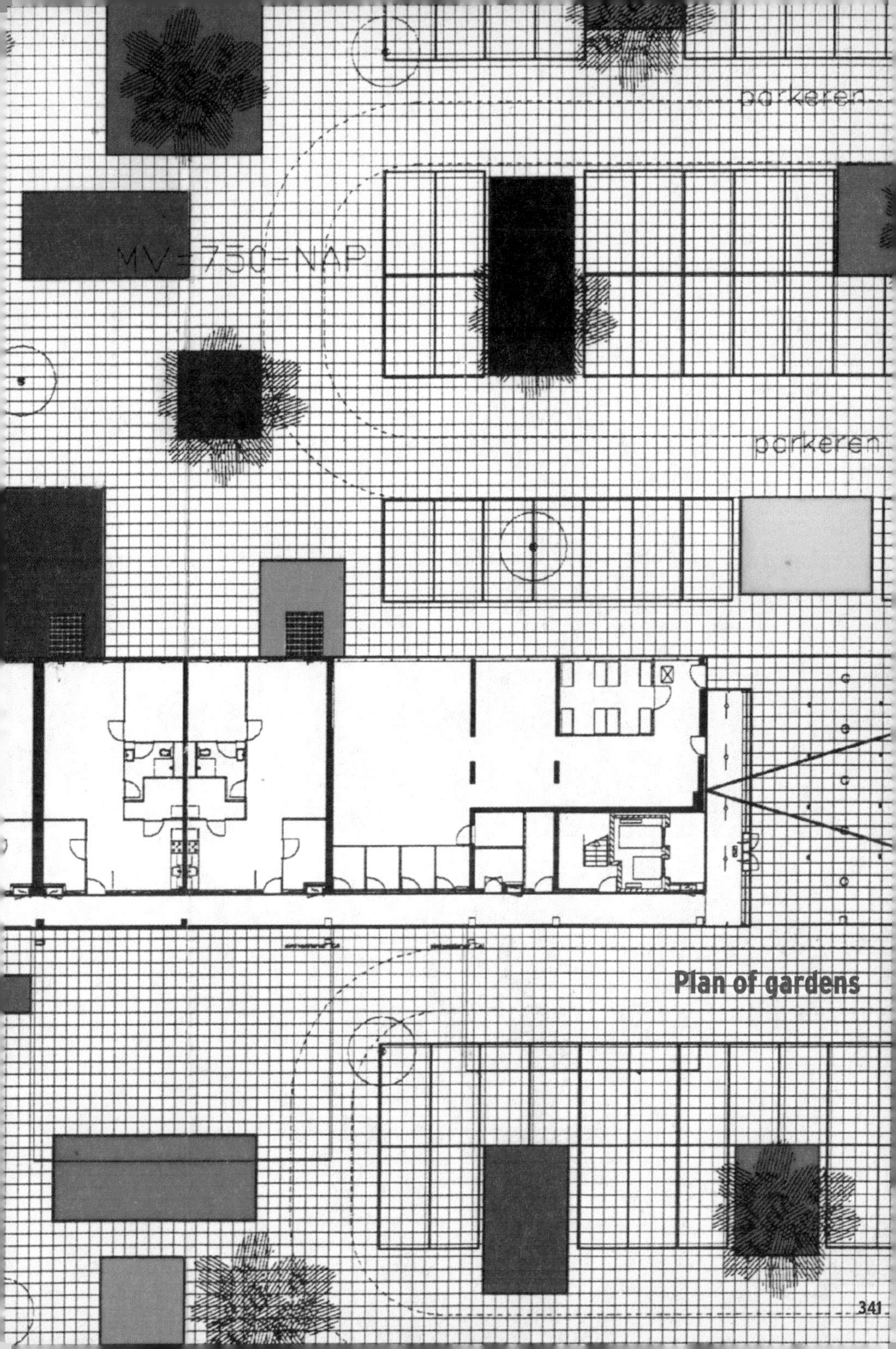

Plan of gardens

ESSO

RELATIVITY

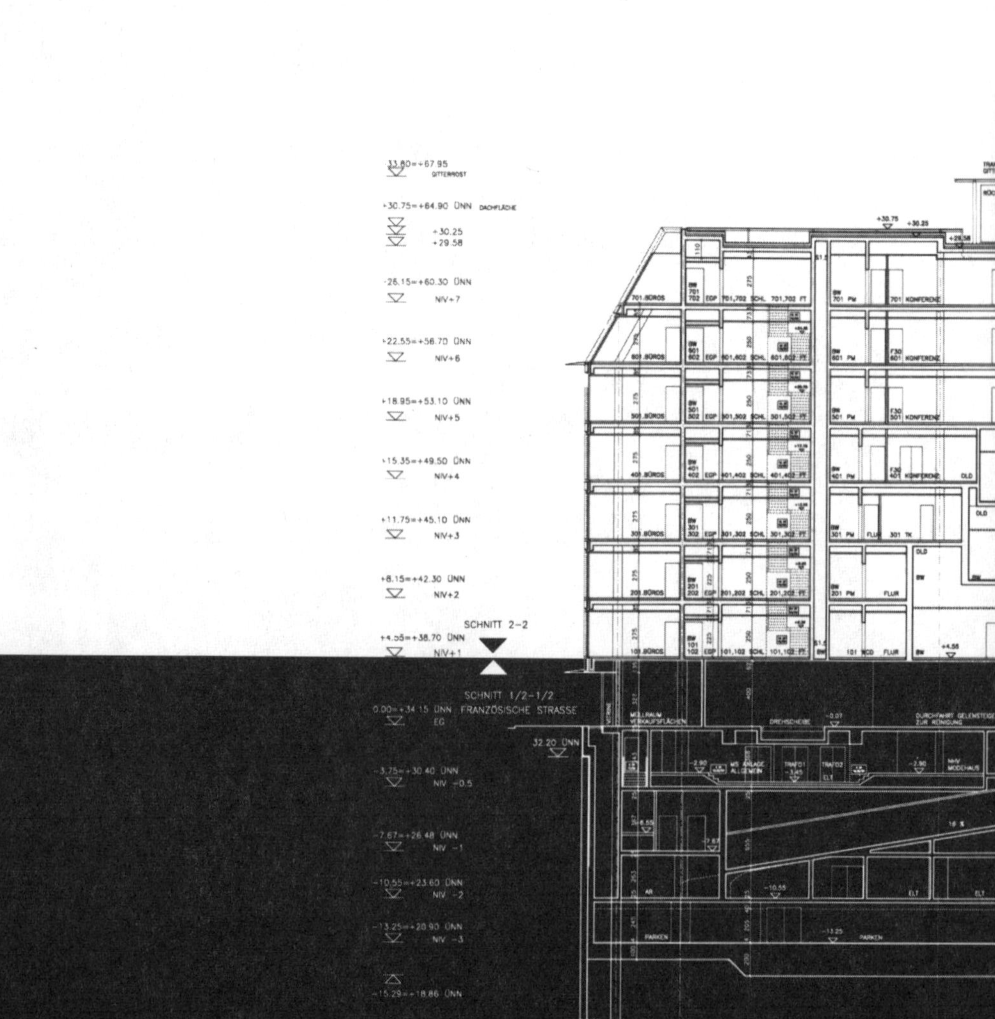

33.80=+67.95
GITTERROST
+30.75=+64.90 ÜNN DACHFLÄCHE
+30.25
+29.58
+26.15=+60.30 ÜNN
NIV+7
+22.55=+56.70 ÜNN
NIV+6
+18.95=+53.10 ÜNN
NIV+5
+15.35=+49.50 ÜNN
NIV+4
+11.75=+45.10 ÜNN
NIV+3
+8.15=+42.30 ÜNN
NIV+2
SCHNITT 2-2
+4.55=+38.70 ÜNN
NIV+1
SCHNITT 1/2-1/2
0.00=+34.15 ÜNN FRANZÖSISCHE STRASSE
EG
32.20 ÜNN
-3.75=+30.40 ÜNN
NIV -0.5
-7.67=+26.48 ÜNN
NIV -1
-10.55=+23.60 ÜNN
NIV -2
-13.25=+20.90 ÜNN
NIV -3
-15.29=+18.86 ÜNN

Icebergs

Text

1995

Winy Maas and Jacob van Rijs

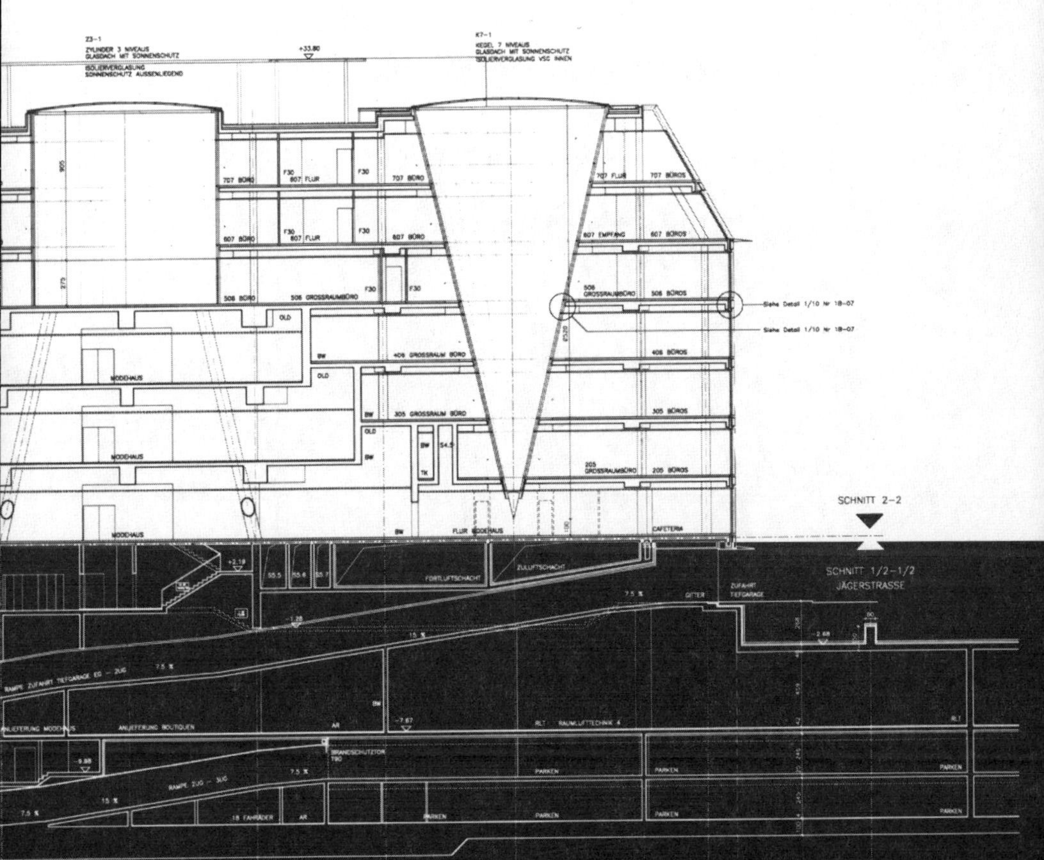

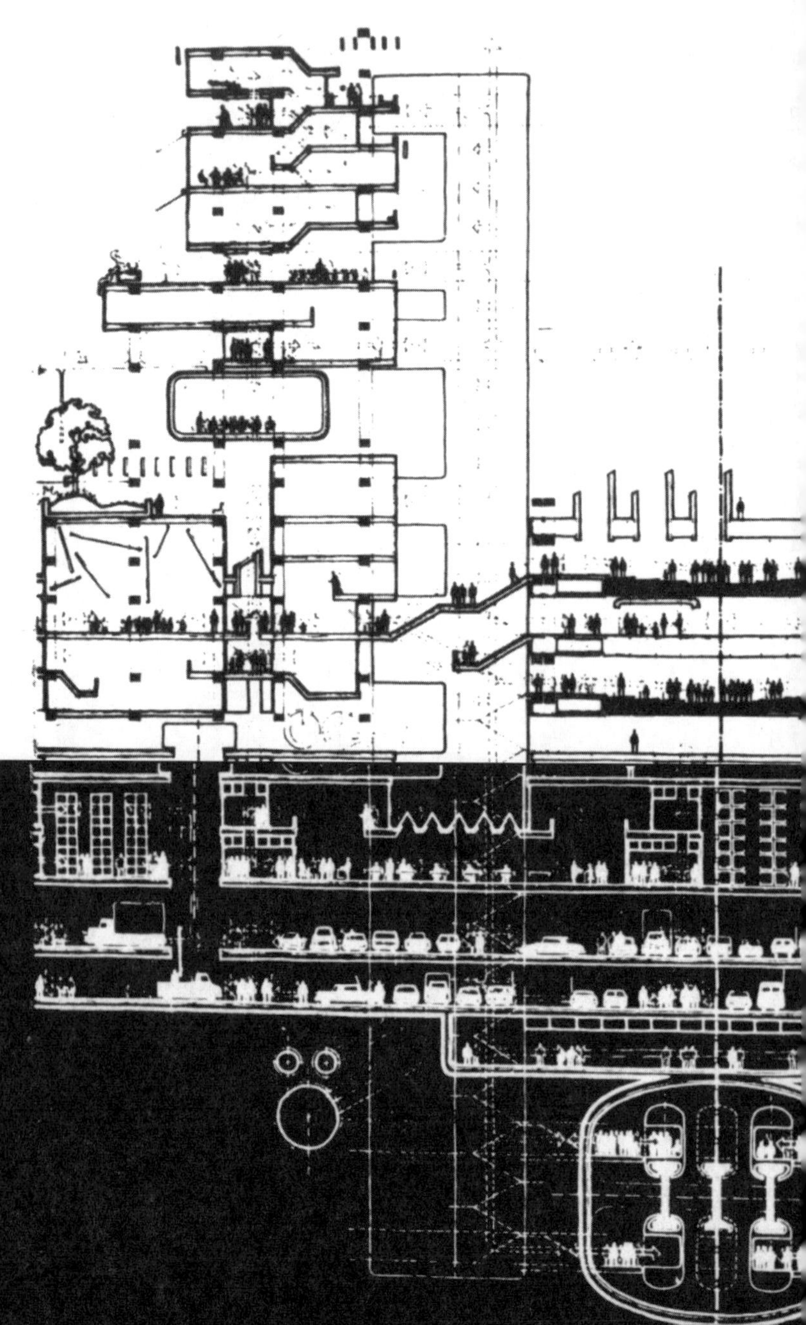

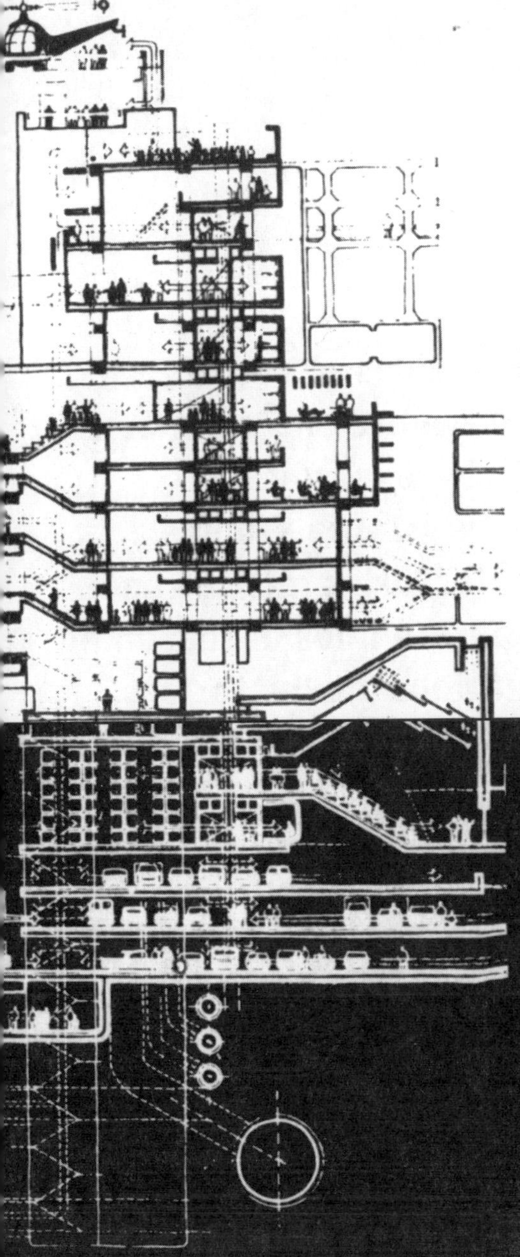

Within the densifying conditions of society, vast amounts of programme are more and more being pushed underground. Water reservoirs, electricity plants, parkings, storage rooms, archives, leisure spaces, factories, offices and even houses. - Quite disparate lines of reasoning such as monument regulations and historical sentiments, ecological notions and security objectives seem to be behind this process. - It is almost as though the ideological notion of 'the deck', the modernist level-in-the-air, has gradually found its position and is going to be realized - at zero level. - In doing so, the

existing earth is going to be loaded with underground programmes, with the more acceptable parts of modern society on top, like the peaks of icebergs. - Can we accept this phenomenon and explore it as an enormous potential reservoir? Can we adjust life to its logic which is mainly defined by technical and logistic parameters? - How can one live within this claustrophobia, the lack of light, the difficulties of escape? What type of behaviour or orientation can be imagined in these places without context, without reference? How would we imagine an underground termite life to be?

sección transversal aa. zonas a y b / zones a and b

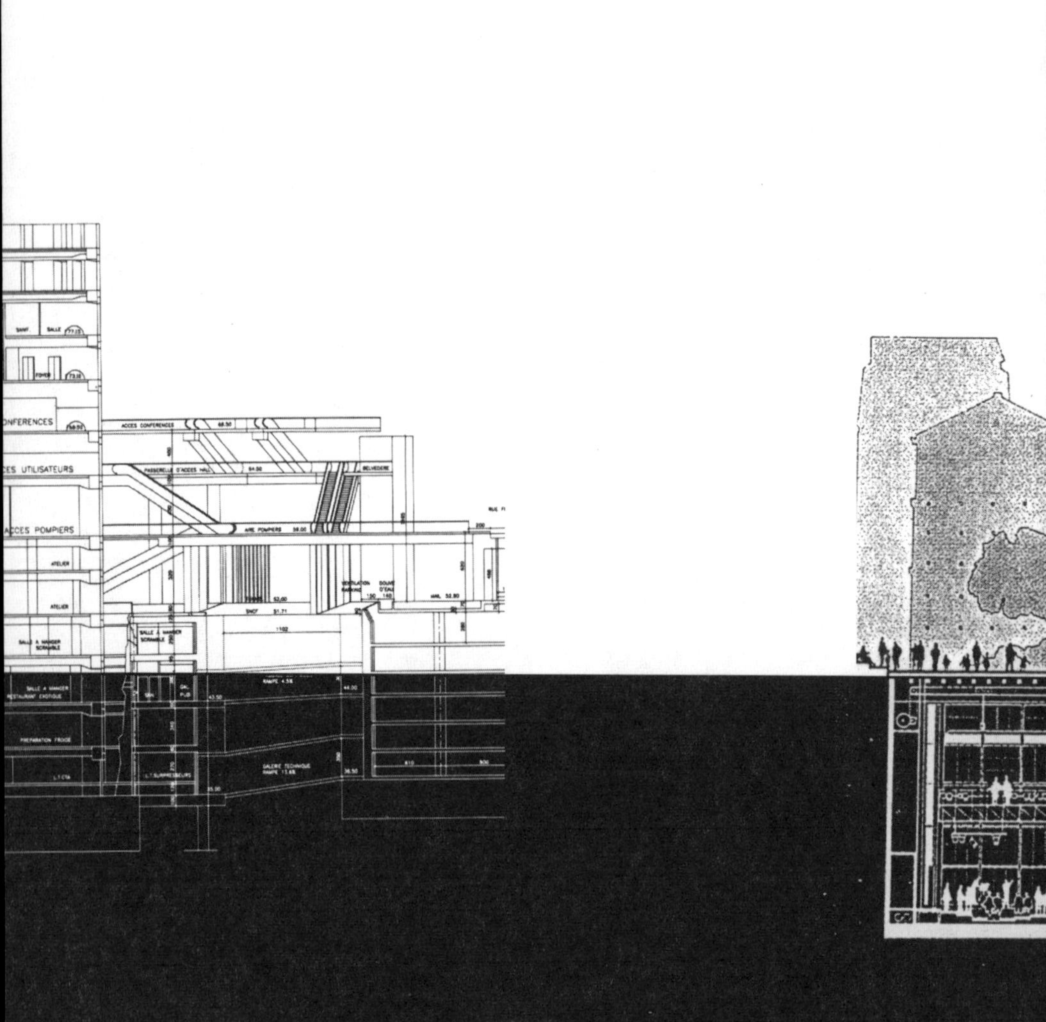

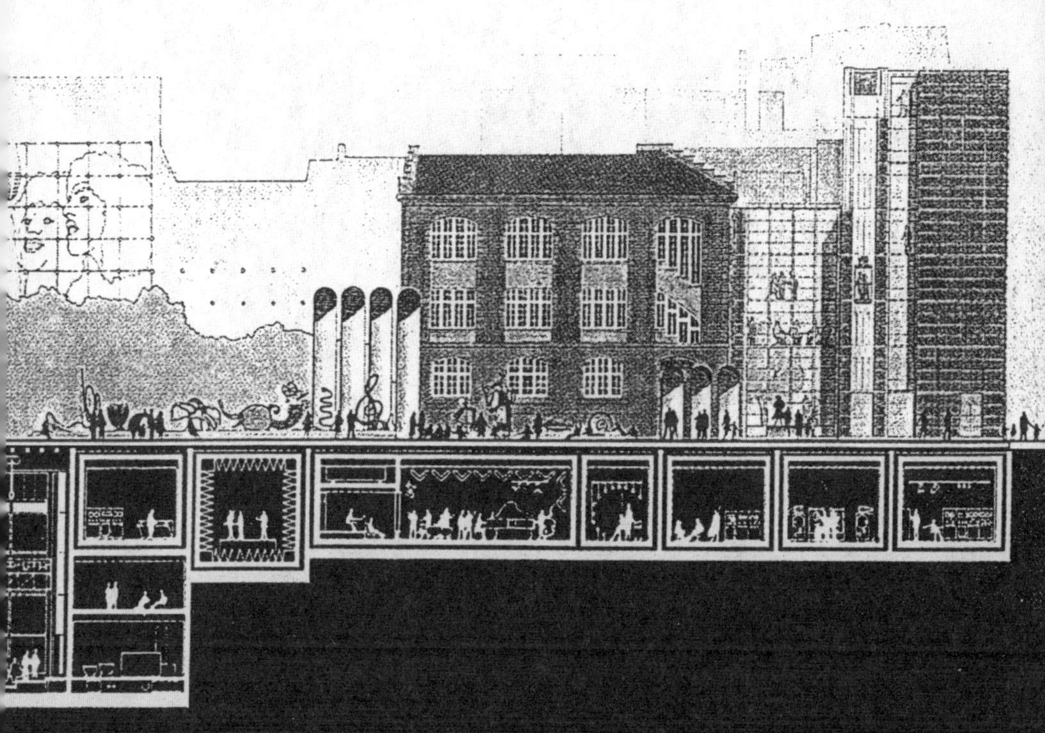

Darklands

Photographic study for underground life

1995

Indesem group

In a total darkness,
light is like a shadow to the sun.

In these Darklands all relation with time is lost.

A day could last for 30 hours in this autonomous wonderland.

With an immense freedom in all its dimensions.

HANDLUNGSABLAUF
Auf

Aren't we already accepting situations
with less natural light?
ATHLETES WORLD

Aren't we already adapting our habits?

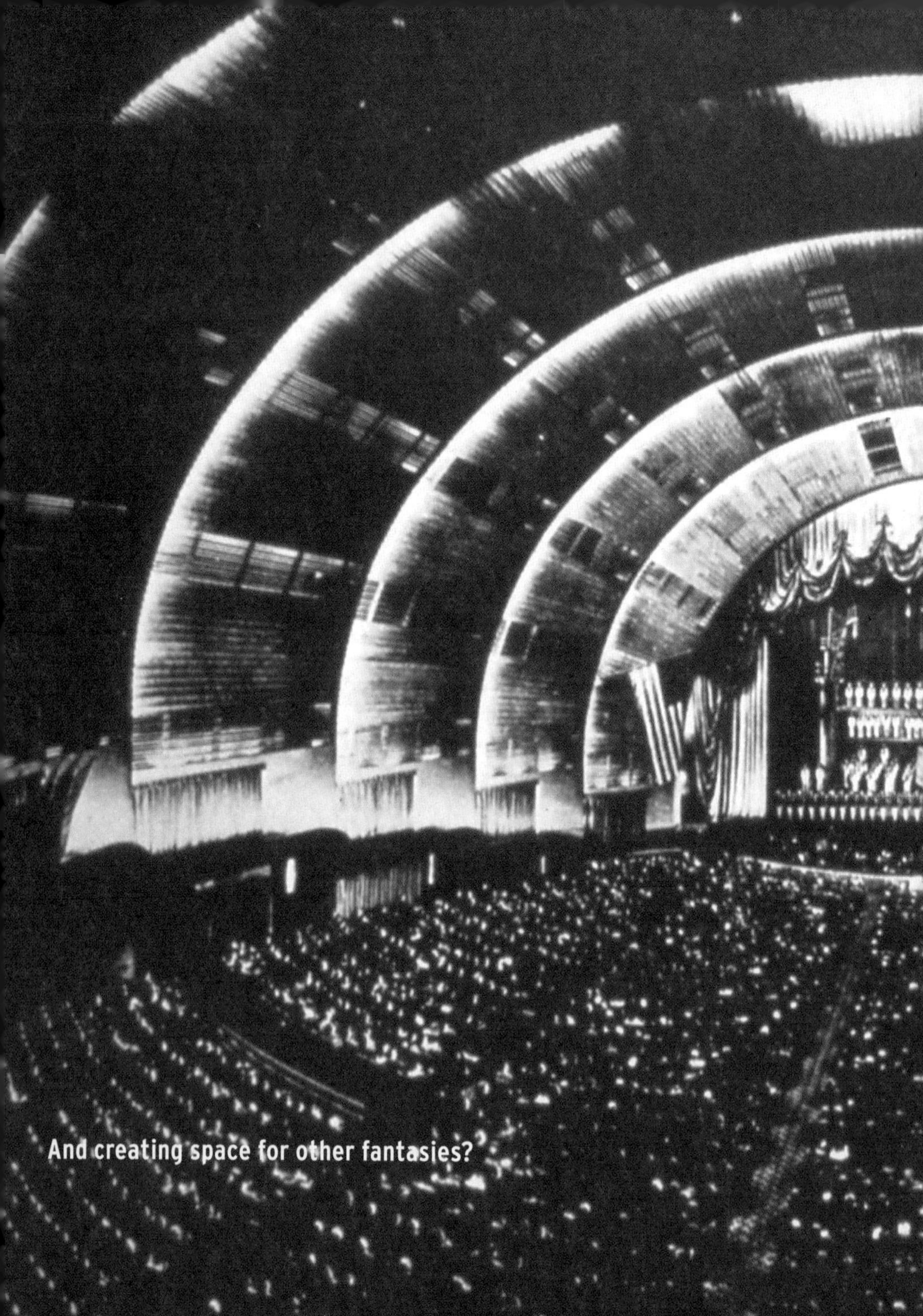

And creating space for other fantasies?

PAN AM

Chrysler & Friends

Extension to Chrysler Building, New York, U.S.A.

1995

Jago van Bergen and Evert Kolpa

**New York City has no obvious monuments.
Its cathedrals and piazzas are lost in the density of the city. The Chrysler Building is one such monument. How are we to celebrate it, but in a European way? The Chrysler Building can be seen as an American cathedral that deserves 'space'. Abounding space would make it a Rockefeller-like attraction. Because of the plaza, a rare and therefore attractive presence, new building programmes - the friends of Chrysler - appear as sunflowers on the horizon around Chrysler and, paradoxically, make it appear denser. - The Chrysler Building preens itself in the mirror, a square that covers up its depth with theatres, cinemas, parkings and shops. A network of circulation veins penetrates the collective space connecting these friends with 135 Lexington. - All the friends of Chrysler share its prestigious address and entrance lobby from where visitors choose their gate number, pass a security lock and either disappear into the Chrysler Building or descend via escalators to one of Chrysler's friends, from where they have a splendid backward view of the Chrysler Building, doubled in size by the reflecting plaza.**

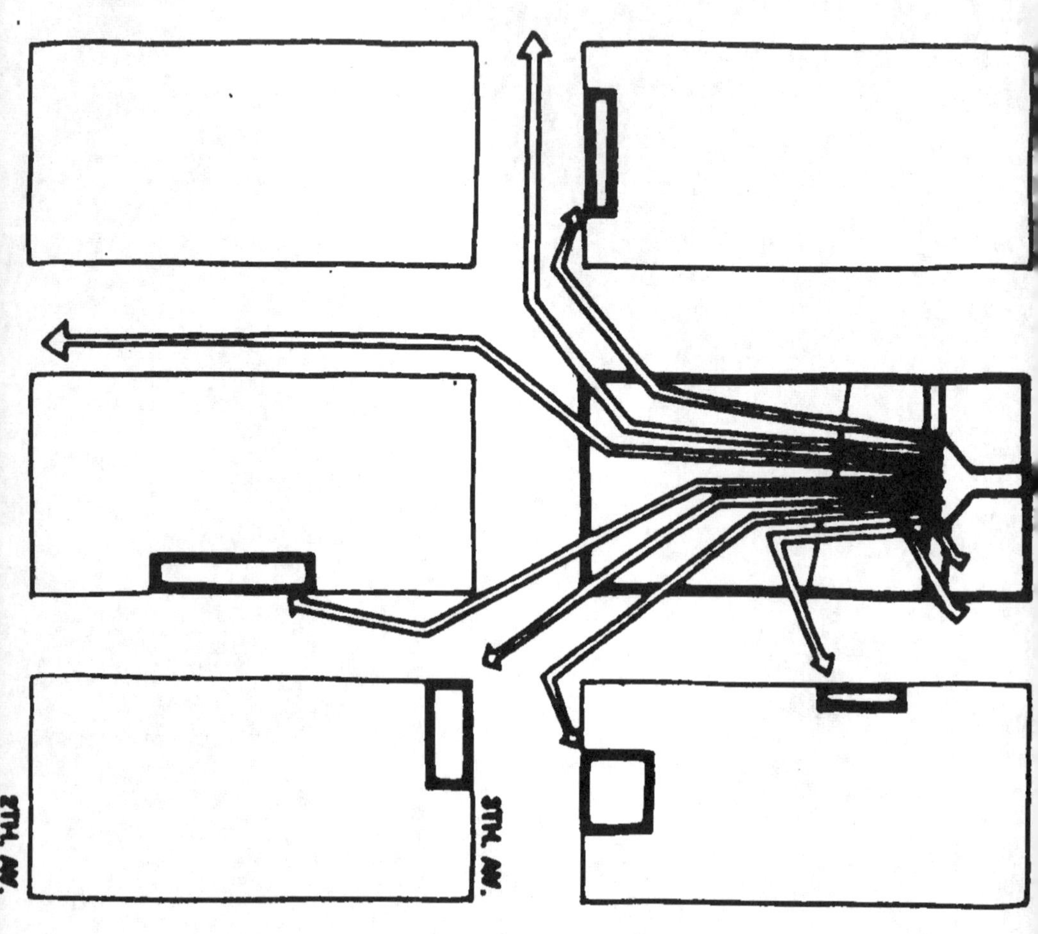
5TH. AV.
5TH. AV.

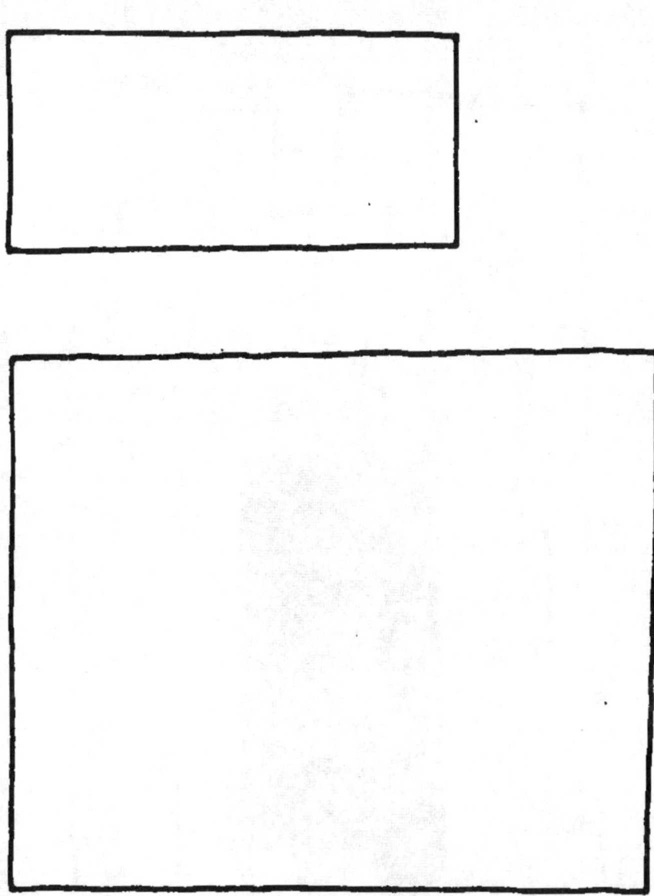

One address

Detail section

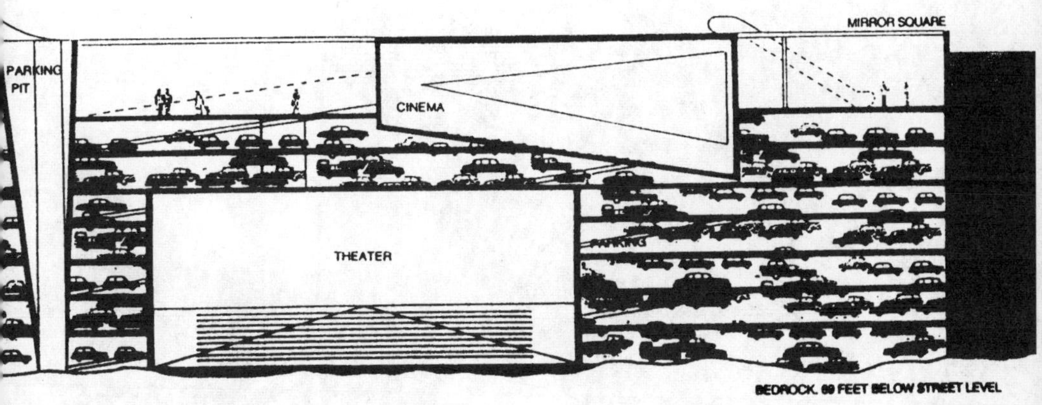

View from underneath the glass plaza.

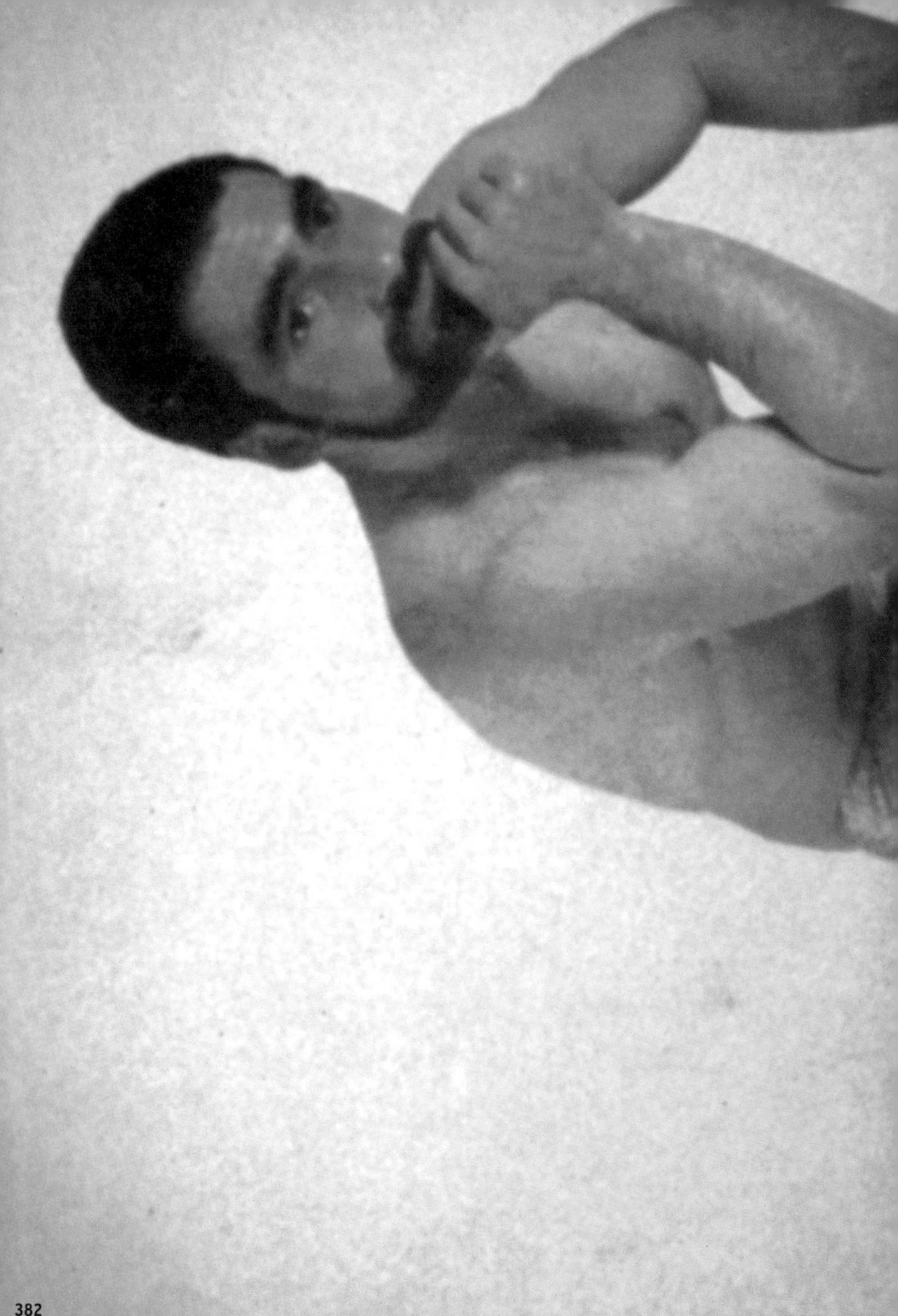

Parkhouse/Carstadt

Shopping Mall, Amsterdam, The Netherlands

1995

Pieter Bannenberg and Kamiel Klaasse

Vital urban programmes are essential to prevent historic centres from being reduced to cultural theme parks. The shopping area of Amsterdam city centre attracts 14 million visitors per year, which amounts to the total population of the Netherlands. 40,000 fun shoppers a day are squeezed into ten metre wide alleys in a very small part of town. The Economic pressure turns every square metre of street level facade into shop windows, leaving large parts of the upper floors empty and unused due to the retail rules which state that only the lowest floors have economic value.
A sloping sandwich of parking areas and directly accessible shopping areas incises these upper floors, enlarging their economic potential.
It turns the block into a 'sponge' of accessibility, where valuable display frontage can be encountered everywhere, even in the interior. The journey between the narrow streets becomes a pleasant ride over 'hills' of programme, affording spectacular views across the historic city.

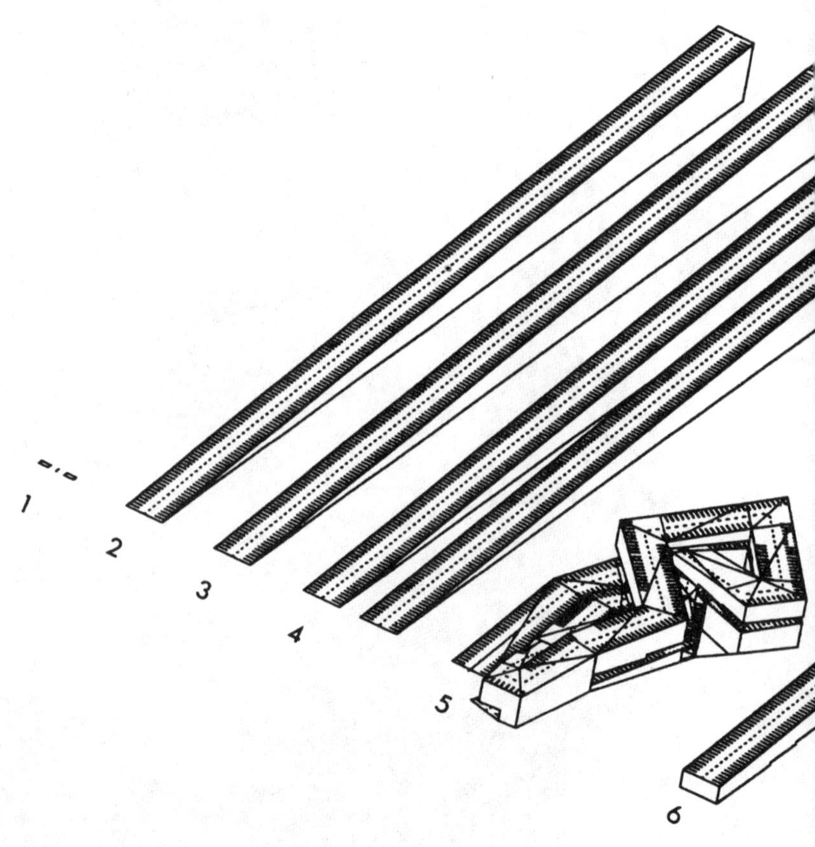

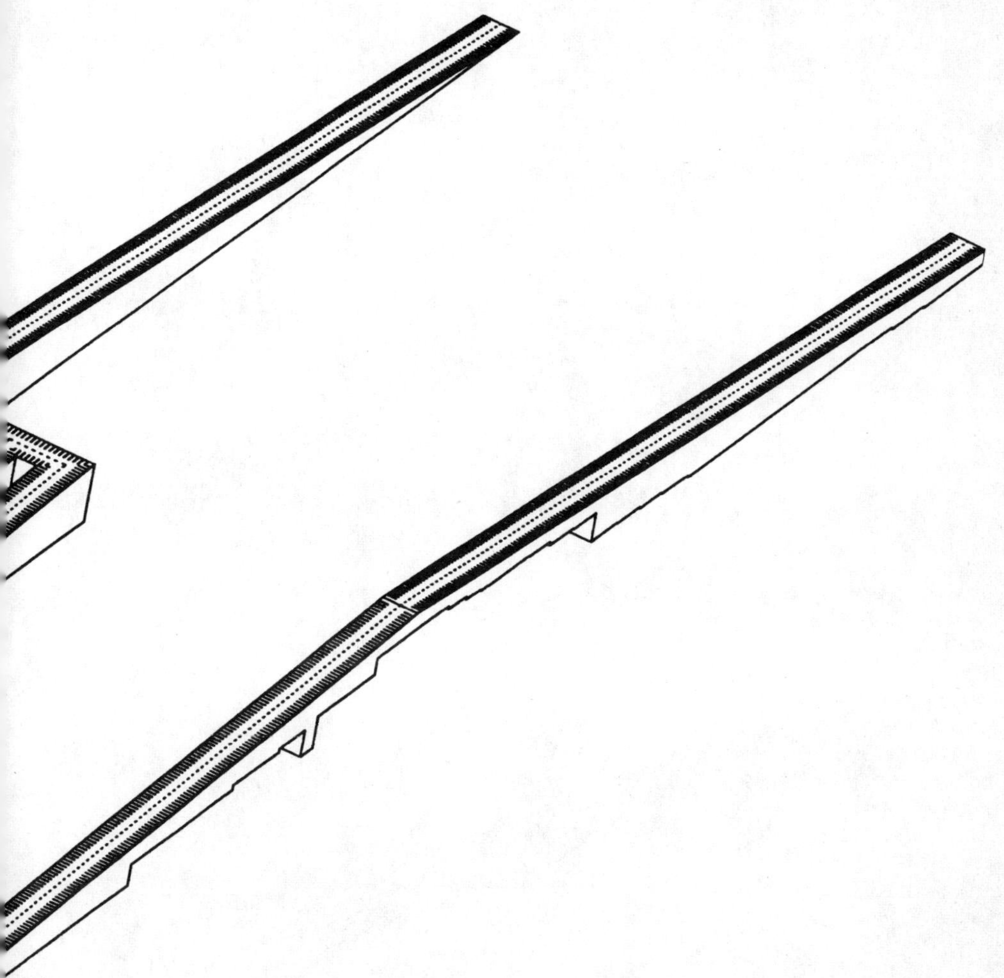

Asphalt, n. A black, sticky substance like coal-tar used for making roofs etc. waterproof, and mixed with gravel or crushed rock to make road surfaces.

Plan

V34 · Fax
DACOM
Gold Card
Gold Card
HOME

Aerial view

Spatial components

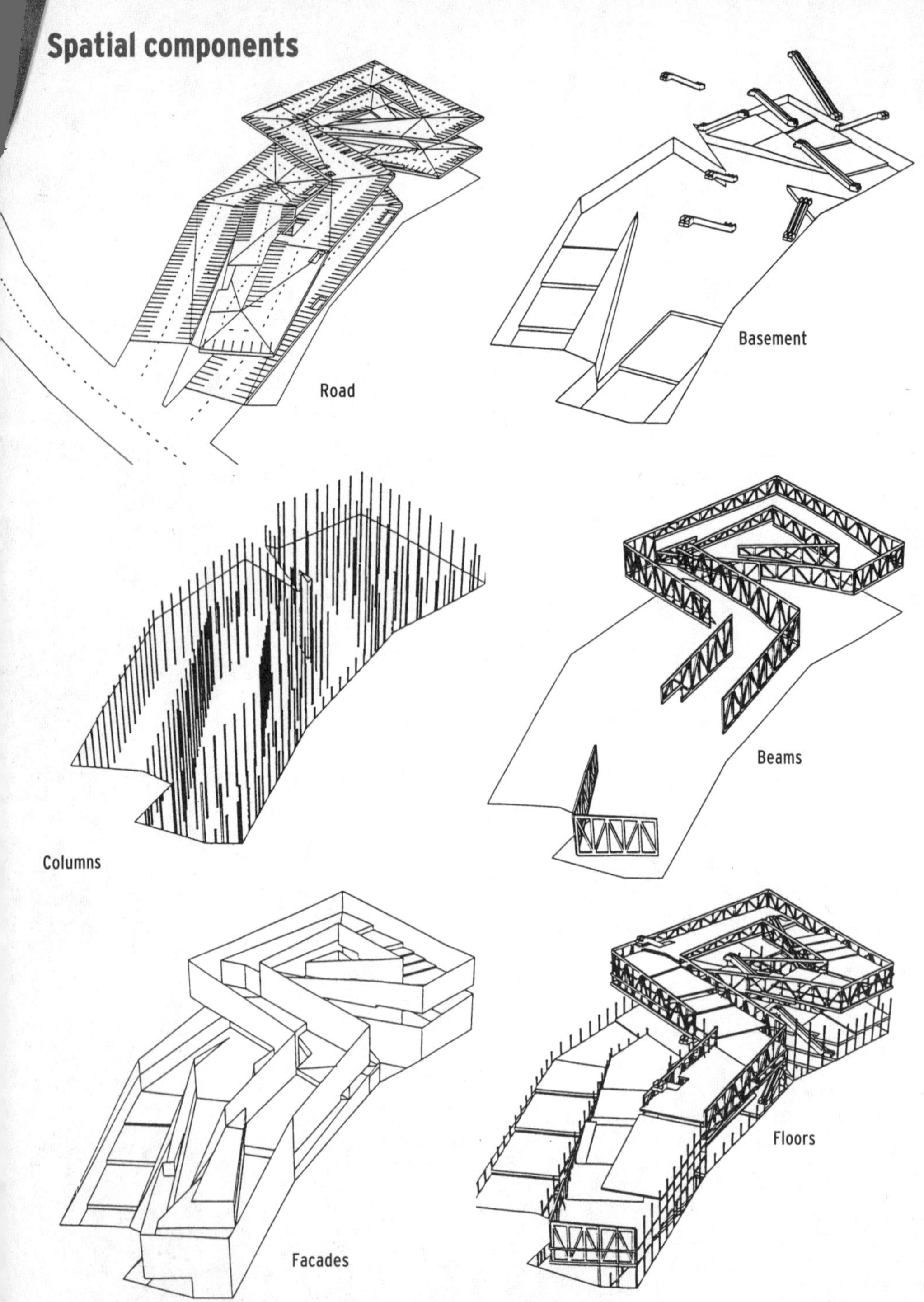

HOME
V34 + Fax
DACOM
Gold Card
Gold Card
58001
STOP
WAIT
GO
MOVE
MOVE
Gold Card
LIGHT
WAIT
Gold Card

Detail

Z-Mall

Main centre for the new district of Leidschenveen, The Netherlands

1997

MVRDV

In the drive for density, not only houses or offices should be stacked. Factories, agriculture, parks and retail would accelerate this imagined 3-D life. How can one in this respect generate, on a modest lot, a vertical city centre in which complete automobile accessibility can coexist with a promenade where cars are prohibited?

Incising and stretching the parking volume required in the brief, carves out enormous 'recesses' between the parking layers, offering space for shops, supermarkets, medical facilities, a social/cultural centre, a library, a church, a sports hall and some eighty houses.
The result is an unbroken rising public parking zone with a continuous urban floor above it.
The diversity of slope percentages encourages a like diversity of uses: from terrace landscapes with market stalls, through platforms for the sale of food, streets for selling non-food products, slopes with tiers of seats in the sports hall and valleys containing auditoria, to a level expanse of patio houses.
Variation in the building's width enables the capacity of the urban floor to mesh with demands made by the programmes and adapt parking needs to suit the programmes located above. This will generate a crystalline terrace-like facade on the park side.
The building's main form will become a beacon for this low-rise city, a latter-day cathedral.

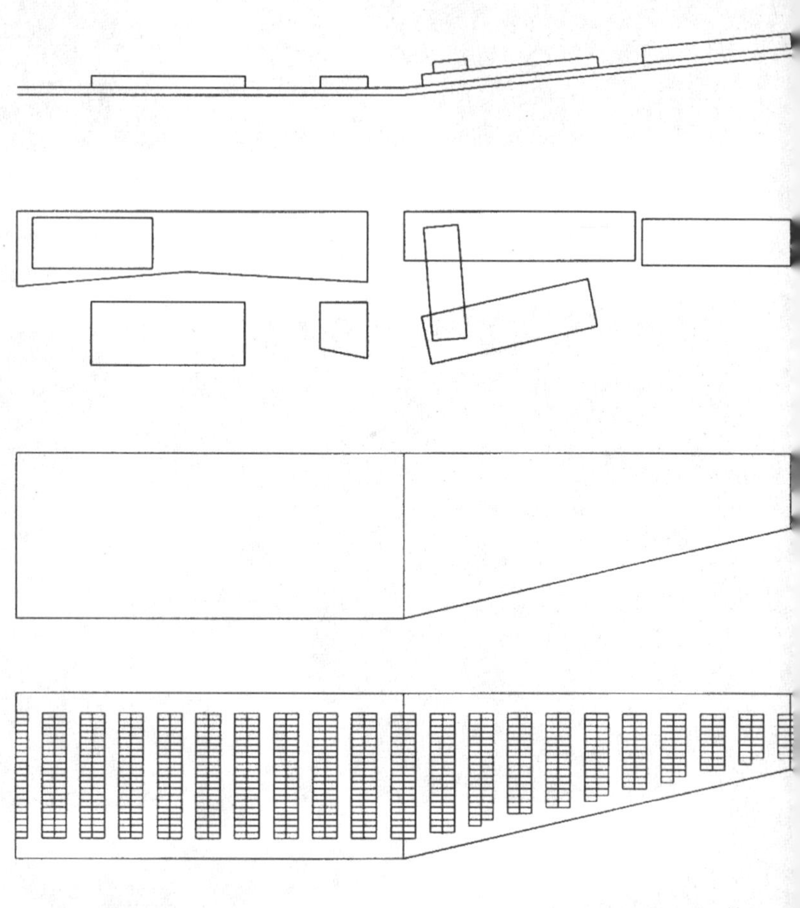

FOODNON FOODLIBRARY

PARK

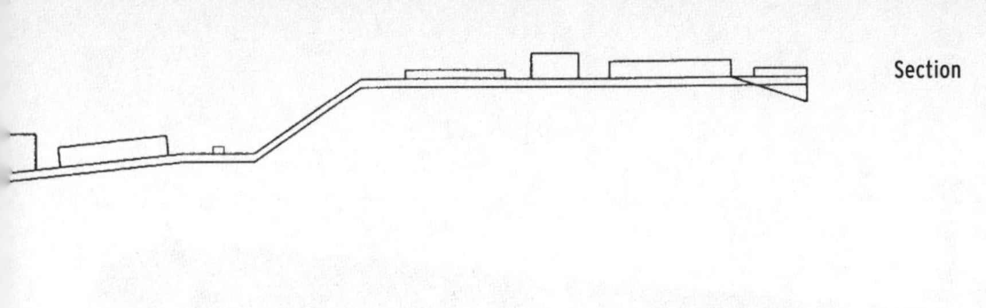

Section

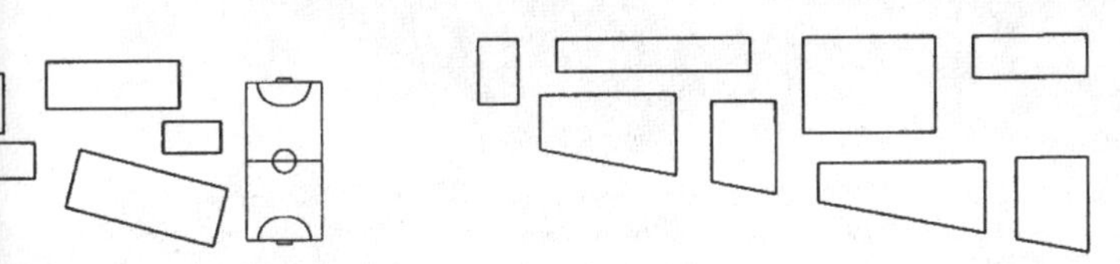

Volumes

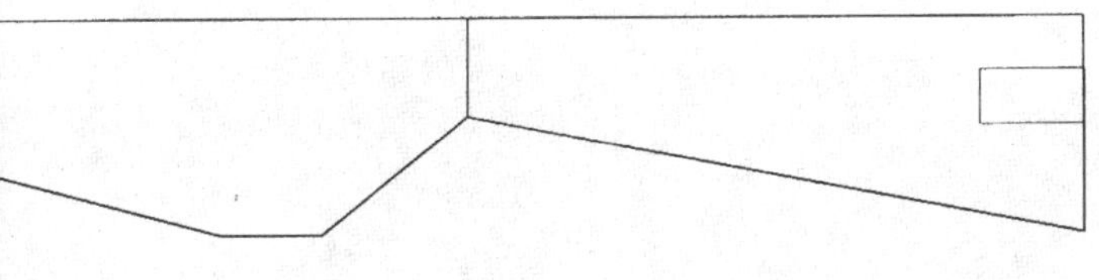

Promenade

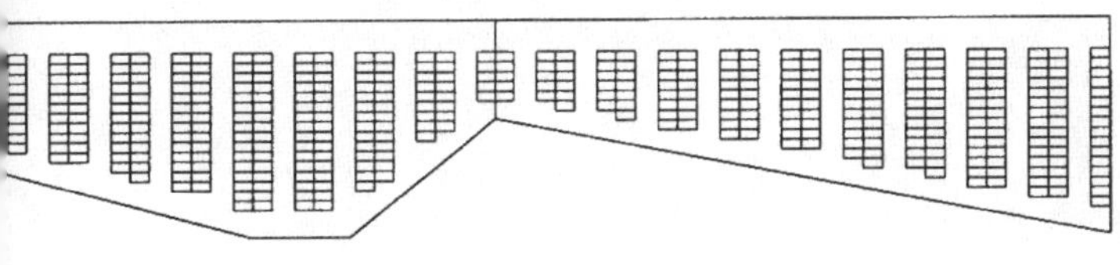

Parking

Programme

FICESSPORTSHOUSING

KING

East

South

West

North

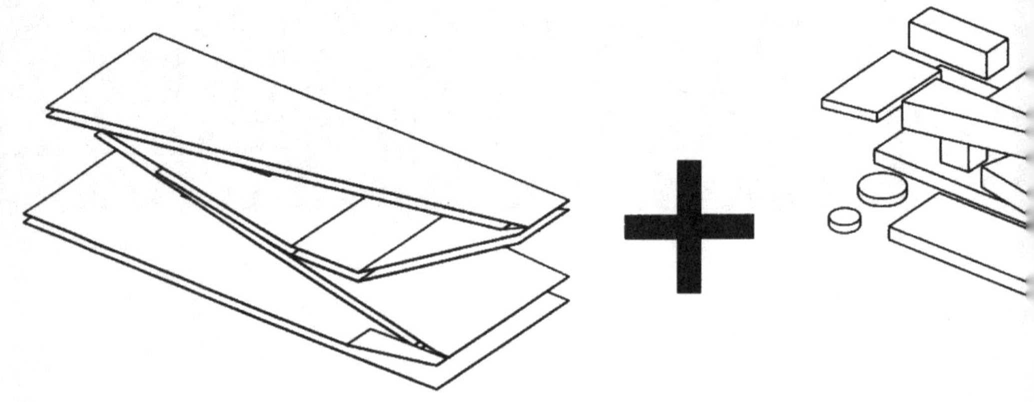

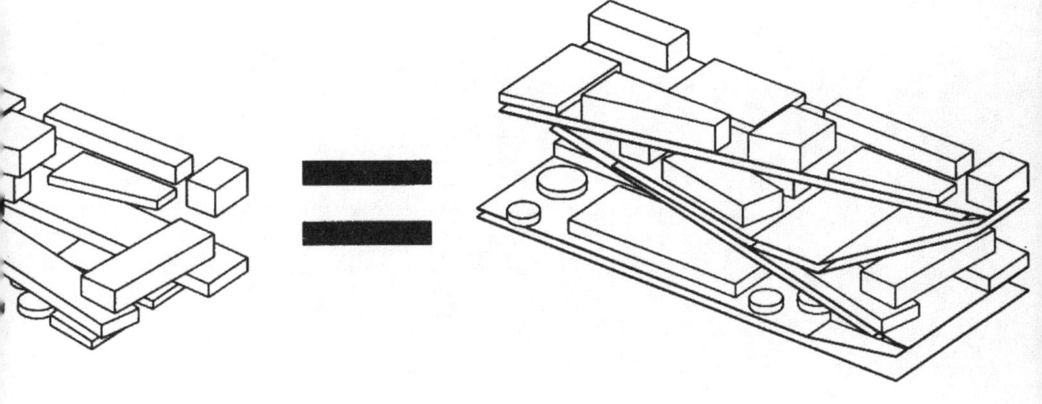

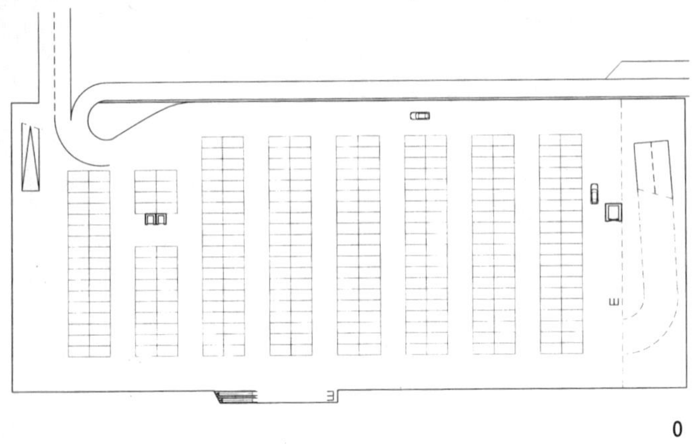

0

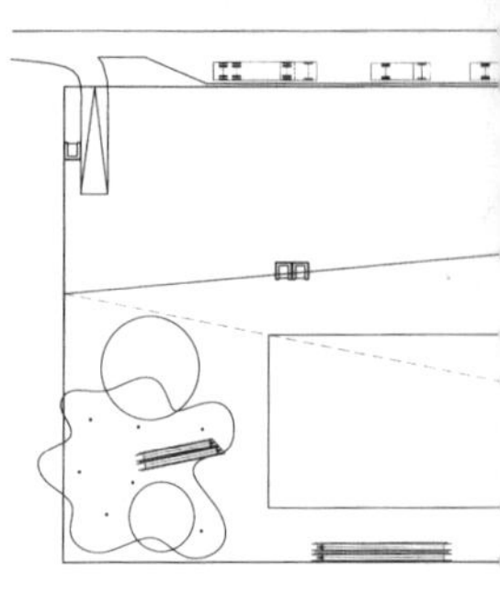

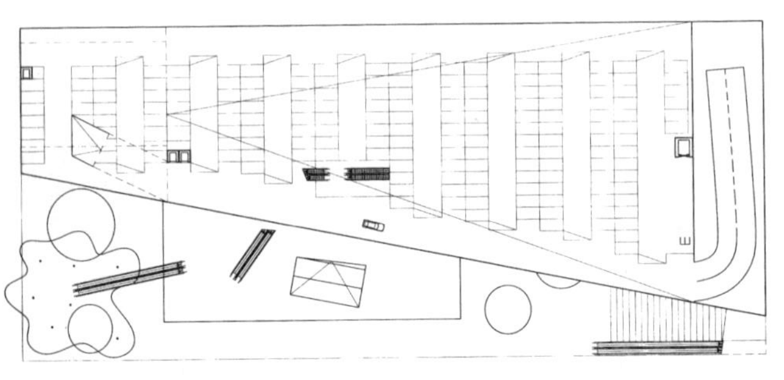

2

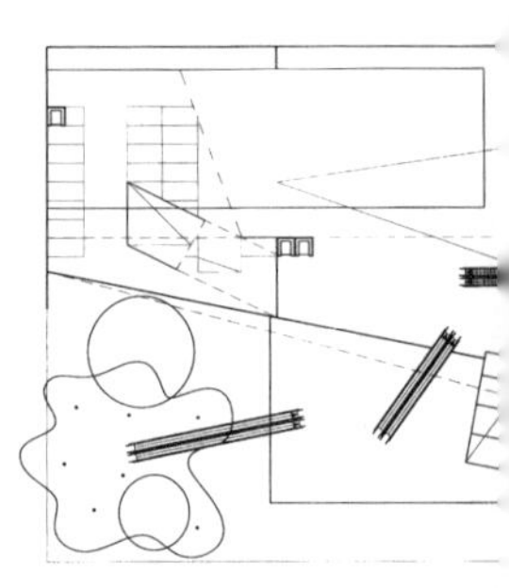

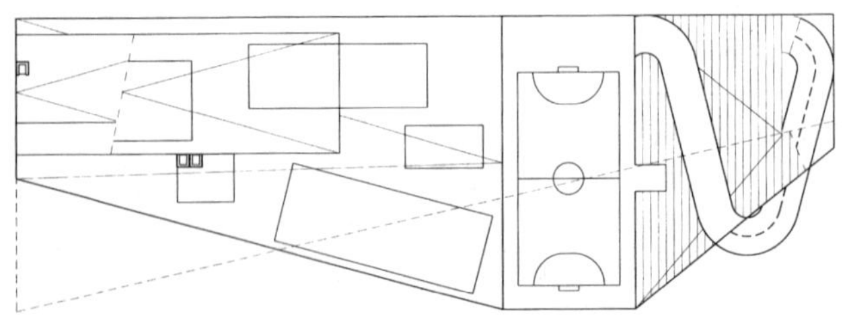

5

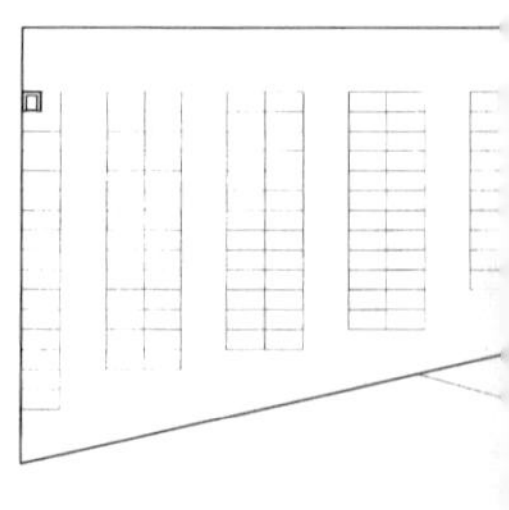

Plans

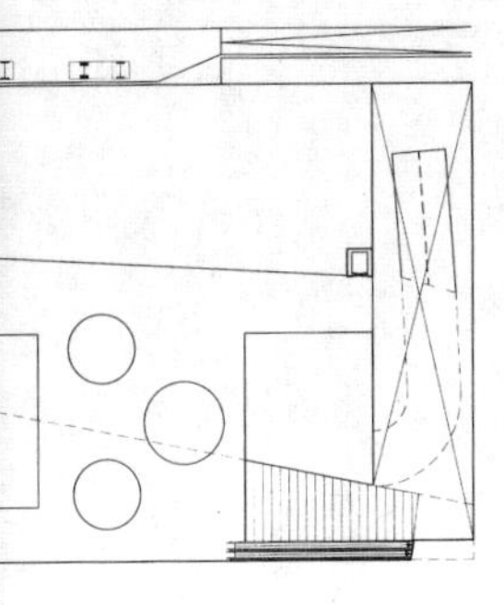

1

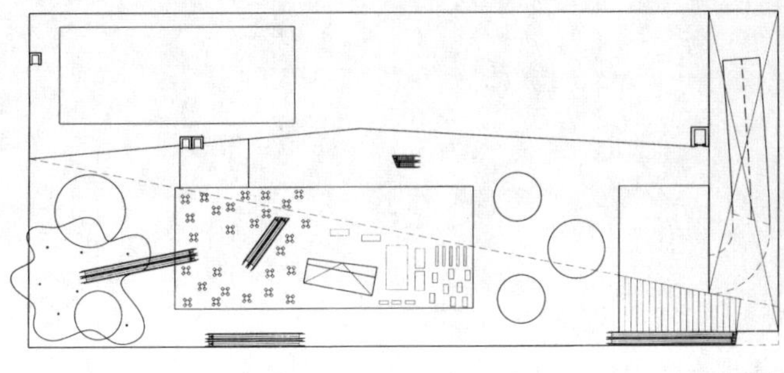

1a

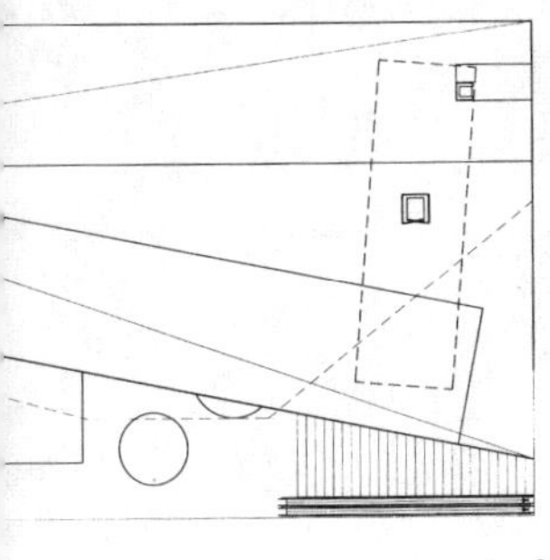

3

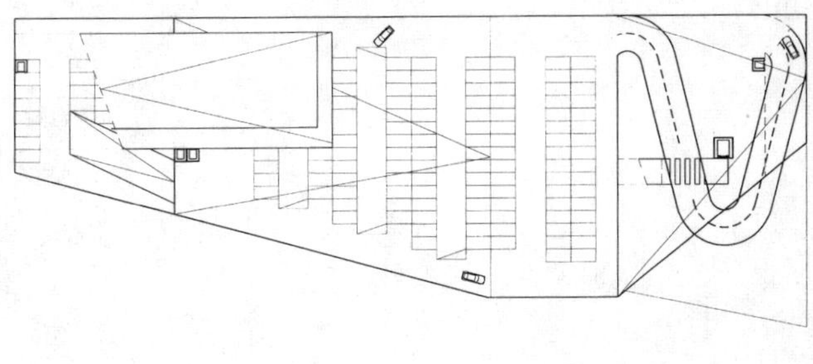

4

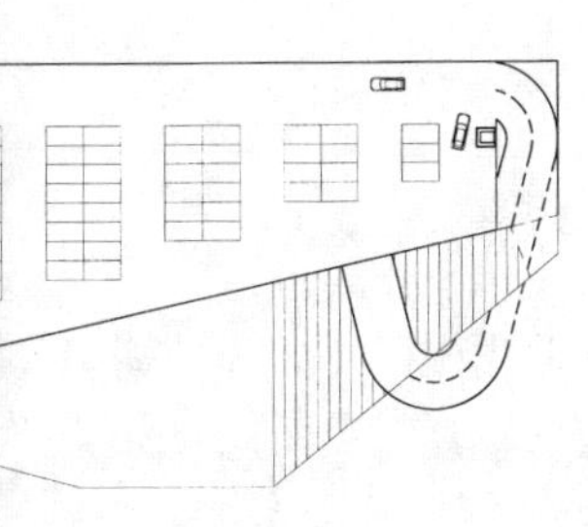

6

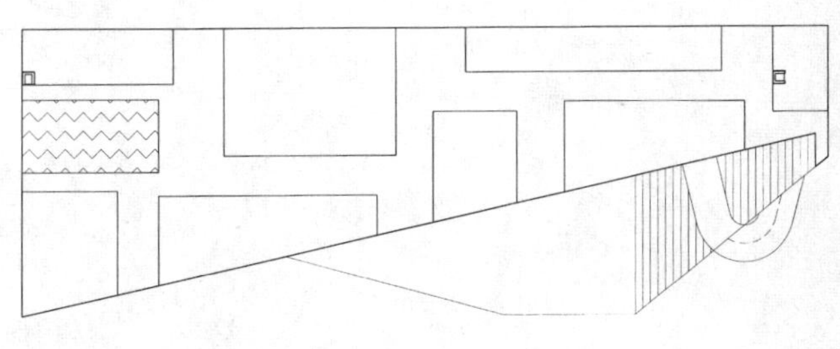

7

Park view

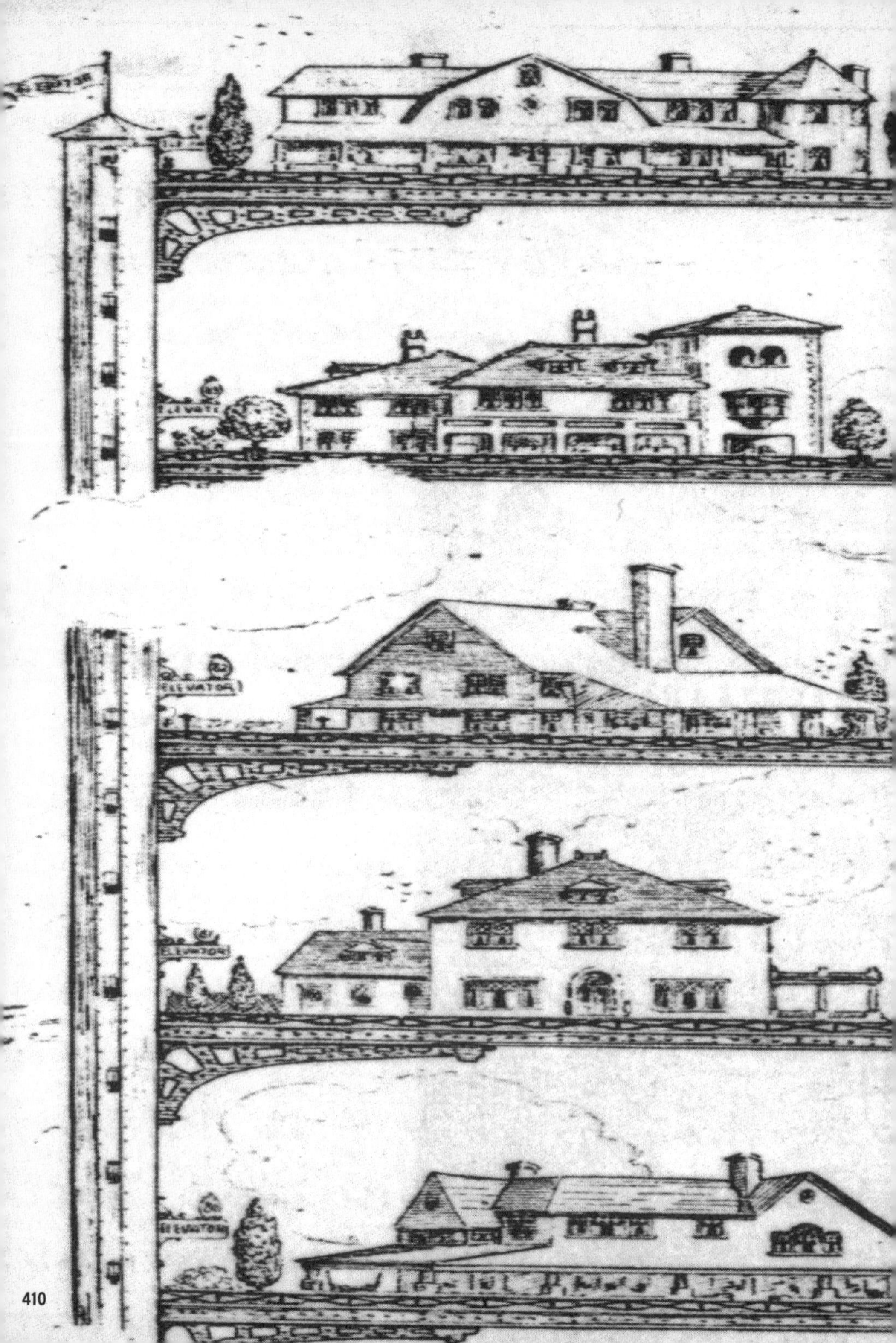

Stack Attack

Central park of the new town of Leidschenrijn, The Netherlands

1997

MVRDV

Can the increasing densification proceed in concert with the increase in the quality of life, is a question that is often asked, with 'nature' featuring as one of the key conditions for that quality.
Clearly 'nature' is retained in the zones beyond the densified zones.
But what role will Nature - in its broadest sense - play within the bounds of such densification? Might this be such a thing as a 'New Nature'?

Should we define "nature" in terms of gradients and difference, then a stacking (quite literally) of different natures would be the most ultimate nature.
Park-buildings, with football pitches on the third level, a wood of beeches on the tenth and a ski-slope on the thirteenth. Where you can swim or play golf on the twentieth floor with a view out over the surroundings. Where you can take the lift to the woods or to one's personal vegetable patch. Where you can even finally transcend the earth in the ultimate cemetery. Where every possible artificial condition can be exacted by means of lamps, types of ground and wind- and heat-proof screens, so that you can even wander between the crocuses in winter and ski amongst Madagascar flora in summer.

We propose a wildy contrasting series of levels housing a kaleidoscope of recreational functions and activating a kaleidoscope of 'natures'.
Differences between levels are brought out by differences in construction, in infrastructure, ground types, water treatment and provision of energy.

The wood room, then, is supported on timber columns, the cave room built up of vaults, the rain room columnless, the glass nursery room a vierendeel girder, the mushroom room built of solid brick, the paddyfields of rippling corrugated sheet, rocks in the alpine room, and so on. A literal stacking pushed to the limit.

The visitor wanders by way of a sequence of small stairs through the paddyfield room, an incline in the ramp room, a mountain path in the alpine room, an escalator in the woods, a lift in the sports rooms, a platform lift to the cemetery. A route architecturale constructed from the differences between levels.

Classic grounds such as clay, sand or peat alternate with more modern ones, clay granules for instance; water and air currents are there to nurture plants and natures. By mixing these 'grounds' with species of worms and insects other biotopes are born.

An unbroken stream of water from the fountain on the roof, water basins with hydrophyte filters, sieves that cause indoor showers of rain, waterfalls along the facades, veils of mist on the forest floor, streams of condensation at extremely low levels with a higher air pressure, flows of droplets over the cave walls, marshes and pressure vessels - all these combine to sustain a cyclic system. The watery masses can be mixed with fizzy lemonade: it's so clean that you can drink it anywhere you choose!

Deploying windmills on the roof or as a separate turbo-floor, watermills, floors filled with energetic biomasses, stairs that 'tap' the energy of the visitors and pressure vessels that pump the water back up, the building can be conceived of as an energetic self-supplying or even energy-producing machine. That way it can freely 'waste' energy: the facades can consist of heat curtains, gauze or plants or just fencing, thus fully safeguarding the public character. Even the roof can consist of a heat shield: high pressure air currents of 200 degrees Celsius melt even the coldest snow and dispose of the hardest rainfall. Enter such possible sublime combinations as nude recreation in the icy cold or sunbathing in the grey autumn drizzle!

The nett result is a building type that literally saves and expands (public) space, one that also saves energy, time, water and infrastructure.
A mini-ecosystem. An oxygen machine. A survival kit.

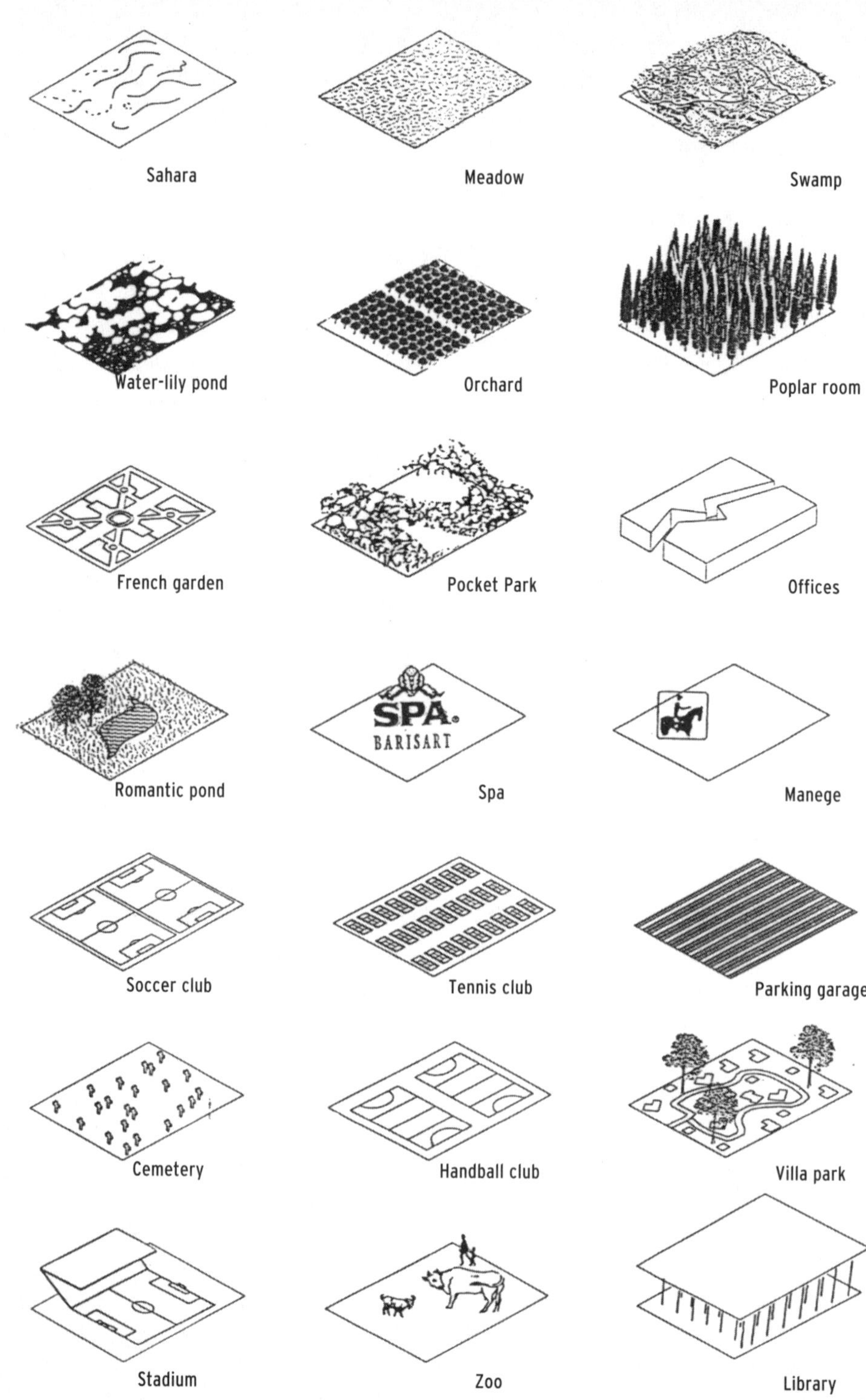
Sahara
Meadow
Swamp
Water-lily pond
Orchard
Poplar room
French garden
Pocket Park
Offices
Romantic pond
SPA
BARISART
Spa
Manege
Soccer club
Tennis club
Parking garage
Cemetery
Handball club
Villa park
Stadium
Zoo
Library

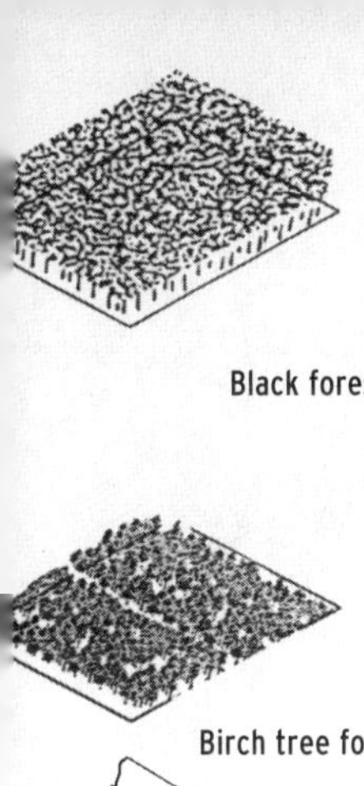

Black forest

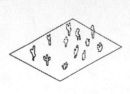

Cactus garden

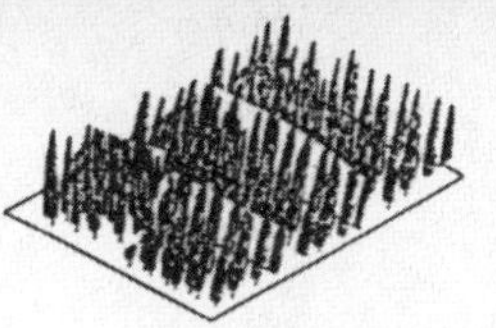

Cypress city

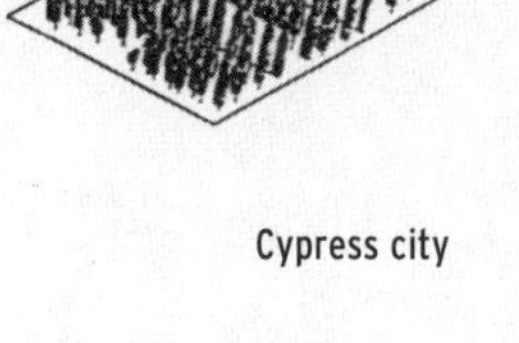

Birch tree forest

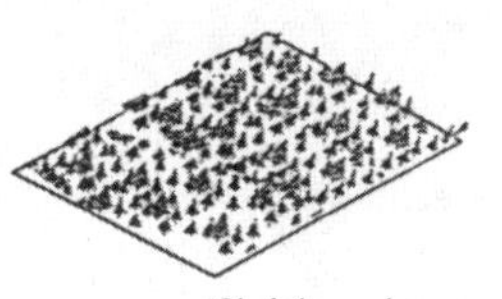

Christmas trees park

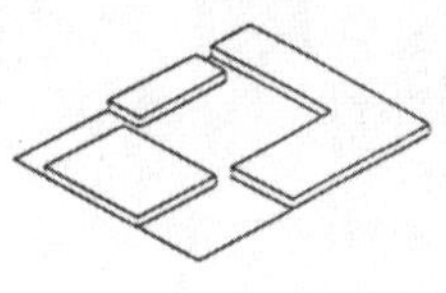

Shopping mall

Ski club

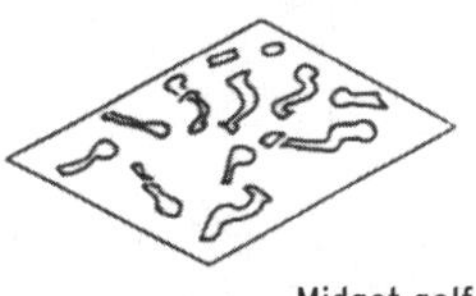

Midget golf

Sports club

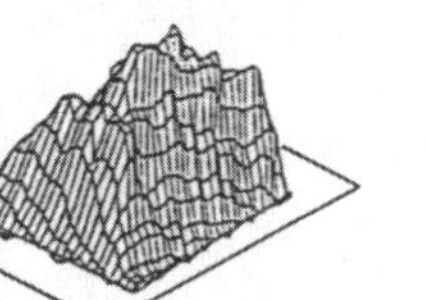

Alpine hotel

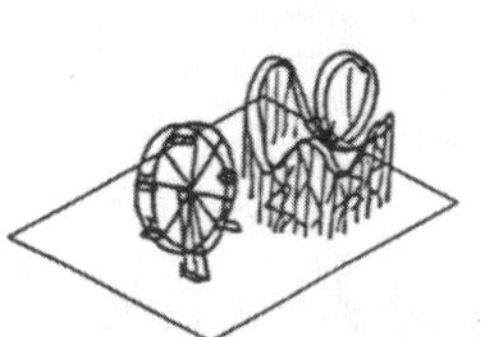

Lunapark

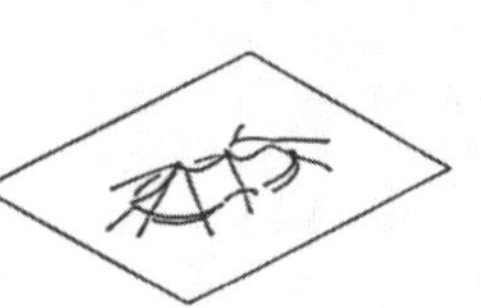

Manifestations

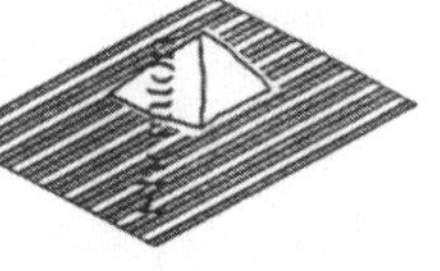

Mall

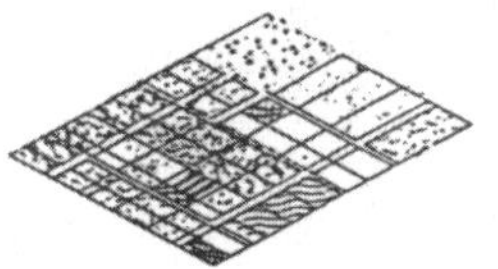

Allotment gardens

Swanlake

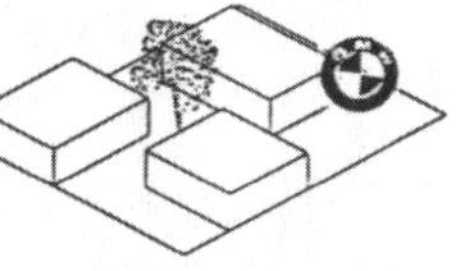

Car repair

Patio houses

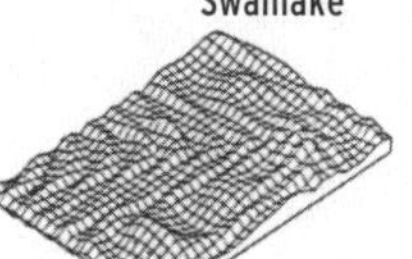

4 wheel drive club

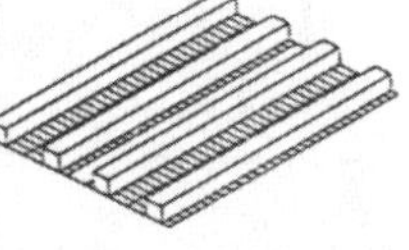

Row houses

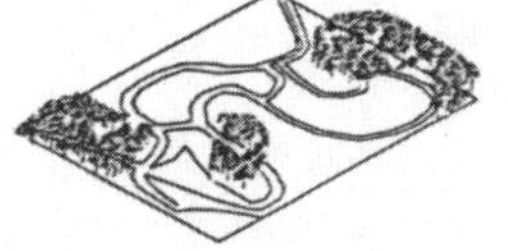

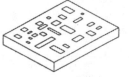

English garden

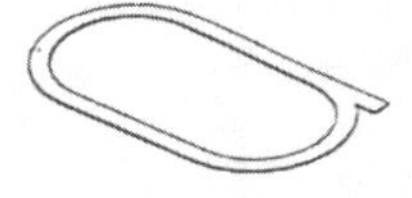

Athletics club

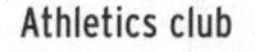

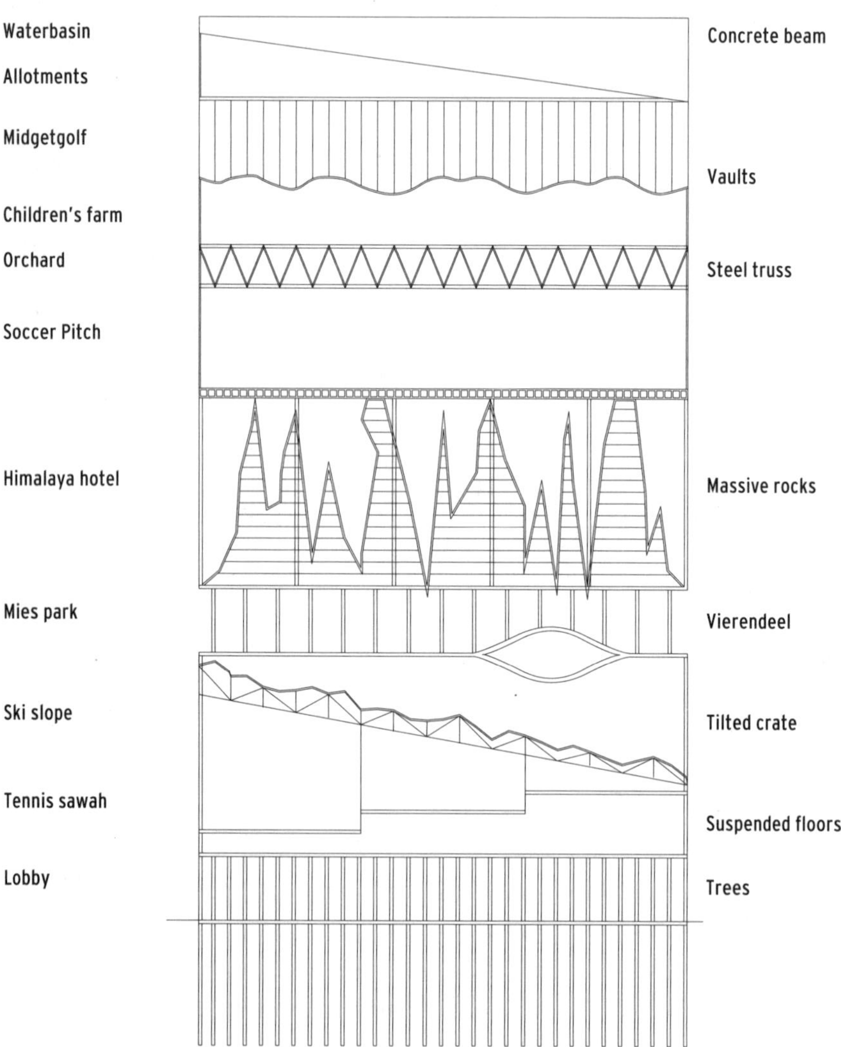
Program
Structure
Waterbasin
Allotments
Midgetgolf
Children's farm
Orchard
Soccer Pitch
Himalaya hotel
Mies park
Ski slope
Tennis sawah
Lobby
Concrete beam
Vaults
Steel truss
Massive rocks
Vierendeel
Tilted crate
Suspended floors
Trees

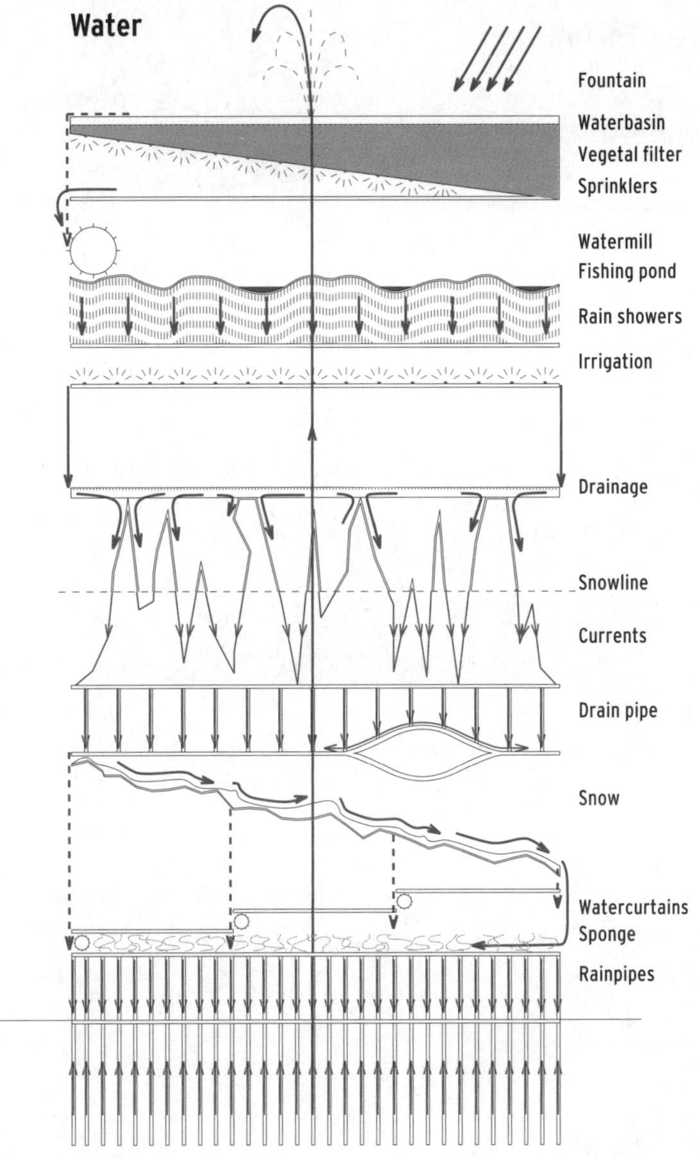
Water
Fountain
Waterbasin
Vegetal filter
Sprinklers
Watermill
Fishing pond
Rain showers
Irrigation
Drainage
Snowline
Currents
Drain pipe
Snow
Watercurtains
Sponge
Rainpipes

Energy

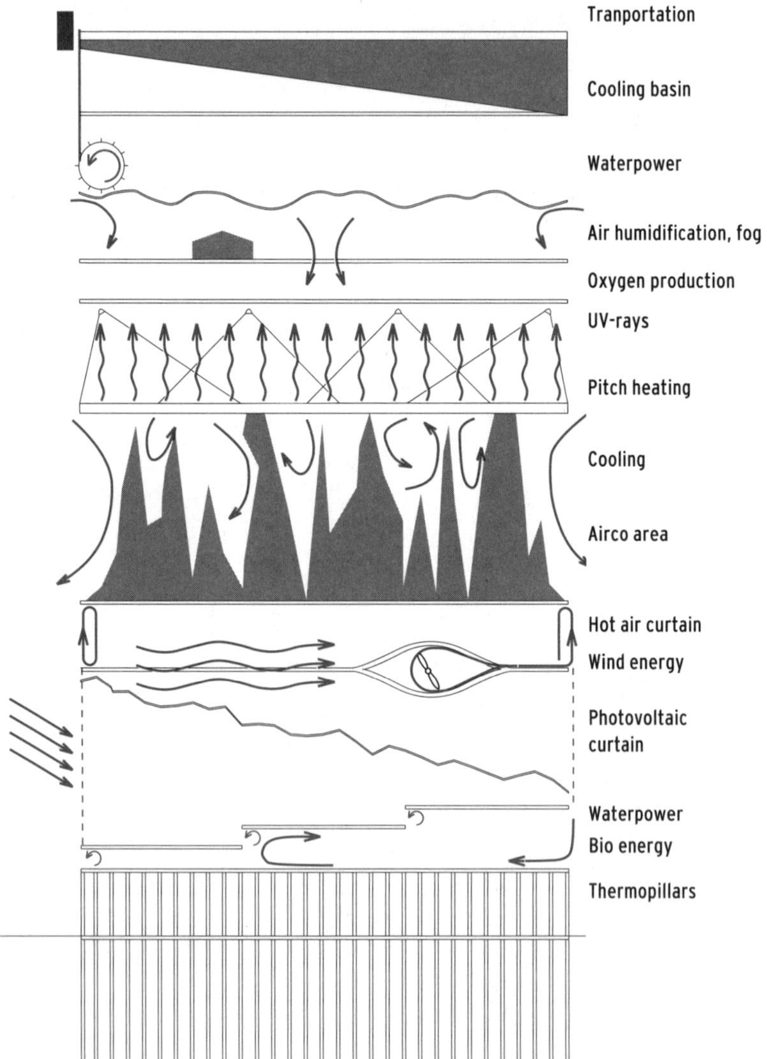

Tranportation
Cooling basin
Waterpower
Air humidification, fog
Oxygen production
UV-rays
Pitch heating
Cooling
Airco area
Hot air curtain
Wind energy
Photovoltaic curtain
Waterpower
Bio energy
Thermopillars

Circulation

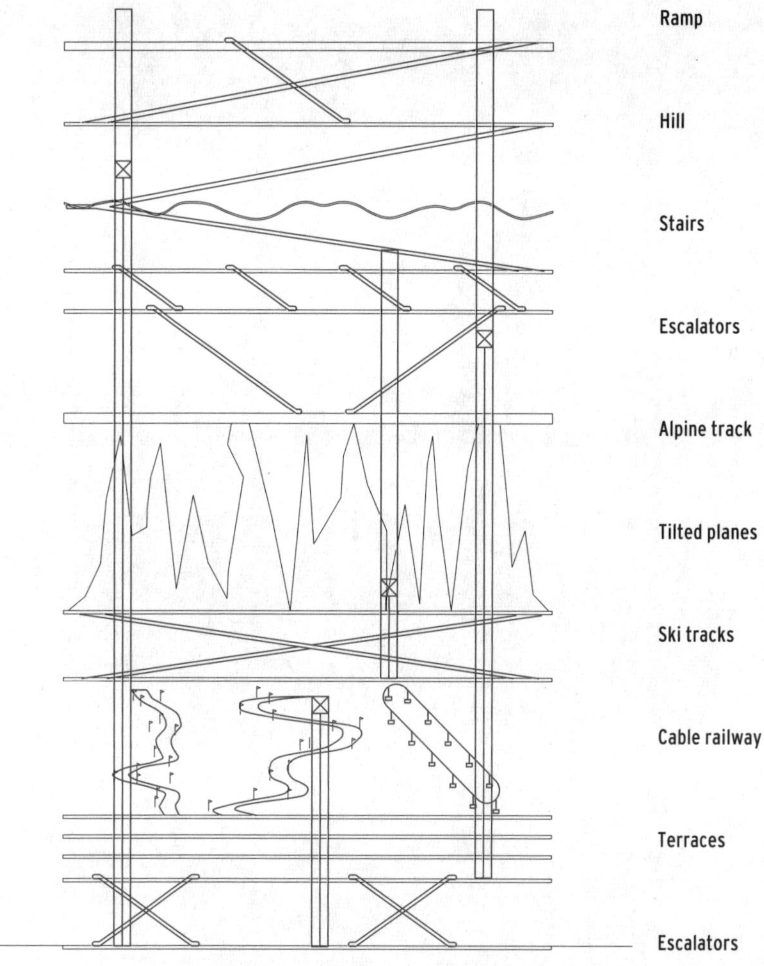

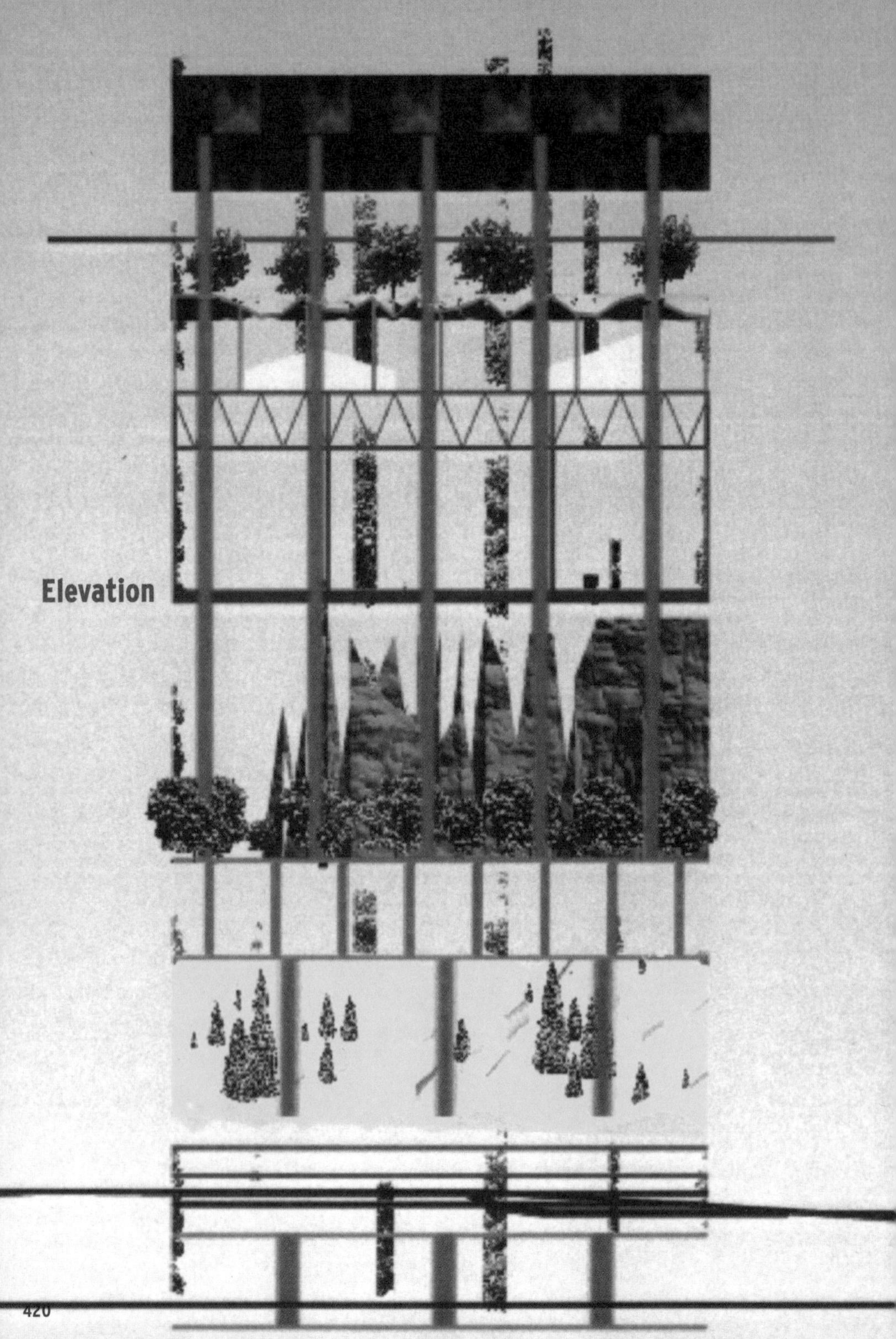
Elevation

Street view

Stacked park

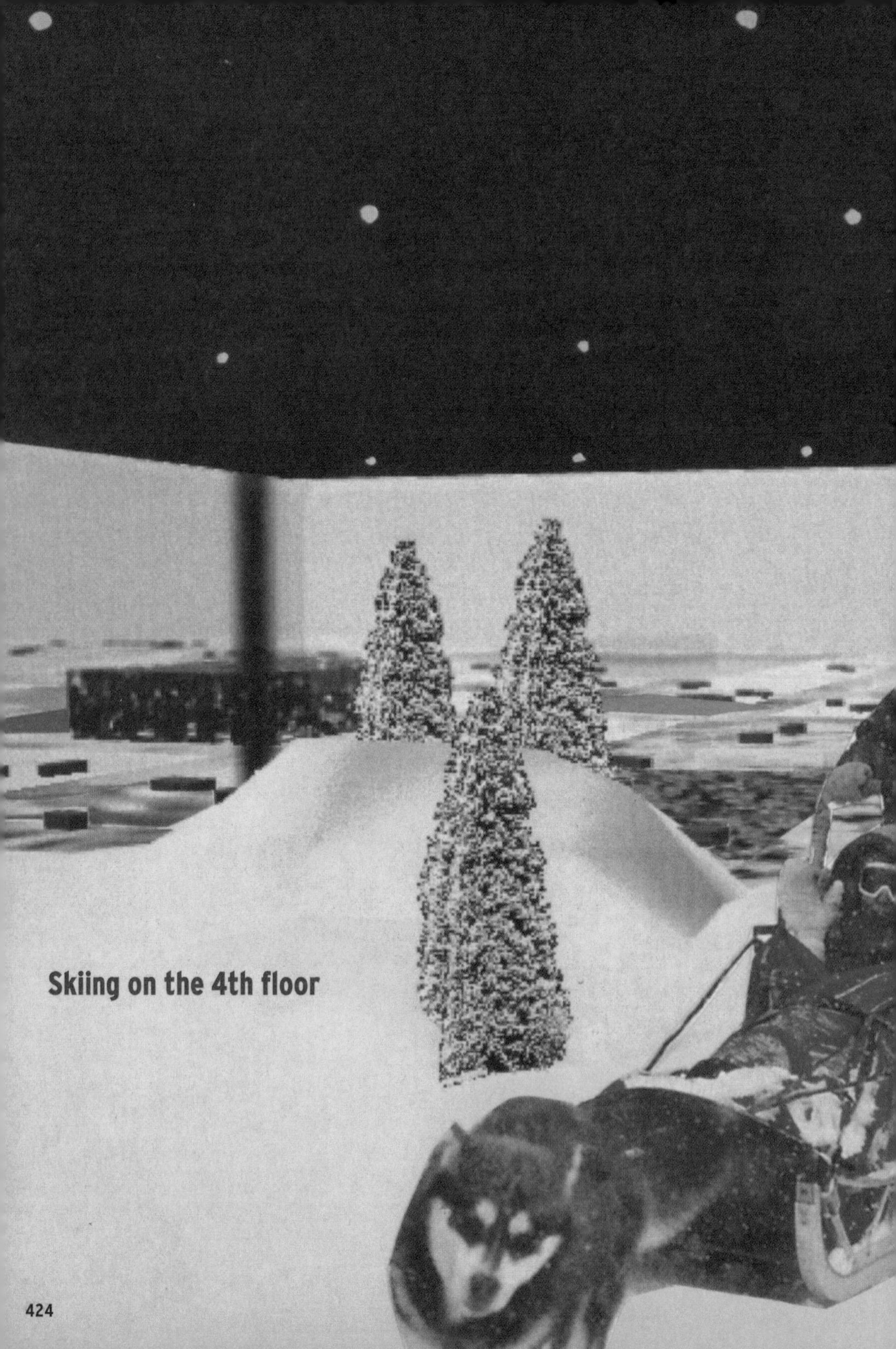

Skiing on the 4th floor

INFRASTRUCTURE

Mainstreet

Town planning study for development of Almere, The Netherlands

1996

MVRDV

A6 boulevard Would it be a viable proposition in the coming decades to radically strengthen the green image of Almere, the most successful new Dutch polder town, and pair it with the required growth by an extra 20,000 to 30,000 houses in the period 2005-2015, by concentrating this growth in the existing urban area?

And would it be feasible also to fill Almere with a new, inner urban environment, thereby avoiding overcapacity of the existing daily living environment? Could we then bring about a fusion of periphery and centre by celebrating rather than avoiding the hindrance zones of the urban programme?

The key to this hypothesis lies in the position of the A6 highway.

If urban corridors elsewhere are found in the periphery, in Almere such a corridor pierces the heart of the town. By siting most of the building programme in this zone, a 'boulevard' could emerge where dwelling and work have more than local significance by their position on the A6. It would give Almere a Mainstreet.

Downtown Almere In transforming the required expansion of the A6's traffic capacities into through and local lanes there could be more slipways, generating a series of such 'addresses'. By having these parallel lanes meander both existing and new addresses could be strung together. Unsuspecting places in Almere could suddenly find themselves endowed with regional significance.

A mosaic of plots and addresses then emerges, that can be construed as a single dwell-work city, a single 'downtown'. It might grow into the Sunset or Sunrise Boulevard of Almere, depending on the traffic direction.

A radical coordination of 'normal' and exorbitant programmes, of intensive and extensive infills, from Business Districts to villa parks, Chinatowns to valleys of industrial hangars, from Lido to IJsselmeer Strand, from fishing village to Lake Shore Drive - this coordination would transform that mosaic into a contemporary parkway.

Extending the local lake (Weerwater) to the south of the A6 would turn coastal Almere Haven to face the heart of the town, provide sand for infrastructural works, enlarge the recreational potential, retain views and make it more attractive for businesses to set up branches there.

A rapid rail link and a loop round Weerwater would build on operations to establish a local urban centre and tie these to the A6. The result would be a tight weave between existing polynuclear urban areas and the new town.

Placing parts of the housing programme outside the noise zone would make space for more open 'sinusoid' motorway plazas surrounded by businesses.

In the remaining zones the noise level would be tempered by a series of measures: dikes to create fortified settlements, mixed blocks with office 'shields' to create scenes reminiscent of Hamburg's Wasserstadt, a local arch over the A6 to throw up a residential mound ('Belmonte') with views across Weerwater, and patio villas strung together to generate 'massifs' with personal acoustic baffles on the roof.

Weerwaterstad Weerwater, the central lake, is reconfigured and expanded by the Loop into an urban quarter where daily living programmes and urban services meld into a single central archipelago, like an Almerian version of Stockholm. A 'void' as centre, with the various urban components of Almere putting on a brave face in its direction.
Utterly disparate neighbourhoods take up a position here, strung together by the Loop, by bus lines, watertaxis and a monorail. We find successively along the banks of the lake a 'Lake Shore Drive' of apartments on an urban beach, a 'Barceloneta' of ground-accessed housing in a taut setting, a 'Village' fronting Almere Haven with mixed block development and a villa park. Enlarging the lake generates, among other things, a park-island of condominiums, an 'Ile de la Cité' with apartment buildings à la Petersburg, an island of patio houses and a 12 metre high residential mound (Belmonte) of compact ground-accessed houses.
This mound is primed to receive commercial services and parking garages. Here the A6 has its own slipway and a 'pitstop' generating the conditions for a Mall of regional potential. At the crest of the mound is a deck spanning the A6 that is able to accommodate offices with a view out across lake and town. This archipelago is completed by the remaining urban services.
A crematorium stands on the 'Isola Bella'. The Lido amusement park lies in friendly proximity to a Drive-In Beach and the new stadium for Almere football club with additional space for exposition and congress facilities. The roof of this hall can be folded back, transforming the hall into stands overlooking the field and the town. A power station can warm up the lake for use all year round. An artificial ice rink can be moored there in a cloud of steam. The position of the swimming pool, executed as a floating tray, can be changed to suit the demand. Its grass roof, which can be slid away, can act as a sunbathing area in summer, an observation platform in winter.
The vistas can double as courses for rowing and waterskiing. Zones outside the vistas can be fleshed out as carpets of waterlilies and reeds.

The environs This concentrated injection means that the existing environs can be kept free of urbanization and can even become a string of parks of a more long-term and permanent nature.

Further growth When further intensifying the A6 zone with an extra 20,000 houses, the existing rail link can be transformed into a more lightweight, inner urban loop. This can be achieved by reserving the central berm of the A6 for intercity trains with a central station in Belmonte, in the heart of Weerwaterstad (and consequently Almere). The result? A tight-knit, compact city, a monolith in the landscape of the Flevopolders.

Almere 1996

Almere 2030?

A6 boulevard

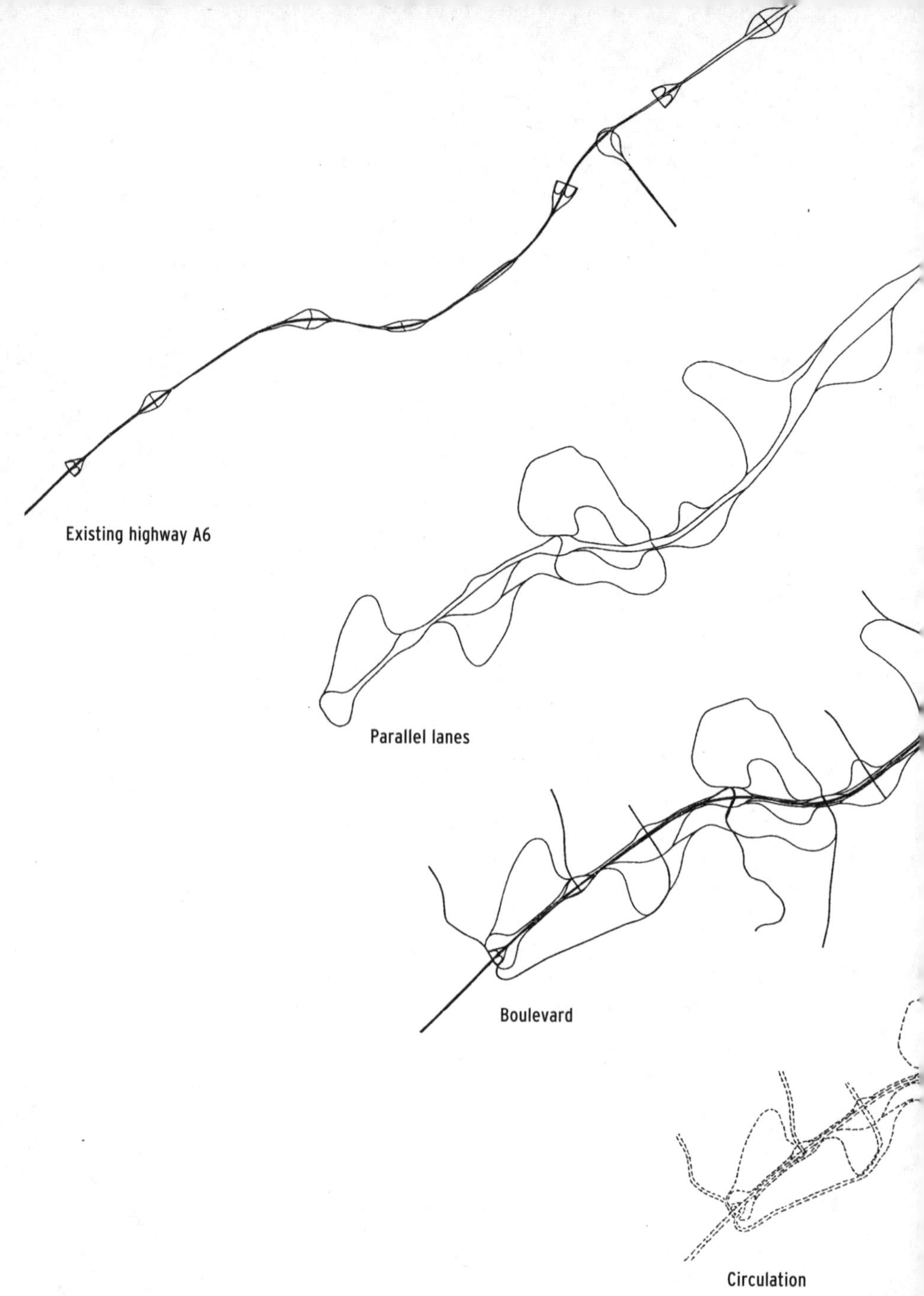
Existing highway A6
Parallel lanes
Boulevard
Circulation

Traffic

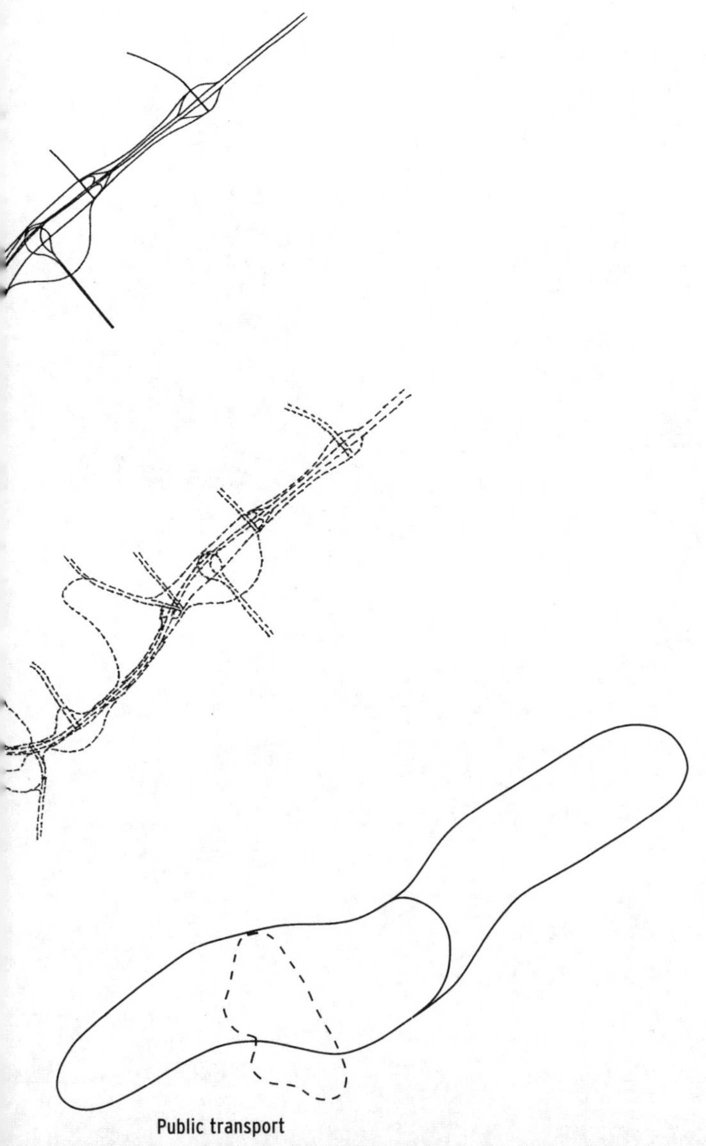

Public transport

Addresses

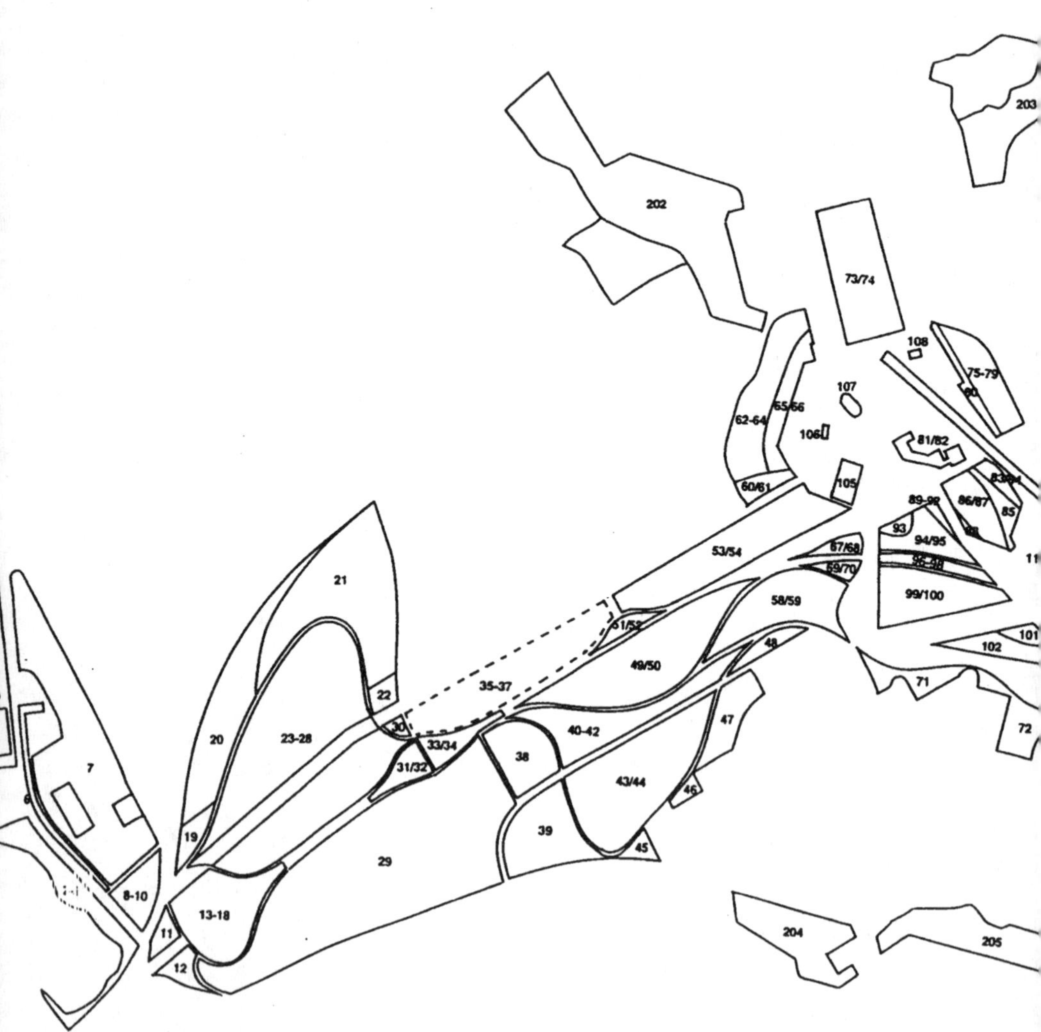

203
202
73/74
108
75-79
107
65/66
62-64
106
81/82
105
60/61
86/87
85
93
94/95
53/54
67/68
69/70
99/100
21
58/59
51/52
101
102
48
49/50
35-37
71
22
72
47
30
40-42
20
23-28
33/34
7
31/32
38
43/44
6
46
19
39
45
29
8-10
13-18
204
205
11
12

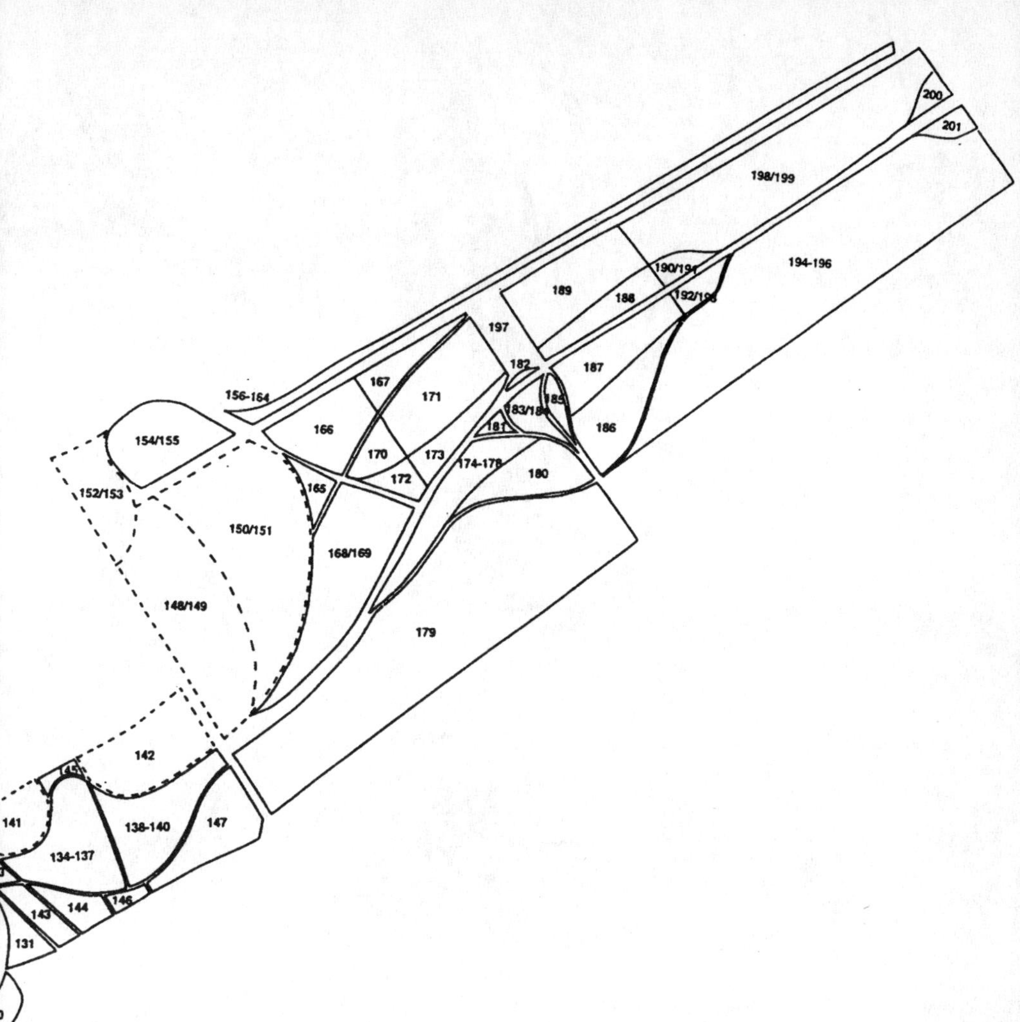
200
201
198/199
190/191
194-196
189
188
192/193
197
182
187
156-164
167
171
185
183/184
166
181
186
154/155
170
173
174-178
180
172
165
152/153
150/151
168/169
148/149
179
142
145
141
138-140
147
134-137
33
144
146
143
131
30

Plots

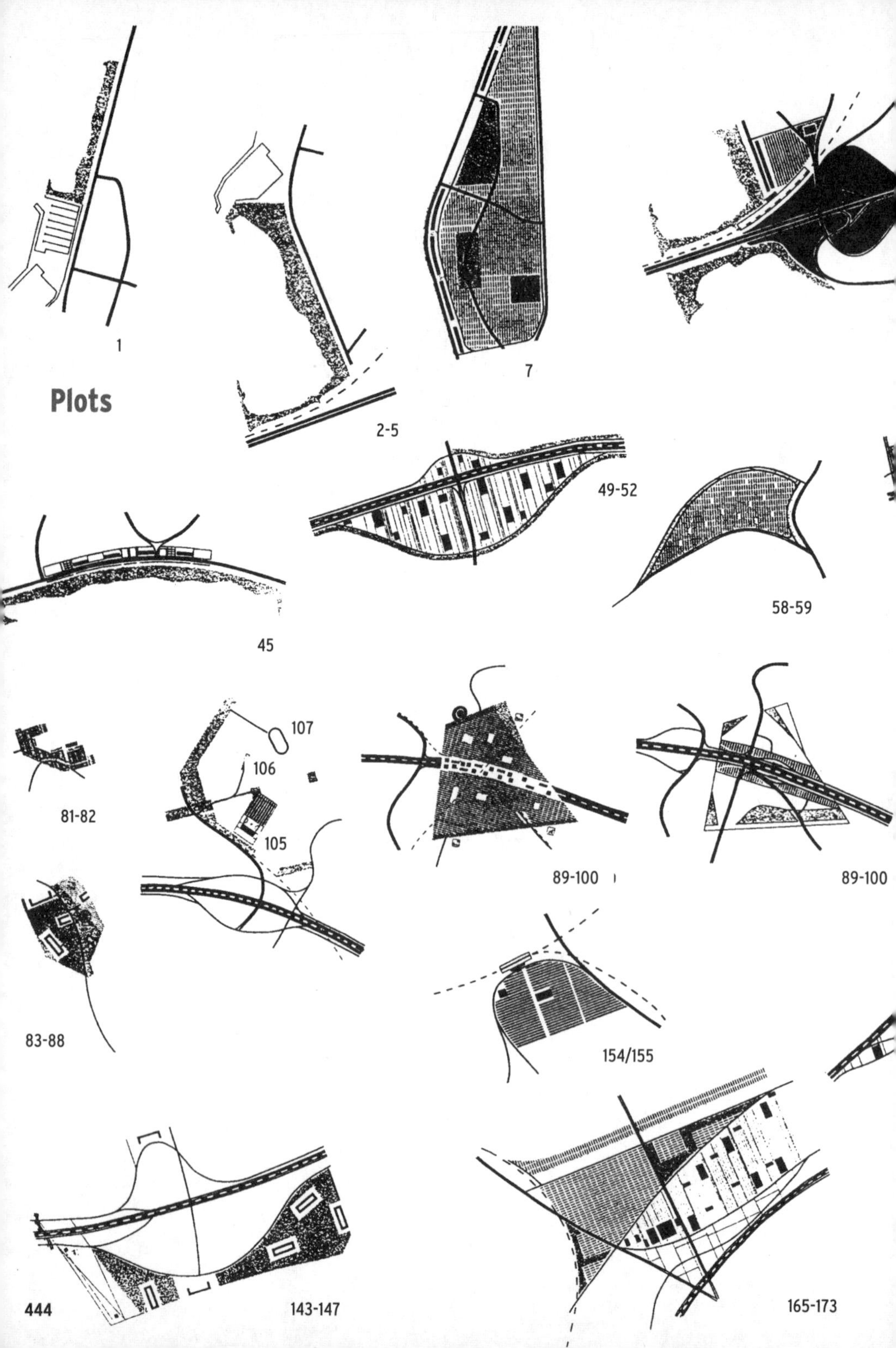

1
2-5
7
49-52
58-59
45
81-82
107
106
105
89-100
89-100
83-88
154/155
143-147
165-173

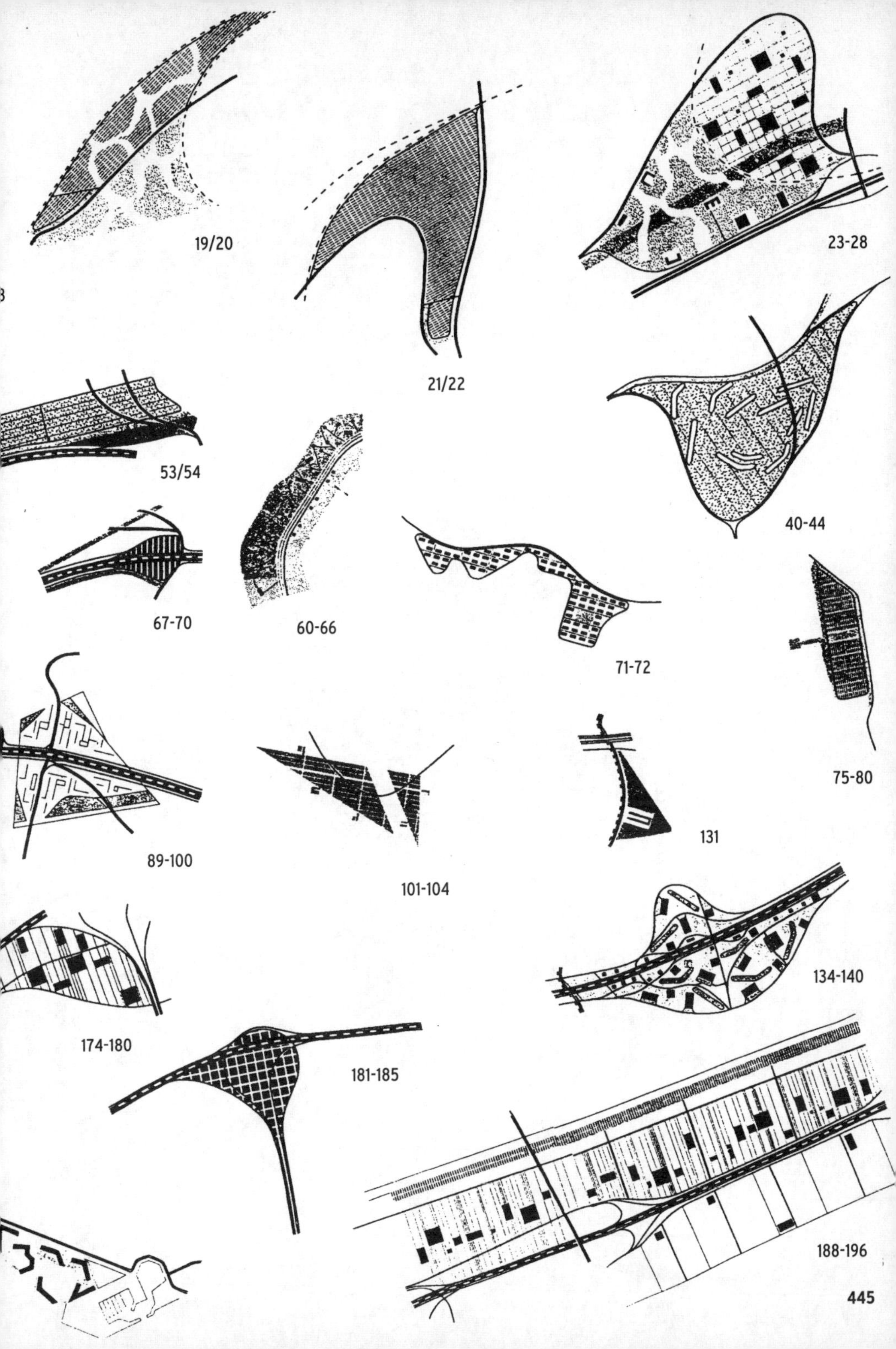
19/20
21/22
23-28
40-44
53/54
67-70
60-66
71-72
75-80
89-100
101-104
131
134-140
174-180
181-185
188-196

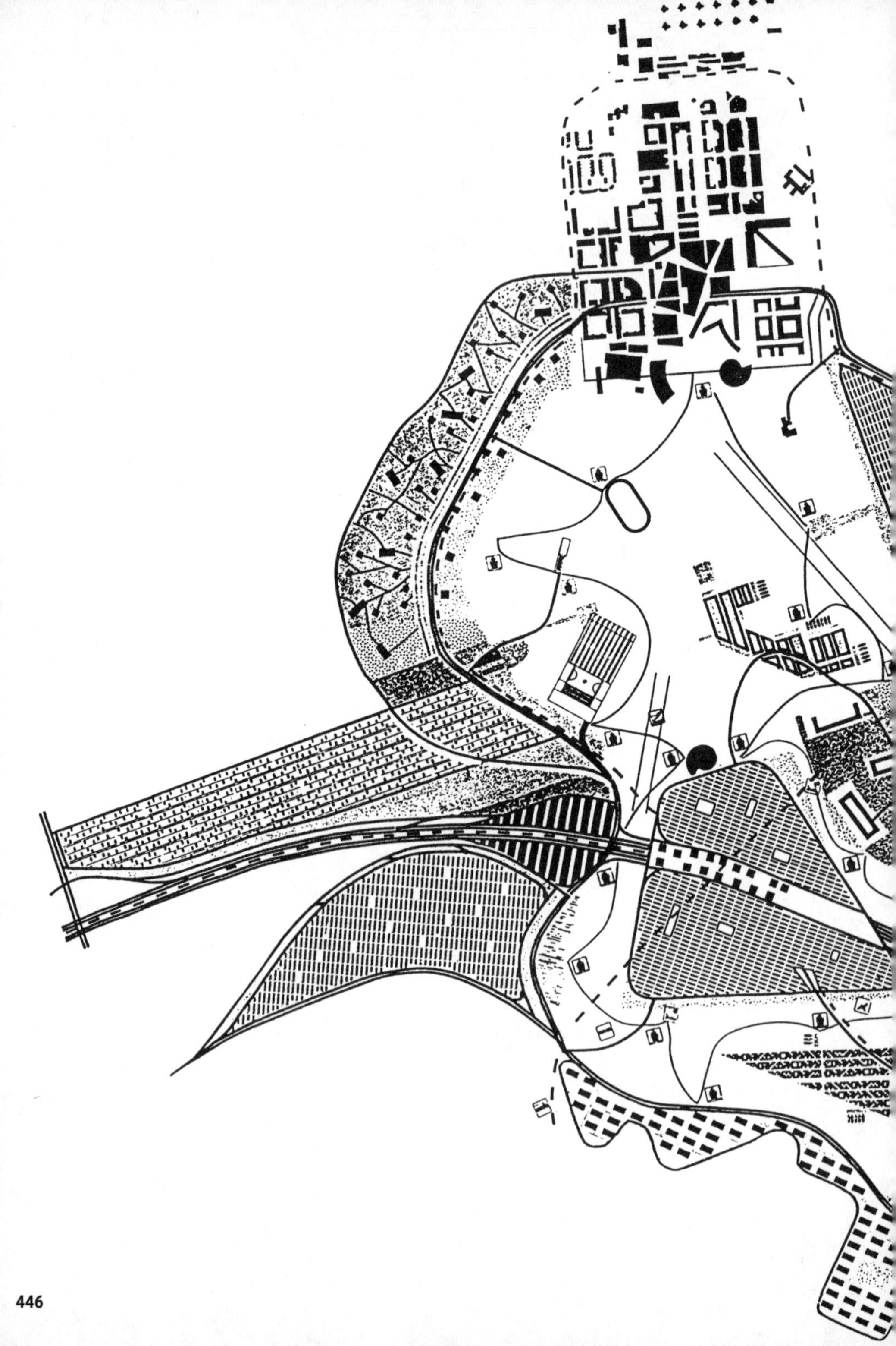

Centre

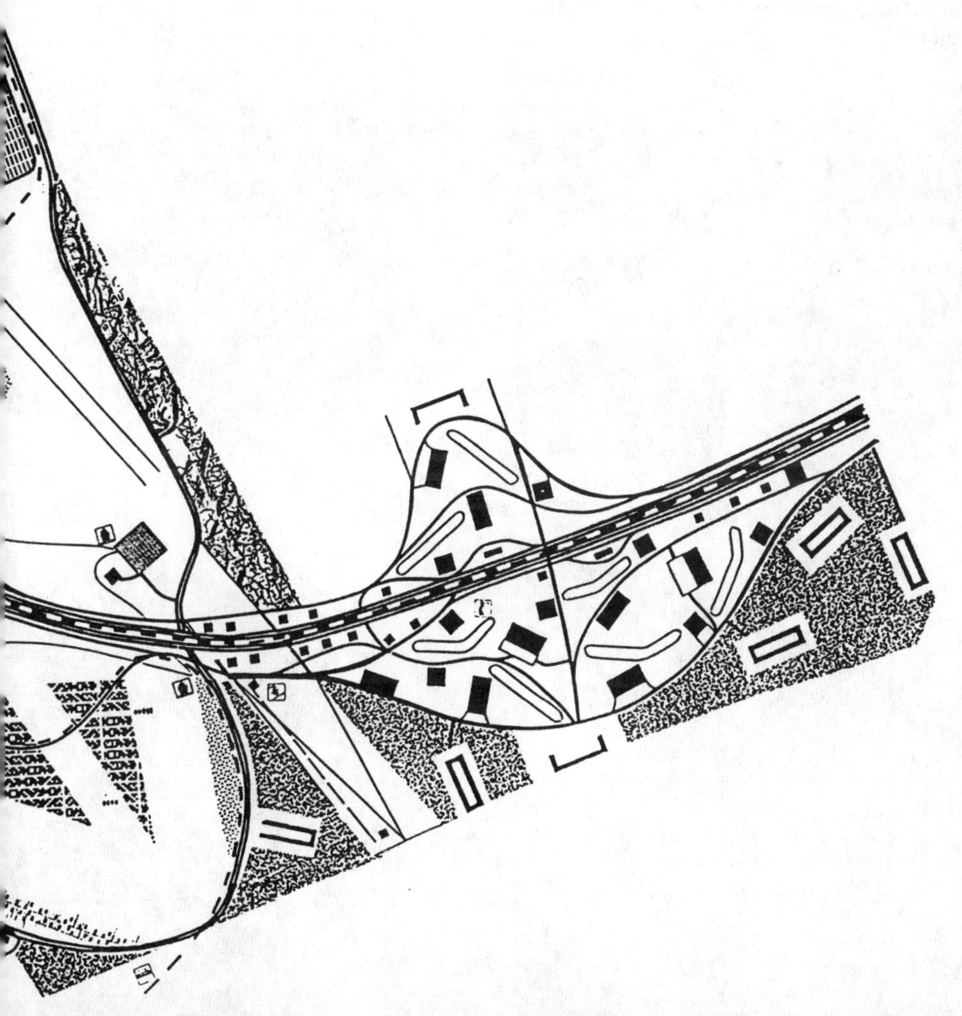

Mainstreet

The scenic driveway

Lace

Study of mobility scenarios in The Netherlands

1997

MVRDV

Individual modes of transport seem to continue playing a dominant role in our society, no matter how hard we keep stimulating public transport, or try to subdue the automobile with higher taxes, more expensive petrol and planning measures. It might be more plausible to develop an energy-saving, relatively quiet car, to solve the unpleasant aspects of automobility as energy consumption, pollution and noise, instead of punishing the desired freedom. Couldn't we force things to move in such a direction, by stimulating automobility instead of taming it? Couldn't we aim for a more apocalyptic approach, that initially would make congestion skyrocket thereby increasing cries for a solution?

In this light perhaps we should be deploying the motorways to intensify, and to densify. Instead of building extra motorways, the existing ones could be concentrated. Leftover noise zones round these roads are earmarked for development precisely because of their extreme (potential) accessibility. The shield culture that is thrusting the motorways into dehumanized 'tunnels' can be stemmed.

These freeways can be transmuted into urban boulevards, particularly those in urban areas, and added to the city as a new brand of urban district. Radical reflection is of the essence, it seems, if these zones are to become accessible. Which traffic-related strategy and scale should we deploy to achieve intensive use of such zones (known to us from, say, Porte de Bagnolet in Paris), zones where you can drive into your house or office at 120 km per hour, at an address literally on the A10 or A20?

Could these urban freeways be revamped using a refined system of parallel lanes and slipways into bona fide city streets linking rather than cleaving apart neighbouring city areas?

By transforming the expansions required for such urban highways into through and local lanes we can provide more slipways, thereby generating a string of motorway 'addresses'.
The various driving speeds, and their attendant design parameters of radii and sliproad/lane interchange can give rise to a 'Brussels lace' of roads. Configuring the parallel lanes in one-way systems makes for smoother circulation and permits relatively higher speeds, so that the lanes can be more fully exploited. At the same time, pedestrians can cross them with greater ease and the lots can accept more traffic, increasing their economic potential.
Stretching this lacework pattern creates space for pockets of preexisting landscape elements or for bigger programmes and both new and existing addresses can be strung together. The most unexpected places all at once take on regional significance.
On narrower stretches of the trajectory this system can be transmuted into a vertical bundle of roads, a 'roulade' with which higher physical levels can also be accessed. A vertical brand of urbanism attains to the realms of the possible.

Weaving zones

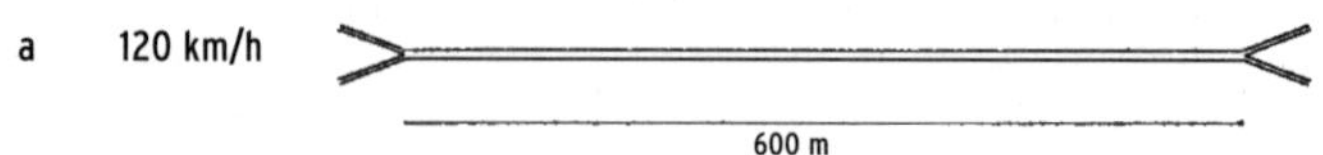

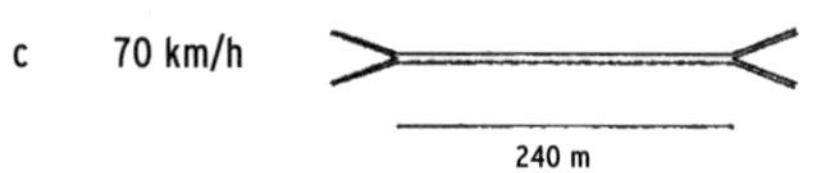

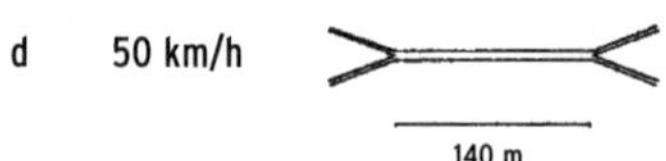

Exits

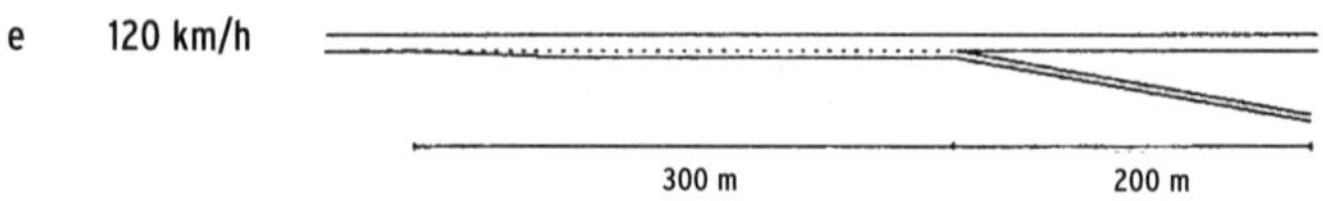

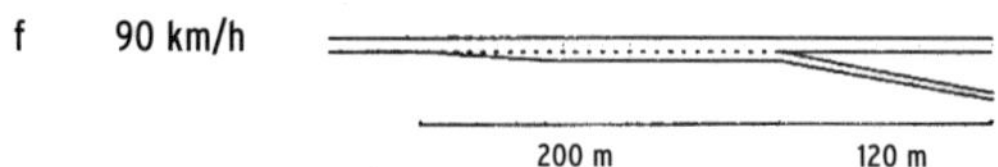

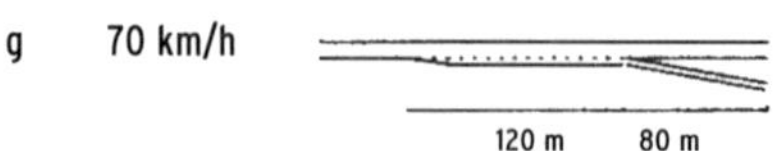

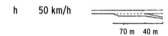

h 50 km/h

70 m 40 m

Horizontal curves

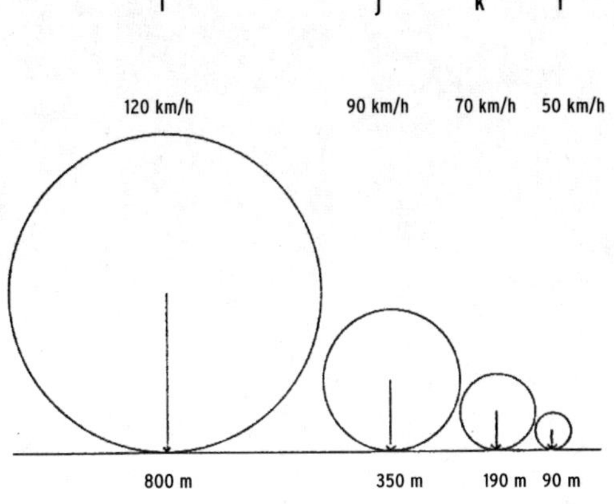

Vertical curves

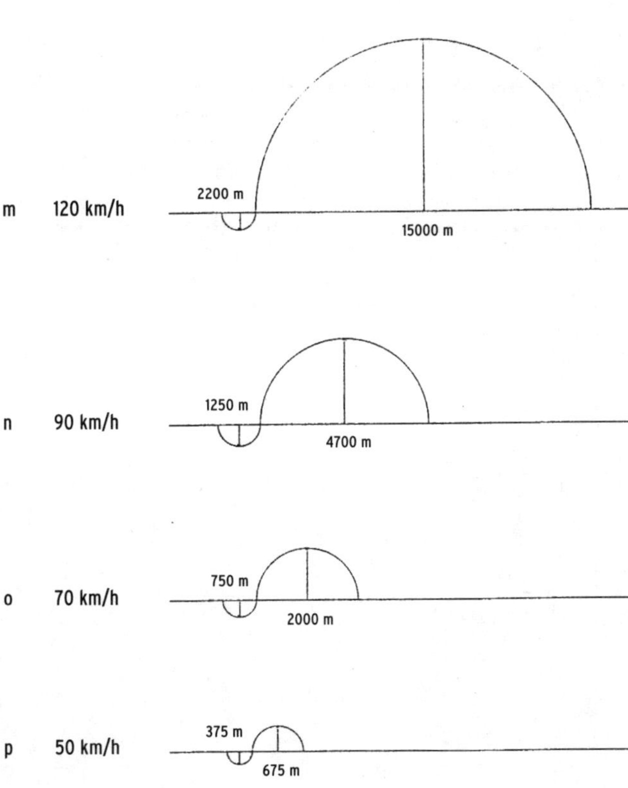

Twinning

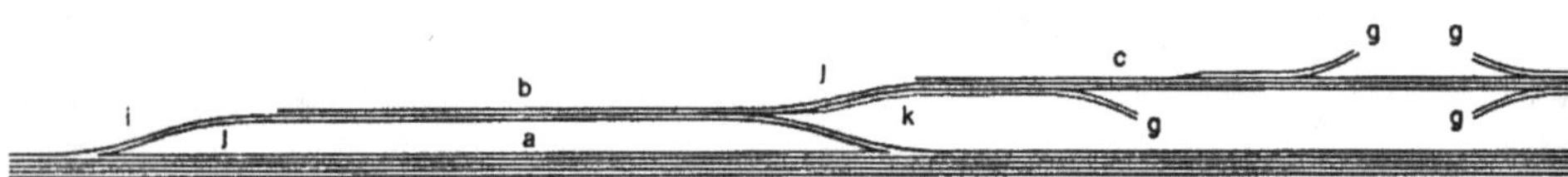

120 km/h	120 km/h	120-90 km/h	90 km/h
	weaving: 600 m + n* 300 m	reducing speed: 100 m + n* 250 m	weaving: 400 m + n* 200 m

N = N addresses = N x (1 exit + 1 entrance)

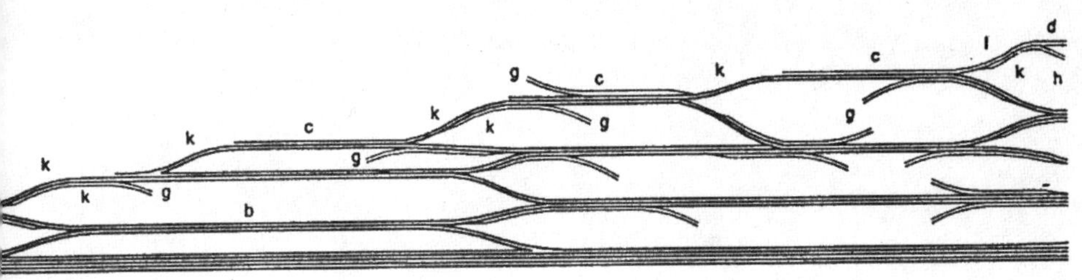

90-70 km/h	70 km/h	70-50 km/h	50 km/h
educing speed: 125 m + n* 150 m	weaving: 240 m + n* 120 m	reducing speed: 25 m + n* 90 m	weaving: 140 m + n* 70 m

Lace

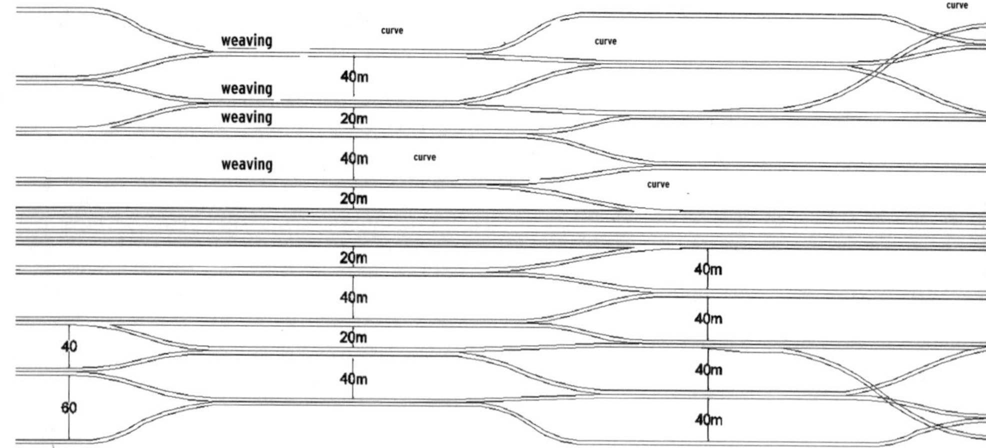

curve
weaving
curve
curve
40m
weaving
weaving
20m
weaving
40m
curve
curve
20m
20m
40m
40m
40m
40
20m
40m
60
40m
40m

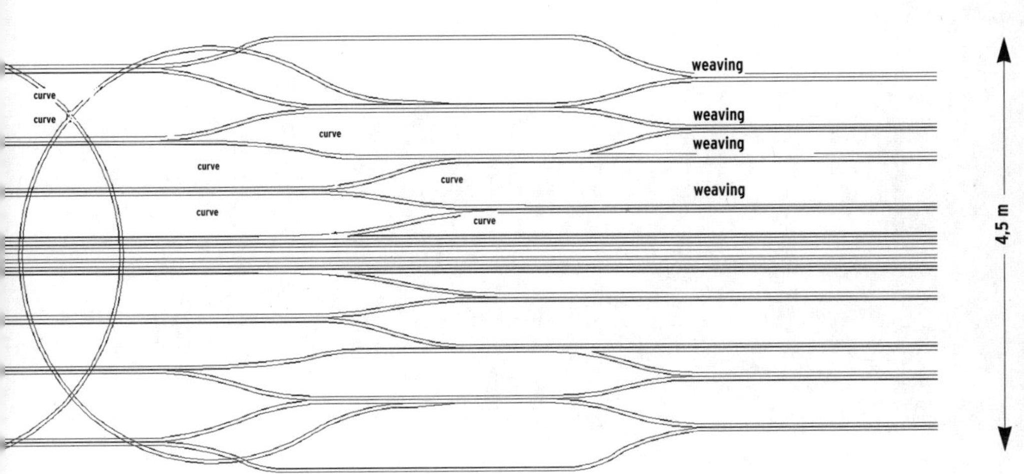

measurements in metres

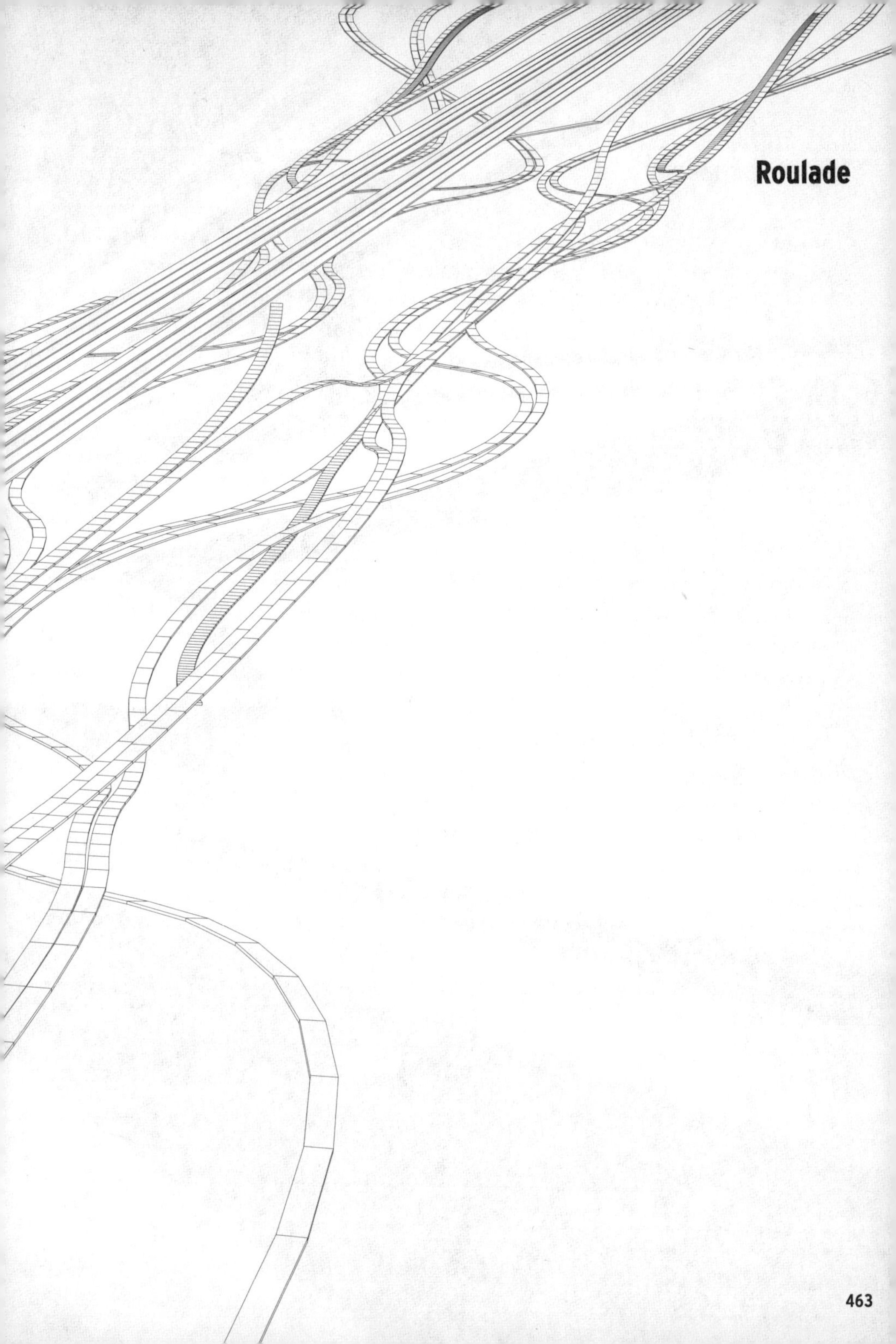

Roulade

Highway space

Vertical Urbanism

Urban boulevard

Highway habitat

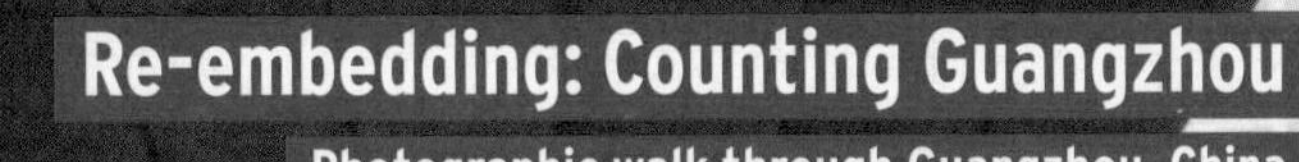

Re-embedding: Counting Guangzhou

Photographic walk through Guangzhou, China

1998

Bart Lootsma

Re-embedding: Counting Guangzhou You're not in a jam, you are the jam.[1]

In his essay 'Living in a Post-Traditional Society', the British sociologist Anthony Giddens describes the effects of the rise of what he calls 'abstract systems'.[2] These are institutional networks of specialists who found their decisions and authority on scientific facts and methods. These abstract systems penetrate all layers of society, at a global level as well as at that of the everyday life of the individual. According to Giddens, in this phase of modernity we all continuously form part of experiments, some large, some small, whose outcome is as open and uncertain as the great modernist experiments which were concerned with humanity as a whole. Technology, in the general sense of the word, has a determining influence both materially and in the form of specialized social expertise.

The effects of this can be seen all over Asia in far more literal and extreme forms than in the West. If there is one thing that expresses the quintessence of contemporary Asia, it is numbers. This, of course, primarily relates to the population growth, migration from the country to the city, and the economy. The evidence of these phenomena is almost entirely numerical, though this has resulted in numbers being given a cultural value and, conversely, being able to express these values. That most of Asian architecture and urban design appear to us to be so unashamedly direct does not mean that it is without culture. On the contrary, it is precisely this that makes it an expression of the essence of our times. Numbers have become a universal language, allowing us to connect the most disparate of phenomena and distil patterns from them. The knowledge of these patterns and the values attached to them thus make it possible to operate using complex systems of laws and technical interventions.

With 6.5 million inhabitants, Guangzhou is the largest city on the Pearl River Delta. Unlike most cities in the region, which have grown up from practically nothing, Guangzhou has a long history. The city used to be called Canton and the city's centre still has retained a largely traditional character - small streets designed for pedestrian traffic and a highly densified colonial centre. The city is growing extremely rapidly however. 'The expansion of the built-up area corresponds with the increase in total population or, more accurately, with the size of the working population. The total number of workers employed by the industrial enterprises soared from 107,596 in 1949 to 704,035 in 1982 and the latest figure recorded 833,000 in the year ending 1992.' Between 1982 and 1993 the density of the population, measured in terms of the number of people per km^2, has almost doubled, growing from 478 to 839.[3] Furthermore, the 'floating population' of migrants rose from 306,000 in 1980 to 1.3 million in 1989. With the growth and density of Guangzhou's population, the amount of traffic has naturally also increased. Between 1990 and 1993 the number of motorized vehicles swelled from 251,000 to more than 290,000, the number of bicycles from 2.52 million to 2.8 million and through traffic from 80,000 to 100,000.[4] Although no figures are available, it is clear that since 1993 the number of cars in particular has risen enormously. The average speed of public transport has dropped from 17 kmph to less than 10 kmph since the 1960s. The city practically grinds to a halt during the rush hour. All these facts are constantly being measured. Throughout the city, day in, day out, there are men perched on top of viaducts counting the number of vehicles that pass beneath them. To alleviate the congestion, numerous infrastructural projects ranging from bridges and (ring) roads to an underground system have been developed. However, most characteristic of the city are the enormous viaducts that run either above an existing road, thereby multiplying the road's surface area, or along existing riverbeds. Here the abstract system of traffic literally solidifies into what MVRDV would call a datascape.[5] Numbers take on a material form and give rise to a new and artificial landscape above the existing cityscape that attempts to connect with a much larger regional and supraregional scale. Not unusual in itself, perhaps, but the speed of developments and the contrast with the existing landscape has brought a spectacular quality to Guangzhou. One experiences this mainly below the new roads where - for the time being - the traditional city and traditional life continue to exist in some form as a kind of underworld. According to Anthony Giddens, the creation of abstract systems is the reason why traditional ways of life are being disembedded, deprived of their original social embedding. We are now in a phase in which these ways of life are re-embedded.[6] This is literally visible in the riverbed at Guangzhou. Below, in the underworlds, traditional life carries on in the markets, temples and small streets, where goods for the market are still partly delivered by boat. Above are the new roads that carry their users far away in no time at all. Shipping, pedestrian and motor traffic all use the same embedding, but, being much larger systems, they embed the area around the riverbed in entirely different ways. Steadily we see buildings lining the main roads wither and already, every so often, modern high-rise looms up.

As if in a strange dream, I remember a journey by autorickshaw in the evening rush hour during which I suddenly realized that the wide avenue along which we were driving was so crowded you could have crossed it over the heads and roofs of the rest of the traffic, and which was surrounded by buildings at least five storeys high and covered entirely in concrete panels. The dusk was not simply due to the lateness of the hour; the sun simply couldn't penetrate down to the street below. The hallucinatory nature of the roar of traffic was caused by the reverberations inside this gigantic concrete arena.

This article was first published in Dutch and English in Archis, no. 4, 1998 (English translation by Annabel Howland).

NOTES: 1. Quoted in Ulrich Beck, 'The reinvention of politics' in Ulrich Beck, Anthony Giddens and Scott Lash, Reflexive Modernization. Politics, tradition and aesthetics in the modern social order, Cambridge 1994. 2. Anthony Giddens, Living in a Post-Traditional Society, see note 1. 3. Roger C.K. Chan and Chaolin Gu, 'Forms of Metropolitan Development in Guangzhou Municipal City', in S. MacPherson and J.Y.S. Cheng, Economic and Social Development in South China, UK 1996. 4. See note 3. 5. See also Luis Moreno Mansilla+Emilio Tuñon, 'The Space of Optimism' and Bart Lootsma, 'Towards a reflexive architecture', both in El Croquis, 1997, special issue: MVRDV 1991-1997; Bart Lootsma, 'Datascapes', AA News, Autumn 1997, 150th Anniversary Issue. 6. See notes 2 and 3.

厂价直销
18

Doubledecker

Traffic study for Rotterdam centre, The Netherlands

1995

Mark Verheijen

Re-editing: MVRDV

Densification leads to an enlargement of the number of activities and therefore of movements. But is it possible to make a meaningful estimate of the increase in the number of movements? How large, for instance, would the Coolsingel, the main street in Rotterdam, have to be if the area were to have more than twice the density it has now?
Each function has its own special traffic production and traffic attraction. 'Dwelling', for example, with its social and shopping patterns generates three times as much movement as 'work'. Depending on the existing programmatic division, an increase in density can produce more than just linear increase or decrease as a result of programmatic shifts. For instance, a constant density with a shifting programme can effect a change in movements. A shift in the ratio dwelling-work from 20:80 to 80:20 at constant density can double the number of movements!
An increase in the number of activities does, however, produce a synergetic transposition effect which enhances the efficiency of the traffic component. For a low density with few mixes of function the dwelling-work movement pattern is unambivalent and direct: dwelling-work-dwelling.
For higher densities and a greater mix of functions this pattern is ambivalent and complex: dwelling-crèche-breakfast café-work-copyshop-library-homeworking-lunch-work-restaurant-cinema-café-dwelling. This synergetic effect is as yet difficult to estimate.
The average distance of movement decreases as density increases. There will be a great number of 'criss-cross' relations: multiple successive movements over short distances.
This increase in the number of short distance movements in particular influences the choice of transportation mode; the modal split (i.e. the division among the various modes of transport for the movements) changes. This choice is contingent upon speed, comfort and cost.
The current modal split consists of 40% car, 40% public transport and 20% bicycle. Should the density become slightly more than double (from FAR 2.8 to FAR 6). Then we might consider the following traffic scenarios:

Scenario 1: Public transport city

This scenario is predicated upon a policy geared to suppressing use of the car and stimulating the use of public transport and the bicycle.
The infrastructure for cars is not expanded. 66% of this infrastructure is

exploited at present. Car traffic can accordingly increase by 50%. Bicycle traffic will double. The remaining growth will be absorbed by public transport. The following modal split emerges: 14% car, 76% public transport and 10% bicycle. In this scenario the car traffic still uses the existing 2x2 lanes. The number of metro lines will have to become five times as many, each with double the use of the present lines. The increase in pre- and post-transport movement will bring five times as many pedestrians to the street, necessitating a pedestrian area three times as large as the current one.

Scenario 2: Continuing as at present

Here the current modal split would be maintained: 40% car, 40% public transport and 20% bicycle. All forms of infrastructure would need expanding. Everything becomes more. The Coolsingel gets 2x6 motorized traffic lanes. Despite this increase, there are still several tailbacks a day. The number of public transport lines will triple proceeding from a doubly intensive use of the present lines.

Scenario 3: Car city

This scenario proceeds from an increase in car traffic. This might be acceptable if solutions were found for the disadvantages of present car traffic: i.e. a virtually noiseless, clean mode of transport. This would optimize individual transportation. Current exploitation of public transport is far from maximum. It can increase by some 50%. As use of the car becomes attractive, use of the bicycle will decrease by about 50%. The modal split is now 84% car, 14% public transport and 2% bicycle. The Coolsingel gets 2x12 lanes to allow for an acceptable circulation all day. The speed in the central lanes is high; that in the side lanes containing much entering and exiting is low. All slipways and intersections need to be split level. Pedestrian movement takes place inside the buildings, between parking lot and destination. The existing tramline will disappear from ground level. The existing metro line will be packed all day.

	now	scenario 1	scenario 2	scenario 3
car	23,000	34,500	97,759	204,125
public transport	23,000	186,870	97,759	34,500
bicycle	11,500	23,000	4,887	45,750

Existing situation

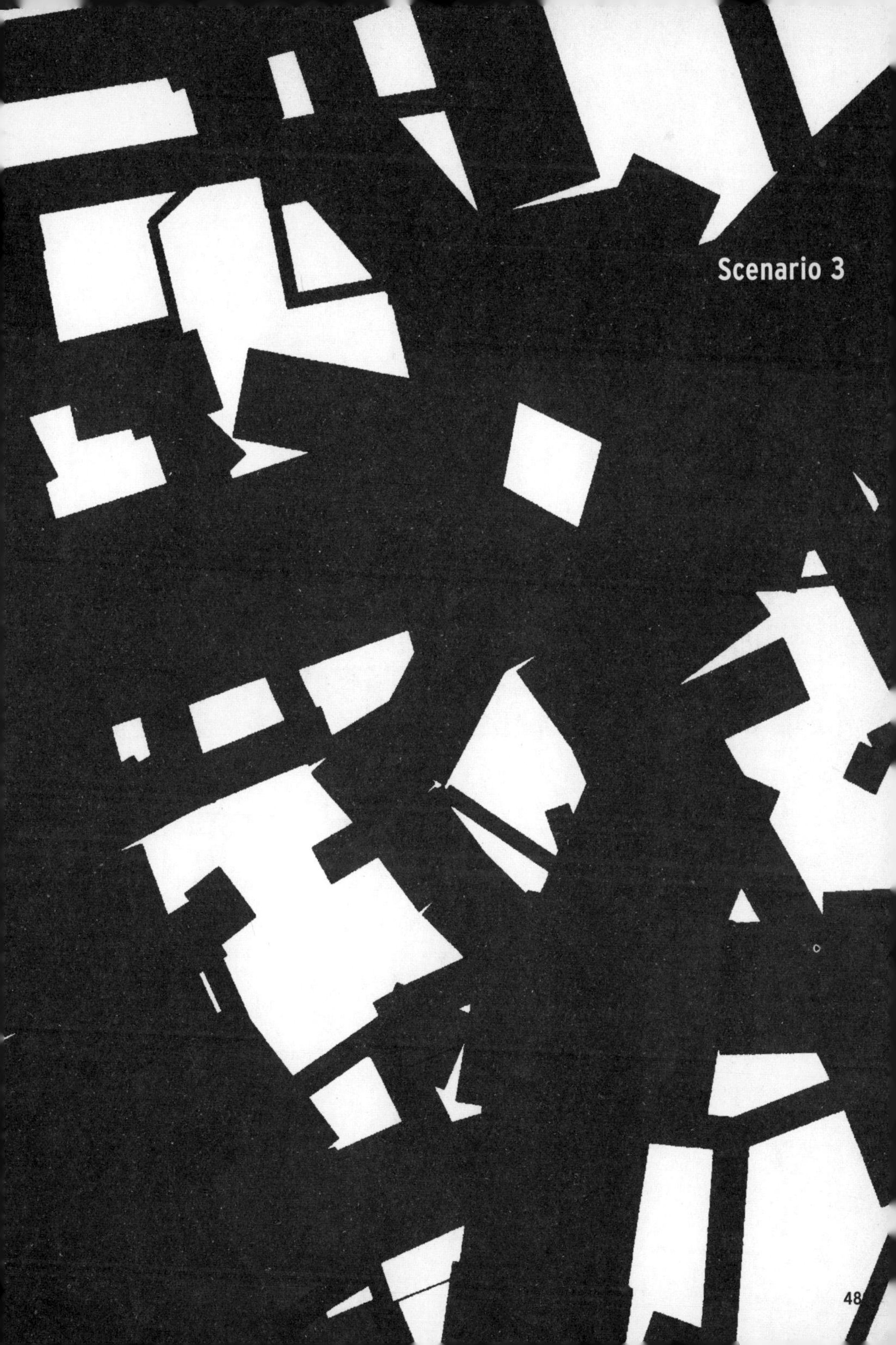

Scenario 3

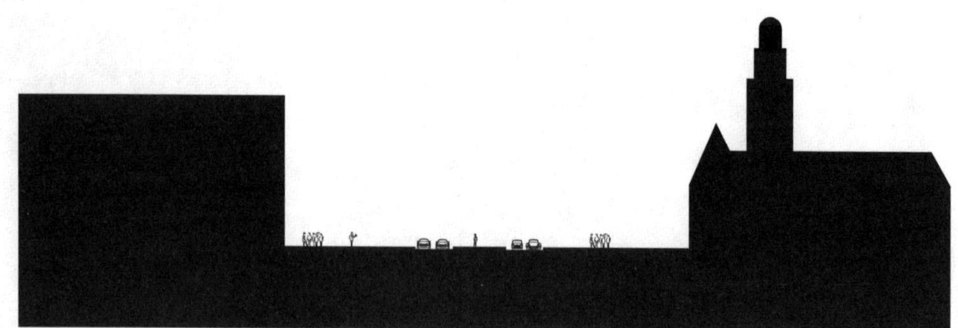

Existing situation

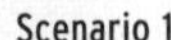

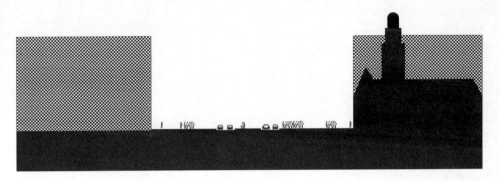

Scenario 1

Scenario 2

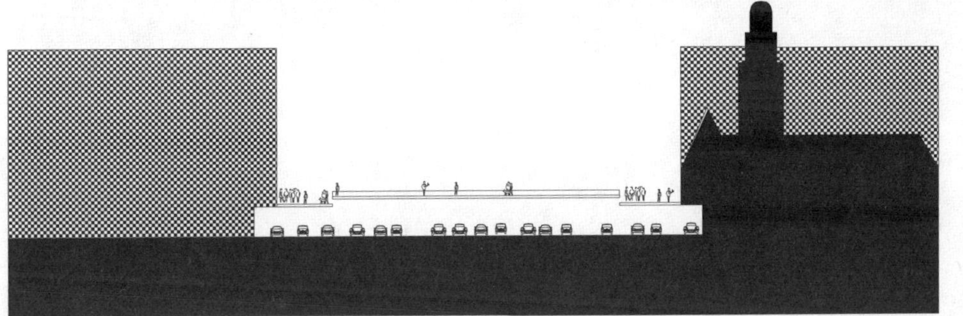

Scenario 3

Noise scape

Datascape

1997

Penelope Dean

Re-editing: MVRDV

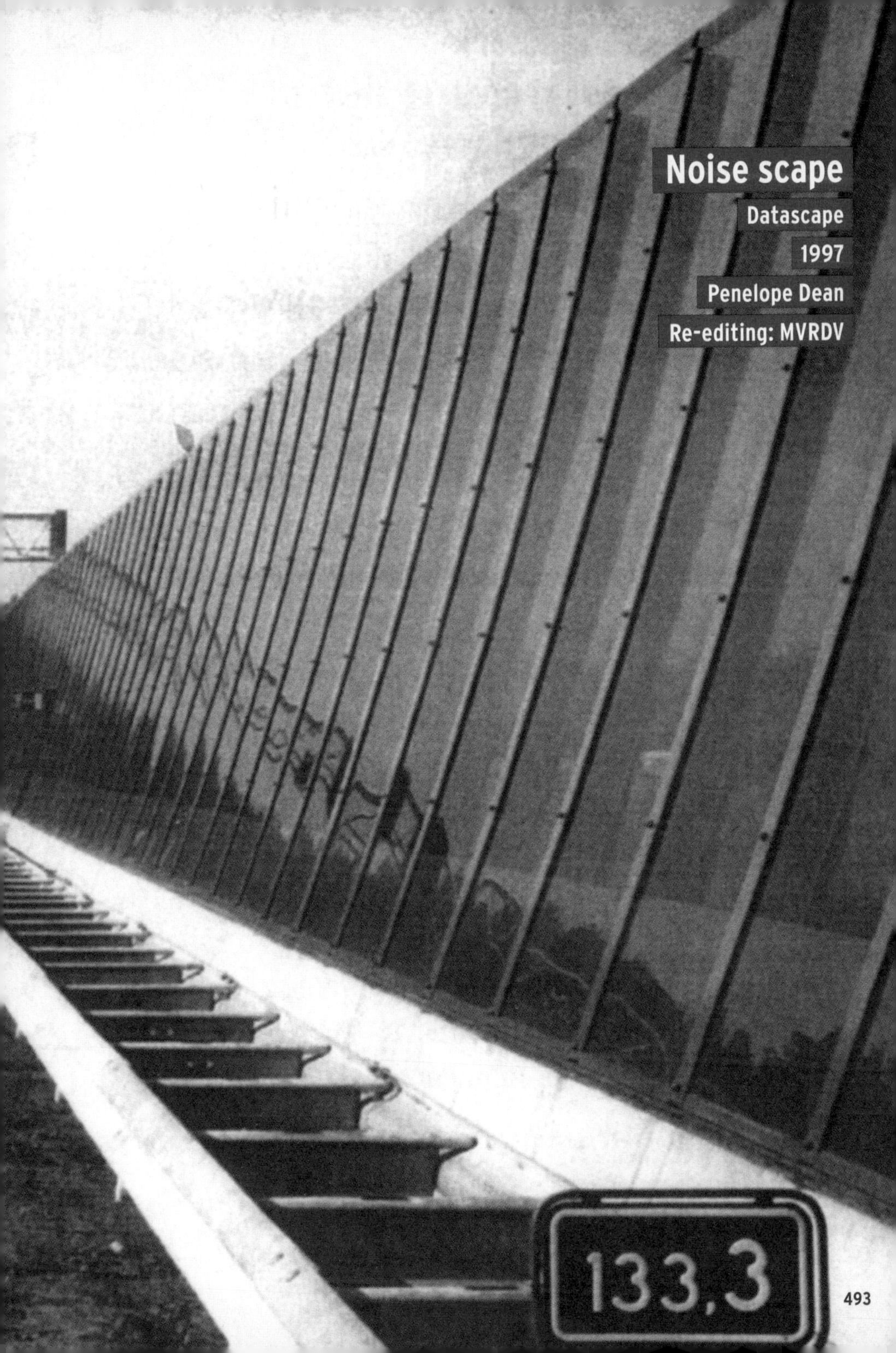

If we wish to deploy the motorways for further densification, then we will have to spend the time ahead developing a way of dealing with this noise. Familiar solutions are of course to screen it behind noise baffles or behind relatively noise-insensitive functions such as offices and commercial activities.
It is clear that a surrounding or oversailing shield dampens all noise. But just how attractive is such a walling-in or tunnel for the road user, for the fire brigade, for the potentials of the site and for the city? Is it possible to develop a relatively open city street that can even include housing? Should we wish to live on the motorway without screens so that we could simply open the windows and sit on the balcony without being inconvenienced by the noise of its traffic, then this can be done at a distance that is variable both in height and in the flat surface. If we were to impose a far-reaching urbanization on such an area, then these contour lines would show up as expansive paddyfields that together shape an acoustic 'cave' of John Portmanesque potential.

Data design

Noise Source

1.	source	moving unconfined locality 0.75m above ground
2.	freeway	20m wide 8 lanes of two way traffic symmetrical lane configuration infinite length (calculations derived from 1000m length)
3.	traffic	speed of 120 km/hr intensity of 4000 vehicles/hr (500 vehicles per lane per hour or one vehicle per lane per 7.2 seconds) vehicles: 25% light, 25% medium, 25% heavy, 25% motorbikes
4.	road	asphalt
5.	ground	absorptive
6.	emission	as per Wegverkeerslawaai SRM 2

Obstacle

1.	dimensions	5 x 200 x 100m obstacle adjacent to freeway edge
2.	programme	car park 15000 sqm
3.	effect	contours derived for 65 dB(A), 67 dB(A), 70 dB(A), 75 dB(A) at heights of +1.5m, +25m, +50m, +75m, +99.9m as per Wegverkeerslawaai SRM 2 calculation programme dgmr V1 version 5.1/b

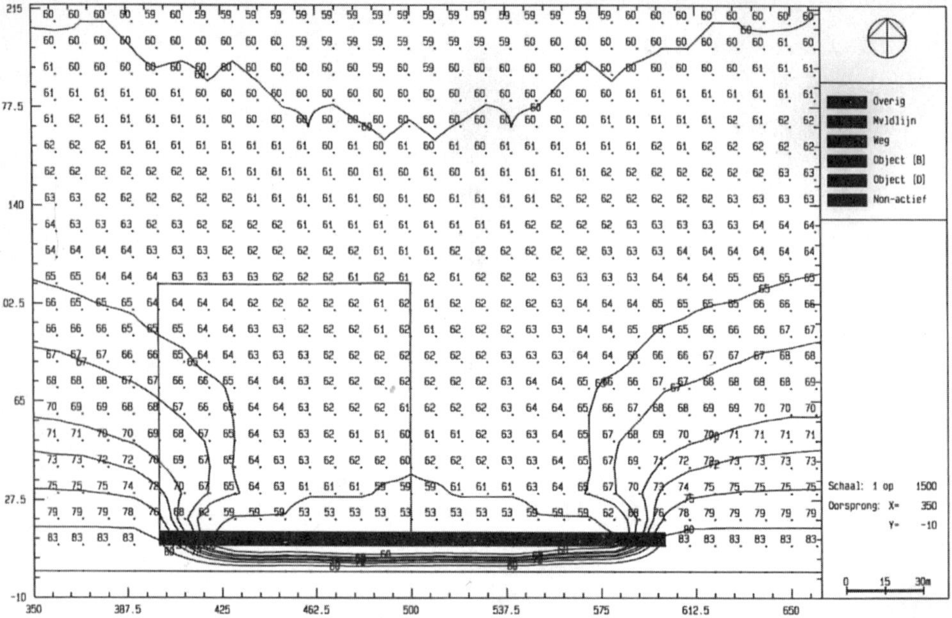

Overig
Mvldlijn
Weg
Object [B]
Object [D]
Non-actief

Schaal: 1 op 1500
Oorsprong: X= 350
Y= -10

0 15 30m

Leeg

Nachtwaarden in dB(A)

TEST
Figuur

Receiver height of 50 meters

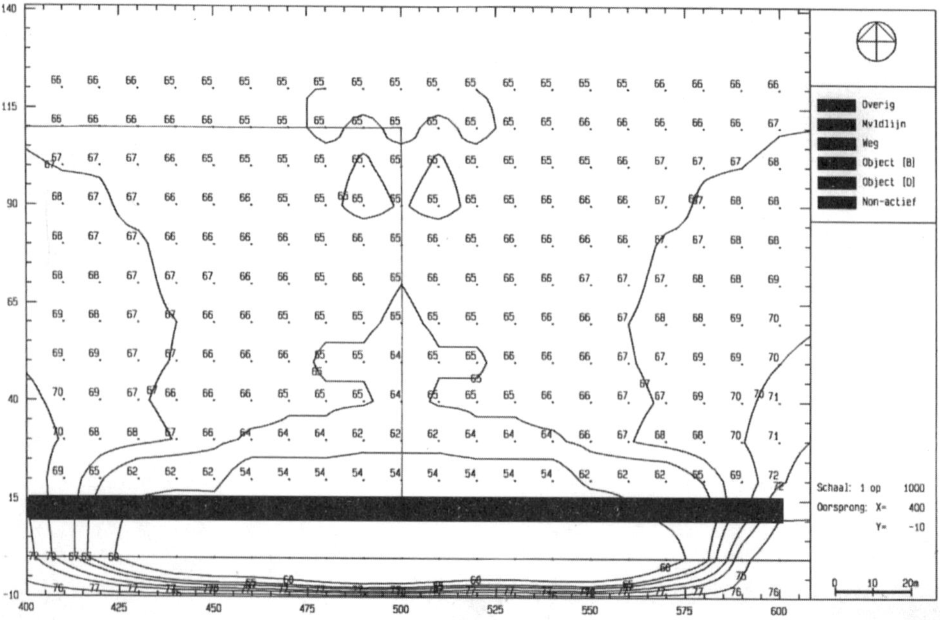

Overig
Mvldlijn
Weg
Object [B]
Object [D]
Non-actief

Schaal: 1 op 1000
Oorsprong: X= 400
Y= -10

0 10 20m

Leeg

Nachtwaarden in dB(A)

TEST
Figuur

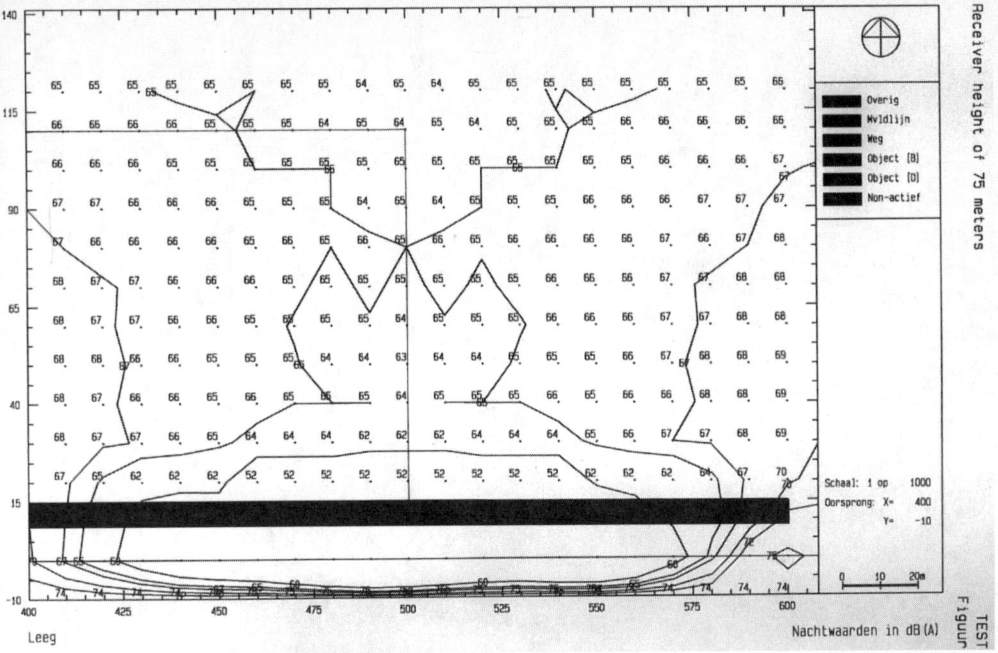

Receiver height of 75 meters

Overig
Mvldlijn
Weg
Object [B]
Object [D]
Non-actief

Schaal: 1 op 1000
Oorsprong: X= 400
Y= -10

0 10 20m

Leeg

Nachtwaarden in dB(A)

TEST
Figuur

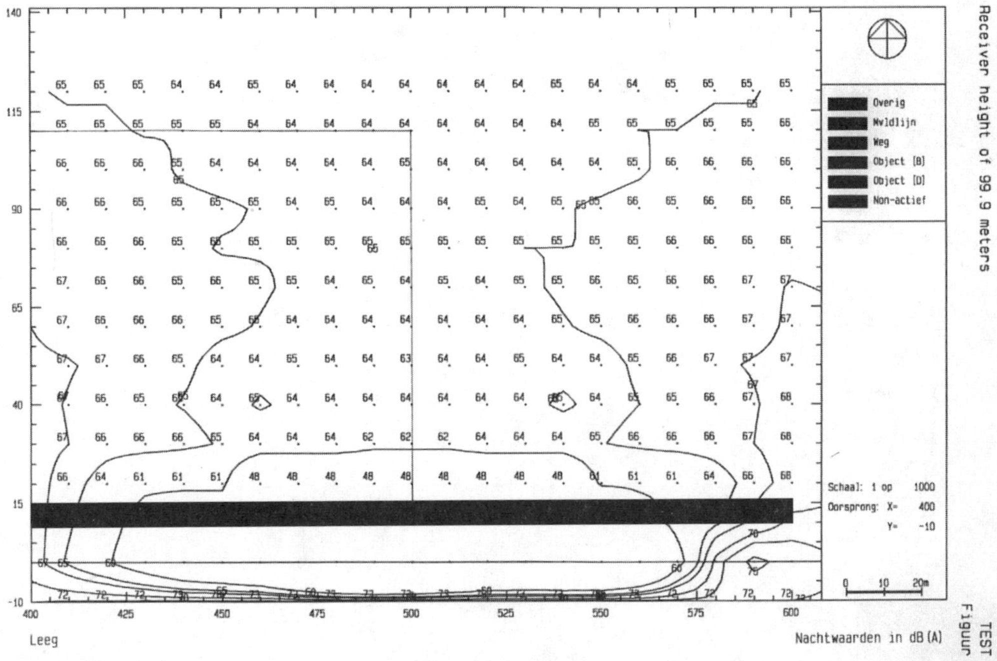

Receiver height of 99.9 meters

Overig
Mvldlijn
Weg
Object [B]
Object [D]
Non-actief

Schaal: 1 op 1000
Oorsprong: X= 400
Y= -10

0 10 20m

Leeg

Nachtwaarden in dB(A)

TEST
Figuur

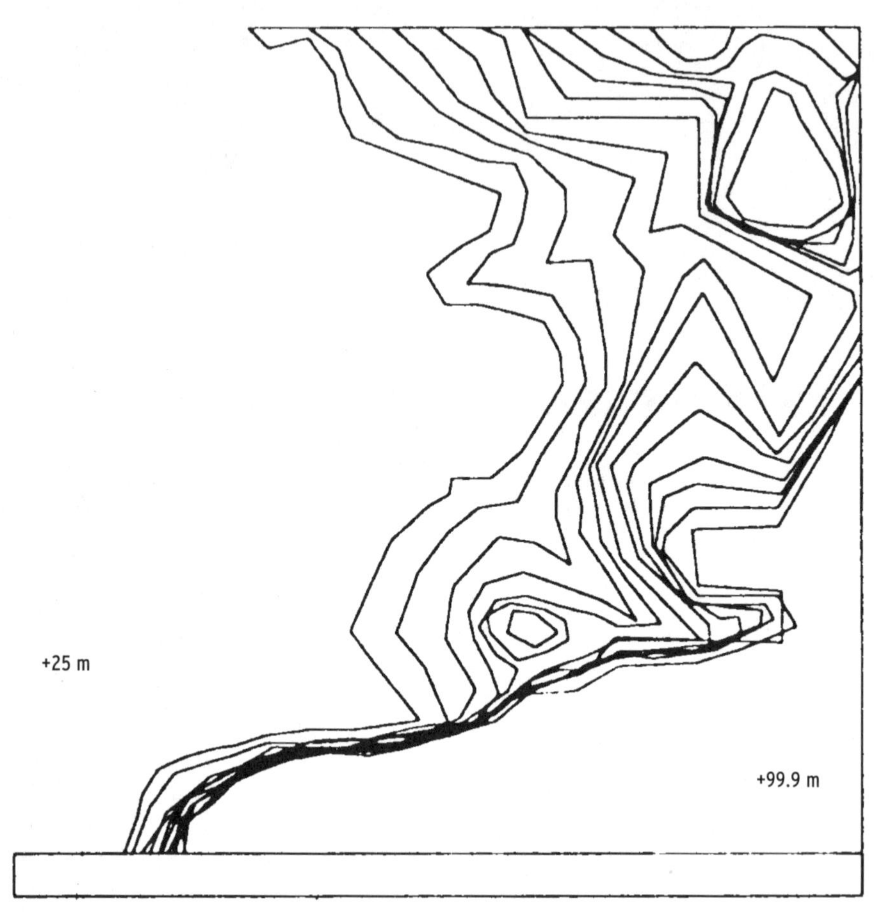

Housing 65 dB(A) and less

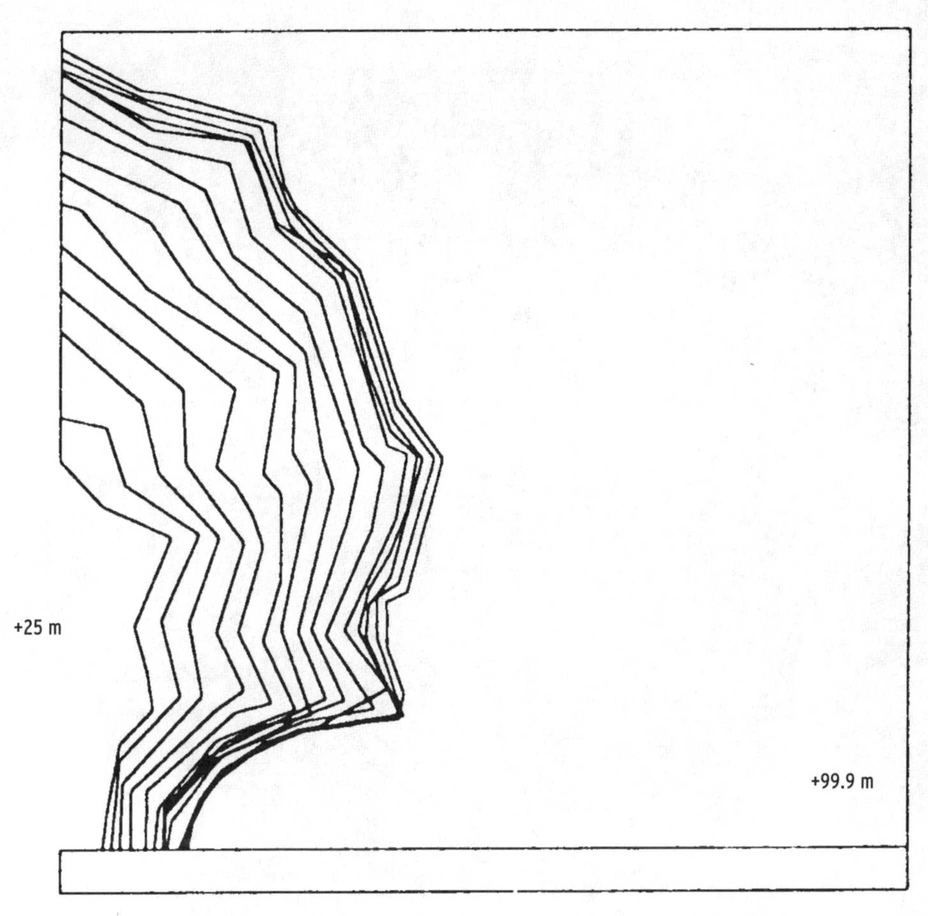

Offices 67 dB(A) and less

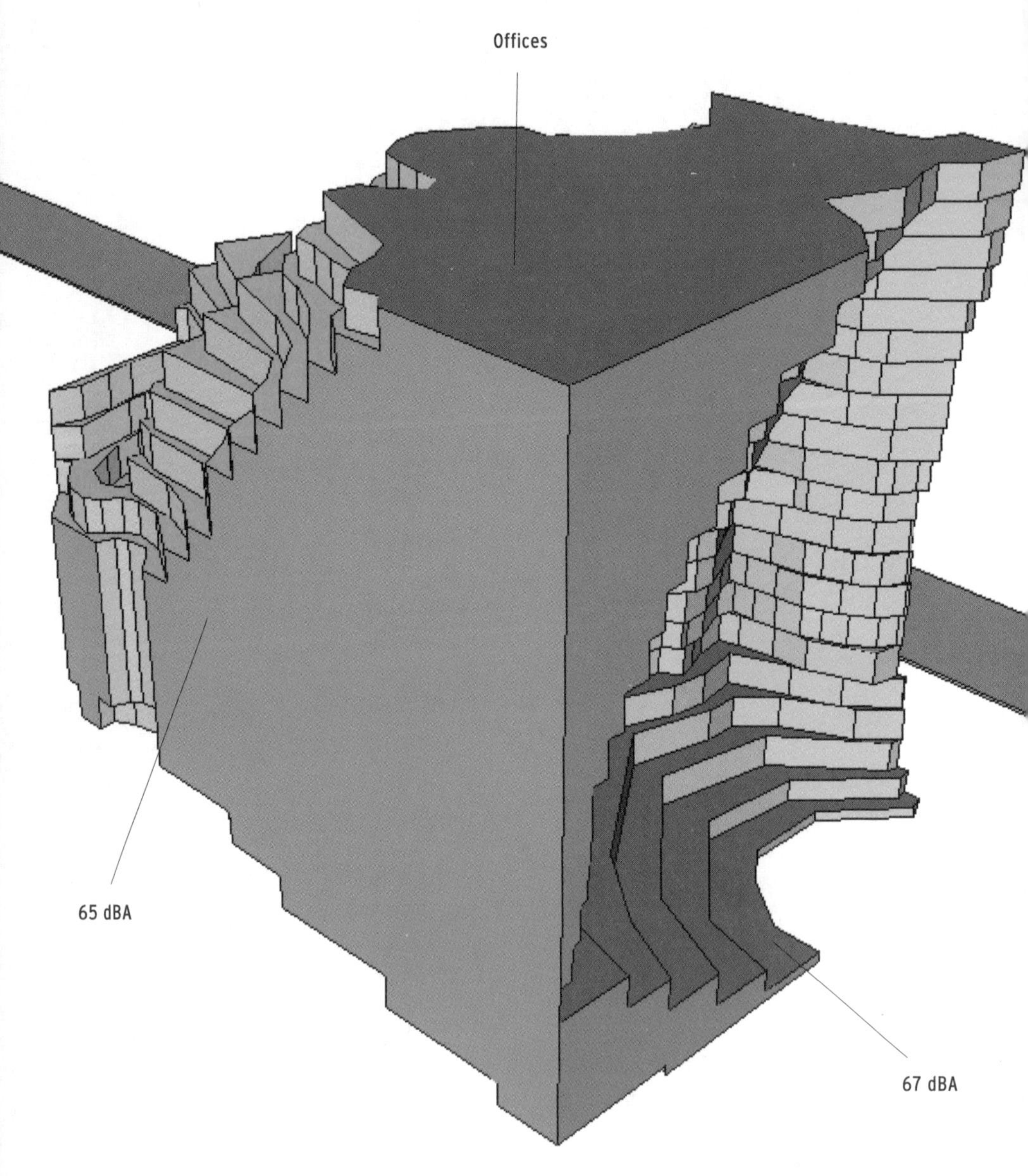
Offices
65 dBA
67 dBA

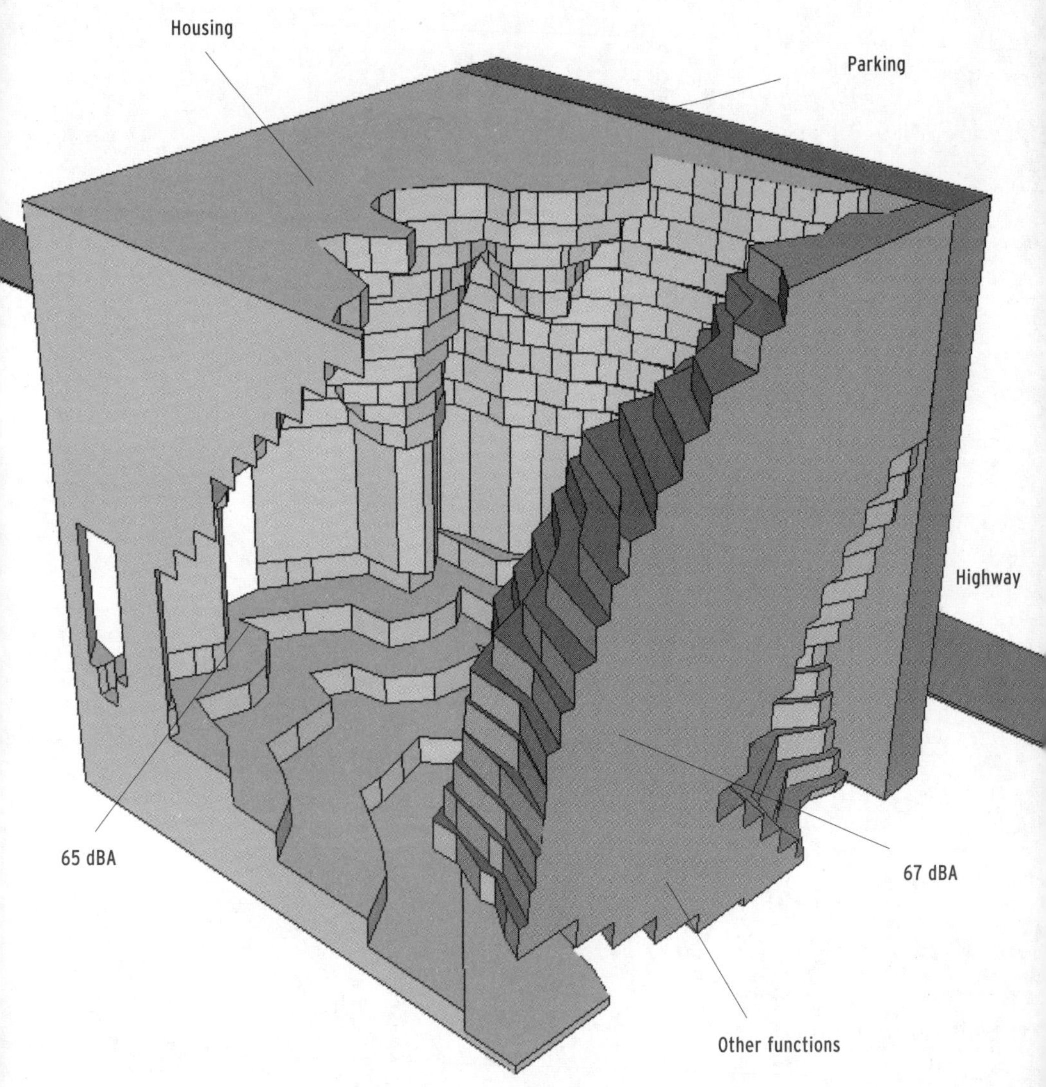
Housing
Parking
Highway
65 dBA
67 dBA
Other functions

Housing sawas

Plan of noise contours

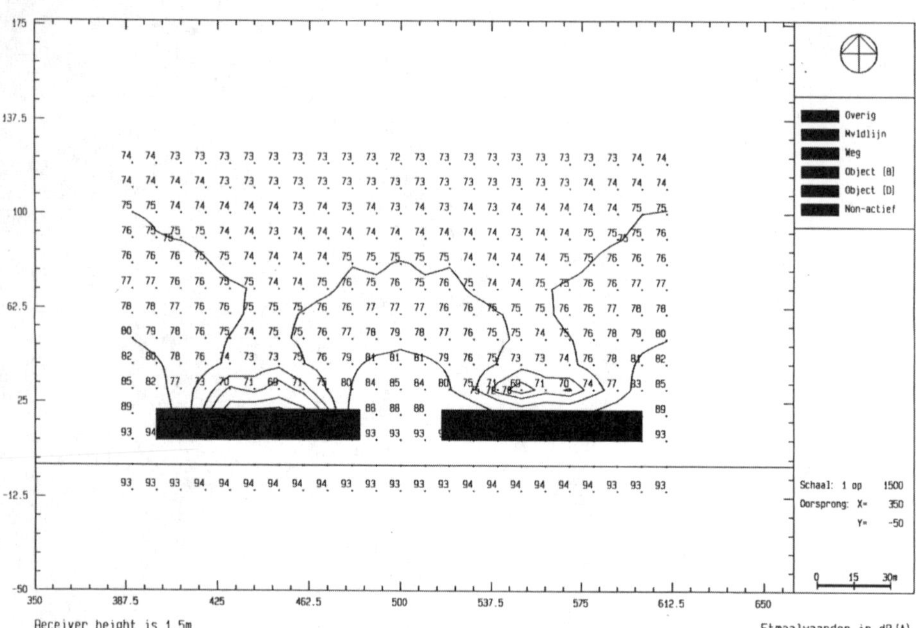

Receiver height is 1.5m

Etmaalwaarden in dB(A)

Overig
Mvldlijn
Weg
Object (B)
Object (D)
Non-actief

Schaal: 1 op 1500
Oorsprong: X= 350
Y= -50

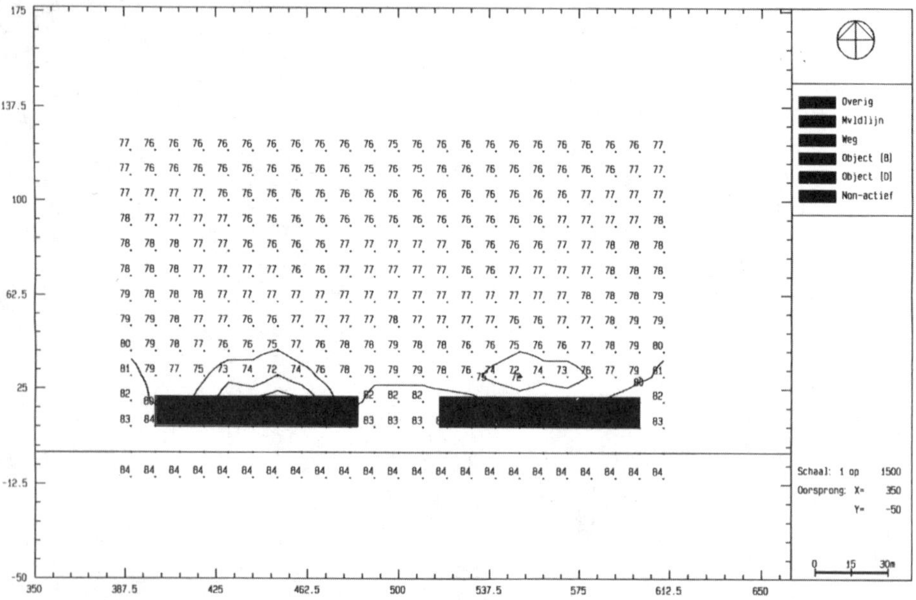

Receiver height is 75m

Etmaalwaarden in dB(A)

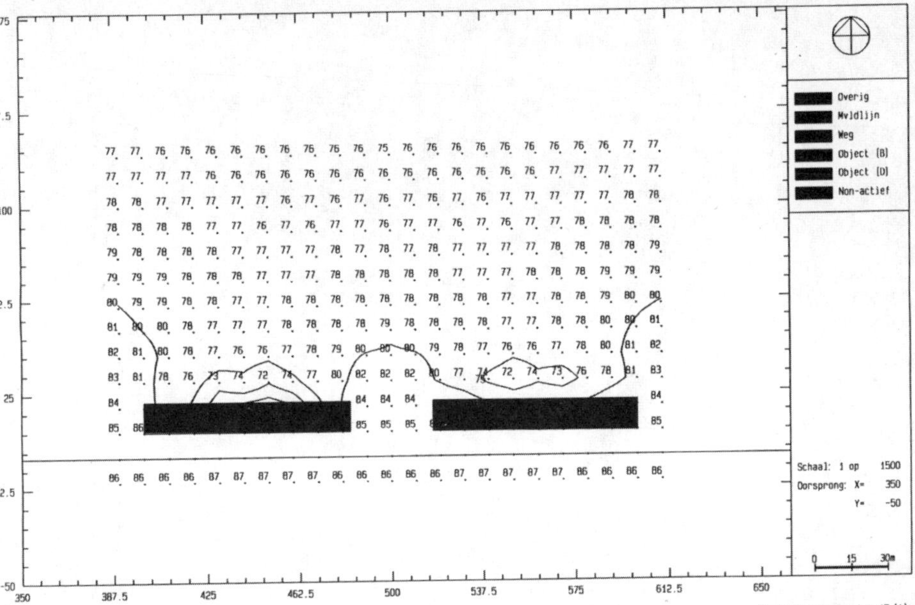

175
137.5
100
62.5
25
-12.5
-50

350 387.5 425 462.5 500 537.5 575 612.5 650

Overig
Mvldlijn
Weg
Object (B)
Object (D)
Non-actief

Schaal: 1 op 1500
Oorsprong: X= 350
Y= -50

0 15 30m

Receiver height is 50m

Etmaalwaarden in dB(A)

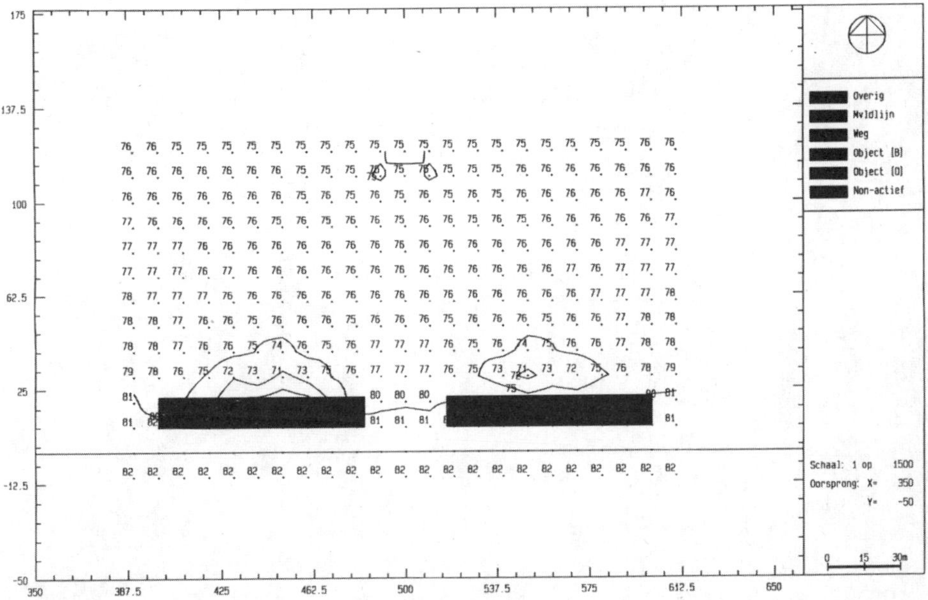

175
137.5
100
62.5
25
-12.5
-50

350 387.5 425 462.5 500 537.5 575 612.5 650

Overig
Mvldlijn
Weg
Object (B)
Object (D)
Non-actief

Schaal: 1 op 1500
Oorsprong: X= 350
Y= -50

0 15 30m

Receiver height is 99.9m

Etmaalwaarden in dB(A)

Acoustic cave

DISTRIBUTION

h.
m.

Stourhead revisited

Town planning design for a Neighbourhood of 1800 houses along the Amsterdam IJ channel, The Netherlands

1994

MVRDV

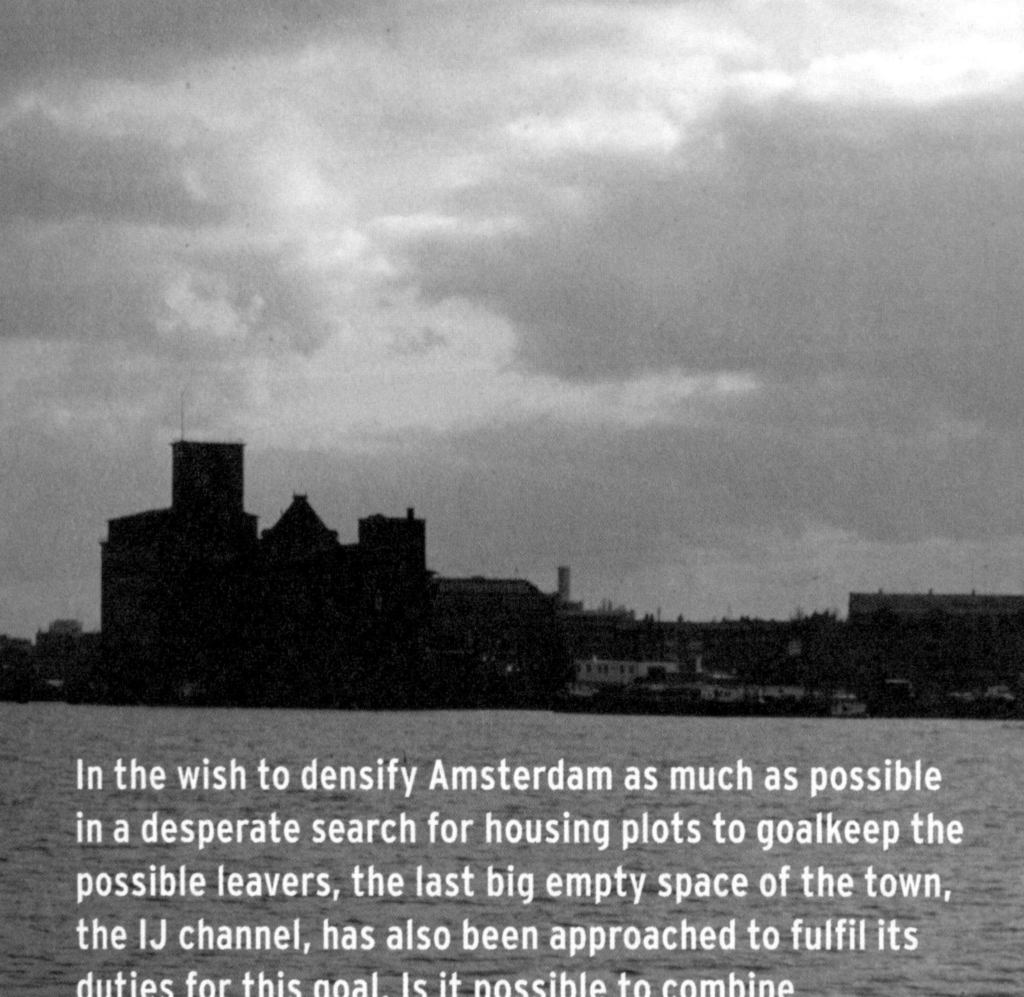

In the wish to densify Amsterdam as much as possible in a desperate search for housing plots to goalkeep the possible leavers, the last big empty space of the town, the IJ channel, has also been approached to fulfil its duties for this goal. Is it possible to combine densification with an enlargement of the spatial experience? Can we keep this part of the IJ - the greatest flat expanse in Amsterdam - as wide and open as possible, by densifying groups of dwellings into condominiums of about 120 houses each.
The condominiums are placed at different positions in

the water, that can be regarded as public space. - The blocks obtain their character from their position, their programme and the definition of their collective 'interior' space: a balcony, a parterre, a giant hall, a stair, a grotto, a garden, and so on. - Cars will be parked in the blocks and on San Marco-like squares along the waterfront. - The composition of the blocks generates a series of perspectives that visually accentuates the width of the IJ, transforming it into a Dutch Venice of water-alleys and Canal Grandes.

Densification act

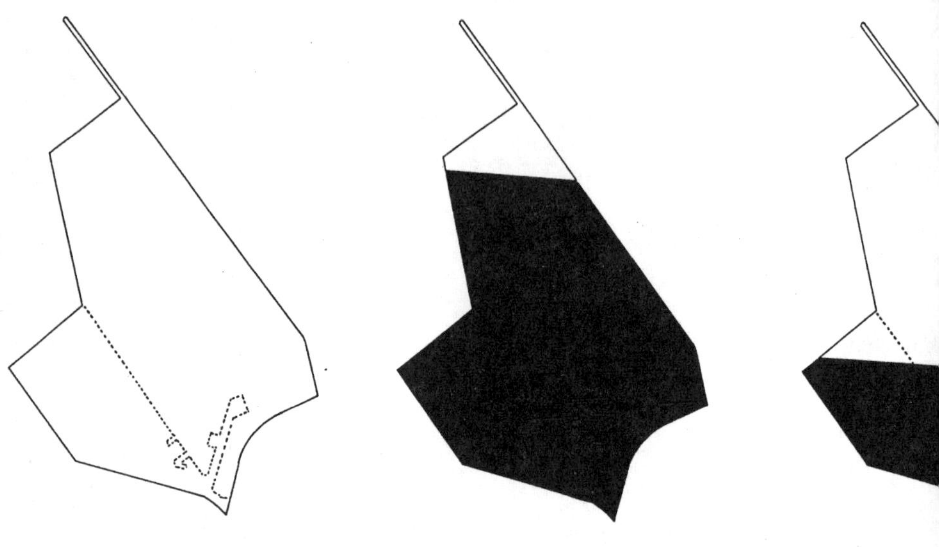

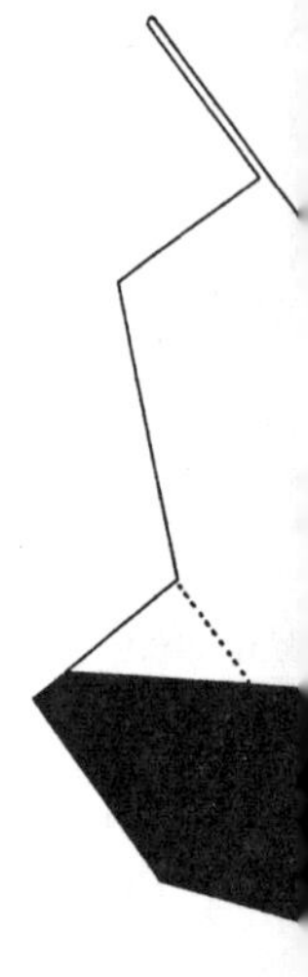

Planning zone: 67.6 ha open space

Suburb: 7.6 ha open space

Patio blocks: 4

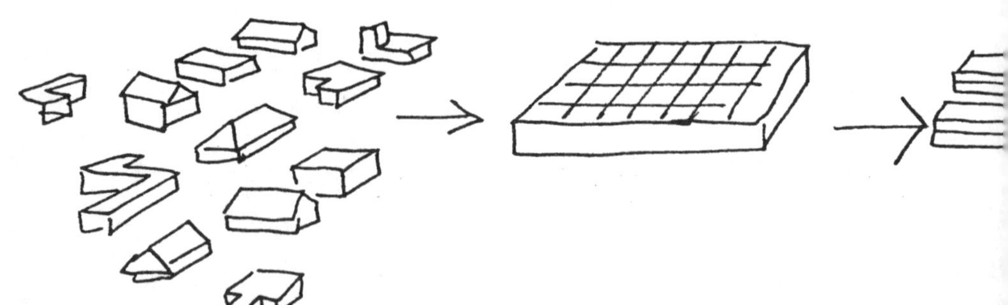

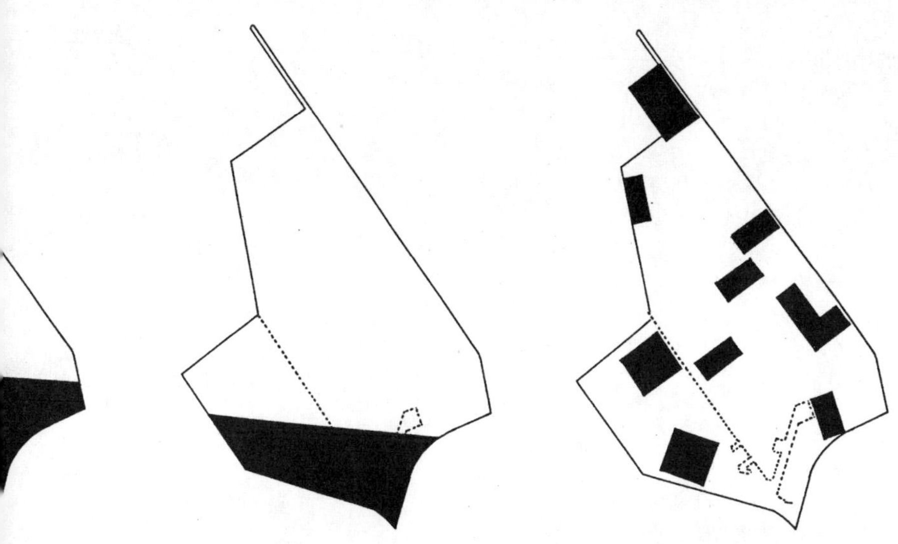

a open space

Massiveness: 55.6 ha open space

Condominiums: 52.6 ha open space

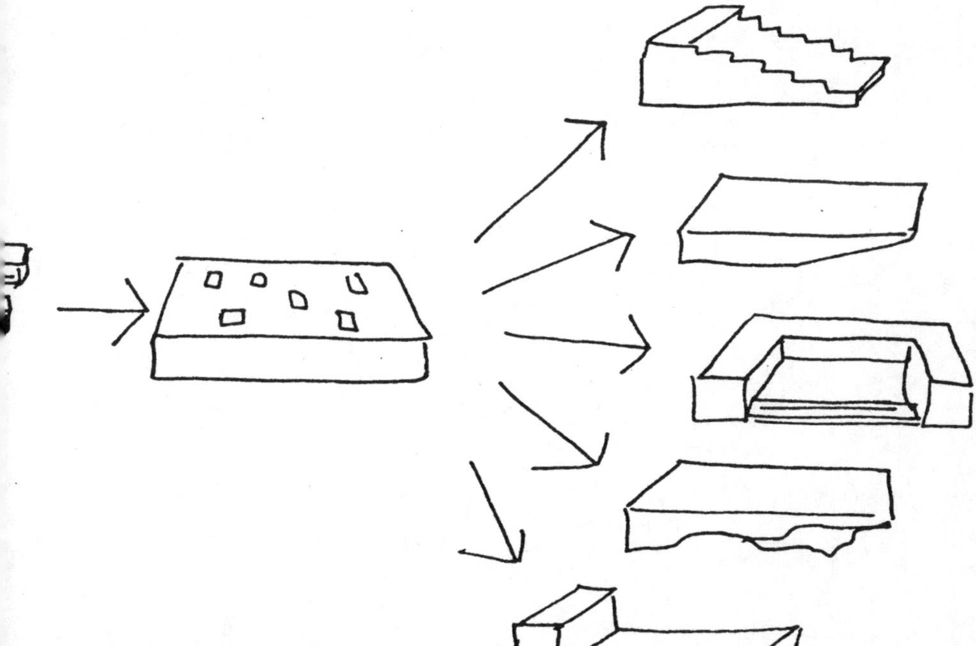

Condominiums

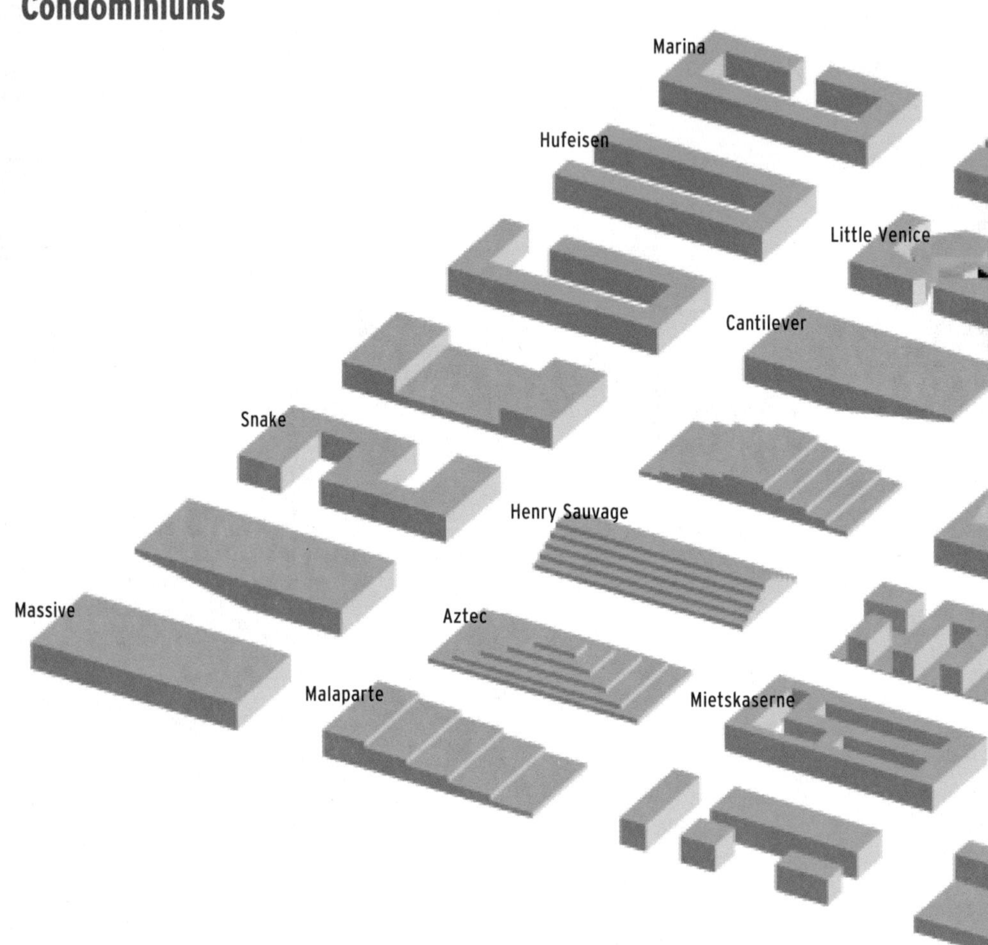

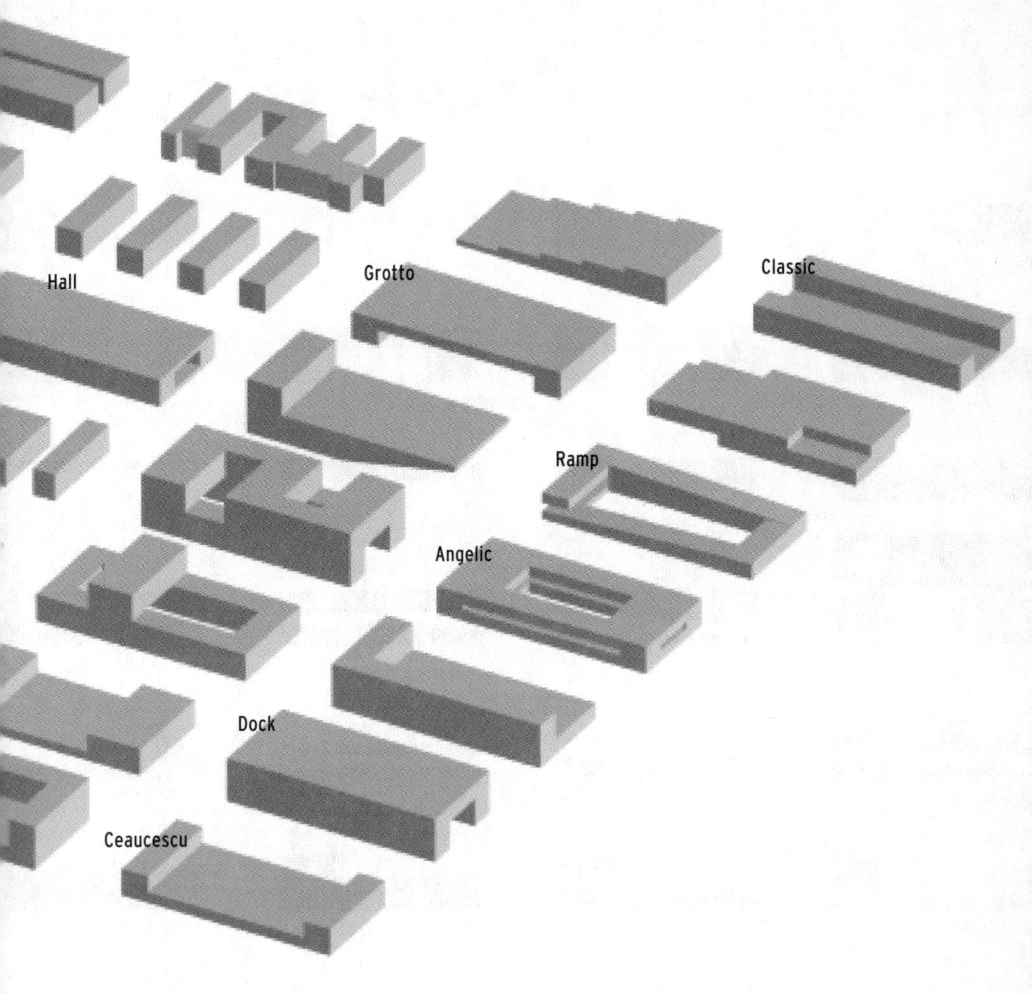
Hall
Grotto
Classic
Ramp
Angelic
Dock
Ceaucescu

Sections

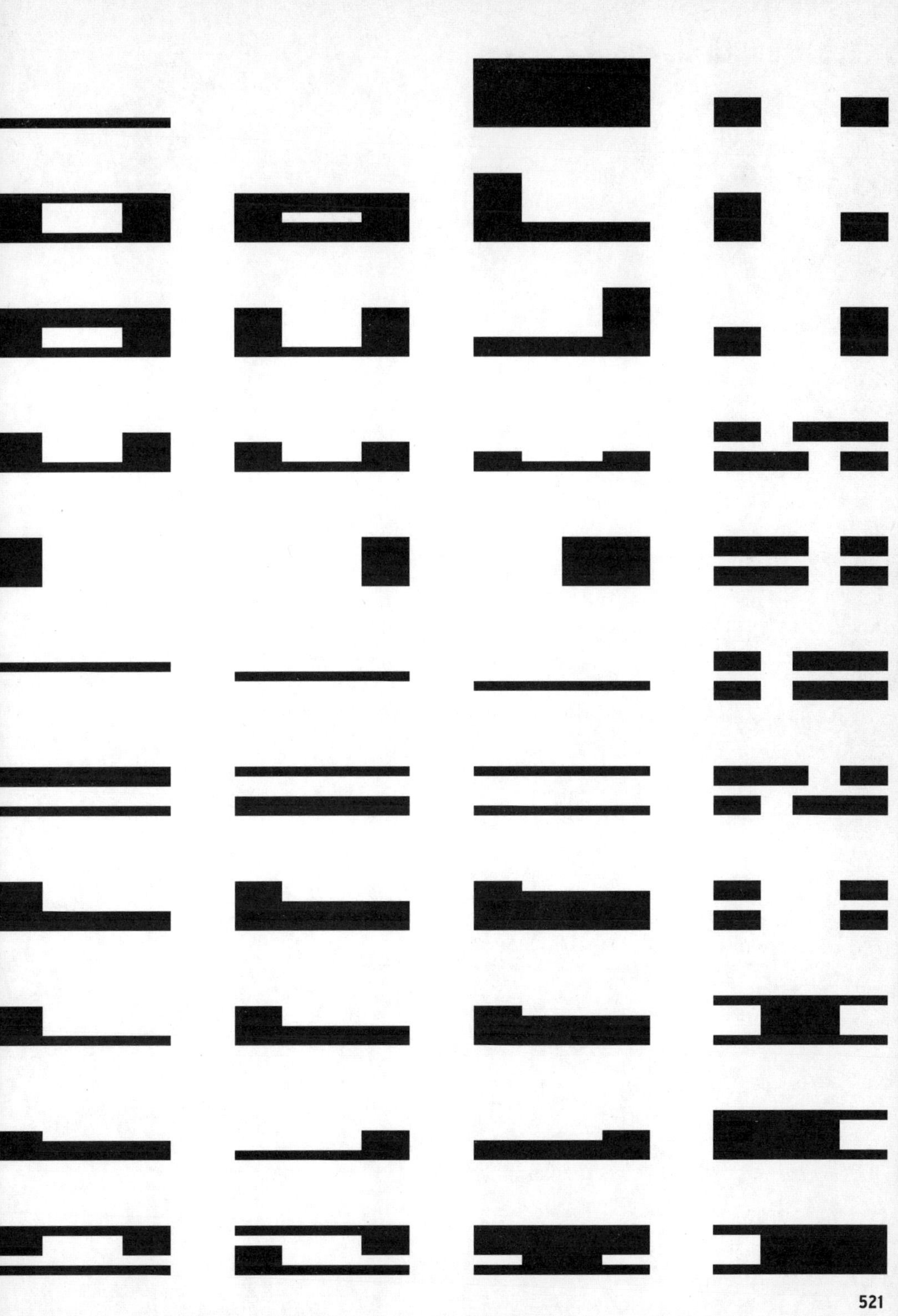

Scheme with viewlines

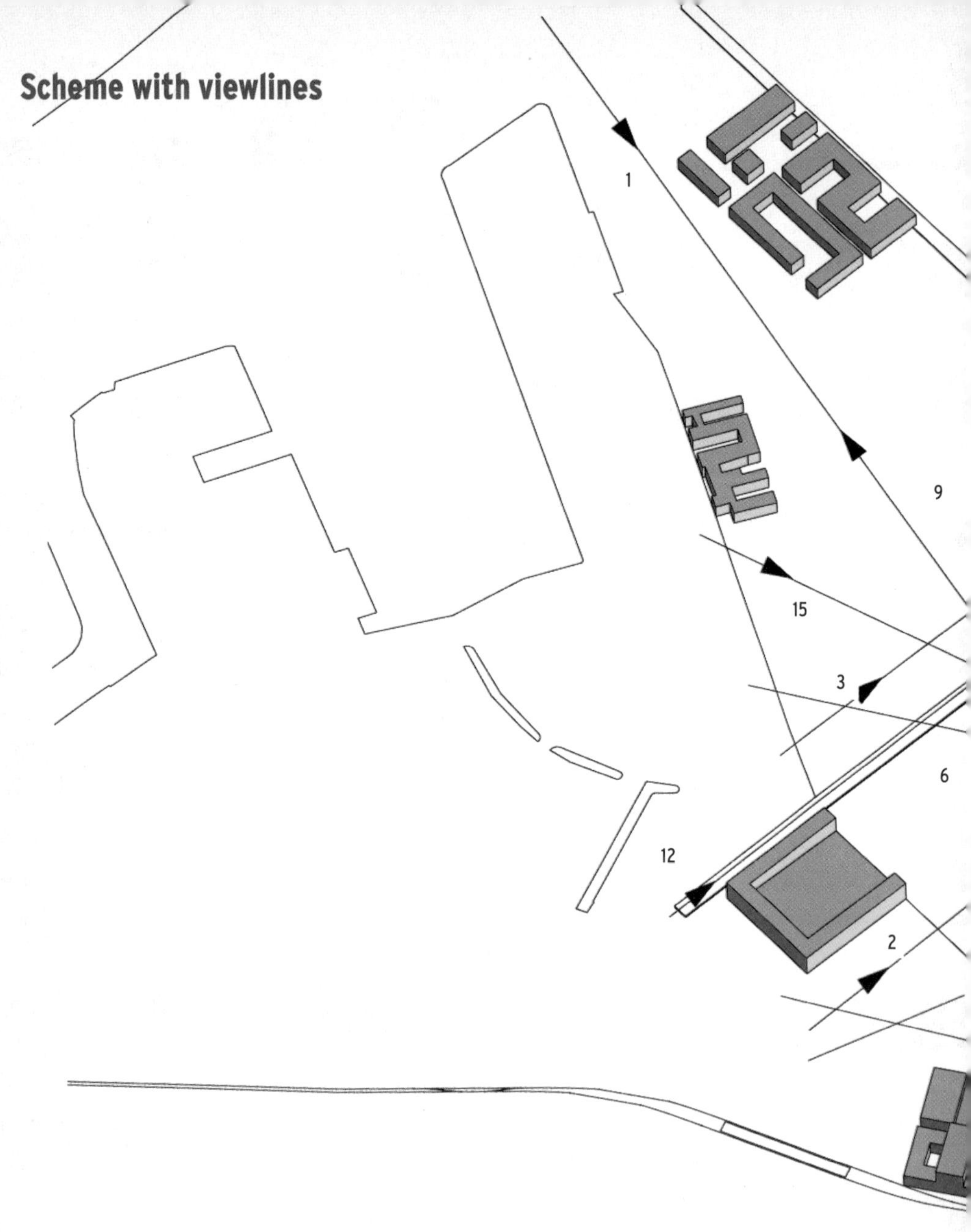

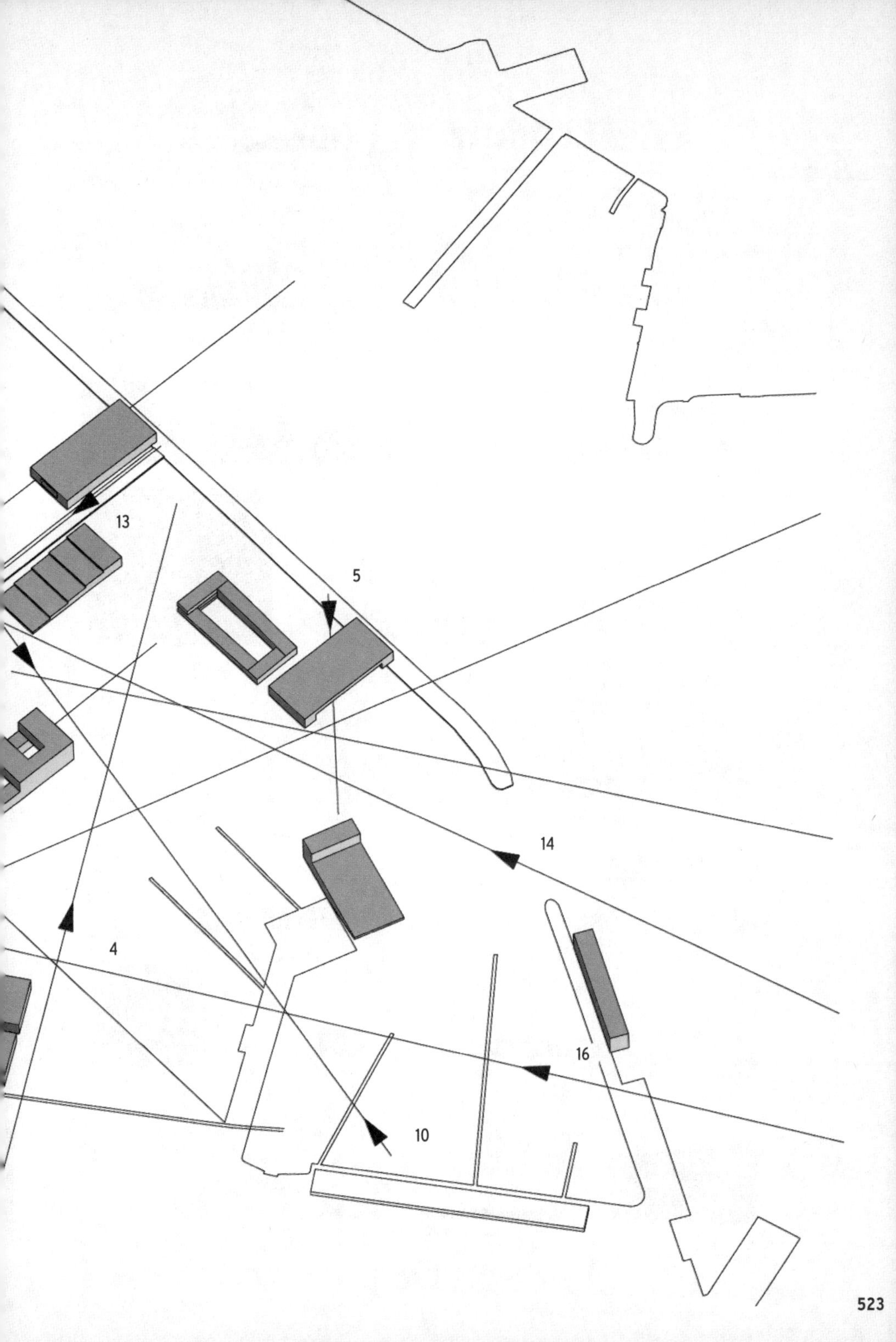
13
5
14
4
16
10

Views

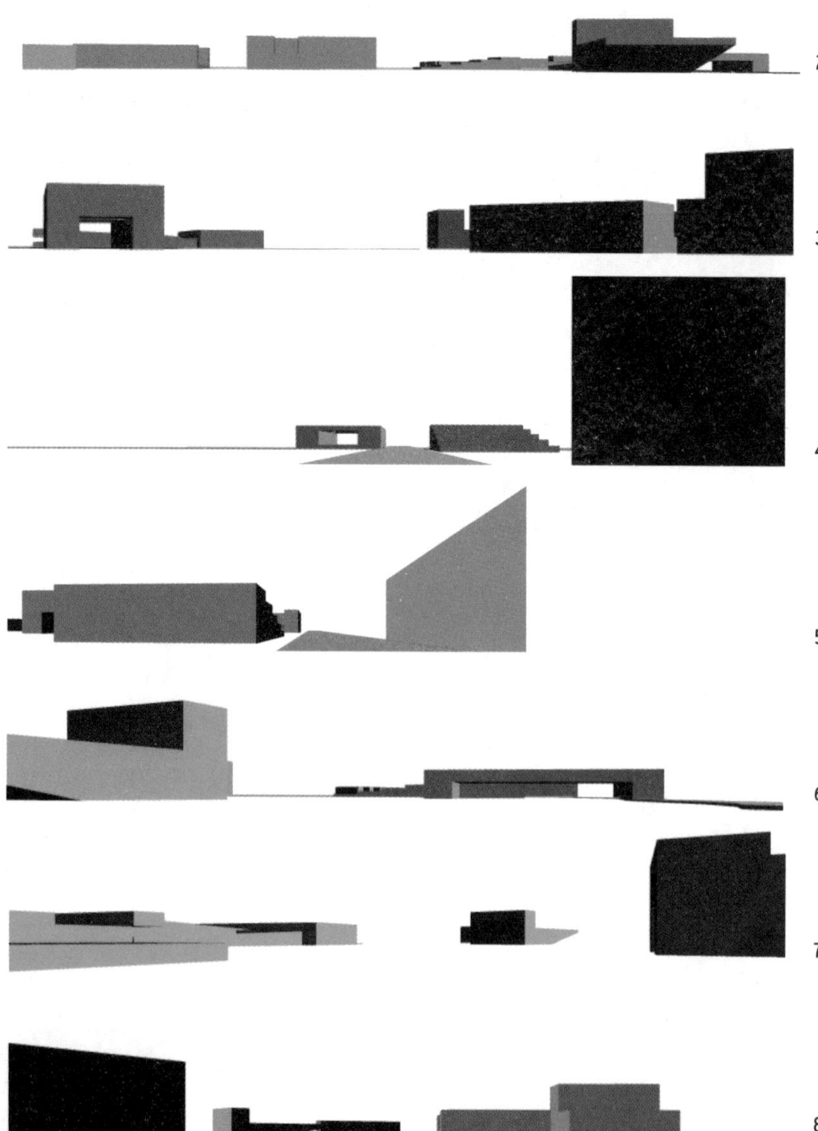

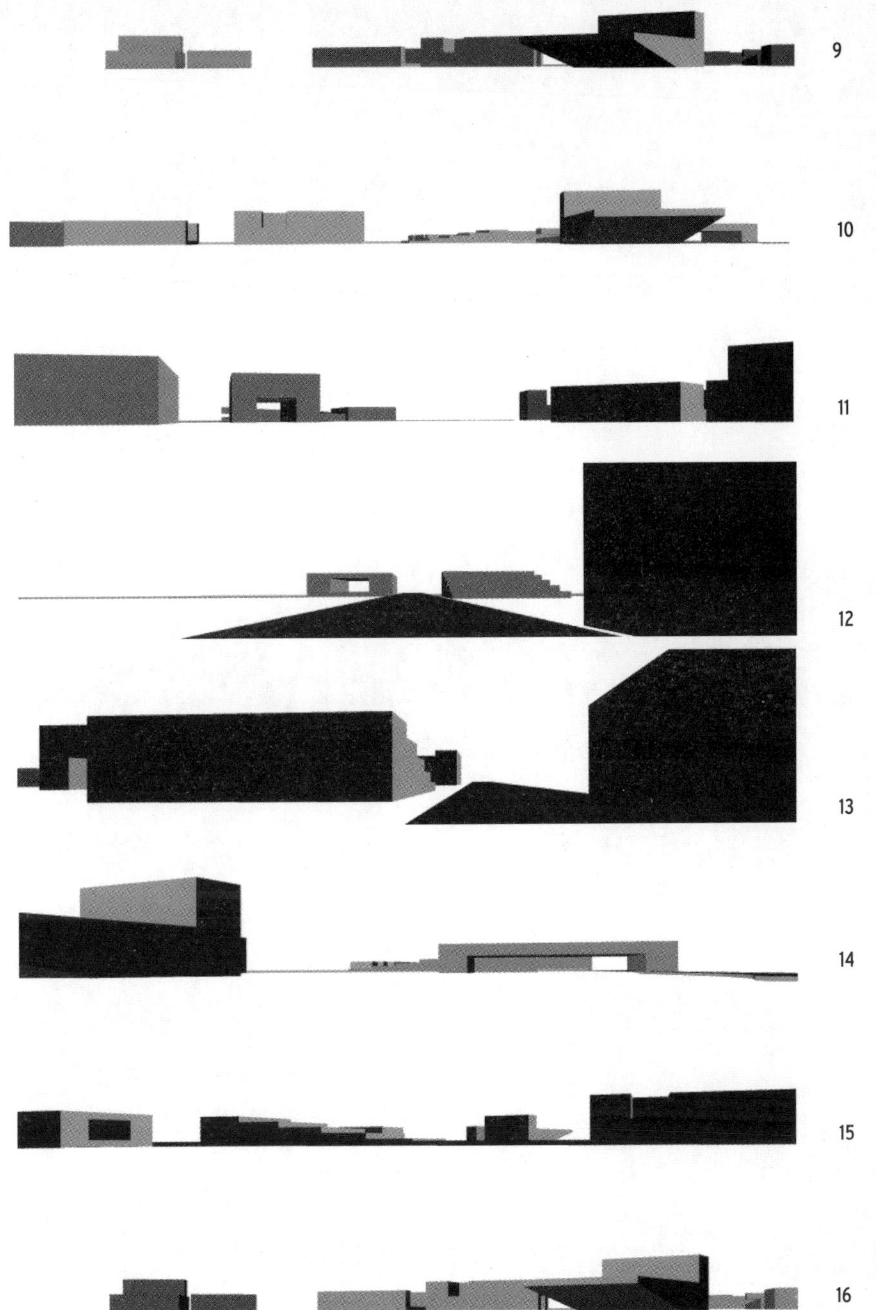
9
10
11
12
13
14
15
16

View 10

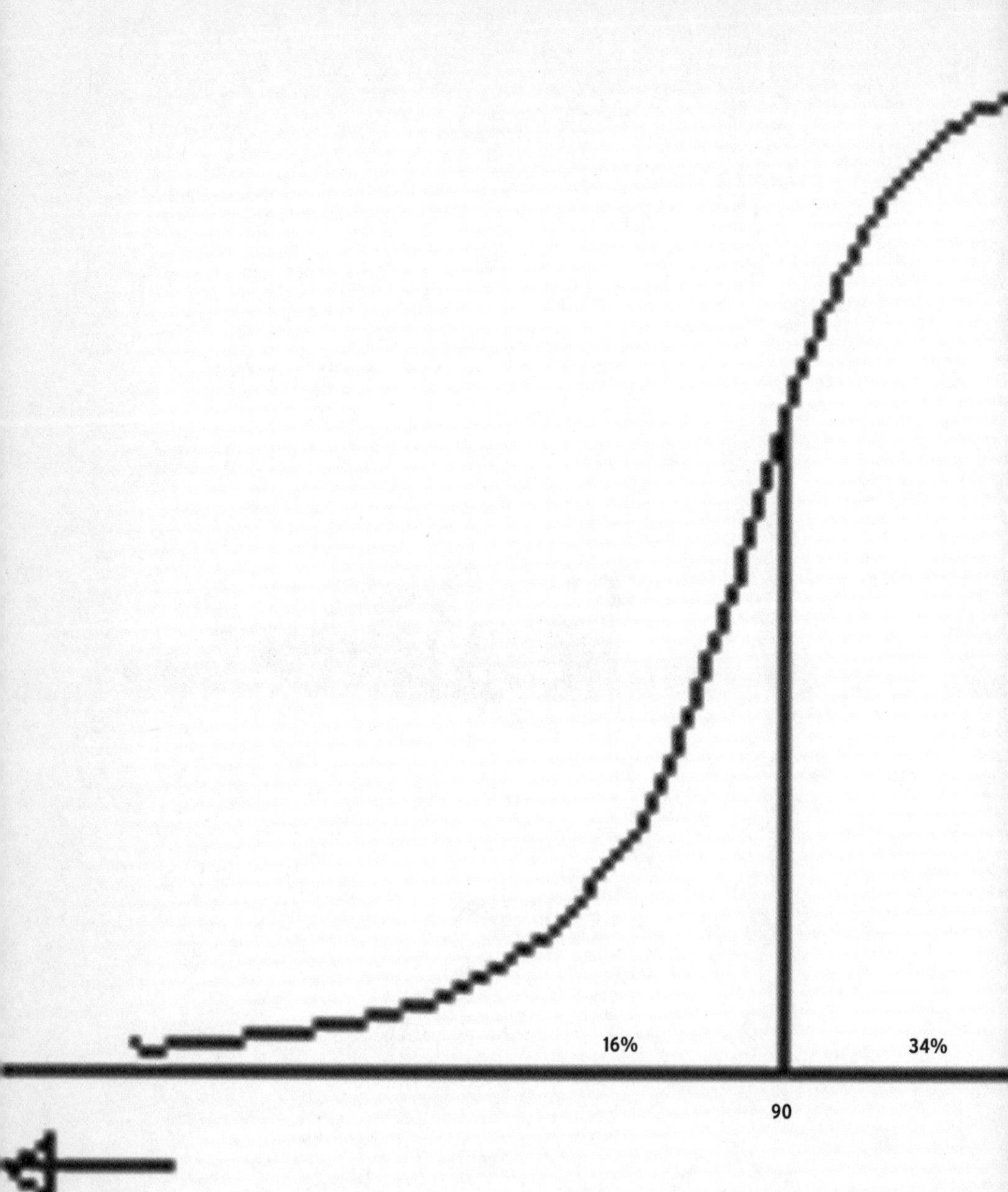
16%
34%
90

The world according to Gauss

Text

1996

Hans Krijnsen

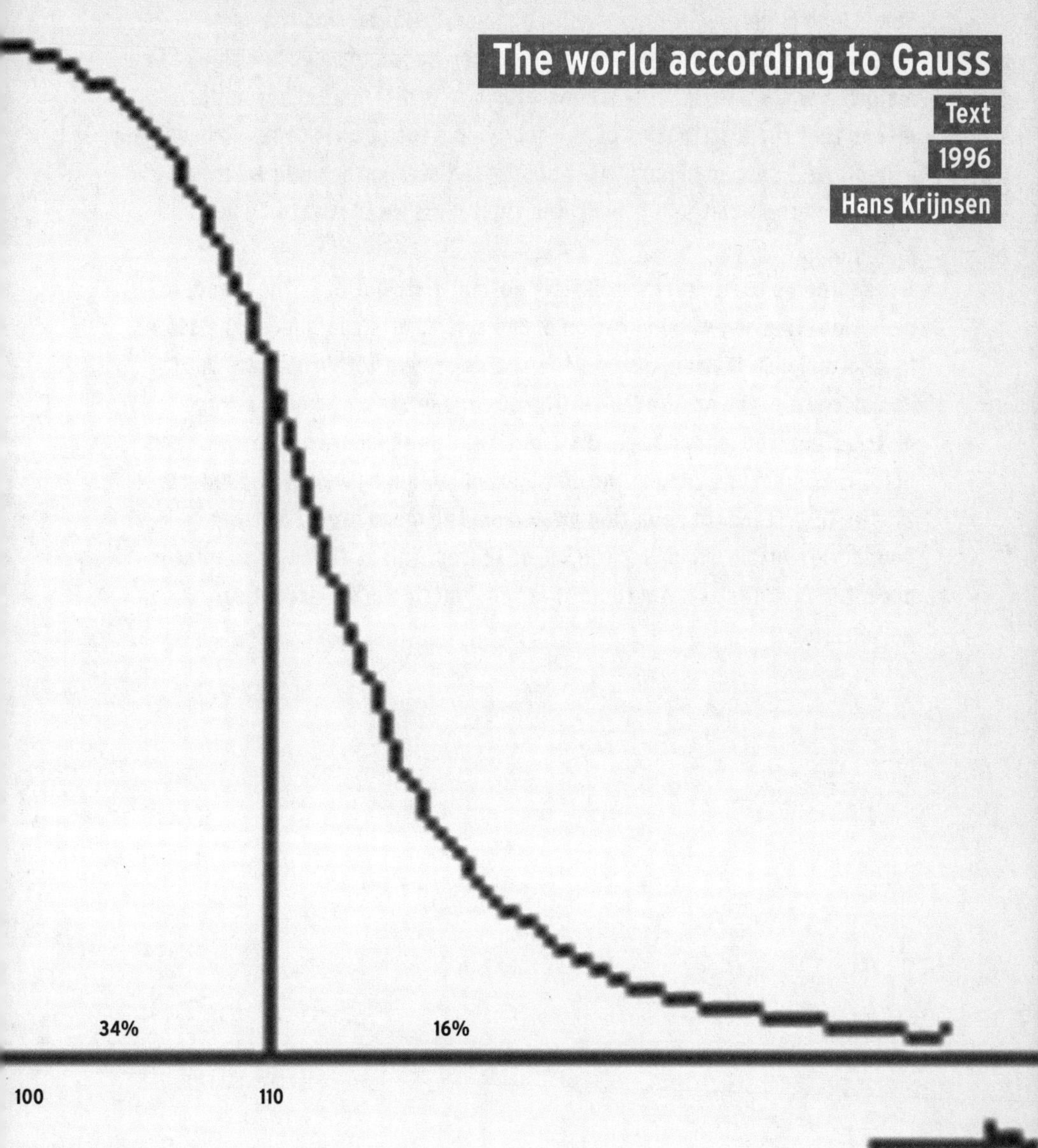

In statistics there is no literal definition of 'normal', only a description and a formula.
Something is normal if it belongs to a majority possessing the same properties; a number of exceptions can then be found on either side of this majority. When a variable or a characteristic is distributed normally, it means that the distribution of the scores in a research is symmetric and has a single bell-shaped 'hump'. Most scores register in the middle with as many deviations to the left as to the right. This we illustrate by means of the Gauss curve.
A resource we use to further classify normal distribution is the standard deviation. This gives an indication of the spread or dispersion of the scores. In a normal distribution, 68% of the scores remain within one standard deviation from the middle (the arithmetic mean). In a standard normal distribution (the most normal distribution), the standard deviation at this point is 1. Examples include the distribution of human weight and length. One further standard deviation away from the mean produces two boundaries within which occur 95% of scores. This is the limit to what is accepted in statistics. Anything that falls outside is an 'exception' or an 'extreme'.

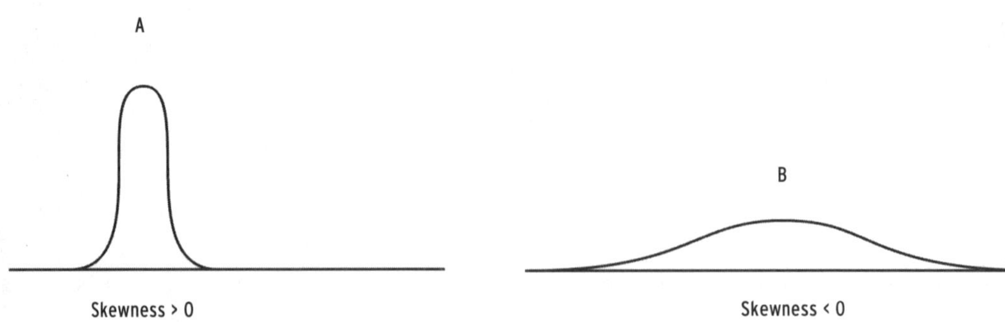

Of course, the computed distribution can deviate dramatically from the normal distribution; it can be 'flat' and/or 'skewed'.
The degree of flatness is illustrated by what is called kurtosis.
A negative kurtosis means a flat distribution. This happens when, for example, every imaginable score occurs equally often. Then there is a maximum standard deviation and a maximum spread. This is rendered as a horizontal line.
When all respondents have the same score, there is no spread. There is then no difference between the answers. The standard deviation is zero. The distribution has maximum 'peakedness': a vertical line. This kurtosis is extremely positive and in fact is impossible to calculate. A sudden craze is a good case in point.

If the distribution is asymmetric, then there are relatively many scores on one side of the mean. Examples of such asymmetry include the distribution of wealth and the outlay of sickness benefit per person.
This asymmetric state is rendered in degrees of 'skewness'; this is positive with relatively many extremely high scores and negative with relatively many extremely low ones.

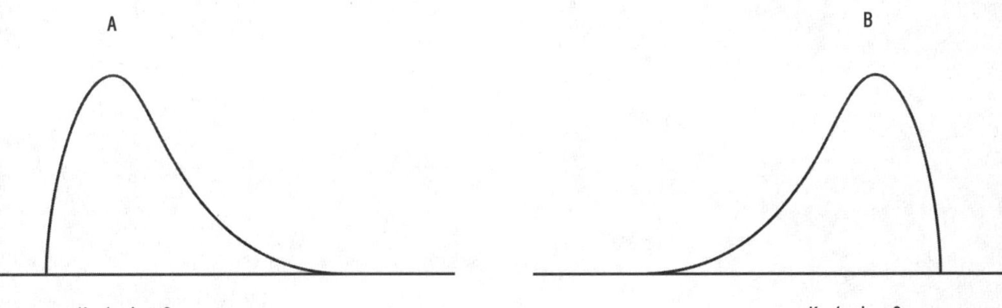

Mixed bloc

Negotiations in a housing silo

165 dwellings and business units on a jetty in the Amsterdam IJ channel, The Netherlands

1995/-

MVRDV

In times of uncertain economies building production becomes more and more phasable. That results in small buildings which have to be 'multifunctional' and therefore general in concept. At such times the realization of a condominium with its critical size and specific social ambitions is a sensible task that can almost only be achieved by gathering together different clients putting them under conditions so pressurized as to promote interdependencies.
Here a mixed programme of 160 houses, offices, work spaces, commercial spaces and public spaces has been squeezed into a given tight urban envelope. These elements were covered by four different clients: a housing developer, a housing corporation, a developer of workspaces and the City of Amsterdam.
The extreme variety of wishes has been addressed by finding the 'common size' within the programme: a series of 'mini-neighbourhoods' which, as a reaction to the increasing individualization, try to create a more social and safer living environment.
Each neighbourhood gets its own collective access principle according to its requirements: a hall, a tall corridor, a large balcony, an alley, a garden, a patio - these generate a specific housing type, structure and facade.
By stacking them independently next to and on top of each other, a system of public routes through the building emerges. When mixed with workspaces and open zones, a vertical neighbourhood is the result, one that tries to give the apartments equivalents of the house-with-a-garden feeling.
At the position of the main entrance, a part of the building is shifted

out over the water to form a public balcony filled with a restaurant offering a panoramic view back across the waters of the IJ towards the old centre. This restores the lost character of the jetty: a 270 degree perspective.

In a series of meetings, the qualities, quantities and positions of each of the neighbourhoods were presented to the participants. The possible desire for a monoculture by one of them was immediately tackled by another, one's possible wish for separation was at once confronted with the paradigm of the other.

It is unthinkable that in Amsterdam the higher floors are used only for the more expensive apartments, so that the 'rich are sitting on top of the poor'!

Again, it is unbearable to imagine that the less-rich social types would be separated from the rich by putting them in discrete towers like a form of Apartheid!

For once, architecture was saved by ancient social democratic ideals that obliged the participants to work together on the mix, as if a reflection of the celebrated characteristics of Amsterdam society.

In order to protect this process from going out of economical control, we set up a desired optimum division of dwelling sizes described by a 'gauss curve', so that in this series of meetings the potential cacophony could be tied to economical considerations.

The building can be seen as a 'frozen' result of the negotiations and therefore as a mirror of the political and economical situation in Amsterdam at the end of the twentieth century.

Mini neighbourhoods

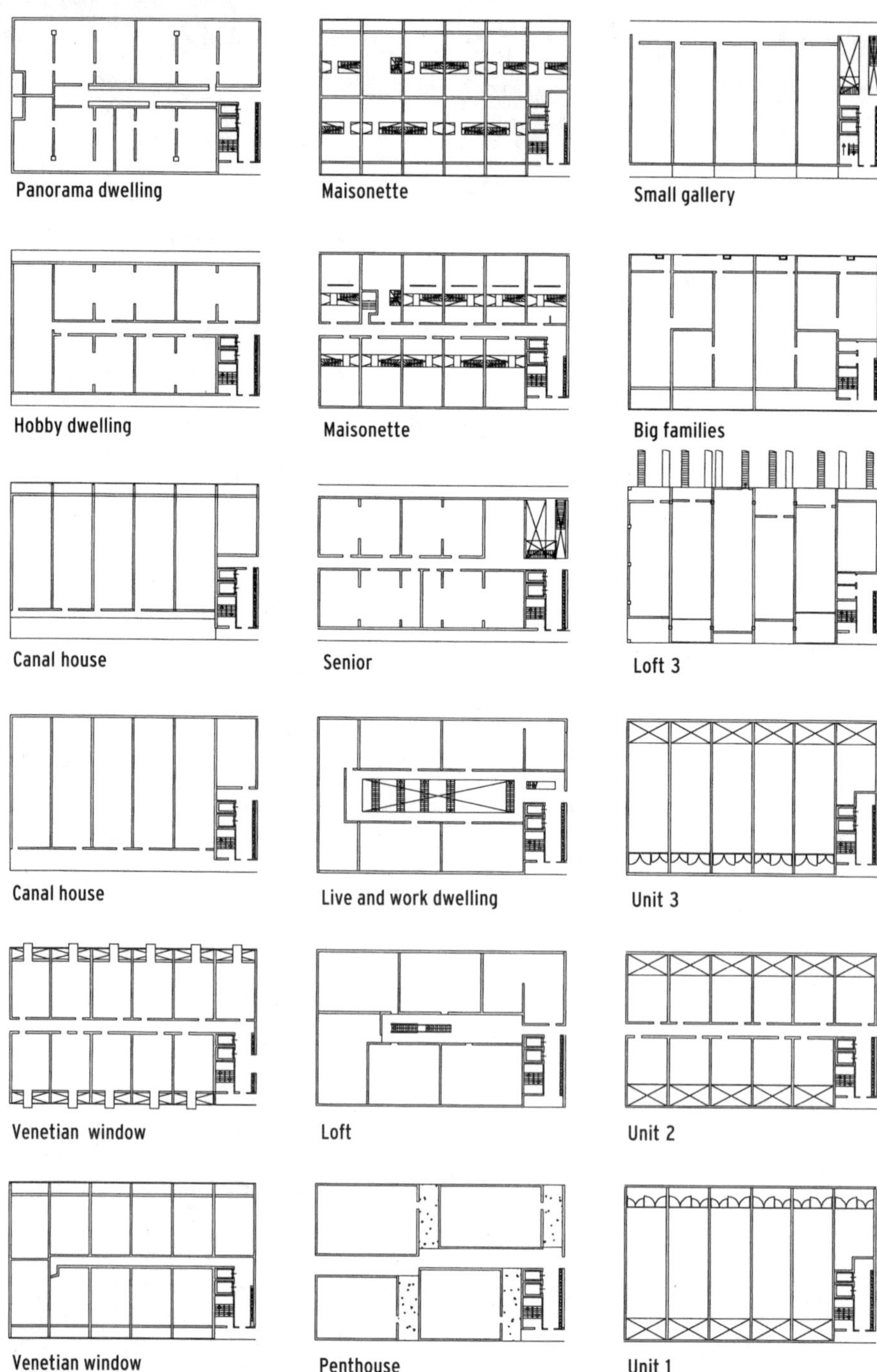
Panorama dwelling
Maisonette
Small gallery
Hobby dwelling
Maisonette
Big families
Canal house
Senior
Loft 3
Canal house
Live and work dwelling
Unit 3
Venetian window
Loft
Unit 2
Venetian window
Penthouse
Unit 1

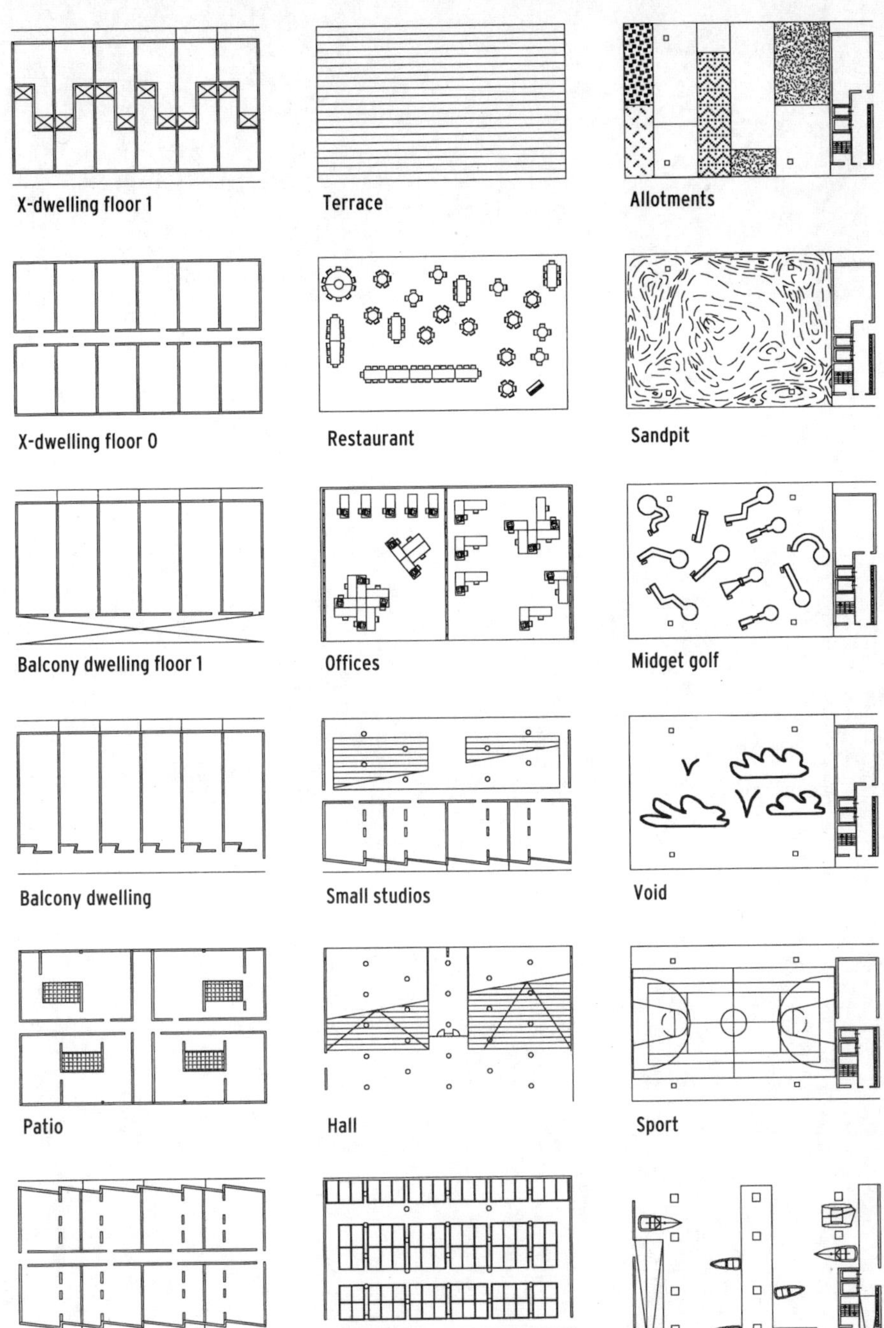
X-dwelling floor 1
Terrace
Allotments
X-dwelling floor 0
Restaurant
Sandpit
Balcony dwelling floor 1
Offices
Midget golf
Balcony dwelling
Small studios
Void
Patio
Hall
Sport
Small studios
Storage
Marina

Political negotiations

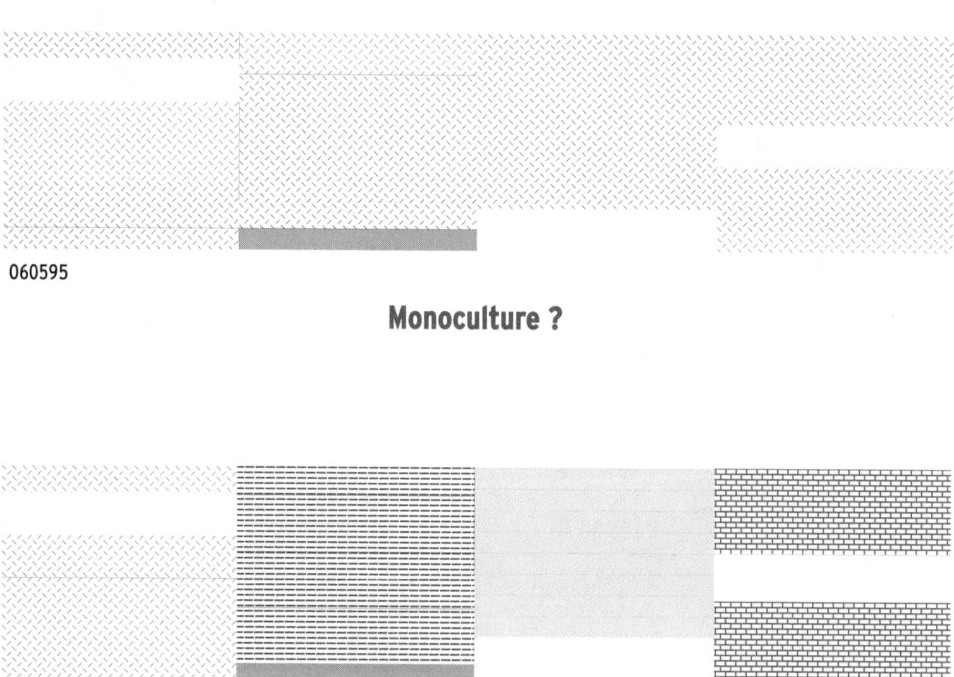

060595

Monoculture ?

130595

Apartheid ?

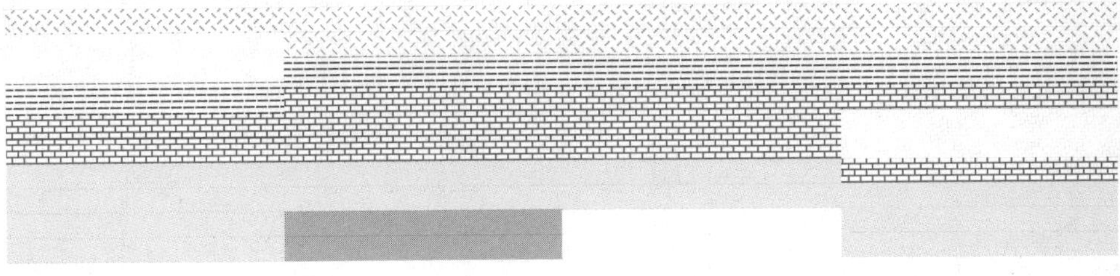

160595

Social stratification ?

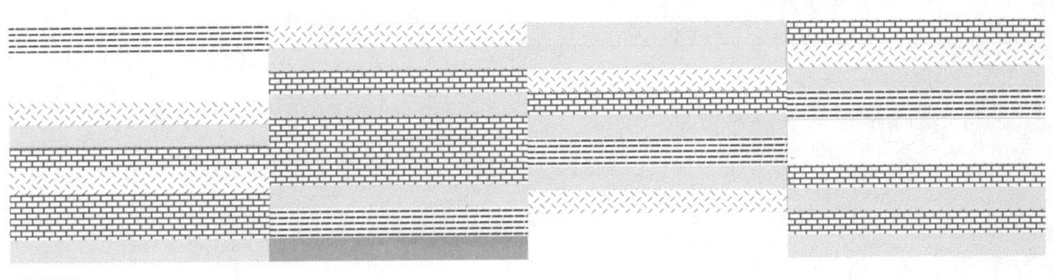

200595

Mix ?

Cheap category housing | Middle category housing | Expensive category housing | Offices and workshops | Entrance and storage

Economical negotiations

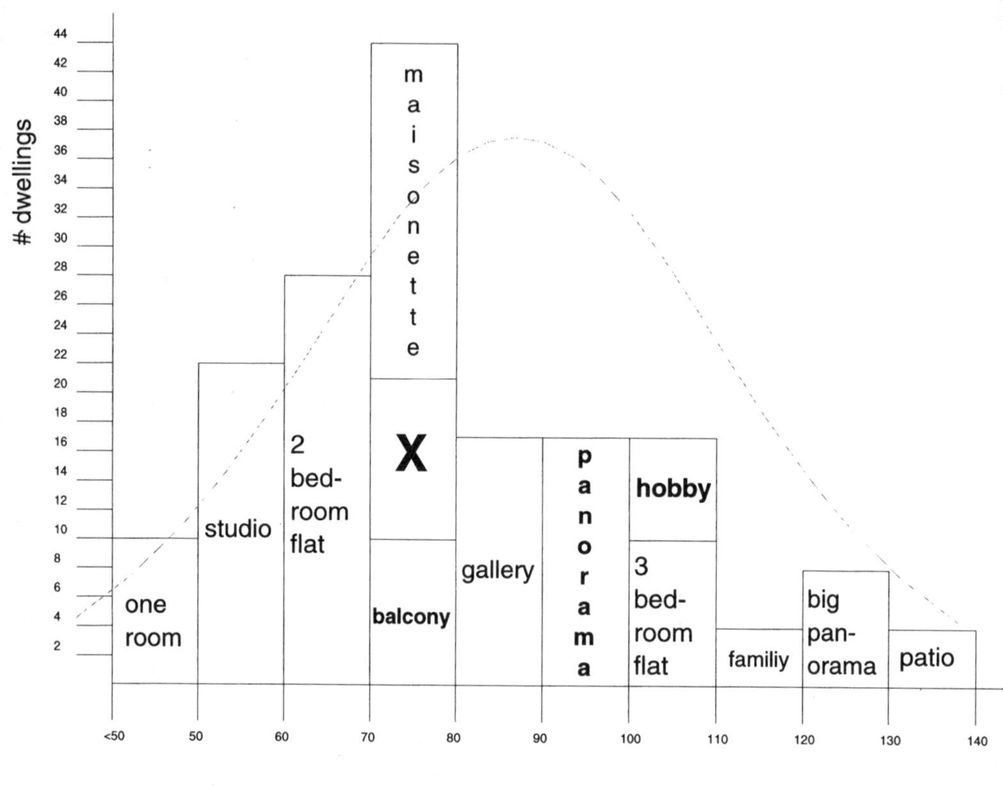

240595

OFFICES
GYMNASIUM
PANORAMA
BIG PANORAMA
PANORAMA
BIG PANORAMA
GALLERY
MAISONETTE

PATIO
HOBBY
FAMILY
STUDIOS
HOBBY
STUDIOS
STUDIOS
STUDIOS
HALL+ TRAY
STORAGE

PATIO
X-HOUSE
BALCONY
OFFICES
MAISONETTE
MARINA

2 BEDROOM FLAT
3BEDROOM FLAT
2 BEDROOM FLAT
OFFICES
SANDPIT
3 BEDROOMFLAT
2 BEDROOMFLAT
2 BEDROOMFLAT
GALLERY

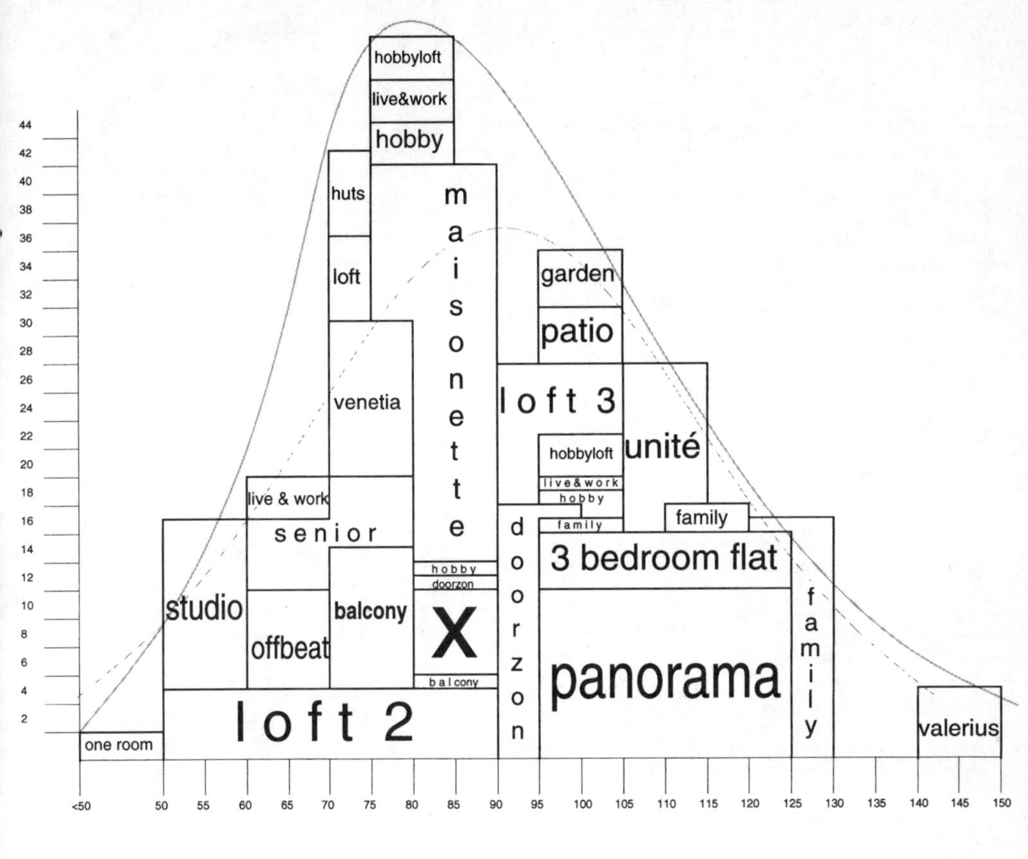

270995

LOFTS	HUTS	PATIO	MAISONETTE
GYMNASIUM	HOBBY	X-HOUSE	OFF-BEAT 3 ROOM
PANORAMA	UNITE	BALCONY	PANORAMA
PANORAMA	SENIOR	SENIOR	GARDEN HOUSE
HOBBY	STUDIOS	LIVE & WORK	DOORZON
VALERIUS PLEIN	STUDIOS	WORKLOFT	3 BEDROOMFLAT
VENETIAN WINDOW	HALL+ TRAY	MARINA	FAMILYHOUSE
	STORAGE		LIVE & WORK LOFT

Economical fine-tuning

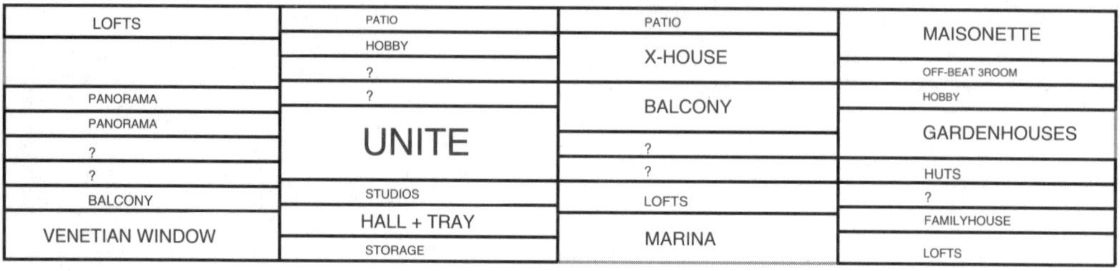

LOFTS	PATIO	PATIO	MAISONETTE
	HOBBY	X-HOUSE	OFF-BEAT 3ROOM
PANORAMA	?	BALCONY	HOBBY
PANORAMA	?	?	GARDENHOUSES
?	UNITE	?	HUTS
?	STUDIOS	LOFTS	?
BALCONY	HALL + TRAY	MARINA	FAMILYHOUSE
VENETIAN WINDOW	STORAGE		LOFTS

290895

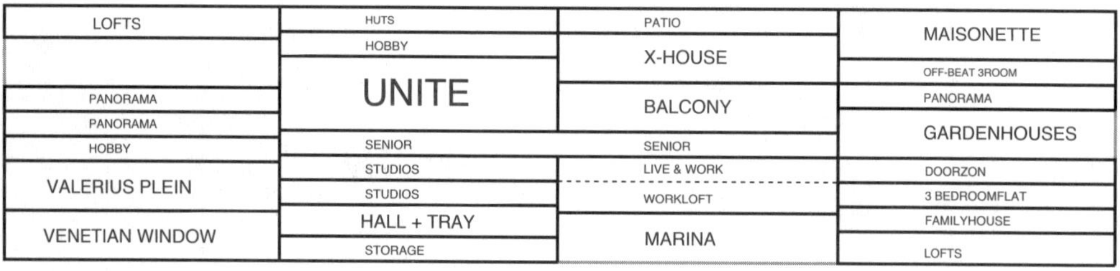

LOFTS	HUTS	PATIO	MAISONETTE
	HOBBY	X-HOUSE	OFF-BEAT 3ROOM
PANORAMA	UNITE	BALCONY	PANORAMA
PANORAMA	SENIOR	SENIOR	GARDENHOUSES
HOBBY	STUDIOS	LIVE & WORK	DOORZON
VALERIUS PLEIN	STUDIOS	WORKLOFT	3 BEDROOMFLAT
VENETIAN WINDOW	HALL + TRAY	MARINA	FAMILYHOUSE
	STORAGE		LOFTS

270995

LOFTS	PATIO	PATIO	PENTHIOUSE
	HOBBY	X-HOUSE	PANORAMA
PANORAMA	UNITE	MAISONETTE	PANORAMA
PANORAMA	SENIOR	SENIOR	UNITE
HOBBY	STUDIOS	LIVE & WORK	DOORZON
VALERIUS PLEIN	STUDIOS	WORKLOFT	3 BEDROOMFLAT
VENETIAN WINDOW	HALL + TRAY	MARINA	FAMILYHOUSE
	STORAGE		LOFTS

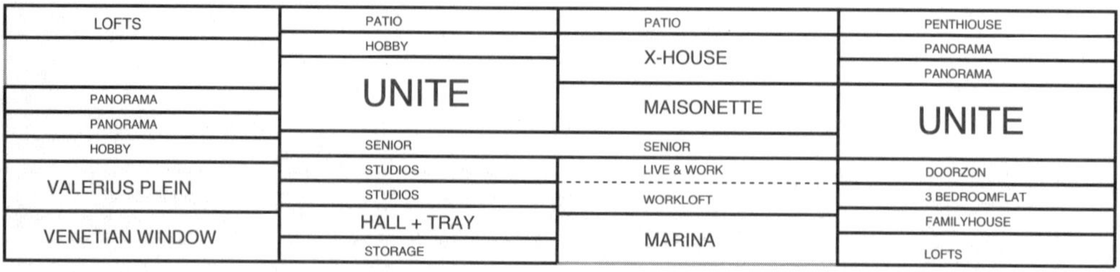

201295

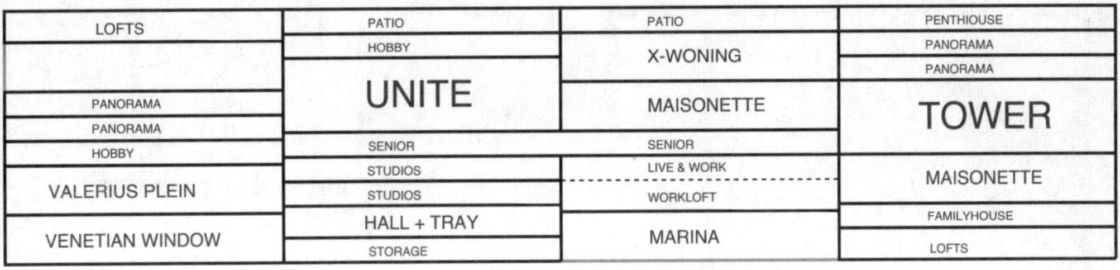

LOFTS
PANORAMA
PANORAMA
HOBBY
VALERIUS PLEIN
VENETIAN WINDOW

PATIO
HOBBY
UNITE
SENIOR
STUDIOS
STUDIOS
HALL + TRAY
STORAGE

PATIO
X-WONING
MAISONETTE
SENIOR
LIVE & WORK
WORKLOFT
MARINA

PENTHIOUSE
PANORAMA
PANORAMA
TOWER
MAISONETTE
FAMILYHOUSE
LOFTS

120196

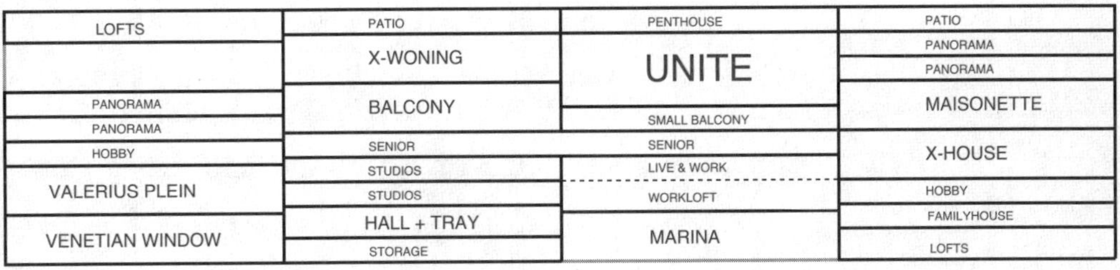

LOFTS
PANORAMA
PANORAMA
HOBBY
VALERIUS PLEIN
VENETIAN WINDOW

PATIO
X-WONING
BALCONY
SENIOR
STUDIOS
STUDIOS
HALL + TRAY
STORAGE

PENTHOUSE
UNITE
SMALL BALCONY
SENIOR
LIVE & WORK
WORKLOFT
MARINA

PATIO
PANORAMA
PANORAMA
MAISONETTE
X-HOUSE
HOBBY
FAMILYHOUSE
LOFTS

260397

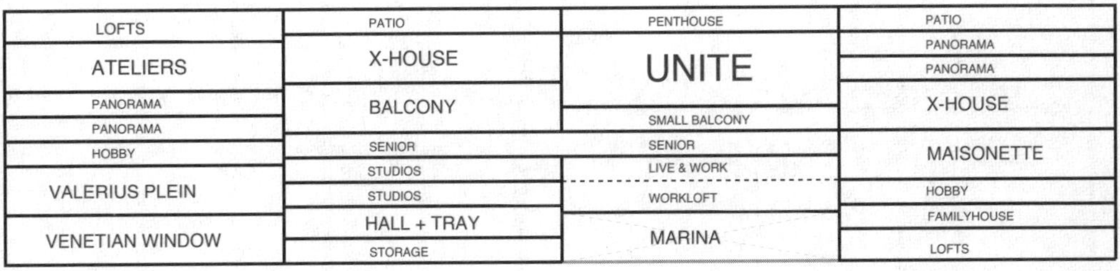

LOFTS
ATELIERS
PANORAMA
PANORAMA
HOBBY
VALERIUS PLEIN
VENETIAN WINDOW

PATIO
X-HOUSE
BALCONY
SENIOR
STUDIOS
STUDIOS
HALL + TRAY
STORAGE

PENTHOUSE
UNITE
SMALL BALCONY
SENIOR
LIVE & WORK
WORKLOFT
MARINA

PATIO
PANORAMA
PANORAMA
X-HOUSE
MAISONETTE
HOBBY
FAMILYHOUSE
LOFTS

270897

Collage of mini-neighbourhoods

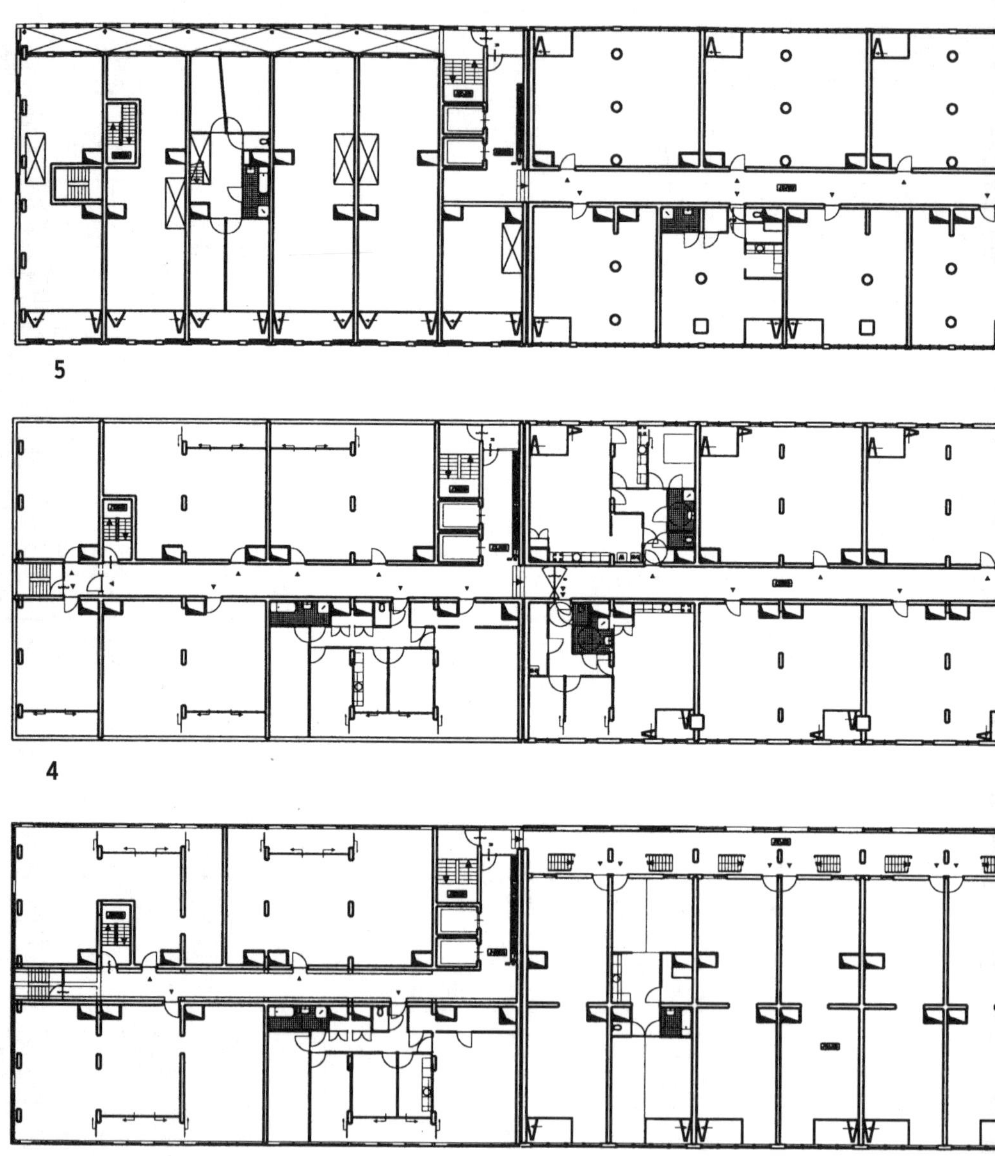

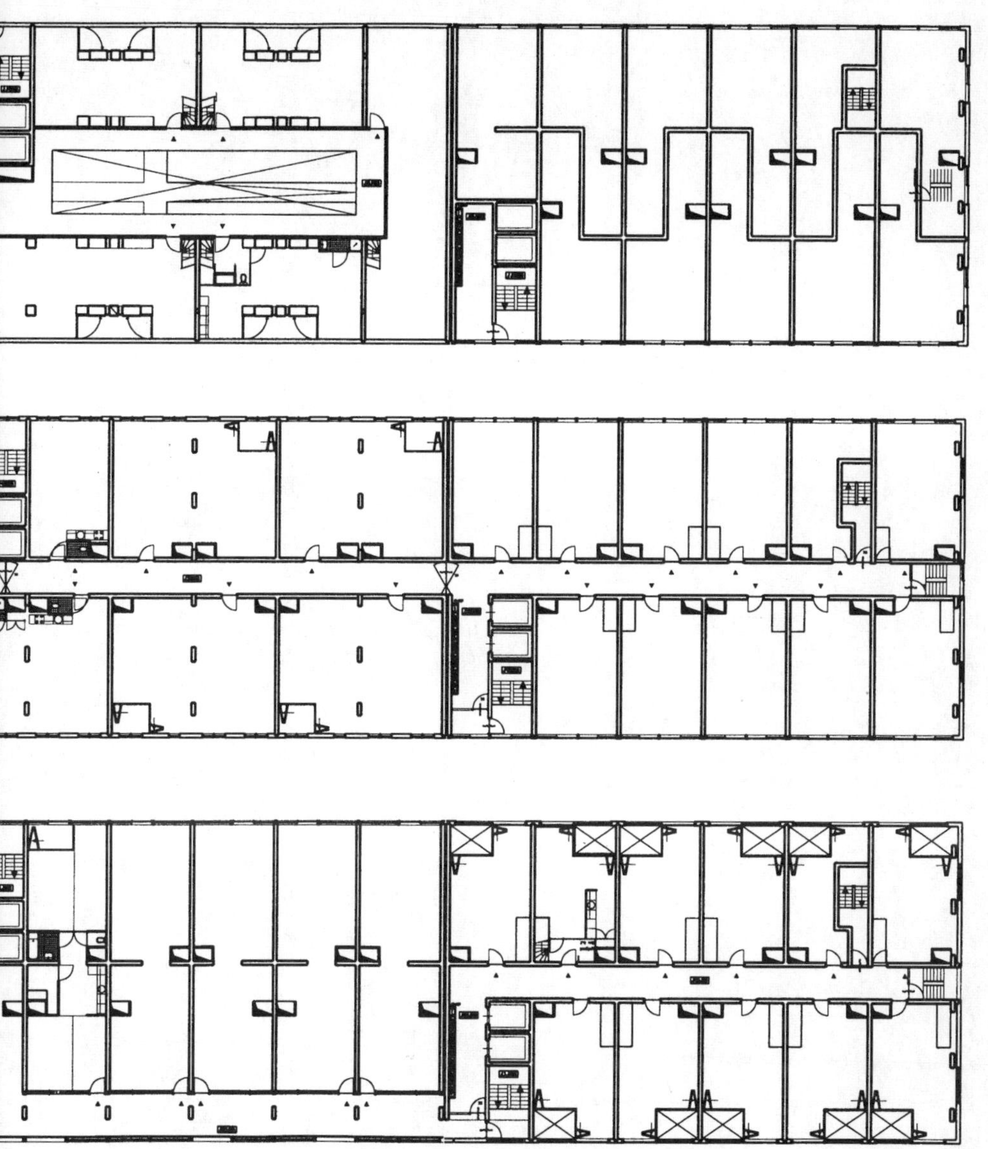

Plans

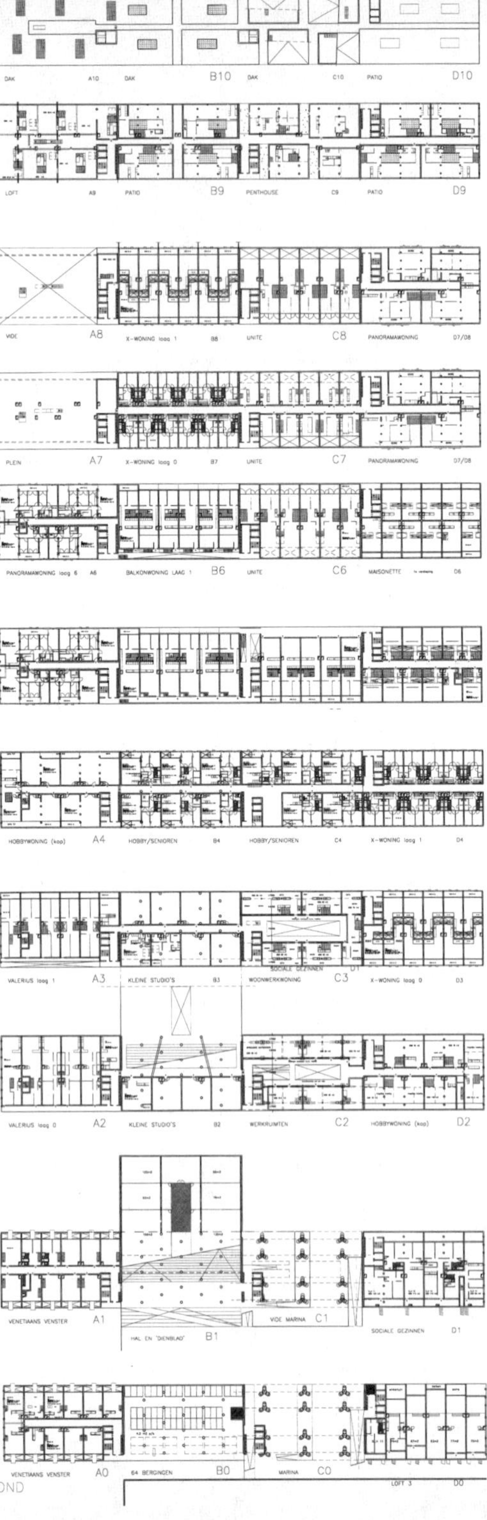
DAK A10 DAK B10 DAK C10 PATIO D10
LOFT A9 PATIO B9 PENTHOUSE C9 PATIO D9
VIDE A8 X-WONING laag 1 B8 UNITE C8 PANORAMAWONING D7/D8
PLEIN A7 X-WONING laag 0 B7 UNITE C7 PANORAMAWONING D7/D8
PANORAMAWONING laag 6 A6 BALKONWONING LAAG 1 B6 UNITE C6 MAISONETTE D6
HOBBYWONING (kop) A4 HOBBY/SENIOREN B4 HOBBY/SENIOREN C4 X-WONING laag 1 D4
VALERIUS laag 1 A3 KLEINE STUDIO'S B3 WOONWERKWONING C3 X-WONING laag 0 D3
SOCIALE GEZINNEN D1
VALERIUS laag 0 A2 KLEINE STUDIO'S B2 WERKRUIMTEN C2 HOBBYWONING (kop) D2
VENETIAANS VENSTER A1 HAL EN 'DIENBLAD' B1 VIDE MARINA C1 SOCIALE GEZINNEN D1
VENETIAANS VENSTER A0 64 BERGINGEN B0 MARINA C0 LOFT 3 D0
GROND

Public routes

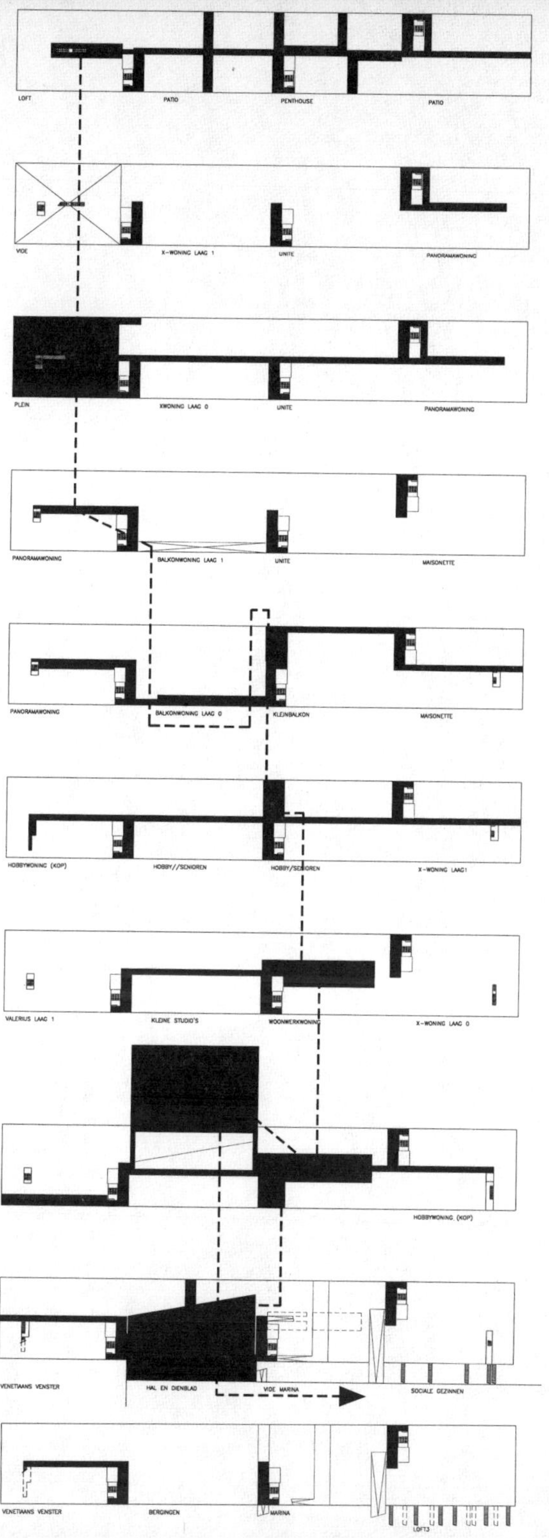
LOFT
PATIO
PENTHOUSE
PATIO
VIDE
X-WONING LAAG 1
UNITE
PANORAMAWONING
PLEIN
XWONING LAAG 0
UNITE
PANORAMAWONING
PANORAMAWONING
BALKONWONING LAAG 1
UNITE
MAISONETTE
PANORAMAWONING
BALKONWONING LAAG 0
KLEINBALKON
MAISONETTE
HOBBYWONING (KOP)
HOBBY//SENIOREN
HOBBY/SENIOREN
X-WONING LAAG1
VALERIUS LAAG 1
KLEINE STUDIO'S
WOONWERKWONING
X-WONING LAAG 0
HOBBYWONING (KOP)
VENETIAANS VENSTER
HAL EN DIENBLAD
VIDE MARINA
SOCIALE GEZINNEN
VENETIAANS VENSTER
BERGINGEN
MARINA
LOFT3

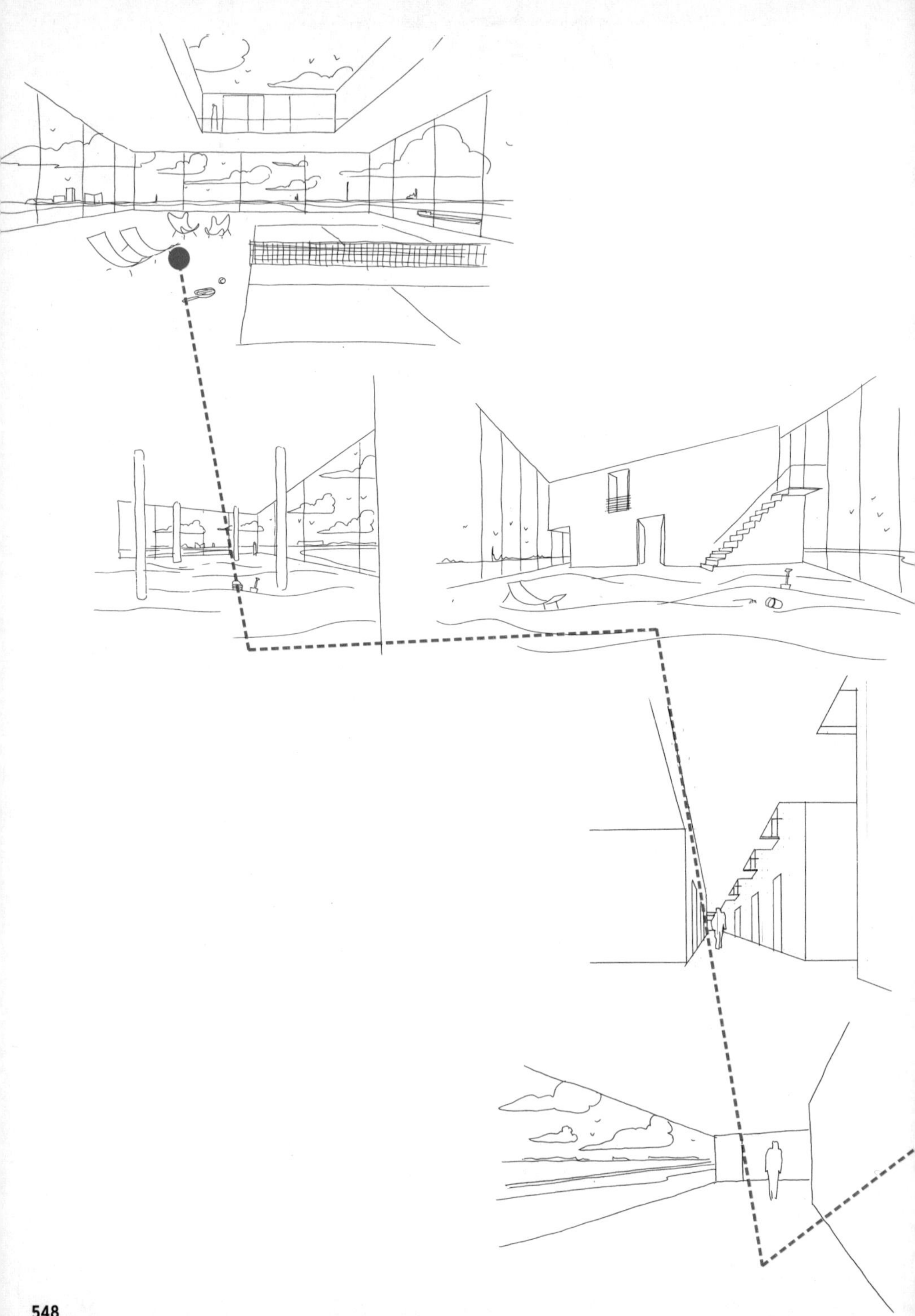

Public route

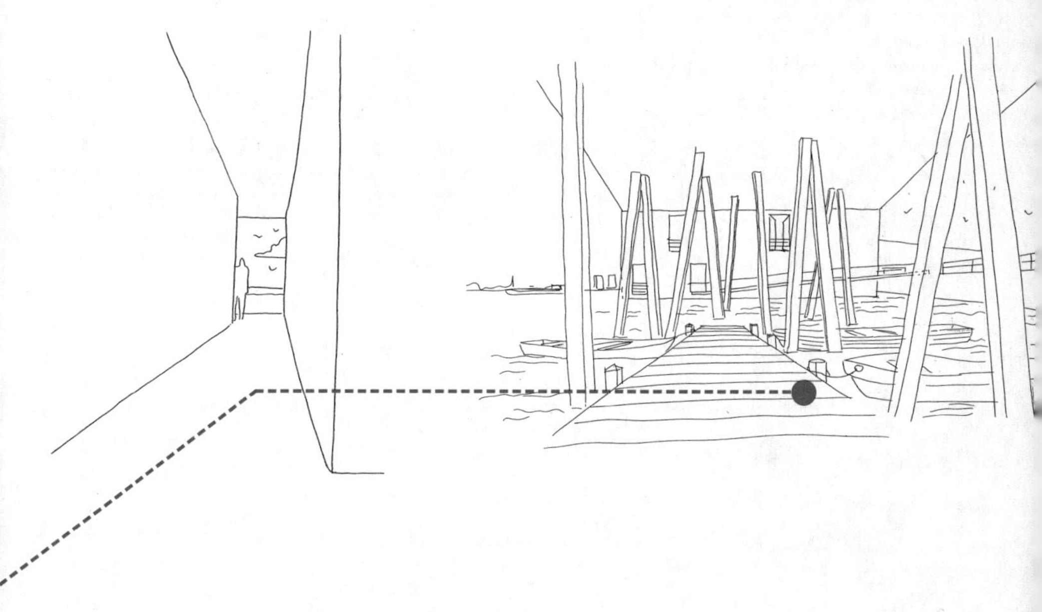

Elevations

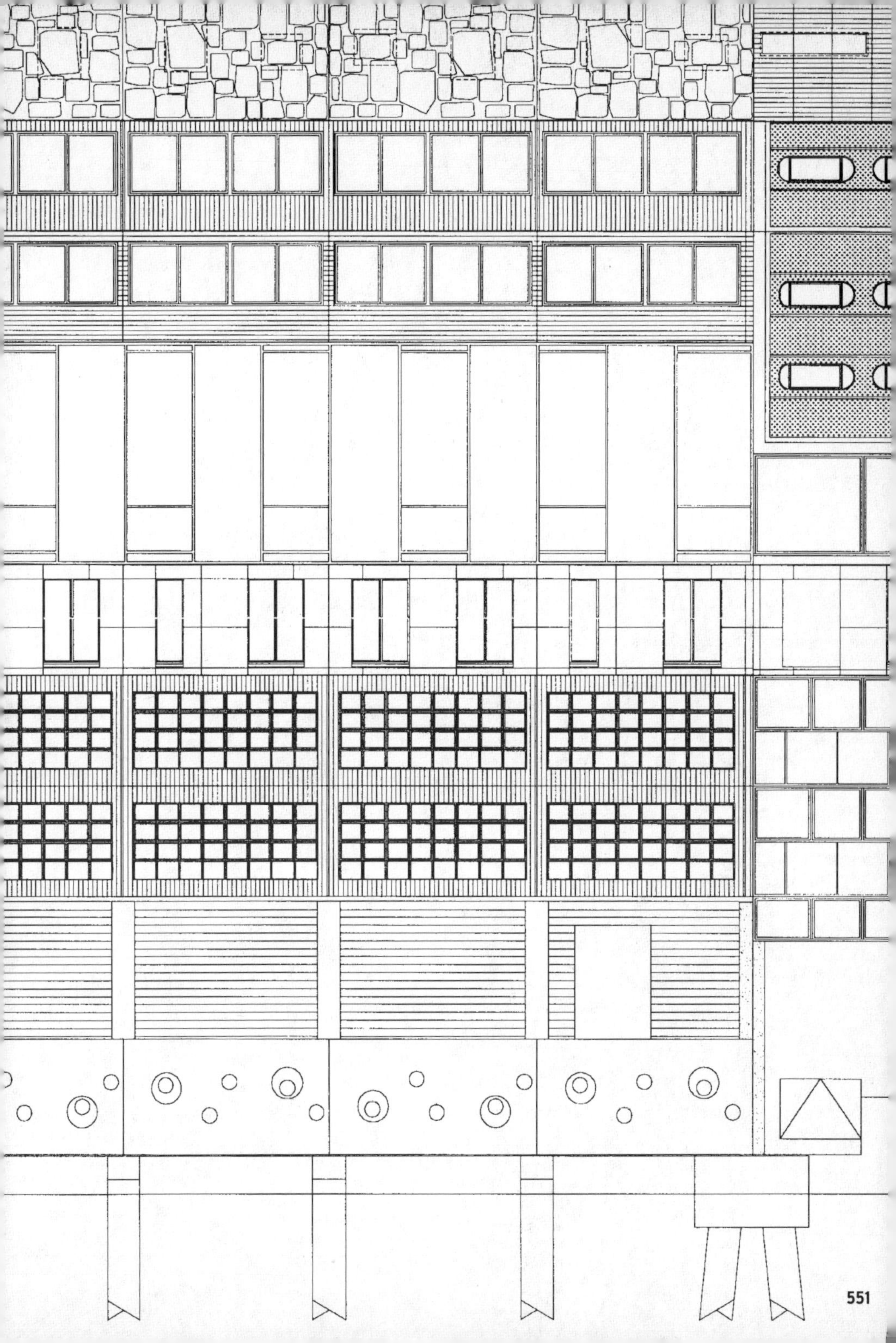

Entrance

Housing silo

Proximity

284 houses in Berlin-Prenzlauerberg, Germany

1991

MVRDV

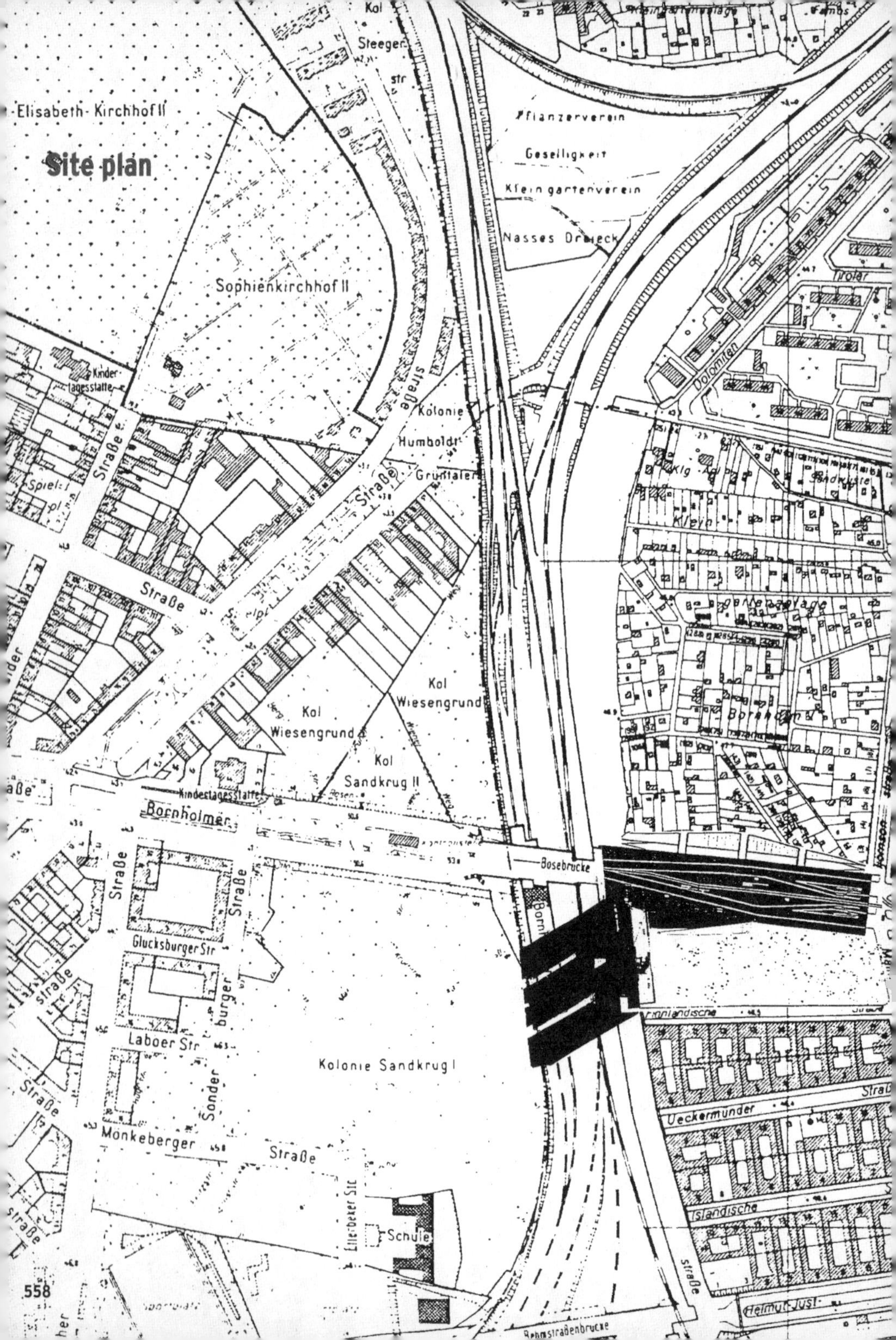
Elisabeth-Kirchhof II
Sophienkirchhof II
Kol
Steeger
str
Pflanzerverein
Geselligkeit
Kleingartenverein
Nasses Dreieck
Tiroler
Dolomiten
Kinder-
tagesstätte
Straße
Spielpl.
Straße
Straße
Kolonie
Humboldt
Grüntaler
Straße
Kol
Wiesengrund
Kol
Wiesengrund
Kol
Sandkrug II
Kindertagesstätte
Bornholmer
Bösebrücke
Klein
gartenanlage
Bornholm
Straße
Straße
Glücksburger Str
burger
Laboer Str
Sonder
Kolonie Sandkrug I
Mönkeberger
Straße
Straße
Straße
Schule
Ueckermünder
Straße
Isländische
Straße
Helmut-Just
Behmstraßenbrücke

Site plan

Straße
Andreas-Hofer-Platz
Brenner
Toblacher
Esplanade
Lagerplatz
Baustelle
Baustelle
Stavanger
Westerland
Halland
Andersen Straße
Bergener Straße
Nordkap Straße
Alesunder Straße
Stavanger
Gotland Straße
Paul-Robeson-
Willi-Bredel-
Amimplatz
Kugler
Straße
Wisbyer
Erich-Weinert
Rodenberg

With the Wall torn down and East and West Berlin recently reunited, the central government proposed organizing a competition for the infill of a left-over space in the nineteenth-century Prenzlauerberg district, a former Russian checkpoint next to the old Wall zone.
284 houses and 30,000 m² of commercial space are to be placed so as to give this area a shot of 'progress'. How are we to show these aspirations? Should the former envelope be respected, so that East Berlin continues to withdraw into the world of inhuman tenement blocks (Mietskasernen)? Or could this building stand proudly, encouraging literal connections between these Mietskasernen and other 'grosshäuser' on the horizon, so that Berlin could enjoy the large-scale cohesion worthy of a capital city?
A 'flipped' Mietskaserne could be erected to meet these aspirations, while saving enough of the existing voids of the former wall zone to reserve it for public functions. It could then display its contents to the outer world as a vertical neighbourhood packed with 'ideals'. For the organizers, being of a progressive persuasion, requested the ideal house.
Since modernist times every architect seems to feel obliged to design the ideal house. But is there such a thing as the ideal place?

'On the beach, beyond the sandy concrete walk, moms under beach umbrellas lie fast asleep on their heavy sides, arms flung over sleeping babies. Secretaries with a half day off to start the long weekend are lying on their bellies, shoulder to shoulder, chatting, winking and smoking cigarettes in their two-pieces. Tiny, stick-figure boys stand bare-chested at the margins of the small surf, shading their eyes as dogs trot by, tanned joggers jog and elderlies in pastel garb stroll behind them in the fractured light. Here is human hum in the barely moving air and surf-sigh, the low scrim of the radio notes and water subsiding over words spoken in whispers. Something in it moves me as though to a tear (but not quite); some sensation that I have been here, or nearby, been at dire pains here time-ago and am here now again, sharing the air just as then. Only nothing signifies, nothing gives a nod. The sea closes up, and so does the land.
'I am not sure what chokes me up: either the place's familiarity or its rigid reluctance to act familiar. It is another useful theme and exercise of the Existence Period, and a patent lesson of the reality profession, to cease sanctifying places - houses, beaches, home-towns, a street corner where you once kissed a girl, a parade ground where you marched in line, a courthouse where you secured a divorce on a cloudy day in July but where there is now no sign of you, no mention in the air's breath that you were there or that you were ever, importantly you, or that you even were. We may feel they ought to, should confer something - sanction, again - because of events that transpired there once; light a warming fire to animate us when we're well nigh inanimate and sunk. But they don't. Places never cooperate by reverting you back when you need it. In fact, they almost always let you down, as the Markhams found out in Vermont and now New Jersey. Best just to swallow back your tear, get accustomed to the minor sentimentals and shove off to whatever's next, not whatever was. Place means nothing.'

Richard Ford, Independence Day, page 151-152, 1995

Given the increase in the number of times we move house these days (from 2.2 times per person per lifetime in 1950 to 7.8 in 1994), the feeling that a house is a temporary place to stay in increases with it. The house has become part of our 'dwelling-career' with the longing-for diversity seemingly paramount: everyone should have lived in a loft at one time, in a house on the lake, in a squat, a bungalow, a commune, alone, with kids.... The demand for a greater variety and even more extreme dwelling forms is gaining momentum. The ideal home doesn't exist anymore, there are thousands of ideal homes. The permanent ideal has been supplanted by the temporary.

It seems as though we buy homes instead of houses, rather than making them ourselves.

This opens up unprecedented opportunities for the role played by home catalogues. The cultivation of a maximum choice of housing types fulfils the wishes of the potential client, and covers the uncertainties of the market. This extention of the known ideals can be set up through a series of extended or extrapolated 'permutations' of the average house: this would lead from the straightforward front-to-back type to the stair type, the house with the superwindow, the house with no roof, the house with no walls, to the pit house, the catholic house, the house with the towers, the disconnected house, etcetera. All specific and characteristic spaces that wait to be inhabited, to be urbanized, to be appropriated, time and again. The housing block can be constructed as a Chinese puzzle of these ideals. But the placement of these ideals within the building envelope causes in-between houses with even more unexpected spaces and qualities. Is unexpectedness not the sublime goal of one's 'dwelling career'?

The concrete walls and floors absorb through modern technology almost every possible contact between the neighbours. It stimulates anonymity. This leaves a new role for the visual. Through this Chinese puzzle of houses, the neighbour is not visually hidden but present. Could this stimulate a certain social awareness and security?

This puzzle evokes a curiosity as to how your neighbour's house will be, and your neighbour's neighbour's house and your neighbour's neighbour's neighbour's house....

284 'ideals' are shown to the east and west (of Berlin) in a frozen composition of well-known and newly-discovered dwelling types.

Flipped Mietskaserne

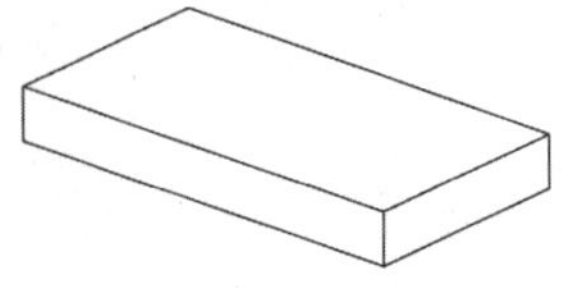

Existing envelope

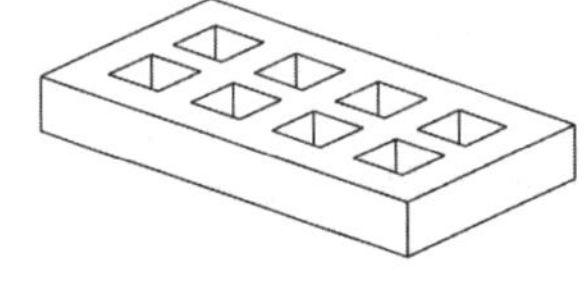

Mietskaserne?

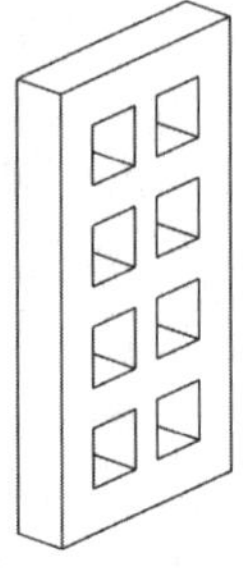

Flipped
Mietskaserne

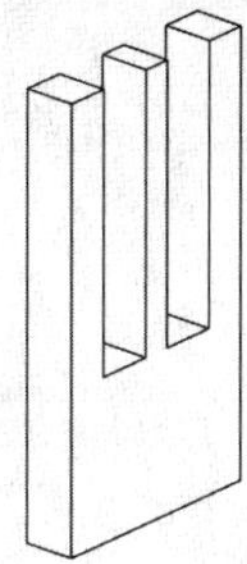
Light slots

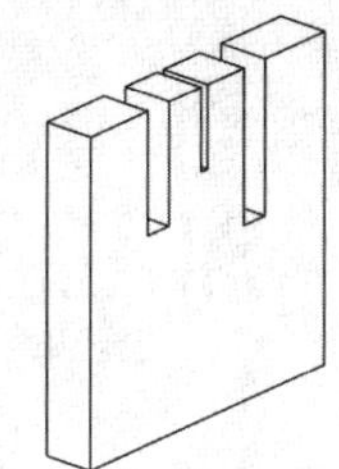
Height possibilities

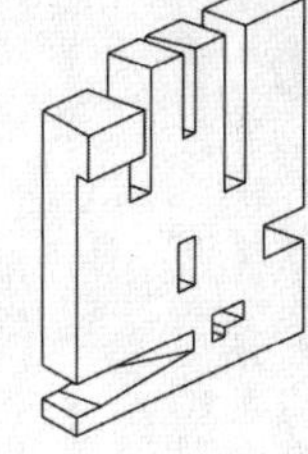
Urban voids

Exposed neighbourhood

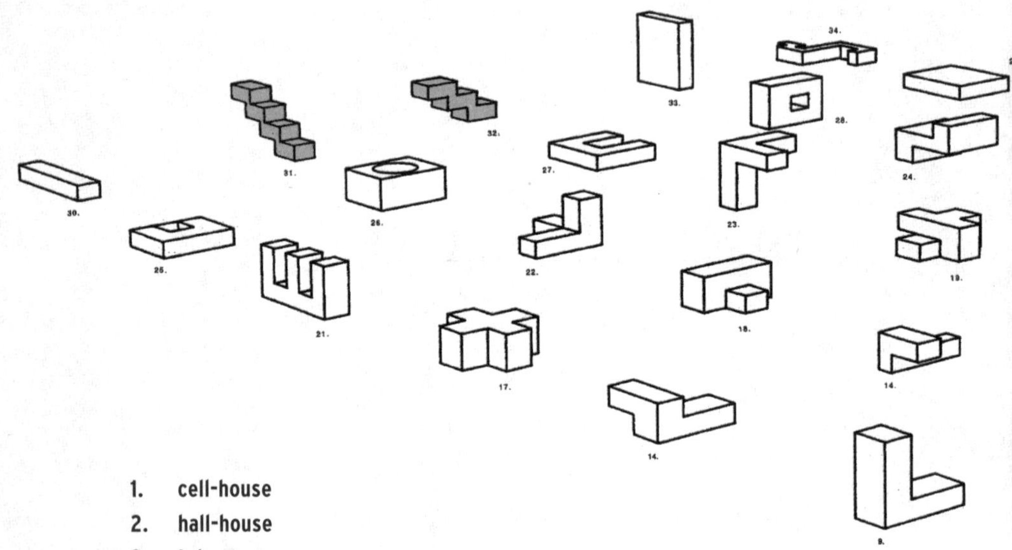

1. cell-house
2. hall-house
3. L-house
4. snake-house
5. Z-house (vertical)
6. Z-house (horizontal)
7. zino the dino-house
8. loop-house
9. lower-house
10. pit-house
11. T-house
12. disconnected-house
13. grotto-house
14. hallsnake-house
15. bügel-house
16. terrace-house
17. church-house
18. chapel-house
19. leapfrog-house
20. cross-house
21. cactus-house
22. XYZ-house
23. ZYX-house
24. zigzag-house
25. patio-house
26. dome-house
27. U-house
28. hole-house
29. loft-house
30. long-house
31. stair-house (north/south)
32. stair-house (east/west)
33. slab-house
34. corridor-house

Housing ideals

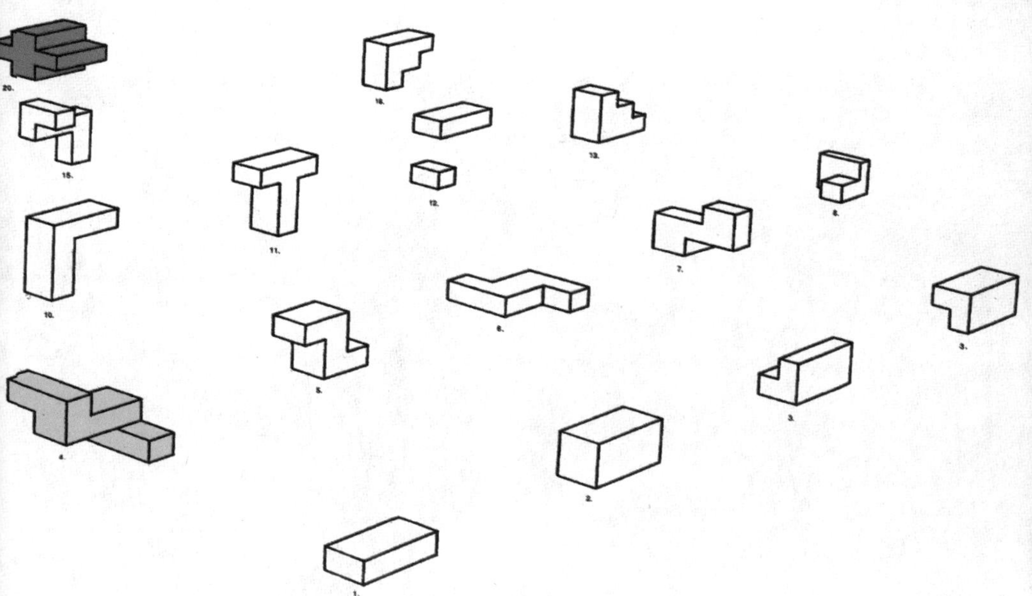

Permutations of
the ideal
pure stairhouse
pure snakehouse
stairhouse in column zone
snakehouse in column zone
decorated stairhouse
decorated snakehouse

pure crosshouse

crosshouse in column zone

decorated crosshouse

Plans of floors 19, 20, 21

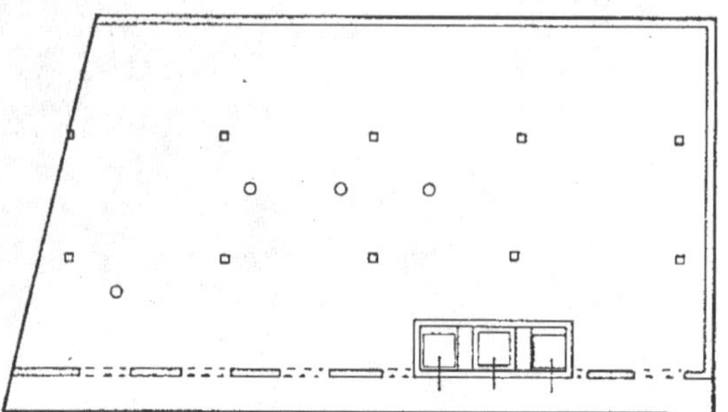

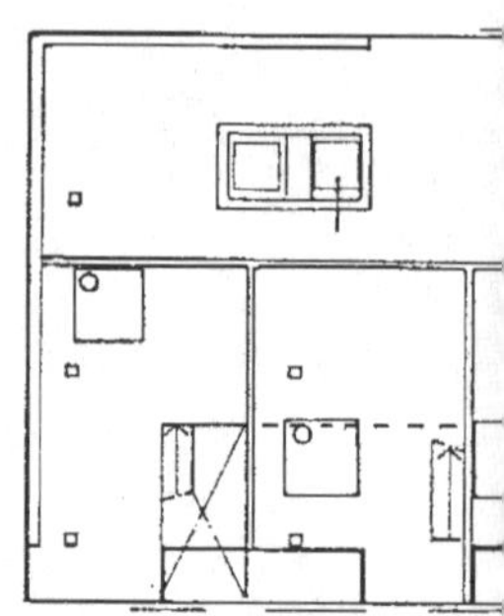

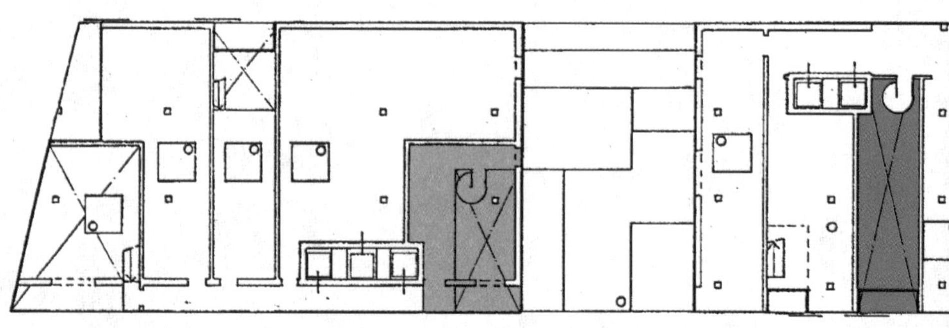

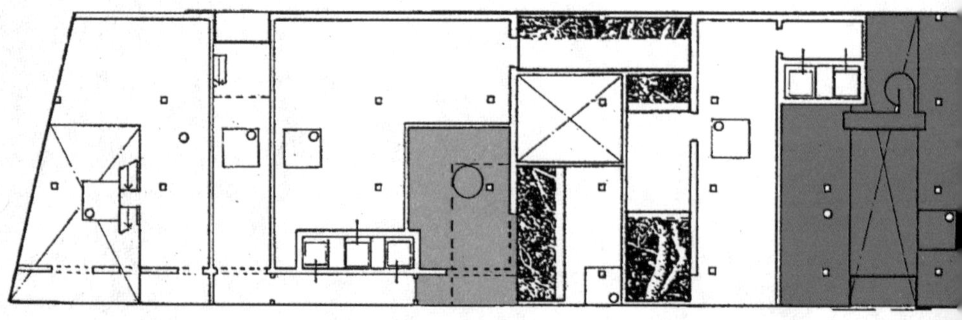

Stair-house

Cross-house

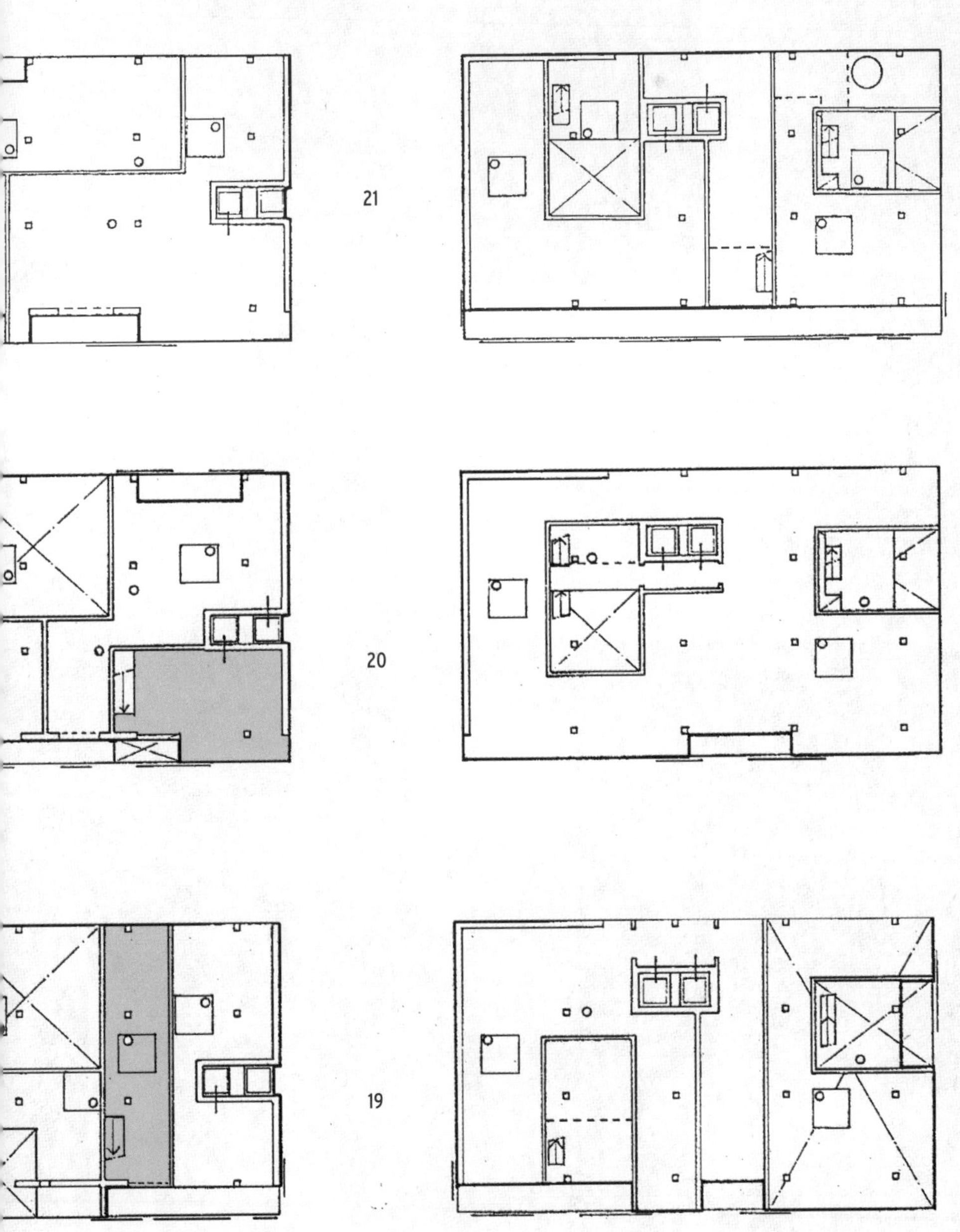
21
20
19

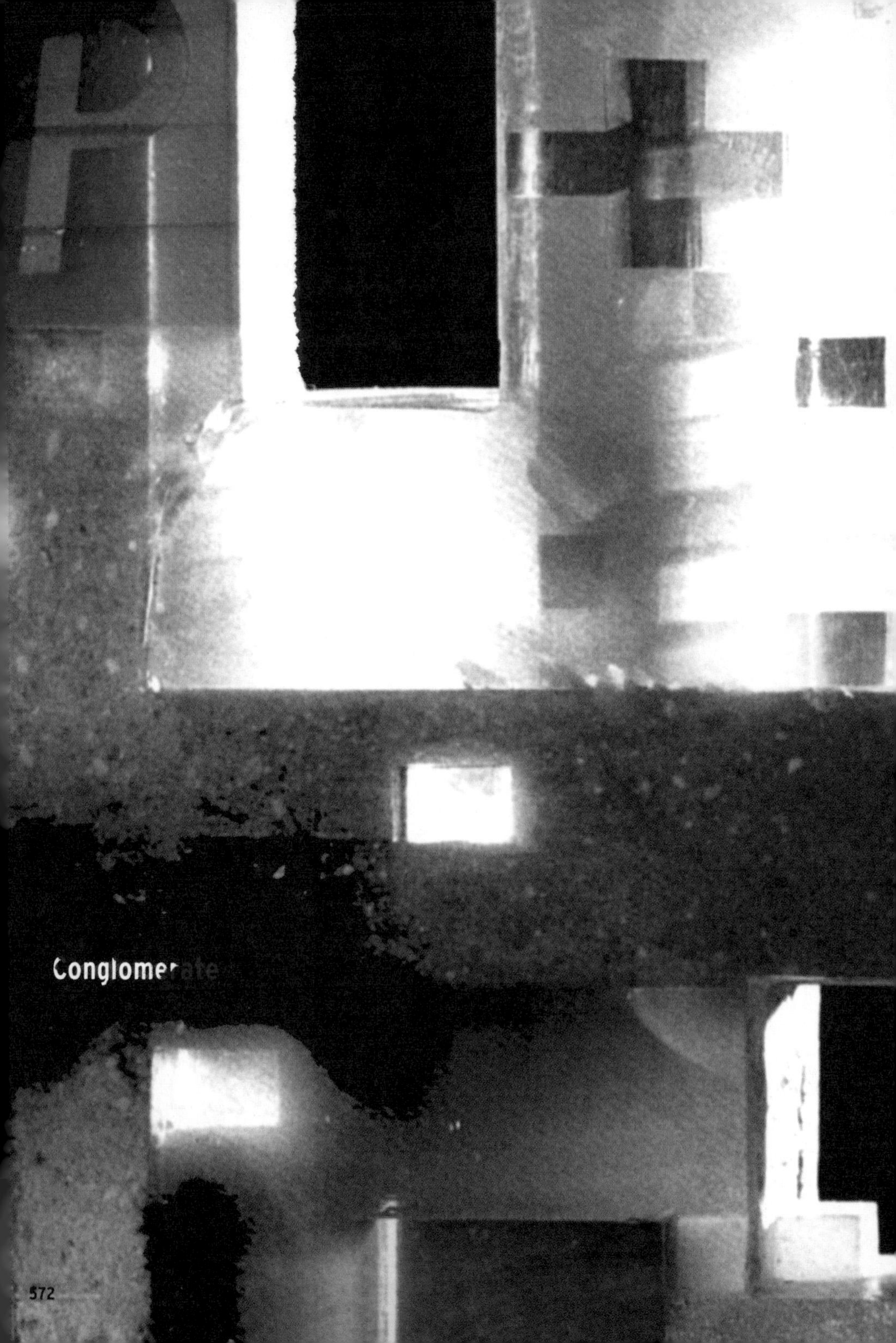

Conglomerate

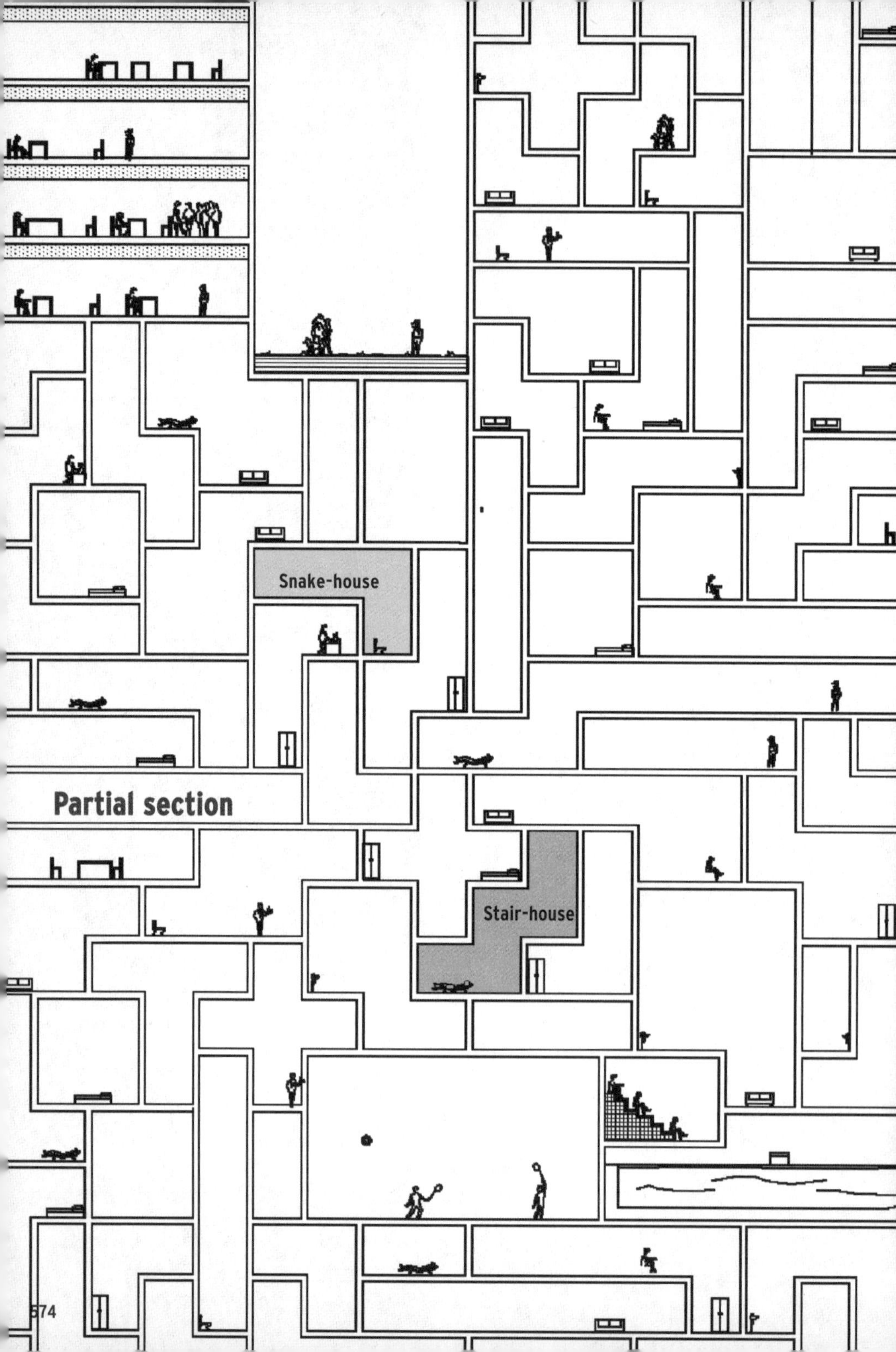
Snake-house
Partial section
Stair-house

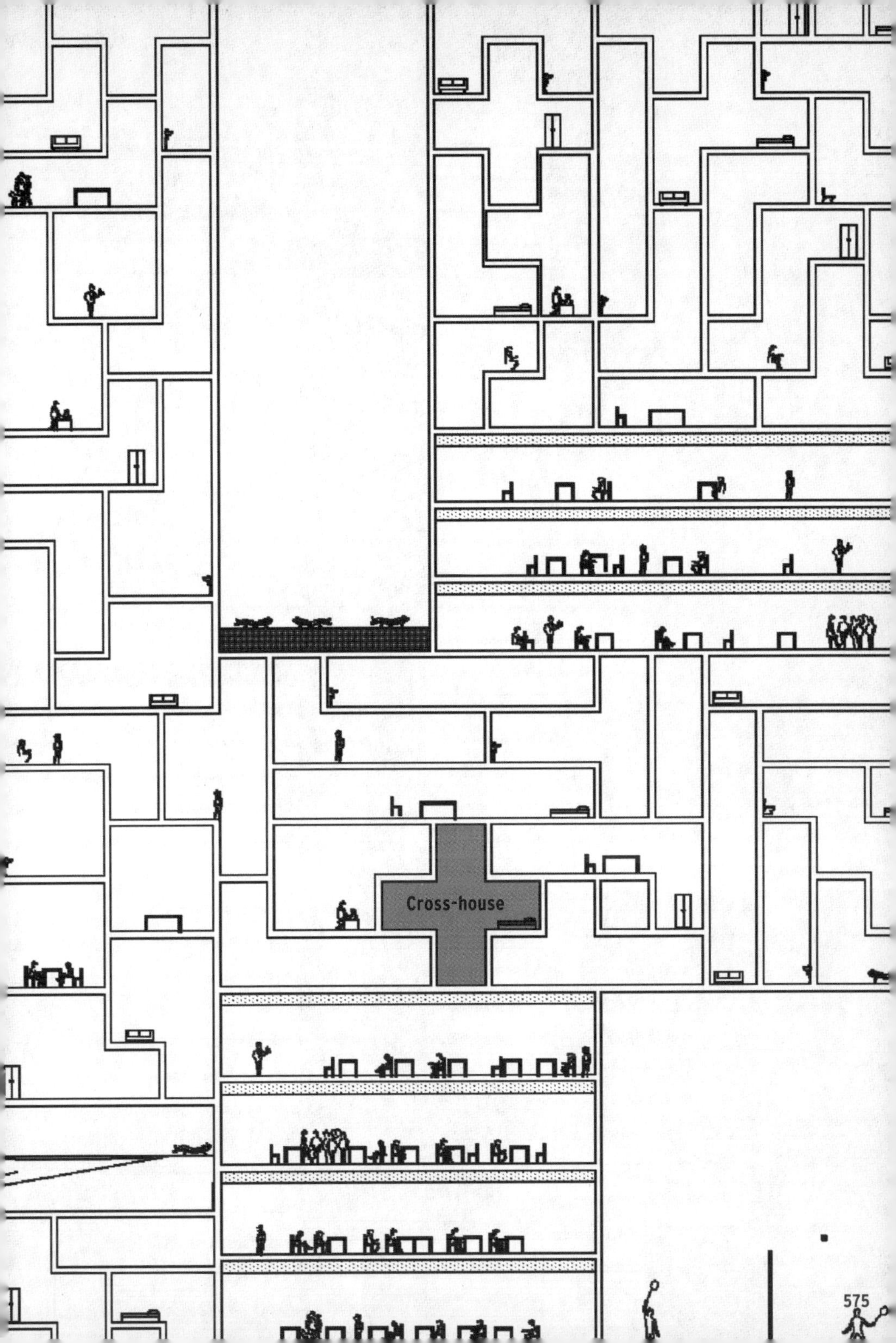
Cross-house

Chinese puzzle

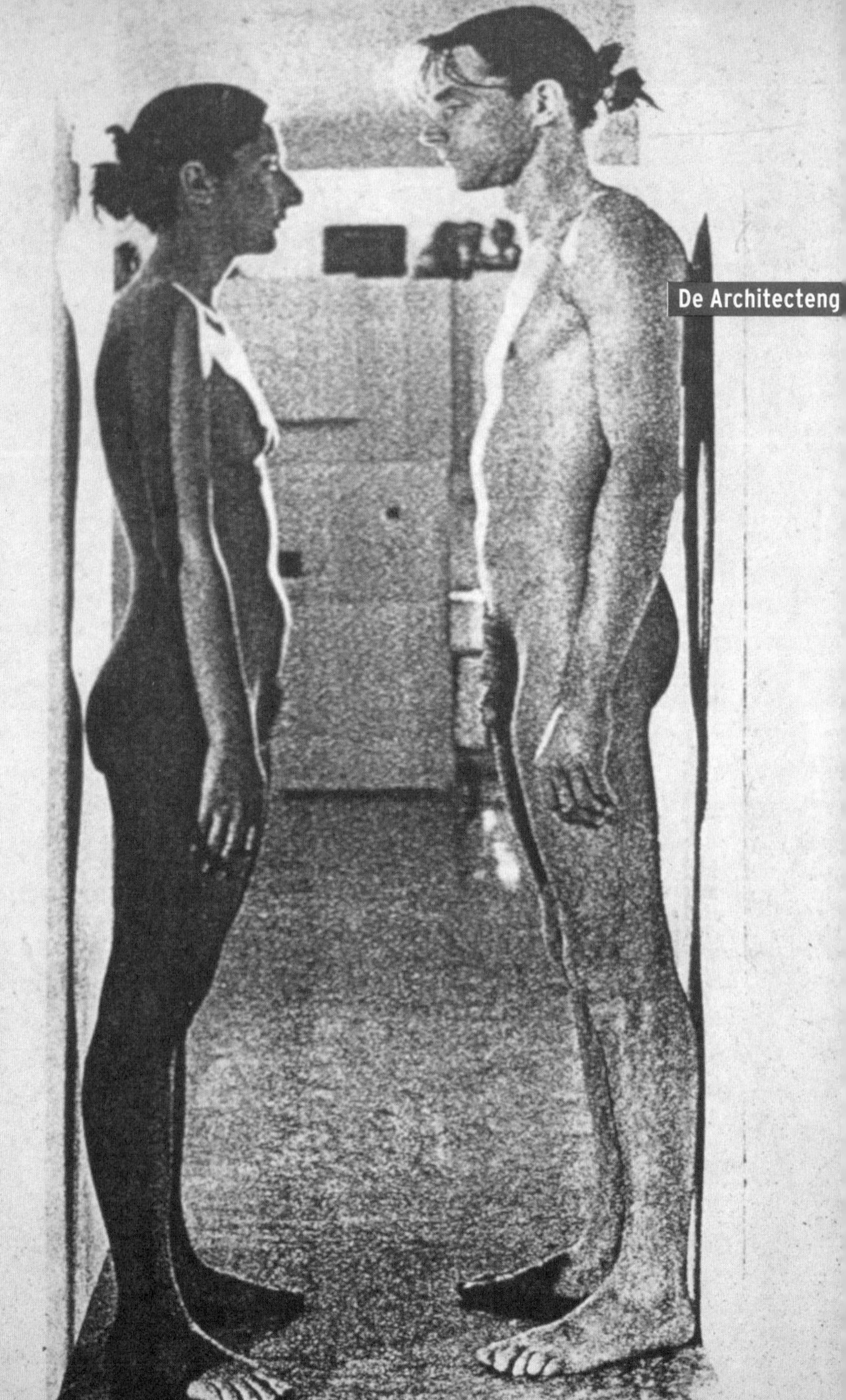

De Architecteng

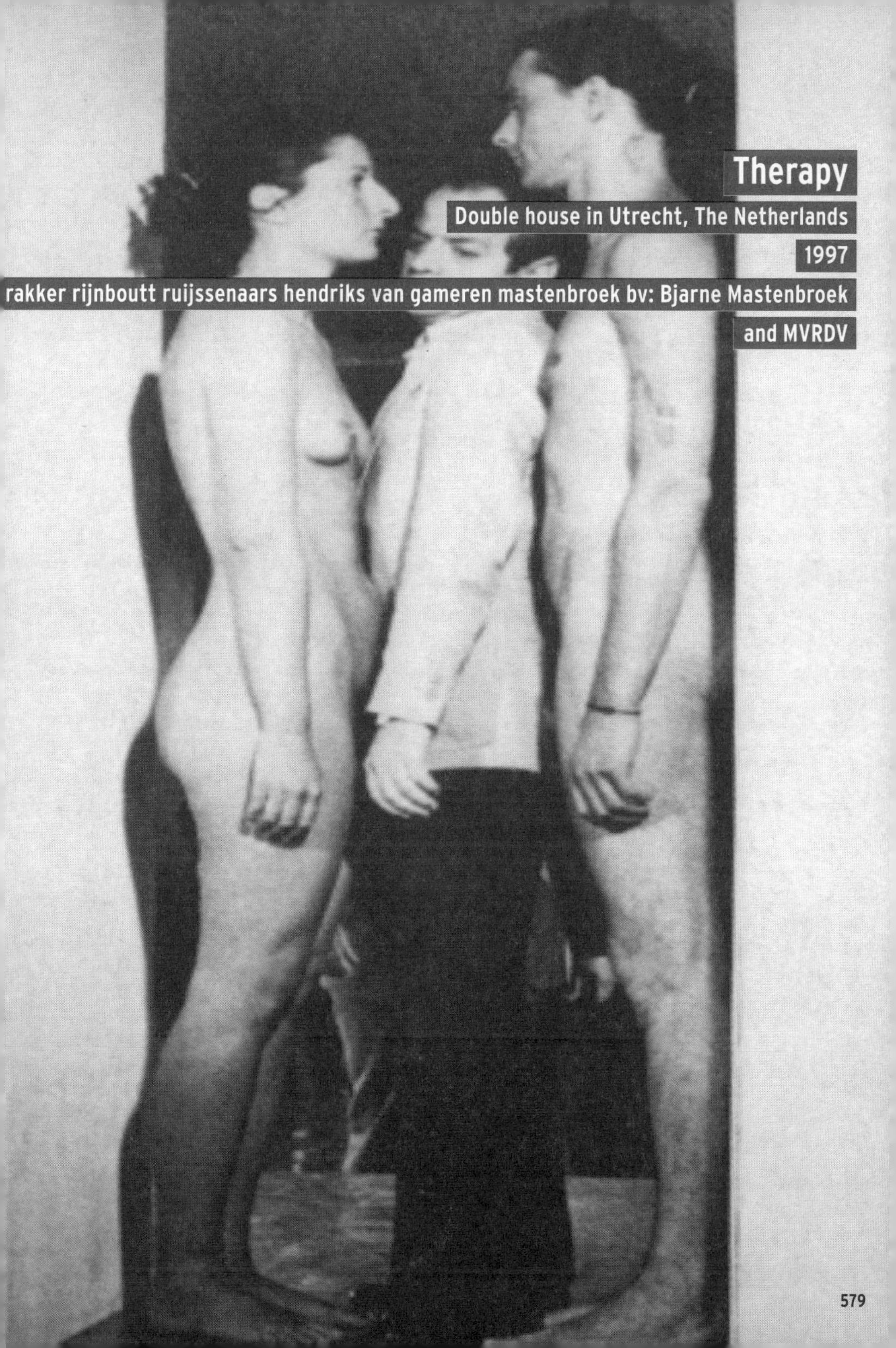

Therapy

Double house in Utrecht, The Netherlands

1997

rakker rijnboutt ruijssenaars hendriks van gameren mastenbroek bv: Bjarne Mastenbroek

and MVRDV

Neighbours

The villa, the specially designed private house, was long synonymous with the ultimate home. Often this personal and distinctive space was unambivalent, ushering in such classic one-liners as the Palladian dome, the Wrightian salon or the Miesian hall.
Under the present densifying circumstances the need for personal houses is being challenged by ever more intense negotiations with the city, civil servants, amenities authority, fire brigade, acoustical engineers, neighbours, ecologists.
But all this enforced negotiating, in which the architect is finding himself more and more in the role of a middle-man or a therapist, has given rise to spaces that are more opulent, more unexpected and therefore more extreme that the classic paradigms.
There is now the 'remainder-house', or the 'result-house': the house that contorts its way through the prevailing conditions like a latterday version of the Roman poché and where the unexpected aspects of this process are uppermost.
In a row of town houses opposite a splendid nineteenth-century park in Utrecht, the missing link in the chain has been forged by two families. Both wish to combine the finest view of the park with easy access to the garden and the roof.
By proposing the house with the least imaginable depth, the programme can be 'stretched' up to four or five storeys while keeping the garden as big as possible.
At the same time, a 'town house' can be designed as can vie with the surroundings. Interpreting the partition wall between neighbours as a 'therapeutic first move' towards negotiations has given birth to two interlocking dwelling-volumes, each richer than the premise underlying them both.
The bedrooms are incorporated in the meandering heads as houses-in-a-house. Here extreme differences can coexist: where the one occupant wants to be surrounded by the garden, the other can withdraw to the piano nobile. Where the one chooses a salon just past the children's playrooms, the other opts for a work- cum bedroom upstairs, and so on.
Their reciprocal dependence threatened to paralyse them. But as in the parable of the lame and the blind, together they were more than they could have possibly imagined themselves being as individuals.

161094

2 Storeys 14 deep

231194

4 Storeys 7 metres deep

No wide views to park

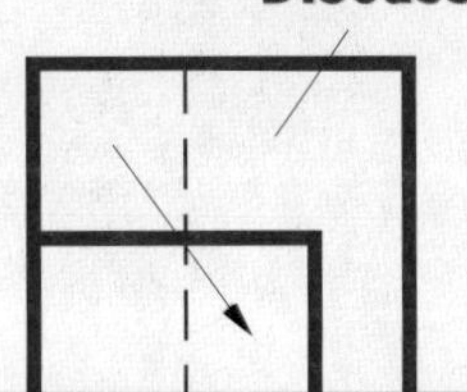

141294

House in a house

No roof access house 1

Small garden access house 2

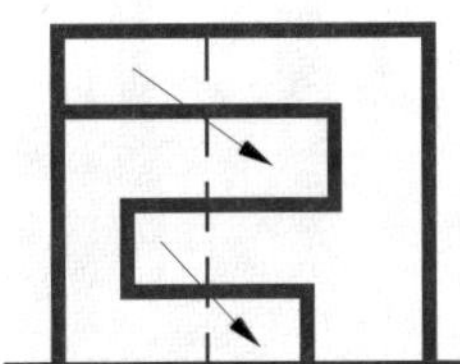

231295

Alternating floors 1

No roof access house 1

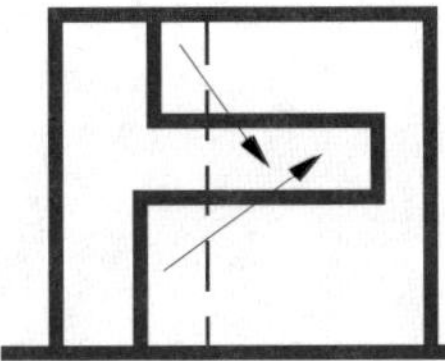

040194

Alternating floors 2

Too little garden access for house 1

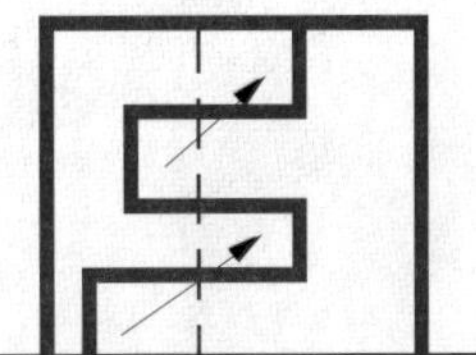

120195

Alternating floors 3

Too little garden access for house 1

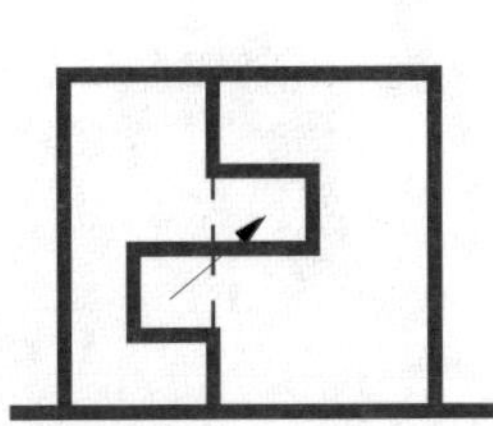

200295

Alternating floors 4

Includes garden access + roof access

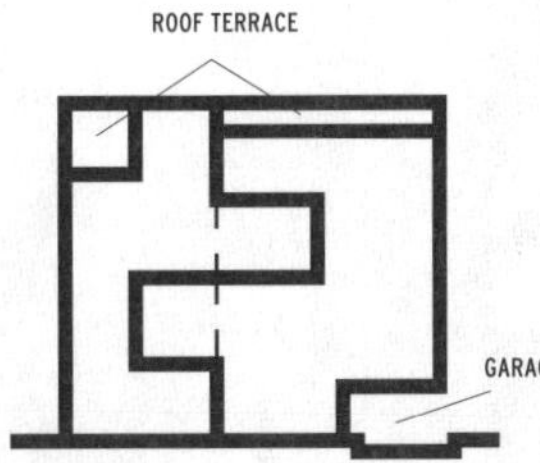

090395

Outdoor space

Roof terrace house 1

Garage + roof terrace house 2

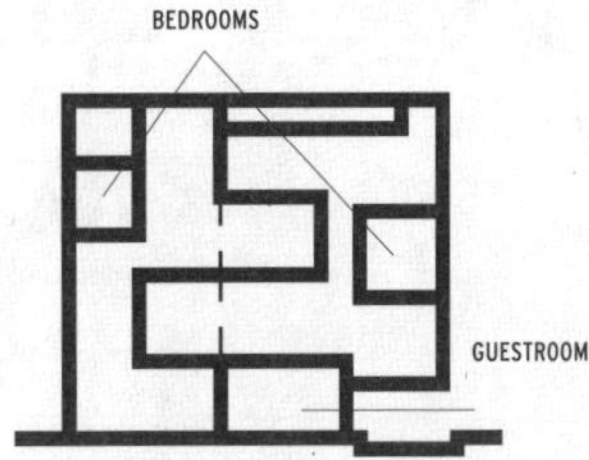

130495

Final result

Bedrooms in 1 + 2

Pianoble house 2

Incl. fire regulations

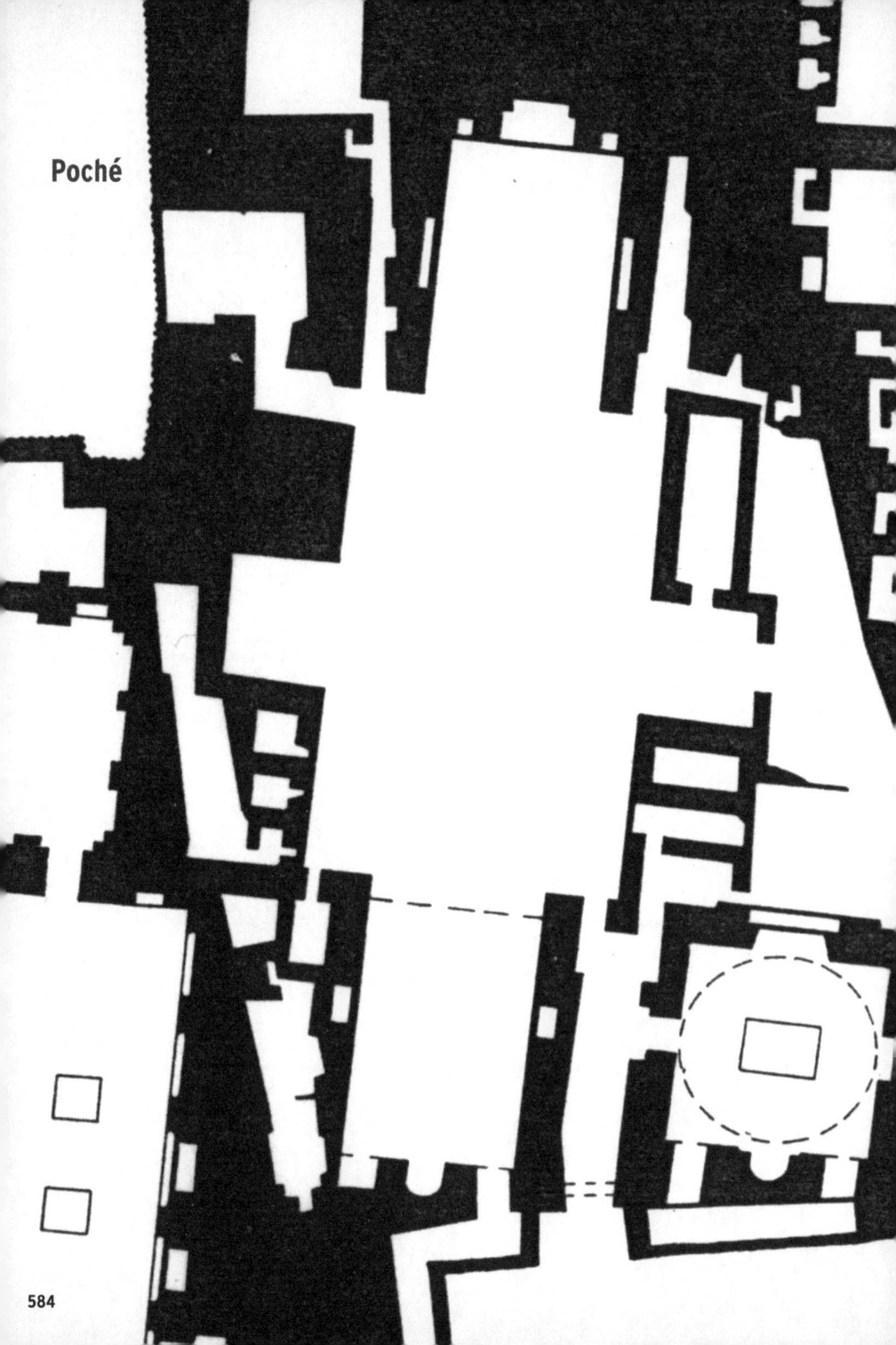

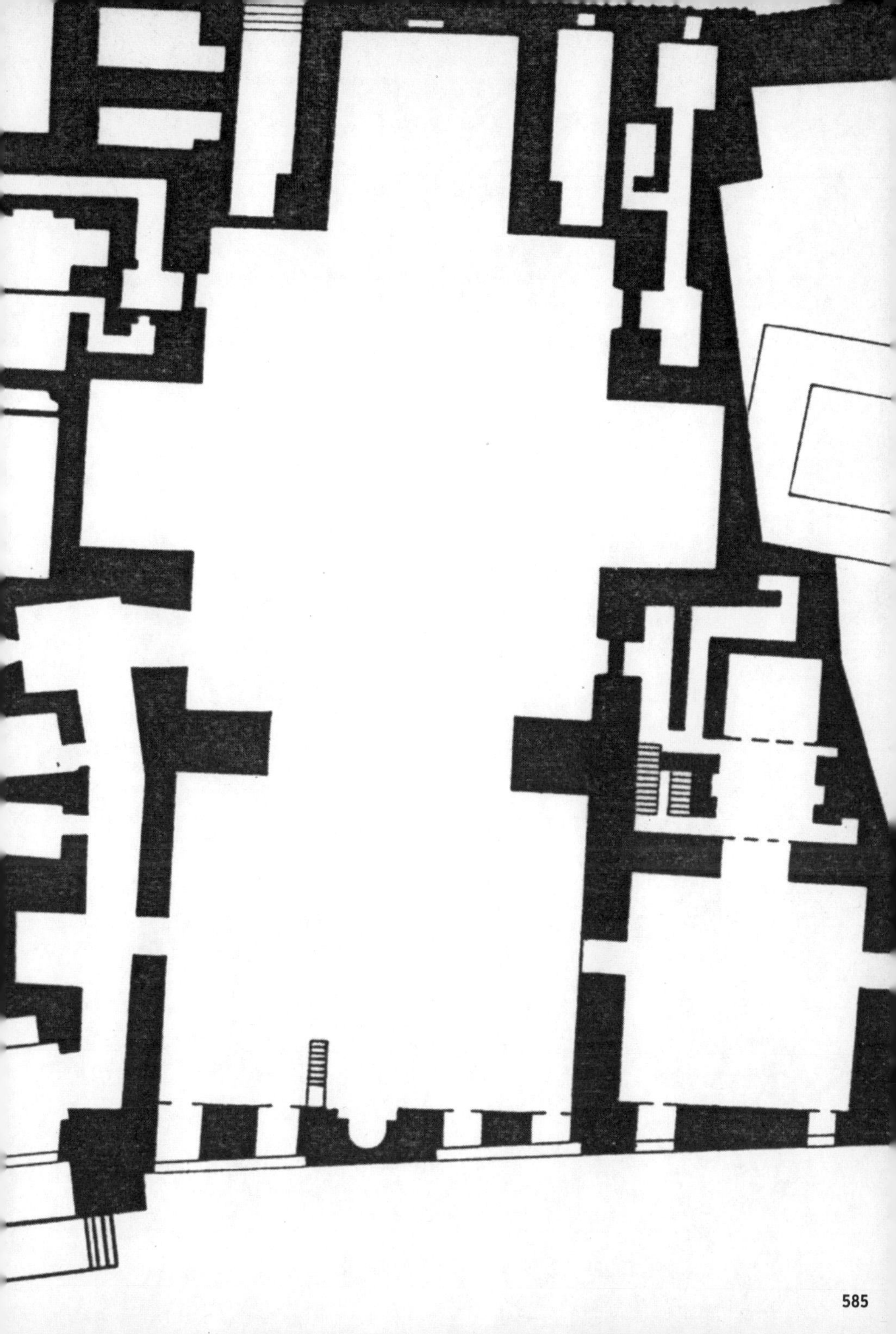

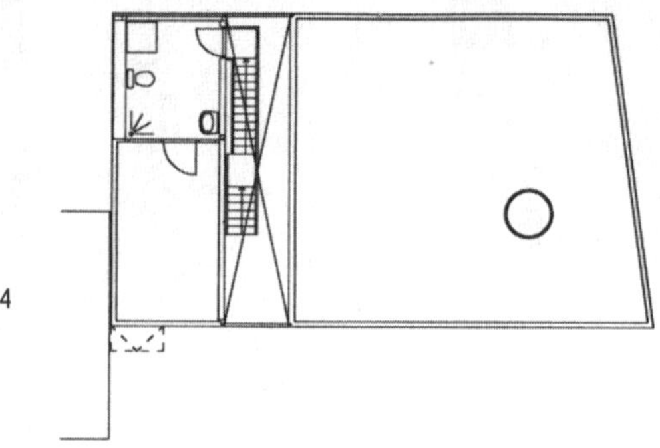

Plans

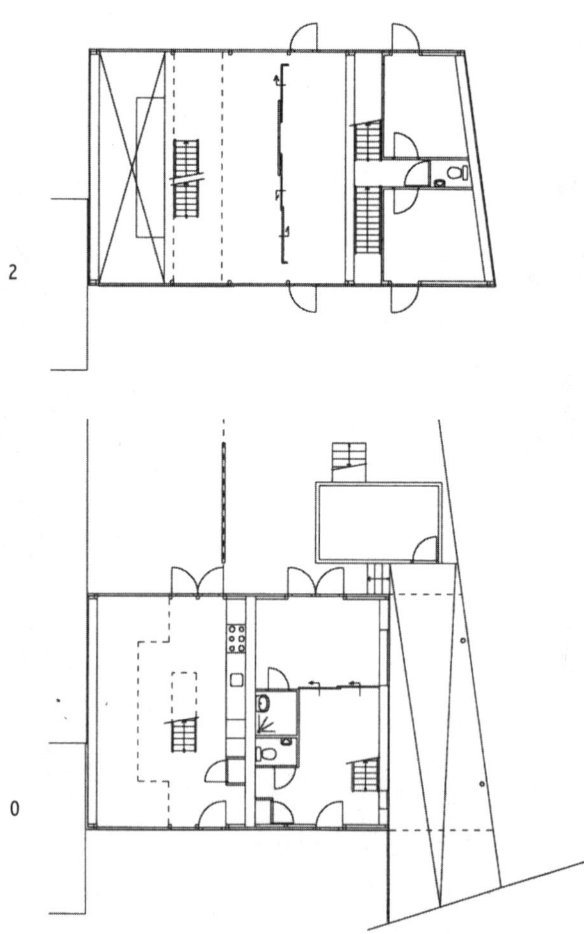

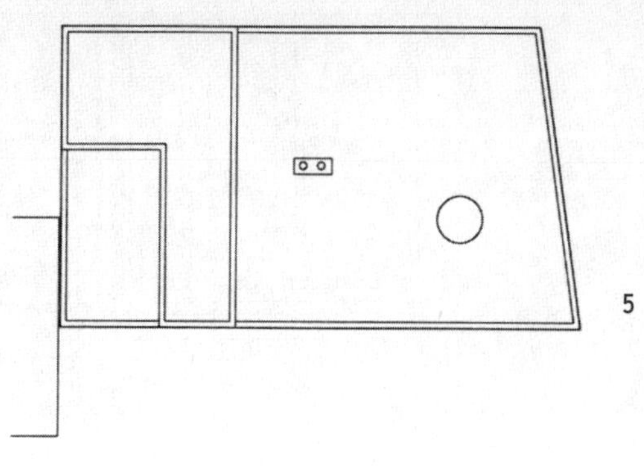
5

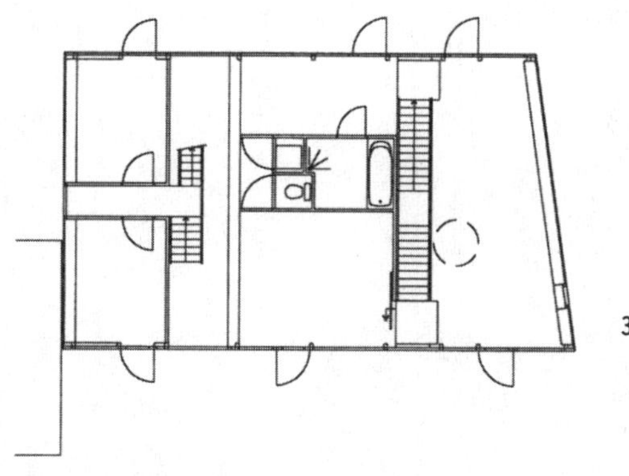
3

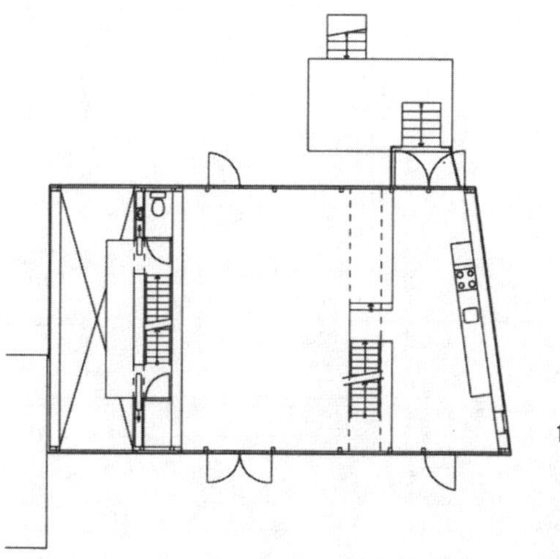
1

Section

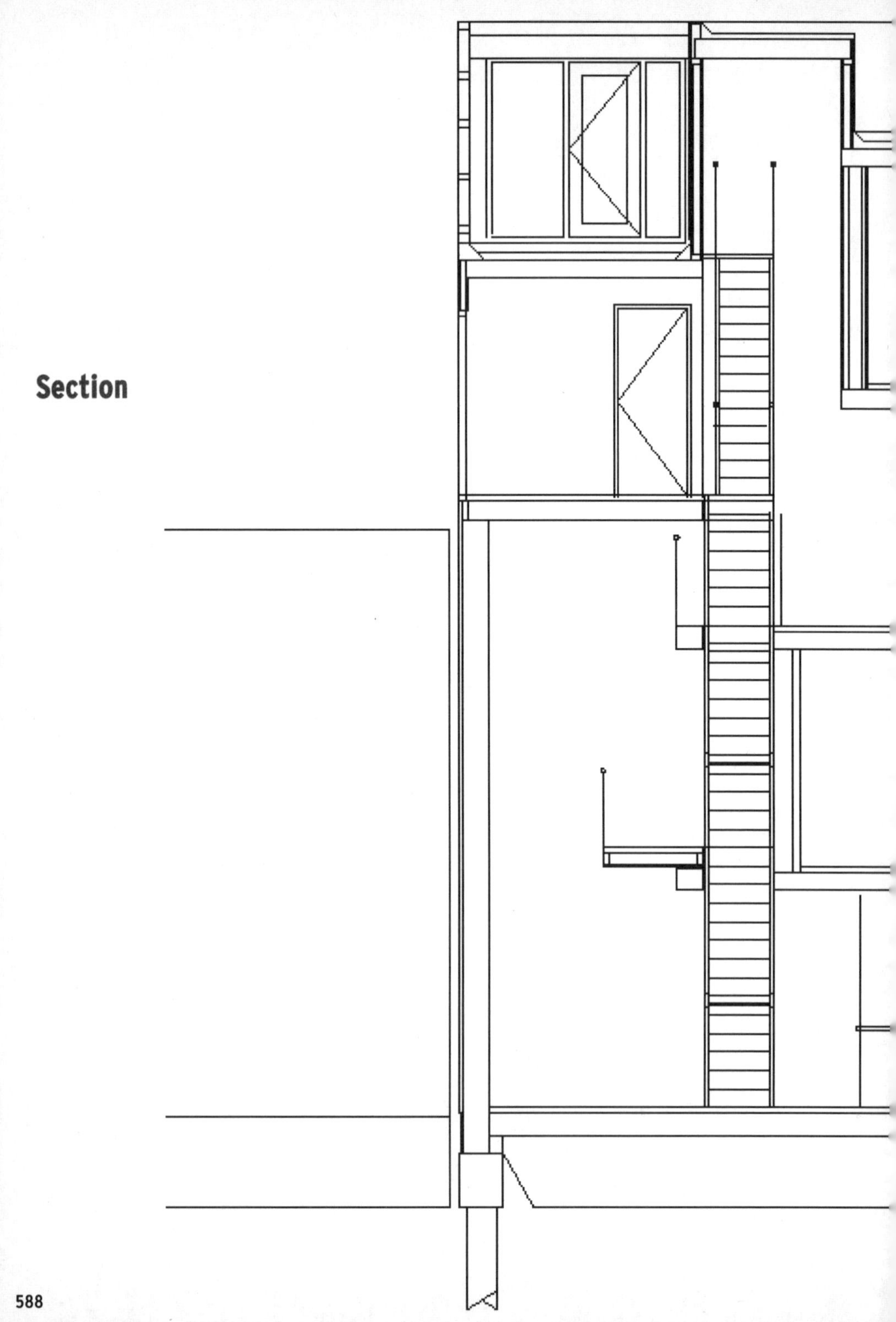

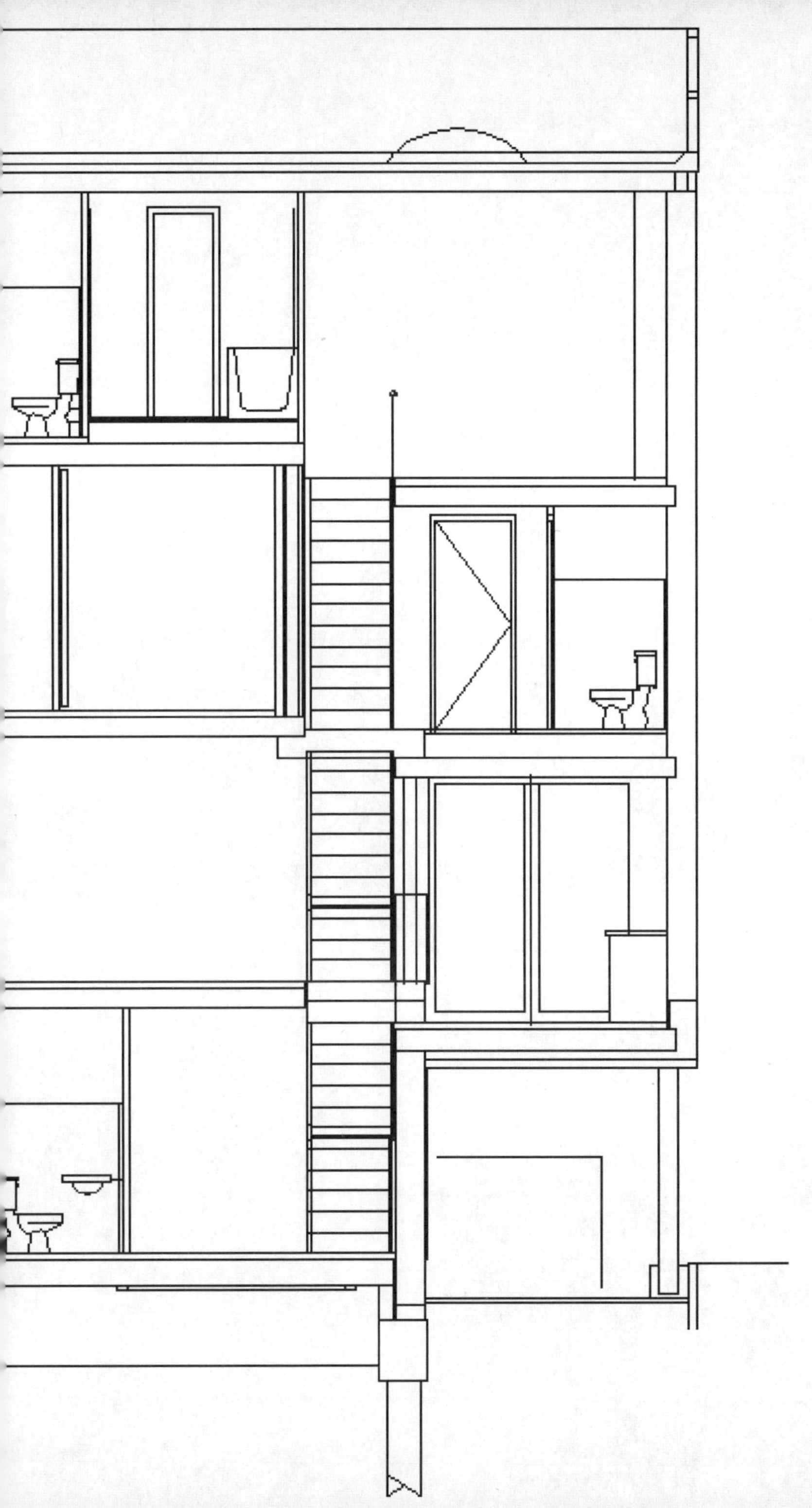

Street view

Shallow

High

Wide

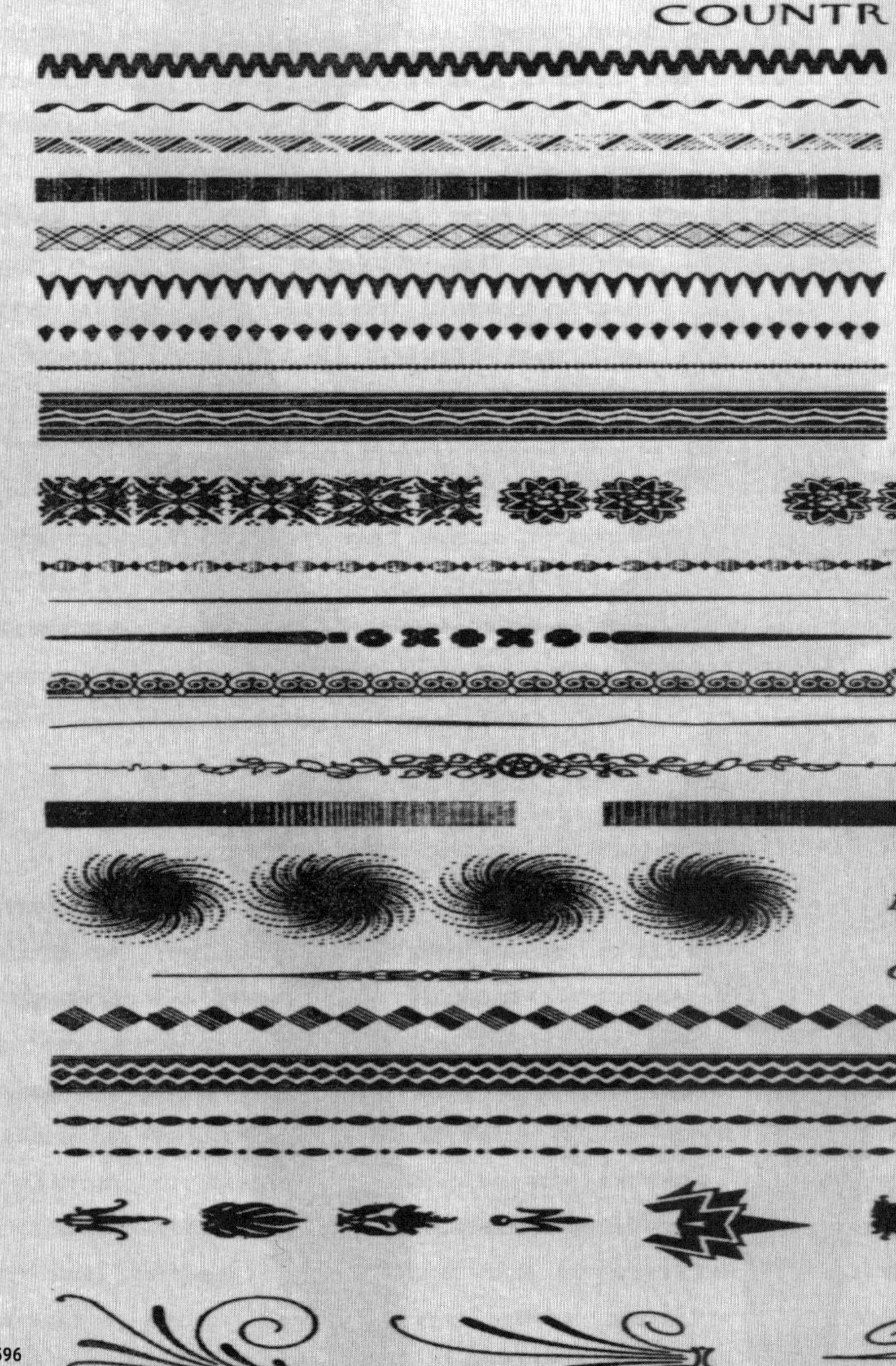

Statistic suspense

Study for a development of 750 houses in Delft, Hoornse Kwadrant, The Netherlands

1992

MVRDV

NOISES

Phone rings

Phone rings in TV drama

Phone rings in house across the road

Furnace

Refrigerator

Lawnmower

Small plane

T.W.A. from Paris to Kennedy

Dishwasher

Cricket

Electric clock

Car

Truck

Dead leaves cross the road

Mosquito

Paper uncrumples in wastebasket

Willow

oon?

of drawers creaks

Frog

Woodpecker

Rain on roof

Rain on deck

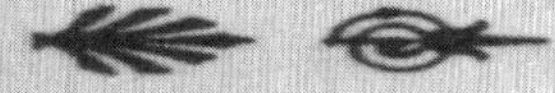

Blue jay

Catbird

Difference as parameter - Due to the tight budgets allotted to housing, the programme for residential areas has been rendered as an 'urbanism of percentages', i.e. the combination of economy and social obligations lead to strict maximum percentages for dwelling types (100 m^2 with a maximum of three storeys, ground-access), gardens (40 m^2 per house), parking places (1.2 cars per house), pavement (30 m^2 per parking place, including roads) and greenery (5 m^2 per house). - In order to address the demand for individuality and variety - seemingly the only architectural tools for mass housing (and therefore overused) - the planning area in Delft has

been organized in bands set in a parking field, the one element with strict measurements. - By composing each band differently from elements of the 'percentages' programme, the confrontation between all these bands - from intelligent to absurd - turns the built area into a kashbah-like labyrinth. - The neighbourhood takes on adventurous qualities in which the unexpected features prominently. - To escape the claustrophobic aspect of this 'tapestry', every dwelling sports a tower-room or a patio. The public space has been given a mound on top of the supermarket and the sports hall - with a public view over this 'housing-carpet' towards the sea.

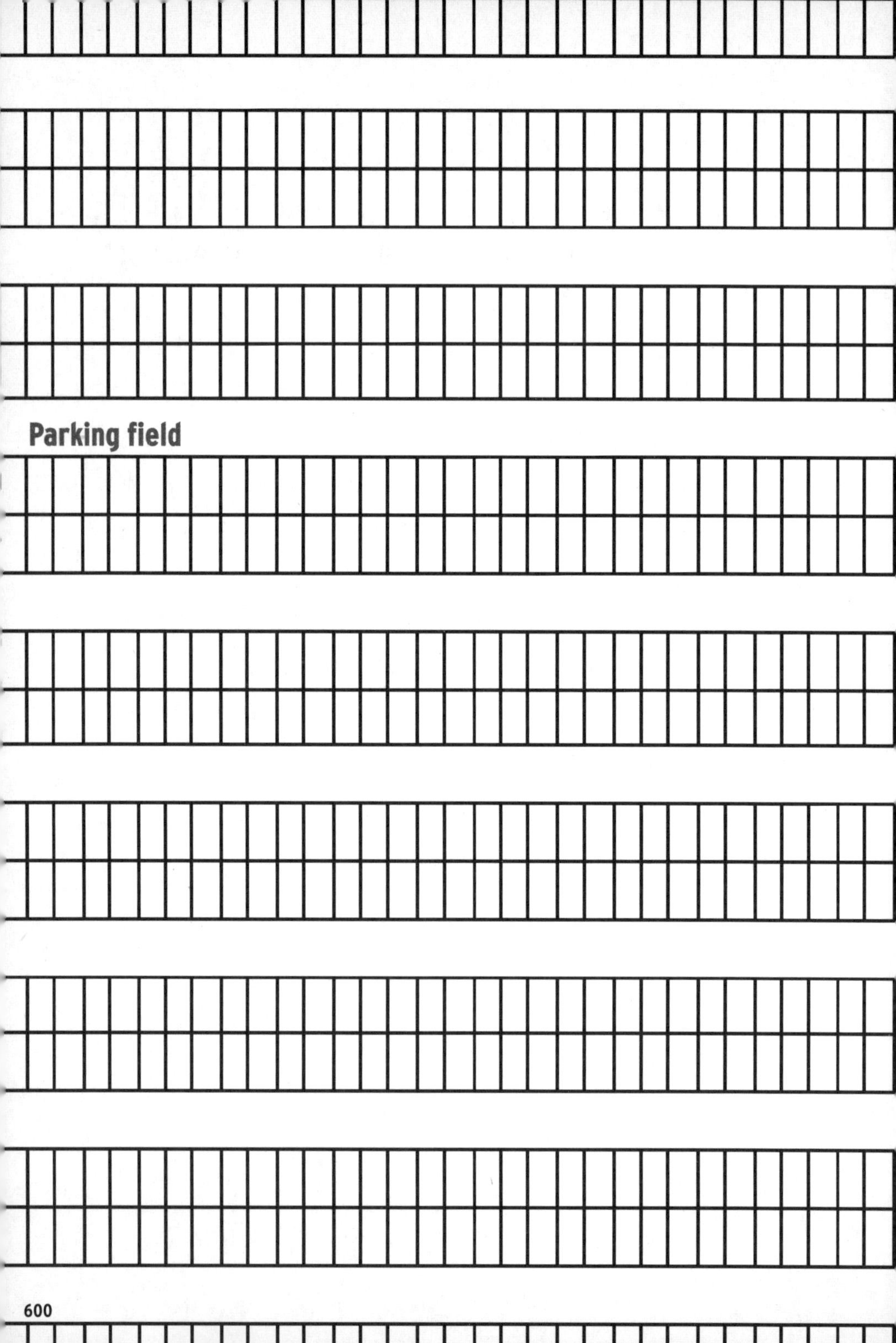

Parking field

Programmatic elements

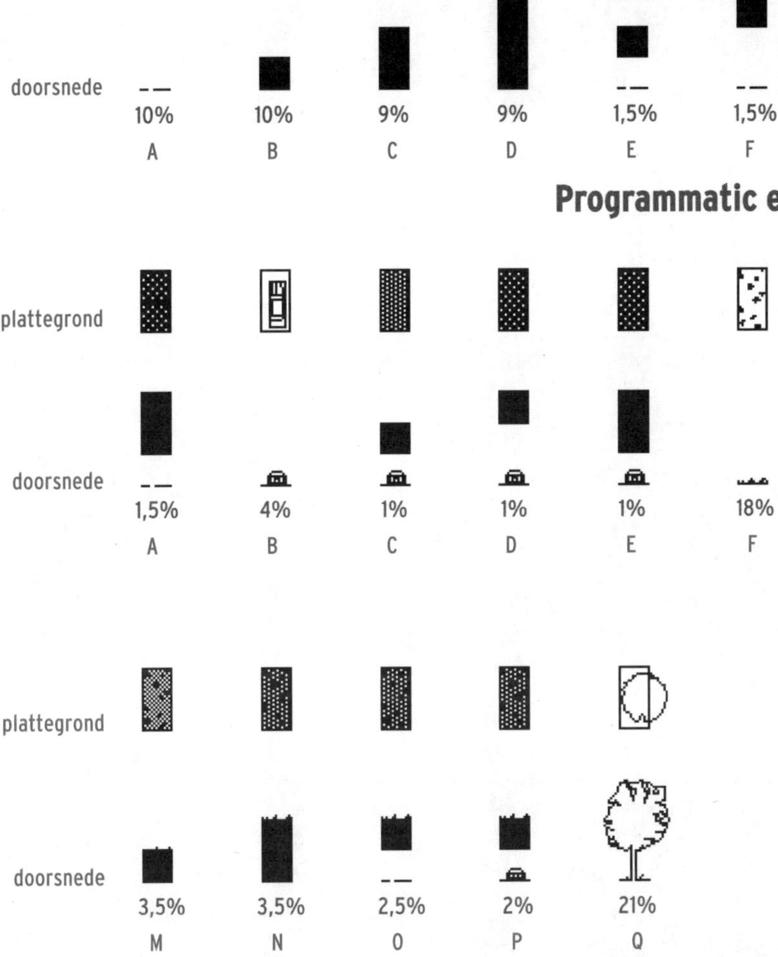

A. road **B]** single storey house **C.** double storey house **D.** triple storey house **E.** bridge house on second floor **F.** bridge house on third floor **G.** double bridge house **H.** parking lot **I.** bridge house on second floor with carport **J.** bridge house on third floor with carport **K.** double bridge house with carport **L.** garden on ground floor **M.** garden on first floor **N.** garden on second floor **O.** garden on second floor with street underneath **P.** garden on second floor with carport underneath **Q.** public greenery

Distribution

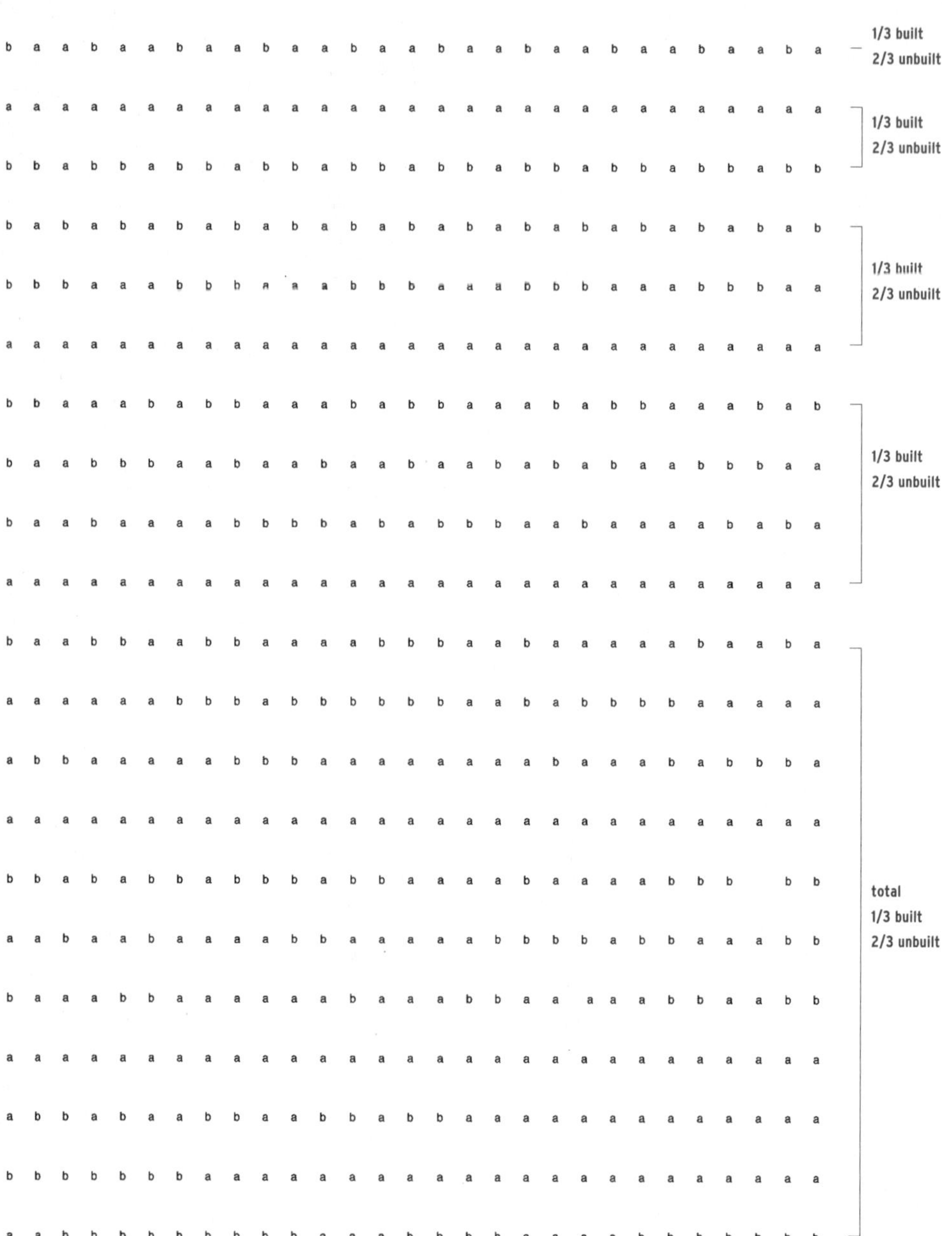

Pattern of lowrise houses

Plan

J
I
H
G
F
E
D
C
B
A
1 2 3 4 5 6 7 8 9 10 11 12 13 14 15 16 17 18 19 20 21 22 23 24 25 26 27 28 29 30

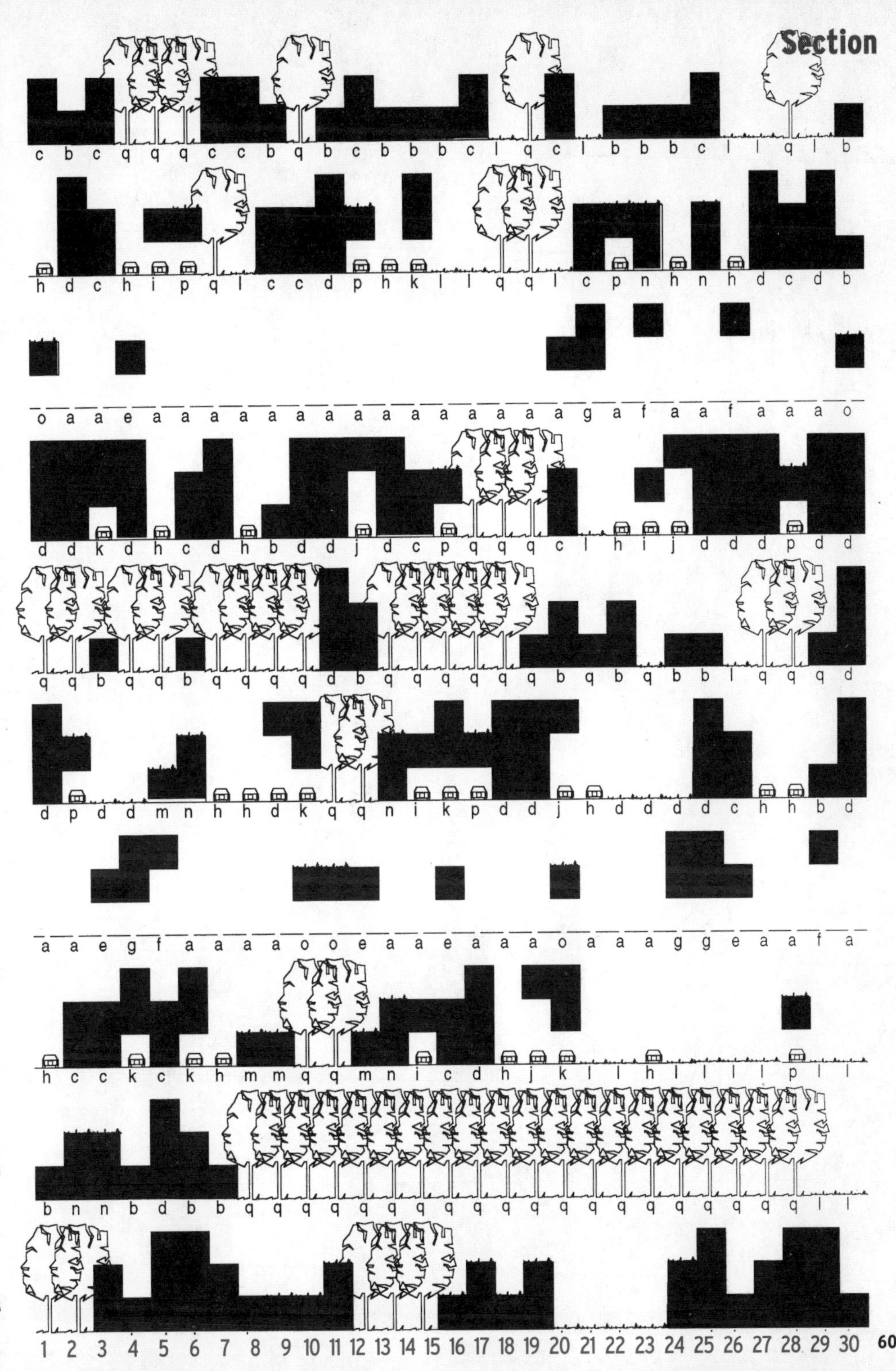
J
c b c q q q c c b q b c b b b c l q c l b b b c l l q l b
I
h d c h i p q l c c d p h k l l q q l c p n h n h d c d b
H
o a a e a a a a a a a a a a a a a a g a f a a f a a a o
G
d d k d h c d h b d d j d c p q q q c l h i j d d d p d d
F
q q b q q b q q q q d b q q q q q q b q b q b b l q q q d
E
d p d d m n h h d k q q n i k p d d j h d d d d c h h b d
D
a a e g f a a a a o o e a a e a a a o a a a g g e a a f a
C
h c c k c k h m m q q m n i c d h j k l l h l l l l p l l
B
b n n b d b b q q q q q q q q q q q q q q q q q q q q q l l
A
1 2 3 4 5 6 7 8 9 10 11 12 13 14 15 16 17 18 19 20 21 22 23 24 25 26 27 28 29 30

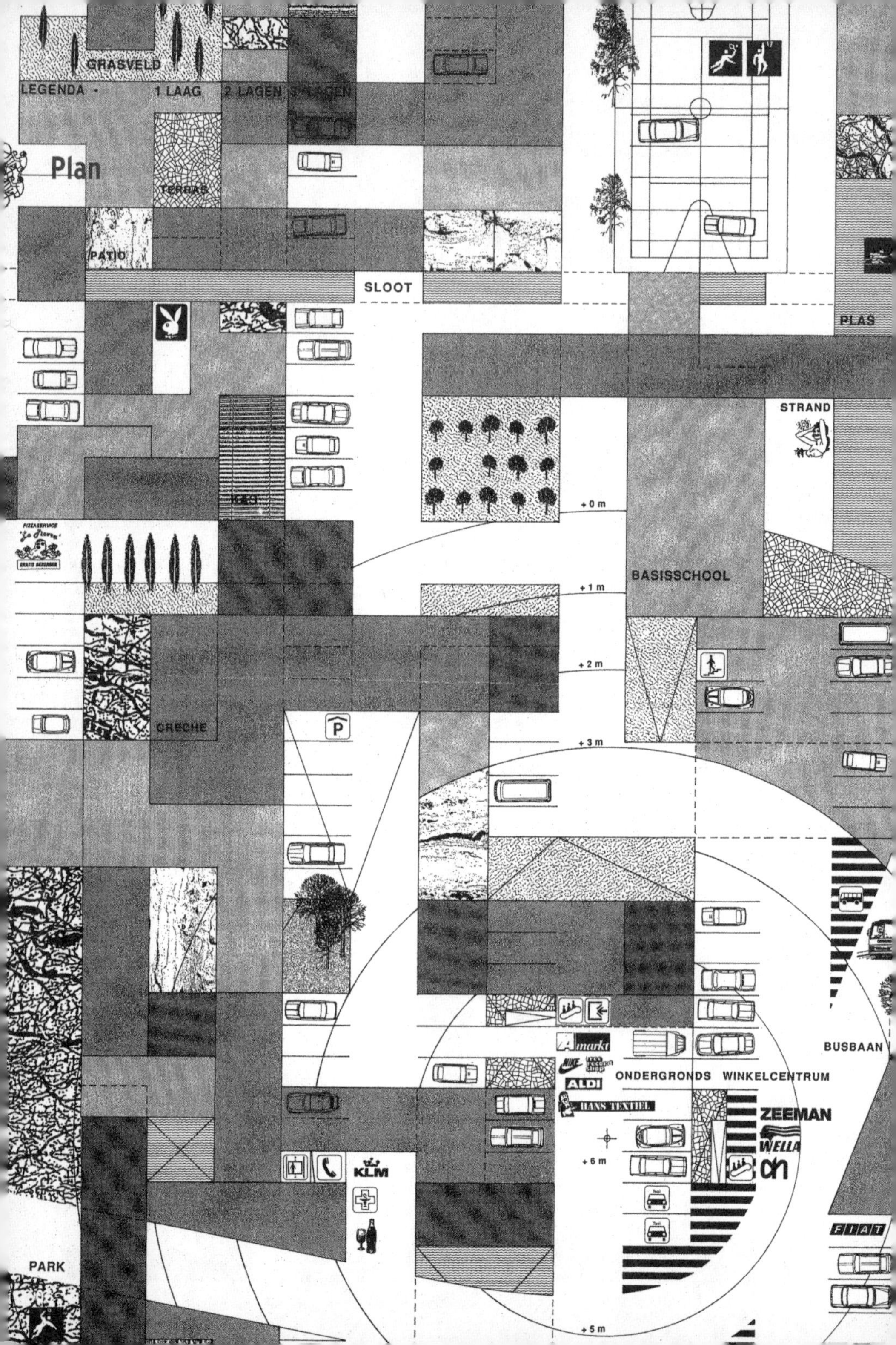
GRASVELD
LEGENDA
1 LAAG
2 LAGEN
Plan
TERRAS
PATIO
SLOOT
PLAS
STRAND
+0 m
BASISSCHOOL
+1 m
+2 m
CRECHE
+3 m
BUSBAAN
ONDERGRONDS WINKELCENTRUM
ALDI
HANS TEXTIEL
ZEEMAN
WELLA
KLM
+6 m
FIAT
PARK
+5 m

View

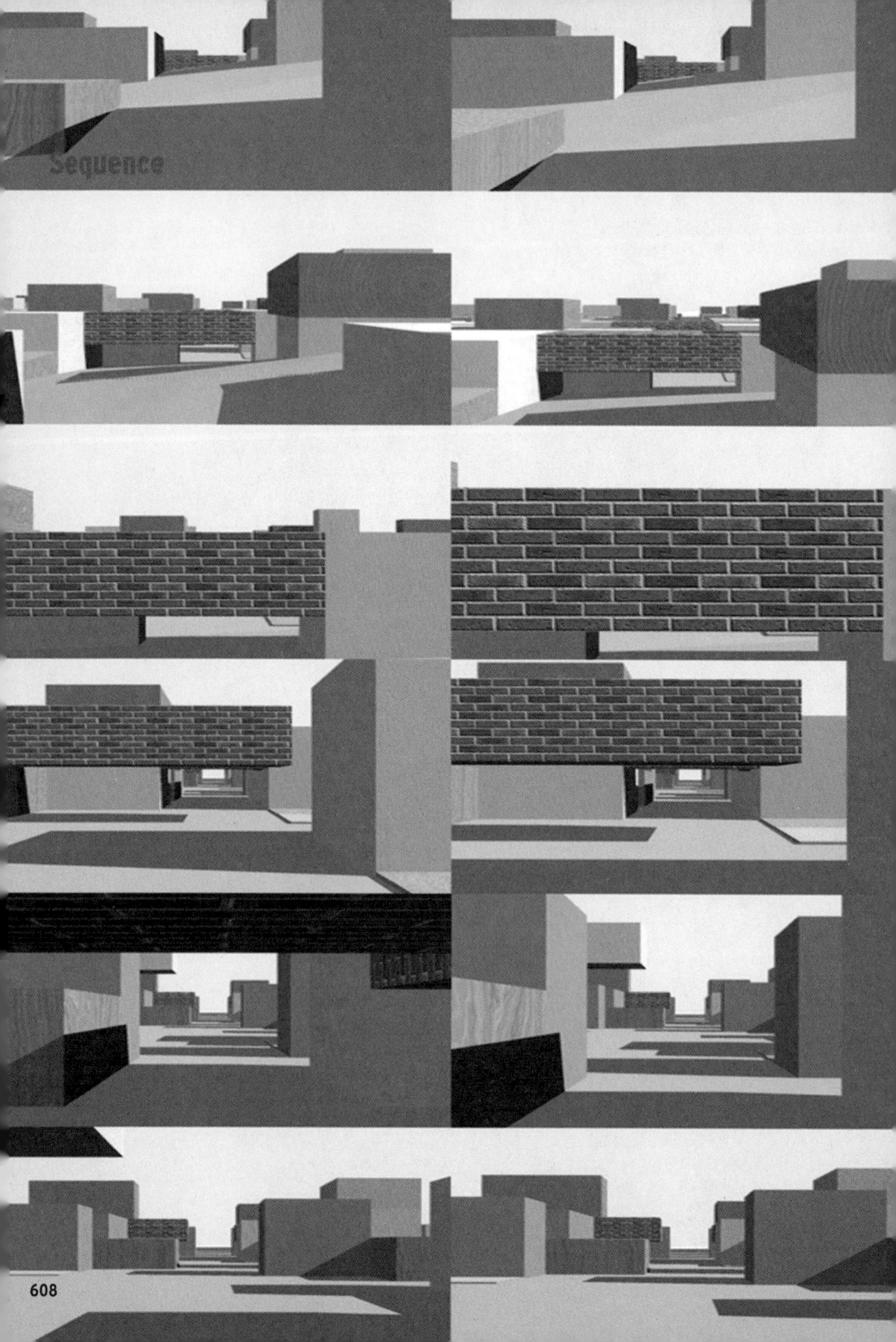
Sequence

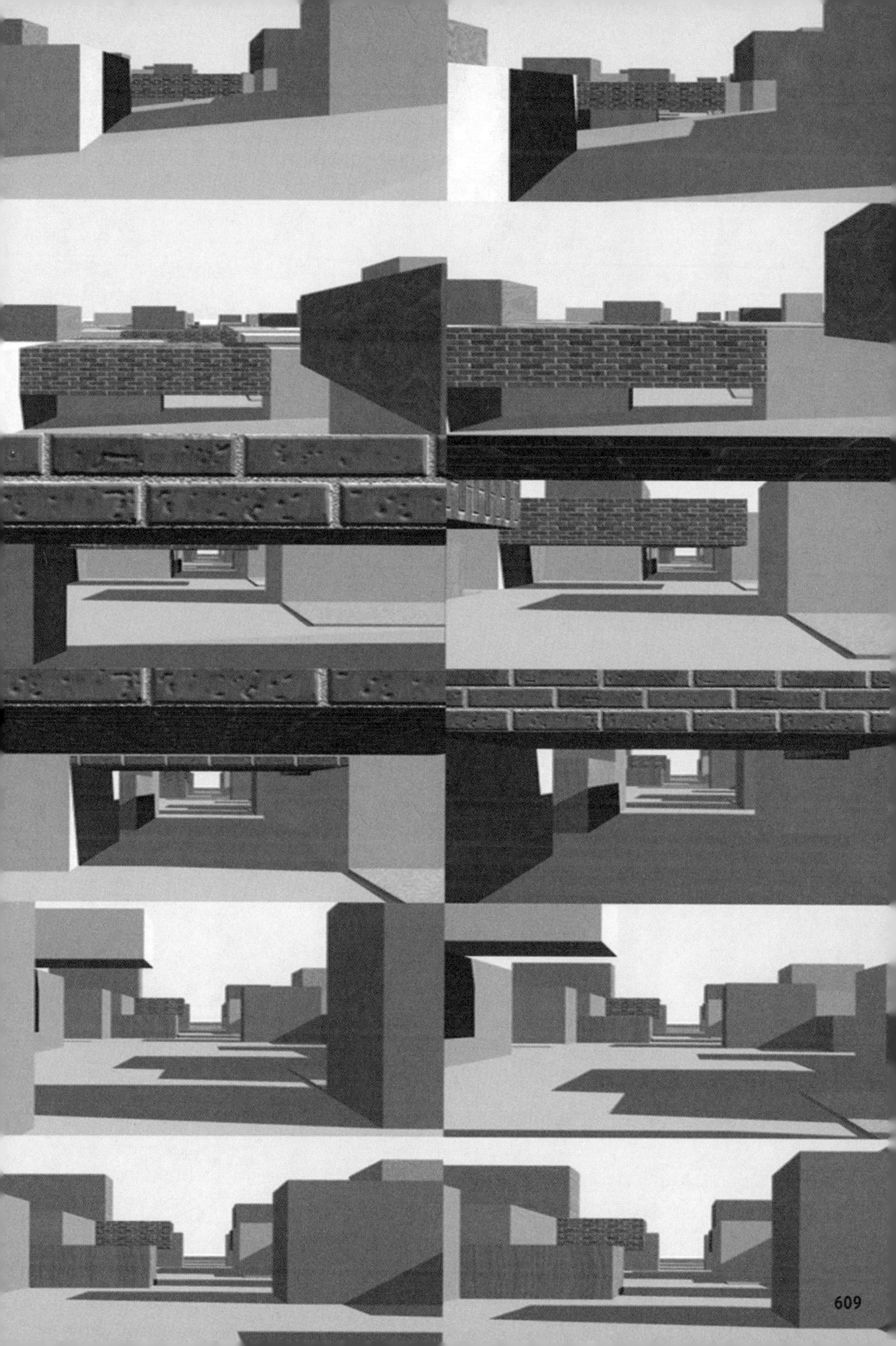

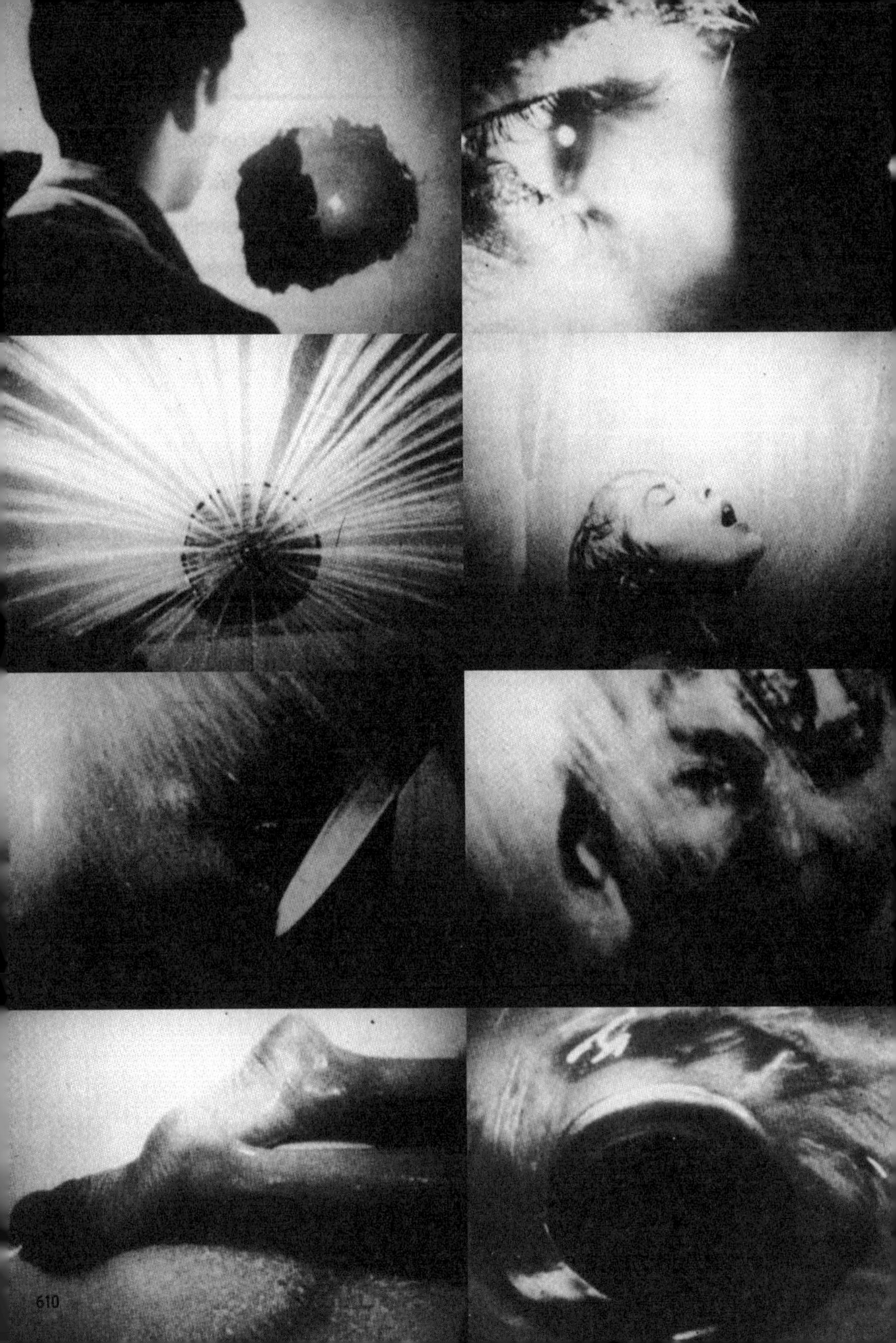

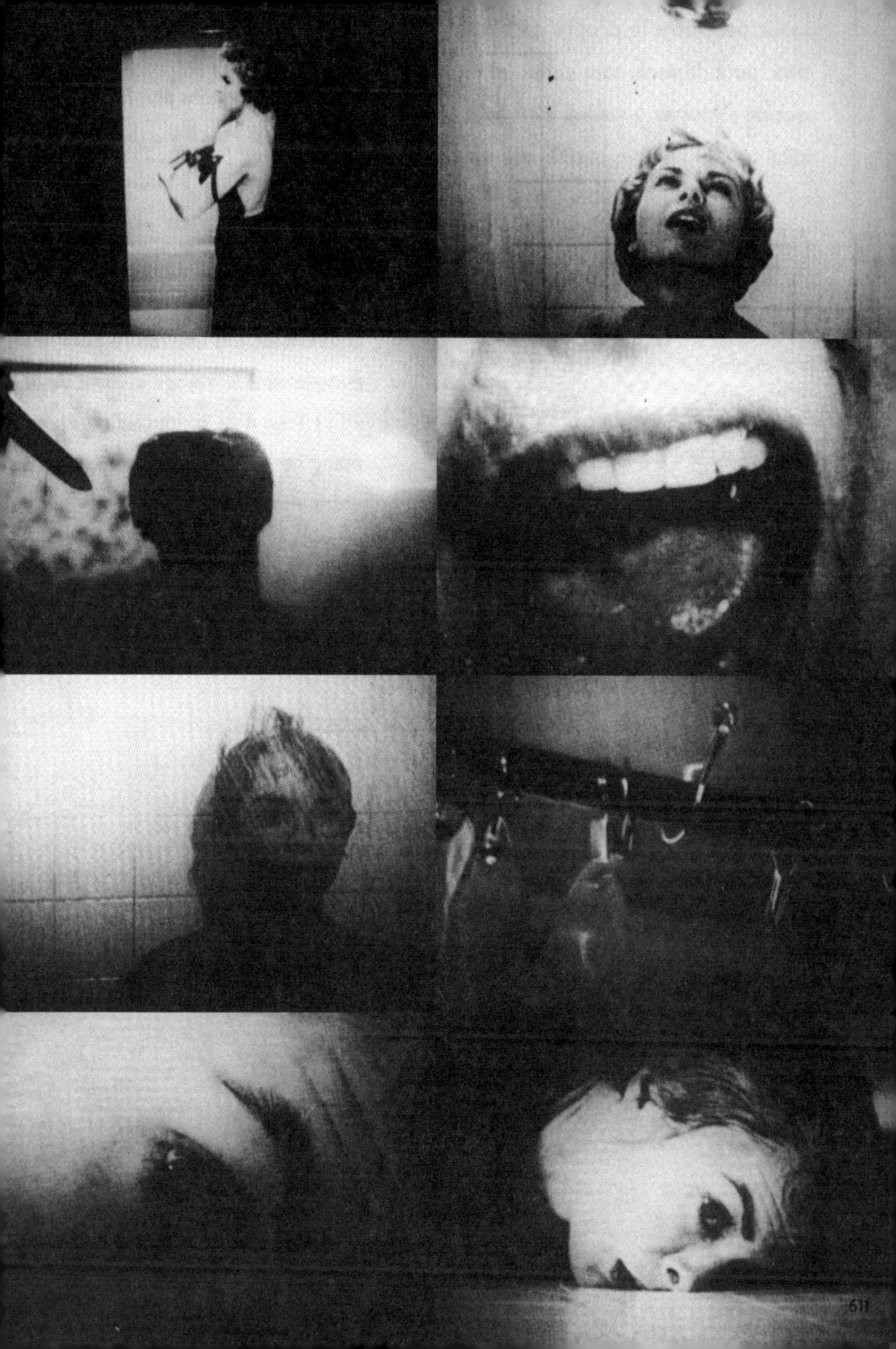

Roof view

MUSIC

Massive pluralism

Text

1996

Winy Maas

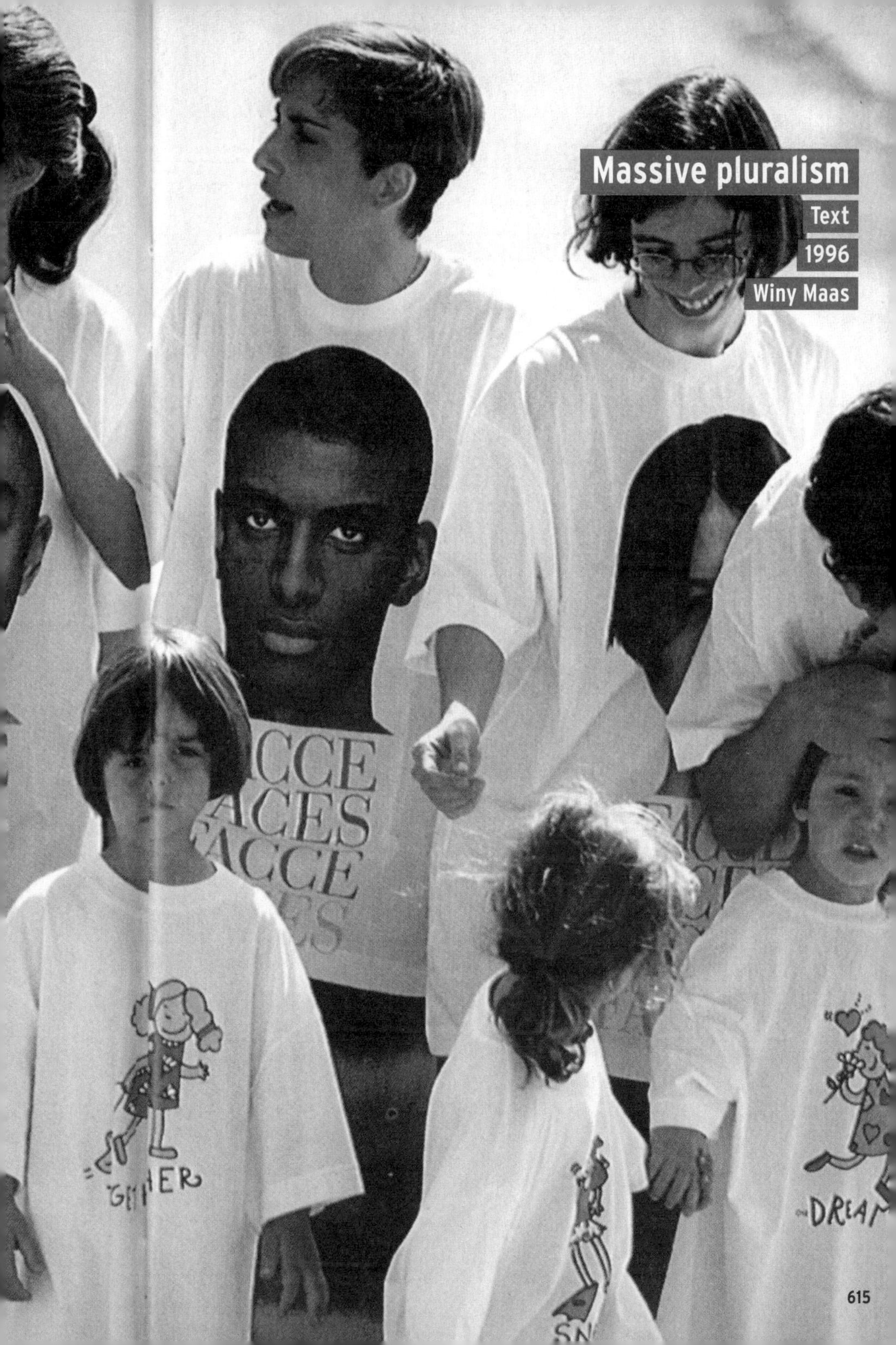

Rough clashes between extreme cultures generate a society that cannot be defined by words like 'harmony' or 'pure stability'.
A continuous change of positions turns our society into a condition of relativities.
The question of 'how to do it' has turned into one of 'should we do it' or 'where to do it' or 'for how long shall we do it'.
This field of interchanging positions has its own logic, its own rules, its own "ecologies". It is a field that cannot be covered by any suggestion of unity - that would be a total denial of the multicoloured aspects of modern society and would discourage us from studying it. In order to understand the possibilities of this field, we can unfold it and explore it through an all-out stimulation of pluralism.
A maximum of difference turns the town into a pixel-city composed of a 'lava' of programme that obtains its coherence simply through its differences.

Its lack of hegemony or leadership might lead to a delicate balance in which these differences attain a certain 'gravity' because of their numerical aspects.
This gravity can be compared with the awareness of watching the same television programme together with two million invisible fellow-viewers; it focuses the totally different views of the spectators in one direction.
If we are to understand this gravity and manipulate it we have to study the rules of pluralism. Rules that can be distilled from analyses of the sudden craze or mass hysteria, analyses of their successes and failures.
Maybe we can start to test this by making space for the opinions and desires of all those hundreds involved in realizing large-scale operations, and literally lining them up. By so combining the demand for a diversity of ideals and pumping these up to a critical level, this multiformity will gel, will even itself become a presence an object of intense and dense difference.

Competition

Plant City

or Town plan and landscape design for the Bundesgartenschau 2001 in Potsdam, Germany

1997

MVRDV

The last buga How long are we going to continue with the current BUGA concept in times of travel and digital information exchange? In this era of individualization, the making of the public park ceases to exist. Malls, holiday parks, leisure centres, natural reserves, National Parks, roads and theme parks seemingly and involuntarily take over the role of the traditional public park. Can this process be considered as one of the reasons for the decay of traditional town planning, which used the park for structuring new urban developments? In such a process, garden exhibitions become one of the last tools to make a public park. In an overwhelming battle, comparable with the competition for the Olympic Games, municipalities try to obtain such an exhibition, that gives so much media attention during the festival and creates a public leisure zone afterwards. It has led to an impressive collection of parks throughout Germany, Holland and England, that reflect the thinking in landscape architecture of the past decades.

In Potsdam we seized upon the Bundesgartenschau (Buga) of 2001 to develop a new city district afterwards. A district intended to reinterpret the famous garden suburbs that have sprung up in and around Berlin this century.

In its quest for originality, we wondered how long the concept of garden exhibitions will endure in times of travel and digital information exchange.

Are we heading for an epoch without 'exhibitions'? Will this be one of the last BUGAs? Has the time arrived for us to consider an exhibition that sets out to summarize the exhibition concept? An exhibition so overwhelming that one questions the need for a successor?
This notion coincides with the moment when landscape architecture is entering an era of doubt. After conquering the doom and pessimism of the seventies with an ecological response and meeting the economic boom of the eighties and nineties with 'design', the profession is now confronted with the issue of how to address the daunting quantity of paradoxical demands made by the contemporary landscape around us. How to embody plural culture and multiplicity in a profession that engages historically with the paradigms of 'nature', 'beauty', 'purity', 'harmony' and 'nobility'. How to escape from the 'innocence' to which the profession has been politically condemned and with which it has been misused.

Is it conceivable to make a park where all demands, every imaginable paradox, all garden elements, all styles, all issues are unceremoniously gathered together in an 'e-quality' that avoids morality and prejudice, one where every element can have the space to show its beauty and its power?

Can we amass a collection of elements and issues that can be seen as the status quo at century's end and be considered as a contemporary Noah's Ark for the coming generations?
This park accordingly transforms into an exhibition where, instead of the widely divergent demands being camouflaged, this diversity itself becomes the object.
No species or style should then be excluded. Neither marigold nor geranium, forsythia nor fern should be forbidden because of its composition or quality. No commercial entry or ecological thought should be excluded. All together in one pluralistic 'Benettonesque' garden.

Plant city The available space will be partitioned into plots or gardens of 20 by 50 metres. This module can efficiently accept both trees and bulbs, both parking places and sports fields. It gives the correct size for accommodating groups of row houses, villas and apartment buildings after the BUGA closes.
The short side of the fields are east-west oriented so that the longest on-site line of vision takes in the maximum number of plots. This results in a distinction between the avenues and the street, with an existing historical road operating as a nostalgic Broadway in Plant City, this vegetal Manhattan. The strict north-south direction gives it a 'global' character.

In order to avoid any preference, all these elements acquire the same plot type, the same amount of space. Placed in alphabetical order, any 'artistic composition' will be avoided. And everything can be found easily.
Plants, recreational elements (such as a Ferris wheel, trampoline field, beach-volleyball field, pool, children's playground, midget golf and minigolf areas), decorative elements (vases garden, benches garden, chair garden, light garden), national gardens (French, Zen, Chinese, Japanese, Italian, Nigerian), theme gardens, ecological experiments, the designers' collections - all are placed from A to Z so that the maximum number of combinations can

be met. Here surprise combines with logic.
Since some of the plant families have more than one species, parts of the exhibition transform into larger elements: 6 species of Erica together constitute a large field of heather, 5 species of Ilex turn that area into an Ilex forest, 10 species of pruned Ligustrum give a tea-plantation aspect to that zone.
The latest entries can be found under N (new) or L (late arrivals), and the industries under I.

The 3.5 metre wide paths that divide the gardens and sections can be used after the exhibition as streets for the housing areas.

Silicon valley The humus can be removed by clearing the ground to a depth of 1 metre. This improves the soil condition for maintenance-free greenery. It also creates a uniform soil for planting, which makes for flexibility and provides conditions for comparison if scientific research is done.
The amount of soil accumulated from this excavation can be used to erect a forty metre high 'James Turrell' hill on the edge of the BUGA terrain.
Being surrounded by three hills, the exhibition field can be seen as a vegetal 'Silicon Valley'.
In order to use the hills to the maximum, the summits are accessed by escalators placed between the trees on the slopes. The views from the peaks visually tie together all the elements of the park.
Restaurants can be placed next to these peaks with elongated terraces. Every dining table gives a panoramic view across the valley. A private telescope with taped explanations rounds off the menu. You are therefore able to 'visit' the exhibition without physically entering the park.

Screen Each field will be illuminated by one light mast placed at its northeast corner.
A computerized system makes it possible to turn the lights on and off individually. It converts the park into a single large horizontal screen, where all kind of texts and messages, commercial, educational, informational and cultural, can be shown to visitors to the terraces and to airplanes passing by the site. BUGA 2001, WELCOME TO POTSDAM, MONEY CREATES TASTE, CONIFERS NOW 3DM ONLY, JOHANN (3 JAHRE) SUCHT SEINE ELTERN, BUY SEEDS FROM.....
This way, the valley transforms into one big Land Art project.

Post-buga: pixel city After the BUGA, the fields with the most expensive maintenance costs can be used to receive 2000 houses and attendant facilities such as schools, shops, parking areas and personal allotments.
A whole host of different housing types can easily be allocated there: row houses, villas, patio houses, apartment buildings, condominiums.

The houses absorb or adopt the found BUGA elements: this could result in houses round a Japanese garden, houses in a mini-forest, houses surrounded by roses, etcetera. A maximum of personal connotations becomes possible. Since all houses will be surrounded by planting, a true garden city will emerge.

The BUGA becomes a basis for this housing area, and as such will determine its character. It will be as if the BUGA has petrified, turned to stone; the next sustained memory of the history of this place.

In that respect even the graves are spread out individually throughout the area, so that the personality developed in life can continue after death. Life and death once again acquire a meaningful and visible link.

The ruthless but flexible combination and variety of plantings, sports equipment, leisure elements, parking solutions and different types of housing, turn the field itself into an object: the variety will be so great that the boundaries between built and not-built will dissolve in a single 'Pixel City'.

Corridor or valley

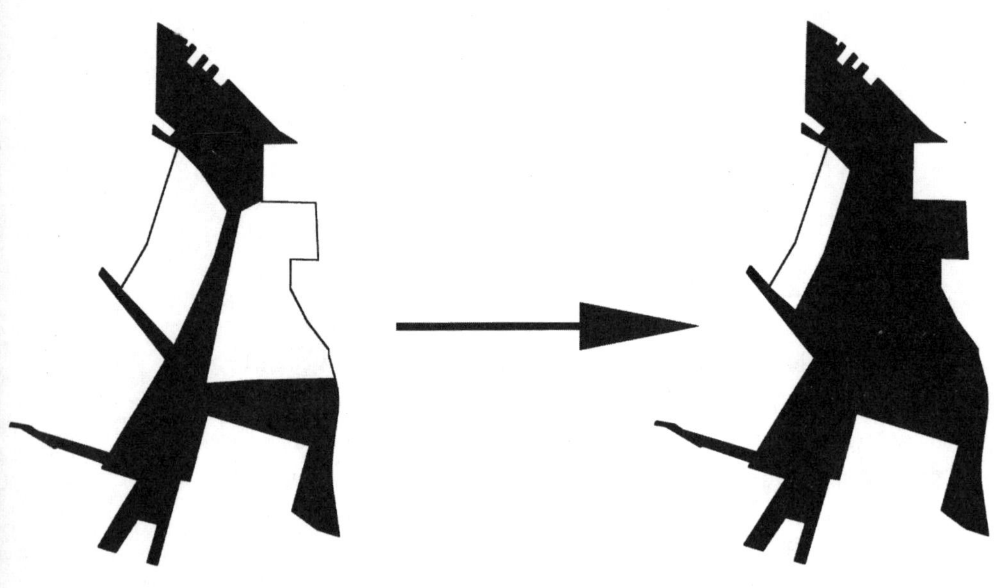

Living next to a park

Living in a park

Vegetal Manhattan

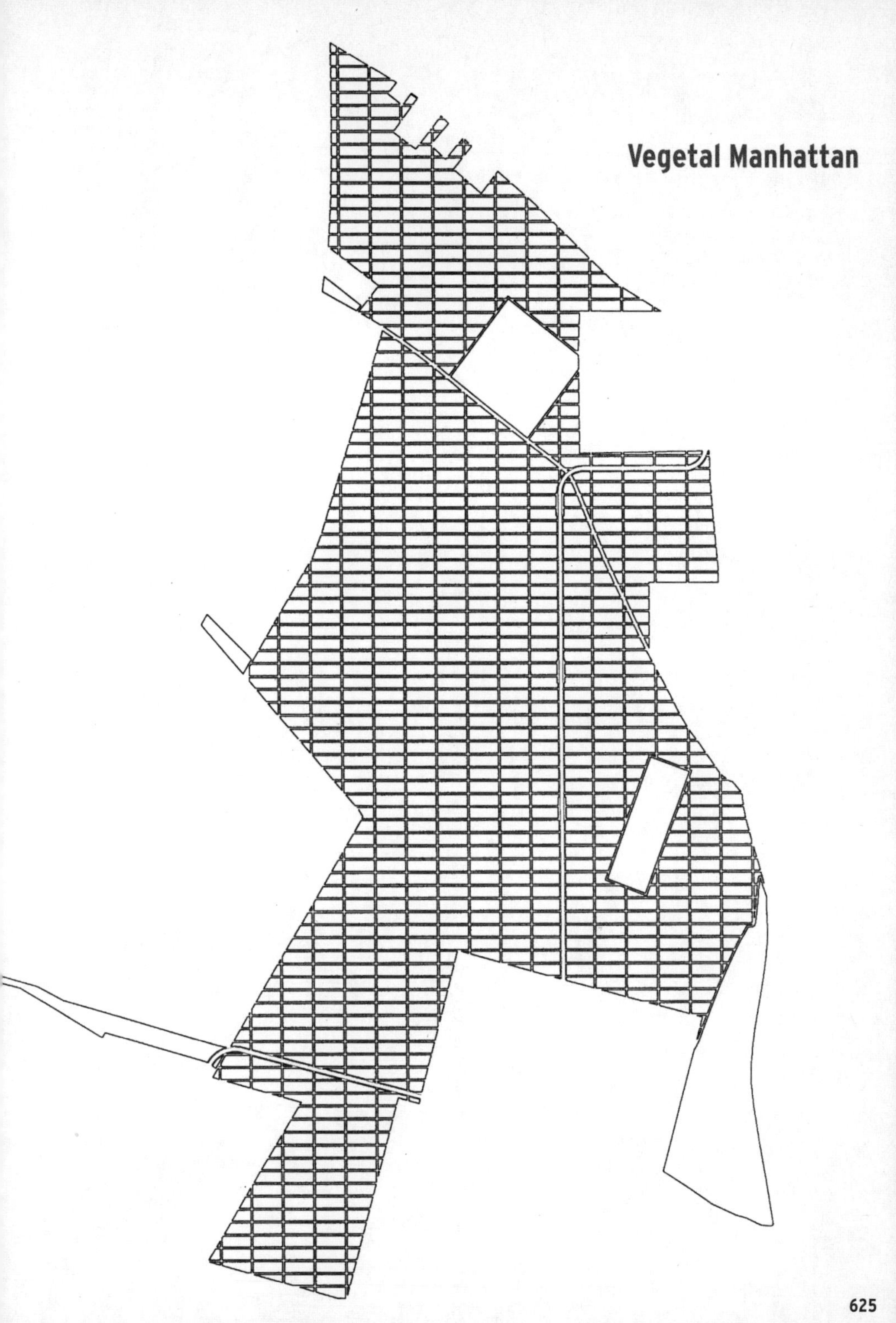

Collection

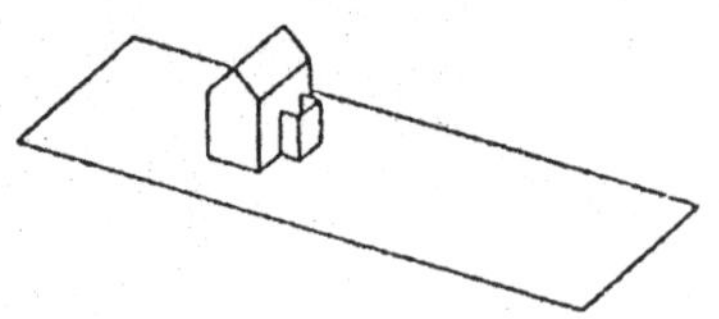
Villa

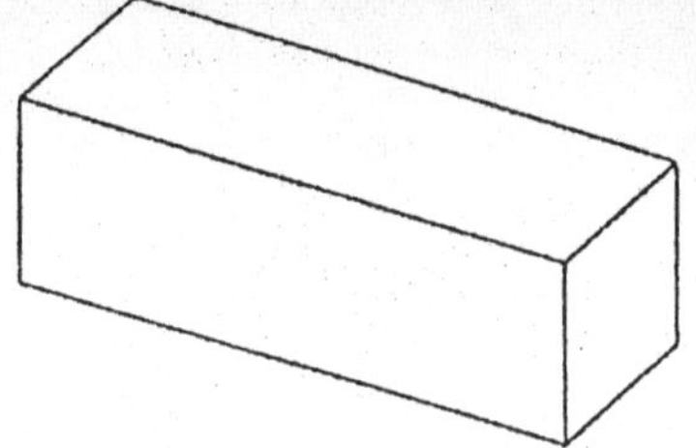
Apartment block

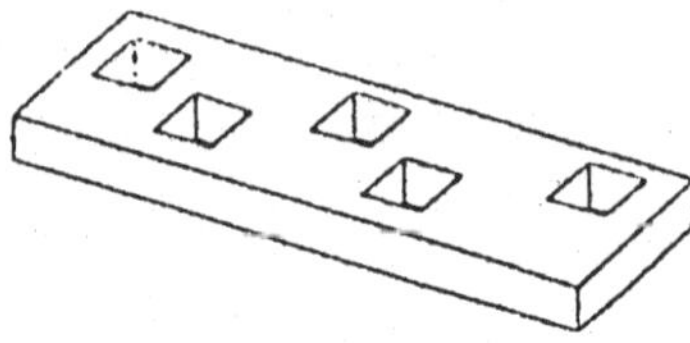
Birkenwald

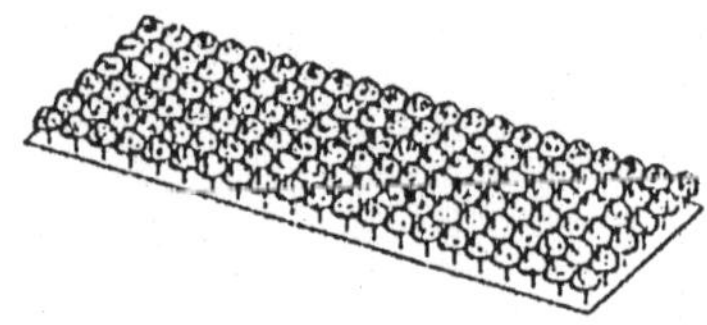
Fruittrees

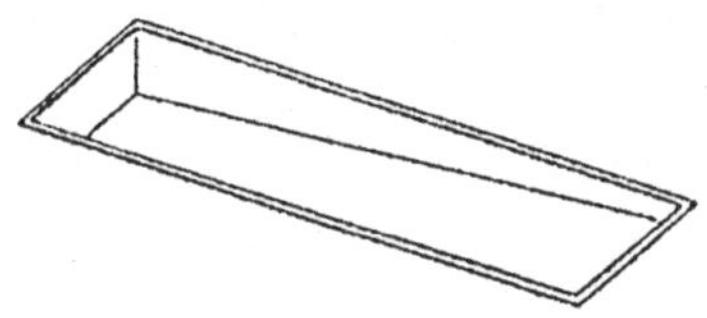
Swimming pool

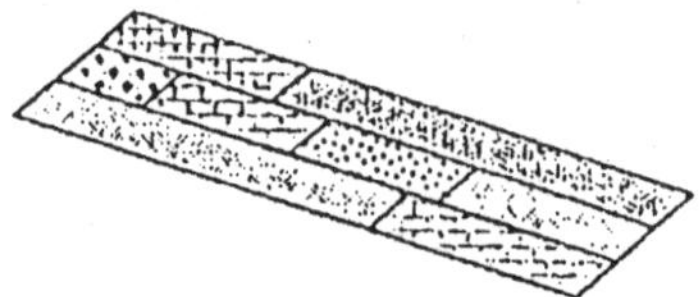
Experimental gardens

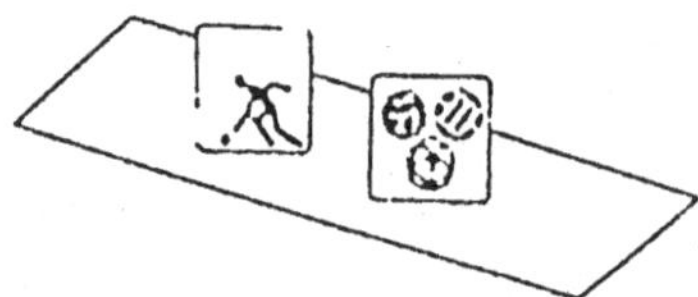
Sport

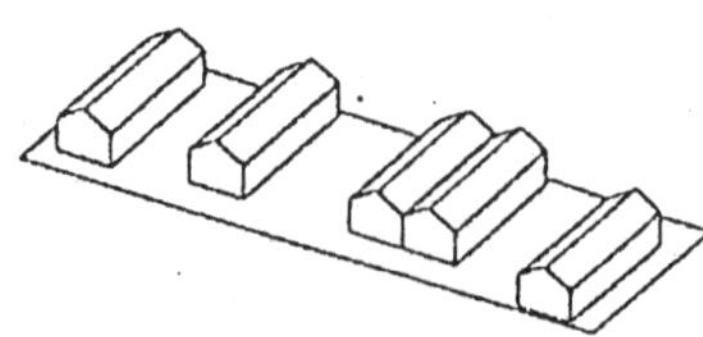
Gardencenter

Ponyfield

Childrensfarm

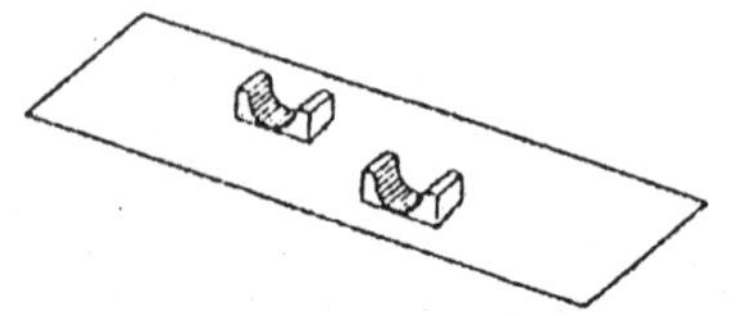
Halfpipe

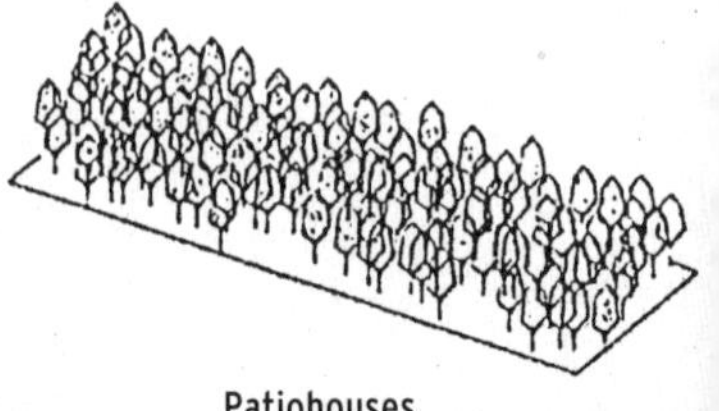
Patiohouses

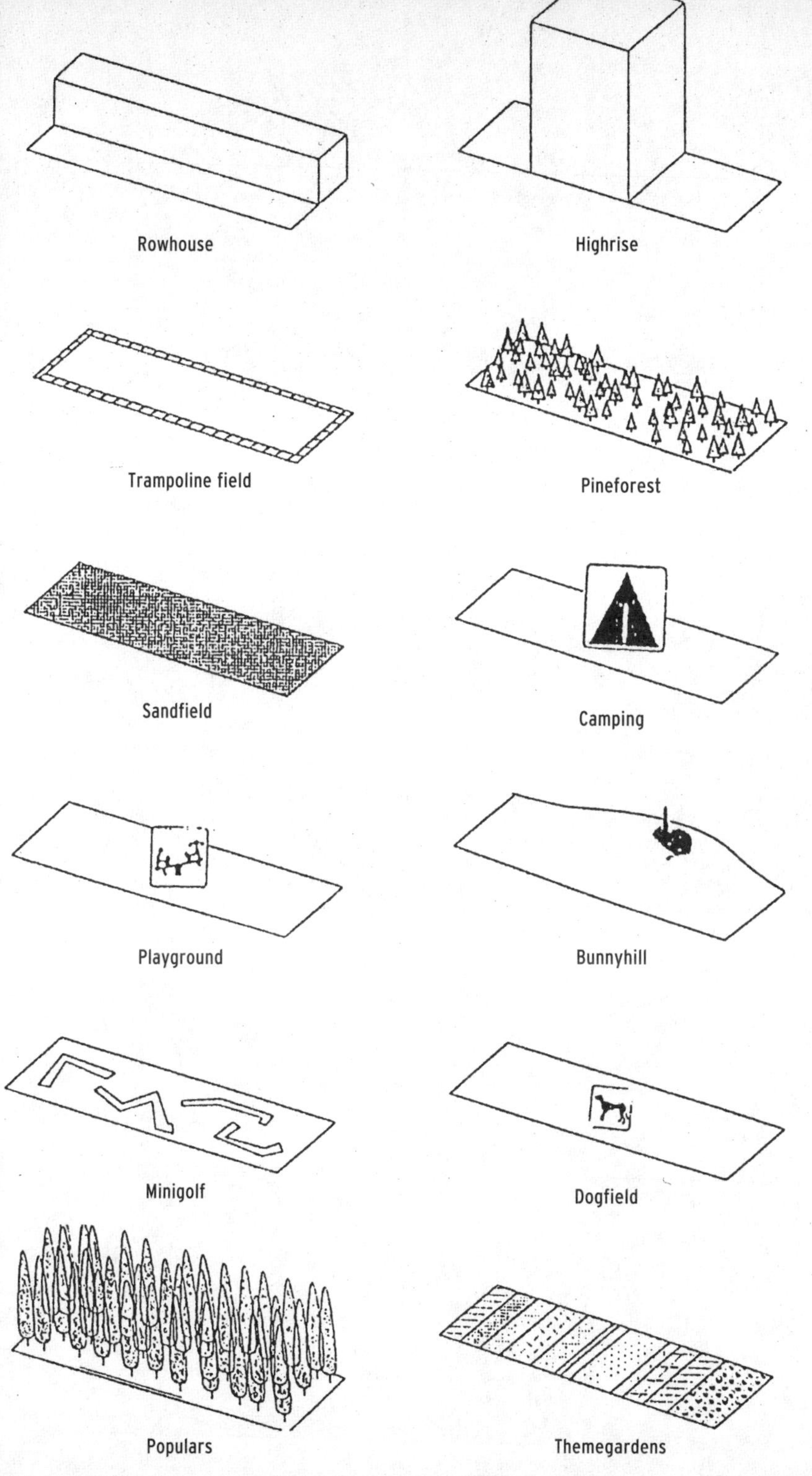
Rowhouse
Highrise
Trampoline field
Pineforest
Sandfield
Camping
Playground
Bunnyhill
Minigolf
Dogfield
Populars
Themegardens

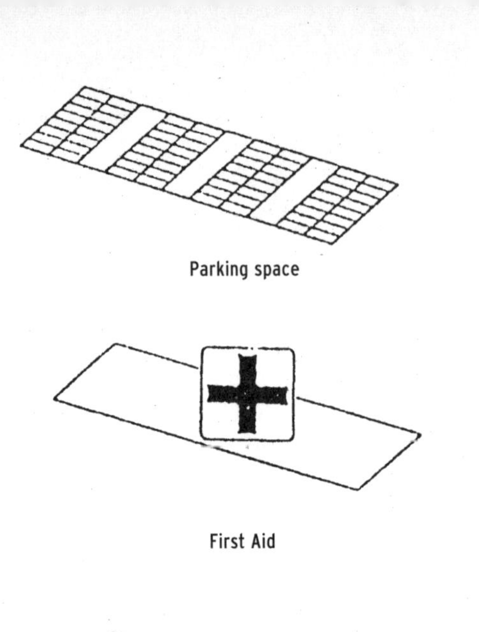

Parking space

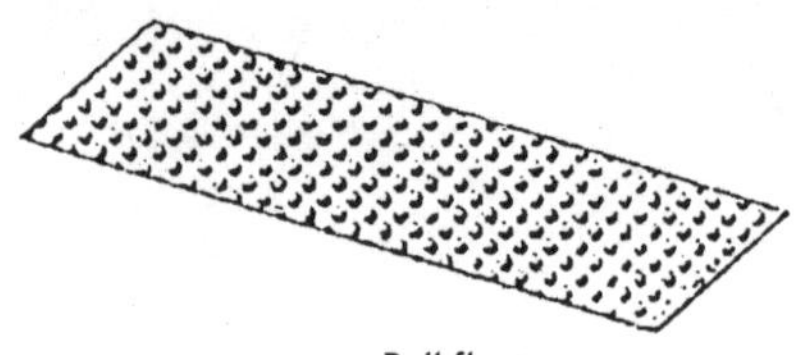

Bulbflowers

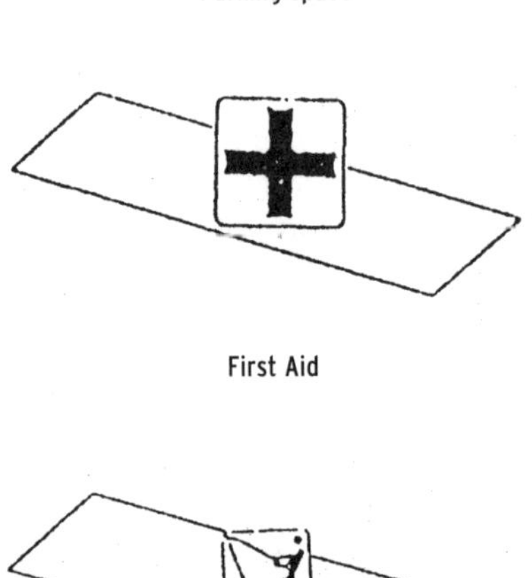

First Aid

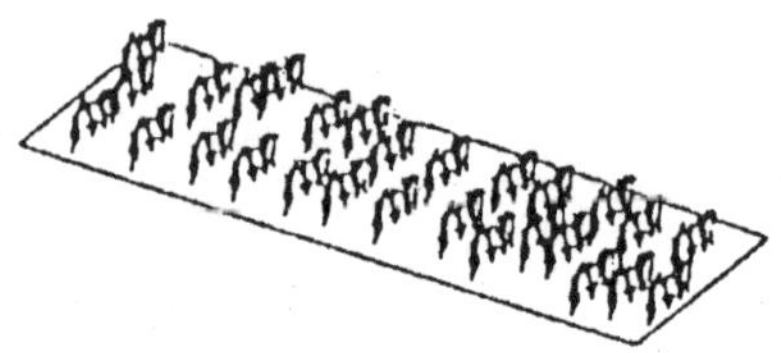

Climb plants

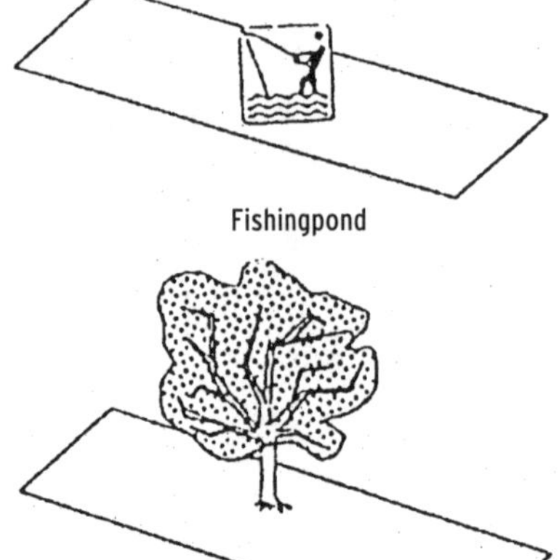

Fishingpond

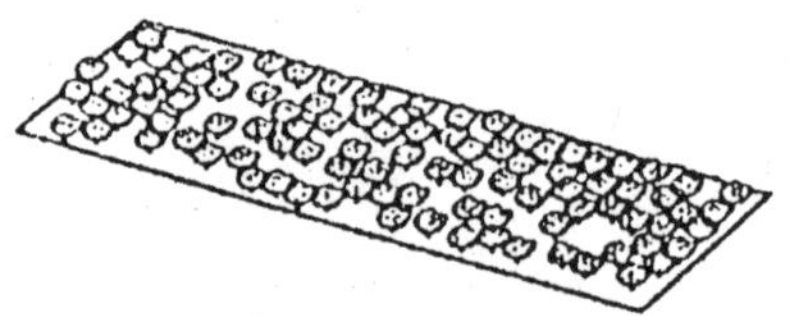

Bushes

Holy oak

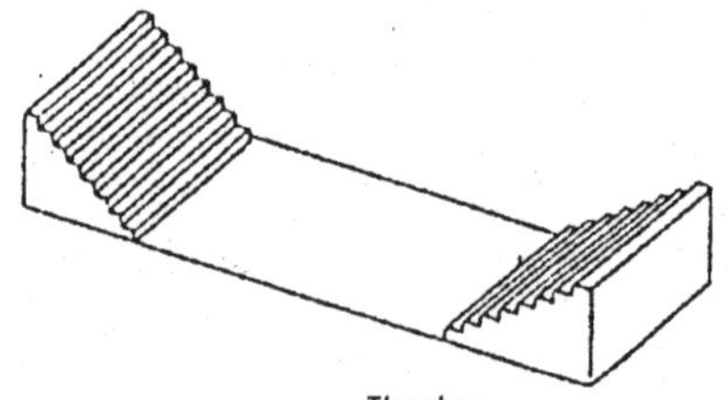

Theater

Benches

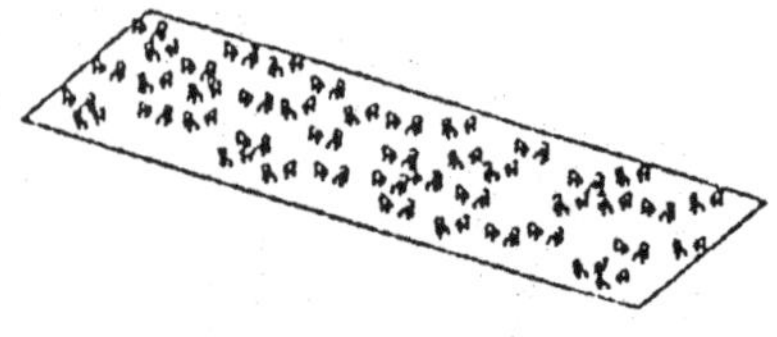

Chairs

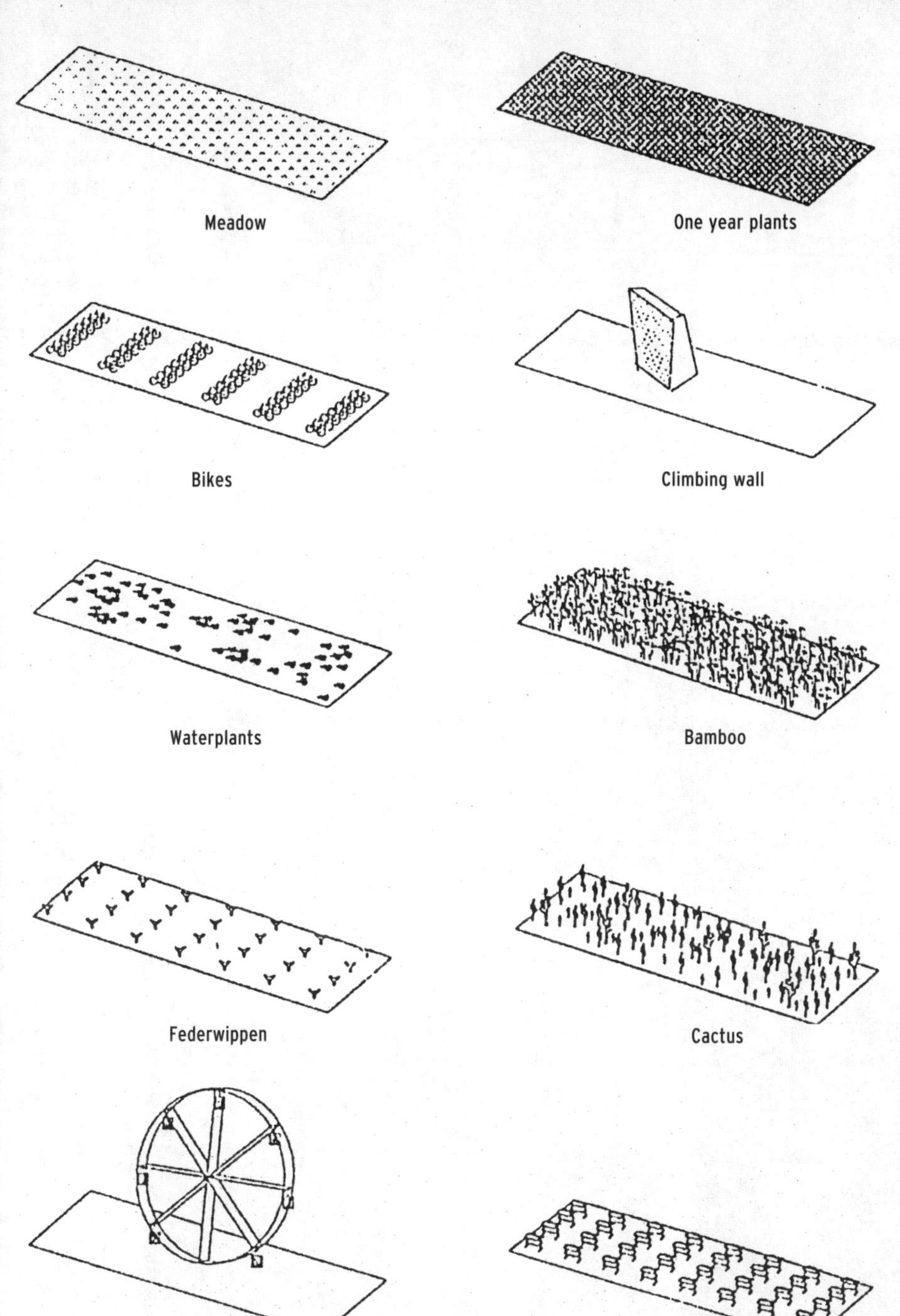
Meadow
One year plants
Bikes
Climbing wall
Waterplants
Bamboo
Federwippen
Cactus
Giant wheel
Info center

GRUND
SCHULE
KITA

KITA
SCHULE

Views

Code	Type of planting
v	= perennials
w	= waterplants
g	= grasses/bamboos
k	= herbs
va	= ferns
b	= tree
c	= conifers
bb	= coverplants
klpl	= climbers
1j	= seasonal plants
bk1	= bulbs, extensive
bk2	= bulbs, intensive
h1	= shrubs, extensive
h2	= shrubs, intensive
h3	= roses
pot	= containerplants
s	= clipped plants
g1	= grass, mown 1x per year
g2	= grass, mown 1x per month
g3	= grass, mown 1x per week
1	= intensive maintenance
2	= Extensive maintenance

COLLECTION

name	code
Abeliophyllum	h2
Abies alba	c
Abies basamea	c
Abies concolor	c
Abies grandis	c
Abies koreana	c
Abies lasiocarpa	c
Abies nordmanniana	c
Abies pinsapo	c
Abies procera	c
Abies veitchii	c
Acaena buchananii	v
Acaena microphylla	v
Aceana sanguisorbae	v
Acanthopanax	h2
Acanthus	pot
Acer campestre	b
Acer japonicum	b
Acer palmatum	b
Acer pensylvanicum	b
Acer platanoides	b
Acer pseudoplatanus	b
Acer rubrum	b
Acer ruvinerve	b
Acer saccharinum	b
Acer saccharum	b
Acer zoeschense	b
Achillea filipendulina	v
Achillea millefolium	v
Achillea ptarmica	v
Achillea taygetea	v
Acorus	w
Actinidia	b
Aesculus carnea	b
Aesculus hippocastanum	b
Aesculus octandra	b
Aethionema	v
Agapanthus	pot
Ageratum	1j
Agrimonia	v
Ailanthus	b
Ajuga	v
Akebia	klpl
Alchemilla mollis	v
Alisma	w
Allium	bk
Alnus cordata	b
Alnus cordinca	b
Alnus glutinosa	b
Alnus incana	b
Alnus rhombifolia	b
Alnus spaethii	b
Alopecurus	g1
Alstroemeria	bk
Althaea	v
Alyssum montanum	v
Alyssum saxatile	v
Amelanchier	b
Ampelopsis	v
Amorpha	k
Anaphalis	v
Anchusa	v
Andromeda	h2
Anemone hepatica	v
Anemone hybrida	v
Anemone pulsatilla	v
Anemone Blanda	bk
Antennaria	v
Anthriscus	v
Aquilegia	v
Aralia	h1
Arabis	v
Araucaria	c
Arctostaphylos	v
Aristolochia	k
Armeria maritima	v
Armeria pseudomaritima	v
Armoracia	k
Aronia	h1
Arrhenatherum	g1
Artemisia	k
Arum	v
Aruncus dioicus	v
Aruncus sylvester	v
Arundinaria	g1
Asarum	v
Asclepias	v
Asperula	v
Aster amellus	v
Aster dumosus	v
Aster novae-angliae	v
Aster novi-belgii	v
Aster sedifolius	v
Aster tongolensis	v
Astilbe astilboides	v
Astilbe chinensis	v
Astilbe japonica	v
Astilbe thunbergii	v
Astilboides	v
Aubretia	v
Aucuba	h1
Avena	g1
Azalea japonica	h2
Azalea mollis	h2
Azalea occidentalis	h2
Azalea pontica	h2
Azalea rustica	h2
Azalea viscosa	h2
Bambusa	g1
Bambusgarten	
Berberis candidula	h1
Berberis darwinii	h1
Berbaris frikartii	h1
Berberis gagnepainii	h1
Berberis interposita	h1
Berberis julianae	h1
Berberis koreana	h1
Berberis linearifolia	h1
Berberis lologensis	h1
Berberis media	h1
Berberis mentorensis	h1
Berberis ottewansis	h1
Bergenia	v
Berggarten	
Betula alleghaniensis	b
Betula costata	b
Betula ermanii	b
Betula jacquemontii	b
Betula lenta	b
Betula maximowicziana	b
Betula medwediewii	b
Betula nana	b
Betula nigra	b
Betula papyrifera	b
Betula pendula	b
Betula populifolia	b
Betula pubescens	b
Bienengarten	
Biogarten	
Blechnum	va
Bonsai	s
Broussonetia	h2
Bruckenthalia	v
Brunnera	v
Buddleia	h1
Bungee Jumping	
Burago	1j
Butomus	w
Buxus	s
Calla	w
Callicarpa	h2
Calluna vulgaris	v
Calluna vulgaris 'Alba'	v
Calluna vulgaris 'Carl'	v
Calluna vulgaris 'Wanderer'	v
Calluna vulgaris 'Hollandia'	v
Caltha	w
Calycanthus	h2
Camasia	bk
Camellia	h2
Campanula carpatica	v
Campanula garganica	v
Campanula glomerata	v
Campanula lactiflora	v
Campanula latiloba	v
Campanula persicifolia	v
Campanula portenschlagian	v
Campanula porscharskyana	v
Campsis	klpl
Caragana	h2
Carex	g1
Carpinus betulus	b/s
Caryopteris	h2
Castanea	b
Catalpa	b
Catanache	v
Cedrus atlantica	c
Cedrus deodara	c
Cedrus libani	c
Celastrus	h2
Celtis	h2
Centaurea dealbata	v
Centaurea macrocephala	v
Centaurea montana	v
Centranthus	v
Ceonothus	h2
Cephalanthus	h2
Cephalotaxus	h2
Cerastium	v
Ceratostigma	v
Cercidiphyllum	b
Cercis	b
Chaenomeles californica	h1
Chaenomeles cathayensis	h1
Chaenomeles clarkiana	h1
Chaenomeles japonica	h1
Chaenomeles speciosa	h1
Chaenomeles superba	h1
Chaenomeles vilmoriniana	h1
Chamaecyparis lawsoniana	c
Chamaecyparis nootkatensis	c
Chamaecyparis obtusa	c
Chamaecyparis pisifera	c
Chamaedaphne	h2
Chamaenerion	v
Chelidonium	v
Chinanthus	h2
Chidnodoxa	bk
Choisya	h2
Chinesischer Garten	
Chrysanthemum frutescens	v
Chrysanthemum hortorum	v
Chrysanthemum koreanum	v
Chrysanthemum maximum	v
Chrysanthemum rubellum	v
Cimicifuga	v
Clematis	klpt
Clerodendron	h2
Clethra	h2
Clivia	pot
Colocasia	w
Coleus	1j
Colutea	h2
Consolido	1j
Convallaria	v
Cornus alba	h1
Cornus alternifolia	h1
Cornus amomum	h1
Cornus baileyi	h1
Cornus drummondii	h1
Cornus florida	h1
Cornus glabrata	h1
Cornus kousa	h1
Cornus mas	h1
Cornus nuttalli	h1
Cornus pumila	h1
Cornus racemosa	h1
Cornus rugosa	h1
Cornus stolonifera	h1
Cornus walteri	h1
Coronilla	h2
Coreopsis grandiflora	v
Coreopsis lanceolata	v
Coreopsis verticillata	v
Coronaria	v
Cortaderia	g1
Corydalis	v
Corylopsis glabrescens	h1
Corylopsis pauciflora	h1
Corylopsis spicata	h1
Corylopsis willmottiae	h1
Corylus avellana	h1
Corylus colurna	h1
Corylus maxima	h1
Cosmea	1j
Cotinus	h2
Cotoneaster adpressus	h1
Cotoneaster ballatus	h1
Cotoneaster conspicuus	h1
Cotula	v
Crataegus laevigata	b
Crataegus lavalei	b
Crataegus monogyna	b/s
Crataegus mordenensis	h1
Crataegus pedicellata	h1
Crataegus pinnatifida	h1
Crataegus prunifolia	b
Crocosmia luc.	1j
Cryptomeria	c
Cupressocyparis leylandii	c
Cupressocyparis notabilis	c
Cydonia	v
Cytisus	h1
Daboecia	v
Daphne	h2
Davidia	h1
Decaisnea	h2
Delphinium belladonna	v
Delphinium hybrida	v
Delphinium pacific giant	v
Delphinium ruysii	v
Desmodium	h2
Deutzia elegantissima	h1
Deutzia gracilis	h1
Deutzia hybrida	h1
Deutzia kalmiaeflora	h1
Deutzia lemoinei	h1
Deutzia magnifica	h1
Deutzia ningpoensis	h1
Deutzia rosea	h1
Deutzia scabra	h1
Deutzia taiwanensis	h1
Dhalia 'Butterball'	bk
Dhalia 'Evening Mail'	bk
Dhalia 'Hamari Bride'	bk
Dhalia 'So Dainty'	bk
Dhalia 'Wootton Cupid'	bk
Dianthusalpinus	v
Dianthus deltoides	v
Dianthus plumarius	v
Dicentra	v
Digitalis	v
Diervilla	h2
Dipsacus	v
Doronicum caucasicum	v
Doronicum plantagineum	v
Draba	v
Drachensteigerfeld	
Dryopteris	va
Duchesnea	v
Echinops	v
Eleagnus	h1
Elsholtzia	h2
Empetrum	bb
Englischer Garten	
Enkiathus	h2
Epilobium	v
Epimedium alpinum	v
Epimedium rubrum	v
Epimedium versicolor	v
Eranthus	bk
Eremurus	pot
Erica carnea	v
Erica carnea 'Heathwood'	v
Erica carnea 'Vivellii'	v
Erica ciliaris	v
Erica cinerea darleyensis	v
Erica erigena	v
Erica hibernica	v
Erica mackaiana	v
Erica praegeri	v
Erica terminalis	v
Erica tetralix	v
Erica vagans	v
Erica williamsii	v
Erigeron	v
Erlebnispark für Kinder	
Erodium	v
Eryngium oliverianum	v
Eryngium planum	v
Escallonia viragat	h2
Escallonia 'Red Elf'	h2
Escallonia 'Victory'	h2
Escholzia	1j
Eulalia	g1
Euonymus alatus	h1
Euonymus americanus	h1
Euonymus bungeanus	h1
Euonymus europaeus	h1
Eonymus phellomanus	h1
Euonymus pauciflorus	h1
Eupatorium	v
Euphorbia	v
Exochorda	h2
Fagus sylvatica	b/s
Fagus sylvatica'asplenifolia'	b
Fagus sylvatica'pendula'	b
Fagus sylvatica'purpurea'	b
Fagus sylvatica'purp. pendula'	b
Filipendula	v
Forsythia intermedia	h1
Forsythia ovata	h1
Forsythia suspensa	h1
Forsythia volunteer	h1
Fothergilla	h1
Fragaria	v
Französischer Garten	
Fraxinus excelsior	b
Fraxinus ornus	b
Fraxinus oxycarpa	b
Fraxinus pennsylvanica	b
Freilichtbühne	
Fritlaria	bk
Früchtegarten	
Fuchsia magellanica	v
Fuchia	pot
Galanthus	bk
Gemüsegarten	
Genista	h1
Gaulnettya	h2
Gaillardia	v
Gaultheria miqualiana	bb
Gaultheria procumbens	bb
Gaultheria shallon	bb
Gentiana acaulis	v
Gentiana clusii	v
Gentiana sino-ornata	v
Geranium	
endressii	v
Geranium grandiflorum	v
Geranium platypetalum	v
Geranium prichardii	v
Geranium sanguineum	v
Geranium	1j
Gerste	1j
Geum	v
Ginkgo	b
Gladiolen	bk
Glasgarten	
Glechoma	v
Gleditsia	b
Gras,1x pro jahr	g1
Gras, 1x pro monot	g2
Gras, 1x pro woche	g3
Großblütenrosen	h3
Gynerium	v
Gypsophila paniculata	v
Gypsophila repens	v
Halesia	h2
Halimodendron	h2
Hamamelis intermedia	h1
Hamamelis japonica	h1
Hamamelis mollis	h1
Hamamelis virginiana	h1
Hebe	h1
Hedera colchica	bb
Hedera helix	bb
Hedysarum	h2
heidengarten	
Helenium autumnale	v
Helenium hybrida	v
Helianthemum	v
Helianthus multiflorus	v
Helianthus superbus	v
Heliantus 'L's pink'	1j
Heliantus 'Orange D'	1j
Heliantus 'Ruth'	1j
Heliantus 'Snow Q'	1j
Heliantus 'Yellow D'	1j
Helictotrychon	g1
Heliopsis	v
Helleboris hybridus	v
Helleborus niger	v
Hemerocallus	v
Heracleum	v
Heuchera	v
Heucherella	v
Hibiscus syriacus	h2
Hieracium	v
Hippeastrum	pot
Hippophae	h1
Holländischer Garten	
Holcus	g1
Holodiscus	h2
Hosta fortunei	v
Hosta sieboldiana	v
Hosta undulata	v
Hottonia	w
Humulus lupulus	klpl
Hutchinsia	v
Hydrangea arborescens	h2
Hydrangea aspera	h2
Hydrangea heteromalla	h2
Hydrangea involucrata	h2
Hydrangea macrophylla	h2
Hydrangea paniculata	h2
Hydrangea petiolaris	h2
Hydrangea quercifolia	h2
Hydrangea serrata	h2
Hydrangea villosa	h2
Hyacint	bk
Hydrocharis	w
Hypericum androsaemum	h1
Hypericum beannii	h1
Hypericum calicinum	h1
Hypericum forestii	h1
Hypericum 'Hidcote'	h1
Hypericum hircinum	h1
Hypericum kalmianum	h1
Hypericum moserianum	h1
Hypericum patulum	h1
Hypericum prilificum	h1
Hypericum pseudohenryi	h1
Hyssopus	k
Iberis	v
Ilex altaclarensis	h1
Ilex aquifolium	h1
Ilex crenata	h1
Ilex vertcillata	h1
Incarvillea	v
Indigofera	h1
Indonesischer Garten	
Internationaler Markt	
Inula ensifolia	v
Inula orientalis	v
Iris germanica	v
Iris kaempferi	v
Iris pseudacorus	v
Iris sibirica	v
Iris	pot
Itea virginica	h2
Japanischer Garten	
Jasminum	klpl
Jazzgarten	
Juglans nigra	b
Juglans regia	b
Jungle	
Juniperus chinensis	c
Juniperus communis	c
Juniperus hoizontalis	c

Juniperus media	c
Juniperus sabina	c
Juniperus squamata	c
Juniperus virginiana	c
Kaktusgarten	
Kaninchenhügel	
Kalmia angustifolia	h2
Kalmia latifolia	h2
Kalmia polifolia	h2
Kalopanax	b
Kartoffel	1j
Kerria	h1
Kieselgarten	
Kindergarten	
Kletterrosen	klpl
Klee	1j
Kniphofia	v
Koeleria	g1
Koelreuteria	b
Kolkwitzia	h1
Konzertgarten	
Kniphofia	v
Kräutergarten	
Kupfergarten	
Krokus	bk
Laburnum alpinum	b
Laburnum anagyroides	b
Laburnum watereri	b
Lamiastrum	v
Lamium	v
Larix	c
Lavandula angustifolia	v
Lavandula intermedia	v
Ledum	h2
Leontopodium	v
Lesegarten	
Lespedeza	h1
Leucothoe	h2
Levisticum	k
Leycesteria	h2
Liatris	v
Libocedrus	c
Ligularia	v
Ligustrum amurensi	h1
Ligustrum dalavayanum	h1
Ligustrum ibolium	klpl
Ligustrum obtusifolium	h1
Ligustrum ovalifolium	h1
Ligustrum quihoui	h1
Ligustrum sinense	h1
Ligustrum tschonoskii	h1
Ligustrum vicaryi	h1
Ligustrum vulgare	s
Liliums	bk
Limonium	v
Linum	v
Liquidambar styraciflua	b
Liriodendron tulipifera	b
Lonicera alpigena	h1
Lonicera amoena	h1
Lonicera bella	h1
Lonicera chaetocarpa	h1
Lonicera fragrantissima	h1
Lonicera involucrata	h1
Lonicera	
korolkowii	h1
Lonicera ledebourii	h1
Lonicera maackii	h1
Lonicera morowii	h1
Lonicera netida 'Elegant'	h1
Lonicera pileata	h1
Lonicera quinquelocularis	h1
Lonicera ruprechtiana	h1
Lonicera syringantha	h1
Lonicera tatarica	h1
Lonicera xylosteum	h1
Lotus	v
Lupinus arboreus	v
Lupinus polyphyllus	v
Luzula	g1
Lychnis chalcedonica	v
Lychnis coronaris	v
Lychnis viscaria	v
Lycium	h2
Lysichiton	
Lysimachia	v
Lythrum	v
Magnolia kobus	h2
Magnolia liliiflora	h2
Magnolia loebneri	h2
Magnolia sieboldi	h2
Magnolia soulangiana	h2
Magnolia stellata	h2
Mahoberberis aquisargentis	h1
Mahoberberis miethkeana	h1
Mahoberberis	h1
Mahonia aquifolium	h1
Mahonia bealei	h1
Mahonia japonica	h1
Mahonia media	h1
Mahonia wagneri	h1
Maianthemum	v
Majorana	k
Malus baccata	b
Malus coronaria	b
Malus floribunda	b
Malus halliana	b
Malus hupehensis	b
Malus pumila	b
Malus sargentii	h1
Malus sieboldii	b
Malus tschonoskii	b
Malva alcea	v
Malva moschata	v
Märchengarten	
Matteuccia	va
Melissa	k
Mentha	k
Menyanthes	w
Mespilus	b
Metasequoia	c
Microbiata	c
Mimulus	v
Miniaturrosen	h3
Minigolf	
Miscanthus	g1
Monarda	v
Morus alba	b
Morus nigra	b
Mountainbike Track	
Myosotis	w
Myrica gale	h2
Myrica pensylvanica	h2
Narcis Actaea	bk
Narcis February Gold	bk
Neillia affinis	h2
Neillia ribesioides	h2
Neillia thibetica	h2
Nepeta	v
Nicotiana	1j
Nothofagus antarctica	b
Nothofagus obliqua	b
Nothofagus procera	b
Nuphar	w
Nymphaea	w
Nymphoides	w
Oenotera	v
Omphalodes	v
Osmanthus decorus	h1
Osmanthus heterophyllus	h1
Osmunda	va
Ostrya carpiniflora	b
Pachysandra	bb
Paoenia officinalis	v
Paoenia suffruticosa	v
Papaver	1j
Parthenocissus	klpl
Parrotia persica	b
Passiflora	klpl
Paulownia tomentosa	b
Peltiphyllum	v
Pennisetum	g1
Pernettya mucronata	v
Periploca	v
Perovskia	b
Persischer Garten	
Petasites	v
Petunia	1j
Phalaris	g
Philadelphus coronarius	h1/s
Philadelphus delavayi	h1
Philadelphus intectus	h1
Philadelphus microphyllus	h1
Phillyrea	h2
Photinia beauverdiana	h2
Photinia koreana	h2
Photinia villosa var. laevis	h2
Phlox amoena	v
Phlox decussata	v
Phlox divaricata	v
Phlox paniculata	v
Phlox pyramidalis	v
Phlox subulata	v
Phyllitus	va
Phylostachys	g
Physalis	v
Physostegia	v
Physocarpusamurensis	h2
Physocarpus monogynus	h2
Physocarpus opulifolius	h2
Phytolacca	v
Picea abies	c
Picea glauca	c
Picea mariana	c
Picea omorika	c
Picea orientalis	c
Picea pungens	c
Pieris floribunda	h2
Pieris japonica	h2
Pinus cembra	c
Pinus densiflora	c
Pinus griffithii	c
Pinus heldreichii	c
Pinus mugo	c
Pinus nigra	c
Pinus parviflora	c
Pinus strobus	c
Pinus sylvestris	c
Pimpinella	k
Platanus acerifolia	b
Platanus orientalis	b
Platycodon	v
Pleione	v
Plumbago	v
Podocarpus	c
Polemonium	v
Polygonum affine	v
Polygonum sinensis	v
Polygonum spicata	v
Polygonatum	v
Polygonum	v
Poncirus	h2
Pontederia	w
Populus acuminata	b
Populus alba	b
Populus berolinensis	b
Populus candicans	b
Populus canescens	b
Populus euramericana	b
Populus interamericana	b
Populus koreana	b
Populus lasiocarpa	b
Populus nigra	b
Populus nigra 'talica'	b
Populus simonii	b
Populus tacamahaca	b
Populus tremula	b
Populus tremuloides	b
Populus trichocarpa	b
Populus wilsonii	b
Poterium	v
Potentilla	h2
Potentilla atrosanguinesa	v
Potentila nepalensis	v
Potentilla recta	v
Primula denticulata	v
Primula japonica	v
Primula pubescens	v
Primula rosea	v
Primula vulgaris	v
Primula	1j
Prunella	v
Prunus 'Accolade'	b
Prunus amygdalo-persica	b
Prunus avium	b
Prunus blireiana	b
Prunus cerasifera	b
Prunus cerasus	b
Prunus cistena	b
Prunus glandulosa	b
Prunus gondouinii	b
Prunus hillierii	b
Prunus laurocerasus	b
Prunus laurocerasus	h1
Prunus mahaleb	b
Prunus pumila	h2
Prunus serotina	h1
Prunus serulata	b
Prunus serrulata	b
Prunus tenella	h2
Prunus triloba	h2
Prunus yedoensis	b
Pseudosasa	g1
Pseudotsuga	c
Ptelea	h2
Pterocarya	b
Pulmonaria	v
Pyrethrum	v
Pyracantha	h1
Pyrus	b
Quercus cerris	b
Quercus coccinea	b
Quercus frainetto	b
Quercus palustrus	b
Quercus robur	b
Quercus rubra	b
Ranunculus	v
regenwald	
Rhamnus	b/s
Rheum	v
Rhododendron ferrugineum	h2
Rhododendron hippophaei.	h2
Rhododendron hirsutum	h2
Rhododendron impeditum	h2
Rhododendron luteum	h2
Rhododendron ponticum	h2
Rhododendron williamsian.	h2
Rhododendron yakusiman.	h2
Rhodotypos	h2
Rhus	h1
Riesenrad	
Ribes alpinum	h1
Ribes aureum	h1
Ribes carrierei	h1
Ribes fasciculatum	h1
Ribes glutinosum	h1
Ribes hirtellum	h1
Ribes montigenum	h1
Ribes orientale	h1
Ricinus	1j
Robinia hillierii	b
Robinia hispida	b
Robinia kelseyi	b
Robinia pseudoacacia	b
Rodgersia	v
Rogge	1j
Rollschuhbahn	
Rosa canina	h2
Rosa carolina	h2
Rosa glauca	h2
Rosa hugonis	h2
Rosa moyessii	h2
Rosa multiflora	h3
Rosa nitida	h2
Rosa pimpinellifolie	h2
Rosa pisocarpa	h2
Rosa rubiginosa	h2
Rosa rugosa	h2
Rosa villosa	h2
Rosa virginiana	h2
Rosa woodsii vendleri	h2
Rosenkohl	1j
Rosmarinus	k
Rotkohl	1j
Rubus arcticus	h1
Rubus cockburnianus	h1
Rubus deliciosus	h1
Rubus idaeus	h1
Rubus lasiostylus	h1
Rubus odorates	h1
Rubus phoenicolasius	h1
Rubus tridel	h1
Rudbeckia daemii	v
Rudbeckia purpurea	v
Rudbeckia speciosa	v
Russischer Garten	
Ruta	k
Sagina	v
Sagittaria	w
Salix alba	b
Salix balfourii	h1
Salix caesia	h1
Salix caprea	h1
Salix chaenomeloides	h1
Salix cottettii	h1
Salix dasyclados	h1
Salix koten	b
Salix matsudana 'Pandula'	b
Salix nigra	h1
Salix purpurea	h1
Salix repens	h1
Salix rubens	b
Salix seringeana	h1
Salvia	v
Salvia	1j
Sambucus nigra	h1
Sambucus pubens	h1
Sambucus sibirica	h1
Sandgarten	
Sanguisorba	v
Santolina	v
Saponaria	v
Sarcococca	h2
Satureja	k
Saxifraga arendsii	v
Saxifraga umbrosa	v
Scabiosa	v
Schmetterlingsgarten	
Schwimmbad	
Sciadopitys	c
Scirpus	w
Sedum acre	v
Sedum album	v
Sedum cauticolum	v
Sedum kamtschaticum	v
Sedum spectabile	v
Sedum spurium	v
Sedum telephium	v
Semiarundinaria	g1
Sempervivum	v
Senecio	v
Sequoiadendron	c
Shepherdia	
Sidalcea	v
Sinarundinaria	g1
Skimmia japoniva	h2
Skimmia 'Foremanii'	h2
Skimmia 'Rubella'	h2
skulpturengarten	
Solidago	v
Sonnenblume	1j
Sophora	b
Sorbaria	b
Sorbus americaba	b
Sorbus arnoldiana	b
Sorbus cashmiriana	b
Sorbus decora	b
Sorbus hostii	b
Sorbus hupehensis	b
Sorbus thibetica	b
Sparganium	w
Spargel	1j
Spartium	v
Spielgarten	
Spiraea albiflora	h1
Spiraea arguta	h1
Spiraea bumalda	h1
Spiraea canescens	h1
Spiraea fritschiana	h1
Spiraea nipponica	h1
Spiraea tomentosa	h1
Spiraea wilsonii	h1
Stachys	v
Staphylea	
Statice	v
Steingarten	
Stephanandra	h2
Strandvolleyballveld	
Stranvaesia	h2
Styrax	
sumpfgarten	
Südafrikanischer Garten	
Symphoricarpos	h2
Syringa amurnsis	h2
Syringa persica	h2
Syringa prestoniae	h2
Syringa swegiflexa	h2
Syringa fulgaris	h2
Tagetus patula	1j
Tamarix odessana	h2
Tamarix pentandra	h2
Tamarix tetrandra	h2
Taxodium distichum	c
Taxodium nutans	c
Taxus baccata	c/s
Taxus cuspidata	c
Taxus media	c
Teucrium	v
Thalictrum	v
Thuja occidentalis	c
Thuja orientalis	c/s
Thuja plicata	c
Thujopsis	c
Thymus citriodorus	v
Thymus serpyllum	v
Tiarella	v
Tiergarten	
Tilia americana 'Nova'	b/s
Tilia euchlora	b
Trampolinfeld	
Tradescantia	v
Tritoma	v
Trollius	v
Tsuga canadensis	c
Tsuga heterophilla	c
Tulipa ' Ancilla	bk
Tulipa 'Ballade'	bk
Tulipa 'Monta Carlo'	bk
Tulipa 'Oranje Nassau'	bk
Tulipa 'Plaisir'	bk
Tulipa 'Princes Irene'	bk
Tulipa 'Red Rid. Hood'	bk
Typha	w
Ulex europaeus	b
Ulmus carpinifolia	b
Ulmus elegantissima	b
Ulmus glabra	b
Ulmus hollandica	b
Vaccinium corymbosum	h2
Verbascum	v
Veronica longifolia	v
Veronica prostrata	v
Veronica spicata	v
Veronica teucrium	v
Viburnum betulifolium	h1
Viburnum bodnantense	h1
Viburnum bracteatum	h1
Viburnum burkwoodii	h1
Viburnum carlesii	h1
Viburnum henryi	h1
Viburnum lentag	h1
Vuburnum plicatum	h1
Viburnum rhytidocarpum	h1
Viburnum rhytidophyllum	h1
Viburnum sieboldii	h1
Viburnum utile	h1
Vinca major	h1
Vinca minor	h1
Viola	v
Viola	1j
Vitex	h2
Vitis	klpl
Viscaria	v
Waldsteinia	v
Weigelia florida	h2
Weigelia venusta	h2
Weizen	1j
Wisteria	klpl
Wüstengarten	
Yucca	v
Zantedeschia aethiop.	bk
Zantedeschia elliottia.	bk
Zantedeschia rehmannii	bk
Zelkova serrata	b
Zen garten	
Zenobia pulverulenta	h2
Zuckerrübe	1j

A-Z

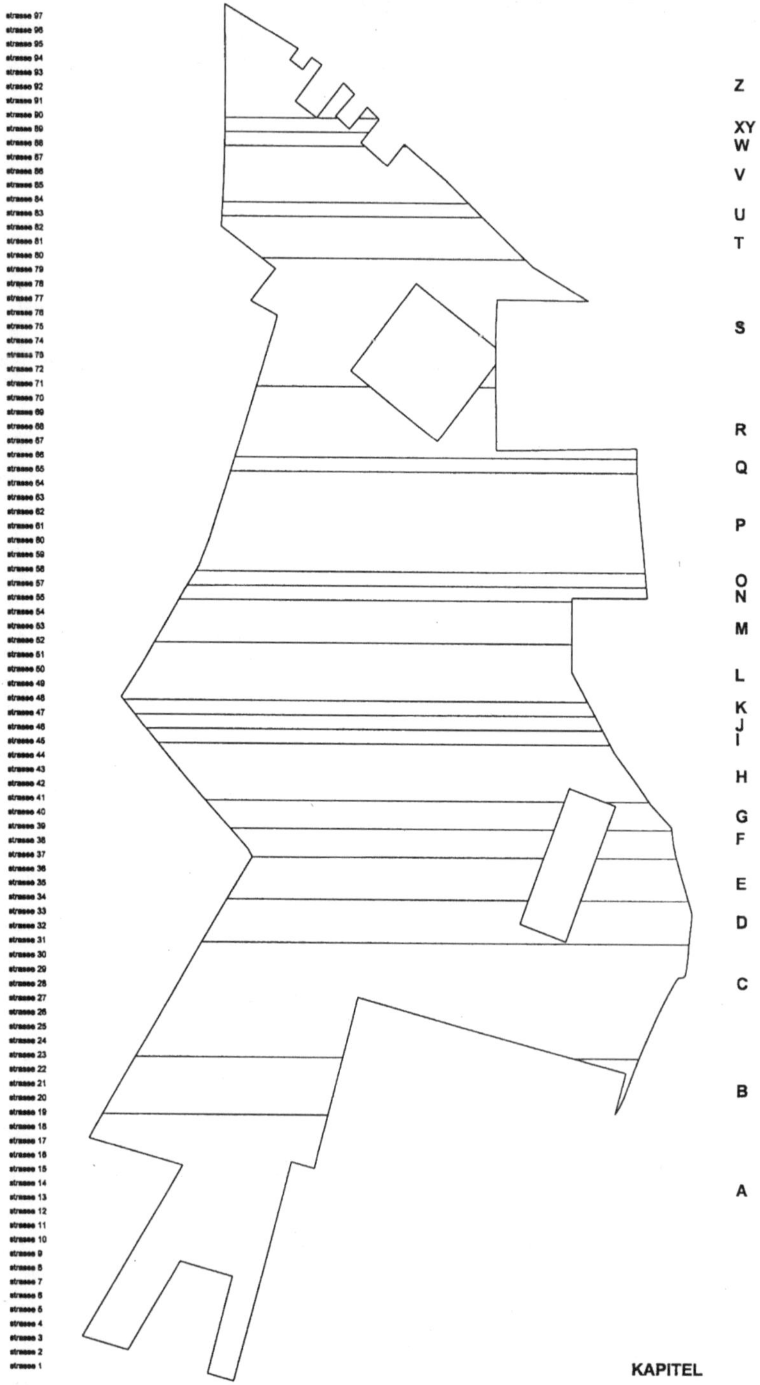

strasse 97
strasse 96
strasse 95
strasse 94
strasse 93
strasse 92
strasse 91
strasse 90
strasse 89
strasse 88
strasse 87
strasse 86
strasse 85
strasse 84
strasse 83
strasse 82
strasse 81
strasse 80
strasse 79
strasse 78
strasse 77
strasse 76
strasse 75
strasse 74
strasse 73
strasse 72
strasse 71
strasse 70
strasse 69
strasse 68
strasse 67
strasse 66
strasse 65
strasse 64
strasse 63
strasse 62
strasse 61
strasse 60
strasse 59
strasse 58
strasse 57
strasse 55
strasse 54
strasse 53
strasse 52
strasse 51
strasse 50
strasse 49
strasse 48
strasse 47
strasse 46
strasse 45
strasse 44
strasse 43
strasse 42
strasse 41
strasse 40
strasse 39
strasse 38
strasse 37
strasse 36
strasse 35
strasse 34
strasse 33
strasse 32
strasse 31
strasse 30
strasse 29
strasse 28
strasse 27
strasse 26
strasse 25
strasse 24
strasse 23
strasse 22
strasse 21
strasse 20
strasse 19
strasse 18
strasse 17
strasse 16
strasse 15
strasse 14
strasse 13
strasse 12
strasse 11
strasse 10
strasse 9
strasse 8
strasse 7
strasse 6
strasse 5
strasse 4
strasse 3
strasse 2
strasse 1
Z
XY
W
V
U
T
S
R
Q
P
O
N
M
L
K
J
I
H
G
F
E
D
C
B
A
KAPITEL

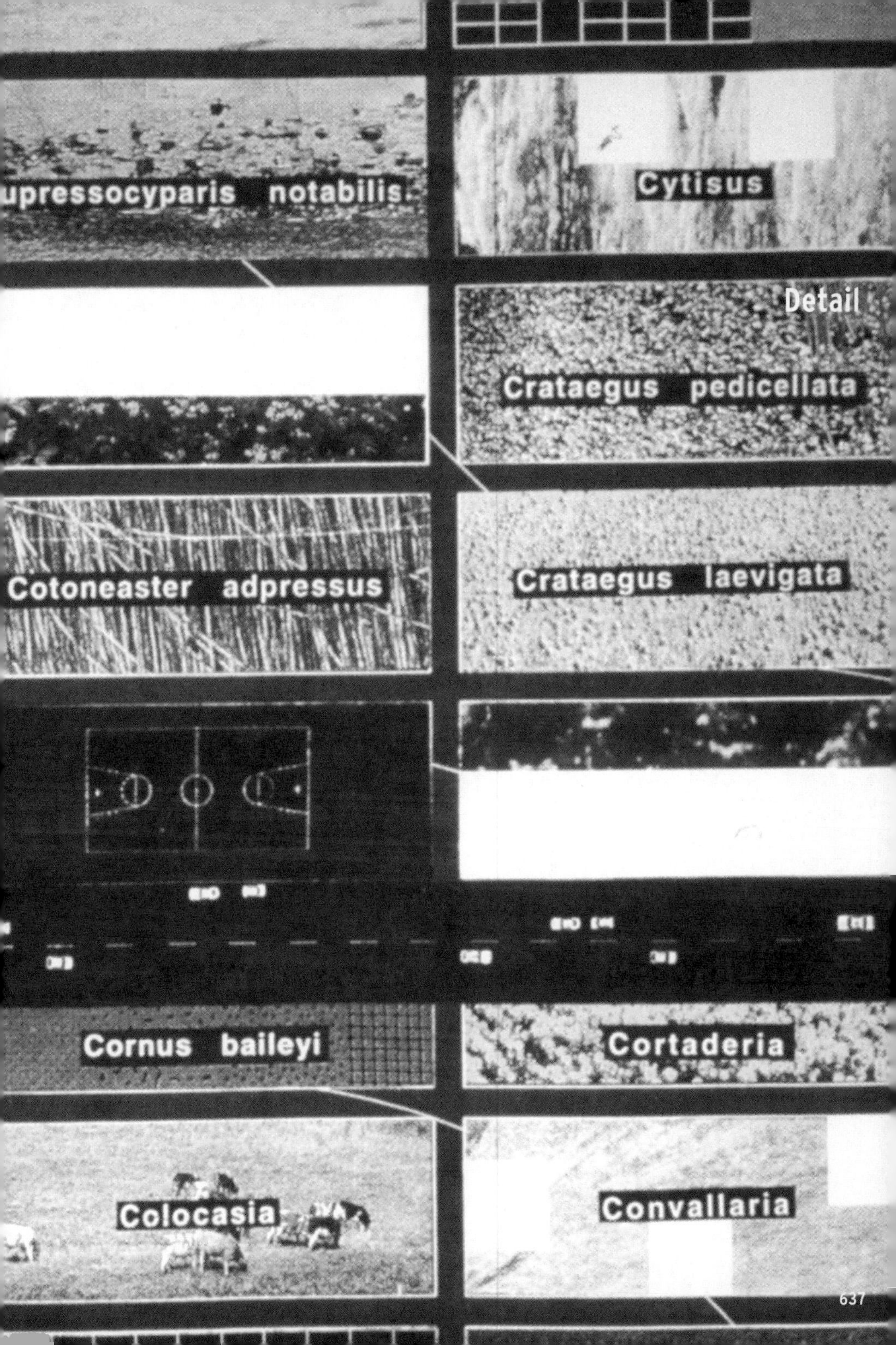

upressocyparis notabilis
Cytisus
Detail
Crataegus pedicellata
Cotoneaster adpressus
Crataegus laevigata
Cornus baileyi
Cortaderia
Colocasia
Convallaria

Programmatical exchange

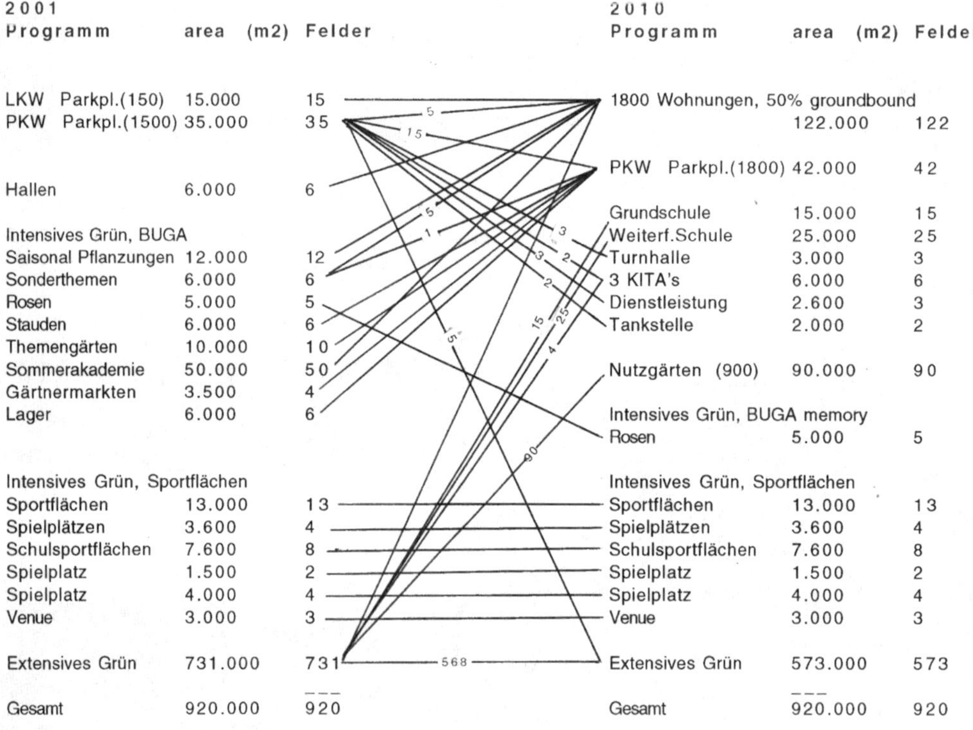

2001
Programm area (m2) Felder
LKW Parkpl.(150) 15.000 15
PKW Parkpl.(1500) 35.000 35
Hallen 6.000 6
Intensives Grün, BUGA
Saisonal Pflanzungen 12.000 12
Sonderthemen 6.000 6
Rosen 5.000 5
Stauden 6.000 6
Themengärten 10.000 10
Sommerakademie 50.000 50
Gärtnermarkten 3.500 4
Lager 6.000 6
Intensives Grün, Sportflächen
Sportflächen 13.000 13
Spielplätzen 3.600 4
Schulsportflächen 7.600 8
Spielplatz 1.500 2
Spielplatz 4.000 4
Venue 3.000 3
Extensives Grün 731.000 731
Gesamt 920.000 920
2010
Programm area (m2) Felder
1800 Wohnungen, 50% groundbound
122.000 122
PKW Parkpl.(1800) 42.000 42
Grundschule 15.000 15
Weiterf.Schule 25.000 25
Turnhalle 3.000 3
3 KITA's 6.000 6
Dienstleistung 2.600 3
Tankstelle 2.000 2
Nutzgärten (900) 90.000 90
Intensives Grün, BUGA memory
Rosen 5.000 5
Intensives Grün, Sportflächen
Sportflächen 13.000 13
Spielplätzen 3.600 4
Schulsportflächen 7.600 8
Spielplatz 1.500 2
Spielplatz 4.000 4
Venue 3.000 3
Extensives Grün 573.000 573
Gesamt 920.000 920
568

Park and neighbourhood

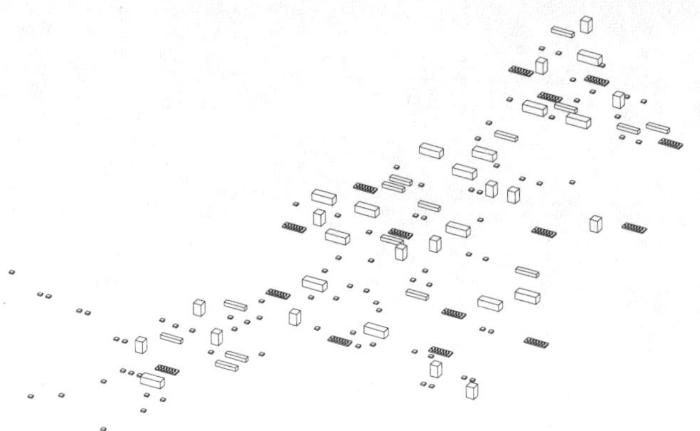

housing 2005

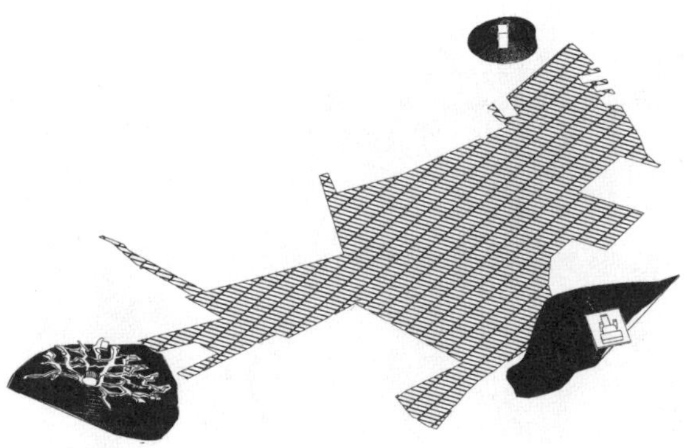

buga 2001

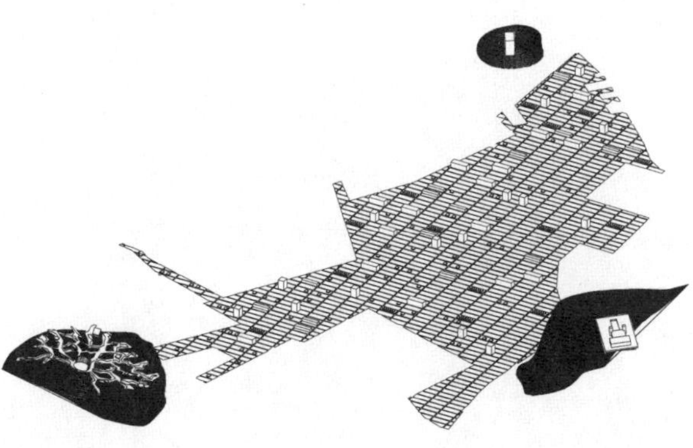

park and neighbourhood 2005

Housing

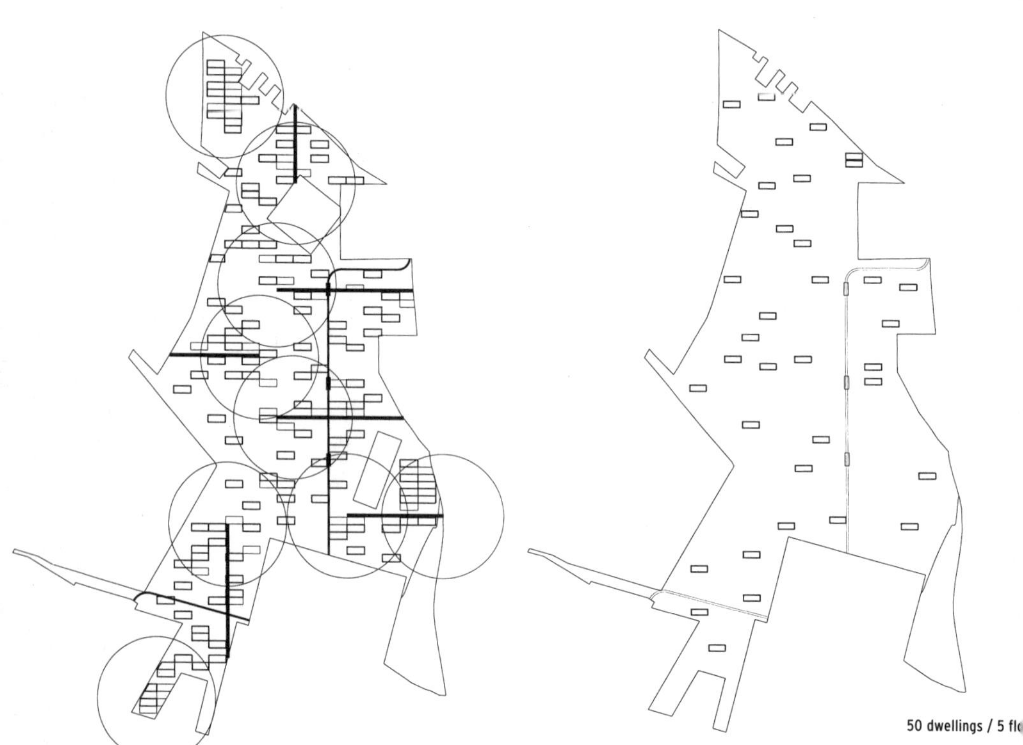

access

100% apartments

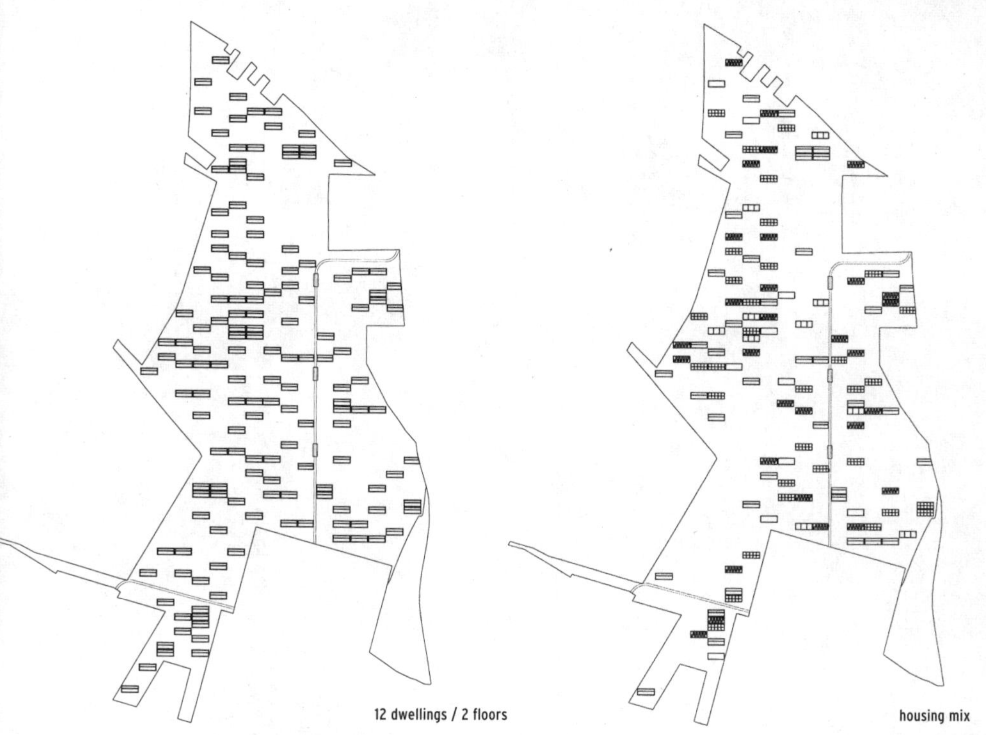

100% row houses

mix

Plan

Aerial view

Hill view

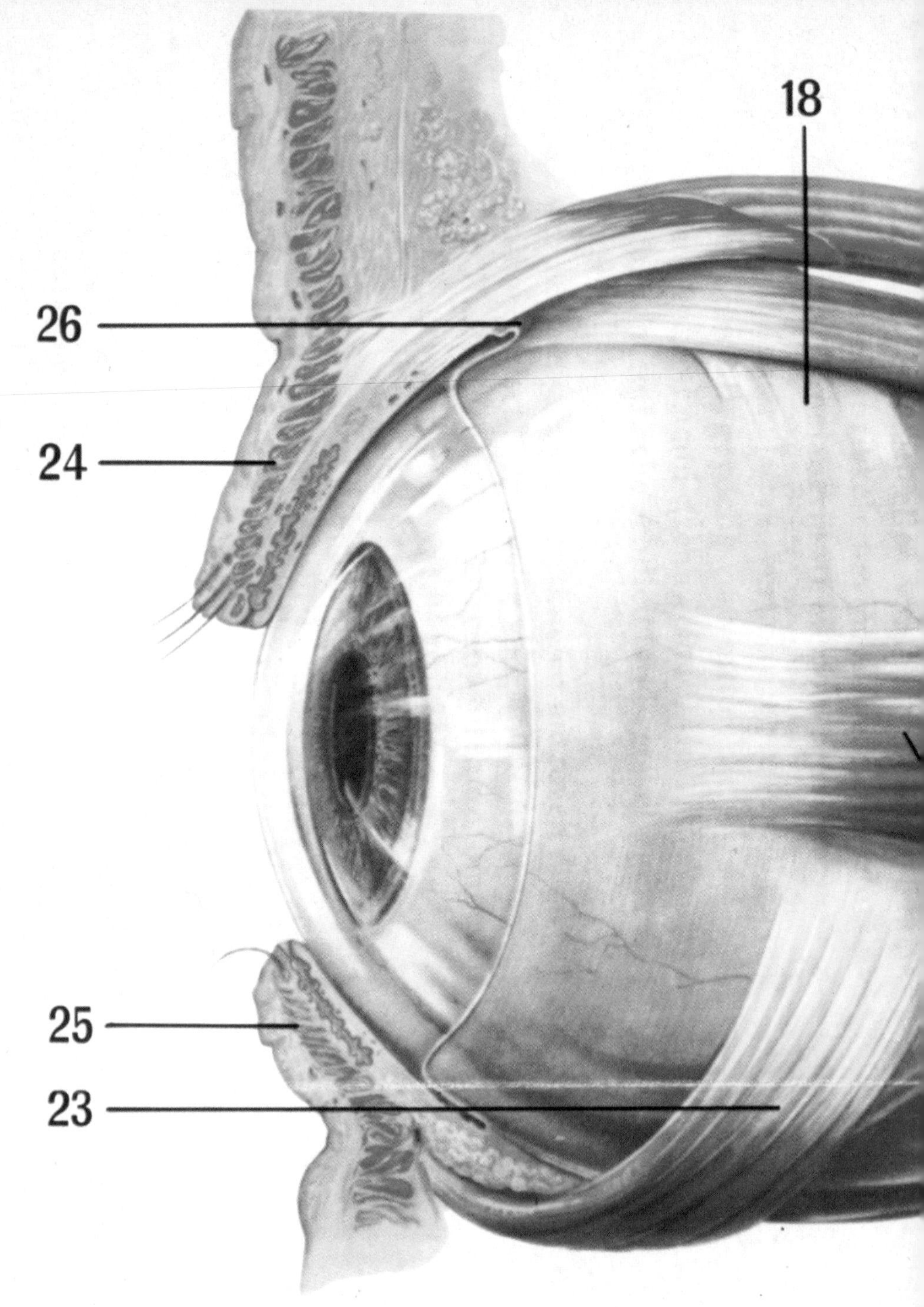
18
26
24
25
23

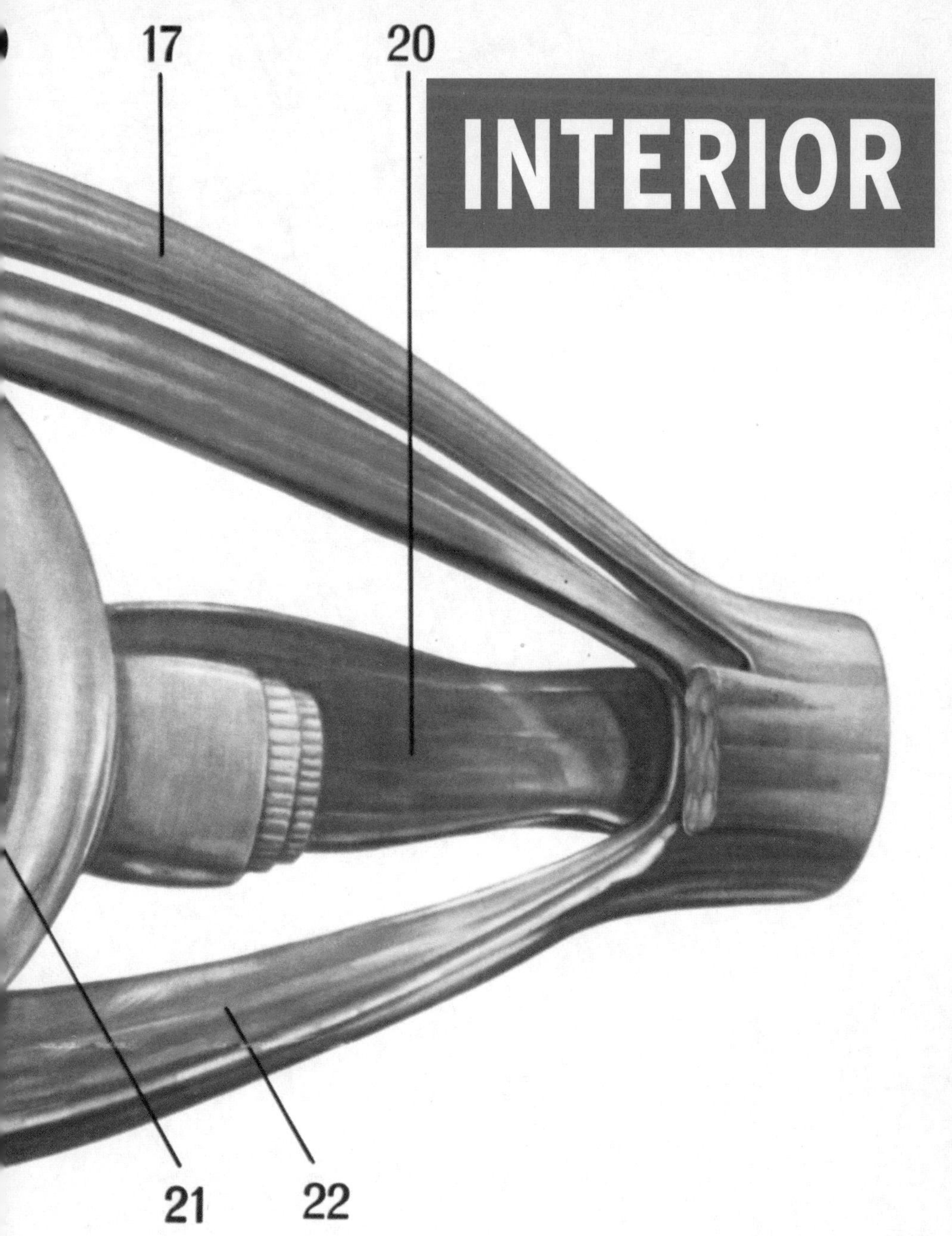
17
20
INTERIOR
21
22

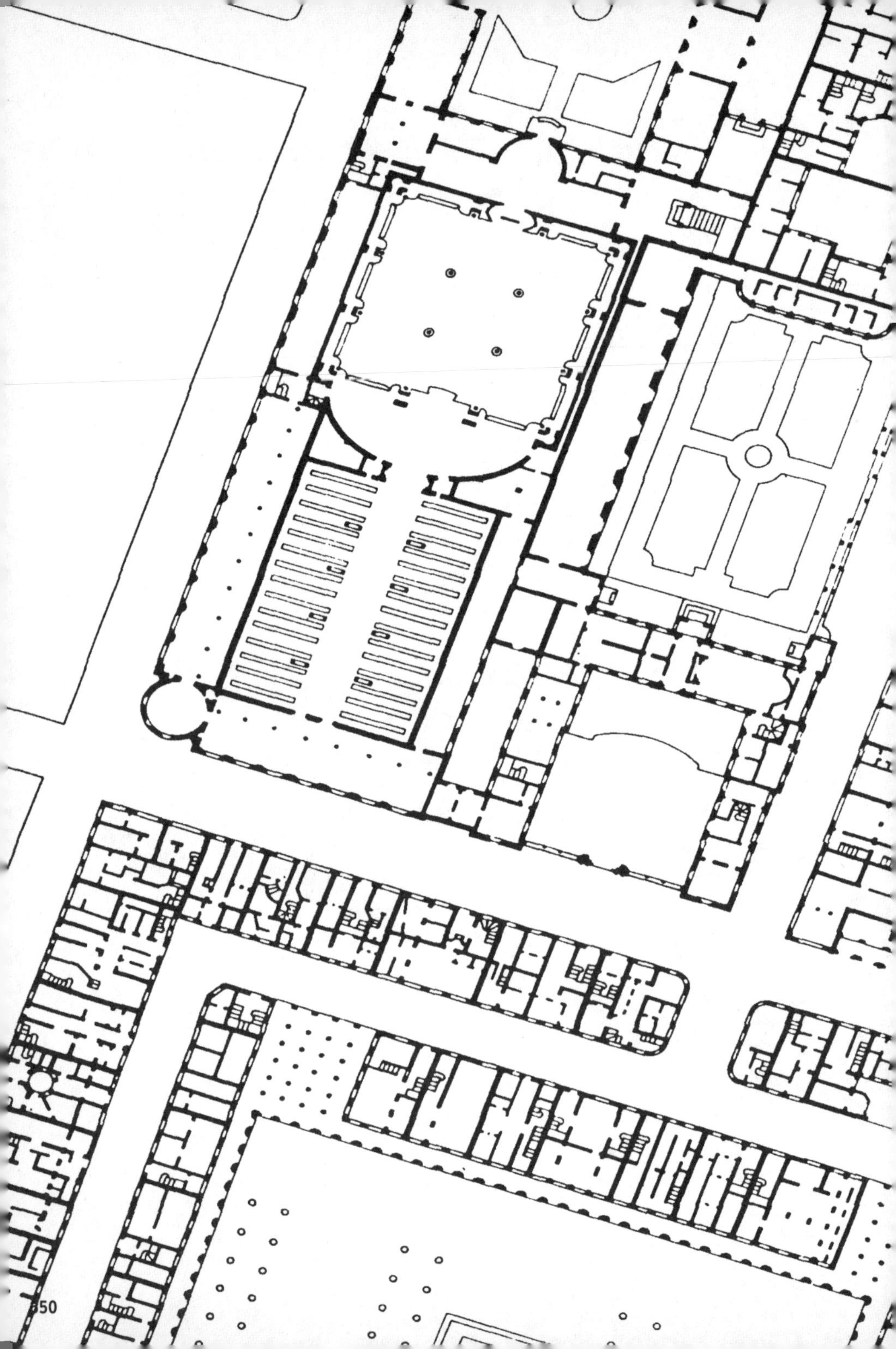

The continuous interior

Text

1996

Winy Maas

Increasingly, buildings are being placed in closer proximity, so that the one interior is literally touching the other. Under these circumstances, the reduced public space in between is subjected to a more focused attention. It has been rescued in the last decades by more and more 'design'. The public space has consequently lost its innocence and its freedom. It has been 'colonized' as a part of our built environment, itself becoming a sort of interior. - How are we to work within these constraints? Does the notion of the street and the plaza still exist? Or has everything become street or plaza? - This mix of the private with the public is emphasized by our behaviour nowadays. Personal declarations of love are shown on television, private phone calls are held on zebra crossings, homeless people live on the pavements, personal identification numbers are everywhere. - In this situation, public space ceases to exist. It appears as a 'sea' of possible meetings or - articulated by confessions, sermons, advertisements, readings, voices - a continuum of 'interiors'. - The world appears as one interior, as a fluid of information. A moving melting plasma as a contemporary variant on Nolli's maps: 'Interior City'. This city cannot be studied or notated only in terms of shape or form, nor in terms of geometry or composition. In order to understand this massive plasma and to address or discuss its wide-ranging directions, we need to apply other scientific methods that come from worlds beyond architecture: social observation, statistics, psychology, organization analyses and so forth.

1001. INSERT (34 Sek.)
Eine Hand, die auf ein Blatt
Papier schreibt:

Als das Kind Kind war,
wusste es nicht,
dass es Kind war,
alles war ihm beseelt,

ABBLENDE

DAMIELS STIMME:
Als das Kind Kind war,
ging es mit hängenden Armen,
wollte, der Bach sei ein Fluß,
der Fluß sei ein Strom
und diese Pfütze das Meer.
Als das Kind Kind war,
wußte es nicht, daß es Kind war,
alles war ihm beseelt,
und alle Seelen waren eins.
Als das Kind Kind war,
hatte es von nichts eine Meinung,
hatte keine Gewohnheit,
saß oft im Schneidersitz,
lief aus dem Stand,
hatte einen Wirbel im Haar
und machte kein Gesicht beim Fotografieren.

1002. TITELSEQUENZ (1 Min. 16 Sek.)
ROAD MOVIES BERLIN
und
ARGOS FILMS PARIS
zeigen

als
DEUTSCH-FRANZÖSISCHE
GEMEINSCHAFTS-PRODUKTION

EINEN FILM
von
WIM WENDERS

mit
BRUNO GANZ
SOLVEIG DOMMARTIN
OTTO SANDER
CURT BOIS
und als Gast
PETER FALK

Kamera
HENRI ALEKAN

Art Direction
HEIDI LÜDI SFK

Regie-
assistenz
CLAIRE DENIS

Schnitt
PETER PRZYGODDA

Musik
JÜRGEN KNIEPER

Herstellungs-
leitung
INGRID WINDISCH

Drehbuch
WIM WENDERS
in Zusammenarbeit mit
PETER HANDKE

DER HIMMEL
ÜBER BERLIN

4

Darunter blendet auf:
1003. TOTAL, außen, tags (8 Sek.)
Ein Wolkenhimmel
ÜBERBLENDUNG

1004. INSERT (2 Sek.)
Ein Auge
ÜBERBLENDUNG

1005. TOTAL, außen, tags (20 Sek.)
(Flugaufnahme) Die Stadt aus der Vogelperspektive
ÜBERBLENDUNG

1006. HALBTOTAL, außen, tags (8 Sek.)
Der Engel Damiel, auf dem offenen Turm der Gedächtniskirche

1007. TOTAL, außen, tags (5 Sek.)
Von oben gesehen: Fußgänger, die die Straße überqueren. Ein Kind bleibt mitten auf der Straße stehen und schaut hoch.

STIMMENGEMURMEL, aus dem aber nichts Deutlic[h] herauszuhören ist.

1008. TOTAL, außen, tags (3 Sek.)
Der Turm der Gedächtniskirche aus der Sicht des Kindes. Obenauf die Figur des Engels

1009. HALBTOTAL, außen, tags (3 Sek.)
Das kleine Mädchen, das nach oben schaut, näher als in 1007.

1010. HALBTOTAL, außen, tags (5 Sek.)
Zwei Mädchen in einem Bus.
Das eine sieht nach oben und stößt dann das vor ihr sitzende an. Beide schauen hoch. Der Bus fährt aus dem Bild.

MÄDCHEN: Guck mal!

1011. TOTAL, außen, tags (8 Sek.)
(Fahraufnahme) Die Kamera entfernt sich von der Gedächtniskirche. Oben erkennt man nach wie vor klein die Gestalt des Engels, der herunterblickt.
ÜBERBLENDUNG

2. INSERT (1 Sek.)
Flügelschlag
RBLENDUNG

3. TOTAL bis HALBNAH, außen, tags (7 Sek.)
anbewegung) Aus größerer Höhe sinkt die
nera herab auf die Augenhöhe eines jungen
nnes, der mit seinem Kind in einem Tragesack
dem Rücken spazierengeht. Das Kleinkind
aut hoch in den Himmel:

Aus dem Stimmengewirr löst sich eine einzelne Stimme heraus:

GEDANKENSTIMME MANN MIT BABY:
Die Labsal, den Kopf zu heben zum Licht hier draußen,
im Freien, die Labsal
der von der Sonne

4. TOTAL, außen, tags (8 Sek.)
Vogel im wolkenlosen Himmel

durchleuchteten
Farben der Augen der Menschen.

5. HALBTOTAL, außen, tags (5 Sek.)
allelfahrt) Eine Frau auf einem Fahrrad, auf
Kindersitz hinter ihr ein kleines Mädchen, das
nfalls zum Himmel hochschaut.

GEDANKENSTIMME FRAU AUF DEM FAHRRAD:
Endlich verrückt,
endlich nicht mehr allein.
Endlich verrückt,
endlich erlöst.
Endlich verrückt,

1016. TOTAL, außen, tags (4 Sek.)
Ein Flugzeug in der Luft, aus der Sicht des Kindes

endlich ruhig.
Endlich ein Narr,
endlich ein inneres Licht.

27. TOTAL, außen, tags (42 Sek.)
lugaufnahme) aus der heraus der Berliner
nkturm auftaucht. Nach einem Halbkreis um
n Funkturm überfliegt die Kamera das Messe-
lände und nähert sich einer Häuserzeile von
tbauten auf der anderen Seite der Stadtautobahn.

MONTAGE VON RADIOSTIMMEN: ... brings you updates throughout the weekend, AFN, Berlin ... entertainment ... RIAS Berlin, eine freie Stimme der freien Welt ... from the wires of the AP and UPI ... des Erich Honnecker, der am Vormittag ... an den Kontrollpunkten starker Ausreiseverkehr ...

28. TOTAL bis HALBNAH, innen, tags (21 Sek.)
amerafahrt zurück und Schwenk) Auf das Messe-
lände und die Stadtautobahn schauend, fährt
e Kamera rückwärts »durch das Fenster« in
e Altbauwohnung. Hinter einem Sofa sitzt ein
nge, der fernsieht. Eine blinde Frau richtet sich
f, als ob sie die Anwesenheit des Engels
r Kamera) spürte.

GEDANKENSTIMME JUNGE VOR FERNSEHER:
Jetzt warten wir schon eine Stunde! Immer noch nichts Vernünftiges im Fernsehen.
GEDANKENSTIMME BLINDE FRAU:
Ihr habt zu viele Farben, um euch in der Zeit auszukennen. Ihr stolpert über eure Farben und seid nie pünktlich.

29. HALBNAH, innen, tags (11 Sek.)
amerafahrt zurück) Von einem Kofferradio auf
m Fensterbrett fährt die Kamera zurück in einen
aum, in dem eine Frau damit beschäftigt ist, eine
and abzuschleifen. Sie hält in der Arbeit inne
d betrachtet ihr neues Reich.

GEDANKENSTIMME FRAU:
Das ist noch kleiner, als ich am Anfang dachte. Wie kriege ich alles rein? Waschmaschine, Kühlschrank ... Ach! ich muß mir was einfallen lassen.

30. TOTAL bis HALBNAH, innen, tags (36 Sek.)
n junger Mann in einem Trenchcoat, eine Reise-
che in der Hand, tritt in einen Raum, das
hnzimmer seiner verstorbenen Mutter. Auf
m Boden sind Briefe und Photos ausgebreitet,
es säuberlich in Kästen und Umschlägen geord-
t. Der junge Mann durchquert den Raum und
zt sich in einen Sessel. Die Kamera schwenkt auf
en Flügel im Vordergrund, auf dem Photos
sgebreitet liegen, darunter auch ein Kinderbild
s Mannes.

GEDANKENSTIMME »HEIMKEHRER«:
Es riecht noch so ... nur staubiger ... Hat sie alles gesammelt ... Rabattmarken, Ansichtskarten, U-Bahn-Tickets.
Nie was weggeworfen, konnte sie nicht ... Mutter! Meine Mutter ... war sie nie. Mein Vater, mein Vater war mein Vater. Sie ist tot. Keine Träne, kein Schmerz ... Vielleicht später.
Gott! Bin ich schon alt! Meine Schwester kommt ... Ich muß weg hier, ganz schnell. Raus hier!

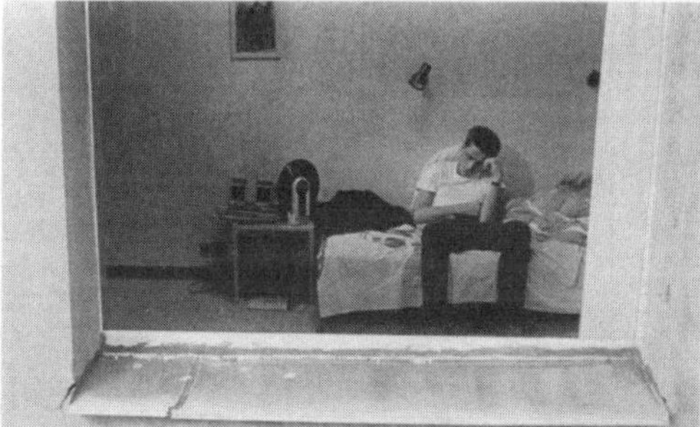

1031. HALBNAH bis TOTAL bis HALBTOTAL, außen, innen, tags (36 Sek.)
(Kamerafahrt und Schwenk) Die junge Frau, die eben die Wand abgeschleift hat, steht jetzt an eine Leiter gelehnt und raucht. Die Kamera fährt rückwärts aus dem Fenster heraus in den Hinterhof und schwenkt nach unten, wo ein paar Kinder Fangen spielen. Dann schwenkt sie wieder hoch und fährt auf ein Fenster im gegenüberliegenden Haus zu. Aus dem Zimmer dringt laute Musik. Ein junger Mann sitzt auf der Kante seines Bettes und starrt vor sich hin.

SPIELENDES KIND: Mich kriegst du nicht!
GEDANKENSTIMME JUNGER MANN AUF BETTKANTE:
Sie hat dich nie geliebt. Und du tust auch nur so als ob! Sei doch froh, daß sie dich vergessen haben. Endlich bist du frei! »Ich möchte auf der Stelle sterben und dann immer weiterleben«, hat sie gesagt ...

1032. HALBNAH bis NAH, innen, tags (34 Sek.)
(Kamerafahrt und Schwenk) Von einer Tür mit einem Schild RUHE, durch die die laute Musik des jungen Mannes herausschallt, fährt die Kamera zurück und schwenkt über einen dunklen Raum, in dem ein älterer Mann vor dem Fernseher sitzt und grübelt. Die Kamera hält schließlich genau in der Blickachse des Alten an, der in die Kamera hineinschaut wie in den Fernseher.

GEDANKENSTIMME GROSSVATER:
Was soll det bloß mit dem Jungen werden? Der hat nur die Musik im Kopf. Also nein, det halt ich nicht mehr aus. Was will der denn nun noch? Hab ich ihm schon eine Gitarre gekauft. Will er noch ein Schlagzeug? Ein Geld kostet det alles, nee! Langsam wird det mir zu ville, ick weeß nich. Kommt der nie zur Vernunft? Nee, also, jetzt langt mir det.

1033. INSERT (3 Sek.)
Der Fernseher. Großaufnahme einer Frau, die ihr Geld zählt.

FRAU IM FERNSEHER: Und als ich dann das Wechselgeld in der Hand hatte, habe ich mir wirklich jedes Stück ganz genau angesehen, ob es ein Markstück, ein Zehner oder ein Fünfer war ...

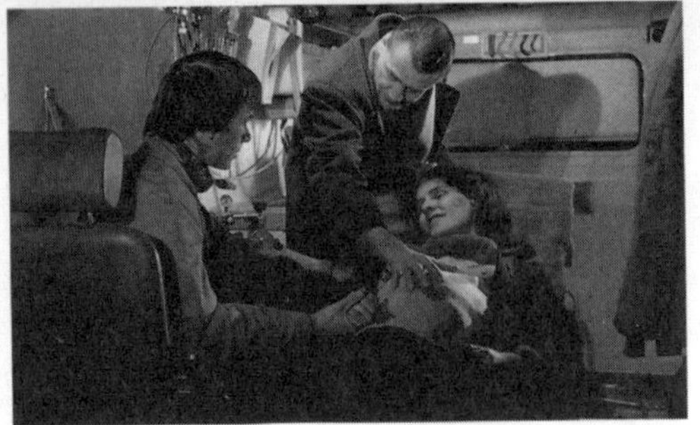

1042. TOTAL, außen, tags (10 Sek.)
(Flugaufnahme) In einem großen Bogen fliegt die Kamera über die Häuserzeile, die wir eben durchquert haben, und nähert sich von oben langsam dem Krankenwagen, der mit Blaulicht und Martinshorn auf der Stadtautobahn fährt.
ÜBERBLENDUNG

der Ich bin, nicht mehr der,
der Ich bin, sein werde.
EIN BABYSCHREIEN

1043. HALBNAH bis NAH, innen, tags (20 Sek.)
(Kamerafahrt) Im Inneren des Krankenwagens: auf der Bahre liegt eine junge Frau in den Wehen. Ihr Mann sitzt neben ihr und hält ihre Hand. Die Kamera fährt vor, bis die Rundung des Bauches das Bild füllt. Damiels Hand legt sich auf die Bauchkuppel. Die Kamera fährt zurück: Damiel steht zwischen dem Mann und seiner Frau, deren Schmerzen jetzt nachlassen und die ihrem Mann zulächelt.

GEDANKENSTIMME WERDENDER VATER:
Hoffentlich hast du es bald, Lotte. Kann überhaupt nicht helfen. Am liebsten hätte ich selber die Schmerzen. Denk daran, bald ist es soweit. Jetzt haben wir es gleich, Lotte. Bald haben wir's durchgestanden.

GEDANKENSTIMME SCHWANGERE FRAU:
Ich muß im Bauch atmen! Das Kind braucht den Sauerstoff! Ganz tief, ganz tief im Bauch atmen! Oh, tut das weh! Ah ja! Jetzt ist es gleich vorbei. Jetzt haben wir es gleich geschafft. Ja, jetzt läßt es nach. Echt, Würmchen, ich freue mich so auf dich. Ich bin ja so gespannt, wie du aussiehst.

1044. HALBTOTAL, außen, tags (3 Sek.)
(Fahraufnahme) Der Krankenwagen auf der Stadtautobahn, von vorn.

1045. HALBNAH, außen, tags (4 Sek.)
(Parallelfahrt) Neben einem Volkswagen Cabriolet: Die Frau auf dem Beifahrersitz schlägt auf den Mann am Steuer ein, dann bricht sie schluchzend an seiner Schulter zusammen.

GEDANKENSTIMME MANN AM STEUER:
Du wirst noch mal zugrunde gehen an den Frauen

WEINENDE FRAU: Du Scheißkerl, du!

1046. HALBNAH, außen, tags (5 Sek.)
(Parallelfahrt) Neben einem Mercedes: Am Steuer eine ältere Dame, neben ihr auf dem Beifahrersitz ein große schwarze Dogge.

GEDANKENSTIMME FRAU MIT HUND:
Ich glaube, Blacky, jetzt habe ich mich verfahren. W wollen doch zum Waldfriedhof. Da waren wir scho lange nicht mehr, Blacky, weißt du noch?

1047. HALBNAH, außen, tags (6 Sek.)
(Parallelfahrt) Langsam einen anderen Mercedes überholend: Eine türkische Familie, drei Kinder und drei Erwachsene.

TÜRKISCHER VATER: Arabada sakın boynunuzu düsareye cıkarmayın dogru oturun.

1048. HALBNAH, innen, tags (19 Sek.)
(Kamerafahrt) Damiel auf dem Beifahrersitz eines offenen Wagens, eines BMW-Cabriolet, der in einer Verkaufshalle ausgestellt ist. Die Kamera sieht ihn zunächst nur undeutlich hinter den auf der Windschutzscheibe reflektierenden Neonlichtern, dann deutlicher, als sie in einem Viertelkreis um den Wagen herumfährt und Damiel schließlich im Profil von der Seite zeigt. Er schließt die Augen.

1049. HALBNAH, innen, tags (10 Sek.)
(Kamerafahrt) Eine ähnliche Bewegung um die Windschutzscheibe auf der anderen Seite. Wir entdecken Cassiel. Cassiel zieht sein Notizbuch hervor.

DAMIEL (OFF): Und?

1050. HALBTOTAL, innen, tags (33 Sek.)
Beide Engel, von vorn durch die Windschutzscheibe gesehen. Cassiel liest aus seinem Notizbuch vor.

CASSIEL: Sonnenaufgang 7.22; Sonnenuntergang 16.28; Mondaufgang 19.04; Monduntergang, Wasserstand von Havel und Spree ... Vor zwanzig Jahren stürzte ein sowjetischer Düsenjäger nahe der Spandauer Heerstraße in den Stössensee.
Vor fünfzig Jahren war ...
DAMIEL: ... die Olympiade.
CASSIEL: Vor zweihundert Jahren überflog Nicolas François Blanchard die Stadt in einem Heißluftballon.
DAMIEL: Das haben die Flüchtlinge neulich auch getan.
CASSIEL: Und heute ...

Damiel weist mit dem Finger nach draußen ...

1051. TOTAL, außen, tags (7 Sek.)
[illegible] Schaufenster umarmt sich ein Liebespaar.

In der Lilienthaler Chaussee ist einer gegangen, ist dann immer langsamer geworden und hat dann über die Schulter ins Leere geschaut ...

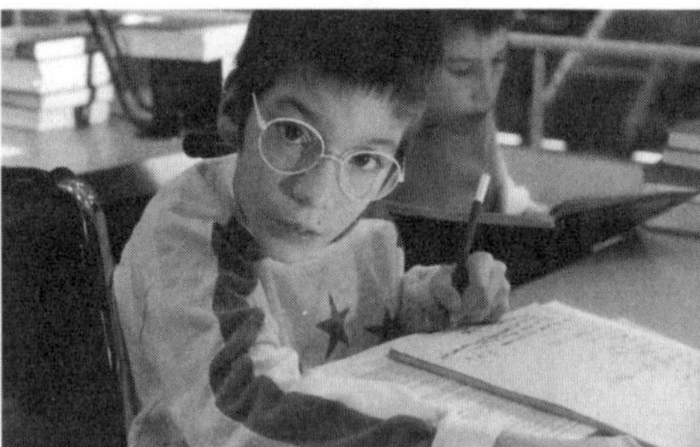

1074. NAH, innen, tags (4 Sek.)
Der Junge schaut auf und blickt erstaunt in die Kamera.

1075. NAH, innen, tags (6 Sek.)
Damiel lächelt dem Jungen zu, dann schaut er ...

falls überhaupt eine existiert, etwa:
$-\frac{a}{2} \ldots$
$+ \sqrt{\frac{a^2}{4}} - b.$

1076. HALBTOTAL, innen, tags (8 Sek.)
... zu dem Tisch vor ihm, an dem gerade ein Student seinen Platz wieder einnimmt. Der freundliche Engel, der dort saß, ist aufgestanden und wendet sich einer anderen Leserin zu.

1077. TOTAL bis HALBNAH bis HALBTOTAL innen, tags (39 Sek.)
Damiel geht weiter durch die Staatsbibliothek. Zwei männliche Engel, die auf einer Brüstung sitzen, grüßen ihn. Die Kamera verläßt Damiel und schwenkt über die Reihen von Lesenden auf der anderen Seite der Empore, die wir in zwei Etagen übereinander sehen können. Dann gleitet der Blick wieder herunter über die Lesenden im Vordergrund. Ein weiterer weiblicher Engel grüßt lächelnd in die Kamera.

So einfach ist das.
ZEHNTER LESENDER:
Bereschit bara elohim et ha'aretz . Weha'aretz hajet tohuwawohü.
ELFTE LESENDE:
Ich liebte dich: vielleicht ist noch bis heute / In mei Brust dies Feuer nicht verglüht; / Doch will ich nic daß sie dein Schmerz erneute – / Nichts soll fortan erregen dein Gemüt! / Ich liebte dich mit hoffnung losem Schweigen, /Bald schüchtern, bald durch Eif sucht betrübt; / Ich liebte dich so innig, so treueige Gott gebe, daß ein andrer dich so liebt!
ZWÖLFTER LESENDER:
Temple crouched against the door, clutching her co about her. She could hear him back there in one of stalls. She opened the door and peered out, at the h in the bright May sunshine, the sabbath peace, and thought about the girls and men leaving the dormit

in their new spring clothes strolling along the shaded streets toward the cool, unhurried sound of bells. She lifted her foot and examined the soiled sole of her stokking, brushing at it with her palm, then at the other one.

DREIZEHNTER LESENDER:
Draußen im Garten schlüpfte ein Vogel, däumlingshaft, in den finsteren, menschhohen Eibenkegel und kam aus dem Dickicht nicht wieder hervor. Das Gebrumm der einmotorigen Flugzeuge über der Landschaft erinnerte an Alaska, und auch das sonore Tuten der Züge, die in einem Bogen die Stadt umkurvten, kam wie aus einem wasserreichen Land. Deutlich ließ sich am Horizont momentlang das Aufrumpeln der Räder auf eine Gleisbrücke hören, und zugleich kratzte sich am Fuß der Treppe das Haustier und erklirrte der Kühlschrank in der Speisekammer. Der Schriftsteller begoß, schon zum zweiten Mal an diesem Tag, die Pflanzen im Flur, welche diesem, zusammen mit der Glaswand, den Anschein eines Gewächshauses gaben, fütterte noch einmal die Katze und putzte zuletzt sämtliche Türklinken. Es drängte ihn, gleichwem einen Brief zu schreiben, aber nicht daheim, sondern später, irgendwo in der Stadt.

VIERZEHNTER LESENDER:
Nächstens will ich mit dem Engel reden,
ob er meine Augen anerkennt.
Wenn er plötzlich fragte: Schaust du Eden?
Und ich müßte sagen: Eden brennt
Meinen Mund will ich zu ihm erheben,
hart wie einer, welcher nicht begehrt.

Ein Greis bin ich
mit einer brüchigen Stimme
aber die Erzählung
hebt immer noch an
aus der Tiefe
und der leicht geöffnete Mund
wiederholt sie, so mächtig,
wie mühelos,
eine Liturgie,
bei der niemand eingeweiht
zu sein braucht,
wie die Wörter und Sätze
gemeint sind.

ENDE DES 1. AKTES

…0. HALBTOTAL, außen, tags (4 Sek.)
…merafahrt) Ein einzelner kleiner Junge, an die …nd gelehnt, der zu Damiel schaut und schüch… zurücklächelt.

…1. TOTAL bis HALBNAH bis TOTAL, außen, tags …Sek.)
…wenk und Kamerafahrt) Die Kinder alle im …tergrund, Damiel im Vordergrund schaut in …Luft nach einem vorüberfliegenden Flugzeug. … Kamera schwenkt von ihm fort und bewegt … durch den dunklen Tunnel der Toreinfahrt auf … Ausgang des Hinterhofes zu. Dort steht, in … Ferne, auf einem leeren Feld, ein Zirkuszelt. … Elefant wird gerade über den Platz geführt.
…RBLENDUNG

GEDANKENSTIMME EINSAMER JUNGE:
Ich bin so allein,
ist das nicht gemein?
Zu dreien,
das wäre fein.

Aber: ich bin ja trotzdem allein,
ist das nicht gemein?
Zu dreien,
das wär' fein!

VIERTER JUNGE: Tu mal deine Schnürsenkel richtig machen.
DRITTER JUNGE: Und dann ein ganzes Leben …
FÜNFTER JUNGE: Und vor fünf Jahren …
VIERTER JUNGE: Und sie lebten glücklich bis an ihr Leben …

1052. HALBTOTAL (wie 1050) (25 Sek.)
Cassiel liest weiter aus seinem Notizbuch vor.

Im Postamt 44 hat einer, der heute Schluß machen will, auf all seine Abschiedsbriefe Sondermarken geklebt, auf jede eine andere, und hat dann draußen auf dem Mariannenplatz mit einem amerikanischen Soldaten englisch geredet, zum ersten Mal seit seiner Schulzeit, und zwar fließend! … In der Strafanstalt Plötzensee hat ein Häftling, bevor er mit dem Kopf gegen die Wand gerannt ist, »Jetzt« gesagt.

1053. HALBNAH, innen, tags (12 Sek.)
Näher: die beiden Engel hinter der Windschutzscheibe.

An der U-Bahn-Station Zoo rief der Beamte statt des Stationsnamens plötzlich das »Feuerland« aus! …
DAMIEL: Schön!
CASSIEL: In den Rehbergen las ein alter Mann einem Kind aus der Odyssee vor,
und der kleine Zuhörer, der dabei ganz zu blinzeln aufhörte …
Und du, was hast du zu erzählen?

1054. TOTAL, außen, tags (7 Sek.)
Vor dem Schaufenster: ein Paar, das sehnsüchtig einen der ausgestellten Wagen betrachtet. Der Mann trägt ein in einen silbernen Anorak vermummtes Kind auf dem Arm.

1055. NAH, innen, tags (48 Sek.)
Damiel liest lustlos aus seinem Notizbuch vor, dann unterbricht er seinen Bericht.

DAMIEL: Eine Passantin, die mitten im Regen den Schirm zusammenklappte und sich naß werden ließ … Ein Schüler, der seinem Lehrer beschrieb, wie ein Farn aus der Erde wächst, und der staunende Lehrer … Eine Blinde, die nach ihrer Uhr tastete, als sie mich spürte … Es ist herrlich, nur geistig zu leben und Tag für Tag für die Ewigkeit von den Leuten rein, was geistig ist, zu bezeugen – aber manchmal wird mir meine ewige Geistesexistenz zuviel. Ich möchte dann nicht mehr so ewig drüberschweben, ich möchte ein Gewicht an mir spüren,

Certain American researchers have examined how often phobias and fears occurred in a specific area of the United States. All inhabitants of that area were asked if they had any 'normal' fears in their lives, or whether those fears were acute enough to warrant the term phobia. Here are the results of that investigation, supplemented with figures for the Netherlands.

Slight to substantial fear

		No. in NL	No. worldwide
Snakes	39%	5,850,000	1,560,000,000
Heights	31%	4,650,000	1,240,000,000
Thunderstorms	21%	3,150,000	840,000,000
Flying	20%	3,000,000	800,000,000
Injury	18%	2,700,000	720,000,000
Illness	17%	2,550,000	680,000,000
Death	16%	2,400,000	640,000,000
Confined spaces	12%	1,800,000	480,000,000

From Diagnostic and Statistical Manual of Mental Disorders, 4th impression, American Psychiatric Association, Washington DC 1994.

Phobias

		No. in NL	No. worldwide
Illness and injury	3.1%	465,000	124,000,000
Thunderstorms	1.3%	195,000	52,000,000
Animals	1.1%	165,000	44,000,000
Unfamiliar surroundings	0.6%	90,000	24,000,000
Death	0.5%	75,000	20,000,000
Crowds	0.4%	60,000	16,000,000
Heights	0.4%	60,000	16,000,000

From M. de Wolf and J. Hoevenaars, Met angst en beven, A. Donker, Rotterdam 1991.

Claustrophobia

Interview with Jac Hoevenaars, psychologist-psychotherapist

1996

Winy Maas

What is claustrophobia? Claustrophobia belongs among the group o specific phobias: fear of spiders, height, depth, flying, certain types o spaces. These fears occur in all cultures to an equal degree. I Indonesia there is just as great a percentage of people with a horro of snakes as there is in the Netherlands, although there are almost n poisonous snakes living here in the wild. There are a very small numbe of localities in the world where a phobia has been identified that i quite specific to that area. For instance, in Southeast Asia some me are afraid that their scrotum will shrivel up. This fear has never sprea to other areas and is an example of a phobia that has been isolated i one spot for centuries. Twelve per cent of the world populatio recognize claustrophobic tendencies in themselves. Only a fraction o this figure, one per cent, actually suffers from claustrophobia an seeks treatment. These are usually people afflicted with a combinatio of claustrophobia and agoraphobia. Claustrophobia is a fear tha occurs in confined spaces such as lifts, low cellars, waiting rooms examination rooms in hospitals, changing cubicles in clothes shops and caves. Claustrophobia often occurs in combination wit agoraphobia, the fear of large spaces. Claustrophobia unaccompanie by agoraphobia, when it occurs, usually does so in pubert Agoraphobia by contrast in found among among young people betwee twenty and thirty. Agoraphobia is currently defined as a fear of eithe empty spaces or social spaces, i.e. spaces full of people. The latte meaning has come down to us from the ancient Greeks, who define agoraphobia as the fear of speaking in public. All spaces experience as being unsafe are termed claustrophobic or agoraphobic spaces There are places where sufferers feel that they cannot count o getting help, or from which they couldn't escape if something scar morbid, deadly or threatening should happen. Thus they feel more i at ease in an express train than in one that stops at every station. deserted beach can likewise be experienced as threatening; after al there is no-one there to come to your aid. Examples of agoraphobi spaces include football stadiums and shopping centres. Cinemas ca also be claustrophobic and agoraphobic spaces. Obviously you ca leave them but not that easily. Agoraphobics or claustrophobic therefore prefer to sit at the open end of a row. Other potentia 'dangerous spaces' include the queues at the cash point in supermarket, and also motorways which you can't leave that easil either and where in principle everyone just keeps driving. Tunnels ar notorious places for causing attacks of agoraphobia or claustrophobia Take the case of a woman who when in a tunnel has the terrifying ide that she wouldn't be able to move in either direction should the ca have to stop. Following the traffic forwards wouldn't work, as her nerve has gone, and reversing out would be impossible due to the oncoming traffic behind her. She only feels safe again if she somehow manages to make it out of the tunnel. There at least she can pull in to the hard shoulder and recover her composure. People suffering from acute agoraphobia or claustrophobia feel safe only with the telephone close at hand, or another person. Some don't dare to leave the house, or even their room. When they visit the toilet, someone must accompany them. And then of course the door has to remain unlocked; imagine if the lock were to jam. When agoraphobics or claustrophobics have a panic attack, they imagine they are about to die. Such an attack is often confused with a heart attack. Such sufferers are invariably brought to the cardiology department of a hospital where they are told that 'nothing' is wrong. The panic attack does look very much like a heart attack. Hyperventilation sets in almost immediately, your whole body and heart start pumping like mad, all your muscles tense. Only occasionally do attacks like these lead to aggression or suicide. The odd tram door may get kicked open for purposes of escape, but in actual fact such reactions are few and far between. In most cases self-control prevails, and the victim tries to calm down by, say, standing for a while at the side of the road. Freud or genes? Freud's theory on the source of fears and phobias states that people suppress their life instincts whenever these are a threat to their integrity. This threat can be external, but may also come from inside (i.e. the conscience). When real or supposed danger threatens, recognition of this danger causes fear, which sets the process of suppression in motion. Freud identifies the phobias as a distinct category of fears: they have a specific cause, such as fear of sexual or aggressive feelings, but that fear is transferred to random objects in the outside world (e.g. snakes) or to features of the outside world (such as confined spaces). It is this act of transferring that makes the fear seem completely unfounded to others. Other researchers feel that there are strong indications that phobias have nothing to do with the psyche but stem from the biological make-up. There is something in our genes that makes all of us sensitive to height, depth, unpredictable spatial conditions and certain animals such as spiders, mice and snakes. Some people appear extra prone to these and develop real fears. For instance, research with victims of manic-depressive psychosis has shown that it is possible to predict from a person's genes whether he may later suffer from manic depression. A third theory states that fears are a spin-off of stress due to marriage problems, hormones, arguments with the neighbours, problems at work and suchlike. The fear would gradually subside if this stress were to be avoided in some way. This theory i based on the fact that man can be conditioned, relatively independentl of genetic make-up and psychoanalitical processes. Remedy Therapy i a way of dealing with claustrophobic or agoraphobic complaints. I takes ten to twenty treatments for claustrophobia or forty fo agoraphobia for patents to learn to live with their affliction. This is no just a question of talking about it, there are exercises as well. The learn how to keep their bodies under control, how to relax and preven their imagination from running away with them. Airline companies us more or less the same techniques to help passengers overcome thei fear of flying. There are also medicines to combat agoraphobia. Ho these work exactly is not known. They are not tranquillizers, but ac on the central nervous system, on the neurotransmitter system in th synapses between two nerve cells. Unfortunately these medicines ar not without side-effects. They are necessary all the same, as there ar not enough psychologists and psychiatrists to treat all 150,00 agoraphobics in the Netherlands. Research into agoraphobia an claustrophobia has been steadily gathering momentum, especiall since the discovery of reasonably successful methods of treatment i the seventies and the concensus about the same time as t classification of the complaint. These days, there are protocol pertaining to general practitioners and others that give the preferre researches and methods of treatment for claustrophobia an agoraphobia. This is not to say, however, that all that research give all the answers to how and why such complaints arise. The results o all these investigations are often contradictory and confusing Research into claustrophobia and agoraphobia is hardly top priority After all, they don't kill you. Yet it is important that we gain mor facts about these phobias, if only in view of the great expense c treating those afflicted by them. It used to cost much more, in th days when agoraphobics were locked away in asylums. The presen treatment with medicines and therapy is certainly cheaper but it doe take a year or so. And with 150,000 agoraphobics in this country tha means spending a small fortune. And now let us look at the problen from the other side, so to speak. When designing buildings we shoul certainly take account of potential complaints of claustrophobia. I helps if, say, there is a camera installed in the lift or the shoppin centre. Air ducts with grilles in full view are another way of puttin people at their ease and lessening the fear of suffocating if somethin goes wrong. A simple thing like a telephone or a small window in th lift gives the idea that direct contact can be made with the outsid world in the case of an emergency. Mobile phones, however, hav proved to be a questionable solution. Those things have a habit of not working when you need them most. During a recent power, there was panic among the city's agoraphobics who claimed that their mobile phones had stopped functioning. Scepticism regarding the effectiveness of this contraption increased as a result. So it is best to use mobile appliances at the start of therapy only, as their powers of reassurance are merely temporary.How does this relate to density? During my years of researching and treating claustrophobia and agoraphobia I was confronted with the following case. There was a woman who had one of these long narrow gardens. Once she had dreadful arguments with her neighbours who had planted a complete hedge of conifers. Whereupon she sawed down the lot. The neighbours took her to court and during the hearing the woman gave to understand that she suffered from claustrophobia. The judge wondered whether the hedge could in fact conjure up claustrophobic feelings. If so, he would take it into consideration when giving his verdict. I was asked to look into the matter. In Germany there has already been research done into the relation between the size of cities and claustrophobia and agoraphobia. There they compared the occurrence of the two morbid complaints in large, medium and small cities and villages. Their conclusion was that there is no relationship between the occurrence of claustrophobia and agoraphobia and the size of the place of residence. The complaints say more about the person than the culture or the habitat. More and more tower blocks are being built at present for working and living, which obviously means that more and more people are occupying them. We can therefore expect an increasing number of claustrophobics. A percentage of this growth is temporary only. More and more of these sufferers will tackle their claustrophobia themselves and get it under control. After a certain period during which acclimatization sets in, the size of the group seeking help will stabilize. To begin with, such phenomena as the growing number of claustrophobics will get broad coverage in the media. A club will be founded and if this gets sufficient attention in papers, on the radio or on TV, a great many people will identify with the situation and apply for membership. When the initial rush is past its peak, the problem will be handed on to bodies that don't cost the government money, such as insurance companies and charity organizations offering DIY therapy. Another point is that there are people suffering from agoraphobia who are only too glad to hear the neighbours. They know that there is someone around that they can turn to in an emergency. These people are very much in favour of densification and contraction.

Claustro city

Datascape

1997

Sven Grooten and Chris Rankin

The causes of claustrophobia within the human population are many and varied. More importantly, they seem not to be measurable in a way that could be extrapolated into three dimensional form.

A solid cube, 100x100x100 metres of continuous programme, is divided into the mixed programme of a 'normal' town: 30% dwellings, 15% offices and workshops, 10% parking, 5% retail. The remaining 40%, consisting of public space, infrastructure and leisure, are used to carve out a public space from the masses that have been constructed using a combination of chosen 'anti-claustrophobic' parameters: a combination of current fire regulations and direct sunlight delivered into these emergency facilities at moments of expected use. These parameters generate a fluid and connective space, where every possible claustrophobia through monotony and repetition is avoided.

Fire escape regulations

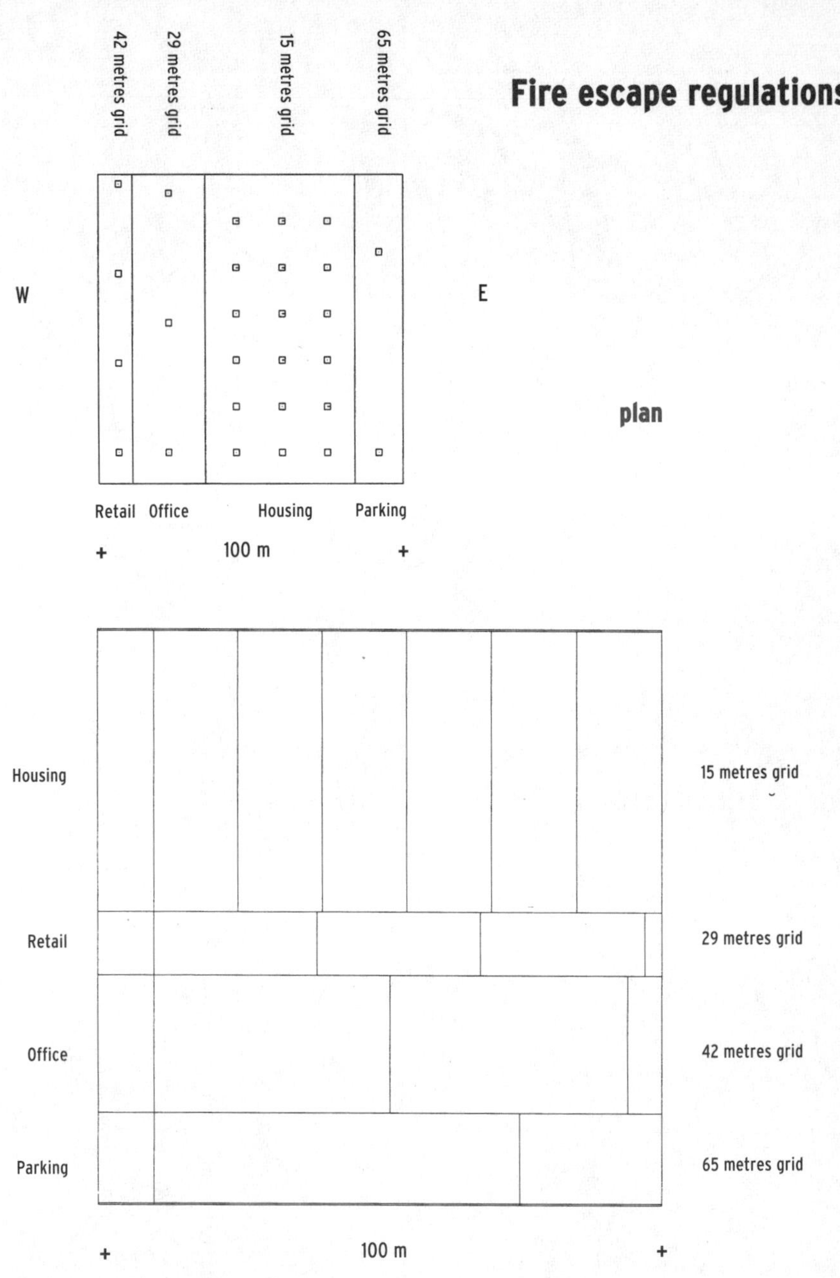

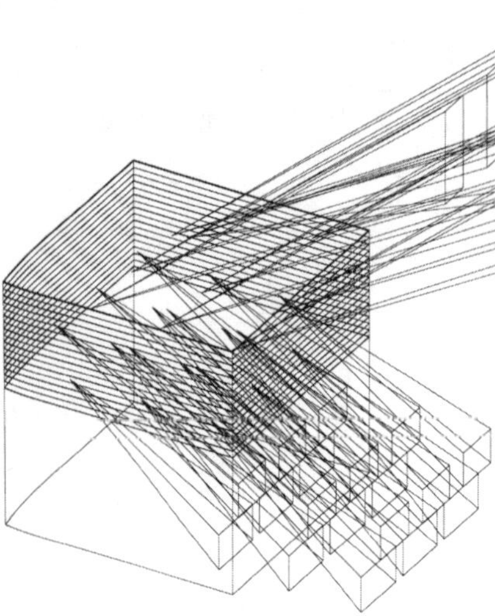

housing

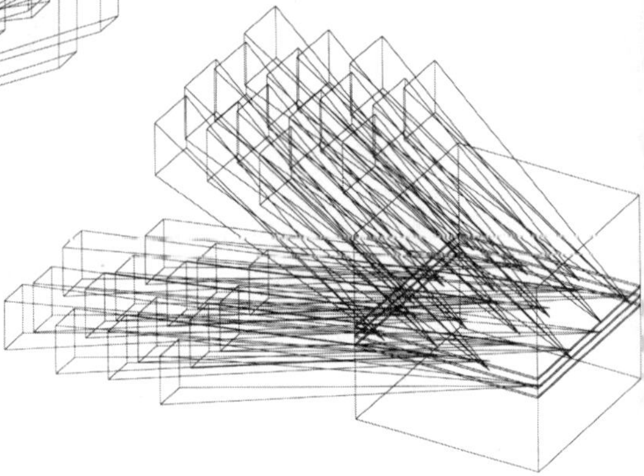

retail

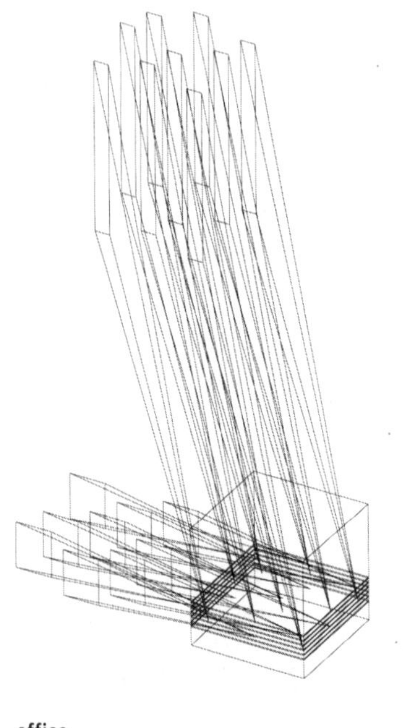

office

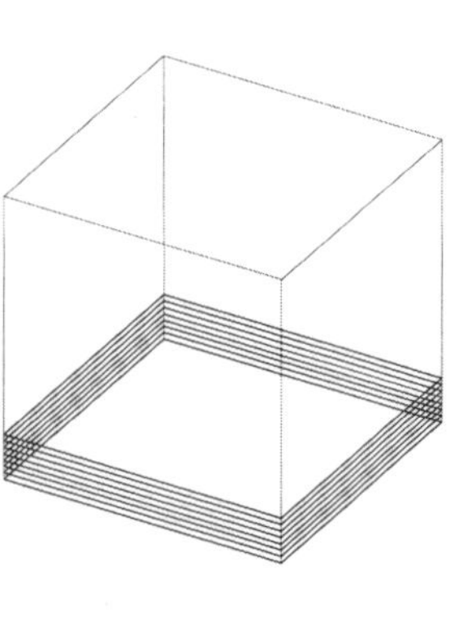

parking

Sun cones

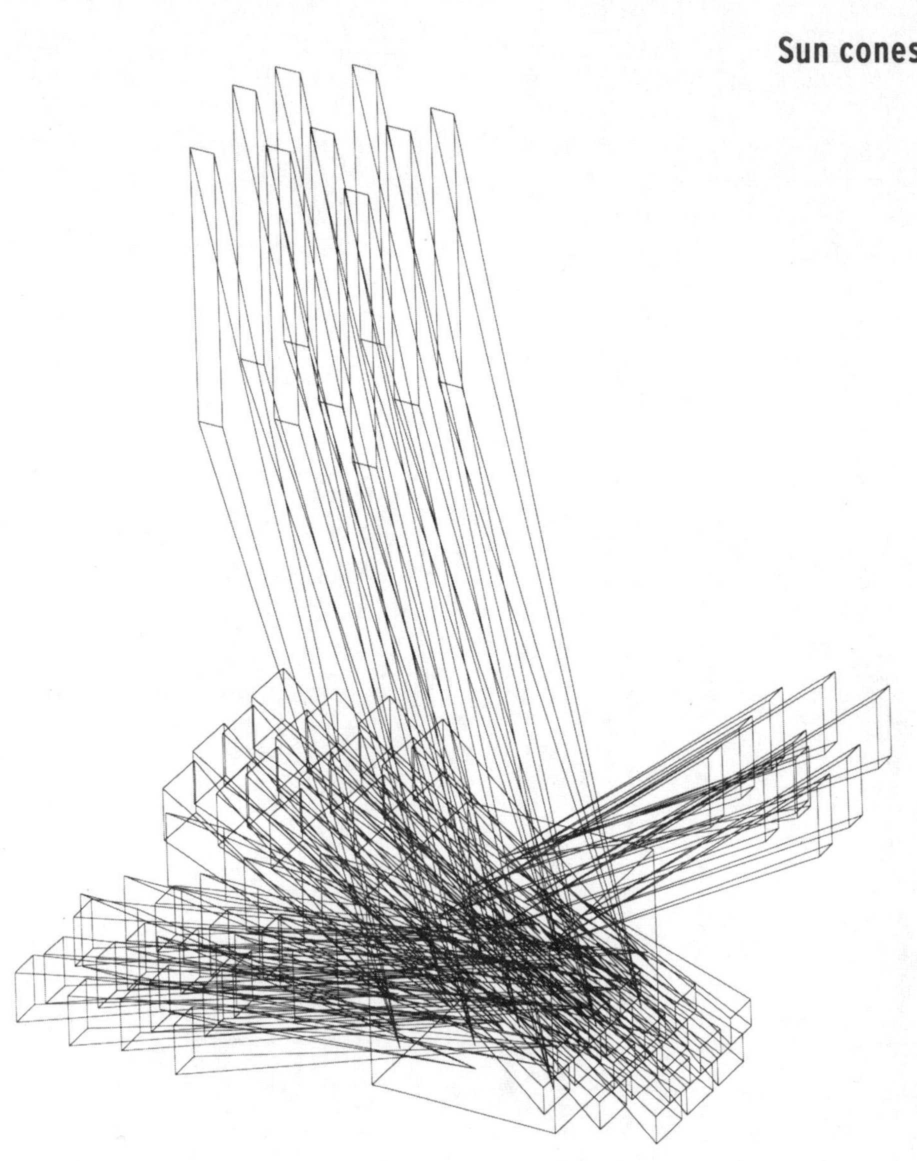

all sun cones

Sun cones

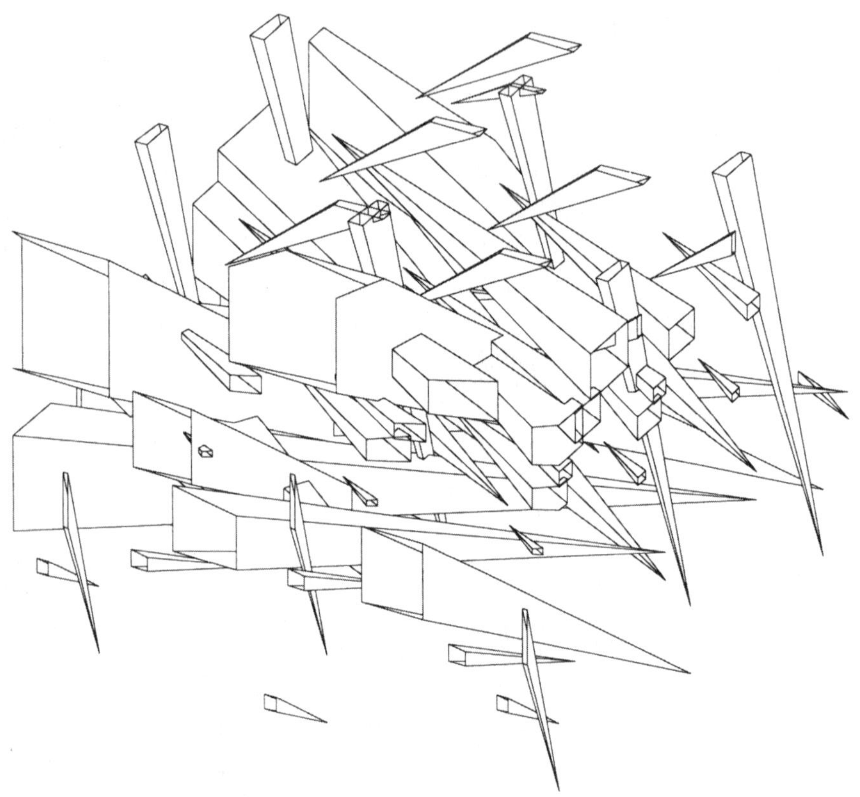

Possible mass

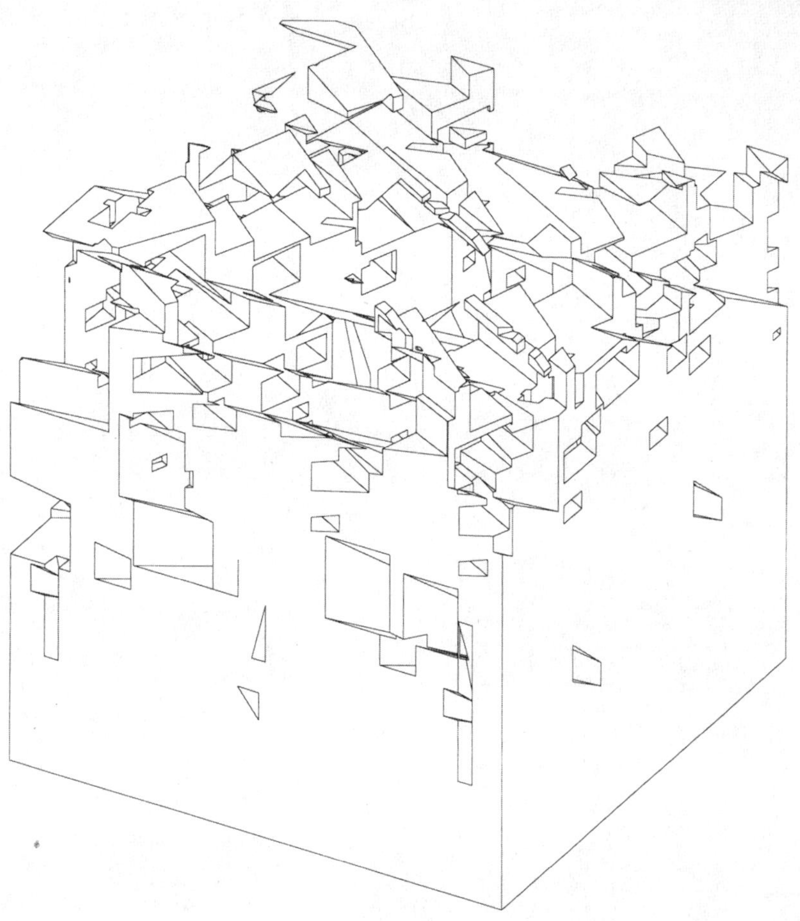

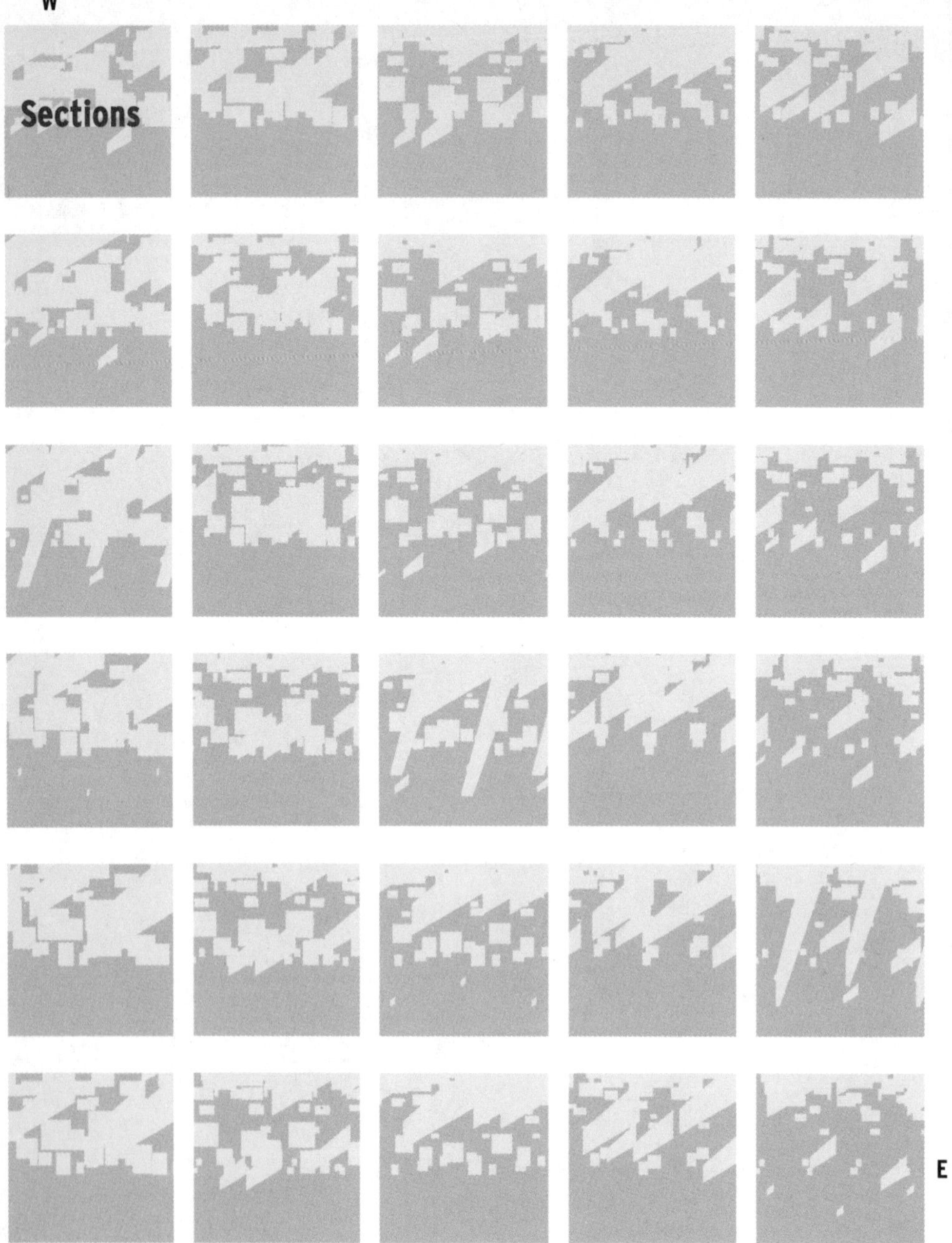
W
Sections
E

Plans

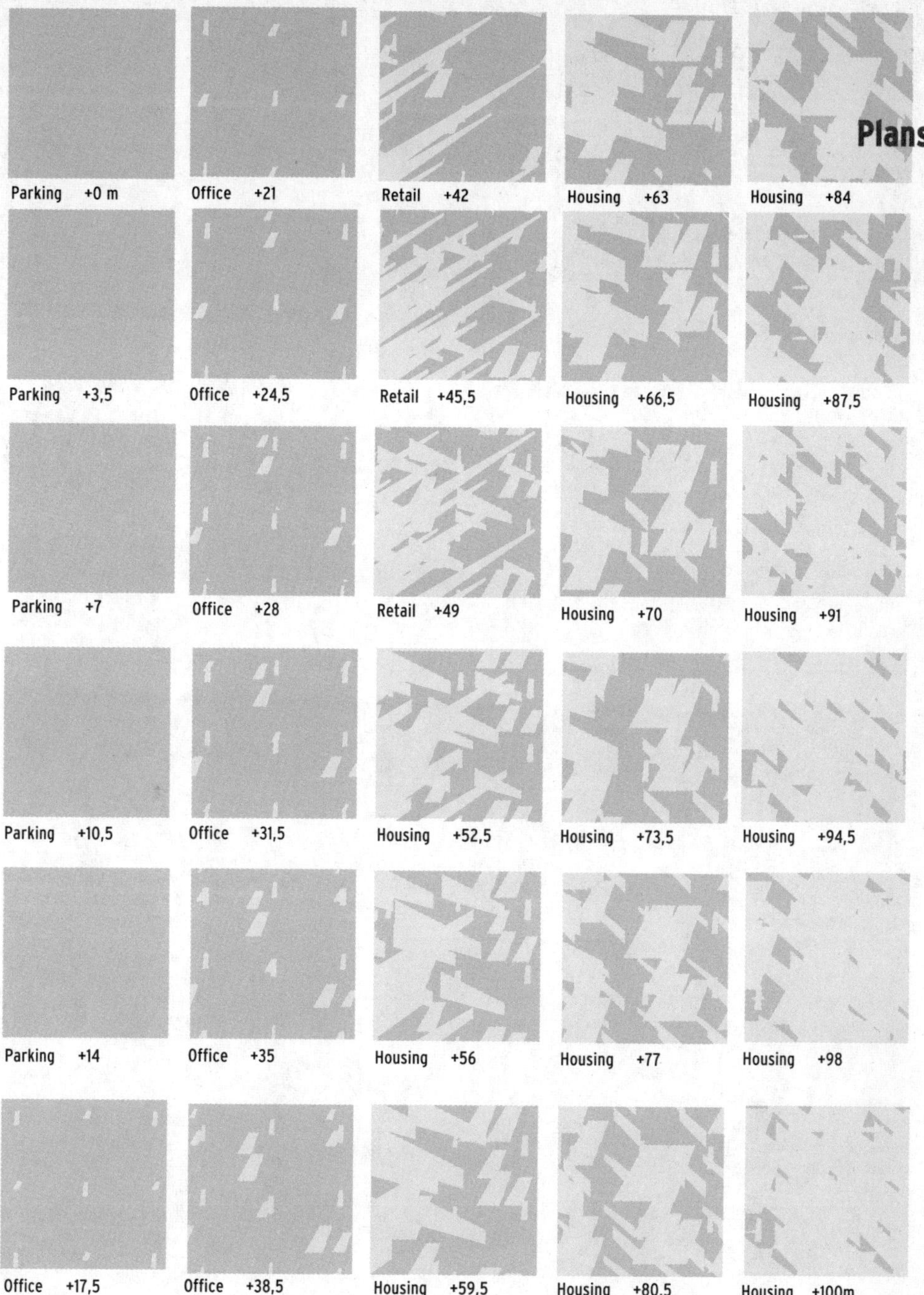

Parking +0 m
Office +21
Retail +42
Housing +63
Housing +84
Parking +3,5
Office +24,5
Retail +45,5
Housing +66,5
Housing +87,5
Parking +7
Office +28
Retail +49
Housing +70
Housing +91
Parking +10,5
Office +31,5
Housing +52,5
Housing +73,5
Housing +94,5
Parking +14
Office +35
Housing +56
Housing +77
Housing +98
Office +17,5
Office +38,5
Housing +59,5
Housing +80,5
Housing +100m

7.00AM

Day cycle

5.00PM

1.00PM
7.00PM

The metropolis (the western model) is a 'dipolis' whose form is determined by the public-private dichotomy. The government puts public property at the service of the private domain and fills in public space with infrastructure and, if very rarely, with places to stay for a longer or shorter period of time. This dipolis consists of a three-dimensional body shaped by the erections created with capital from the private sector and coloured in with shopping malls and residential tower blocks. However, this urban mass is cut to ribbons by the public traffic infrastructures: public space desperately trying to denigrate urban design to two dimensions.

The non-Western metropolis seems only too willing to model itself on the example of the Western city; but this is merely a superficial perception. The non-Western megacity is a dipolis consisting of an informal city and a formal city. Two polarities that hold each other in equilibrium, each trying to deny the existence of the other. The informal city consists of self-build quarters and slums, the formal of shopping centres and business centres. Capital (i.e. property developers) gives shape to the formal city, thereby shouldering the responsibility of binding together its vital organs. The design has but one function: 'Moving people, as many and as fast as possible'.
A logical spin-off is the designing of traffic flows in a three-dimensional composition identical to that of the business centres. Public space no longer represents knife wounds in the three-dimensional body of the inner city: public space is a three-dimensional interurban mass.

Wayfinding

Text

1997

Machiel van Dorst

In a city where movement dominates the public space, the need to be localized no longer presents itself: 'Where am I?' is not a relevant question in the three-dimensional body we call city. Orientation in the entirely filled space is relative to the movement. Absolute orientation makes way for a relative orientation (wayfinding): 'Where do I go?' On route from A to B by car or metro, orientation is utterly dependent on B. Put your trust in the route, as urban mass makes absolute orientation impossible. This experience is comparable with the orienting capacities of a metro passenger in a strange city.

Under these circumstances, entirely filled space acquires the same quality as its opposite, entirely empty space. Space and mass effectively become interchangeable. Seen thus, it is utterly logical that aboriginals in the desert (the empty space) have no absolute orientation. What they do possess is the finesse of relative orientation; 'songlines' tell them which direction to take. 'Where am I?' is superceded by 'Where do I go?' When Western man is likewise able to effortlessly trade in the need for space for an all-encompassing urban mass and kick the habit of absolute orientation, it is time for large-scale densification to begin.

Imploded exterior

ter and studios for the VPRO public broadcasting company in Hilversum, The Netherlands

1993/1997

'Office work' has become an umbrella term for a great variety of activities. Some of these are specific, others very much related to everyday acts such as reading, discussing, talking and so on.
Increasing numbers of people are working at home for part of the time. This means that more spaces might have a double or even triple function, since they could be used by more part-time workers. Smaller office buildings are becoming a viable prospect.
The use of computers and the increased importance of communication with its demand for teamwork offices and meeting rooms, is leading to broader buildings with more extended open plans.
Office buildings can therefore become more compact, creating space that can be used for communication or leisure purposes, which could once again encourage use of the office. These processes have been examined in the VPRO headquarters building.
For the VPRO, the Dutch 'artistic' broadcasting company, a new building means leaving the present accommodation of some eleven separate villas. Villas, which throughout the years have played a vital role in the identity of the VPRO. People who used to work in suites of rooms, attics, conservatories and bel-étages will have to find their niche in a new and truly office-like environment.
Can the present situation with its improvised use of space, which often has had an influence on the programmes that were produced there, be combined with the required 'efficiency' of a modern organization?
And can this relaxed character be reinstated even under the circumstances of enlargement? Can the metaphor of the villa still exist in our epoch?
The villa can be characterized by compactness (the absence of long corridors), by stacking different types of spaces and by its relation with the surrounding landscape.
This compactness has, given the urban constraints, led to the 'deepest' or widest office building in Holland.
A 'precision bombardment' of snake-like holes makes it possible to combine light and air with views of the surroundings. The result is a literal *bürolandschaft* where the difference between outside and inside blurs.
The existing nature of the given site is to be replaced by an elevated heather-covered roof, under which are laid out a series of 'floors' much like a geological formation. These floors are interconnected by various spatial

means: ramps, monumental stairs, mini-hills, grand stairs, slopes, so forming a route leading from the surroundings up to the roof, one that aims to stimulate communication patterns within the building.
It constructs a continuous interior in which differences in height combine the specific (the place) with the general (the continuous floor).
These floors can be 'urbanized' by the changing demands of the company: a range of office typologies such as the salon, attic, corridor, patio and terrace offices presents a retrospective revue of the existing villas.
The floors are supported by a forest of columns and minimal bracing so as to keep the planes as open as possible.
The technique is totally hidden from view in hollow floors much like those in ancient Rome so that the staff members are not distracted from their tasks.
Beside an individually adjustable technique, spartan concrete floors put the smoothed-out, servile aspects of comfort into perspective. The slopes, stairs and hills introduce an athletic 'fatigue' to these overly comfortable conditions.
In its materiality the villa echoes the present villas: no false lowered ceiling systems but a 'real' stone ceiling, no clicking wall systems but 'real' walls with sliding doors, no computer floors but a stone one, covered by a collection of Persian rugs instead of standard 'project tapestry', no windows but full-height glass sliding doors opening onto balconies.
We have tried to avoid an omnipresent facade, to keep the view towards the surrounding nature as open as possible.
We initially proposed a system of megastore heaters as entryways, so that the difference between inside and outside would be climatic only. Birds could easily fly in. 'Air' would become the main building material.
Since this suggestion wasn't legally allowed, the facade is now composed out of thirty-five types of glass, since the different heights and positions cause different heat loads and make cooling demands on the glass elements. The spatial conditions of the interior will thus be reflected by this 'rose-window' of glass types.
The facade has become a 'result', a datascape of demands. It borders the endless interior as requirements demanded. In a building whose activity is mainly expressed by other media, any representation in the facade has been avoided. Interior design has become architecture again.

Office usage

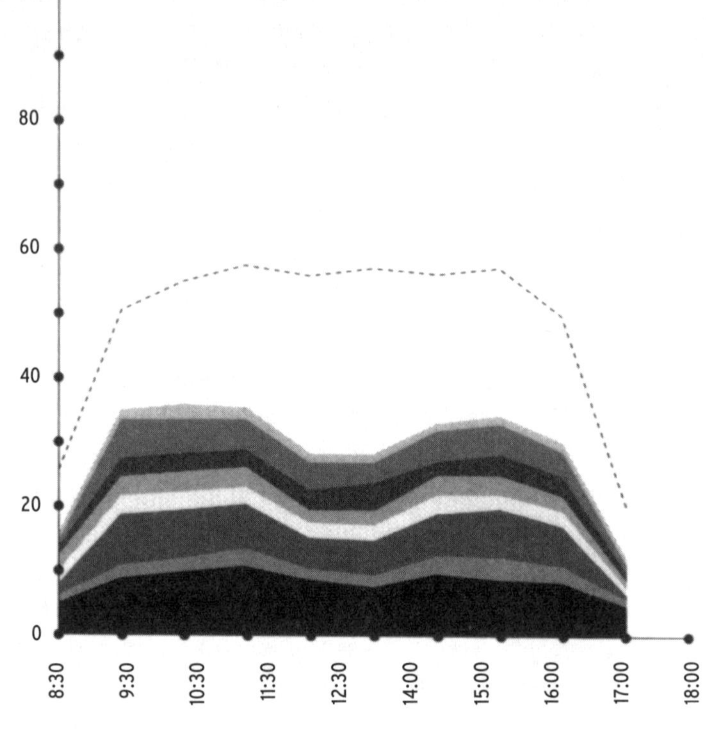

Source: DEGW-London, 1995

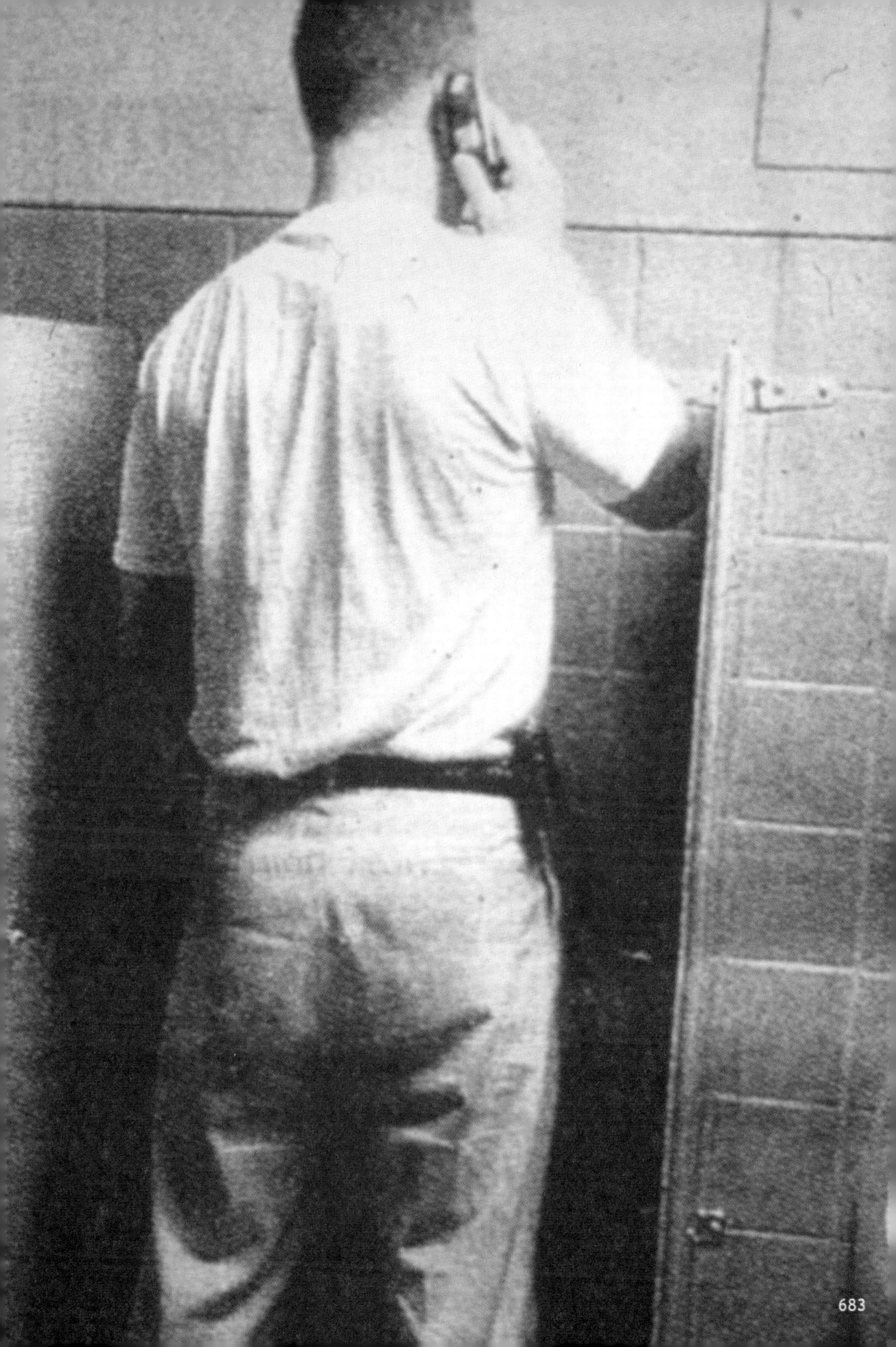

Compactization

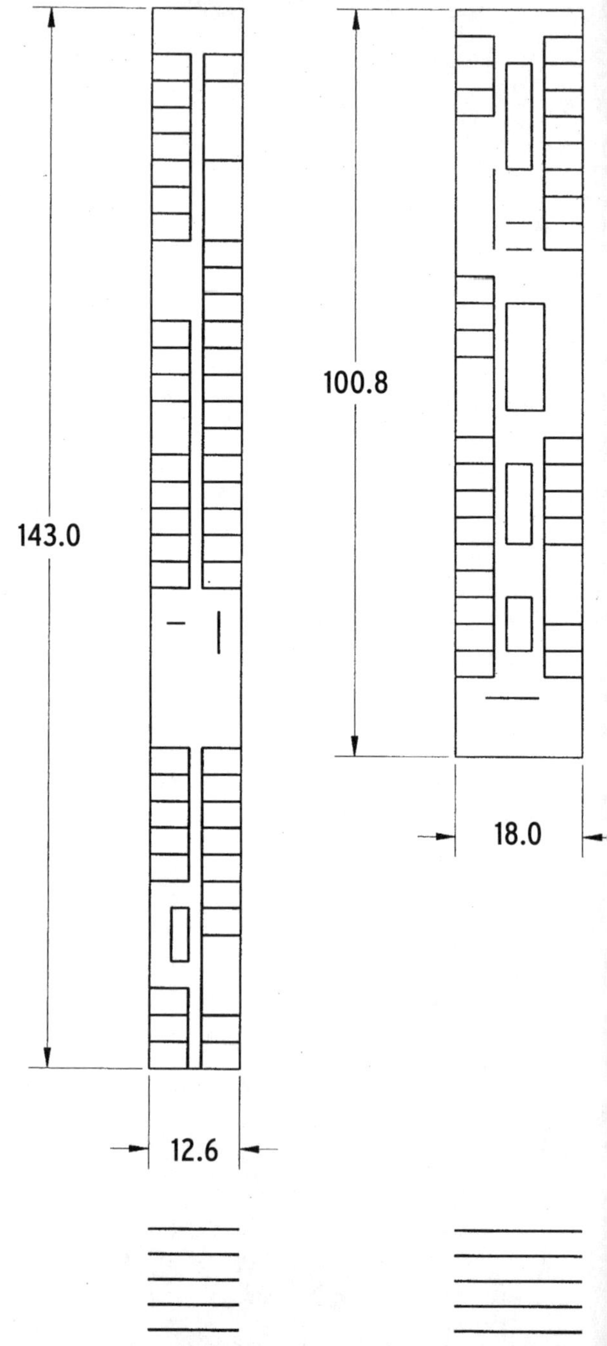

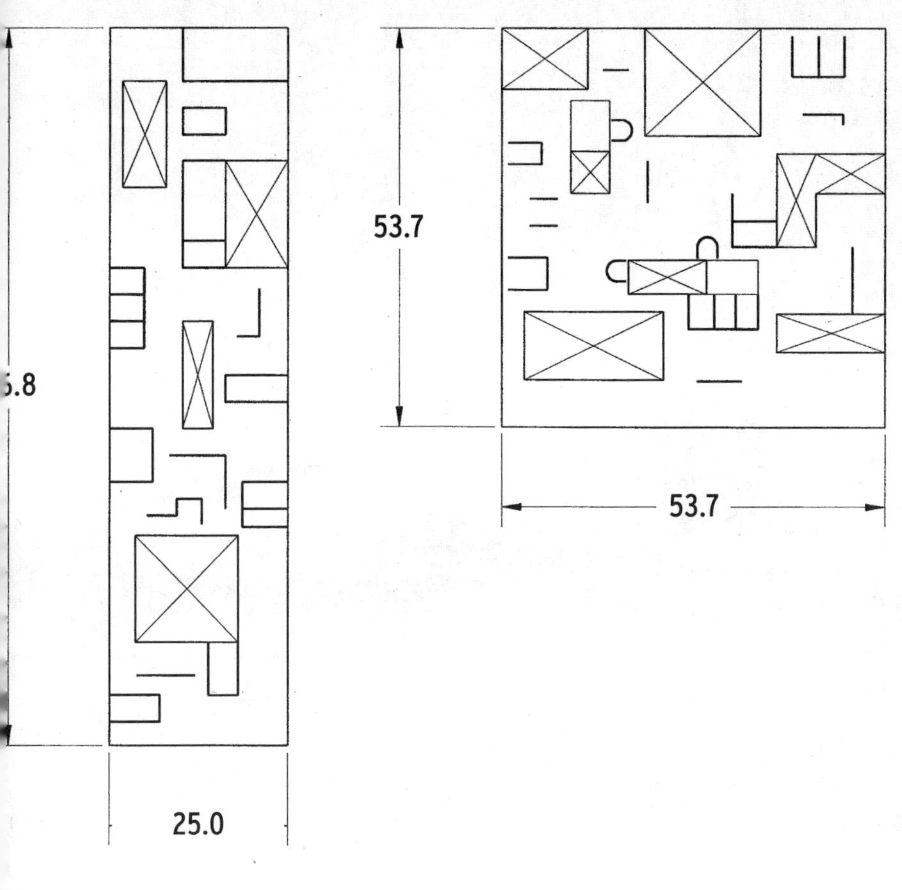

.8
25.0
53.7
53.7

Connected floors

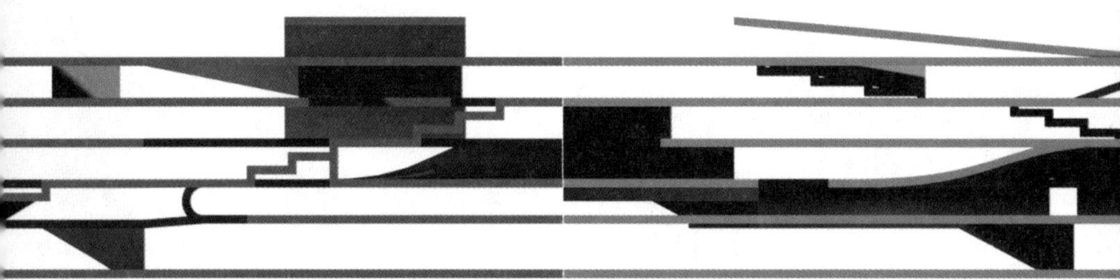

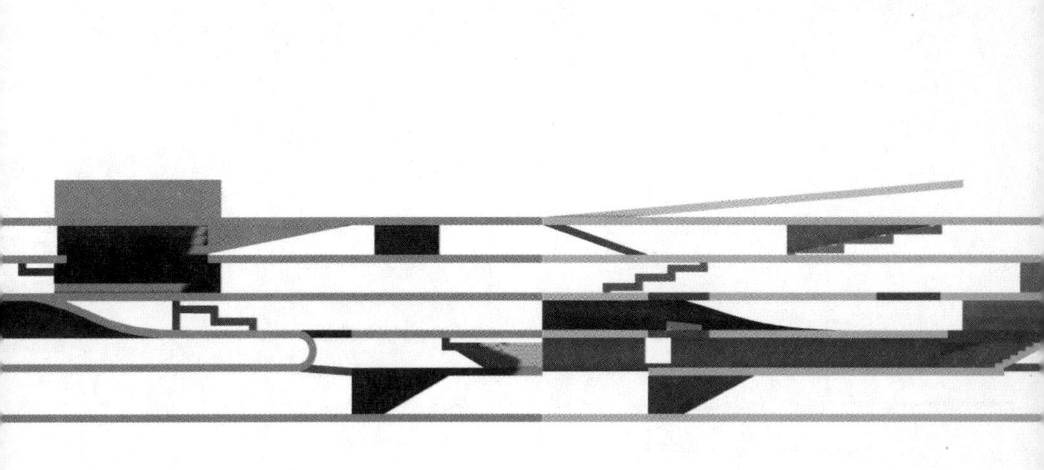

View compensates daylight

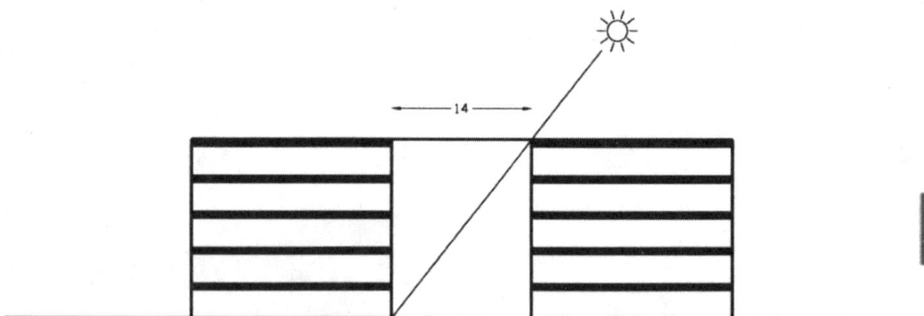

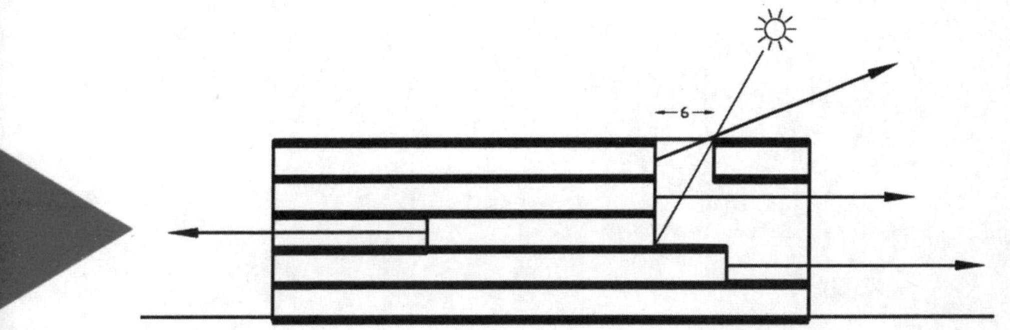
6

Patios

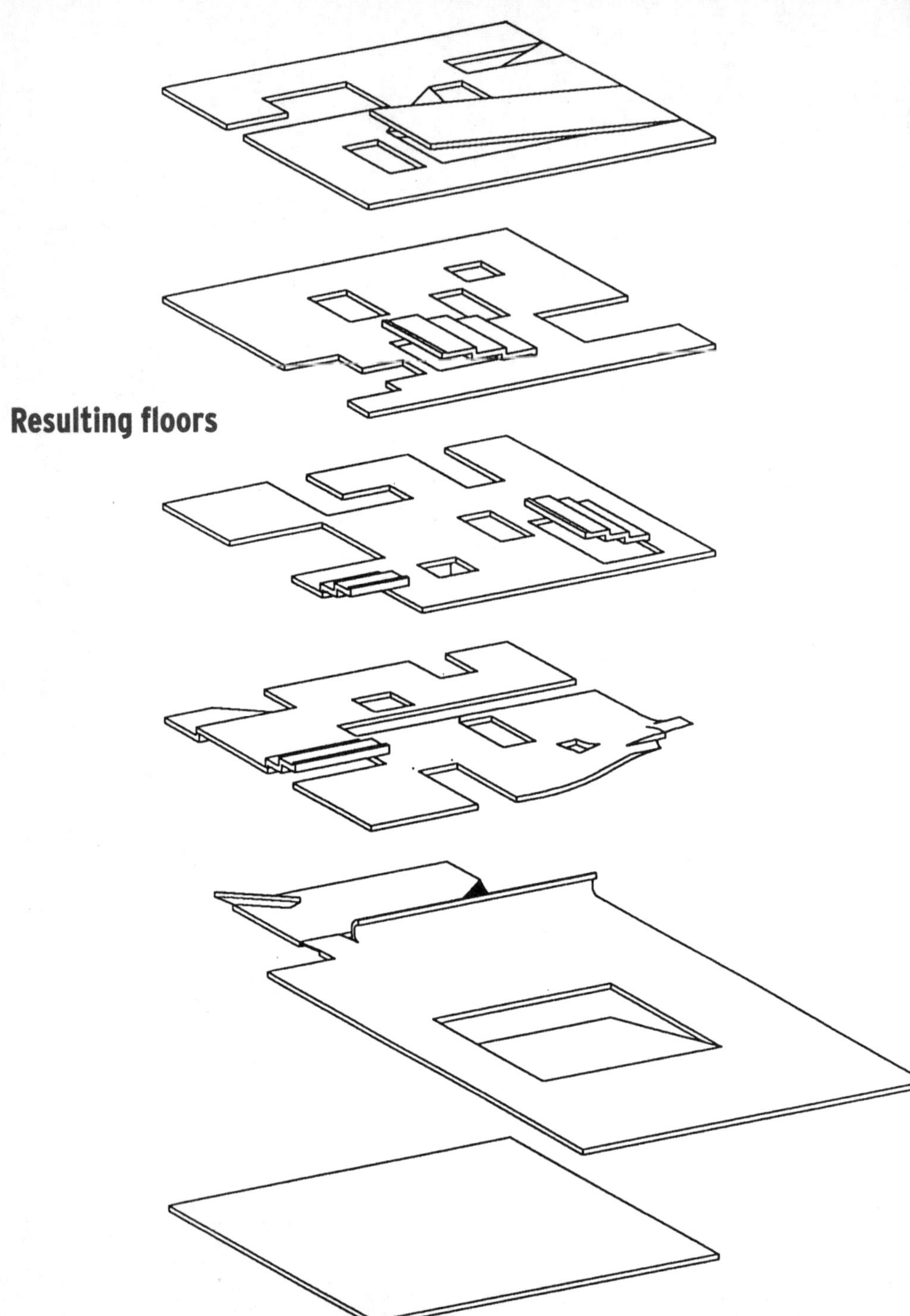
Resulting floors

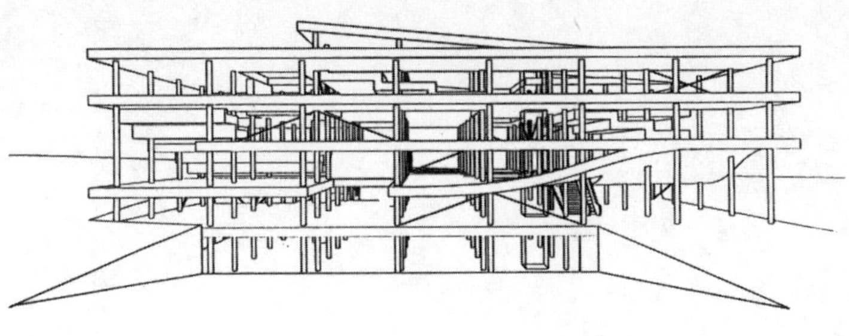

Elevations

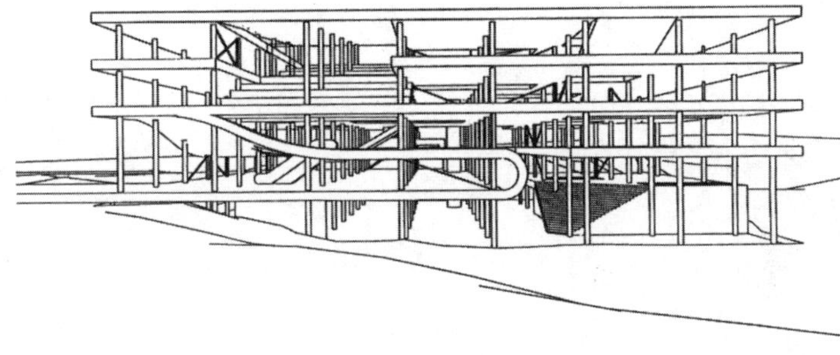

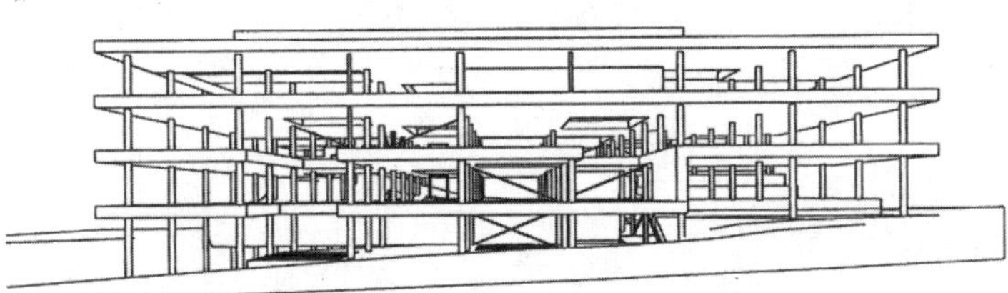

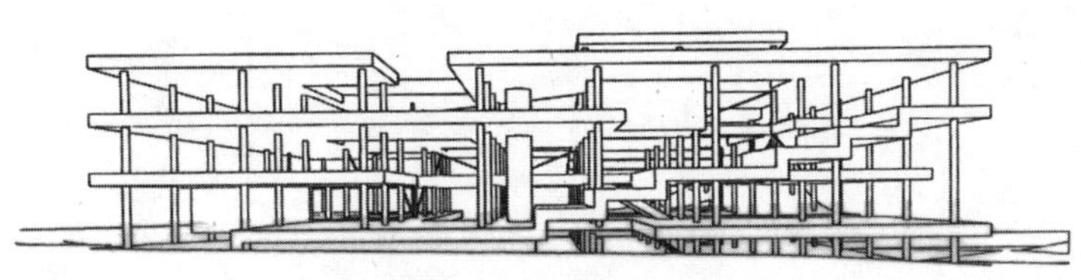

Promenade

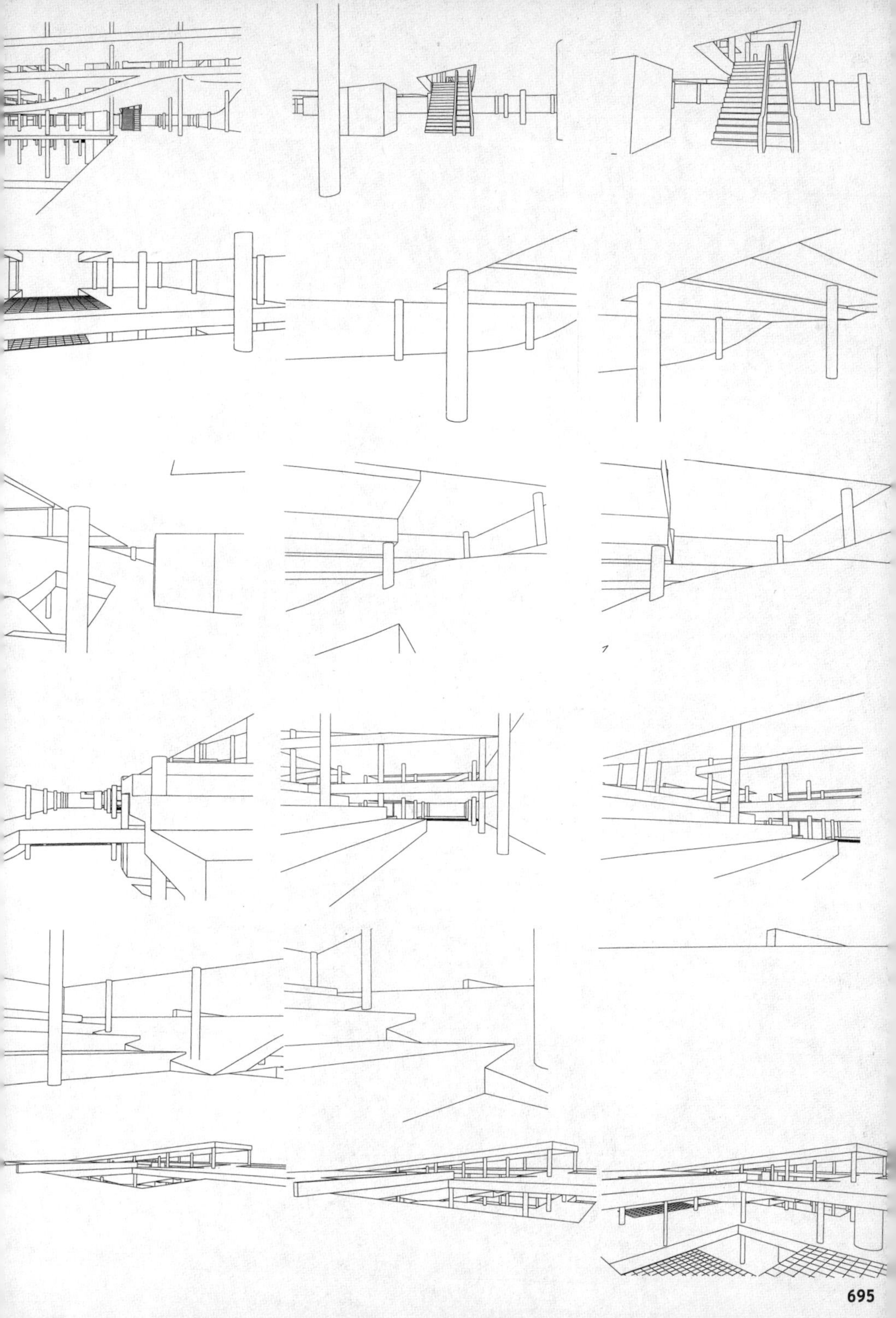

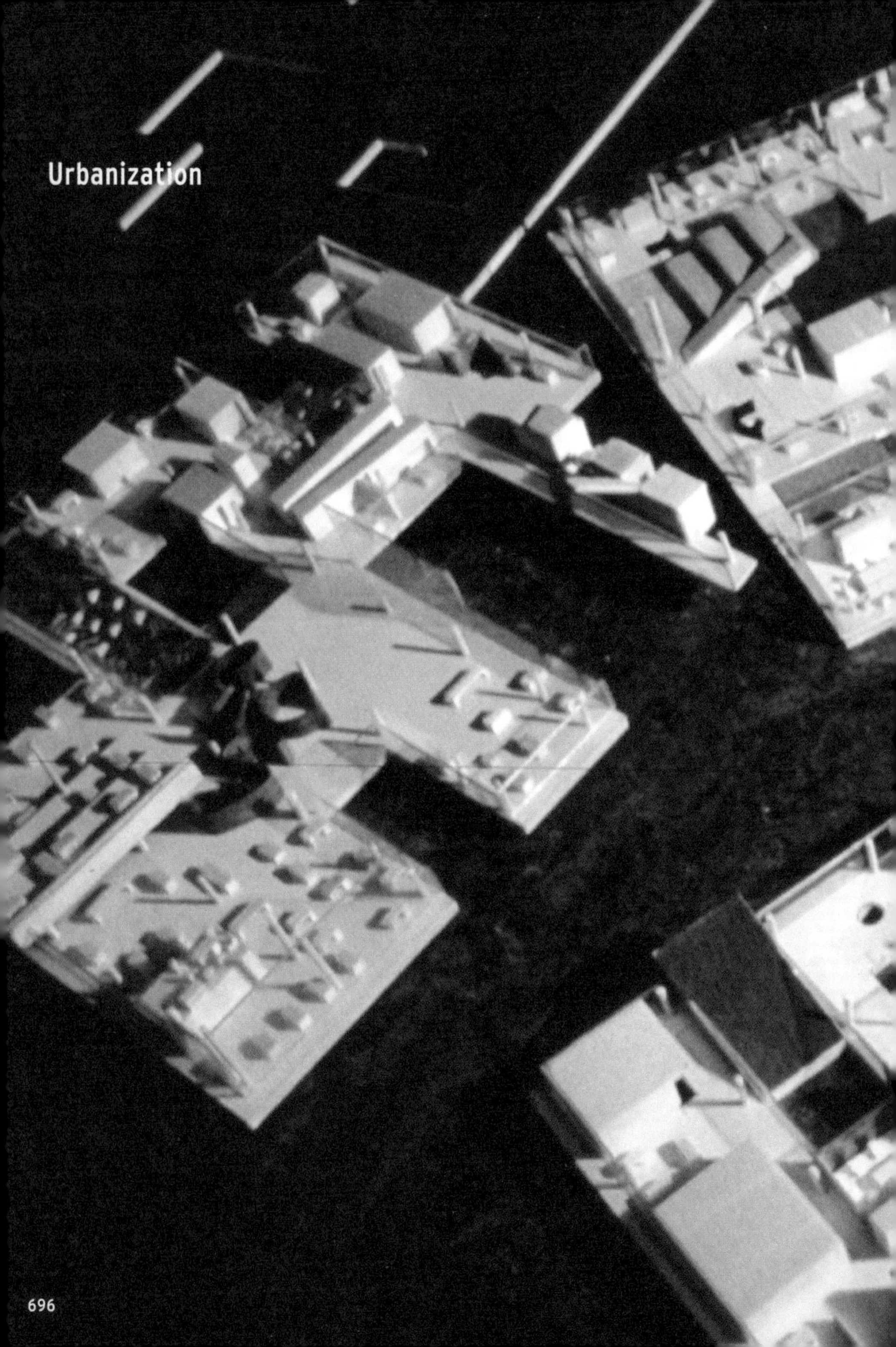

Urbanization

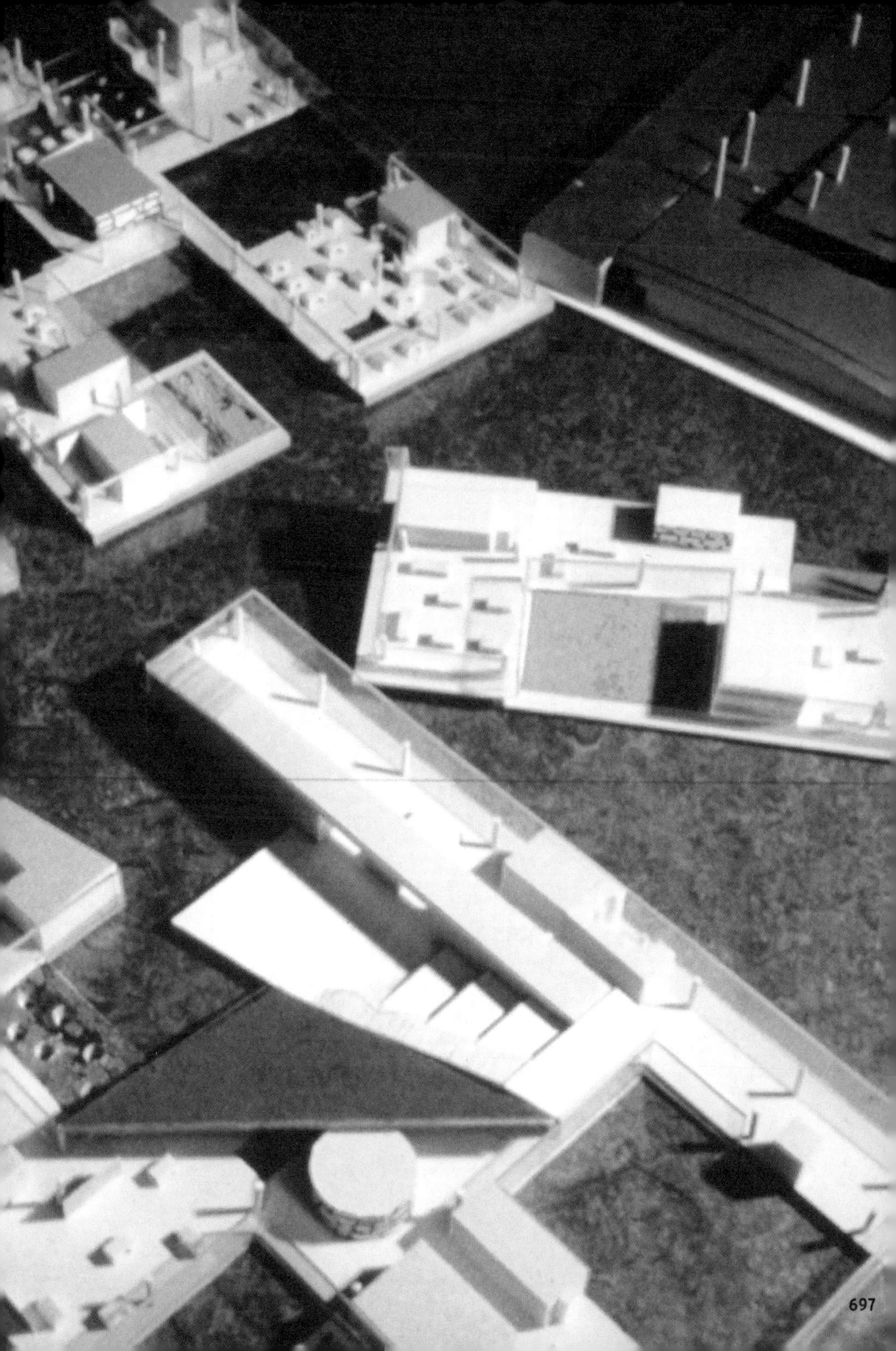

Plans

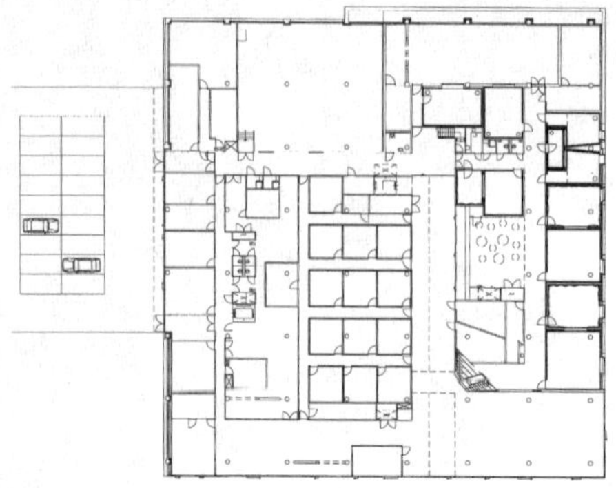

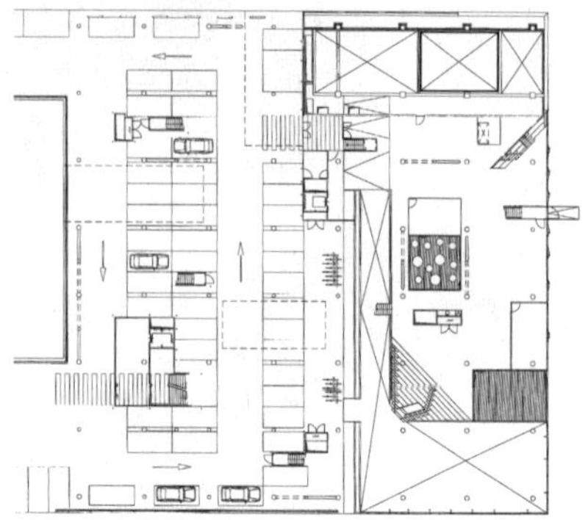

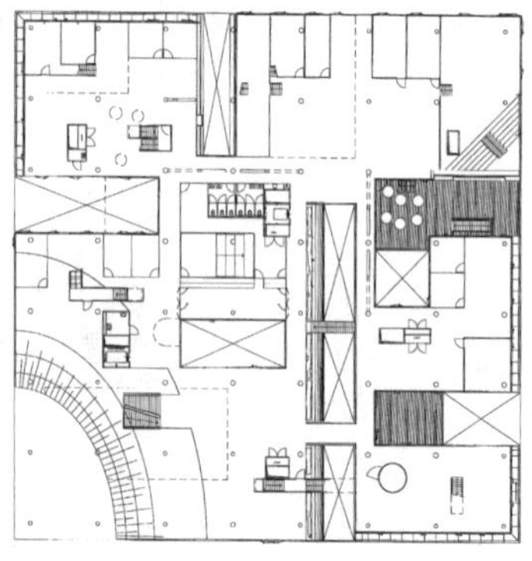

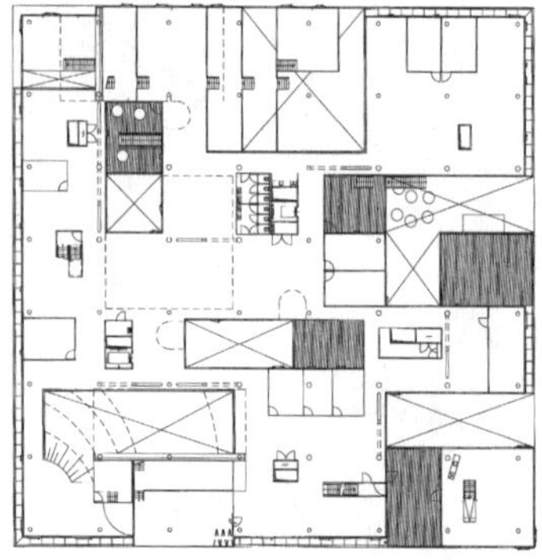

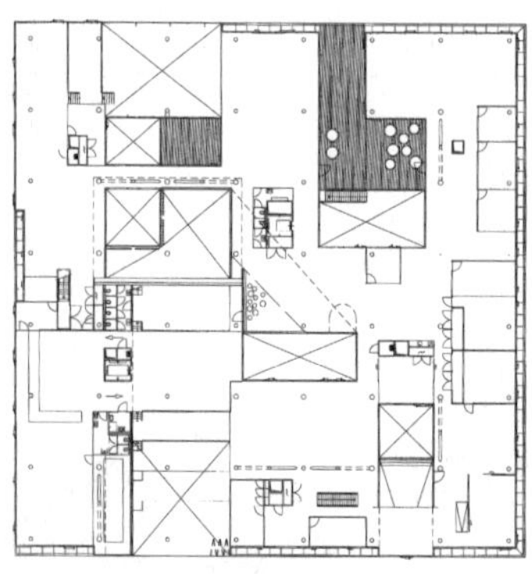

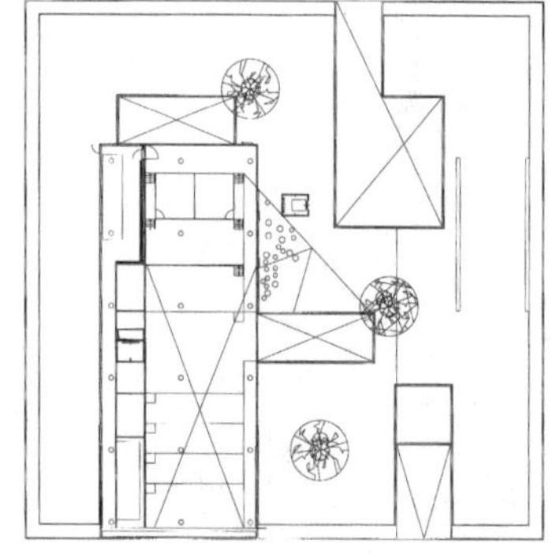

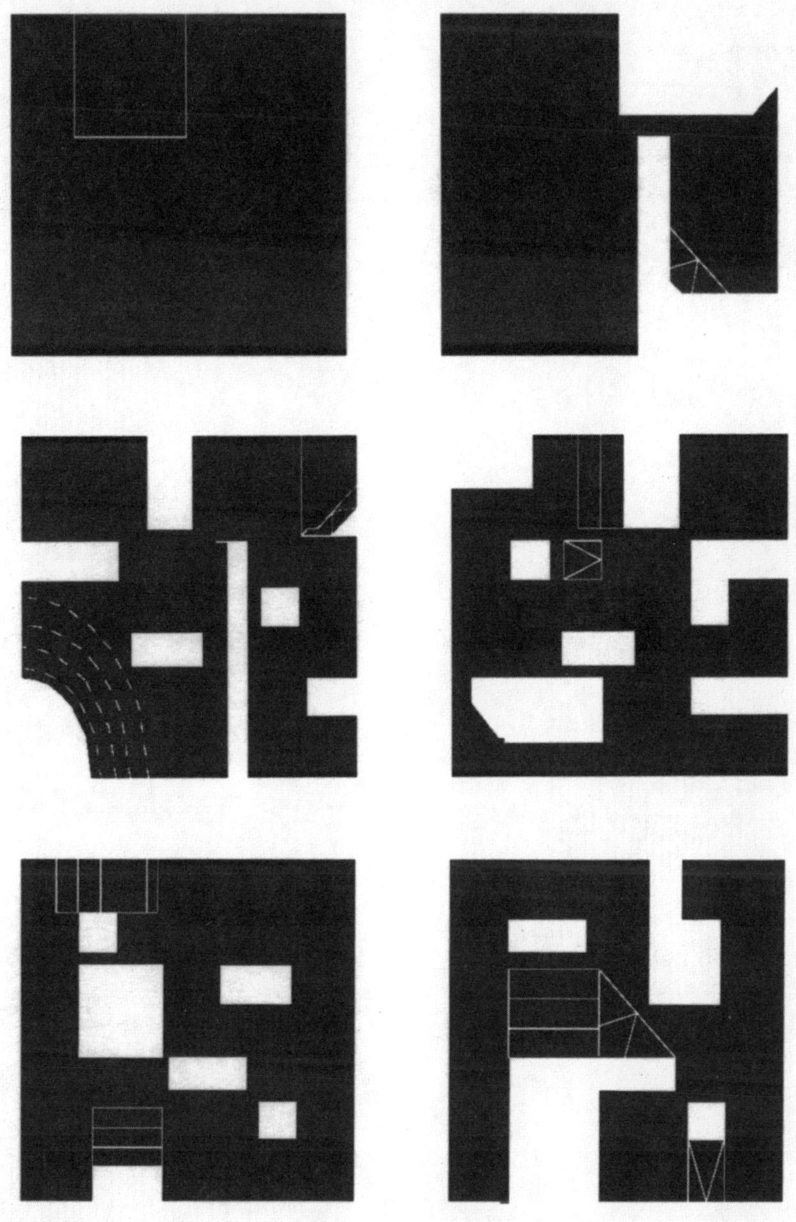

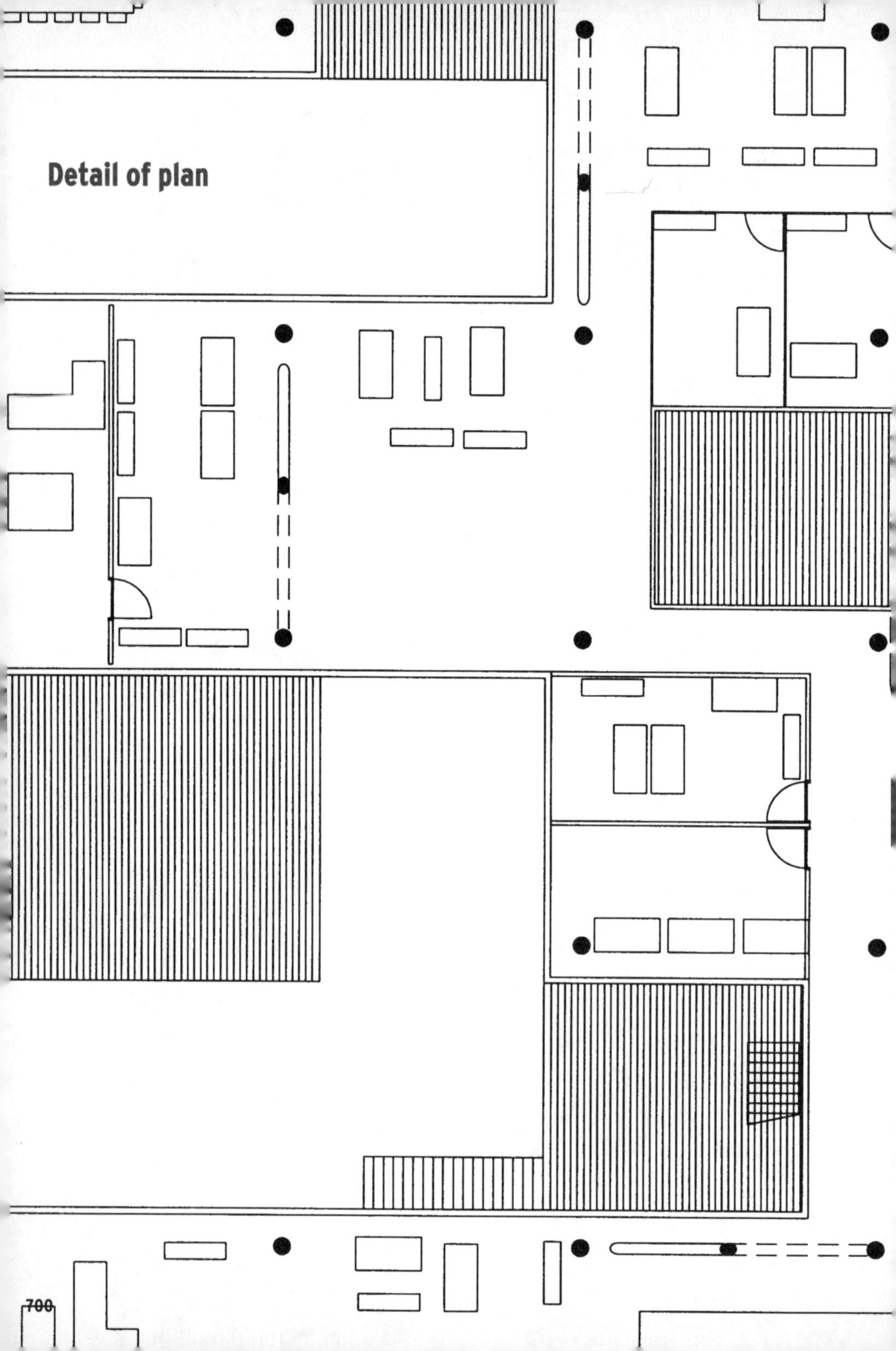
Detail of plan

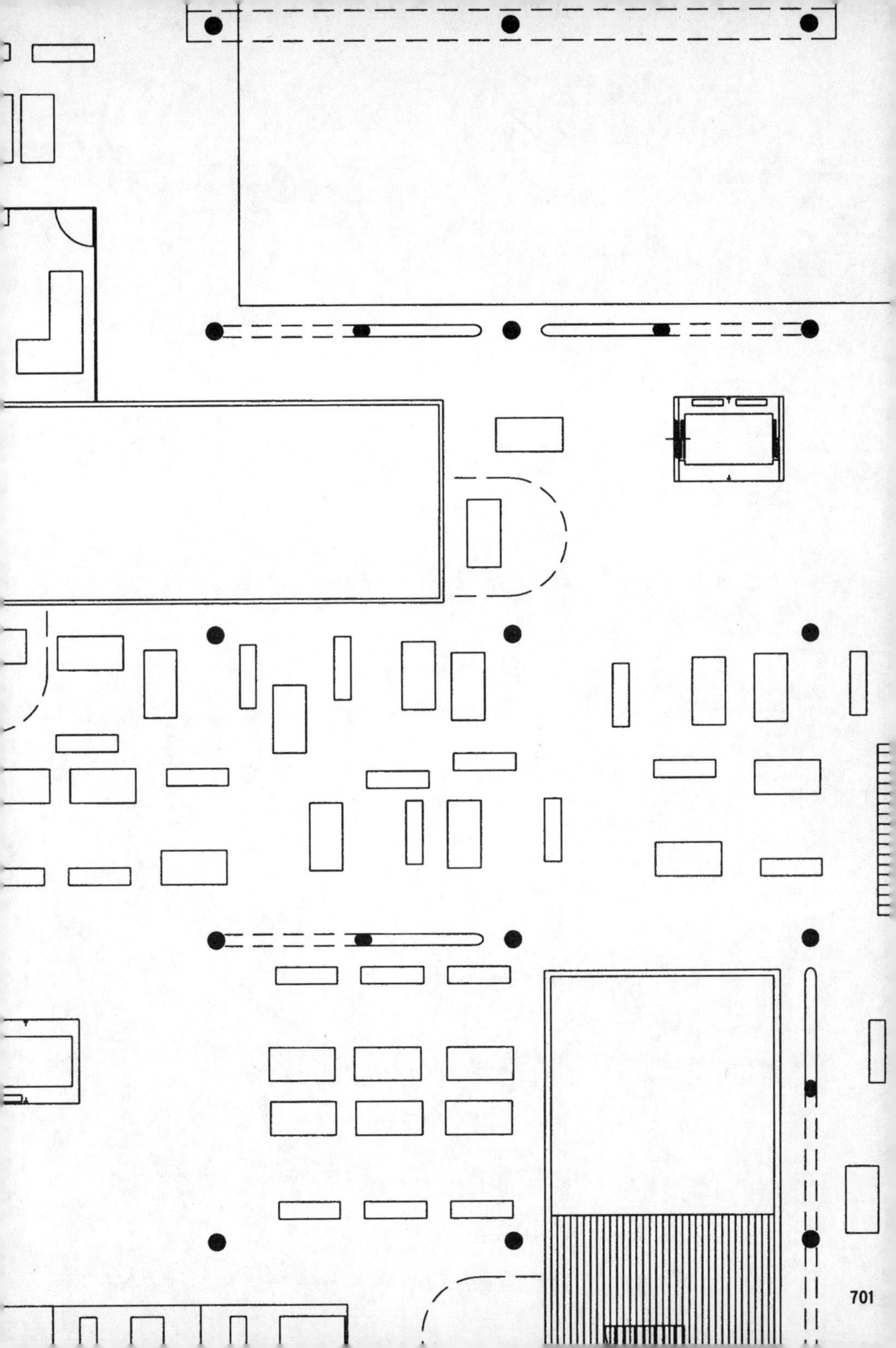

North elevation

South elevation

Credits

Definition of FAR • 1997 • Author: Richard Koek, Winy Maas and Jacob van Rijs

FAR Catalogue • 1997 • Author: MVRDV: Winy Maas, Jacob van Rijs and Nathalie de Vries with Tom Mossel and Joost Grootens

Greyness on the Dutch Mesa • Text • 1994 • Author: Richard Koek, Winy Maas and Jacob van Rijs with Tom Mossel • Source: Dutch Density Image made by MVRDV based on research by Buro Schie, Rotterdam

Permanence • Town planning study for the manifestation 'Rotterdam 2045' on the future development of the Rotterdam region, The Netherlands • 1995 • Design: MVRDV: Winy Maas, Jacob van Rijs and Nathalie de Vries with Tom Mossel, Joost Grootens, Ruby van den Munckhof and Joost Kok • Client: City of Rotterdam, Municipal Department of Urban Planning and Housing/Rotterdam 2045 Foundation • Location: Midden-IJselmonde, Rotterdam, The Netherlands • Project size: 12,000 houses • Ecological research: Architectenbureau J. Kristinsson, Deventer • Sociological research: Arnold Reijndorp and Vincent Kompier, Reijndorp bv Rotterdam

Dutch tendencies • Statistics • 1996 • Design: MVRDV: Winy Maas, Jacob van Rijs and Nathalie de Vries with Bas van Neijenhof • Source: CBS, Arnold Reijndorp and Vincent Kompier, Reijndorp bv Rotterdam

Campingland • Text • 1997 • Author: Arnold Reijndorp and Vincent Kompier, Reijndorp bv Rotterdam

Villageland • Text • 1997 • Author: Arnold Reijndorp and Vincent Kompier, Reijndorp bv Rotterdam

Lelyland • Study for the development of Lelystad, The Netherlands • 1994 • Design: Tom Mossel • Institution: Delft University of Technology • Tutors: Winy Maas and Endry van Velzen • Re-editing: MVRDV: Winy Maas, Jacob van Rijs and Nathalie de Vries with Joost Grootens • Article: Bas Blokker, 'Slack Water in Overpriced Lelystad', NRC Handelsblad, 24 July 1996, p. 1,3.

Landscape • Text • 1995 • Author: Winy Maas

Datascape • Text • 1996 • Author: Winy Maas

Emptyscape • Locus seminar • 1992 • Design: Patricia Bijvoet, Winy Maas and Christian Zalm • Re-editing: MVRDV: Winy Maas, Jacob van Rijs and Nathalie de Vries with Bas van Neijenhof, 1997

Windscape • Case study on the location of windmill parks in The Netherlands • 1997 • Design: MVRDV: Winy Maas, Jacob van Rijs and Nathalie de Vries with Carolien Ligtenberg, Frans de Witte and Joost Glissenaar • Client: E-connection • Location: 6 locations in The Netherlands

When dense, when lite? • Text • 1997 • Author: Harm Tilman

Rat tests • Opinions • 1997 • Collector: MVRDV: Winy Maas, Jacob van Rijs and Nathalie de Vries with Tom Mossel • Sources: P.J.A. Timmermans, Social Behavior in the Rat, (J.L. van Kaauwen and Th.J. Fuchten) 1978

Who is afraid of massiveness? • Global statistics • 1996 • Author: MVRDV: Winy Maas, Jacob van Rijs and Nathalie de Vries with Bas van Neijenhof and Frank van Manen • Sources: Hans Krijnsen, Rotterdam, CBS, G.T. Kurian, The New Book of World Rankings, New York, etc. (Fact on File) 1991

Climate • Statistics • 1996 • Author: MVRDV : Winy Maas, Jacob van Rijs and Nathalie de Vries with Bas van Neijenhof • Source: DGMR, Arnhem

And Holland? • Statistics • 1996 • Author: MVRDV: Winy Maas, Jacob van Rijs and Nathalie de Vries with Bas van Neijenhof • Source: CBS

KWC FAR 12 • Kowloon Walled City Density study • 1995 • Author: Laurence Liauw • Images: HK Government (156, 162, 164, 166 pp), Laurence Liauw (168, 172, 174 pp top left/middle/middle left), extracts from An Architectural Study of the KWC by Suenn Ho 1993 (170, 174 pp bottom left) and Greg Girard (p. 174 top right; bottom right; p. 176)

Far East • HongKong Tower typology • 1998 • Author: Jacob van Rijs • Source: Property Times, November 1997

Aztecs! • Light rules • 1997 • Author: MVRDV: Winy Maas, Jacob van Rijs and Nathalie de Vries with Tom Mossel Source: Based on a study project by Piet Knepper and Martin Loenen, 1995 • Institution: Academy of Architecture, Rotterdam • Tutors: Richard Koek, Winy Maas and Jacob van Rijs

Holland city • Calculation • 1997 • Author: MVRDV: Winy Maas, Jacob van Rijs and Nathalie de Vries with Tom Mossel, Bas van Neijenhof and Bart Reuser • Source: CBS

Meteorite city • Light rules • 1997 • Author: Eric Drieënhuizen • Institution: Academy of Architecture, Rotterdam • Tutors: Richard Koek, Winy Maas and Jacob van Rijs • Re-editing: MVRDV: Winy Maas, Jacob van Rijs and Nathalie de Vries with Tom Mossel and Bart Reuser

Castle Maker • The ultimate light formula • 1995 • Author: Ronald Wall with Rafael Seidle • Institution: Academy of Architecture, Rotterdam • Tutors: Richard Koek, Winy Maas and Jacob van Rijs • Re-editing: MVRDV: Winy Maas, Jacob van Rijs and Nathalie de Vries with Joost Grootens, 1997

Shadowtown • Competition design for the railway station area in Bergen op Zoom, The Netherlands • 1993 • Design: MVRDV: Winy Maas, Jacob van Rijs and Nathalie de Vries with Frans Blok • Organizer: PPP Foundation, Roosendaal • Location: Bergen op Zoom, The Netherlands

Gothics • Design study for densification of the centre of Amsterdam, The Netherlands • 1996 • Design: MVRDV: Winy Maas, Jacob van Rijs and Nathalie de Vries with Tom Mossel • Source: Based on TUD Indesem workshop 1994 • Institution: Delft University of Technology • Tutors: Jean Attali, Winy Maas and Jacob van Rijs

Pompeiian Carpet • Urban study for Molensloot, The Hague, The Netherlands • 1994 • Design: MVRDV: Winy Maas, Jacob van Rijs and Nathalie de Vries with Elaine Didyk, Fokke Moerel and Jaap van Dijk • Client: Molensloot Foundation, The Hague • Location: The Hague, The Netherlands • Project size: 140 houses

Trojan Extrusion • Densification study for Rotterdam centre, The Netherlands • 1995 • Design: Mark Verheijen • Institution: Academy of Architecture, Rotterdam • Tutors: Richard Koek, Winy Maas and Jacob van Rijs • Re-editing: MVRDV: Winy Maas, Jacob van Rijs and Nathalie de Vries with Joost Grootens and Tom Mossel

New! New Babylon • Densification study for Rotterdam centre, The Netherlands • 1995 • Design: Ronald Wall • Institution: Academy of Architecture, Rotterdam • Tutors: Richard Koek, Winy Maas and Jacob van Rijs • Re-editing: MVRDV: Winy Maas, Jacob van Rijs and Nathalie de Vries with Joost Grootens and Tom Mossel

The Cantilever • 100 apartments for elderly people in Amsterdam-Osdorp, The Netherlands • 1997 • Design: MVRDV: Winy Maas, Jacob van Rijs and Nathalie de Vries with Willem Timmer, Arjan Mulder and Frans de Witte• Merkelbach Award 1997, Amsterdam Fund for the Art • Client: Housing corporation Het Oosten, Amsterdam • Location: Amsterdam-Osdorp (Ookmeerweg), The Netherlands • Project size: 7,500 m^2 • Facilitary office: Bureau Bouwkunde, Rotterdam • Structure: Pieters Bouwtechniek, Haarlem • Building physics: DGMR, Arnhem • Contractor: Intervam, Amsterdam

Icebergs • Text • 1995 • Author: Winy Maas and Jacob van Rijs • Drawings: Jean Nouvel and Renzo Piano

Darklands • Photographic study for underground life • 1995 • Author: Indesem group 1995: Alesandra Gvera, Pedro Costa, Tom Bergevoet, Joost Mulders, Tomaso Pini, Ruben Smudde, Rik Splinter, Daan Zandbelt, Aleksander Ignjatovic, Larisa Blazic, Sonja Mertel, Inez Zimmer and Svetislav Bankerovic • Institution: Delft University of Technology • Tutors: Winy Maas and Jacob van Rijs • Photographers: Indesem group, Winy Maas, Peter Seidel, Frankfurt am Main 1993

Chrysler & Friends • Extension to Chrysler Building, New York, U.S.A. • 1995 • Design: Jago van Bergen and Evert Kolpa • Institution: Academy of Architecture, Rotterdam • Tutors: Winy Maas and Jacob van Rijs

Parkhouse/Carstadt • Shopping Mall, Amsterdam, The Netherlands • 1995 • Design: Pieter Bannenberg and Kamiel Klaasse • Institution: Delft University of Technology • Tutors: Bernard Leupen and Winy Maas

Z-mall • Main centre for the new district of Leidschenveen, The Netherlands (Preliminary design) • 1997 • Design: MVRDV: Winy Maas, Jacob van Rijs and Nathalie de Vries with Tom Mossel, Stefan Witteman, Bernd Felsinger and Marco De Francesco • Client: Ontwikkelingsbedrijf Leidschenveen, Leidschendam and Mabon, Rijswijk • Location: Leidschendam, The Netherlands • Project size: 13,000 m^2 shops, 15,000 m^2 parking, 150 houses and various public services

Stack Attack • Competition entry (invited) for the central park of the new town of Leidschenrijn, The Netherlands • 1997 • Design: MVRDV: Winy Maas, Jacob van Rijs and Nathalie de Vries with René Marey, Joost Glissenaar, Tom Mossel, Bas van Neijenhof, Marco De Francesco and Bernd Felsinger • in collaboration with Katie Tedder, landscape architect, The Hague • Hans Venhuizen, artist, Arnhem • Jeroen van Herk, ecologist, Grontmij Waddinxveen• Louis Broersma, hydrologist, Grontmij De Bilt • Arno van der Mark, artist, Amsterdam • Harm Tilman, architectural critic and editor of the magazine 'De Architect', The Hague • Bruno Felix, documentary producer, VPRO Hilversum • Dick Rijken, media advisor and lecturer at the Sandberg Institute Amsterdam • Ton Matton, urban planner specialized in sustainability, Buro Schie Rotterdam • Joep Lax, traffic advisor, Arend en Samhout Utrecht • Client: Project Bureau Leidschenrijn, Vleuten de Meern • Location: Vleuten de Meern and Utrecht, The Netherlands • Project size: 300 ha park with football fields, gardens, gym, ecological areas, nature and water

Mainstreet • Town planning study for development of Almere, The Netherlands • 1996 • Design: MVRDV: Winy Maas, Jacob van Rijs and Nathalie de Vries with Tom Mossel, Lukas Felder, Frank van Manen, Eline Strijkers, Alex Brouwer and Grisha Bourbouze • Client: Municipality of Almere/BVR, Utrecht • Location: Almere, The Netherlands • Project size: 20,000 houses, 500,000 m^2 other programme • Model: Parthesius & de Rijk, Rotterdam • Photographer: EASAN (Pictures) Edgar Cleijne, Rotterdam

Lace • Study of mobility scenarios in The Netherlands • 1997 • Design: MVRDV: Winy Maas, Jacob van Rijs and Nathalie de Vries with Carolien Ligtenberg, René Marey, Tom Mossel, Bas van Neijenhof, Willem Timmer, Frans de Witte, Duzan Doepel and Bernd Felsinger • Client: Ministry of Housing, Spatial Planning and Environment, The Hague • Location: A20, Rotterdam, The Netherlands • Acoustical research: DGMR, Arnhem • Traffic research: Arend en Samhout, Utrecht

Re-embedding: Counting Guangzou • Photographic walk through Guangzou, China • 1998 • Bart Lootsma

Doubledecker • Traffic study for Rotterdam centre, The Netherlands • 1995 • Author: Mark Verheijen • Institution: Academy of Architecture, Rotterdam • Tutors: Richard Koek, Winy Maas and Jacob van Rijs • Re-editing: MVRDV: Winy Maas, Jacob van Rijs and Nathalie de Vries with Joost Grootens and Tom Mossel

Noise scape • Datascape • 1997 • Author: Penelope Dean • Institution: The Berlage Institute, Amsterdam • Tutors: Winy Maas and Jacob van Rijs with Tom Mossel, Patrick Schuhmacher, Brett Steel and Elia Zenghelis • Acoustical research: DGMR, Arnhem • Re-editing: MVRDV: Winy Maas, Jacob van Rijs and Nathalie de Vries with Tom Mossel

Stourhead revisited • Town planning design for a neighbourhood of 1,800 houses along the Amsterdam IJ channel, The Netherlands • 1994 • Design: MVRDV: Winy Maas, Jacob van Rijs and Nathalie de Vries with Ruurd Gietema and Edzo Bindels • Client: City of Amsterdam, Physical Planning Department • Location: Amsterdam, The Netherlands

The world according to Gauss • Text • 1996 • Author: Hans Krijnsen

Negotiations in a housing silo • Competition design for 165 dwellings and business units on a jetty in the Amsterdam IJ channel, The Netherlands • 1995/- • Competition design: MVRDV: Winy Maas, Jacob van Rijs and Nathalie de Vries with Tom Mossel, Joost Glissenaar, Alex Brouwer, Ruby van den Munckhof and Joost Kok • 1st prize • Design: MVRDV: Winy Maas, Jacob van Rijs and Nathalie de Vries with Willem Timmer, Frans de Witte, Duzan Doepel and Bernd Felsinger • Client: Rabo Real Estate, Utrecht and housing corporation De Principaal, Amsterdam • Location: Amsterdam, The Netherlands • Project size: 19.500 m^2 • Facilitary office: Bureau Bouwkunde, Rotterdam • Structure: Pieters Bouwtechniek, Haarlem • Building physics: Cauberg Huygen, Rotterdam • Image: Theorem, 1909

Proximity • Europan-2 competition design for 284 houses in Berlin-Prenzlauerberg, Germany • 1991 • Design: MVRDV: Winy Maas, Jacob van Rijs and Nathalie de Vries • 1st prize • Organizer: Europan • Location: Bornholmerstraße, Berlin, Germany • Project size: 284 houses and 10,000 m² other programme • Model: Parthesius & de Rijk, Rotterdam and Herman Helle, Rotterdam • Cad images: Frans Parthesius • Photographer: Pieter Vandermeer

Therapy • Double house in Utrecht, The Netherlands • 1997 • Design: De Architectengroep loerakker rijnboutt ruijssenaars hendriks van gameren mastenbroek • bv: Bjarne Mastenbroek with Floor Arons and Michiel Raaphorst • And MVRDV: Winy Maas, Jacob van Rijs and Nathalie de Vries with Mike Booth and Joost Glissenaar • Client: Anonymous • Location: Utrecht, The Netherlands • Project size: 300 m² • Structure: ABT Velp • Building physics: DGMR, Arnhem • Contractor: Tiggelman bv, Spaarndam • Fire consultant: Fred Redeker

Statistic suspense • Study for a development of 750 houses in Delft, Hoornse Kwadrant, The Netherlands • 1992 • Design: MVRDV: Winy Maas, Jacob van Rijs and Nathalie de Vries • Client: Delft Department of Urban Planning and Centrum Herengracht, The Hague • Location: Delft, The Netherlands • Project size: 750 houses

Massive pluralism • Text • 1996 • Author: Winy Maas

Plant City • Competition entry for town plan and landscape design for the Bundesgartenschau 2001 in Potsdam, Germany • 1997 • Design: MVRDV: Winy Maas, Jacob van Rijs and Nathalie de Vries with Tom Mossel, Bernd Felsinger, Eline Strijkers, Frans de Witte and Carolien Ligtenberg • in collaboration with Hemprich/Tophof Architekten, Berlin • Katie Tedder, landscape architect, The Hague • Harm Tilman, architectural critic and editor of the magazine 'De Architect', The Hague • Bruno Felix, documentary producer, VPRO Hilversum • Dick Rijken, media advisor and lecturer at the Sandberg Institute, Amsterdam • Ton Matton, urban planner specialized in sustainability, Buro Schie, Rotterdam • Oranjewoud, Almere • Honourable mention • Organizer: Entwicklungsträger Bornstedter Feld/Treuhänder der Stadt Potsdam • Location: Potsdam, Germany • Photographer: Hans Werlemann

The continuous interior • Text • 1996 • Author: Winy Maas • Source: Stills from 'Himmel über Berlin', Wim Wenders

Claustrophobia • Interview with Jac Hoevenaars, psychologist-psychotherapist, Utrecht University, The Netherlands • 1996 • Author: Winy Maas

Claustro city • Datascape • 1997 • Author: Sven Grooten and Chris Rankin • Institution: The Berlage Institute, Amsterdam • Tutors: Winy Maas and Jacob van Rijs with Tom Mossel, Patrick Schuhmacher, Brett Steel and Elia Zenghelis

Wayfinding • Text • 1997 • Author: Machiel van Dorst • Photographer: Harmen van de Wal

Imploded exterior • Headquarter and studios for the VPRO public broadcasting company in Hilversum, The Netherlands • 1997 • Design: MVRDV: Winy Maas, Jacob van Rijs and Nathalie de Vries with Stefan Witteman, Alex Brouwer, Joost Glissenaar, Arjan Mulder, Eline Strijkers, Willem Timmer, Jaap van Dijk, Fokke Moerel and Joost Kok • Dudok Award 1997, Municipality of Hilversum • Client: VPRO Hilversum • Location: Hilversum, The Netherlands • Project size: 10,500 m² • Facilitary office: Bureau Bouwkunde, Rotterdam • Structure: Pieters Bouwtechniek, Haarlem and Ove Arup & Partners, London • Services: Ketel R.I., Delft and Ove Arup & Partners, London • Building physics: DGMR, Arnhem • Contractor: Voormolen Bouw BV, Rotterdam, • Acoustics: Centrum Bouwonderzoek TNO-TU, Eindhoven • Interior design: MVRDV: Winy Maas, Jacob van Rijs and Nathalie de Vries with Joost Glissenaar and Eline Strijkers • Lighting: MVRDV with Robin Hood • Produkties for a TL-light fixture, 1996/1997 • Sink: Peter Hopman • Pantry: Koot Productie (Jan Koot) and Peter Hopman • Signing: Fred Inklaar • Gardens: MVRDV: Winy Maas, Jacob van Rijs and Nathalie de Vries with Alex Brouwer in collaboration with Heidemij Advies • Contractor Gardens: Hogenbirk, Laren

E-scape • Text • 1996 • Author: Arjen Mulder • Film • 1997 • Author: MVRDV: Winy Maas, Jacob van Rijs and Nathalie de Vries with Joost Grootens and Tom Mossel

Jean Attali • 1950 • Philosopher, Paris • Currently working on his doctoral thesis "le detail"

Pieter Bannenberg • 1959 • Architect • Co-founder of NL Architects, Amsterdam

Jago van Bergen • 1969 • Studying at the Academy of Architecture and Urban Planning, Rotterdam • Working at NeutelingsRiedijk Architecten, Rotterdam

Buro Schie • 1995 • Office for sustainable urbanism, Rotterdam • Founded in 1995 by Ton Matton and Lukas Verweij

Patricia Bijvoet • 1960 • Landscape architect, Amsterdam

Penelope Dean • 1969 • Architect • Studying at the Berlage Institute, Amsterdam

Machiel van Dorst • 1963 • Environmental designer • Director of advies- en ontwerpbureau RUIM, Rotterdam

Eric Drieënhuizen • 1968 • Designer • Studying at the Academies of Architecture and Urban Planning, Rotterdam • Working at Drost + van Veen Architekten, Rotterdam

Ewout Fennis • 1968 • Studying at the Academy of Architecture and Urban Planning, Rotterdam • Working at the Municipality of Waddinxveen

Sven Y.H. Grooten • 1971 • Architect • Studying at the Berlage Institute, Amsterdam

Joost Grootens • 1971 • Architectural and multimedia designer, Amsterdam

Jac Hoevenaars Ph. D. • 1945 • Psychologist-psychotherapist • Director of the Outpatient Clinic Faculty of Social Sciences, Utrecht University, The Netherlands • Senior Psychotherapy Trainer, many publications on anxiety disorders, visiting professor in and out of the Netherlands

Piet Knepper • 1946 • Urbanist and transport planner • Working at the Municipality of Nieuwegein, Department of Urban Planning

Kamiel Klaasse • 1967 • Architect • Co-founder of NL Architects, Amsterdam

Richard Koek • 1960 • Urbanist • Co-director of CH&Partners, The Hague • Tutor at the Academies of Architecture and Urban Planning, Rotterdam and Amsterdam

Evert Kolpa • 1966 • Designer • Working at NeutelingsRiedijk Architecten, Rotterdam

Vincent Kompier • 1967 • Researcher and consultant • Working at Reijndorp bv (stedelijk onderzoek en advies), Rotterdam

Hans Krijnsen • 1951 • Research consultant, Rotterdam

Laurence Liauw • 1964 • Co-founder of GAS KL-London (architecture studio) • Architectural Association Research Fellow

Martin van Loenen • 1970 • Studying at the Academy of Architecture and Urban Planning in Rotterdam • Working at the Ministry of Defense, The Hague

Bart Lootsma • 1957 • Architectual critic and historian, Rotterdam • Editor of Archis, herausgeber Daidalos, visiting professor Berlage Institute, Amsterdam

Winy Maas • 1959 • Architect, landscape designer and urbanist • Co-founder of MVRDV • Co-editor of Forum 1994-1997 • Tutor and Lecturer at, among others, the Architectural Association, London, the Technical University Delft, the Berlage Institute, Amsterdam and the Academies of Architecture and Urban Planning, Rotterdam and Amsterdam

Frank van Manen • 1969 • Studying architecture at the Technical University Delft • Worked at MVRDV

Bjarne Mastenbroek • 1964 • Co-director of the architectengroep loerakker rijnboutt ruijssenaars hendriks van gameren mastenbroek bv in Amsterdam • Tutor and Lecturer at the Academy of Architecture and Urban Planning, Amsterdam

Tom Mossel • 1966 • Architect • Working at MVRDV, Rotterdam • Tutor at the Academies of Architecture and Urban Planning in Tilburg and Rotterdam and the Berlage Institute, Amsterdam

Arjen Mulder • 1955 • Writer and journalist, Amsterdam

Roelof Mulder • 1962 • Graphic designer • Founder of Studio Roelof Mulder, Amsterdam • Winner Rotterdam Design Prize 1993 • Co-editor and designer of Forum 1994-1997 • Tutor at the Academie of fine arts in Arnhem 1994-1997

MVRDV • 1991 • Office for Architecture and Urbanism, Rotterdam • Founded in 1991 by Winy Maas, Jacob van Rijs and Nathalie de Vries • Realizations in Amsterdam, Delft, Hilversum, Otterlo, Arnhem, Hoenderlo, The Hague, Utrecht • Publications in many magazines and newspapers • Merkelbach award for 100 Wozocos in Amsterdam, Dudok award and Concrete award for Villa VPRO in Hilversum • Exhibitions in London, Rotterdam, Amsterdam, Sao Paulo, Vienna, Los Angeles, Hilversum, Graz, Haarlem and Venice

Bas van Neijenhof • 1972 • Studying Town and Country Planning at Rijkshogeschool IJsselland, Deventer • Worked at Buro Schie, Rotterdam and MVRDV, Rotterdam

Hans Oldewarris • 1949 • Publisher • Co-founder of 010 Publishers, Rotterdam

Chris Rankin • 1969 • Landscape architect • Studying at the Berlage Institute, Amsterdam

Arnold Reijndorp • 1948 • Researcher and consultant • Founder of Reijndorp bv (stedelijk onderzoek en advies), Rotterdam

Bart Reuser • 1972 • Studying architecture at the Technical University Delft • Worked at MVRDV

Jacob van Rijs • 1964 • Architect • Co-founder of MVRDV • Tutor at the Technical University Delft, the Academy of Architecture and Urban Planning, Rotterdam and the Berlage Institute, Amsterdam

Rafael Seidle • 1962 • Software programmer, Silicon Valley, California, U.S.A.

Harm Tilman • 1954 • Town planner and architectural critic • Director of the Department of Town Planning at the Academy of Architecture and Urban Planning, Rotterdam • Co-editor of the architectural magazine 'De Architect' • Author of many articles on modern architecture and town planning

Marc Verheijen • 1965 • Infrastructural designer • Working at the Municipality of Rotterdam, Municipal Department of Urban Planning and Housing • Studying architecture and townplanning at the Academy of Architecture and Urban Planning, Rotterdam

Nathalie de Vries • 1965 • Architect • Co-founder of MVRDV • Tutor at the Technical University Delft and the Academy of Architecture and Urban Planning, Arnhem

Ronald Wall • 1966 • Studying architecture and townplanning at the Academy of Architecture and Urban Planning, Rotterdam • Initiator and Project Co-ordinator of the Housing Generator Competition

Hans Werlemann • 1948 • Photographer • Founder of Hectic Pictures, Rotterdam • Tutor at the St. Joost Academy in Breda

Christian Zalm • 1943 • Landscape architect • Working at the Municipality of Rotterdam, Municipal Department of Urban Planning and Housing • Tutor at the Academy of Architecture and Urban Planning,

except: **FAR Catalogue** • page 2 (br) • Frans Parthesius • page 3 (bl) • Almere stad, De Groene Randstad Almere Magazine,7 (1992), frontpage • page 3 (br) • Broadacre City, T. Riley (editor), Frank Loyd Wright architect, New York (The Museum of Modern Arts) 1994 • page 4 (mr) • The Cantilever, MVRDV, Joost Grootens • page 5 (mr) • A contemporary city for 3 million inhabitants, Le Corbusier, 1922 J. Dethier, A. Guiheux (editors), La ville, art et architecture en Europe, 1870-1993, Exhibition Catalogue, Centre Georges Pompidou, Paris, 1994 • page 5 (bl) • Berlin Voids, Pieter Vandermeer • page 7 (mr) • De Resident, The Hague, AVEQ Fotografie-& AV Produkties • page 8 (bl) • Vertical city Ludwig Hilberseimer, 1924, J. Dethier, A. Guiheux (editors), La ville, art et architecture en Europe, 1870-1993, Exhibition Catalogue, Centre Georges Pompidou, Paris, 1994 • page 8 (ur) • Project d'immeubles a gradins en front de Seine, Henri Sauvage, Paris, 1928, J. Dethier, A. Guiheux (editors), La ville, art et architecture en Europe, 1870-1993, Exhibition Catalogue, Centre Georges Pompidou, Paris, 1994 • page 8 (bl) • 'dok' -complex, Louis Kahn, 1956, Trustees of the University of Pennsylvania, Kenneth Framton, Modern Architecture. A critical history, Sun, Nijmegen, 1988 • page 9 (bl) • Landmark Tower, Yokohama. The Stubins Associates, architects, 1993, in association with Mitsubishi Estate Archtectural & Engineering. Nikko Hotels. Institute français d' architecture, Skyscrapers Higher and Higher, Tours (Mame) 1995, p. 189 • page 9 (br) • Nec Super Tower and its urban context. Nikken Sekkei, 1990 © The Japan Architect Co. Institute français d' architecture, Skyscrapers Higher and Higher, Tours (Mame) 1995, p. 151 • **Greyness on the Dutch mesa** • page 18/19 • 'U.S.A. density', Harvard Laboratory, Mieke Zijlmans, Duidelijke taal van een plaatje, De Volkskrant, wetenschap, 7 December, 1996, p.15 • **Liteness** • page 32/33 • 'Moving House', postcard by E. Cocaine, H. Armstrong, Utrecht (A division of Catch Publishing) 1991 • **Permanence** • page 34/35 • Photos, Bart Hofmeester, text by Ivo Blom, Rotterdam Breed Gezien, Phoenix & Den Oudsten B.V., Rotterdam, 1985 • page 36/39 • MVRDV, with Joost Grootens • page 42/43 • Broadacre city T. Riley (editor), Frank Lloyd Wright architect, New York (The Museum of Modern Arts) 1994 • page 46/51 • MVRDV, with Joost Grootens • **Lelyland:** page 80/87 • MVRDV, with Joost Grootens and Tom Mossel • **Datascape** • page 98/99 • Chaos, James Gleick, Contact, Amsterdam, 1987 • **Rat tests** • page 130/131 • 'Caged rats' Dr. Mark Rosenzweig • page 132/133 • 'Rat bites', P.J. A. Timmermans, Social Behavior in the rat , (J.L. van Kaauwen and Th. J. Fuchten) 1978 • **Who is afraid of massiveness?** • page 144/145 • 'Life Expectancy', Hans Krijnsen • page 146/147 • 'Climat Walls', DGMR, Arnhem • **KWC FAR 12** • page 152/173 • Laurence Liauw, Suenn Ho,Greg Girard • **Castle Maker** • page 230/239 • 'Castle Maker', Joost Grootens • **Shadowtown** • page 252/253 • 'Historische prent Bergen op Zoom'. From: Historisch Gem. Archief Bergen op Zoom • page 262/263 • 'Historische prent Bergen op Zoom'. From: Historisch Gem. Archief Bergen op Zoom • **Gothics** • page 266/267 • 'Vendex-driehoek', Photo Dijkstra, Photographer Fred Steenman • **Pompeiian Carpet** • page 274/275 • Egon Ceasar Conte Corti, Pompeii en Herculaneum, hun ondergang en herrijzenis, N.V. Oosthoeks uitgevers maatschappij, Utrecht, 1957 • **Trojan Extrusion** • page 296/297 • Carl W, Blegen, Ancient People and Places, Troy and the Trojans. Thames and Hudson, London, 1963 • page 298/299 • 'Luchtfoto Rotterdam', Gemeente Rotterdam Aeroview • page 302/303 • MVRDV with Joost Grootens • **New! New Babylon** • page 310/311 • "Yellow sector", Constant Nieuwenhuys, 1958, Haags gemeentemuseum, Photo courtesy of the artist • page 318/319 • 'Collage Weena Rotterdam', Joost Grootens • **The Cantilever** • page 320/341 • Thijs Wolzak, Hans Werlemann • **Iceberg** • page 344/345 • section galerias lafayette, R.C. Levene, F.M. Cecilia (ed), "Jean Nouvel 1987-1994", El Croquis, (1994) 65/66. • page 346/347 • New movement cities, Brain Richards, Studio Vista, London/Reinhold publishing corporation, New York, 1966 p.47 • page 350 • section fundation cartier, R.C. Levene, F.M. Cecilia (ed), "Jean Nouvel 1987-1994", El Croquis, (1994) 65/66. • page 351/352 • part of section "Tour sans fin", R.C. Levene, F.M. Cecilia (ed), "Jean Nouvel 1987-1994", El Croquis, (1994) 65/66. • page 353 • section of I.R.C.A.M., Paris Renzo Piano • **Darklands** • page 354/357 • Indesem group 1996 • Tutors; Winy Maas, Jacob van Rijs, Nathalie de Vries, Participants; Alesandra Gvera, Pedro Costa, Tom Bergevoet, Joost Mulders, Tomaso Pini, Ruben Smudde, Rik Splinter, Daan Zandbelt, Aleksander Ignjatovic, Larisa Blazic, Sonja Mertel, Inez Zimmer, Svetislav Bankerovic • page 358/359 • 'Regenwaterreservoir München', © Peter Seidel, Frankfürt am Main, 1993. O. Koekebakker, "Het Onderaardse" Items, 14(1995) 2 • page 360/361 • 'Lokatie van Duitse luchtmacht Mosbach', © Peter Seidel, Frankfürt am Main,1993. O. Koekebakker, "Het Onderaardse"

Items, 14(1995) 2 • page 362/363 • 'Ontsmettingsruimte Prenden', ©Peter Seidel, Frankfürt am Main, 1993. O. Koekebakker, "Het Onderaardse" Items, 14(1995) 2 • page 368/369 • 'Radio City Music Hall', R. Koolhaas, Delirious New York, A Retroactive Manifesto for Manhattan, Rotterdam (010 Publishers) 1994 • **Z-mall** • page 394/395 • 'Tokyo elevated express way', L. Halprin, Freeway, New York (Reinhold publishing Corporation) 1966 • **Infrastructure** • page 426/427 • Interstate #278 Brooklyn Heights, N.Y. Design consultant: Clarke and Rapuano. L. Halprin, Freeway, New York (Reinhold publishing Corporation) 1966 • **Mainstreet** • page 448/449 • EASAN (Pictures) Edgar Cleijne, Rotterdam • page 450/451 • EASAN (Pictures) Edgar Cleijne, Rotterdam, MVRDV • **Lace** • page 452/453 • MVRDV / Dubbeldeks Autosnelweg, Bouwdienst Rijkswaterstaat march 1998 • **Re-Embedding: Counting Guangzhou** • page 472/483 • Photographic walk through Guangzhou, China, 1998, Bart Lootsma, First published in Archis 1998 • **Doubledecker** • page 484/485 • 'Bangkok', Harm van der Wal • **Noisescape** • page 508/509 • Marriott Hotel, Atlanta, Atrium. John Portman & Associates, architects, 1985. Jaime Ardiles-Arce. Institute français d' architecture, Skyscrapers Higher and Higher, Tours (Mame) 1995, p. 48 • **Proximity** • page 556/557 • Pieter Vandermeer • page 564/565 • Frans Parthesius • page 568/569 • Pieter Vandermeer • page 576/577 • Frans Parthesius • **Therapy** • page 578/579 • Performance by Marina Abramovic & Ulay • page 580/581 • Sweethearts, Photo by Oliviero Toscani, E.Prando (ed), "Enemies" United Colors of Benetton, Elcograf 1998 (Publishers of Newsweek, add supplement NRC Handelsblad) • page 590/595 • Christian Richters • page 584/585 • Poché Annelies Siero, Cairo, Madrasah of sultan al-Kãmil, 1225, madrasah and tomb of sultan Barqûq, 1384-86, madrasah and tomb of sultan al-Nãsir Muhammad, 1295-1304, madrasah, tomb and bimaristãn of sultan Qalãwûn, 1284-1285 • **Statistic suspense** • page 596/597 • Country Noises, Saul Steinberg, 1978, ©The New-Yorker, • page 610/611 • Stills from 'Psycho', Alfred Hitchcock, Jean Maheu (ed), "le genie de la ponctuation" Traverses 43, (1988), Centre Georges Pompiou, Paris • **Massive pluralism** • page 614/615 • Photo by Oliviero Toscani, E.Prando (ed), "Enemies" United Colors of Benetton, Elcograf 1998 (Publishers of Newsweek, add supplement NRC Handelsblad) • **Plant city** • page 642/647 • Hans Werlemann • **The continuous interior** • page 650/651 • La Bibliotheque nationale: erstitution cartographique (1855-1865) From: Bruno Fortier, La Metropole Imaginaire. Un Atlas de Paris (Mardaga ed. Liège 1989) p.125 • page 654/657 • Stills from 'Himmel über Berlin', Wim Wenders and Peter Handke, Der Himmel uber Berlin, Suhrkamp Frankfurt am Main 1995 • **Imploded exterior** • page 578/579 • Office usage, E. Veldhoen, B. Piepers, The Demise of the Office, The Digital Workplace in a Thriving Organisation, Rotterdam (010 Publishers) 1995 • page 702/703 • Hans Werlemann • page 704/705 • Christian Richters • page 706 (Top) • Christian Richters • page 706 (Bottom) • Hans Werlemann • page 707 • Hans Werlemann • page 708/717 • Film by Hans Werlemann; Montage by Joost Grootens • **E-scape** • page 732/736 • Film by Joost Grootens and Tom Mossel; Montage by Joost Grootens •

LIFT

E-scape

Text

1996

Arjen Mulder

Film

1997

MVRDV

...can't go on. Because I was happy. Because I didn't want to become what she would make me. Because the room was free. Because I was now going to university. Because it was a golden opportunity. Because I went and sat on the steps of the porch. Because I really thought I could handle it. Because the room was three metres high. Because the corridor ran along the washing line. Because her skirt was hanging on it. Because I recognized her in it. Because I had to pass the canal. Because it gets dark in the evening. Because I couldn't go on. Because I still knew nothing. Your life is lived by forces you have no control over. Is that bad? Very. I thought I could escape. Because her eyes were black. Because there are seven days in a week. Because there are trains. Because I cycled through the rain. Because yellow leaves piled up in the porch. Because it was waiting for me when I arrived home. Because I didn't know anyone. I was a nobody too. When you can finally see how the tree branches, then it's winter. Because I couldn't have gone on. Because I had planned to visit. Because I didn't have her phone number. Because I didn't know her surname. Because I didn't know that this existed. Silly boy. I was just dying and didn't know it. Because I had a daily routine. Because the lectures were compulsory. Because I loved drawing. Because I was much too young. Because I wanted to write a book. Because I thought about logic. Because I had to go down three flights of stairs to the toilet. Because the sink was in the passage. Because I washed behind a screen. Because there was macaroni on the roof outside the window. Because her skirt was back on the line. The way she crossed the square, me dying of happiness. And she? I let it flow away into me. The way the moon appears from behind a cloud. The light reflecting in the evening canal. Because the houses were five storeys high. Because people lived on all those storeys. Because the silence was deafening. Because the face flannel was frozen in the morning. Because my walls were white. Because I had a table and chair. And a bed and a cupboard. Things happen in the attic-room that are too much for the daylight. All because I had looked at her. Because I knew there was a solution. Because no-one had ever died. Because water was solid. Because my soul had gone missing. Oh you poor boy, poor girl. I couldn't go on. She was still breathing, I beyond reach. Because a weekend lasts two nights. Because a bicycle gets no further than the door. Because it wasn't at all far. Because the front garden proved impossible to find. Because she swept her hair to one side as she crossed. That's how awareness happens. Because I had reached the wall. Because the fire was unquenchable. Because I became a dot in the nothingness. Because the gods recognized me. I destroyed the absolute. Because I couldn't go on. And winter came. And I moved house to tiny old premises. And survived. And was nowhere. And nothing more happened for a long time. Give us this day our daily life. Years went by. I became a man. And everything came back. Because I didn't take note. Because I thought this was loving. Because fairytales are fantasy. Because I was trapped in that old place. Because we could get a new house. Because the view was deadening. Because the clouds made up for it all. Because we each had our own room. Because there was a kitchen. Because I didn't know how life worked. Because I thought the right gestures would be enough to conjure up the contents. Because I always take the practical approach. Because the stair was always lit. Because her friends weren't my friends. Because there was no reason to stop. I was happy, wasn't I? My social utopia in the bag. And the holidays were great. Until I walked onto the beach. Because it was too warm for anything else. Because the cafés were fun. Because it was full of people after all those unpeopled mountains. Because she went there every day. Because she had such fine hair. Because she drew down her swimming costume to sunbathe. Because she played with a ball at the water's edge. Because I realized that it was her. The gods don't die, the goddesses. Because I could have held her in my arms. Because we could have been so happy. Because she looked at me when she arrived in the morning. Because she came and lay down near us. Because I knew then what I had missed out on. More than half my soul. My other body. My indescribably beautiful, voluptuous other body. Because it was already too late. Because the city consisted of a house, a café, an office. Because this was supposed to be a life for two. Because I couldn't go on. I sat on the balcony. Once again it had all disintegrated. The sun shone across the roof onto the houses. I could see into ten of them. I went to lie on the tiles of the flat roof. Admit it. Admit it, mate. This time it could really go wrong. You'll never right it again. Because the essential bit's not there. Because you didn't see it. Because you thought you were doing what you had to do. Because life refuses to become real. Because everyone just fools around. Because I am no better and no worse. Because it can go wrong. Admit that you can die. Without having achieved anything. With no reason at all why you said no the first time. Because you were too shy. Because you were too neurotic. Because you were too cackhanded. Because you were chicken. Because you were mortified by her girlfriends. Because you thought you might explode. Because you knew you would love each other too much. Because you would never get out of it again. Because you needed a secret. Because you were nobody. Because your feelings were stronger than that tiny grain of sense you had. Because you couldn't go on. As I can't go on now. I admit things can go wrong. I accept that death can be stronger. Death I accept you, come to me. That's how awareness happens. Because I don't know who I am. Because I don't know how else it could be. Because I am no more than a body. Because I never should have got used to the city. Because I should have stayed among the fields and woods. Despair isn't enough. Because I can't leave. Because nobody misses out if I don't achieve anything. Because I am only my own psychodrama. No-one else is part of it. I am missing from my life. Because I cannot possibly leave. Because the stairwell beckons. The chair is ready at the table. Blue is in the air. Because I won't manage it this time. Death had never anything to do with dying yourself. Death was a powerful force behind all the living. Each inspiration, each sentence I wrote came from that force. Death is dead. Now I can die too. I accepted that on the balcony in the sunlight. On the tiles of the flat roof. I can't go on. I have never been able to. There is someone blocking the way on every route. That's how empty my life is. A bunch of zombies in an empty shed: that's me. I look at the blue sky. Just inside my field of view a crane is erecting high-rise. I hear my neighbour open up a beer. I smell bread baking on the level below. Is it Sunday? I recall sitting on a rock during a mountain walk and thinking: I can't go on. And then I thought: this rock's been here five hundred million years. I'm here such a short time, it will never remember me. Because I'm mortal. Because I am short-lived. Because I won't keep fresh for long. Because I am a self-regulating, self-correcting system. Because I am a node in a social network. One that has fallen away. Because I am dying. What was so wonderful about being lonely? Together charging up the stairs in a state. Because I'm the one lying here. And everything changed. I stand up, take the passage past the rooms, past the kitchen. Out the door and down four flights. A congenial, unique being heads up the street. A summer's evening with people here and there. Past the few tables outside an eating house. Across the bridge with the bottle bank. Past the pavement café for more serious drinking. There it is. In I go. Packet of cigarettes, please. That one. A disposable lighter. Thanks. Bye. Once you yourself have accepted death, there's no reason not to go through with it. Because it's over. Because something else

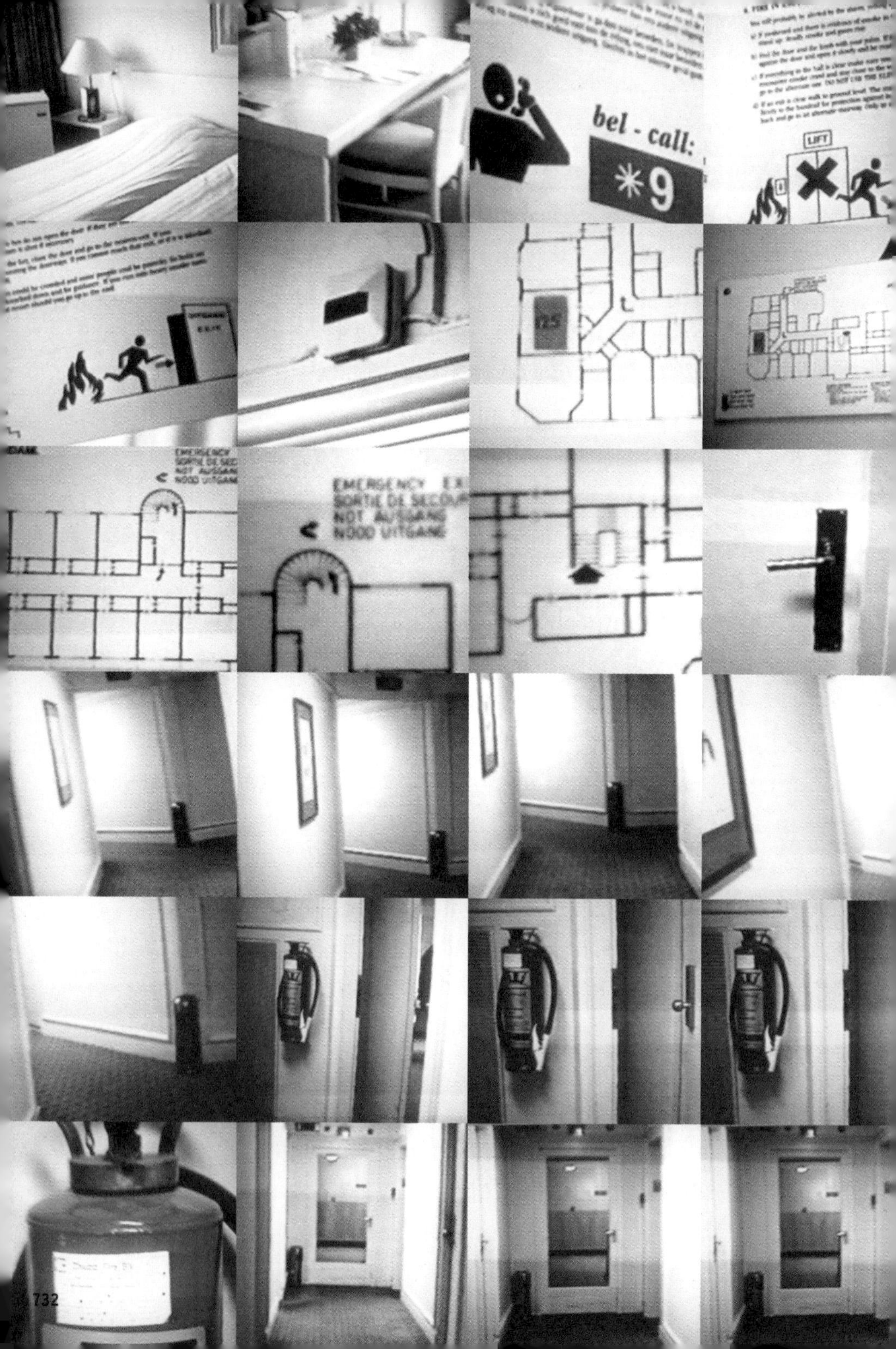
bel - call:
*9
LIFT
EMERGENCY EX
SORTIE DE SECOU
NOT AUSGANG
NOOD UITGANG

BRANDKRAA
BRANDKRAAN
BIJ BRAND
BIJ BRAND
LIFT
HEFVERMOGEN 900 kg
OF 12 PERSONEN
ALARM

brandslang
firehose
alarmknop
firealarm
u bent hier
you are here

vluchtweg
escape-route
BRANDMELDER
NOODUIT
FIRE ES
=ALARM ZONE
TGANG
SCAPE
ANG
APE